TABLE OF CONTENTS

p.5		THE OFFICE AS WE'VE COME TO KNOW IT: A PLAY IN THREE ACTS
p.13		THE WHY, HOW, WHAT OF THIS BOOK
p.19		INFOGRAPHICS

CASES
----

p.36	1895	Reliance Building
p.48	1924	Chilehaus
p.60	1925	Tribune Tower
p.66	1935	Kirovsky District Town Hall
p.68	1938	Palazzo Montecatini
p.80	1940/43	Palazzo della Civiltà Italiana
p.92	1941	Aarhus City Hall
p.108	1953	Secretariat Building
p.116	1955	Rautatalo
p.128	1956	Price Tower
p.132	1956	National Pensions Institute
p.144	1958	Van Leer Headquarters
p.156	1958	Inland Steel Building
p.164	1958	Seagram Building
p.176	1958	Kagawa Prefectural Office
p.188	1960	Pirelli Tower
p.204	1960	Nestlé Headquarters
p.218	1960	Pepsicola Headquarters
p.220	1961	Buch und Ton
p.228	1962	Bell Labs Holmdel Complex
p.240	1962	Tomado House
p.252	1962	Home Federal Savings and Loan
p.260	1962	Enso-Gutzeit Headquarters
p.272	1962	Bank Melli University Branch
p.284	1962	Bacardi Headquarters
p.292	1964	Unilever Headquarters
p.304	1964	Johnson Wax Headquarters Europe
p.306	1964	Erieview Tower
p.308	1964	John Deere Headquarters
p.320	1966	Palaceside Building
p.332	1966	Finnland Haus
p.340	1966	Osram Administration Building
p.352	1966	Meguro City Hall
p.360	1967	Ford Foundation
p.364	1967	Shizuoka Press and Broadcasting Center
p.380	1971	Communist Party Headquarters
p.388	1972	Centraal Beheer
p.400	1973	Uni-Hochhaus
p.404	1973	Chicago Federal Center
p.416	1973	BMW Headquarters
p.428	1978	Danmarks Nationalbank
p.444	1982	Pendorp
p.450	1985	HSBC
p.452	1987	SAS Frösundavik Office Building
p.464	1989	Grande Arche
p.468	1991	Delftse Poort

----

p.483	EXECUTIVE SUMMARY IN SIX POINTS
p.485	1__ How not everything goes according to plan...
p.488	2__ Grids and windows didn't say much, yet remain essential...
p.490	3__ How architect/client commitment enables longevity...
p.500	4__ Keep it clean!
p.508	5__ Following the money...
p.512	6__ ...And the murky life cycles of office buildings demand that we rethink the office of the 21st century...
p.516	CREDITS AND ACKNOWLEDGMENTS

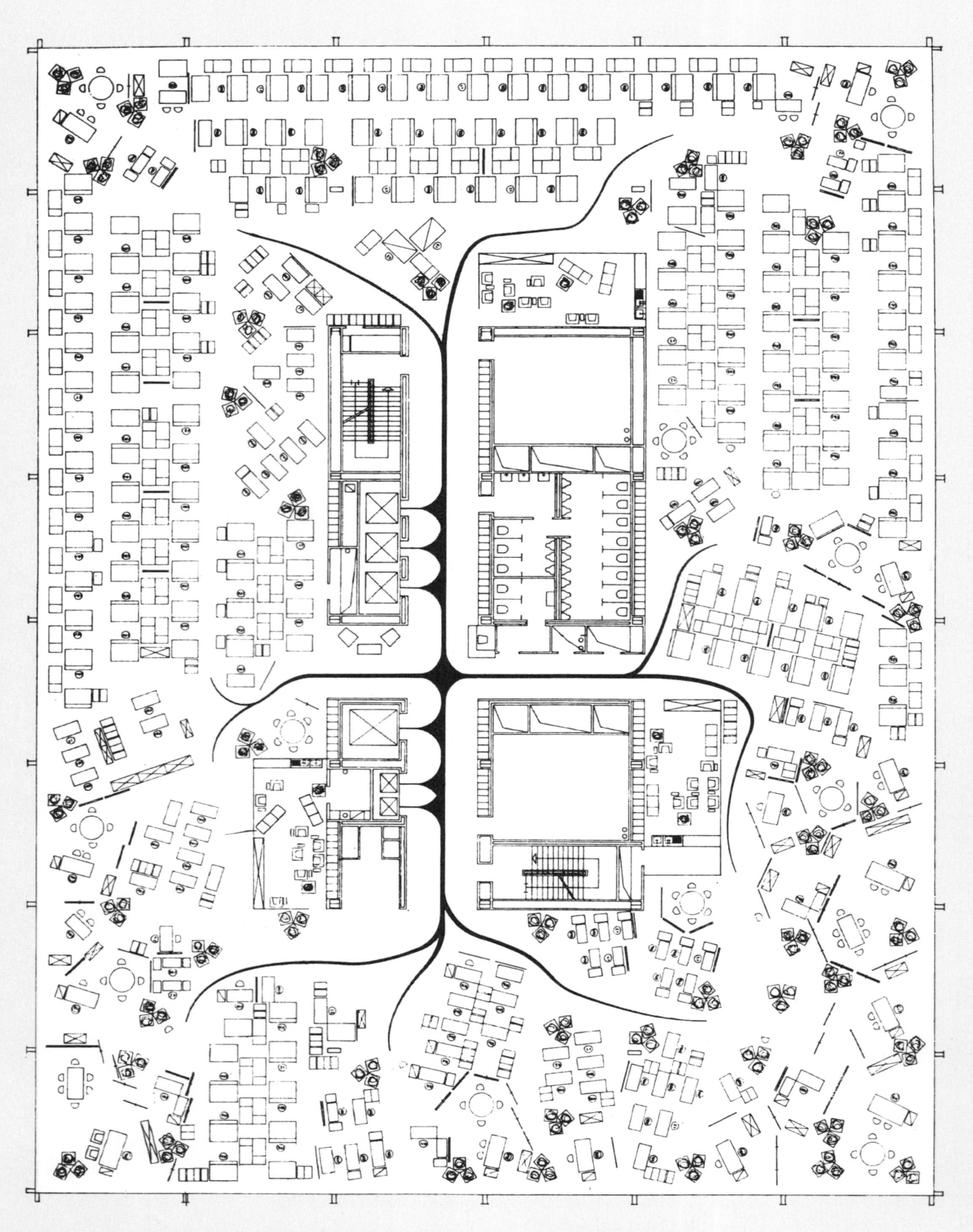

Plan for an office floor at the Krupp HQ building in Rheinhausen (Germany) designed by the Schnelle Organizations Team.
Published in Francis Duffy, "Skill: Bürolandschaft," *The Architectural Review 135*, no. 804 (1964), p.150

THE OFFICE AS WE'VE COME TO KNOW IT: A PLAY IN THREE ACTS

Blessed are the forgetful: for they get the better even of their blunders — Friedrich Nietzsche

Prologue
While the office as we know it (or knew it) is an invention of modernity[1], the COVID-19 pandemic has – almost, and weirdly – returned us to pre-Enlightenment modes of working. Then, like now, the majority of work was done from home. The few spaces outside the house where you might work had something like a hot-desk setup: clerical stations for city administration and archiving; public taverns and city halls for larger meetings; mess halls and libraries functioned something like contemporary co-working spaces. Business travel was only allowed with an official permit granted by a ruler.

The self-evidence of the modern office (prior to COVID-19) hides the fact that within the larger history of buildings and cities it is a newcomer, 150 years old at most. Its initial development stemmed from notably different prototypes in America and Europe. Early European offices were often overlayed on plans of monasteries and palaces with corridor layouts dividing adjacent small private rooms (also known as cellas). Early American offices, unencumbered by previous architectures, were largely based on improvised clerical working areas organised close to, or directly on factory floors. With the further development of industrialisation, that started to change.

Office life remained a practice without a theory until Frederik Taylor (1865–1915) set the stage. He would have a profound impact on how we see work and subsequently indirectly shape its spatial organisation. As a foreman at the Midvale Steel company in Pennsylvania in 1878, he figured that the assembly of foundry parts ran smoother when production was broken down, with specific stages for each constituent part, and with the amount of time each part took to make carefully quantified. This innovation had also been emerging in other industries, but Taylor gave it a name: scientific management. Output increased dramatically at the Midvale Steel plant under Taylor's regime. Eventually, it led to a worldwide rationalisation of production processes, the further specialisation of tasks and skills, the advent of mass production, and a subsequent revolution in spatial organisation, from the kitchen to the workplace. Technological inventions like the steel frame building, the grid, curtain wall, elevator, fluorescent light, and air conditioning gradually gave Taylor's organisational idea spatial expression as the open plan. These wall-less expanses had as few columns as possible, with services and circulation crammed into a structural core. Maximum flexibility was programmed into the architecture, facilitating the flux of capital and the churn of labor.[2] The modern office was born: a blank space for a new class of workers who would be solely active in administrative and service-related functions.

The stage is set
The post-World War II period, with its economic boom and growing business landscape, accelerated the evolution of the office. A break with the Cartesian open plan – and with the orthogonality of modernism – appeared with the Bürolandschaft (office landscape). It was conceived by the Schnelle brothers, Eberhard (37) and Wolfgang (27) in Western Germany. The brothers began as office furniture salesmen for Velox, a factory near Hamburg run by another brother, Klaus, but in 1958, they founded their own consulting group, later known as the Quickborner Team. Their goal: to design offices based on the functions and spatial needs of the worker rather than the organisational hierarchies and prestige of the company. The Schnelle brothers became evangelists for a new mode of working and spread the word through lectures, books, and articles, and through Verlag Schnelle Quickborn, their own publishing house.

Their Bürolandschaft was an open plan typology that proposed a radical rethinking of the American scientific management regime, which served a rigid apparatus of hierarchical control. For the first time, desks – and clusters of desks – deviated from 90-degree angles. While they may have looked haphazard, or organic, the layouts drew from cybernetic analysis of workflows and were precisely organized according to the specific work performed by the company, and by each department, facilitating not just efficiency but improved communication. This more dynamic, collaborative, humane office layout resonated with West Germany's democratic rebirth during the Wirtschaftswunder period, with the country eager for redemption and dissociation from its still-recent past and beginning to welcome new, partly-foreign companies.

In their publications, the Schnelle brothers advocated for an interdisciplinary approach to planning and organisation, venturing into the areas of office psychology, filing systems, light and climate control, office and urban planning, worker safety, and corporate hierarchies.[3] According to Eberhard Schnelle in *Architekt und Organisator: Versuche zu*

Frank Duffy (1940-)

Jack M. Nilles (1932-)

einer komplexen Planungsmethodik (Architect and organizer: Attempts at a complex planning methodology): "the sociological relationships, which make the single-cell office one of the most important badges of honor in the hierarchy of the administration, must be re-examined … The conventional, strictly subdivided office building … sets in stone the hierarchical conditions existing at the planning stage, and by doing this contributes to further bureaucratization".[4] The Schnelles' method, while not always frictionless, was to integrate themselves into their client's corporate structure in order to devise spatial planning that would combine worker wellbeing with operational benefits – all derived from cybernetic analysis of worker functions within the organisation and their immediate needs. Although they consulted for some large international corporations establishing new bases in Germany, their Bürolandschaft projects would largely remain domestic.

Act 1: The golden age

Now, picture four figures – white men all under 50, some in their 20s – entering the stage: a student of architecture, a NASA engineer, and two management consultants. They are key protagonists in the evolution of the workplace that would unfold in the second half of the 20th century up until today; or, more precisely, they represent the constraints within which office life was and is still defined. Think of these men as designers, inventing new ways of (constantly) re-arranging the physical framework (and the philosophy) of the environment that's still inhabited on a daily basis by hundreds of millions. Their story, their style, unsurprisingly began during the peak of modernity and in the 'modernized' world: mid-century America and Europe.

Frank Duffy – early evangelist for the humane workplace and founder of the office consultancy industry

In 1963 Frank Duffy, a 23-year-old English student at the Architectural Association in London, went on a field trip to West Germany. He wanted to study the new wave of recently finished 'democratic' office buildings developed by the Schnelle brothers. Duffy shared his findings in *The Architecture Review* in 1964,[5] enthusiastically noting that the Bürolandschaft could accommodate change by simply moving furniture rather than removing, moving, or building new partition walls (not as easy as it's cracked up to be). He praised the "domestic character" of the spaces versus "inhuman" glass partition cells, and had high expectations of improved acoustics thanks to the low ceilings and carpeted floors.[6] Still, Duffy spotted teething problems, including shortfalls in the technical performance of the new offices, judging it too soon to fully assess their functioning. Duffy felt pity for the supervisors: "[T]he fact that they can be seen makes their subordinates want to unload more decisions on to them than they need to."[7] Duffy's overall impression was that, with a few small organisational adjustments and technological fixes, there would be no way back from life in the Bürolandschaft.

Duffy's visit to West Germany and his witnessing of the Bürolandscaft triggered a career dedicated to analyzing and prophesying the future of the office. While the theory of scientific management had a huge impact on working processes, the workspace itself – as architecture – had not been similarly theorized. Duffy saw an opportunity and became one of the key figures in the development of office consultancy in the second half of the 20th century, founding his own DEGW consultancy and publishing more than ten books, including *Planning Office Space* (1976), *The Responsible Workplace* (1993), *The New Office* (1997), and *Work and the City* (2008). The life of the Bürolandschaft, retrospectively praised by Duffy as "the office as a cybernetic device: an ever-changing, non-hierarchical, empirically accessible network of communications,"[8] proved to be less prosperous, replaced by a more generic arrangements of open and closed spaces on the office floor (see page 220).

Duffy also witnessed the rise of the cubicle in the late 60s. Locked in a curious dialectic with the open plan – enabled by it but fundamentally opposed to its very openness – the cubicle promised maximum, ruthless adaptability (their quantity easily growing or shrinking with staff numbers), while supposedly granting the solidity and dignity of an individual workspace, a personalized fort in the endless, anonymous prairie of the open plan. Yet, the cubicle quickly had the opposite affect, repeated *ad nauseum*, boxing out workers' sense of individuality and freedom (a situation critiqued by any number of movies and pop cultural references).

Duffy lamented such quick-fix spatial arrangements later in his career. He noted how the "deterioration" of (North American) office design could be traced to "a classic example of sub-optimization, i.e. too strong a focus on cost-cutting efficiency" that failed to stretch beyond "the narrow and the purely utilitarian."[9] Beyond the plethora of office designs Duffy advised on, his greater success was trailblazing the global industry of workspace consultants, who skillfully position themselves between corporations and architects.

Jack M. Nilles – WFH prophet who underplayed the social dimension of the office

In 1976, just over a decade after Duffy's initial foray inside the new office landscape, former NASA physicist Jack M. Nilles (47), who was a consultant to Presidents Kennedy and Johnson's Science Advisory Council and responsible for the preliminary design of several space vehicles and communications systems, was one of the first to issue a search warrant – if not a death warrant – for the office itself, cybernetic or otherwise. Within the context of increased awareness

notes

1. Systematic research on the historical development of the pre-modern offices is, accordingly, scarce; the most compelling account is Hans-Joachim Fritz's Menschen in *Büroarbeitsräumen* (Heinz Moos Verlag, Germany, 1982).
2. This was the architecture conceptualized retrospectively as the "Typical Plan" by Rem Koolhaas in *S,M,L,XL*: "[T]he utilitarian is refined as a sensuous science of coordination – column grids, facade modules, ceiling tiles, lighting fixtures, partitions, electrical outlets, flooring, furniture, color schemes, air-conditioning grills – that transcends the practical to emerge in a rarified existential domain of pure objectivity." Rem Koolhaas, Bruce Mau, *S,M,L,XL* (Monacelli Press, 1994) p.338.
3. *Architekt und Organisator* (Verlag Schnelle Quickborn, 1965), *Hierarchische Ordnung im Büro* (Verlag Schnelle Quickborn, 1965), *Entscheidung im Management* (Verlag Schnelle Quickborn, 1966).
4. Eberhard Schnelle, "Architekt und Organisator: Versuche zu einer komplexen Planungsmethodik" in: *Bauen + Wohnen*, 17 (1963) Heft 1. Translation by the author. "Die soziologischen Zusammenhänge, die das Einzelzimmer zu einem der wichtigsten Rangabzeichen der Verwaltungshierarchie machten, müssen durchleuchtet und in die Planung einbezogen werden. … Das herkömmliche, stark untergliederte Bürohaus ..] zementiert die zur Zeit der Planung vorgefundenen hierarchischen Verhältnisse und trägt damit zur Verbürokratisierung bei."
5. Francis Duffy, "Skill: Bürolandschaft," *The Architectural Review* 135, no. 804 (1964), p.148-54. Duffy notes the importance of this visit in the preface to his book *The Changing Workplace* (Phaidon, 1997).
6. Duffy (1964), p.148
7. Duffy (1964), p.154
8. Francis Duffy, "Niels Torp's contributions to office design and urbanism" in *Niels Torp* (Oslo, 2011), p.69
9. Francis Duffy. "The Key to Reinventing the Office," in Chris Grech and David Walters (eds.) *Future Office, design, practice and applied research* (Routledge, 2013). In the article, one of the last Duffy would publish, he examines the "sharp contradiction now existing between the vitality of new office technologies and processes and the inertia of those who design and supply office space." North American office design seems stuck, he says, in "in a cost-cutting time warp with the same stereotypical office design … replicated over and over again, only in cheaper, quicker and, … generally in ever nastier ways." As a way out, Duffy proposes more visionary longterm leadership: a "possible return to the kind of imaginative grasp of what architecture can achieve … depends absolutely upon the systematic measurement of office design against business goals that transcend the short term, the narrow and the purely utilitarian."

surrounding environmental degradation and finite resources – *Clean Air Act* of 1970, the Oil Crisis, the Club of Rome's *Limits to Growth* (1972) – Nilles' 1976 seminal study *The Telecommunications Transportation Tradeoff*, raised the question of whether offices needed to exist at all.[10] Nilles' study coined the terms telecommuting and tele-working and was developed with fellow researchers at the University of Southern California, who employed a barrage of statistics and calculations stacked with dollars, miles, bits and bauds, to convincingly project how a mixture of increased pollution, fuel prices, suburbanisation, and technological advances would inevitably lead to white collar workers working from home in the near future.

As Nilles conducted his research, with the development of the HTTP protocol underway and a worldwide communication data network was within reach, he drew inspiration from science fiction: a 1928 short story "The Machine Stops" by E.M. Forster, which predicted a future where humanity lives in the "Machine," an underground city with a voice-controlled communication network, videophones, central data storage, and high-speed printers. All this was necessary as life above ground had become impossible due to environmental degradation and the collapse of cities.[11]

Nilles analysed the financial and environmental costs and benefits of remote working. He compared the cost-energy ratio of an employee traveling across the US by Boeing 747 for a business meeting with a precursor to video conferencing (facilitated by infrared technology). The video meeting would be 95 times more efficient. Nilles suggested that, from a cost perspective, business travel would quickly become obsolete, consuming too much time and too many resources.

Nilles also surveyed groups of students in California working with an early interactive television system. Their positive feedback on the system, which integrated other functions like entertainment and government services, led Nilles to conclude that, socially, organisations would be perfectly able to survive without an office.

Here, with hindsight, Nilles overlooked the social considerations of office life. As various psychologists have determined since Nilles's study, our actual behavior is shaped more by desire than by rationality. Through the cracks of Nilles' determinism, the reasons why the office survived in the late 20th century – and persists post-pandemic – are clear, and evident in his own survey. The student subjects reported that they wanted to remain close to the campus so they could continue working together and hanging out. Nilles' engineering mindset underestimated that part of his equation.

Tom Peters and Robert H. Waterman Jr. – strategy consultants who celebrated people (well, staff) and helped create a new global corporate culture
1977: A year after the publication of Nilles' work, and following the economic downturn – the oil crisis, plus rising competition from Japan – two San Francisco-based partners in McKinsey, Tom Peters (35) and Robert Waterman Jr. (42) launched a project that would revolutionize management and revive their ailing consultancy firm.

Throughout the mid-20th century, McKinsey had been at the leading edge of a new class of companies full of the engineers and analysts who migrated from banks after the 1929 Wall Street crisis. Part of the US government's response to that crisis required banks to stick to their core task and divest from other activities, which it recognised had been the fuel for the collapse: a toxic collision of financial prowess and industrial knowledge inside a single company structure. The banks had to fire their corps of engineers and business analysts. This was the big bang moment for office consultancy: a profession geared to rationalizing the world's production by mastering efficiency and finding cost reduction – true Miesian corporate modernists. But after nearly 50 years of crafting the immaculate figure of *the man in the flannel suit* selling superior knowledge and fixing bleeding industries, by the mid-70s McKinsey found itself outsmarted by their competitor Booz Allen Hamilton, which had set up shop in Tokyo to learn from Japanese management, in vogue at the time for Americans.

So, in 1977, McKinsey's managing director Ron Daniel launched two projects. The first aimed at solving Business Strategy. This project was allocated to the best and brightest consultants at McKinsey's New York HQ. Little has been recorded about its long term impact. Peters and Waterman's project was the other one. They traveled the world, interrogating business leaders about their organisations. Their aim was to discover just how crucial people are to business success, and to release them from the "tyranny of the bean counters"[12] – the same bean counters McKinsey had previously helped install in countless companies under the earlier regime of efficiency. This radical change unleashed by McKinsey was the postmodern Pruitt-Igoe moment in corporate philosophy.

Peters and Waterman managed to convince the leadership of McKinsey that the company's future was not in optimizing machines and factories, but in optimizing people. Based on this conviction, the two partners developed McKinsey's famed 7S framework: an organization analysis tool focusing on the relationship between structure, strategy, systems, skills, style, staff, and superordinate goals (shared values).

With their 1982 best-selling book *In Search of Excellence*, Peters and Waterman evolved the 7S framework to encourage the development of soft skills, leadership courses, and a culture of training.[13]

McKinsey themselves embraced the approach which helped re-establish their place at the top of the consultancy world. From their perch, they would help shape the corporate world for the rest of the 20th century and beyond. The 7S framework, still in use today, attempts to move away from a fetish for execution towards a larger integrated strategic vision, a "constellation of interrelated factors that influence an organization's ability to change".[14] The first three S's devoted to "hard elements" (strategy, structure, systems) and four "soft elements" (shared values, skills, staff, and style) together created a new corporate culture. As all culture needs a stage, the architecture of the office was called upon to fulfill its goals and project its own importance. Without the office, no stage, and without a stage, no culture.

These four protagonists – Duffy, Nilles, Peters, and Waterman – started a drama that shaped 20th- and 21st-century office life. Consciously and unconsciously, they have defined our sense of place, of belonging, and spatial control in working life. Through his books and his consultancy for large companies over many decades, Duffy amplified the connections between architecture and organisational planning, showing how spatial planning can be used as a tool for organisational development across the globe. Nilles was the first to raise doubts about the office's effectiveness as a space, or the need to have an office at all, leading to regular obituaries for the office typology over the years, an uncertainty that

IN SEARCH OF EXCELLENCE, the 90-minute special based on the best-selling book by the same name written by Thomas J. Peters (l) and Robert H. Waterman, Jr. (r), returns for an encore presentation on public television. The film offers a fascinating tour behind the scenes of eight American businesses. PBS airdate: 9:00 p.m. ET, July 23. (Photo by Stember)

on Channel 3

Thomas J. Peters (1942-), Robert H. Waterman (1936-2022)

has blossomed during COVID-19. But McKinsey mobilized the inherent weakness that Nilles identified in the office – that we know it's all a bit of a performance, that it's a huge consumer of material resources – and used it as an argument for the ennoblement of the office as a stage from which to project (corporate) self-worth, while facilitating the often wrenching changes essential to profit.

Act 2: Tear it up and start again
This book seeks to document the evolution, metabolism, decay, maintenance, and sustainability – beyond carbon calculations – of office spaces born in the 'golden age' of Duffy, Nilles, Peters and Wasserman. What happened to their convictions? How have new ideas, and pragmatism (plain and simple), transformed the array of modern office-temples we survey in these pages?

As an effect of the perceived symbolic and functional importance of the office, in the following decades the stage filled with a growing number of (innovation) consultants, tech companies, interior designers and other strategists, and, to a much lesser degree, architects. Offices interiors churned as a result of rapid technological and economic convulsions – desktop computers, (early) internet, globalization. As staff numbers fluctuated and working methods changed, the cubicle, instead of sustaining – instead of being reuse in other configurations – became the most disposable of office furniture ever.

The drama devolved into a cyclical farce: a parade of brazen, suited (mostly) men alternately prophesize the abolishment of the office, or, with equal confidence, its necessity as a space in which corporate culture can coalesce. Workspace consultants suggest striking new concepts, typically oscillating between advocacy for the open plan and renewed faith in private cells. Open plans foster collaboration and creativity, we were told, while – confirmed in movie after movie – private cells are isolating and inhuman (and expensive).[15] Just as easily, other arguments can be mobilized for the reverse spatial configuration: open plan is distracting, crowded, stressful; private cells promote focus and productivity, and if handled correctly, can confer dignity on their occupants. If not an oscillation, hybrid configurations are suggested – a détente between the open and the closed – designed and installed.

The constant advice and the impulse for frequent change requires endless cycles of demolishing – or at best dismantling – and building afresh, promising the ever-new, continuously turning tons of valuable resources into waste. Since the mid-late 20th century, the office drama assumes that any office is in need of replacement: predictions of its obsolescence range between seven and 10 years.[16] For office consultants, the status quo of an office should never persist, because persistence is fundamentally unsellable. Charging a client for advice to simply leave everything as is, because it works, is impossible. The drama demands obstacles, upheaval, and apparent resolution, only to start over.

The drama has to suggest that the world is changing faster than ever, pushing endless cliffhangers. Godot can never arrive. Anti-clutter agendas require the removal of personal affects, plus objects considered obsolete. Libraries are replaced by library-styled wallpaper or zones for table football. Inevitable as a Nietzschean cycle of everlasting recurrence, these changes will be inverted too. There will be a point in time, maybe not far away, where a new generation will wonder what the beanbag room was all about. The drama operates regardless of direction, apart from suggesting that a new future is always lurking around the corner. Reflecting on the past – including learning from it – risks rejecting the notion of

---

10. Jack M. Niles, *The Telecommunication Transportation Tradeoff: Options for Tomorrow* (John Wiley and Sons, 1976)
11. "Imagine, if you can, a small room, hexagonal in shape, like the cell of a bee. It is lighted neither by window nor by lamp, yet it is filled with a soft radiance. There are no apertures for ventilation, yet the air is fresh. There are no musical instruments, and yet, at the moment that my meditation opens, this room is throbbing with melodious sounds. An armchair is in the centre, by its side a reading-desk – that is all the furniture. And in the armchair there sits a swaddled lump of flesh — a woman, about five feet high, with a face as white as a fungus. It is to her that the little room belongs." Opening paragraph of The Machine Stops, first published in The Oxford and Cambridge Review in November 1909, and later included in Forster's *The Eternal Moment* (Sidgwick & Johnson, 1928 London). The story's influence can arguably be seen on George Orwell's *Nineteen Eighty-Four*, but also Ray Bradbury's *Fahrenheit 451*, and Charlie Brooker's *Black Mirror*. A full version of the text can be found on Project Gutenberg: (https://www.cs.ucdavis.edu/~koehl/Teaching/ECS188/PDF_files/Machine_stops.pdf).
12. Tom Peters, "Tom Peters's True Confessions," *Fastcompany.com*, November 30, 2001 (https://www.fastcompany.com/44077/tom-peterss-true-confessions)
13. Tom Peters and Robert H. Waterman, Jr. *In Search of Excellence* (HarperCollins, 1982)
14. Tom Peters, "The Planning Fetish" op-ed in *The Manager's Journal Wall Street Journal* (July 7 1980). On its website McKinsey still promotes the use and relevance of the 7S system: https://www.mckinsey.com/business-functions/strategy-and-corporate-finance/our-insights/enduring-ideas-the-7-s-framework.
15. Films like Billy Wilder's *The Apartment* (1960), Jacques Tati's *Playtime* (1967), or more recent movies like the Mike Judge's *Office Space* (1999) and Alexander Payne's *About Schmidt* (2002), amongst many others express the monotony and drudgery of the modern office.
16. Seven years has been suggested to the authors in various conversations with industry representatives, mostly from office spatial consultancy and furniture companies. Knoll is one of the few companies who have published about it, in: "Shaping the Dynamic Workplace" (2013), http://www.knoll.com/knollnewsdetail/shaping-the-dynamic-workplace.
17. Based on a survey of the first edition of Ernst Neufert's *Bauentwurfslehre* (1936), the oldest modern guide for standard measurements of architectural elements, with its most recent edition – the 42nd – published in 2019, in which the advised length of a standard desk increased from 156cm to 160cm.
18. Reliable historical research is largely lacking here, but early guides like Neufert's *Bauentwurfslehre*, different international standards, and more recent office planning guides made by office furniture makers and planning agencies show a pattern of shrinkage, mostly in what is already considered minimum standards. More about this development can be found in the executive summary (p.486).

progress. The undecidedness that the future suggests is infinitely more attractive than present reality, history, decay, and details. With eyes fixed forward, the past is mostly a drag, laden with moralism, something to shed. The cult of disruption demands not only that we ignore the past but that we destroy it, in stark opposition to the lifespan of building materials, which can, with proper maintenance and repair, last thousands of years.

The drama hides the fact that the wrenching physical and ideological changes forced on offices perhaps didn't produce the revolutionary affects they claimed, or that they had ulterior motives. Yes, since the days of Duffy and the others, the typewriters are gone, and most of the desktop PCs too, but looking at building standards we see our desks only grew by four centimeters in 70 years.[17] The one thing that shows significant and linear development is the shrinking average floor space per employee, from an estimated 18 square meters in the pre-war single cell office down to a minimum of seven square meters per person.[18] The shrinkage answers to an ultimate motive for most involved in the sector: reducing costs – a structural imperative that no amount of bean bags can cover.

Act 3: We have a choice
Does COVID-19 finally end our drama – proving one side right? Will climate collapse quickly render the drama irrelevant? Is the scarcity of resources influencing the speed of our movements? Or will the show lumber on regardless? A continuation of working from home with some organised moments of interaction? In the wake of the pandemic, real estate brokers immediately prophesied a great bounce back, convinced that the shock-moment - a great reset- in which suddenly new opportunities and directions emerged wouldn't last. Once the theatre opens again, the play will proceed as was. It has to. The typical mingling, wheeling and dealing at Cologne's Orgatec office fair, the Salone del Mobile in Milan, and the luxury real estate brokering at MIPIM in Cannes, all unbearable screen experiences during COVID-19, are making slow steps towards the stage again, determined to resurrect business as usual.

But what show to put on now? Do we have a choice? Subtle, indirect affects are emerging. The office is dressed down further. The power suits on Wall Street are gone – the writing on the wall that management is giving up on its self-created elite image? Real estate holders with less bluster are anxiously exploring building conversion scenarios – from commercial to residential. At the time of writing, it is clear that management is not fully convinced of the first steps back to the office. Office workers have become appreciative of the perks working from home brings. Less commuting, more family presence, more time for small domestic chores during breaks. But they miss some of the social – and status – perks of the office. Affirmation, collaboration, artisan coffee, connection to the outside world. And management itself enjoys the cost-saving of reduced office space. 'Blended' is the new corporate-speak for the emerging regime: WHF + occasional IRL.

This book does not seek to answer the question of whether the future needs offices, nor does it settle, once and for all, the superiority of open plan over cubicles. What it does seek to do is decipher the factors at play when a classic modern office space manages to endure the decades, and the factors that lead to the erasure of the qualities once held by those spaces. What is blatantly clear is that the most sustainable possible thing is to reuse offices buildings – through maintenance, careful adaptation, and reprogramming if necessary – rather than constantly gutting, demolishing, and rebuilding them. Sustainable not only for the planet, but often for the healthy functioning of culture, and capital.

We are slowly realising that our habits cannot last. How much unnecessary pollution and waste is created by runaway office mutations? And what can architects, clients and office workers do about it? What if we don't answer to the market first, but to the environment? Circular design hopes to mitigate the pollution belched out by the office drama, while retaining the possibility for cyclical change. But the intricacy needed to maintain circularity requires a radically new skill set and choreography between different agents for which we have not trained: not as designers, not as researchers, nor as clients and users. While we are eager to learn, or unlearn, what emerges from this research is that we can slow down our cycles.

This book is a simultaneously simple and complex exercise of consciously observing what was, what changed, and figuring out what function(ed), what didn't, why, and how smartly or otherwise it was changed. It celebrates how personalities were able to shape futures: clients, architects, and real estate managers. For architects it shows longitudinal evidence of what most already knew: attention matters, personality matters. For clients it shows that both don't necessarily come at great expense. This book poses a challenge: to confront and build on the past, rather than fixate on the open-endedness of the future. We need to cut our addiction to changing carpet colors and cycling through philosophies of work & space every season and think in new, longer cycles, because paraphrasing Richard Feynman: nature will not be fooled. We only have one planet.

Well? Shall we go? Yes, let's go.
—Samuel Beckett's *Waiting for Godot*, 1952

Ruth Baumeister, Stephan Petermann
Spring 2022

MODERN
OFFICE
BUILDINGS
MICHAEL ROSENAUER,

Bürobauten
Schulze · Krause

the new office
FRANCIS DUFFY

In Search of
EXCELLENCE
Lessons from America's Best-Run Companies
Thomas J. Peters and Robert H. Waterman Jr.

Imma Forino
Uffici
Interni arredi oggetti
Piccola Biblioteca Einaudi

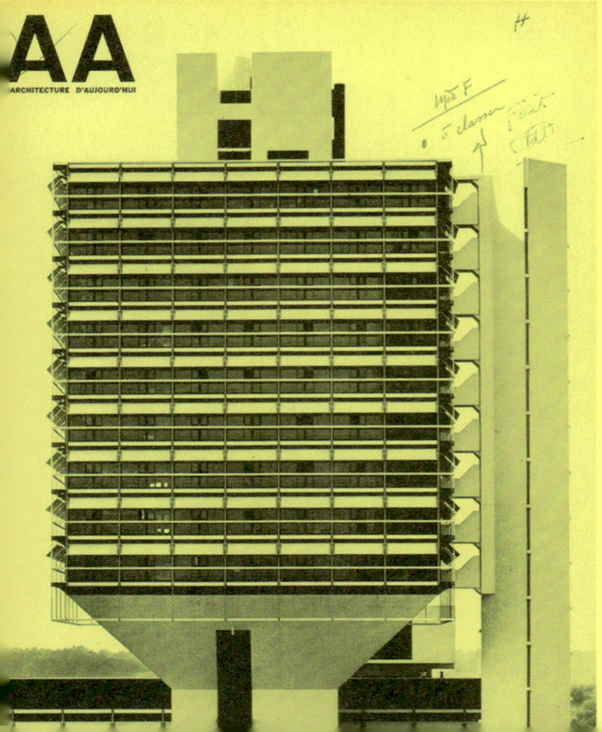
AA
ARCHITECTURE D'AUJOURD'HUI

Reinhold Hohl
Office Buildings
An International Survey

THE WHY, HOW, WHAT OF THIS BOOK

What is this book about?
This book looks at the lives of office buildings after they have been inaugurated. What is presented here can be read as a post-occupancy report, but it also tries to go beyond that. It looks at a multitude of cases within a single typology spread out over different areas in the world across different moments in time. The case studies share a common denominator: many of them are considered modernist classics, from the 'golden age' of the office; all of them were in some way once considered innovative examples to follow.

Why this book?
The work on this book was triggered by a shared concern about the limited use of knowledge gained in historical research to inform design practice. A survey of studies about the workplace, authored by architectural peers and those closely linked to workspace development like real estate managers, furniture designers, tech developers, and office consultants was emblematic of history's absence in the future of the office.[1] The current position of office consultancy perhaps even prevents a historic perspective, as the parties involved are expected (and paid) to come up with something new.

The studies were replete with clichés about generational differences in approaches to work, global change in workforce habits, and desperate calls for increased collaboration on the work floor, while carefully integrating management speak and avoiding specificity. The studies were sometimes data-driven, some with and others without sourcing: average square meters per worker, desk occupancy rates, even ideal office temperatures and how they affect productivity (1-2 percent for every degree higher or lower than 21.6 °C).[2]

But what became obvious were methodological and sourcing challenges in office research: vested industry interests and the inherent privacy of the corporate office make it difficult to gather longitudinal, reliable data. Research results that might point to anything other than increasing turnover would be automatically set aside. Looking towards academia also revealed methodologically-challenged forms of research, especially towards the 'soft' sides of office life, for instance in applied social science research determining the value of different colors in terms of promoting creativity on the work floor.[3] Questions of sustainability were reduced to climate control, material passes, and a building's initial carbon footprint at best. All the studies lacked mechanisms for learning from built results, and culminated in relatively similar generic design proposals.

The term 'sustainability' has, rather predictably, been hijacked by those with an interest in maintaining business-as-usual, and can now mean almost anything. Developers can claim it is "sustainable" to demolish an office building entirely and build a new one from scratch because the new one will use less heating and A/C (never mind the massive amounts of embodied carbon expended in the process, and the deeper ecological impact of all the demolition waste and all the resource extraction for the new materials). With IPCC reports becoming increasingly alarming, it's clear that sustainability, as it's currently conceived and practices, isn't sustainable. It's not enough. Looking at the relentless churn of office buildings and interiors in this book, we hit upon another goal: sustain. We ditched the discredited adjective and went with the verb, since everything is a process and nothing can be confidently declared as 'sustainable.' We mean 'sustain' in the sense of endure. But this does not mean 'stay the same'; sustain encompasses the ability to evolve and adapt – to metabolize over the decades. So: what has lasted in office buildings, how, and why? This was one of our guiding lights throughout the research for this book.

What does post-occupancy mean?
Post-occupancy reporting is not new, but its systematic use remains relatively limited in architecture, especially in Europe.[4] Architects typically understand their work to be finished once the building is inaugurated. Post-occupancy research is widely used in the fields of engineering and social science but is typically perceived as something outside the architects's domain. Within architectural discourse, the study of the life of buildings has either concentrated on documenting individual cases or focused on a more symbolic interpretation of life aimed at developing design strategies. Within the latter, Christian Norberg Schulz's *Genius-Loci*, Aldo Rossi's explorations of historical layering in *The Architecture of the City* (1966), or Eisenmanian palimpsests, share a concern for buildings over time, but fail to go beyond their design idiosyncrasies.[6] Interest in user participation and everyday life led to excavating theories of the 1960s, by Jane Jacobs, George Perec, Team 10, Independent Group, among others. They largely focus on surveys and interviews of potential future users, instead of investigating the buildings themselves, the traces of use, or those who maintain and develop the buildings over time.[6]

It took non-architect Stewart Brand in his seminal *How Buildings Learn* to draw attention to the life of buildings. His work however remains mostly anecdotal and non-systematic, focusing on a variety of building types and documentation forms. It is driven by the author's personal preferences and lacks an analytical eye for architectural quality or thorough critical inquiry.

A 2019 article in *Metropolis* by Lance Hosey suggests that the main reason for the absence of lifetime analysis and post-occupancy studies is because there is no market for it.[7] Owners don't want to pay for them and neither would architects, for fear of exposing shortcomings. The author quotes Z. Smith, a sustainability expert at Eskew+Dumez+Ripple: "As my mom used to say, 'If you look behind the refrigerator, you'll be compelled to clean it.' The fact that positive stories also come to light is often neglected."[8] This was also something Frank Duffy finally realized towards the end of his career in office consultancy: "To invent the future we need to escape from the past and yet paradoxically to escape from the past we have to engage with history to understand it as fully as possible. We need to deploy critical intelligence to understand why office work and the office as a building type developed the way they did, distinguishing between futures that may continue to be valid and those that appear to be rapidly becoming redundant, irrelevant and even downright dangerous. Architects in particular, if we are to be free to invent, need to know where existing office typologies came from, how they have developed and why so many features of conventional office environments are becoming inadequate, dysfunctional and divorced from emerging modes of living and working."[9]

This book attempts to do just that.

How was this book conceived?
In the fall of 2016, the Aarhus School of Architecture hosted their annual start-up workshop for masters' students. Working with 200 students over 10 days, the authors – together with additional teaching staff from the school and external experts – opened a temporary workspace consultancy called *Scrupulous*. Housed in an abandoned warehouse in the city's harbor, *Scrupulous* was organized into 10 departments looking at different elements of the history of offices. Twenty students focused on the aging of office buildings and were tasked with finding out what happened to roughly 50 pre-selected, once historically relevant offices buildings. A follow-up studio was organized in collaboration with the Knowlton School of Architecture in Ohio in 2017, looking at US projects. Finally, a 2020 studio with Waseda University in Tokyo looked at Japanese case studies. These workshops laid the groundwork for the case studies featured in this book. The first milestone of the research was exhibited as a prototype of this book at the 2019 Oslo Architecture Triennale, *The Architecture of Degrowth*. Along the way a number of experts on specfic cases were identified and asked to contribute as well.

Why the emphasis on photos?
The invention of photography dramatically changed how we perceive, represent, and share our built environment. And yet, how photographs inform research in architecture history has gained little attention, with images mainly understood as a means to illustrate text. Most often, buildings are documented at their inauguration, their users waiting in the wings. Today, within a social media culture, the focus is on the new and just-released, rather than paying attention to ongoing inhabitation. Such processes create idealized images of buildings which endure and subsequently become a source of reference and inspiration, even though they have little or nothing to do with the actual performance of a building and the way people use it. This book seeks to challenge conventional modes in historiography,

1928

Gospom
Freedom Square
Kharkiv, Ukraine
Serafimov, Kravets & Felger

1936

Casa del Fascio
Piazza del Popolo 4
Como, Italy
Giuseppe Terragni

1937

Tsentrosoyuz building
Myasnitskaya Ulitsa, 39
Moscow, Russia
Le Corbusier

1956

GM Warren
Technical Center
GM Tech Center Rd
Warren, Michigan, US
Eero Saarinen

notes

1. Twelve future workplace reports studied in 2015 included publicly accessible publications by CISCO, IBM, Accenture, Gensler, HOK, Aecom, JLL, CoreNET, Knoll, and Steelcase, to represent the mainstream thinking in office consultancy. JLL, *Forget the Workplace for now…* (2014); Leesman, *High Performance Workplace* (2014) CISCO, *Cisco Smart+Connected Spaces* (2014); Accenture, *Workplace Transformation Services* (2013) CURE Columbia, *Work and Workplaces in the Digital City* (2013); Gensler, *2013 U.S. Workplace Survey* (2013); HOK, *Workplace Strategies that Enhance Human Performance, Health and Wellness* (2013) Aecom, *Strategy Annual Plus* (2012); CoreNET Global, *Corporate Real Estate 2020* (2012); Knoll, *Shaping the Dynamic Workplace* (2011) Steelcase, *Workplace Case studies* (2011) IBM, *The new collaboration: enabling innovation, changing the workplace* (2009).
2. HOK, *Workplace Strategies that Enhance Human Performance, Health and Wellness* (2013), online PDF p.3
3. See: Iris Bakker, "Maakt het uit of een vergaderzaal rood of blauw is?" (Does it matter if a meeting room is red or blue?, 2011), available in TU Delft library. While the work deserves credit and attention, the simplifications of actual life and the inhibited biases in finding out average conditions leaves us skeptical about the results.
4. The American Institute of Architects' *AIA journal* briefly had a section in the early 70s featuring monthly "evaluations". This started in 1976, and lasted until the end of 1978. No reason is given for its discontinuation.
5. Christian Norberg-Schulz, *Genius Loci: Towards a Phenomenology of Architecture* (Academy Editions, 1979); Aldo Rossi, *The Architecture of the City* (MIT Press, 1982; original in Italian published in 1966); Peter Eisenman, *Eisenman Inside Out: Selected Writings, 1963-1988* (Yale University Press, 2004).
6. The adaptation of buildings over time played an important part in early building conservation theory and history, with extensive documentation on specific monumental buildings. Lacking a shared framework, their significance remains limited to historical documentation. Their work doesn't necessarily require them to learn from them for future development.
7. Steward Brand, *How Buildings Learn What Happens After They're Built* (Phoenix Illustrated, 1995)
8. Brand acknowledges this in the book. More reflections on Brand's work can be found in the final part of this book's executive summary.
9. Lance Hosey, "Going Beyond the Punchlist: Why Architects Should Embrace Post-Occupancy Evaluations" February 6 2019, on *metropolismag.com* https://metropolismag.com/viewpoints/architecture-post-occupancy-evaluations/

attempting to show how designs performed and sustained over time. To catch the process of a building's aging, rather than its birth, we work with comparative analysis: iconic photographs of buildings at time of inauguration are reconstructed today in exactly the same frame. While this before-and-after concept is highly staged – almost a performance – unlike their historical counterparts, the contents of the contemporary photographs are entirely 'natural.' Whatever happens to be in that historical frame that we are replicating is fair game. These images allow multiple readings of success and failure, ranging from the performance and adaptation of the architectural composition, to the materials and the structure, through the behavior of the building's users.

What do you mean with iconic and revolutionary?
The late 1950s and 1960s saw the publication of Micheal Rosenauer's *Modern Office Buildings* (1955), Jürgen Joedicke's *Bürobauten* (1959), and Reinhold Hohl's *Office Buildings* (1968), which focused solely on showing exemplary office buildings. Together with office buildings celebrated in prominent architecture magazines, they were foundational sources for this research.[11] The cases were selected for analysis because they were considered revolutionary, e.g. for their construction method, their sublime detailing, their compositional set-up, their symbolic value. The selection is by no means exclusive and is meant to be understood as open ended. This work is a starting point for a broader and deeper evaluation of how buildings change and why; proving it is possible to study offices over time, hoping others can follow and critically engage with our findings.

We also recognize a marked deviation in the lives of many of our selected offices compared to the overall narrative of how 'standard' offices are supposed to change over time according to office consultancy thinking. Our case studies are not representative of offices as a whole – they are extraordinary buildings, gems of modernism. They are not generic, though they are inspirational. What happens in them isn't what happens in offices generally. Yet they provide us with longitudinal evidence that gives space to elaborate office thinking in general.

The projects are shown in chronological order of their completion date. In some cases due to their unique historical circumstances, these dates are unclear or still a matter of discussion. The names of several buildings also changed over time: we used the name most recognizable to a current audience.

What is not in the book?
Where our initial research started with a mostly western-oriented history – following the geography, politics, and economics of the office typology's development – we tried to expand our list by including Russia, Africa, Asia, and South-America. COVID-19 made some of these ambitions impossible due to difficulty traveling and accessing offices. The book covers several non-Western examples, but not as many as we wanted.

Our wish-list was further whittled down by the availability of historical interior photography of projects. Our research revealed that despite lively debate and reporting on offices specifically in pre-war (architecture) magazines, their attention focused mainly on the external appearance of the office building and much less on plans or interiors.[12]

Gaining access to buildings proved to be challenging. Most requests were greeted with reservation, sometimes hostility. This book is a product of nagging and persistent door-

1957

Connecticut General Life Insurance Company HQ
900 Cottage Grove Rd
Bloomfield, Connecticut, US
SOM

1958

l'Hôtel de Ville
1517 Pl. de l'Hôtel de ville
Le Havre, France
Auguste Perret

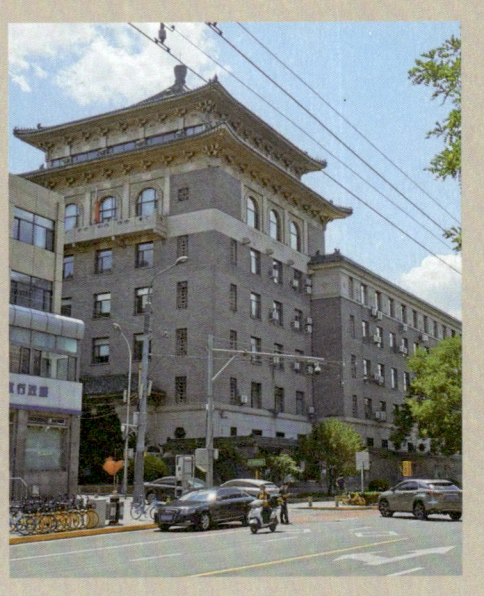

1958

Four Departments and One Meeting office
38 Yuetan South St
Xicheng District, Beijing
Zhang Kaiji

10. Frank Duffy, *Work and the City* (Black dog, 2008) p.8
11. Igea Troiani, Suzanne Ewing's *Visual Research Methods in Architecture* (Intellect Books, 2021) attempts to fill this gap by reviewing research practices traversing design and the humanities, focusing on drawings, diagrams, photographs, film, and new media.
12. Rosenauer, M. (1955). *Modern office buildings*. London: Batsford. Manasseh, L., & Cunliffe, R. (1962). *Office buildings*. New York: Reinhold Pub. Corp. Schulze, S., & Krause, C. (1967). *Bürobauten*. Stuttgart: K. Krämer. Hohl, R. (1968). *Office buildings: An international survey*. New York: Praeger. Gottschalk, O. (1968). *Flexible Verwaltungsbauten; Planung, Funktion, Flächen, Ausbau, Einrichtung, Kosten, Beispiele*. Quickborn: Schnelle.
13. The gradual shift in the representation of office spaces in architecture books and magazine moving from exteriors to interiors is discussed in the text chapter of Oscar Niemeyer's Communist HQ in Paris (p.380).

knocking. It took six weeks to get into the first case we documented, the Bürolandschaft at Bertelsmann. In the case of City (Uni-) Hochaus Leipzig, built in the former GDR, countless requests over several were turned down by the owner, an investment firm. Lloyds of London proved to be impenetrable. The same holds true for Oscar Niemeyer's office buildings in Brazil, Soviet-period buildings in Russia, and Chinese offices. Political circumstances also proved to be a challenge. Le Corbusier's Centrosoyuz in Moscow is now used by the Russian state security agency FSB. Some of the owners also expressed concerns that the exposure of their buildings could lead to them being landmarked and consequently restrict what they can do to them.

What's the take-away from this book?

Each case study can stand on its own, but readers are invited to a concerto, or to connect some of the dots. The book does not require one direction of looking or reading; it can easily be browsed. The more research we did, the more we became aware of parallels and rhythms between cases which over time became harder to ignore. We have condensed our findings into an executive summary in the back of this book where we try to gather and interpret the 'as found' conditions.

1964

The Economist Building
25 St. James's Street
City of Westminster, London, UK
Alison and Peter Smithson

1970

Itamaraty Palace
Zona Cívico-Administrativa BL H
Brasília, Brasil
Oscar Niemeyer

INFOGRAPHICS

1895 Reliance Building Burnham and Root	**1924 Chilehaus** Höger	**1925 Tribune Tower** Howells and Hood	**1935 Kirovsky District Town Hall** Trotsky	**1938 Palazzo Montecatini** Ponti
1956 National Pensions Institute Aalto	**1958 Van Leer Headquarters** Breuer	**1958 Inland Steel Building** Skidmore, Owings & Merril	**1958 Seagram Building** Mies van der Rohe	**1958 Kagawa Prefectural Office** Tange
1962 Tomado House Maaskant	**1962 Home Federal Savings and Loan** Mies van der Rohe	**1962 Enso-Gutzeit Headquarters** Aalto	**1962 Bank Melli University Branch** Utzon	**1962 Bacardi Headquarters** Mies van der Rohe
1966 Finnland Haus Hentrich, Petschnigg & Partners	**1966 Osram Administration Building** Henn	**1966 Meguro City Hall** Murano	**1967 Ford Foundation** Roche and Dinkeloo	**1967 Shizuoka Press Center** Tange
1978 Danmarks Nationalbank Jacobsen	**1982 Pendorp** Bonnema	**1985 HSBC** Foster + Partners	**1987 SAS Frösundavik Office Building** Torp	**1989 Grande Arche** Von Spreckelsen and Andreu

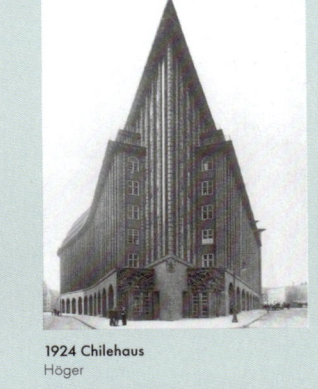

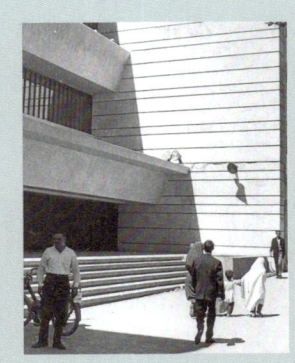

20

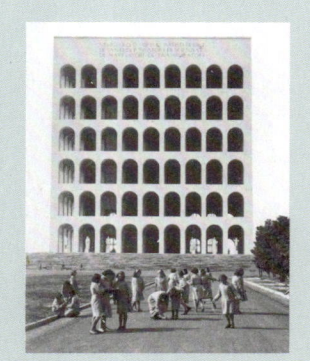

1940 Palazzo della Civiltà Italiana
Guerrini, La Padula and Romano

1941 Aarhus City Hall
Jacobsen and Møller

1953 Secretariat Building
Jeanneret and Le Corbusier

1955 Rautatalo
Aalto

1956 Price Tower
Wright

1960 Pirelli Tower
Ponti

1960 Nestlé Headquarters
Tschumi

1960 Pepsicola Headquarters
Skidmore, Owings & Merril

1961 Buch und Ton
Schnelle

1962 Bell Labs Holmdel Complex
Saarinen

1964 Unilever Headquarters
Hentrich, Petschnigg & Partners

1964 Johnson Wax Headquarters Europe
Maaskant

1964 Erieview Tower
Harrisson and Abramovitz

1964 John Deere Headquarters
Saarinen

1966 Palaceside Building
Sekkei and Hayashi

1971 Communist Party Headquarters
Niemeyer

1972 Centraal Beheer
Hertzberger

1973 Uni-Hochhaus
Henselmann

1973 Chicago Federal Center
Mies van der Rohe

1974 BMW Headquarters
Schwanzer

1991 Delftse Poort
Bonnema

46 ONCE REVOLUTIONARY AND ICONIC OFFICE BUILDINGS...

21

1895 Reliance Building
Burnham and Root

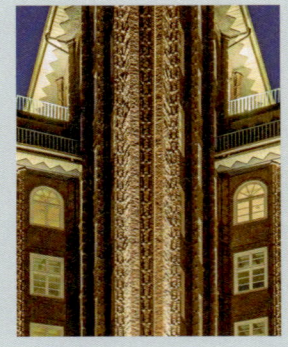

1924 Chilehaus
Höger

1925 Tribune Tower
Howells and Hood

1935 Kirovsky District Town Hall
Trotsky

1938 Palazzo Montecatini
Ponti

1956 National Pensions Institute
Aalto

1958 Van Leer Headquarters
Breuer

1958 Inland Steel Building
Skidmore, Owings & Merril

1958 Seagram Building
Mies van der Rohe

1958 Kagawa Prefectural Office
Tange

1962 Tomado House
Maaskant

1962 Home Federal Savings and Loan
Mies van der Rohe

1962 Enso-Gutzeit Headquarters
Aalto

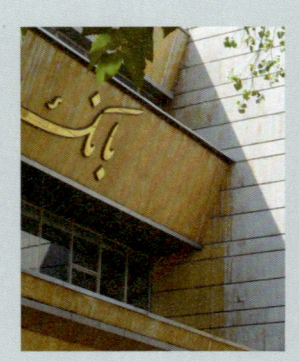

1962 Bank Melli University Branch
Utzon

1962 Bacardi Headquarters
Mies van der Rohe

1966 Finnland Haus
Hentrich, Petschnigg & Partners

1966 Osram Administration Building
Henn

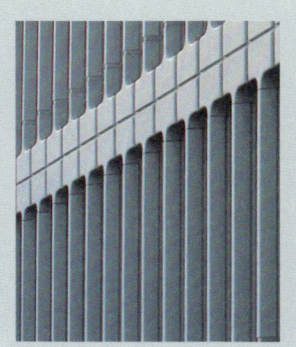

1966 Meguro City Hall
Murano

1967 Ford Foundation
Roche and Dinkeloo

1967 Shizuoka Press Center
Tange

1978 Danmarks Nationalbank
Jacobsen

1982 Pendorp
Bonnema

1985 HSBC
Foster + Partners

1987 SAS Frösundavik Office Building
Torp

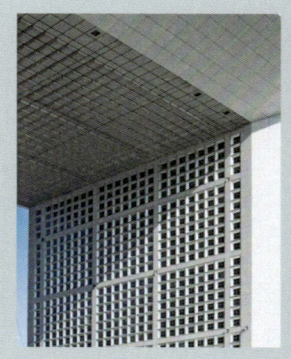

1989 Grande Arche
Von Spreckelsen and Andreu

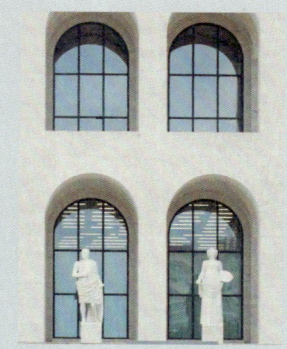

1940 Palazzo della Civiltà Italiana
Guerrini, La Padula and Romano

1941 Aarhus City Hall
Jacobsen and Møller

1953 Secretariat Building
Jeanneret and Le Corbusier

1955 Rautatalo
Aalto

1956 Price Tower
Wright

1960 Pirelli Tower
Ponti

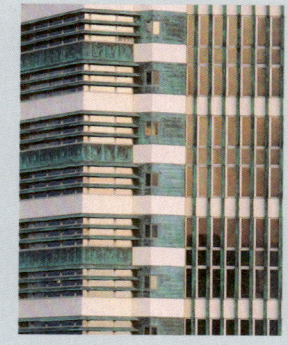

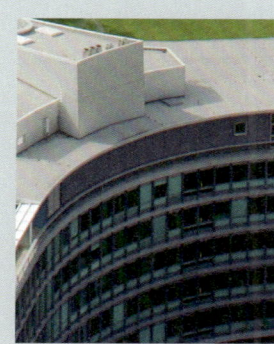

1960 Nestlé Headquarters
Tschumi

1960 Pepsicola Headquarters
Skidmore, Owings & Merril

1961 Buch und Ton
Schnelle

1962 Bell Labs Holmdel Complex
Saarinen

1964 Unilever Headquarters
Hentrich, Petschnigg & Partners

1964 Johnson Wax Headquarters Europe
Maaskant

1964 Erieview Tower
Harrisson and Abramovitz

1964 John Deere Headquarters
Saarinen

1966 Palaceside Building
Sekkei and Hayashi

1971 Communist Party Headquarters
Niemeyer

1972 Centraal Beheer
Hertzberger

1973 Uni-Hochhaus
Henselmann

1973 Chicago Federal Center
Mies van der Rohe

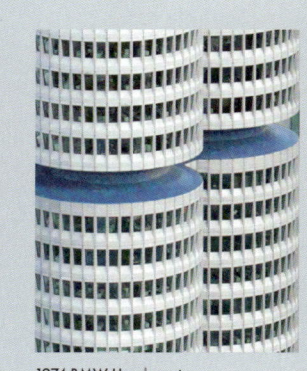

1974 BMW Headquarters
Schwanzer

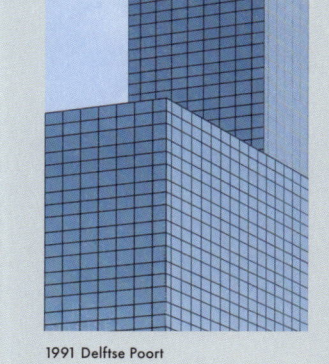

...AND WHAT IS LEFT OF THEM.

1991 Delftse Poort
Bonnema

North America:
1895 Reliance Building, Chicago (IL)
1925 Tribune Tower, Chicago (IL)
1956 Price Tower, Bartlesville (OK)
1958 Inland Steel Building, Chicago (IL)
1958 Seagram Building, New York (NY)
1960 Pepsi-Cola Headquarters, New York (NY)
1962 Bell Labs Holmdel Complex, Holmdel (NJ)
1962 Home Federal Savings and Loan, Des Moines (IA)
1964 Erieview Tower, Cleveland (OH)
1964 John Deere Headquarters, Moline (IL)
1967 Ford Foundation, New York (NY)
1973 Chicago Federal Center, Chicago (IL)

Middle America:
1962 Bacardi Headquarters, Tultitlán (MEX)

Europe:
1924 Chilehaus, Hamburg (DE)
1938 Palazzo Montecatini, Milan (IT)
1940 Palazzo della Civiltà Italiana, Rome
1941 Aarhus City Hall, Aarhus (DK)
1955 Rautatalo, Helsinki (FI)
1956 National Pensions Institute, Helsinki (FI)
1958 Van Leer Headquarters, Amstelveen (NL)
1960 Pirelli Tower, Milan (IT)
1960 Nestle Headquarters, Vevey (CH)
1961 Buch und Ton, Gütersloh (DE)
1962 Tomado House, Dordrecht (NL)
1962 Enso-Gutzeit Headquarters, Helsinki (FI)
1964 Unilever Headquarters, Hamburg (DE)
1964 Johnson Wax HQ's Europe, Mijdrecht (NL)
1966 Finnland Haus, Hamburg (DE)
1966 Osram Administration Building, Munich (DE)
1971 Communist Party Headquarters, Paris (FR)
1972 Centraal Beheer, Apeldoorn (NL)
1973 Uni-Hochhaus, Leipzig (DE)
1974 BMW Headquarters, Munich (DE)
1987 Danmarks Nationalbank, Copenhagen (DK)
1982 Pendorp, Alkmaar (NL)
1987 SAS Frösundavik Office Building, Solna (SE)
1989 Grande Arche, Paris (FR)
1991 Delftse Poort, Rotterdam (NL)

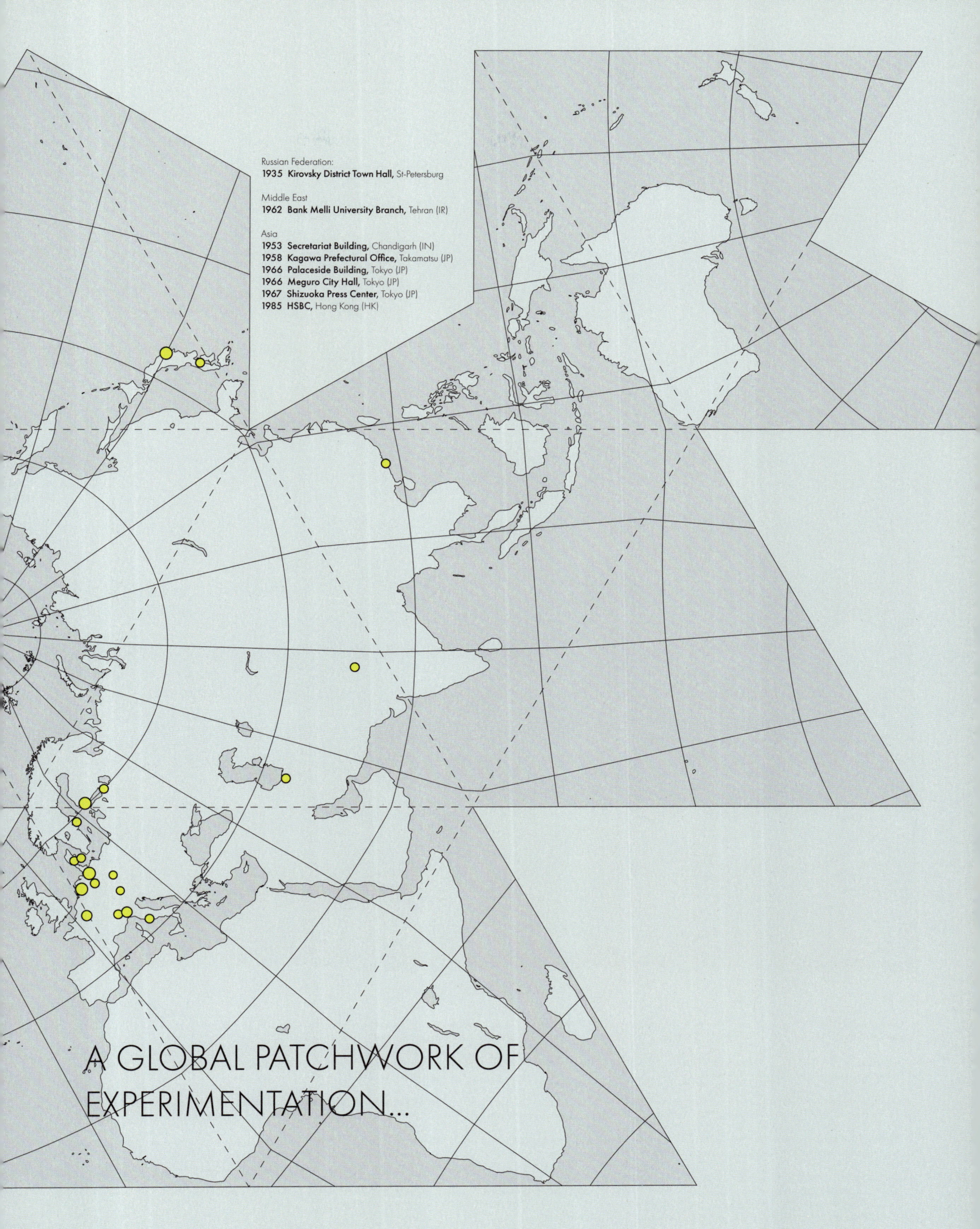

Russian Federation:
1935 Kirovsky District Town Hall, St-Petersburg

Middle East
1962 Bank Melli University Branch, Tehran (IR)

Asia
1953 Secretariat Building, Chandigarh (IN)
1958 Kagawa Prefectural Office, Takamatsu (JP)
1966 Palaceside Building, Tokyo (JP)
1966 Meguro City Hall, Tokyo (JP)
1967 Shizuoka Press Center, Tokyo (JP)
1985 HSBC, Hong Kong (HK)

A GLOBAL PATCHWORK OF EXPERIMENTATION...

...BY ARCHITECTS...

1. **Abe Bonnema (1926–2001)** Pendorp, Delftse Poort | 2. **Wallace Harrison (1895–1981)** Erieview Tower | 3. **Johan Otto von Spreckelsen (1929–1987)** Grande Arche
4. **Karl Schwanzer (1918–1975)** BMW Headquarters | 5. **Norman Foster (1935–)** HSBC | 6. **Ludwig Mies van der Rohe (1886–1969)** Chicago Federal Center
7. **Paul Andreu (1938–2018)** Grande Arche | 8. **Jean Tschumi (1904–1962)** Nestlé Headquarters | 9. **Jørn Utzon (1918–2008)** Bank Melli University Branch | 10. **Bruce Graham (1925–2010)** Inland Steel Building
11. **Hubert Petschnigg (1913–1997)** & 12.**Helmut Hentrich (1905–2001)** Unilever Headquarters, Finnland Haus | 13. **Kevin Roche (1922–2019)** Ford Foundation, Bell Labs Holmdel Complex
14. **Charles B. Atwood (?–1894)** Reliance Building | 15. **Alvar Aalto (1898–1976)** Rautatalo, National Pensions Institute | 16. **Max Abramovitz (1908–2004)** Erieview Tower | 17. **Eero Saarinen (1910–1961)** Bell Labs Holmdel Complex | 18. **Arne Jacobsen (1902–1971)** Aarhus City Hall | 19. **Johann Friedrich Höger (1877–1949)** Chilehaus | 20. **Shoji Hayashi (1928–2011)** Palaceside Building
21. **Daniel Hudson Burnham (1846–1912)** Reliance Building | 22. **John Mead Howells (1868–1959)** Tribune Tower | 23. **Huig Maaskant (1907–1977)** Tomadohuis, Johnson Wax Headquarters Europe
24. **Marcel Breuer (1902–1981)** Van Leer Headquarters | 25. **Hermann Henselmann (1905–1995)** Uni-Hochhaus | 26.**Herman Hertzberger (1932–)** Centraal Beheer
27. **Gio Ponti (1891–1979)** Palazzo Montecatini | 28. **Erik Møller (1909–2002)** Aarhus City Hall | 29. **Noy Abramovich Trotsky (1895–1940)** Kirovsky District Town Hall
30. **Ernesto La Padula (1902–1968)** Palazzo della Civiltà Italiana | 31. **Togo Murano (1891–1984)** Meguro City Hall | 32. **John Dinkeloo (1918–1981)** Ford Foundation, Bell Labs Holmdel Complex
33. **Le Corbusier (1887–1965)** Secretariat Building | 34. **Frank Lloyd Wright (1867–1959)** Price Tower | 35. **Raymond Hood (1881–1934)** Tribune Tower
36. **Pierre Jeanneret (1896–1967)** Secretariat Building | 37. **Kenzo Tange (1913–2005)** Kagawa Prefectural Office, Shizuoka Press and Broadcasting center
38. **Giovanni Guerrini (1887–1972)** Palazzo della Civiltà Italiana | 39. **Walter Henn (1912–2006)** Osram Administration Building | 40. **Walter Netsch (1920–2008)** Inland Steel Building

26

...AND THEIR CLIENTS...

1. Henry Brarens Sloman (1848–1931) Chilehaus | 2. Bernard van Leer (1883–1958) Van Leer Headquarters | 3. Harold C. Price (1888–1962) Price Tower | 4. Robert McCormick (1880–1955) Tribune Tower

5. Reinhard Mohn (1921–2008) Buch und Ton | 6. Jan Carlzon (1941–) SAS Frösundavik Office Building | 7. Phyllis Lambert (1927–) Seagram Building | 8. Joseph Patterson (1879–1946) Tribune Tower
9. Guido Donegani (1877–1947) Palazzo Montecatini | 10. Henry Townley Heald (1904–1975) Ford Foundation

11. Alfred Steele (1900–1959) Pepsicola Headquarters | 12. Jonathan Fletcher (1914–2004) Home Federal Savings and Loan | 13. Clarence B. Randall (1891–1967) Inland Steel Building
14. William A. Hewitt (1914–1998) John Deere Headquarters | 15. Jan van der Togt (1905–1995) Tomadohuis | 16. Jose "Pepín" Bosch (1898–1994) Bacardi Headquarters
17. Masanori Kaneko (1907–1996) Kagawa Prefectural Office

18. Anthony J. Celebrezze (1910–1998) Erieview Tower | 19. François Mitterrand (1916–1996) Grande Arche | 20. William Ellery Hale (1836–1898) Reliance Building

Shizuoka Press and Broadcasting Center 1.493 m² typical floor	**Price Tower** 4.180 m² 7th floor	**Finnland Haus** 8.300 m² typical floor	**Reliance Building** 6.850 m² 10th floor	**Tomadohuis** 4.542 m² 3rd floor	**Communist Party Headquarters** 20.780 m² 5th floor	**Home Federal Savings and Loan** 4.250 m² ground floor	**Rautatalo** 8.480 m² ground floor

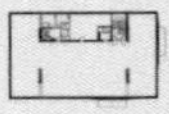

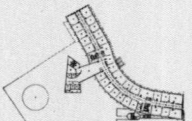

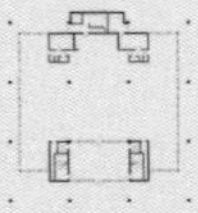

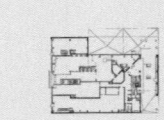

Inland Steel Building 28.768 m² 5th floor	**Enso-Gutzeit Headquarters** 12.000 m² 1st floor	**Ford Foundation** 28.980 m² 5th floor	**Unilever Headquarters** 65.400 m² 18th floor	**Buch und Ton** 5.200 m² 5th floor	**Seagram Building** 78.876 m² typical floor of tower level	**Van Leer Headquarters** 7.770 m² 1st floor

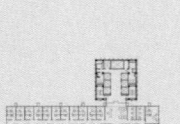

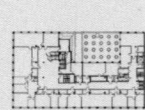

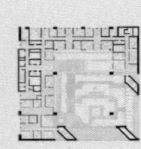

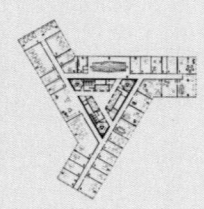

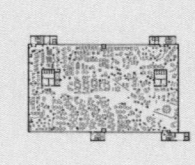

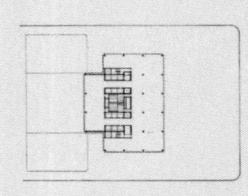

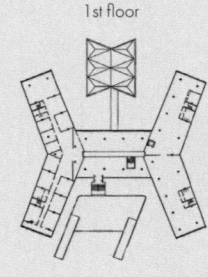

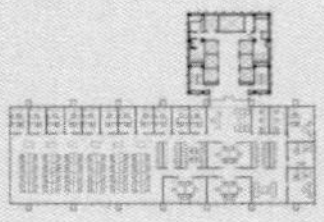

Erieview Tower 65.300 m² typical floor	**Danmarks Nationalbank** 48.131 m² ground floor	**HSBC** 99.000 m² typical floor	**Pirelli Tower** 24.000 m² 3rd floor	**National Pensions Institute** 22.500 m² 1st floor

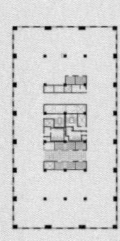

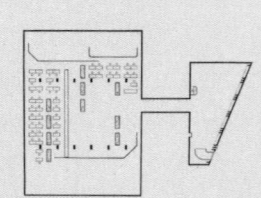

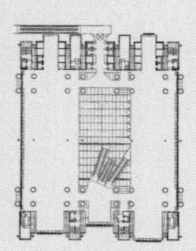

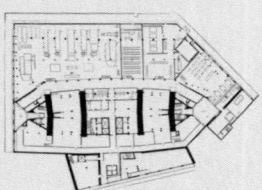

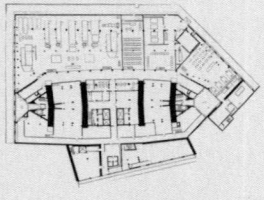

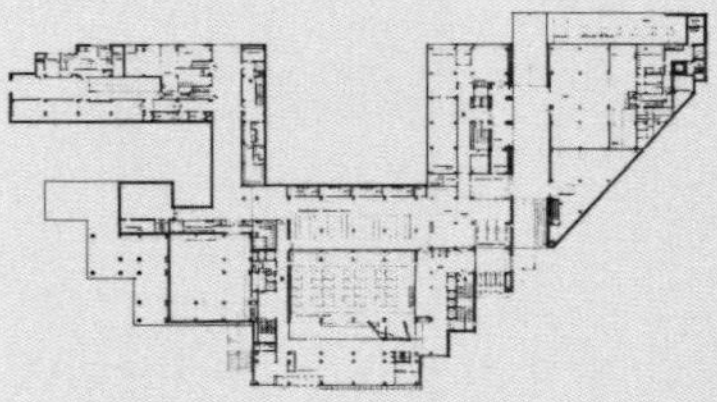

Nestlé Headquarters 60.000 m² typical floor	**Soccer Field** 7.140 m²	**Kirovsky District Town Hall** 35.000 m² 1st floor	**Paraceside Building** 119.625 m² ground floor

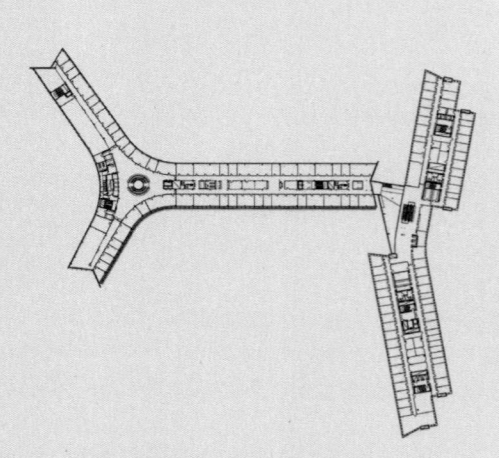

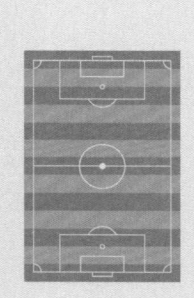

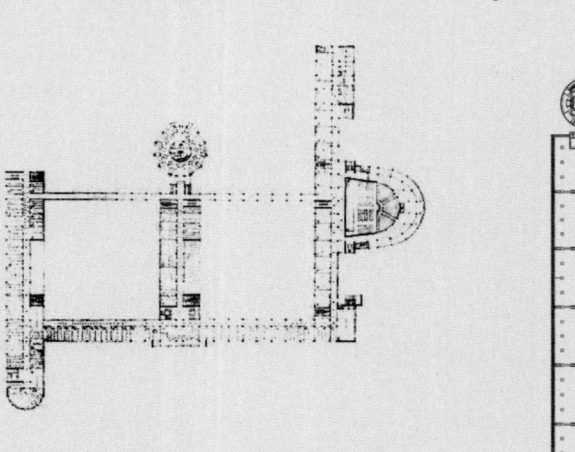

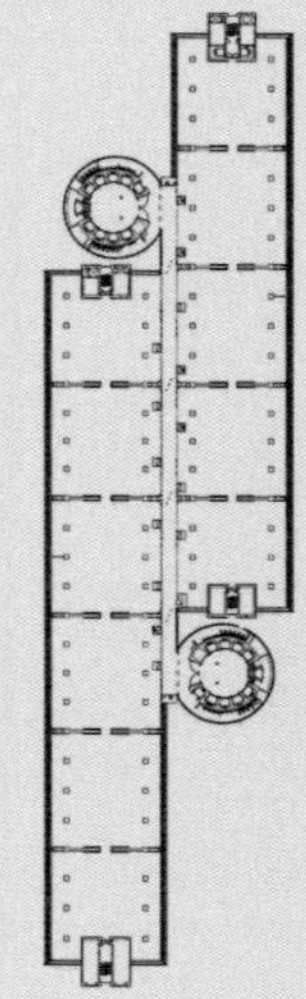

SAS Frösundavik Office Building
54.000 m²
4th floor

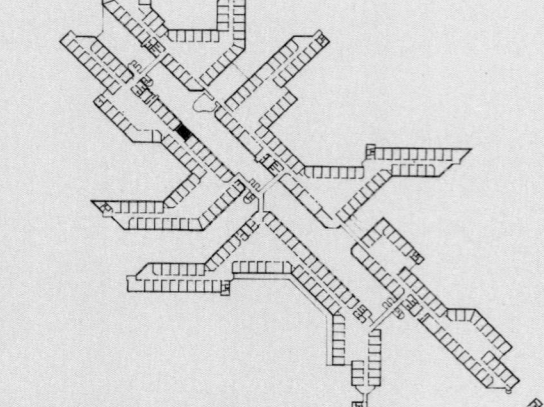

Grande Arche
87.000 m²
top floor

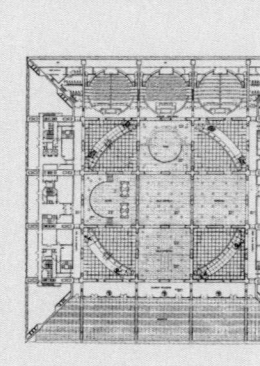

0 50m 100m

Bacardi Headquarters	Pepsi Cola Headquarters	Bank Melli University Branch	Palazzo della Civiltà Italiana	Kagawa Prefectural Office	BMW Headquarters	Tribune Tower
1.655 m²	13.238 m²	3.711 m²	8.400 m²	12.066 m²	72.000 m²	68.500 m²
1st floor	11th floor	ground floor	4th floor	4th floor	typical floor	typical floor

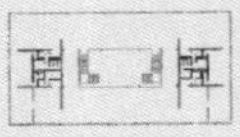

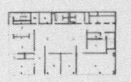

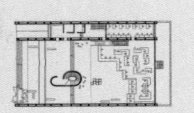

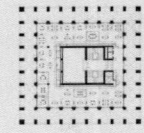

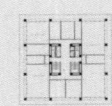

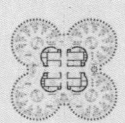

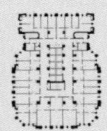

Pendorp	Osram Administration Building	Palazzo Montecatini	Johnson Wax Headquarters Europe	Aarhus City Hall
14.500 m²	22.260 m²	52.132 m²	20.000 m²	19.380 m²
x floor	typical floor	typical floor	1st floor	1st floor

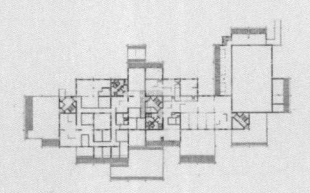

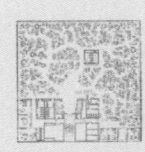

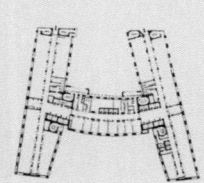

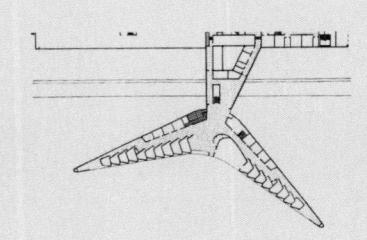

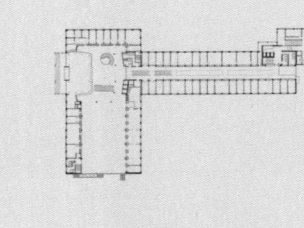

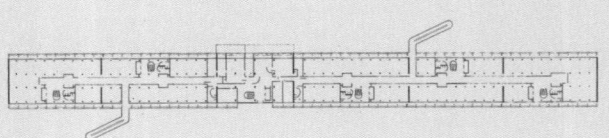

Secretariat Building	Chilehaus	Delftse Poort
44.000 m²	36.000 m²	60.000 m²
typical floor	typical floor	ground floor

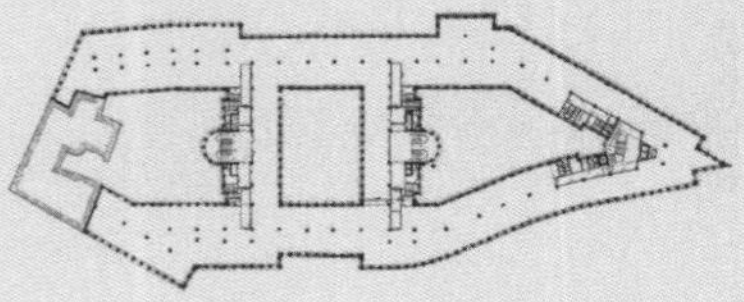

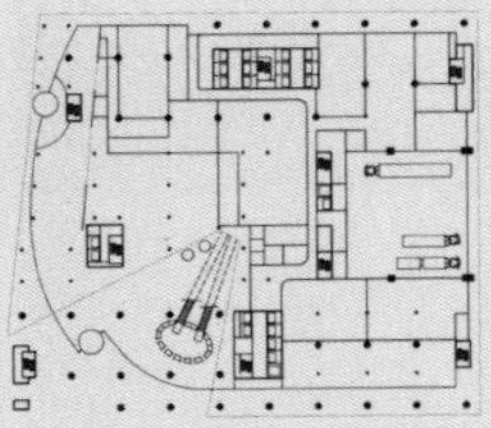

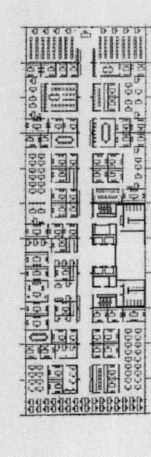

John Deere HQ	Meguro City Hall	Chicago Federal Center	Centraal Beheer
32.541 m²	48.075 m²	268.303 m²	30.536 m²
typical floor	ground floor	ground floor	ground floor

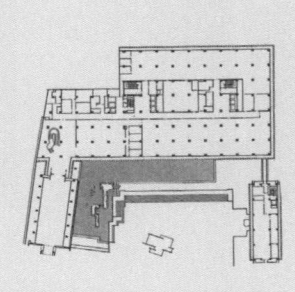

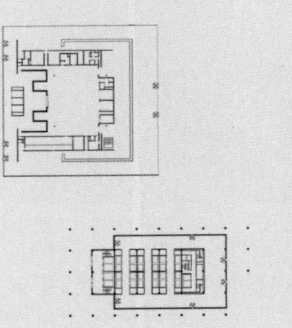

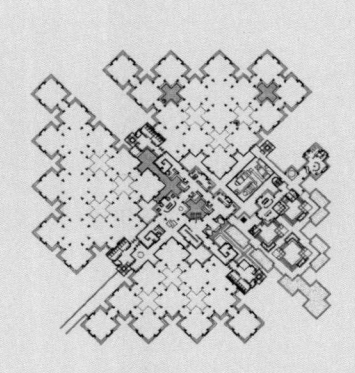

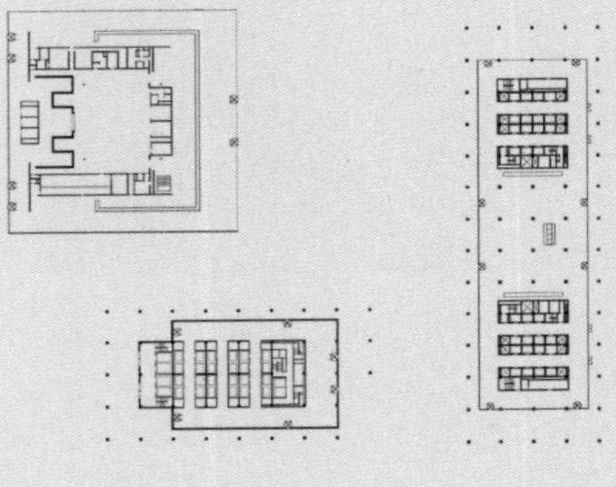

Bell Labs Holmdel Complex
185.806 m²
typical floor

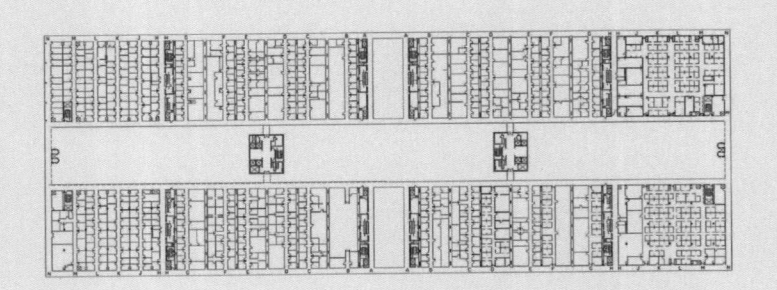

...LEAVING UNIQUE FOOTPRINTS...

Bacardi Headquarters
1962, Tultitlán

Johnson Wax Headquarters Europe
1964, Mijdrecht

Home Federal
Savings and Loan
1962, Des Moines

Buch und Ton
1961, Gütersloh

Bank Melli
University Branch
1962, Tehran

€69.878.317
€3.091 p/m²

Osram Administration
Building
1966, Munich

Nestlé Headquarters
1960, Vevey

Communist Party
Headquarters
1971, Paris

National Pensions
Institute
1956, Helsinki

€146.211.623
€3.046 p/m²

-$732.243.054
-$5.549 p/m²

Rautatalo
1955, Helsinki

Danmarks Nationalbank
1978, Copenhagen

Kagawa Prefectural Office
1958, Kagawa

Kirovsky District Town Hall
1935, St. Petersburg

Finnland Haus
1966, Hamburg

Pepsicola HQ
1960, New York

-$184.071.523
-$991 p/m²

€44.395.405
€2.290 p/m²

Bell Labs Holmdel Complex
1978, Holmdel

Palazzo Montecatini
1938, Milan

Aarhus City Hall
1941, Aarhus

€249.334.054
€3.462 p/m²

$57.705.467
$2.006 p/m²

BMW Headquarters
1973, Munich

Inland Steel Building
1958, Chicago

Unilever Headquarters
1964, Hamburg

Chicago Federal Center
1974, Chicago

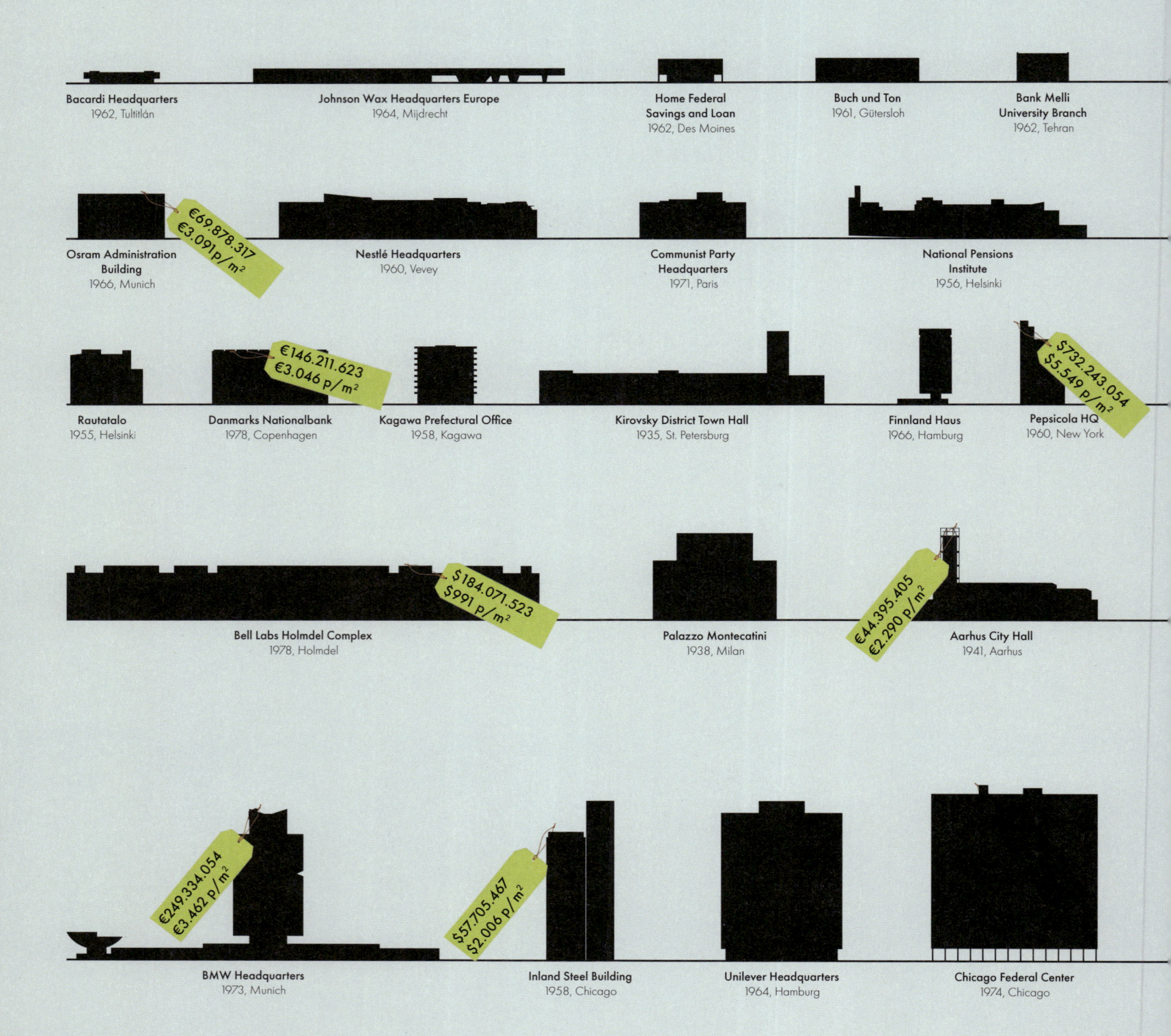

...A SKYLINE OF INVESTMENT IN THE FUTURE...*

*Prices shown are construction costs drawn from historical records in public and private archives, corrected for inflation to 2021 and subsequently converted to Euro and/or US Dollars. Lack of documentation of capital costs, furnishing, and land prices means these figures are a best estimate, providing only a rough guide to the real total cost of each building.

0 50m 100m

Building	Year, City	Price	Price/m²
Pendorp	1982, Alkmaar	€84.550.972	€3.078 p/m²
Centraal Beheer	1972, Apeldoorn	€85.624.304	€3.567 p/m²
Van Leer Headquarters	1958, Amstelveen		
Enso-Gutzeit Headquarters	1962, Helsinki	€11.600.000	€1.506 p/m²
Meguro City Hall	1966, Tokyo		
Tomadohuis	1962, Dordrecht		
SAS Frösundavik Office Building	1987, Solna	€131.121.615	€1.316 p/m²
John Deere Headquarters	1964, Moline	$89.660.645	$2.758 p/m²
Secretariat Building	1953, Chandigarh		
Chilehaus	1924, Hamburg		
Palazzo della Civiltà Italiana	1940/43, Rome		
Price Tower	1956, Bartlesville	$21.459.220	$5.133 p/m²
Shizuoka Press and Broadcasting Center	1967, Tokyo		
Ford Foundation	1967, New York	$133.148.742	$4.607 p/m²
Palaceside Building	1966, Tokyo	$352.862.451	$2.947 p/m²
Reliance Building	1895, Chicago	$165.44.523	$2.415 p/m²
Grande Arche	1989, Paris	€866.090.114	€9.955 p/m²
Delftse Poort	1991, Rotterdam	€146.659.475	€1.397 p/m²
Tribune Tower	1925, Chicago	$135.003.314	$1.971 p/m²
Pirelli Tower	1960, Milan		
Seagram Building	1958, New York	$418.965.735	$6.116 p/m²
HSBC	1985, Hong Kong	$1.725.550.780	$17.429 p/m²
Erieview Tower	1964, Cleveland	$216.083.051	$3.309 p/m²

31

1890 1900 1910 1920

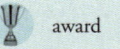

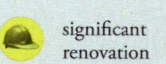

Reliance Building, Burnham and Root
Chilehaus, Höger
Tribune Tower, Howells and Hood
Kirovsky District Town Hall, Trotsky
Palazzo Montecatini, Ponti
Palazzo della Civiltà Italiana, Guerrini, La Padula and Romano
Aarhus City Hall, Jacobsen and Møller
Secretariat Building, Jeanneret, Le Corbusier
Rautatalo, Aalto
Price Tower, Wright
National Pensions Institute, Aalto
Van Leer Headquarters, Breuer
Inland Steel Building, Skidmore, Owings & Merril (SOM)
Seagram Building, Mies van der Rohe
Kagawa Prefectural Office, Tange
Pirelli Tower, Ponti
Nestle Headquarters, Tschumi
Pepsicola Headquarters, Skidmore, Owings & Merril (SOM)
Buch und Ton, Schnelle
Bell Labs Holmdel Complex, Saarinen
Tomado House, Maaskant
Home Federal Savings and Loan, Mies van der Rohe
Enso-Gutzeit Headquarters, Aalto
Bank Melli University Branch, Utzon
Bacardi Headquarters, Mies van der Rohe
Unilever Headquarters, Hentrich, Petschnigg & Partners
Johnson Wax Headquarters Europe, Maaskant
Erieview Tower, Harrison and Abramovitz
John Deere Headquarters, Saarinen
Palaceside Building, Nikken Sekkei and Hayashi
Finnland Haus, Hentrich, Petschnigg & Partners
Osram Administration Building, Henn
Meguro City Hall, Murano
Ford Foundation, Roche and Dinkeloo
Shizuoka Press and Broadcasting Center, Tange
Communist Party Headquarters, Niemeyer
Centraal Beheer, Hertzberger
Uni-Hochhaus, Henselmann
Chicago Federal Center, Mies van der Rohe
BMW Headquarters, Schwanzer
Danmarks Nationalbank, Jacobsen
Pendorp, Bonnema
HSBC, Foster + Partners
SAS Frösundavik Office Building, Torp
Grande Arche, Von Spreckelsen and Andreu
Delftse Poort, Bonnema

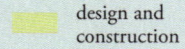

...WHERE WE TRY TO FIGURE OUT WHAT HAPPENED IN THEIR LIFETIME...

design and construction   lifetime   competition   award   significant renovation   demolition

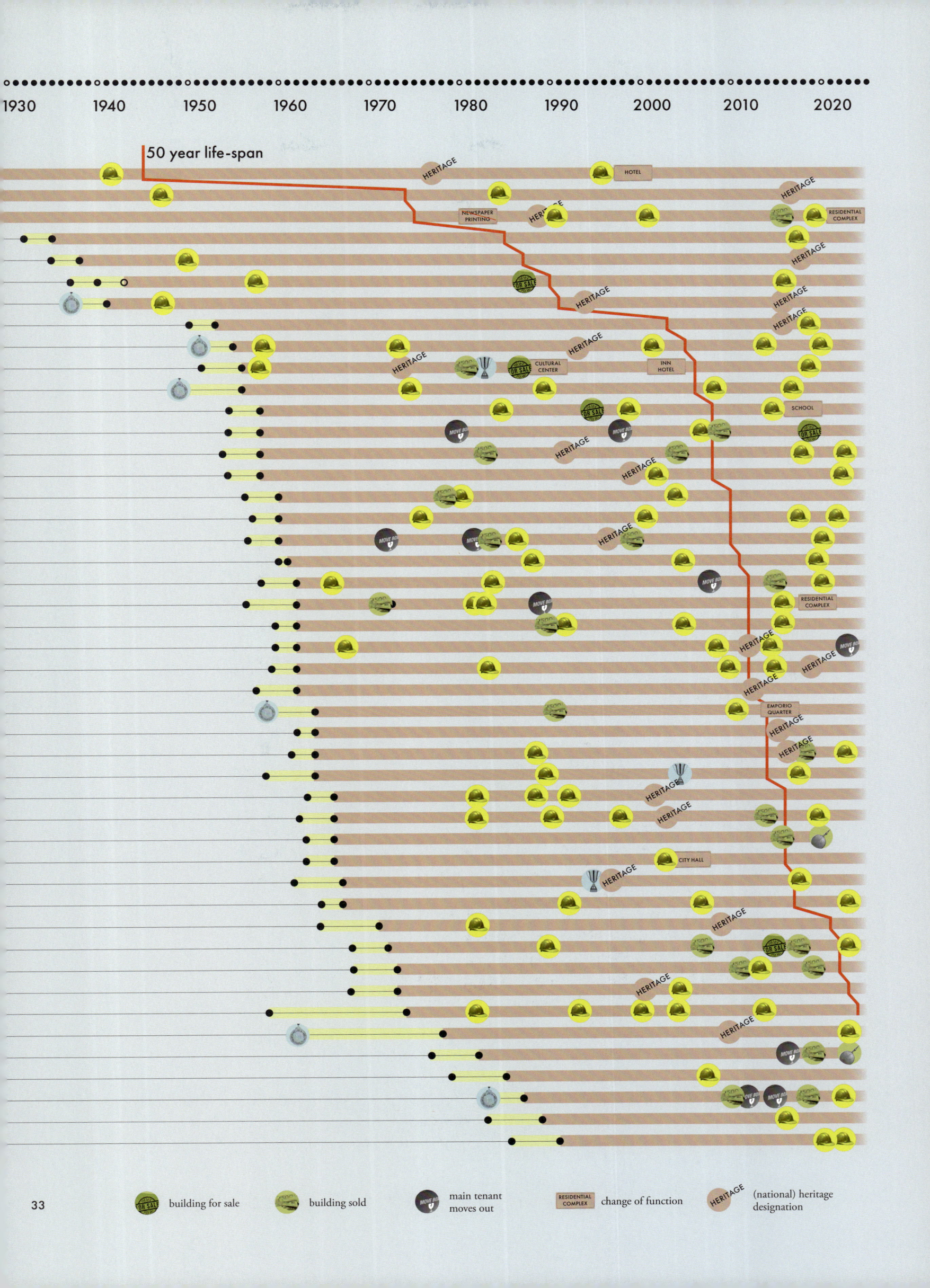

1930 1940 1950 1960 1970 1980 1990 2000 2010 2020

50 year life-span

HERITAGE
HOTEL
NEWSPAPER PRINTING
HERITAGE
HERITAGE
RESIDENTIAL COMPLEX
HERITAGE
HERITAGE
FOR SALE
HERITAGE
HERITAGE
HERITAGE
CULTURAL CENTER
HERITAGE
INN HOTEL
HERITAGE
SCHOOL
MOVE OUT
FOR SALE
HERITAGE
MOVE OUT
HERITAGE
HERITAGE
MOVE OUT
HERITAGE
MOVE OUT
RESIDENTIAL COMPLEX
HERITAGE
HERITAGE
MOVE OUT
HERITAGE
EMPORIO QUARTER
HERITAGE
HERITAGE
HERITAGE
HERITAGE
CITY HALL
HERITAGE
HERITAGE
FOR SALE
HERITAGE
HERITAGE
MOVE OUT
MOVE OUT MOVE OUT

33
- building for sale
- building sold
- main tenant moves out
- change of function
- (national) heritage designation

CASES

1895

RELIANCE BUILDING

Program trumps typology in a tower designed to be open plan but used otherwise

1890 The second, third, and fourth stories of the First National Bank building, on Chicago's Loop – owned by real estate investor William Hale (also founder of the Hale Elevator Company) – are lifted on jackscrews, allowing the first floor to be demolished. John Root designs a new basement and ground floor based on a "floating raft" system – a concrete base with deep caissons. Hale envisions a new 14-story tower rising on top as soon as he can terminate the lease of the First National and evict them from the doomed upper levels.

1891 Root dies of pneumonia. Charles Atwood is hired to design the rest of Hale's new tower. With engineer E.C. Shankland, he proposes a revolutionary agenda: a novel riveted steel-frame superstructure that would clear high-rises of load-bearing

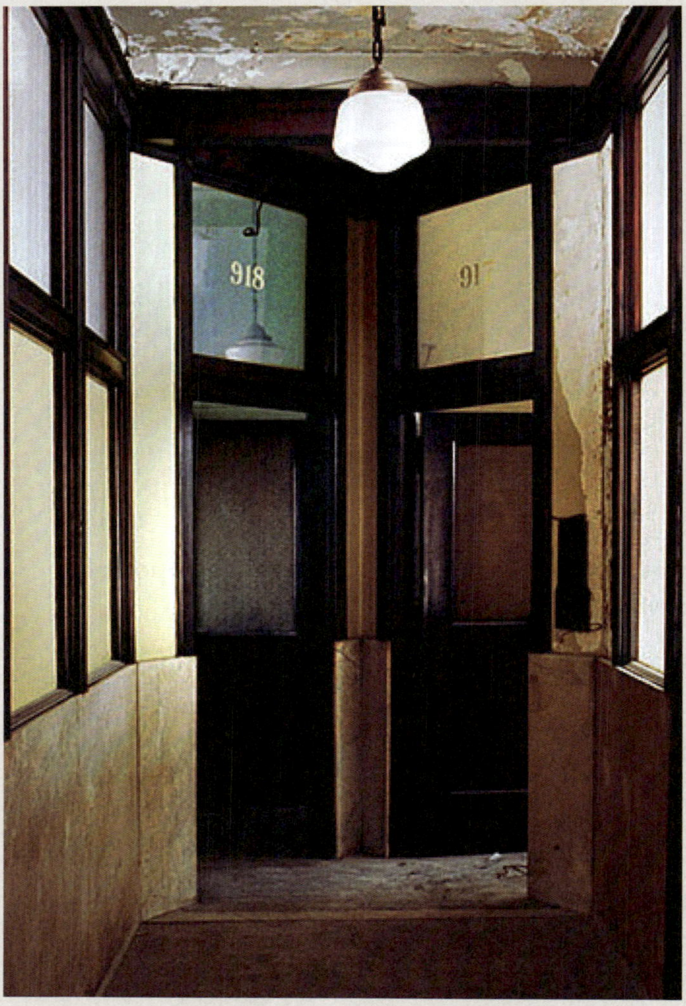
918

interior walls, enabling completely open spaces. The integrated building system would include custom steel members, "self-cleaning" glazed white terra cotta facade tiling, and unusually large sheets of plate glass to flood the interior with natural light.

1895 The Reliance Building's steel frame is erected in 15 days. Within four months the shell is completed. The new construction method limits waste, dust, and much of the usual construction debris, prompting the Chicago Daily Tribune to call its construction magical.[1] (Burnham and Root would repeat this magic a few years later with the Flatiron in New York).

1896... While the steel frame structure eliminated the need for load-bearing walls, the tower's program packs it with partitions walls. The building is marketed as a vertical center for doctors' and dentists' offices, with more than 280 private practitioners renting the now-small spaces (all of them equipped with electricity and phone lines). A dense labyrinthine plan emerges, with around 28 rooms on each floor.

1920 The Reliance reaches peak capacity with more than 300 tenants, all of them linked to medical services. Doctors rent practice spaces by the hour. "Any doctor who wants a downtown office for a few hours a day can have one of these with the use of the reception rooms at so much an hour, a day, or a month. That is, he can use a room say from 9 a.m. to 10 a.m. At 10 o'clock he will pack his medicine chest, depart, and the next doctor will take his place."[2] Its most famous and notorious occupant is Al Capone's dentist.

1930s Parts of the cornice fall to the street below. Occupancy begins to drop due to the emergence of new healthcare practices and hospitals in Chicago's periphery. New occupants begin taking their place: jewelers, photographers, fortune tellers. Several larger companies start using more floor space. The ground floor becomes a patchwork of different storefronts.

1941 Architectural historian Siegfried Giedion identifies Reliance as a milestone in his seminal *Space, Time and Architecture* : "This glass tower is still standing, and, although its glazed white tiles have become encrusted with dirt, its airiness and pure proportions make it a symbol of the spirit of the Chicago School. It is curious that this building too has been left unnoticed in the history of architecture. It has its place there as a witness to the best of the spirit of the nineteenth century." Giedion concludes that the building may be considered "an architectonic anticipation of the future."

1948 Karoll's Men's Shop opens on the lower two floors, erasing the original storefront.

1970 The Reliance is placed on the National Register of Historic Places.

1976 The Reliance is designated, despite its increasingly deteriorating state, a national landmark.

1990s Occupancy: 20 percent. Mayor Richard Daley labels the Reliance a "pigeon haven". City alderman John Steele informs the council, "It is not worth a dime." The City fails to find private developers to give the building a new future.

1994 The City purchases the Reliance for $1.3 million and spends $5.2 million for emergency repairs on the exterior, replacing the terracotta tiles and windows.

1998 The city grants ownership to a group of developers for the sum of $1. In turn, they invest $28 million, on top of the City's total investment of about $11 million, transforming the building into a hotel.[3]

1999 The Hotel Burnham opens, winning numerous awards for its faithful restoration of the Reliance. The building enters into another phase of its remarkable life as the original 250 medical rooms are converted into 122 hotel rooms.

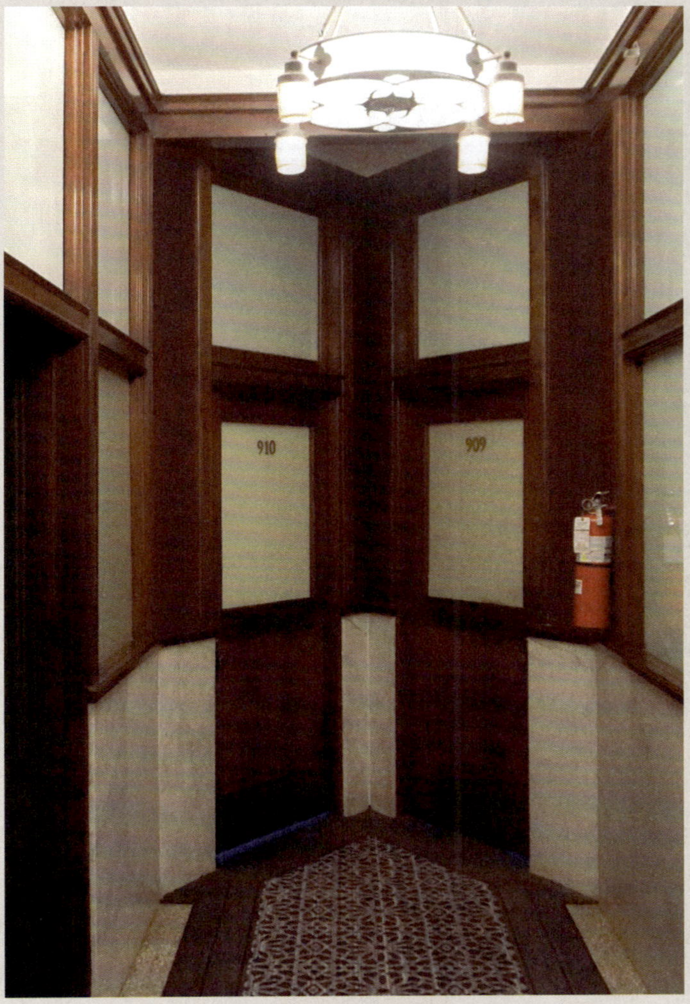
910
909

FOR RENT
OFFICES, HOURS & SALESROOMS
W. E. HALE, 13ᵗʰ FLOOR.

RELIANCE

100 STATE STREET.

2005 The hotel is listed as one of Condé Nast's top 500 hotels in the world.

Present Day Although much of the building appears original, very little (apart from the structure and facade parts) remains. The success of the steel structural system lies in its ability to absorb significant modifications to the core, stairwells, façade, and function, without aesthetic consequence. The hotel is now called the Staypineapple Hotel.

notes

1   "Springs Up By Magic," *Chicago Daily Tribune*, August 26, 1894
2   "Springs Up By Magic."
3   "The Reliance Building Glows Anew," *Chicago Tribune*, September 25, 1999

building credits

client: William Ellery Hale
architect: Daniel Hudson Burnham and John Wellborn Root (1890), Charles B. Atwood (1894)
engineer: E.C. Shankland, Gray Company

photo credits

p.36, 46: from Commision on Chicago Landmarks via McClier Historic Structures Report
p.38, 42 (below), 47 (above): Jay Boersma
p.41, 43, 45: Jared Younger
p.42 (above): ornamental Iron courtest of Winterthur via McClier Historic Structures Report
p.46: from The Winterthur Library Printed Books and Periodical Archive
p.47 (below): Jon Miller

2017

32 S. STREET
CHICAGO, ILLINOIS, US

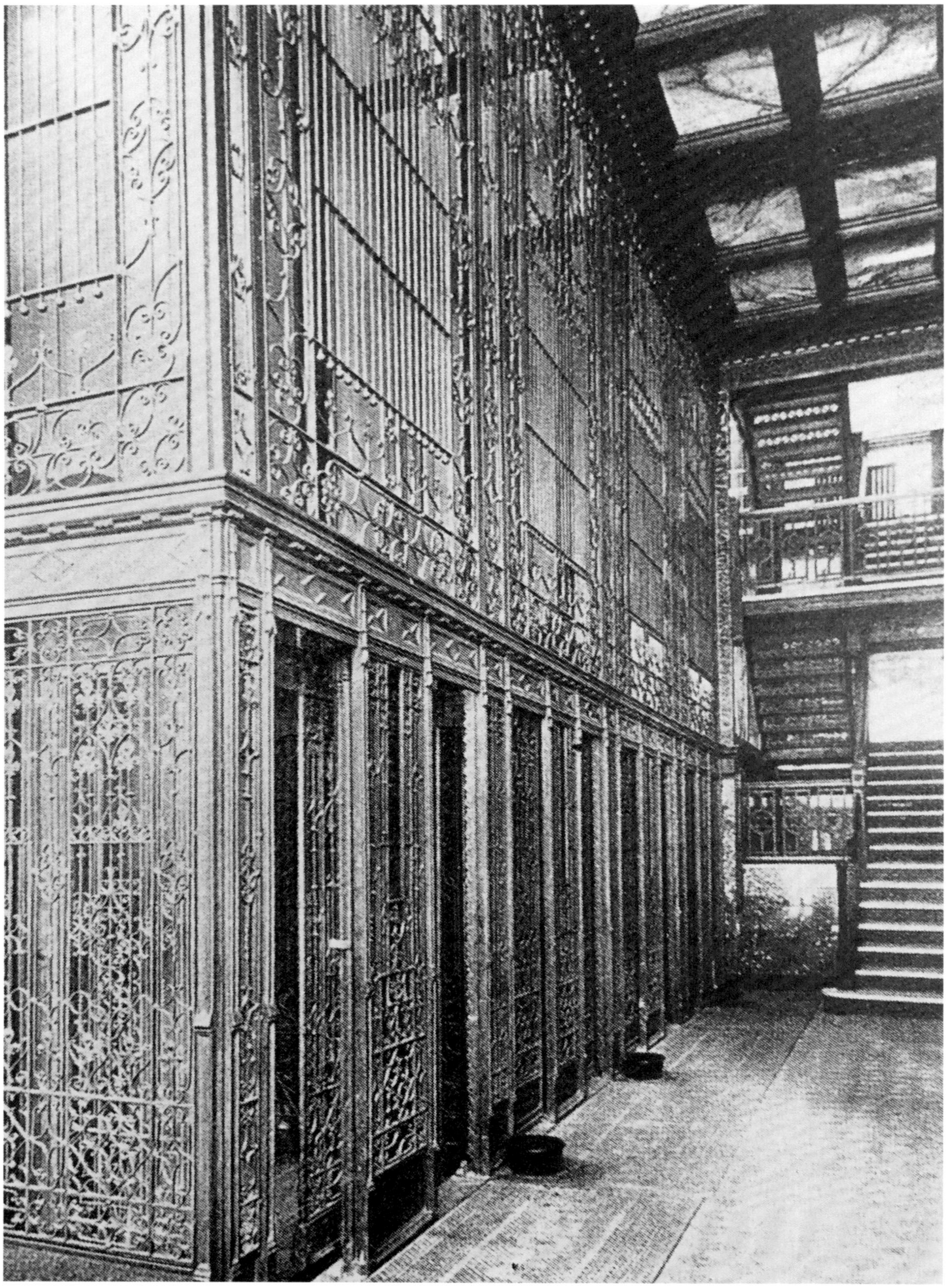

1995

1924

Ruth Baumeister

CHILEHAUS

Rustic brick masterpiece belies a ruthless modernity

Chilehaus is a massive, wedge-shaped, city block-sized, 10-story brick office building in Hamburg with shops on the ground floor and two courtyards. It was designed by architect Fritz Höger (1877–1949) and completed in 1924. The client, Henry B. Sloman, a shipping magnate, had earned his fortune mining saltpeter in Chile, which gave the building its name. In just two years, 4,000 construction workers turned 750 freight wagons of cement, 30,000 cubic meters of gravel, 1,600 tons of round iron, and close to five million Oldenburg bricks into one of Germany's largest and tallest buildings.

What was then, and still is today, celebrated as a masterly achievement – Chilehaus received UNESCO World Heritage status in 2015 – has at least a couple of dark sides to it. After the cholera epidemic in 1892, the city of Hamburg launched on a long-term plan to tear down the Gängeviertel, a large neighborhood in its historic inner city, consisting of half-timbered houses and narrow alleyways. Under the banner of public health, large areas were rebuilt and over 20,000 inhabitants had to be relocated. In the case of Chilehaus, an entire residential neighborhood – 69 buildings in all – was demolished and hundreds of people lost their homes to make space for this behemoth, which formed the core of Kontorhausviertel, a quarter exclusively for commerce in the center of Hamburg.

With his enormous building, Höger managed to polarize his audience: "Chilehaus is not only the biggest house in Hamburg, it is also the most beautiful one. It signifies a milestone in architecture history in general,"[1] stated architect and would-be continental engineer Herman Sörgel[2] shortly after the building's inauguration. However, Swiss critic Peter Meyer's verdict in *Moderne Architektur und Tradition* was more critical, unmasking its blunt strategies: "Chilehaus Hamburg, massively praised as the beginning of a new flourishing in architecture. An office building, covered with bricks in an arts and crafts manner. The overall shape with playful reference to the shape of a ship's bow, pseudo-Gothic verticality. Sacred 'Nordic' for an office building."[3] Indeed, compared to the white cubic architecture of the Neue Sachlichkeit from the 1920s, Chilehaus' expressive brick façade, rhythmically composed of buttresses and white wooden windows, and adorned with sculptural decorations appears unmodern upon first glance. And yet, modern or traditional, Höger managed to create an office building which is still competitive in the market, almost a century after its inauguration.

Today, the building is praised by UNESCO for its iconic form and the expressive use of material. The architect's motivation behind the expressive use of material and form lies in a rather problematic ideology though. Back then, Höger said, "I intentionally chose scrap bricks, which would otherwise only be used for pig stables and paving, for this building." Explained the bricks' intended effect, Höger said: "They gave the gigantic building its vibrancy and took away its earthen heaviness."[4] Höger – promoter of the German *Heimatschutzbewegung*[5] and later a member of the Nazi party and the KDAI (Kampfbund Deutscher Architekten und Ingenieure, a congregation of architects and engineers who decried the "rootless" architecture of the avant-garde) – was making a statement for northern German brick architecture. This was part of a broader effort to cultivate regional cultures and return to the so-called "healthy" traditional values of German arts and crafts. Although Höger claimed that the rough bricks eliminated a sense of heaviness, he still savored their sense of rootedness, being from clay drawn from the German soil; the Gothic-style decorations were, for Höger, an echo of the "glorious times" of the middle age Bauhütten.

It is often argued that when Höger conceived of his building, shortly after Germany lost World War I, he employed the metaphor of Noah's ark to suggest a way out of the crisis. And yet, the building's extraordinary form is first and foremost a result of the problematic geometry of the site, which was divided in half by Fischerwiete, a public street. The architect resolved the problem by proposing to build over it, which would result in additional rentable floor space. Client and architect were not afraid of pushing boundaries to make this gigantic building happen: to get the City's dispensation for changing the building line, 17 separate requests were filed. Hamburg's building archive reveals that administrative costs, fire regulations, and fundamental building laws were negotiated between the city, Sloman, and his architect. Finally, to increase the rentability of the site, dispensation from building regulations was granted to allow Fischerwiete to be built over. The city also relented on the standard permissible building height: client and architect stacked four extra terraced floors on top in order to increase the yield of the site. Clearly, economic factors were allowed to trump planning laws for Chilehaus.

One of the best known and most widely-distributed architecture photographs of the 1920s, by the Dransfeld brothers, represents Chilehaus like an enormous ship's bow rising towards the sky. Subsequently, the Dransfeld brothers' representation of Chilehaus was repeatedly used in popular media e.g. in advertising for the city of Hamburg, Walter Ruttmann's film Berlin: Symphonie einer Grossstadt (1927), and as a postage stamp (1988). The image not only encapsulated the collective memory but also the discourse of Chilehaus in the following decades.

The strong definition of the exterior form suggests a similarly inflexible interior, but here's where the modern kicks in: the loadbearing reinforced concrete columns allow maximal flexibility when it comes to the distribution of the office space inside. The architect's floorplan composition can be read as a direct answer to the demands of the market, which consisted mainly of small businesses, with a high fluctuation rate. To accommodate them, Chilehaus was conceived as one of Germany's first multi-tenant office buildings. Whereas conventional office space in Hamburg tended towards the inflexible and cramped, Chilehaus' relatively open interior spaces could be changed according to tenants' needs. And despite its lack of the signature modern white cube aesthetic, the building proved revolutionary: it was equipped with a low-pressure warm water heating system, paternoster elevators, a mechanical smoke protection system on each level, fire hydrants, safe deposit boxes, a fuel station and an electrical transformer system in the basement.

The first modifications on the ground floor began shortly after inauguration. Höger originally designed the shopfronts behind pedestrian arcades, making it nearly impossible to attach advertising, which would, in Höger's view, degrade the form and expression of the building. This purism did not last very long. The shops were extended outwards, swallowing up the previously exterior arcades. The move added valuable retail space, and broadcasting the shops' wares was now possible.

Subsequently, the building underwent two major renovations. The first one, after World War II, was to fix bomb damage, and the strategy was not to leave any traces of the repair.[6] he second renovation was triggered by a Swedish investor buying the building from Sloman family in 1983. The strategy was founded in a 'Weiterbauprinzip', resulting in a continuous transformation rather than the strict preservation of the historical substance. Restoration to the original state was only applied if authentic substance still existed. Otherwise, only the structural language of the building was followed. Consequently, all shopwindows on the ground floor were replaced with different types. Windows were replaced with double glazing (which nevertheless was intended to resemble the original windows).

The 1980s renovation went much further. After clearing the entire building of asbestos, restoring the roof's concrete structure, and replacing damaged bricks, all office spaces – between 300 and 1,000 square meters – were adapted according to the demands of the tenants (with the possibility of future changes too). Walls, floors, and ceilings were reconstructed according to the original state; paint was removed from ceramic tiles, linoleum floors were refreshed. Paternoster elevators were removed and replaced by contemporary ones. The eastern courtyard was covered with a roof. Retail spaces on the ground and first floors were transformed. Fire regulations were fulfilled by replacing all office doors with fireproof copies (F90) of the originals, and giving House C an additional staircase and a second fire escape route over the balcony.

The monumental character of Chilehaus reaches beyond the building itself and into the design of the Kontorhausviertel, where buildings follow a homogenous structural rhythm and material uniformity in the dark brick façades and white wooden windows on their exteriors. This reciprocity between the architectural object and its urban fabric was decisive for the award of UNESCO World Heritage status. When Chilehaus received this status in 2015, the building's owner, Dr. Reinhard Kutscher of the Union Investment Fond, crowed, "For our investors, and for us as owner and asset manager of Chilehaus, this award is very special. How many people have a World Heritage site in their portfolio, which will generate excellent income for many years?"[7] Kutscher was pointing at what is typically thought of as an antinomy or simply ignored: architecture's capacity for making, rather than only costing money, especially in the long run. The success of Chilehaus as an office building lies in the combination of various aspects: its audacity, its location, and its iconic exterior, suggesting stability while adapting, inside, to the changing needs of the market.

notes

1 Hermann Sörgel, in: *Dekorative Kunst*, Dezember 1924. "Neben den vorbildlichen Staatsbauten Fritz Schuhmachers hebt sich eine zweite Reihe von Geschäftshäusern Fritz Högers heraus, die jetzt durch das Chilehaus, das grösste Haus Hamburgs und somit wahrscheinlich ganz Deutschlands, bekrönt wurde. Das Chilehaus ist nicht nur das grösste Haus Hamburgs, es ist auch das Schönste. Es bedeutet einen Markenstein in der Architekturgeschichte überhaupt."

2 Sörgel spent decades promoting his plans for Atlantropa, a proposal to damn the Mediterranean at several points, creating land bridges from Europe to Africa.

3 Peter Meyer, *Moderne Architektur und Tradition*, Girseberger, Zürich, 1928, appendix, n.p. "Chilehaus Hamburg, als Beginn einer neuen Architekturblüte masslos gepriesen. Ein Bürohaus, äusserlich mit Klinkern in kunstgewerblicher Aufmachung verblendet. Die Gesamtform mit spielerischer Anlehnung an die Form eines Schiffs-Kieles, pseudogotische Vertikalität. Sakrale 'Nordik' für ein Bürogebäude."

4 "Erwähnt sei noch, daß ich für die Fronten des Chilehauses ausgerechnet Ausschußklinker wählte, die sonst normalerweise allenfalls für Schweinställe, Fußböden-Pflasterungen gut genug gehalten würden. Mir aber waren diese deformierten Brocken für meinen Riesenbau gerade so gut, nur durch ihre natürliche Knupperigkeit, so wie sie durch höchste Feuerglut wurden, waren sie mir lieb, nur ihnen verdanke ich einen Großteil der Wirkung des Riesenbaus, durch sie erhielt der Bau seine Beschwingtheit und nahm dem Riesen seine Erdenschwere." Fritz Höger cited in: Piergiacomo Bucciarelli, *Fritz Höger. Hanseatischer Baumeister, 1877–1949* (Vice Versa Verlag, Berlin-Kreuzberg, 1992), p.94. Translation from German by the author.

5 Cultural movement in Germany, founded during the late 19th century to promote national identity and nature, and to criticize industrialization and urbanization.

6 There is no precise record of the war damage, but from photography it seems that the façade was most damaged by fire and many windows were smashed.

7 Dr. Reinhard Kutscher, "Ein Fondsobjekt wird Weltkulturerbe: Hamburger Chilehaus von UNESCO ausgezeichnet," 2015. https://realestate.union-investment.com/de/ueber-uns/meilensteine/ein-fondsobjekt-wird-weltkulturerbe-hamburger-chilehaus-von-unesco-ausgezeichnet.html. Retrieved 1 August, 2021, Translation from German by the author.

building credits

client: Henry Brarens Sloman
architect: Johann Friedrich Höger

photo credits

p.48: Carl Dransfeld
p.53: Michael Valjak
p.54 (left), 56 (left), 58 (all): unknown
p.54 (right), 55, 56 (right), 57, 59 (all): Jens Frederiksen

2020
FISCHERTWIETE 2A
HAMBURG, GERMANY

54

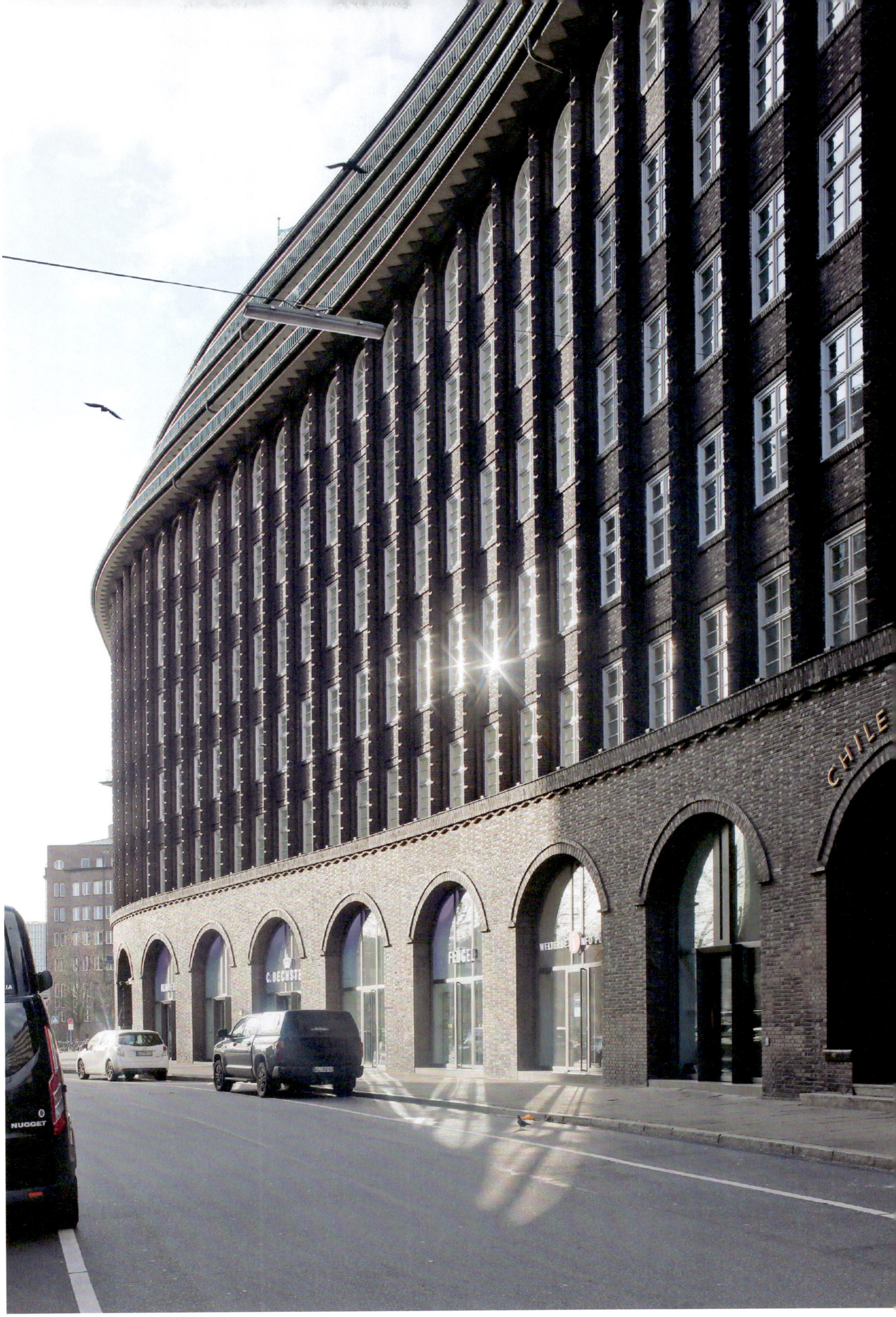
CHILE
C. BECHSTE
NUGGET

56

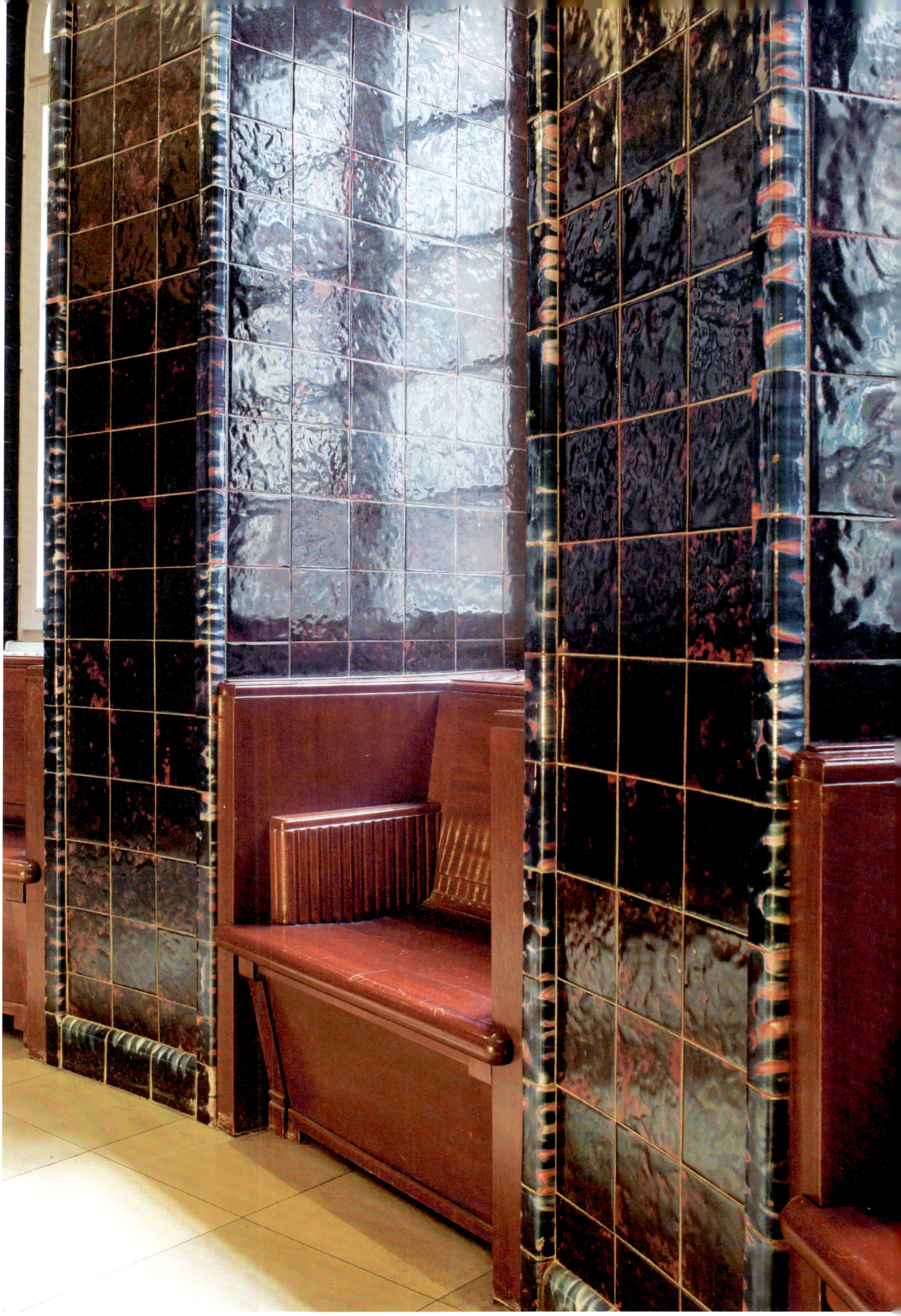

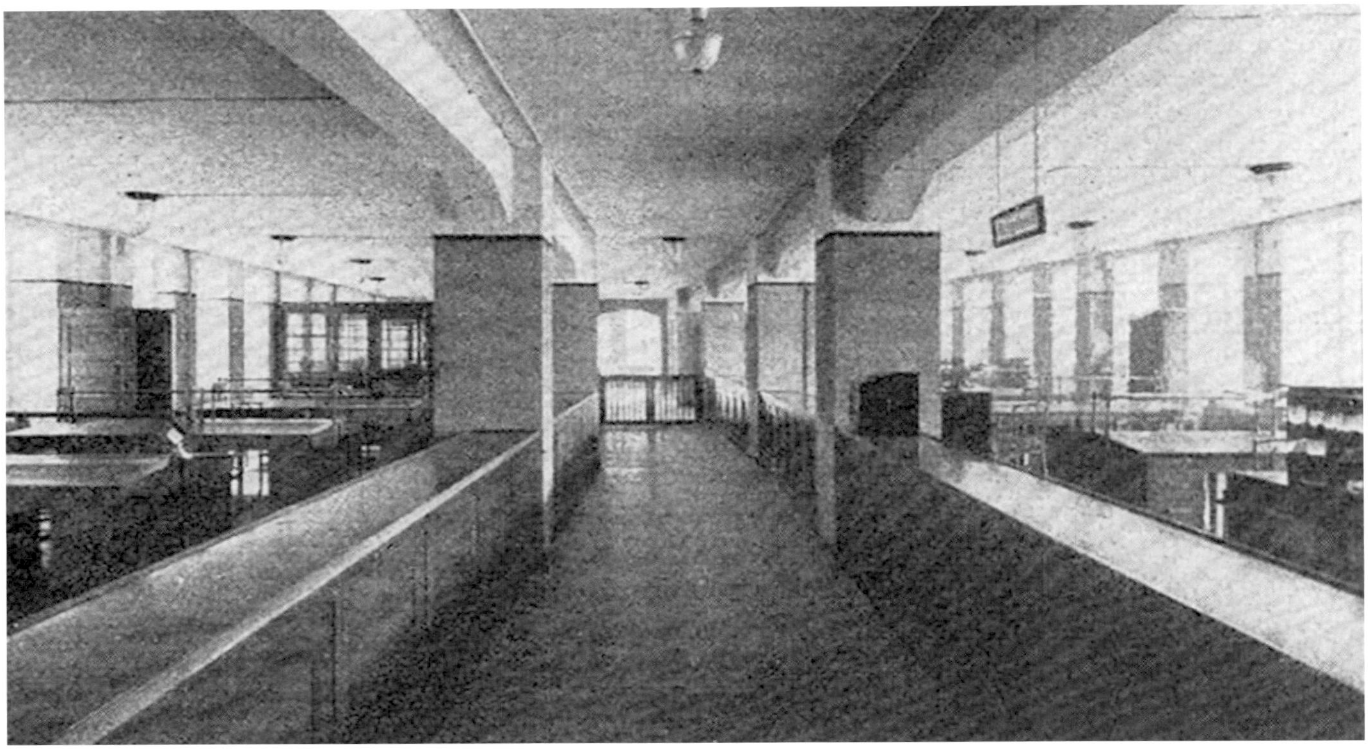

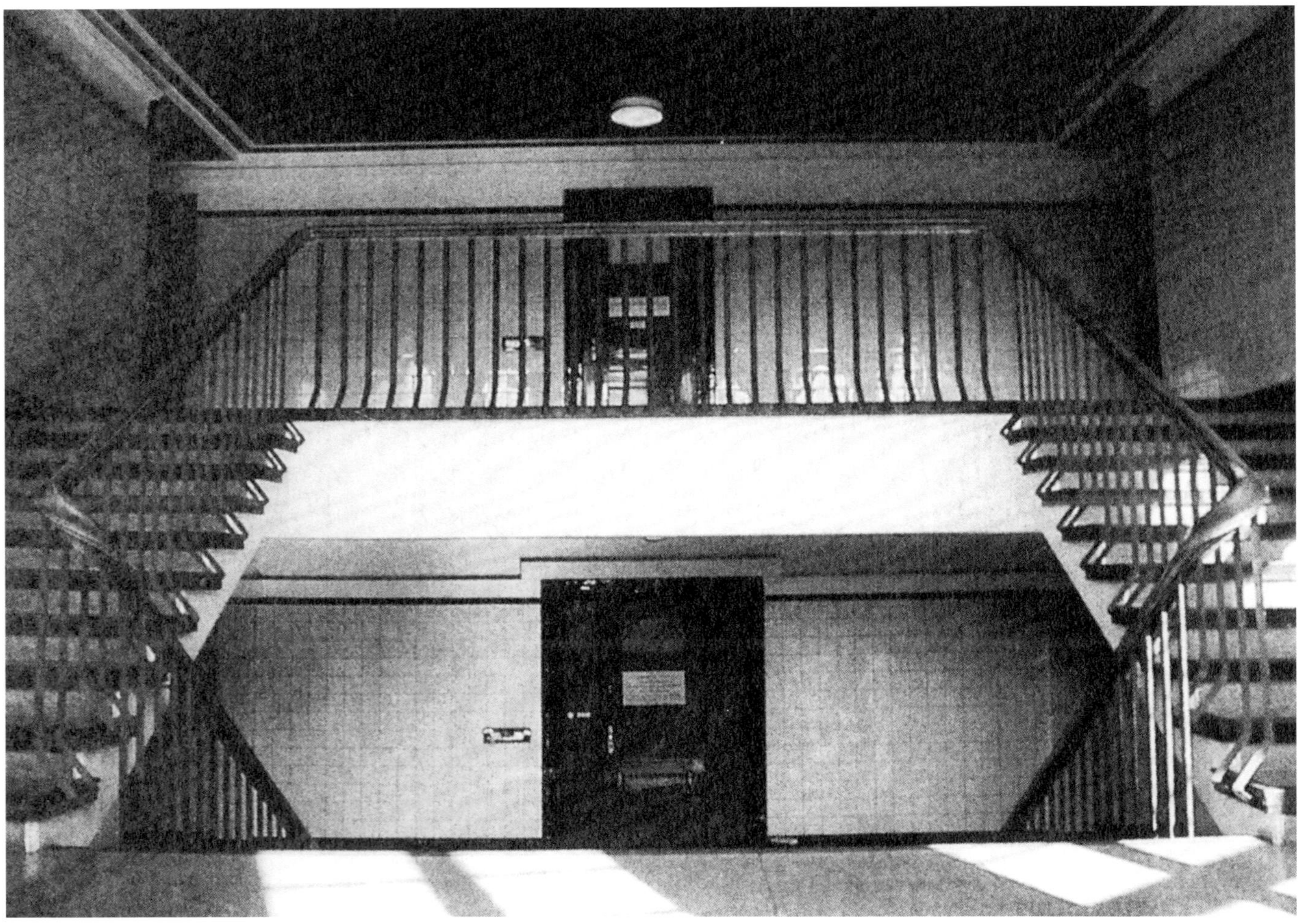

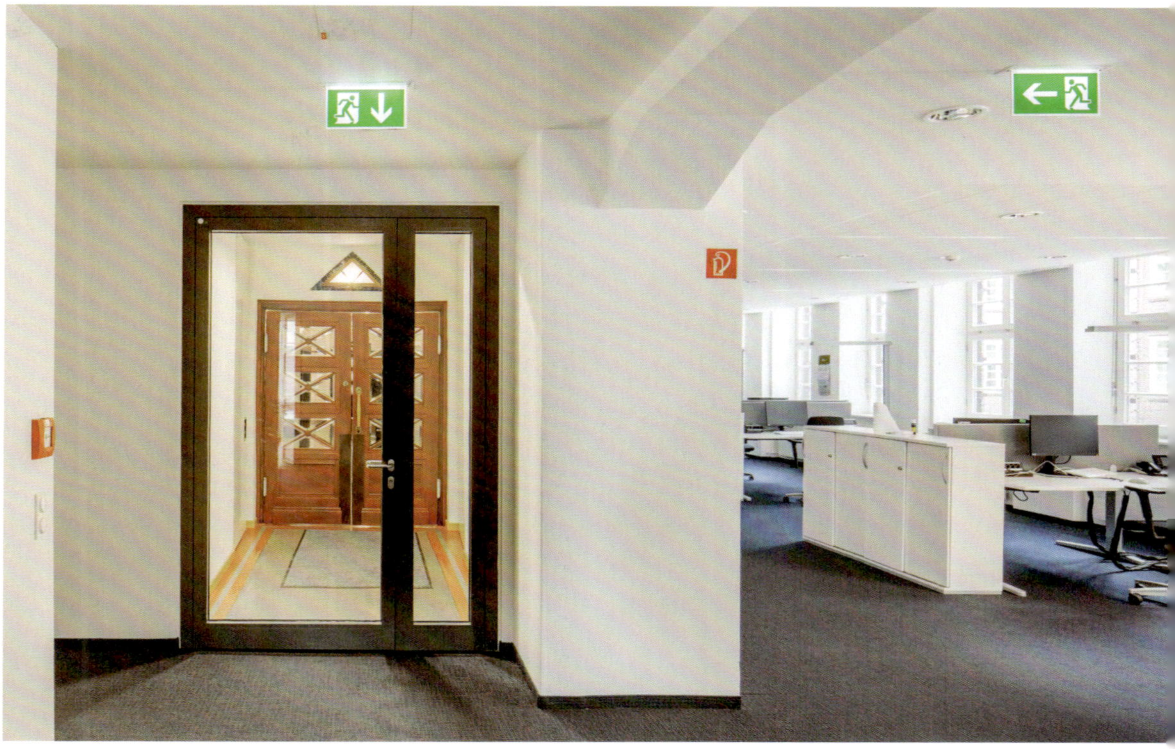

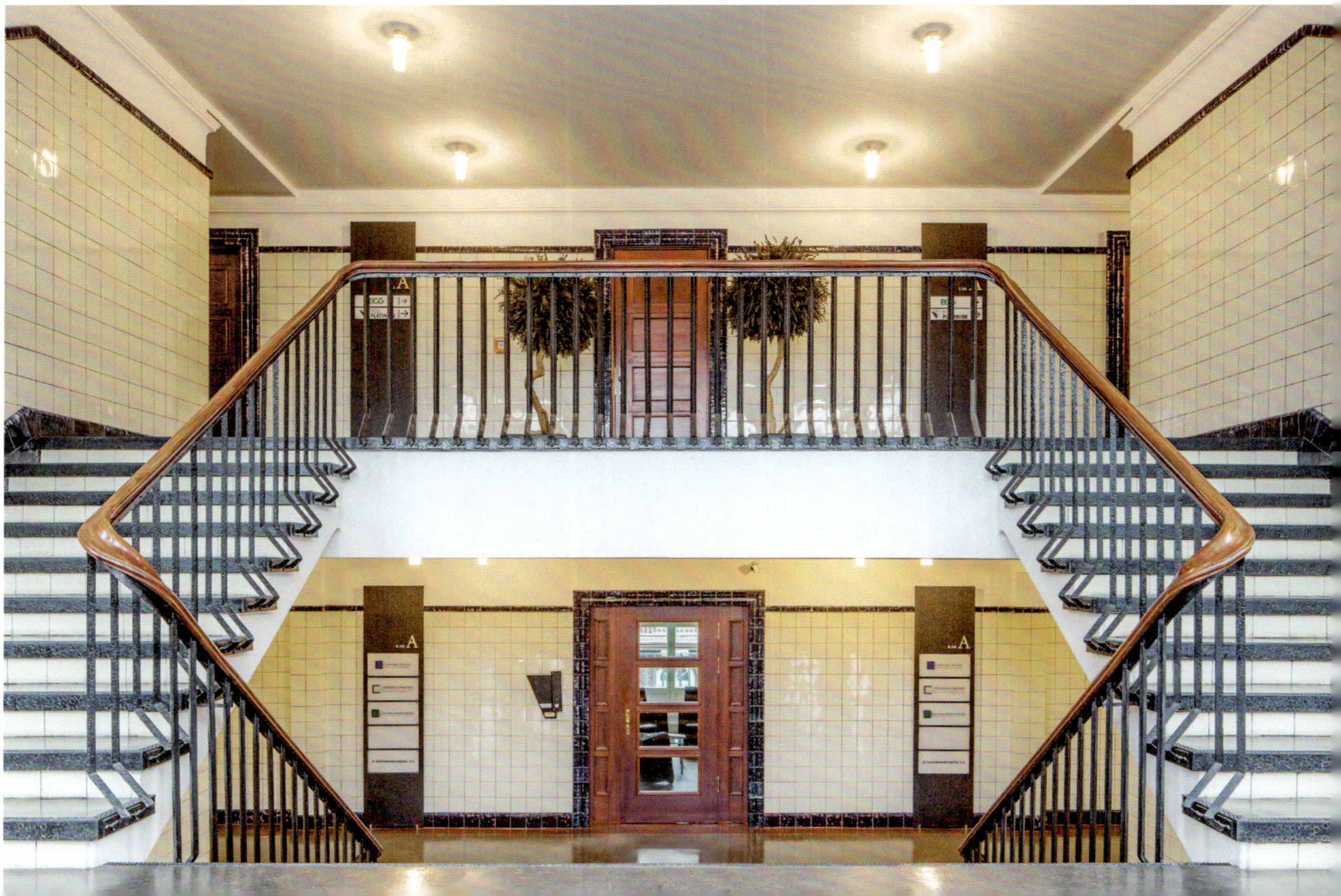

1925

TRIBUNE TOWER

Cathedral for journalism

The Tribune Tower competition was the largest international architecture competition ever launched. In June 1922, the *Chicago Tribune* published an ad in the paper offering $100,000 in prizes to the architects who could full fill three criteria:

1. To adorn with a monument of enduring beauty this city, in which the Tribune has prospered so amazingly
2. To create a structure which will be an inspiration and a model for generations of newspaper publishers
3. To provide a new and beautiful home worthy of the world's greatest Newspaper

Adolf Loos, Bruno Taut, and Walter Gropius were among the 260 entrants, each entering modernist or monumental schemes for towers (Loos proposed a giant Doric column). However the *Tribune's* publisher, Colonel

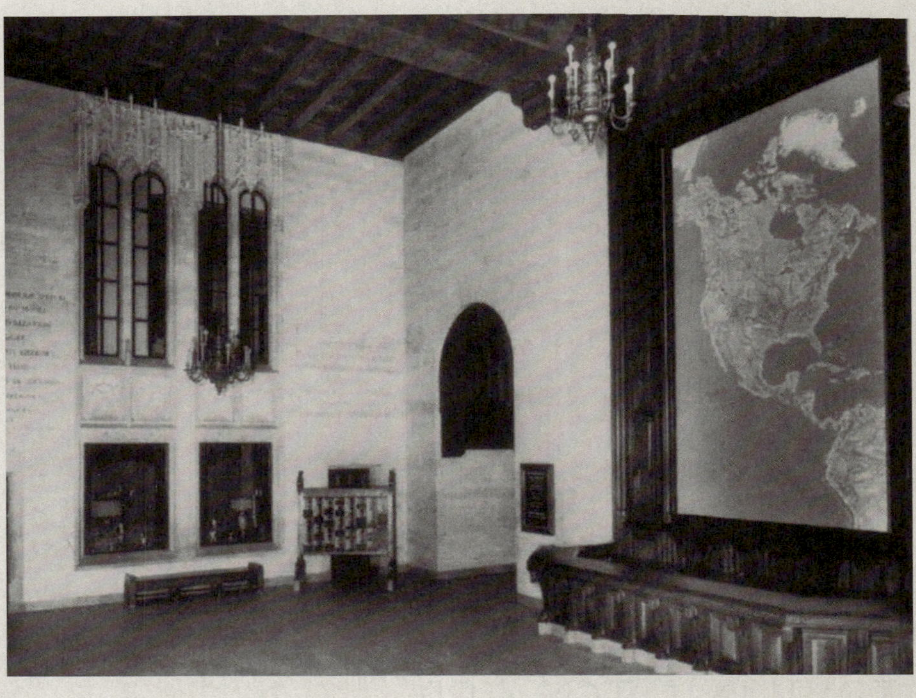

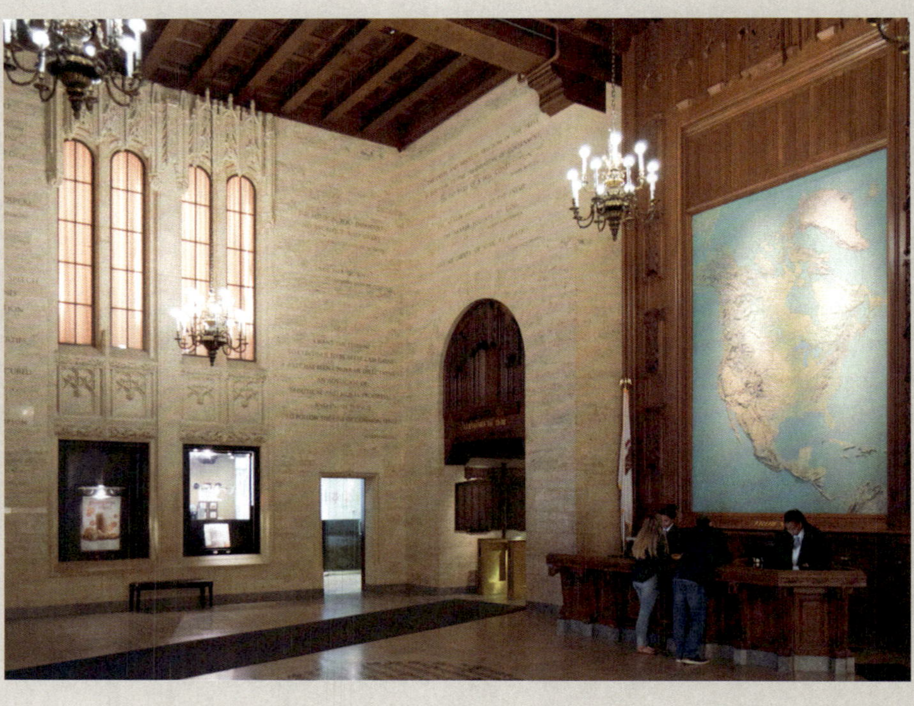

Robert R. McCormick, was a veteran of World War I and having spent time in Europe, he returned with a clear image for the Tribune's future. Articles hinted at a preference for a Gothic inspired design, to endow their paper with an old-world legitimacy and the status of a revered institution: a cathedral for journalism.

On December 23, 1922, an entry by American architects Raymond Hood and John Mead Howells, number 69 – a neo-Gothic 36-floor skyscraper, complete with a crown, buttresses, and gargoyles – won the competition based on a rendering of the exterior. The design amounted to a death knell for the Chicago School. Construction started almost immediately. While the shell was already being constructed, the architects worked to fit all the programmatic requirements into the tower's floor plates, leaving the middle levels of the tower (floors 13-23) for rentable office space. Meanwhile, the newspapers' international reporters were instructed by McCormick to gather – "by honourable means" – fragments from buildings around the world – including Trondheim Cathedral, the Taj Mahal, Hagia Sophia, the Great Wall of China –which would be built into the façade.

Reporters and staff were left in no doubt about the solemnity and dignity of their tasks. The Hall of Inscriptions in the tower's lobby featured quotes on the importance of a free press to a healthy democracy; a massive relief map of North America was installed above the front desk in 1927. But the heart of the newspapers' operations was the newsroom, located on the fourth floor, the only double-height space in the tower, visible to visitors through a gallery. News departments clustered around an editor who was physically and hierarchically at the center. Copy had to be filed by 6 p.m. every day to allow typesetting and printing (in the lower floors on the southeast corner) to be done in time for the morning edition. The materials in the newsroom included white marble, mahogany, and a cork floor. A typewriter sat at every desk, where stories were transcribed from the original handwritten version. Over the decades, technology changed the newsroom space, which became more and more generic – L-shaped desks, half-height partitions, screens everywhere – to the point where it is barely indistinguishable from an advertising agency or an architecture office. In 2018, the Chicago Tribune moved out of what was originally their tower, which was to be converted into 162 condominiums with 56 different layouts. Amid the massive overhaul to the building, scheduled to be finished early 2022, the fate of the newsroom remains unclear.

building credits

client: The Chicago Tribune, Col. Robert McCormick
architect: Raymond Hood and John Mead Howells
building supervisors: Rcbert McCormick and Joseph Patterson

photo credits

p.60: from "Tribune Tower, Chicago." Architectural Forum, vol. 43, Oct. 1925, p.185–198.
p.63 (above): McCormick Research Center, Wheaton, Illinois
p.63 (below), 65: Clark Sabula and Ali Sandu

2017
435 N. MICHIGAN AVENUE
CHICAGO, ILLINOIS, US

1935

2021

PROSPEKT STACHEK 18
ST. PETERSBURG, RUSSIA

KIROVSKY DISTRICT TOWN HALL

Between Cinema Paradiso and Russian Roulette: An iconic Constructivist city hall accrues unexpected functions, granting the building long life (and relevance)

Modernist architecture is known for its purity in structure and material as well as its clarity in composition and program. Kirovsky District Hall, designed by Noi Abramowitsch Trotzki, (1895–1940), with its cubic formal expression, its communist iconography on the façade and the dramatically rising tower is a celebrated example of Constructivist architecture in St. Petersburg. But who would think of programming a cinema, when conceiving a new district hall during the 1930s? And who would imagine the potential this particular program would offer for the longevity of the building? Trotzki's district hall not only marked the district which gave the building its name with a clearly expressed silhouette; intentionally or not, it is also a rare example of a multi-purpose office building, which apart from a large number of cellular offices for the district administration, over time housed a discotheque and a casino with slot machines and roulette tables. More and different screenings to expect in the future…

building credits

architect: Noi Abramowitsch Trotzki

photo credits

p.66 (above): А. Григорьев
p.66 (below): montage, unknown
p.67: Ilya Pilipenko

1938

Manfredo di Robilant

PALAZZO MONTECATINI

A monumental corporate palazzo evolves into a multi-tenant, market-based container

The Montecatini headquarters, in the center of Milan, has an exact date of birth – October 28, 1938 – made official by an instant-book, lavishly illustrated with photos and drawings of the completed building and of the construction process. All the features of the building are illustrated, with emphasis on its elements: façades, stairs, elevators, corridors, windows, walls, roof, and systems – these latter presented as the "nervous system of the building." The book is now a rarity, surprisingly ahead of its time, in its grey tissue cover with a bright yellow window that hosts the title: *Il palazzo per uffici Montecatini* – The palace for the Montecatini offices.

The title reflects the ambition of its architect, Gio Ponti, and its client, Guido Donegani, Montecatini CEO, to insert in the urban scene a perennial architecture, an instant-

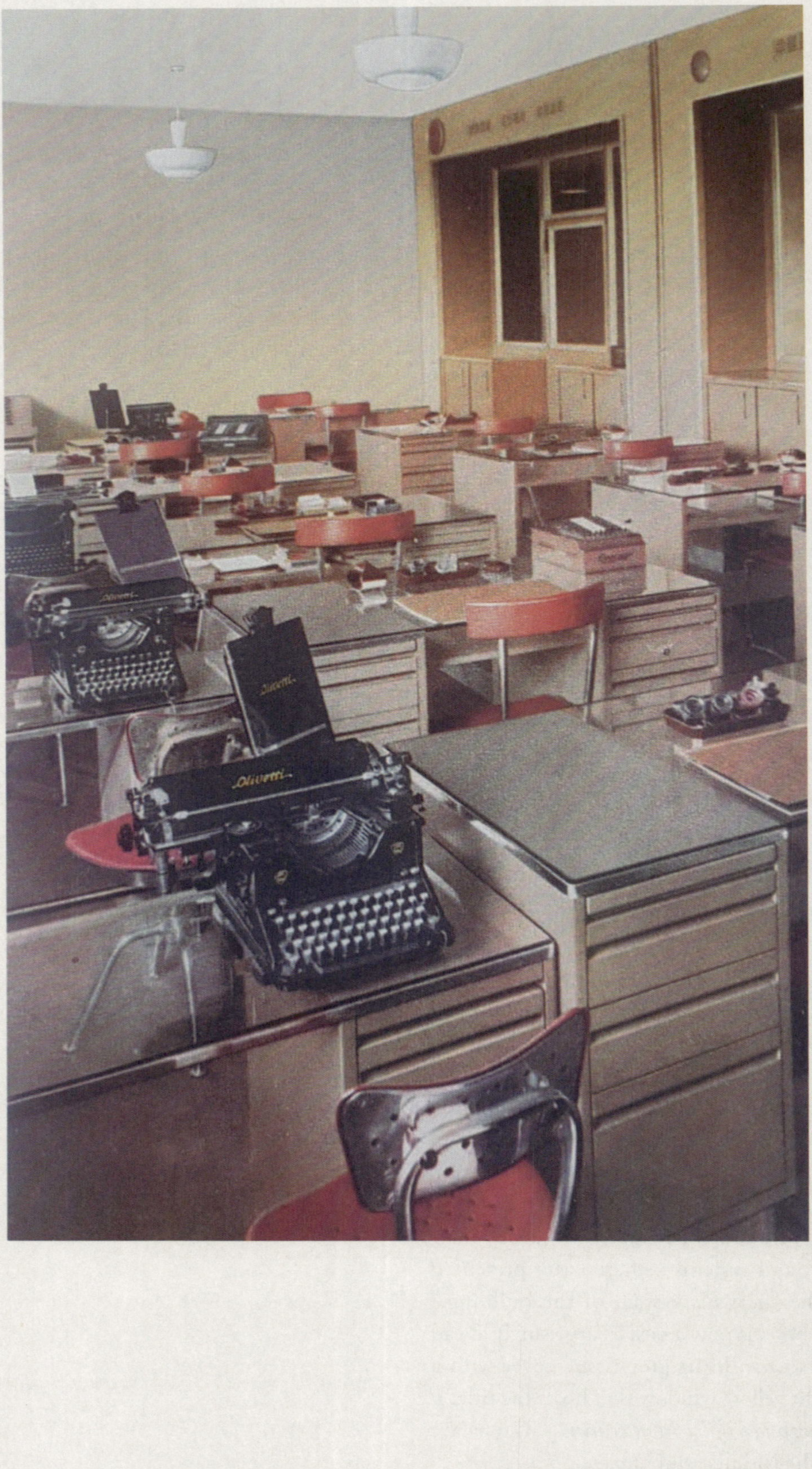
Olivetti
Olivetti

classic that is deserving of the title, palace. With an H-shaped plan, determined by the site, the building's central body of thirteen floors was reserved for the directors and the two lateral wings of eight (then nine) floors for the employees. The layout was based on a square module of 4.2 meters, which in Ponti's understanding corresponded to four desks. The prediction was made true by the fact that Ponti himself designed all the furniture in the Montecatini. Scattered pieces of this 20th-century *Gesamtkunstwerk* for white-collars recurrently appear in international auctions, and a Montecatini chair is today on display in the Denver Art Museum, designed by Ponti himself in the early 1970s.

The Montecatini was and is embedded in a densely built area, but Ponti managed to somehow detach it from the surroundings. The approach to the main entrance is almost processional, passing through a plaza raised slightly above street level and separated from it by a fence. Despite the aspiration, shared by client and architect, to separate the timeless building from quotidian churn outside, the Montecatini headquarters soon underwent changes. The company continued to grow, despite the death of the charismatic Donegani, to whom the street flanking the building is now dedicated. In 1950, a floor was added to each of the side wings, making Ponti furious about the loss of the original proportions. The following year, an additional Montecatini building – again by Ponti – was completed on the opposite site of the road, transforming the area into a small, de facto corporate campus, unusual for the center of an Italian city, even for Milan, the nation's economic capital. The campus also includes the

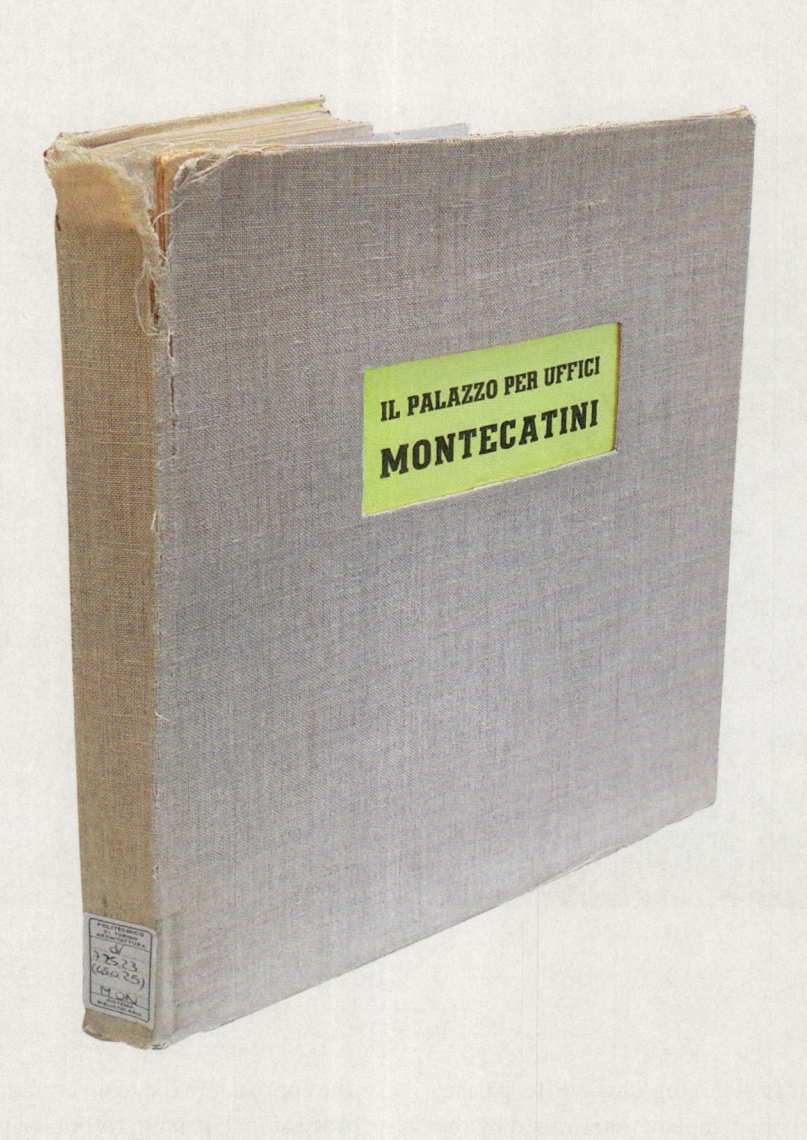

IL PALAZZO PER UFFICI
MONTECATINI

original Montecatini HQ, completed in 1928. The building of 1938 is contiguous and connected to this latter, creating a huge urban wall with a striking contrast between the smoothness of Ponti's façade and the roughness of the other, cladded with rusticated stones and accessorised with columns.

The 1950s were climactic years for Montecatini, the largest chemical company in Italy, producing fertilisers used around the world. But soon the company lost its market share and in 1966 it merged with Edison, an Italian hydroelectric company. Decades of troubled corporate governance were at odds with Ponti's architectural portrait of Montecatini as "a harmonious and disciplined body." Eventually, in 2002, Montedison (the merger company) was dismantled and the campus in Milan abandoned. The Montecatini buildings were put up for sale.

Currently, six companies own the 1938 building. Only one of those operates out of the palazzo; 65 percent is owned by a single real estate company, and five other realtors own and lease the rest of the building. In total there are 22 tenants, inevitably introducing a wide variety of floorplans and interior fit-outs, even though they are all financial companies, with the exception of a cosmetics company and two of Milan's largest notary offices.

The building is managed and run by three different legal entities: two condo associations, and a "super-condo" which bridges them. The budget of the "super-condo" is approximately €1.8 million per year, and the rebuilding cost, estimated for insurance purposes in the event of some disaster, was €60 million in 2018.

The current condition of the building reflects the total disappearance of the original program, as well as the obvious replacement of the original systems that made the Montecatini a frontrunner in Italy for climate control and connectivity. In face of the massive number of systems, Ponti used three different strategies to incorporate them into the architectural composition. In one case he put them on show as *objets trouvés*; in other cases he included them in the architectural design as motifs; in the case of the boilers in the basement, he used bright colors as decoration. The HVAC equipment has been relocated from the basement and the ground floor to the top of the central tower so that the roof – barely visible because of the density of the area – now looks like an involuntary hi-tech tour-de-force of engines and pipes. From the street, the proliferation of window signs broadcasts the multiplicity of tenants, in stark contrast to the windows' obsessive uniformity, intended to project corporate order from the building to the adjacent street.

Visiting the building's common areas while holding in mind the images from its "birth-book", *Il palazzo per uffici Montecatini* would disappoint detail-oriented philologists, but reassure those who think that architecture is definitively and simply about composing volumes and making spaces: from this point of view the work of Ponti is still well recognizable and functioning.

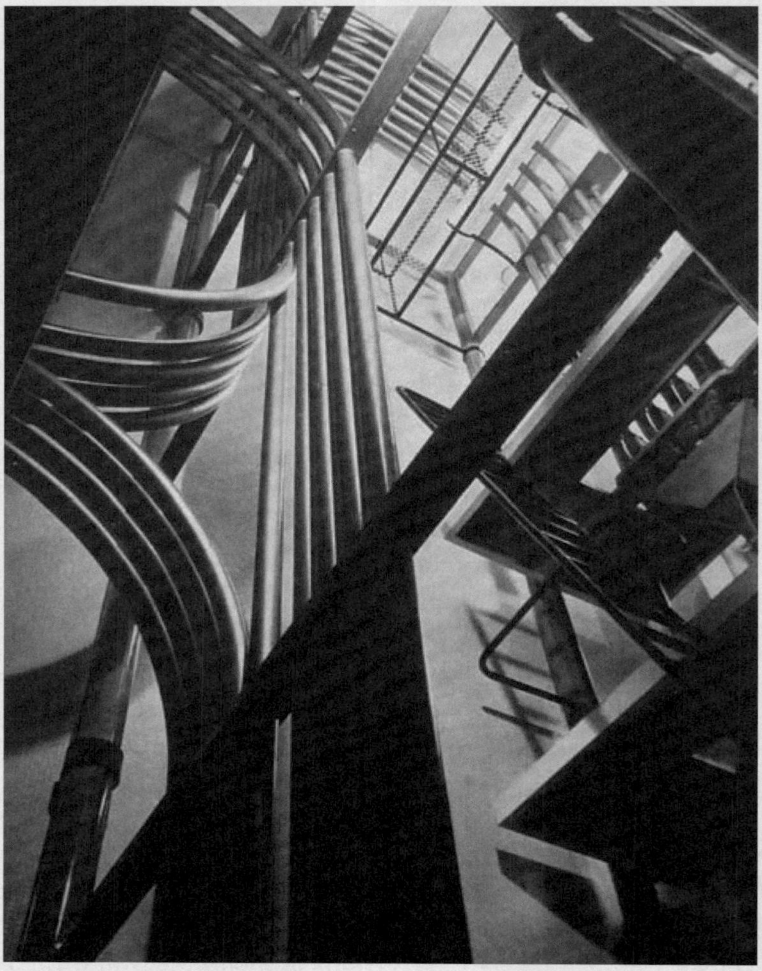

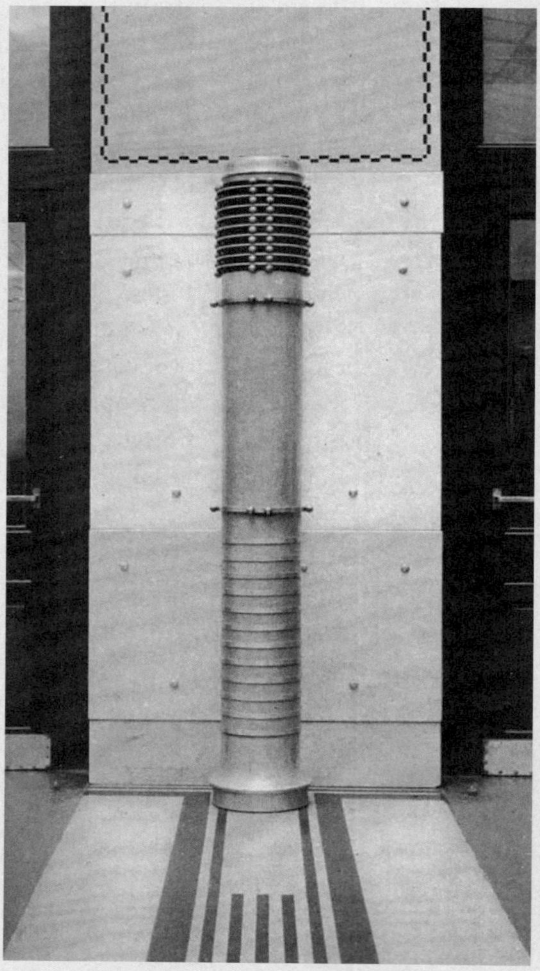

The lobby was completely renovated in the mid-2000s, and it is likely that Ponti – obsessed with interior details – would not appreciate the two garish glass-fountains and the generic marble flooring (the marble that Ponti generously employed throughout the building were from quarries owned by Montecatini, which started, in the late 19th century, as a mining and marble-extraction company). Ponti dedicated careful attention to the marble, employing an unusual crosscut to the raw blocks in order to liberate façade cladding panels from it. Apart from the stairs, rarely used since the building has 19 large elevators, all other interior spaces have been completely transformed. According to Giuseppe Serughetti, a civil engineer who has worked as the building manager since 2018, most tenants opted for open plan layouts, while the original layout was based on a series of corridors.

On a day in mid-August, during lunch break, the building is mostly emptied which is on average 3,000 users per day. On the walkway facing the main façade there is no trace of what Serughetti calls the "guerrilla" parking of scooters.

By chance, "AcomeA", the financial boutique, still maintains a corridor layout. Rocco Lucca, one of the company's leaders, describes the place with enthusiasm, showing the original double-windows, which have been preserved throughout the building, though they have been all sealed because the sills are too low to comply with current safety codes.

The pervasive presence of vertical ducts and risers for mechanical systems hampers the building's adaptability because in case of fire they would convey smoke and heat. The remedy would be isolating each tract of each floor with sealed partitions, but this is a difficult job. Therefore, in some cases waivers based on the "historical" character of the building have been requested, something that usually happens with pre-modern listed buildings – often palaces – now used for public functions.

This may be a paradoxical fulfilment of Ponti's aim of creating a palace, indicating an alternative yet modern path to orthodox functionalism. As for listing, it will probably happen soon: in 2018 the building was surveyed by preservation authorities. Resulting preservation orders may apply to the exterior, to the remaining original parts of the interior, or to the whole building. In this case, every renovation or refit would require a 90-day authorization period, eliminating the flexibility that Ponti infused in his "palatial" architecture. Meanwhile, the Montecatini building continues its day-to-day activity, indifferent to the long term.

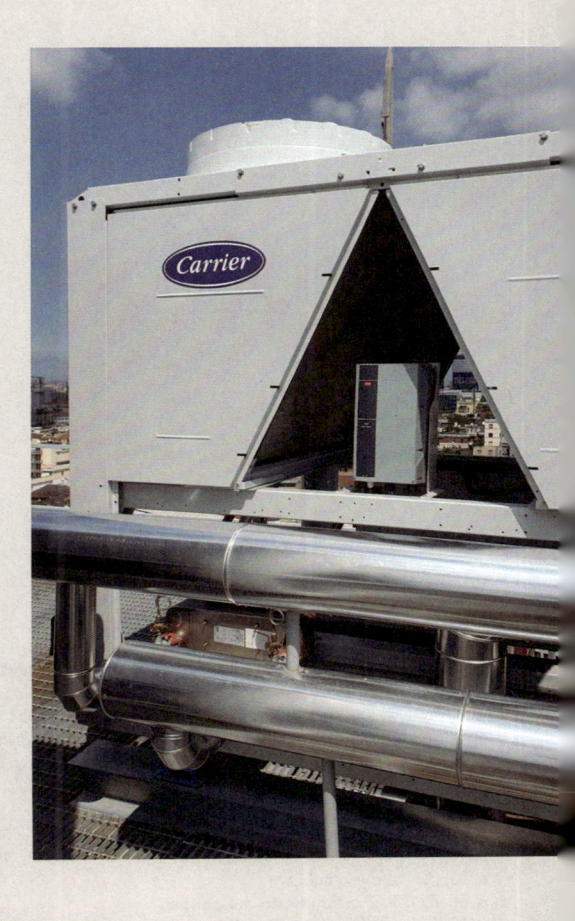

building credits

client: Guido Donegani, president and CEO of the Montecatini group
architect: Gio Ponti
engineering: Eugenio Soncini, Antonio Fornaroli, Montecatini technical office
construction management: Pietro Giulio Bosisio and Mario Gobbi Belcredi

photo credits

p.68, 74 (all), 78: from Il palazzo per uffici Montecatini, 1938
p.70, 72 (above): unkown
p.71, 75, 77, 79: Manfredo di Robilant
p.72 (below): Gio Ponti files, Centro Studi e Archivio della Comunicazione, Università degli Studi di Parma

2019
2. LARGO GUIDO DONEGANI
MILAN, ITALY

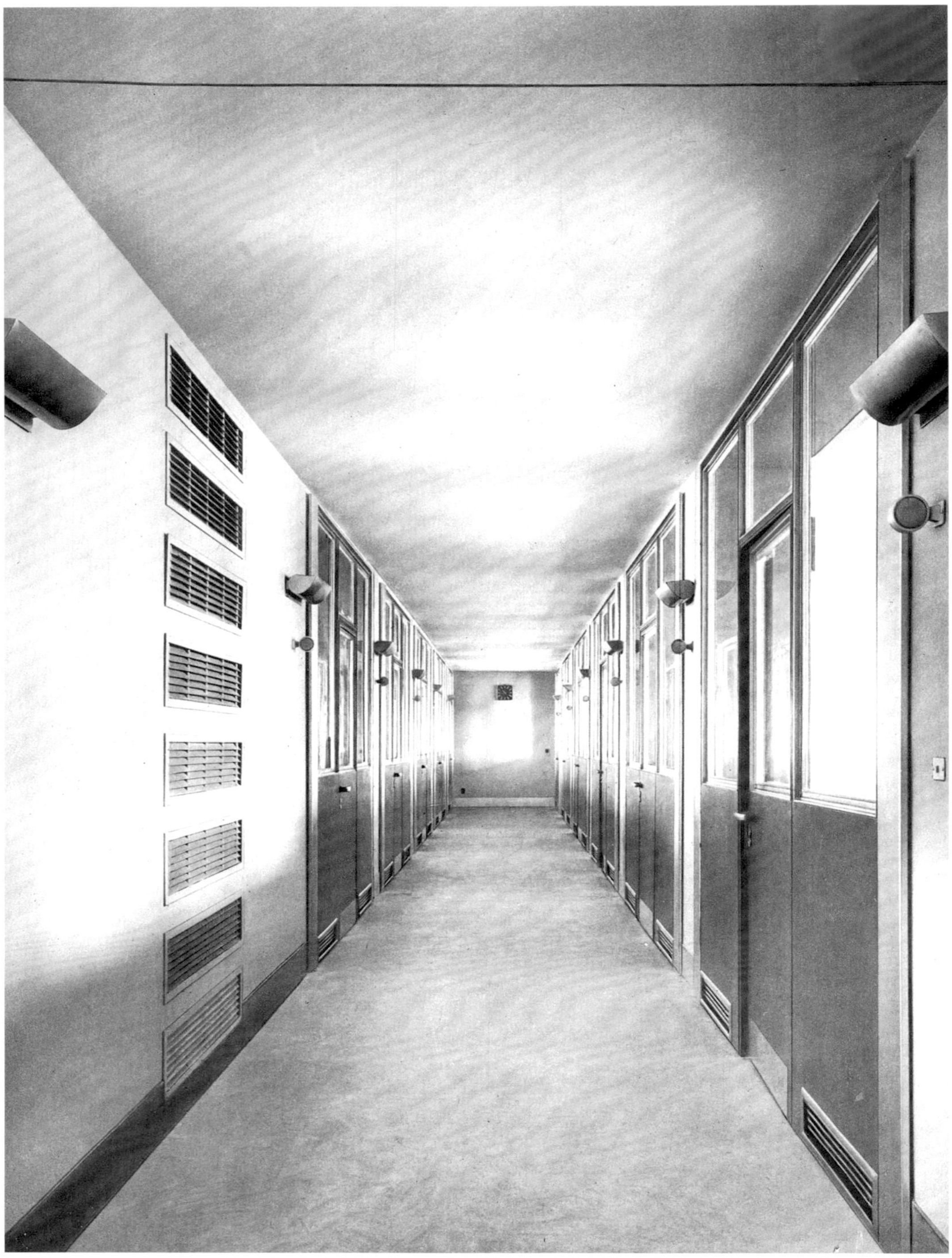

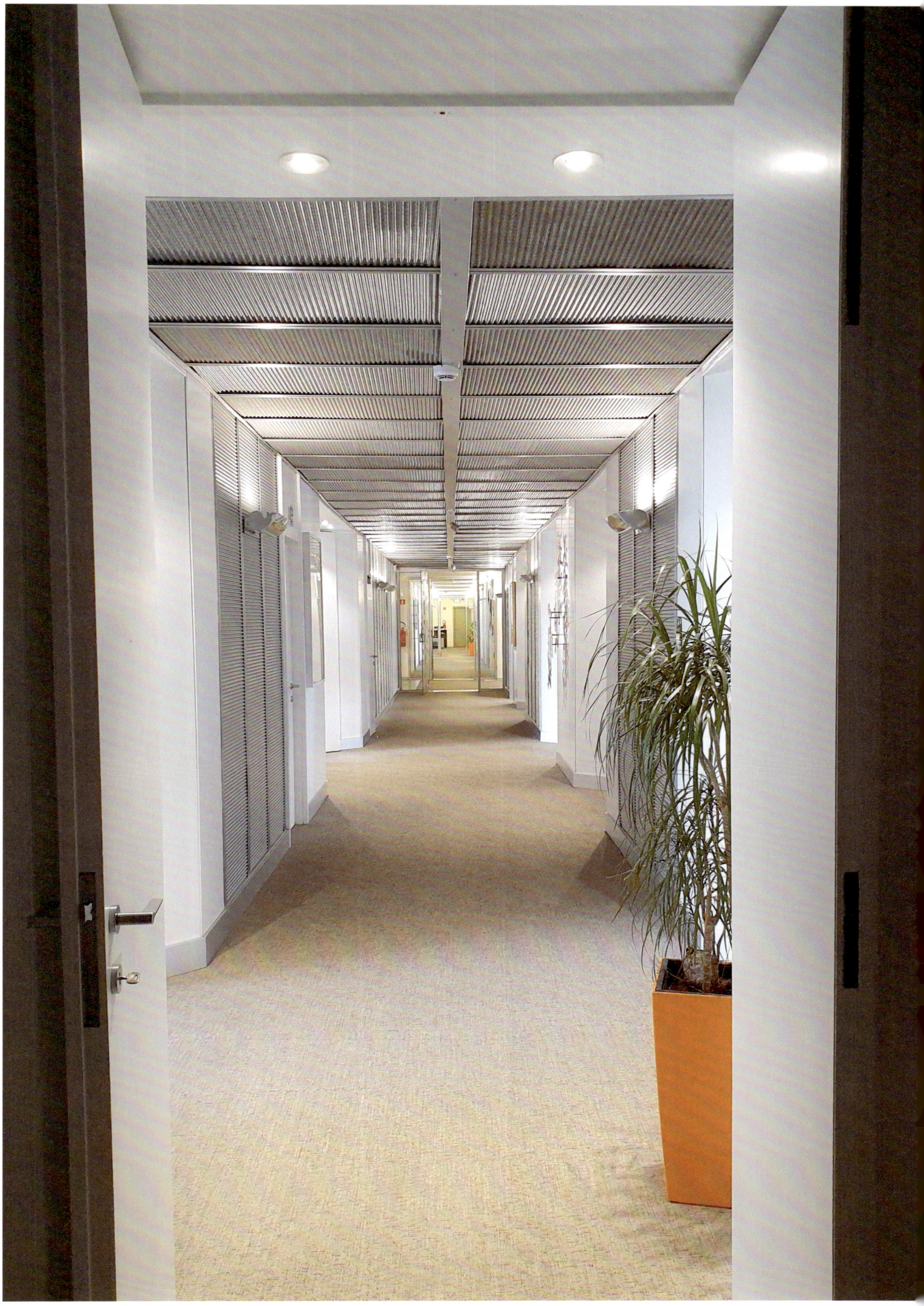

1940/43

Ruth Baumeister

PALAZZO DELLA CIVILTÀ ITALIANA

A fashion house exploits a monument's dubious history, while scaling down its monumental interiors to make it work as a contemporary office

If you land at Fiumicino and take the train to Roma Termini, out of nowhere, you will suddenly spot the impressive mass of a square shaped six-story building. You are in EUR, a business district about 12 km outside the historical center, but you might recall this building from a film you saw once: Julie Taymor's *Titus* (1999); or Peter Greenaway's surrealist tale of an architect searching his himself in the eternal city, *The Belly of an Architect* (1985); or in Italian neorealist masterpieces like Antonini's *Eclipse* (1962); Fellini's *The Temptation of Dr. Antonio* (1962) and *8½* (1963), to name a few. The building looks familiar and yet strange. Its repeated arched openings, covering the entire surface of the building, recall the Colosseum – locals call it Colosseo Quadrato. The perfect grid of arches, identical on all four sides, conveys permanence and rational order. Its simplicity and boldness makes it iconic, unmistakable from far away.

Today, the Colosseo Quadrato houses the headquarters of the luxury fashion house Fendi, founded by Adele Casagrande and Edoardo Fendi in Rome in 1925. For decades, Fendi was operated as a family business by the couple and their four daughters, with Karl Lagerfeld among their chief designers. During the 1990s the company faced a crisis, as opposition grew to wearing fur and counterfeit products took their market share. In 1999, the Fendi daughters sold 51 percent of their stake to Prada and Louis Vuitton Moet Hennessy. LVMH bought all shares in 2001 and expanded the business, opening Fendi stores in London, Paris, Moscow, Dubai, Osaka, and Shanghai, among other cities.

Fendi is known for instrumentalizing cultural heritage for its catwalk shows and advertising campaigns: they launched their Shanghai flagship store with a show on the Great Wall of China in 2007. In 2016, they supported the restoration of the Trevi fountain in Rome, and in return were allowed to present their new collection there the year after. Their choice to move their headquarters from the historical center to the iconic Colosseo Quadrato did not come as a surprise, but it did trigger debate. It is not just another office building, but "the most important modern monument in the city," according to Giorgio Muratore (1946–2017), professor of architecture history at Rome's La Sapienza University.[1]

Before Fendi signed their 15-year lease, the building had stood empty for 30 years. Until 1985, the Federazione nazionale dei Cavalieri del Lavoro – a congregation of chevaliers – occupied the third, fifth and sixth floors. Part of the ground floor, the seventh floor, the attic and the terrace were reserved for Italy's air force and the meteorological institute. The building was named *Tempio di Lavoro* [The Temple of Work] and was instrumentalized as part of the postwar work ethic, which included the state organization of social and cultural activities related to work. The Italian Order of Merit of Labor, granted by the President, was given in a ceremony held at the building – almost exclusively to men – for extraordinary achievement in business. Among the recipients of the order were industrialists like Giovanni Battista Pirelli, Gianni Agnelli, and Silvio Berlusconi.

The monumental building sits on an elevated platform with a broad stair leading up to the entrance. Like many postwar office buildings, it is a box-shaped volume with an unornamented façade. In plan, it is symmetrical, with little usable interior space surrounding the large, six-story central void. A photograph shows a corner office with three workstations that appear lost in the spacious room, with ceilings so high they are not visible in the picture. A reception space in front of the offices is equally generous, equipped with bulky lounge furniture and artworks under a lofty glass ceiling. In both images, there seems to be an error in scale. Fendi's in-house architect, Marco Costanzi, who worked on the redesign of the interior to make it fit for office use[2], solved this problem by introducing a black steel structure. The new is clearly distinguished from the old, historical substance, which is landmarked; and the additional structure provides an office environment that corresponds with the scale of the human body, inside a monumental space that otherwise seems over dimensioned.

Two photographs from the 1950s demonstrate that the building's form and function somehow do not correlate. There is a reason for this. When the Federazione nazionale dei Cavalieri del Lavoro signed the contract with the city, they took over a building which was never completed, had been abandoned for many years, and was in a state of ruin. The condition for the 29-year lease was that the tenant would complete and renovate the building at the same time.

Marcello Piacentini (1881–1960), head of architecture and urbanism at EUR, expressed in a letter to Rome's urban administrative chief his grave concerns about the plans to transform the building, which was supposed to be a center for culture, science, and arts, to something as banal as public and private offices, open to people of low class like the chevaliers. He could not see how offices with partitions measuring about two meters from room to room and from room to corridor could be created in this building.[3] The vision for this building, and for the new EUR district, was a different one. Piacentini himself – in his role as First Architect of State under the Fascist regime – helped conceive the district, which was planned for a large exhibition celebrating the twentieth anniversary of Fascism, in 1942. The plan represented Mussolini's vision of Rome's expansion towards the sea. The Duce's agenda was to connect fascism to antiquity by creating a new architectural style, called La Romanità.

The Palazzo della Civiltà Italiana (Palace of the Italian Civilization) – the original appellation of the *Tempio di Lavoro* – was supposed to be the spiritual center of this new *Roma al mare*. It was designed by three architects, Giovanni Guerini (1887–1972), Ernesto Lapadula (1902–1968) and Mario Romano (1898–1087). Two of them young, all three of them rather unknown, they won the design competition for the project in December 1937. In the plans submitted to competition, the building was eight stories and had 13 arches on each floor. The corner columns were deemed too slender, so the design was modified into a six-story building with nine arches. (The number of arches was now equal to the number of letters in the Duce's name, Benito vertically and Mussolini horizontally.) The first floor was increased in height, and on top of the highest row of arches, a crowning element was added, giving space for the inscription: "A people of poets, artists, heroes, saints, thinkers, scientists, sailors, migrators" – words which Mussolini uttered on October 2, 1935, when calling for a general mobilization against the economic sanctions that were imposed on Italy. Mussolini visited the construction site in April 1939, and in November 1940 the building was inaugurated even though it was not finished. Duting the course of the Second World War, the planned exhibition was canceled. In 1943, German occupying troops used the ground floor for offices.

After the war, EUR and the Palazzo was completed according to the original plans accompanied by a long controversial debate over how to handle the problematic cultural heritage. The controversy flared up again when Fendi moved in. The brand employed the slogan "Made in Italy," and was accused of aligning itself with Fascist rhetoric as it promoted the Palazzo as an ideal representation of Italian civilization from ancient Rome to the 20th century, and used the building as a backdrop for its fashion shows. Was this the celebration of the creative spirit of a nation, or a deliberate and sinister frisson of fascism and fashion? Just how pliable is the original symbolism of the Palazzo given that fascism was (and is) anything but over in Italy?[4] Fendi's chief executive, Pietro Beccari, argued: "For me it [the building's Fascist origins] is a non-issue. For the Romans it is a non-issue. For Italians it is a non-issue. This building is beyond a discussion of politics. It is aesthetics. It is a masterpiece of architecture. To rebuild it today would cost more than €500m."[5]

The building's compelling elegance and monumentality has been used by different actors throughout its history. Italian Cinema discovered the Colosseo Quadrato in 1945. In Rosselini's *Roma Città Aperta* (1945, Rome Open City), the building thrones in the background while partisans hide behind bushes waiting to attack a convoy of German troops and free their prisoners of war. In this scene, the Colosseo Quadrato, erected to symbolize the power of the Fascist regime – and also used by Mussolini in propaganda films – all of a sudden, through its frozen appearance represents the fall of the very regime that conceived of it. The orderly, archaic elegance is completely disconnected from life – the chaotic war happening in front of it. Antonini's *The Lady without Camelia*s (1953) emphasizes the Palazzo's metaphysical character. During Italy's economic rise in the 1960s, Vittorio De Sicca's *Il boom* instrumentalizes the building as a vanishing point at the end of the busy Via Cristoforo Colombo, symbolizing Italy's yearning for modernization.

More recently, Julie Taymor's *Titus* (1999), an adaptation of Shakespeare's tragedy, uses the building as a location, blurring past and present by equipping actors in togas with guns and 20th-century cars. The Colosseo Quadrato acts as a hybrid time machine blending the present with past. Critic Gianni Canova explains the building's enduring appeal, "The Square Colosseum is especially suited as a film set because of its formal and semiotic polyvalence. Because of its capacity to generate the most disparate circuits of meaning. Because it is impossible to definitively pigeonhole it as pertaining to a particular school or trend, and that one alone."[6]

notes

1   "Partys auf dem Denkmal," interview with Giorgio Muratore by Leonardo Lella, in: *Baumeister*, April 2016 (Callwey, München), p.81.
2   Apart from the offices, which occupy most of the building, it also contains design studios, exhibition space, and cafeteria.
3   "Mi permetta che le confessi la mia perplessità di adattare il Palazzo della Civiltà dell'EUR a uffici di destinazione commune e modesta. La grandiosità di questo edificio, il suo carattere modern, ma isperato alle forme classiche, il luogo dove si innalza al disopra di tutti gli altri edificio un ruolo elevato, possibilmente adibendendolo a centri culturali, scientifici, artistici, ecc. non vedrei possible disporre in questo sontuoso edificio uffici qualsiasi aperti a un publico numerosoe di bassa classe, con tramezzature tra camera e camera e tra camera e corridoi, eseguite circa due metri." Lettera di Piaccentini à Testa, 01.12.1955/ EUR, CI, Palazzo della Civiltà , Trattazione generale, cart. 14/4, quoted in Casciato/ Poretti, 2002:116. Translated into English by the author. (Virgilio Testa, 1889–1978, worked in the Capitolinian Administration of the city of Rome and was responsible for the development of EUR between 1951–1973.)
4   See: Owen Hatherley, "Fendi vidi vici: when Fashion flirts with Fascism," *Architectural Review*, March 3, 2015: "However much the architecture of the era can be interesting and attractive, its values were deeply sick. It is right that its architecture remain tainted."
5   Stephanie Kirchgaessner, "Fendi rejects criticism over new HQ in Mussolini propaganda building," *Guardian*, October 22, 2015.
6   Gianni Canova, "Between Proportion and Disproportion: The Square Colosseum on the Silver Screen," in: Mario Piazza: *Palazzo della civiltà italiana* (Rizzoli, 2017), p.85.

building credits

architect: Giovanni Guerrini, Ernesto La Padula and Mario Romano

photo credits

p.80: Cartoni
p.85, 88 (right), 89: Jens Frederiksen
p.86: Paul Roland
p.87: Phillip Sinden
p.88 (left), 90: unknown
p.91 (above): Andrea Jemolo
p.91 (below): Emanuale Scorcelletti

2021
QUADRATO DELLA CONCORDIA 3
ROME, ITALY

1962

VN POPOLO DI POETI DI ARTISTI DI EROI
DI SANTI DI PENSATORI DI SCIENZIATI
DI NAVIGATORI DI TRASMIGRATORI

2015

83

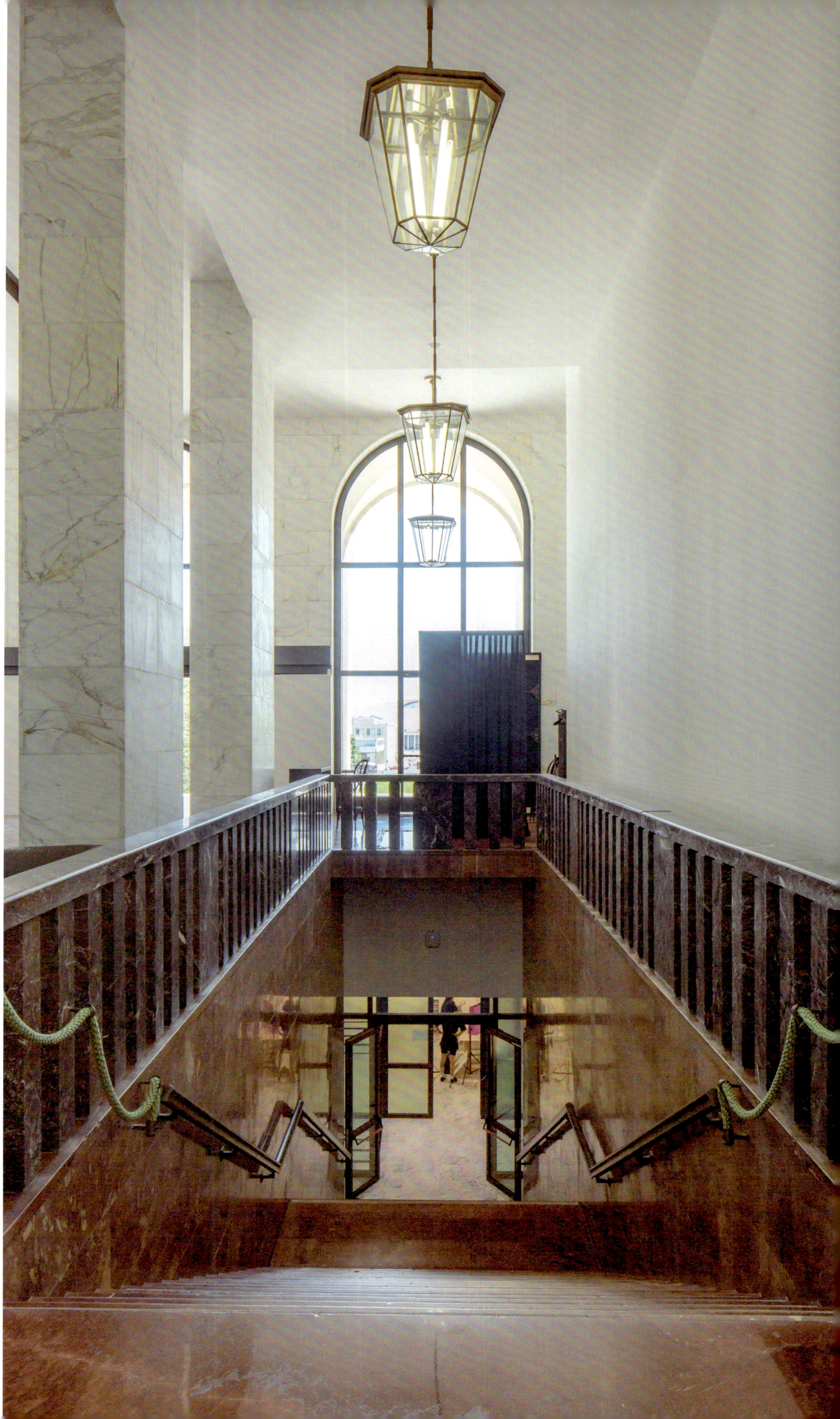

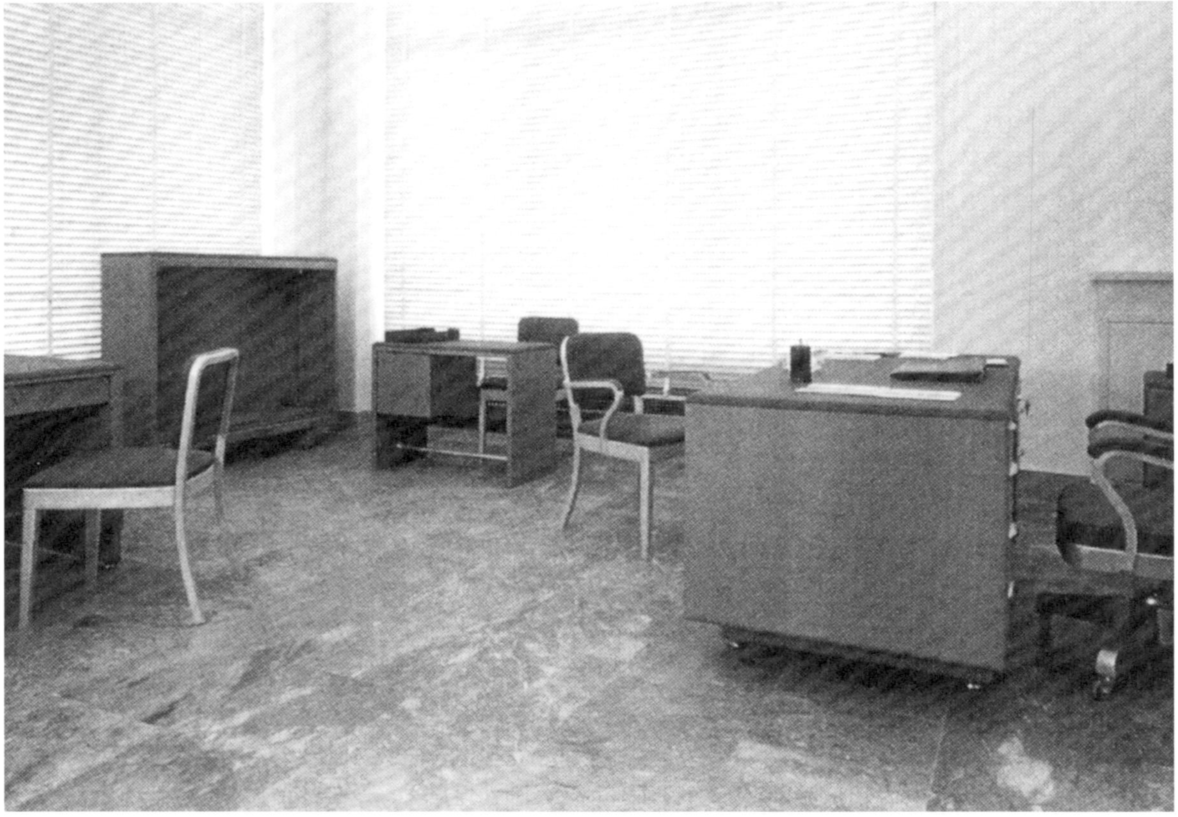

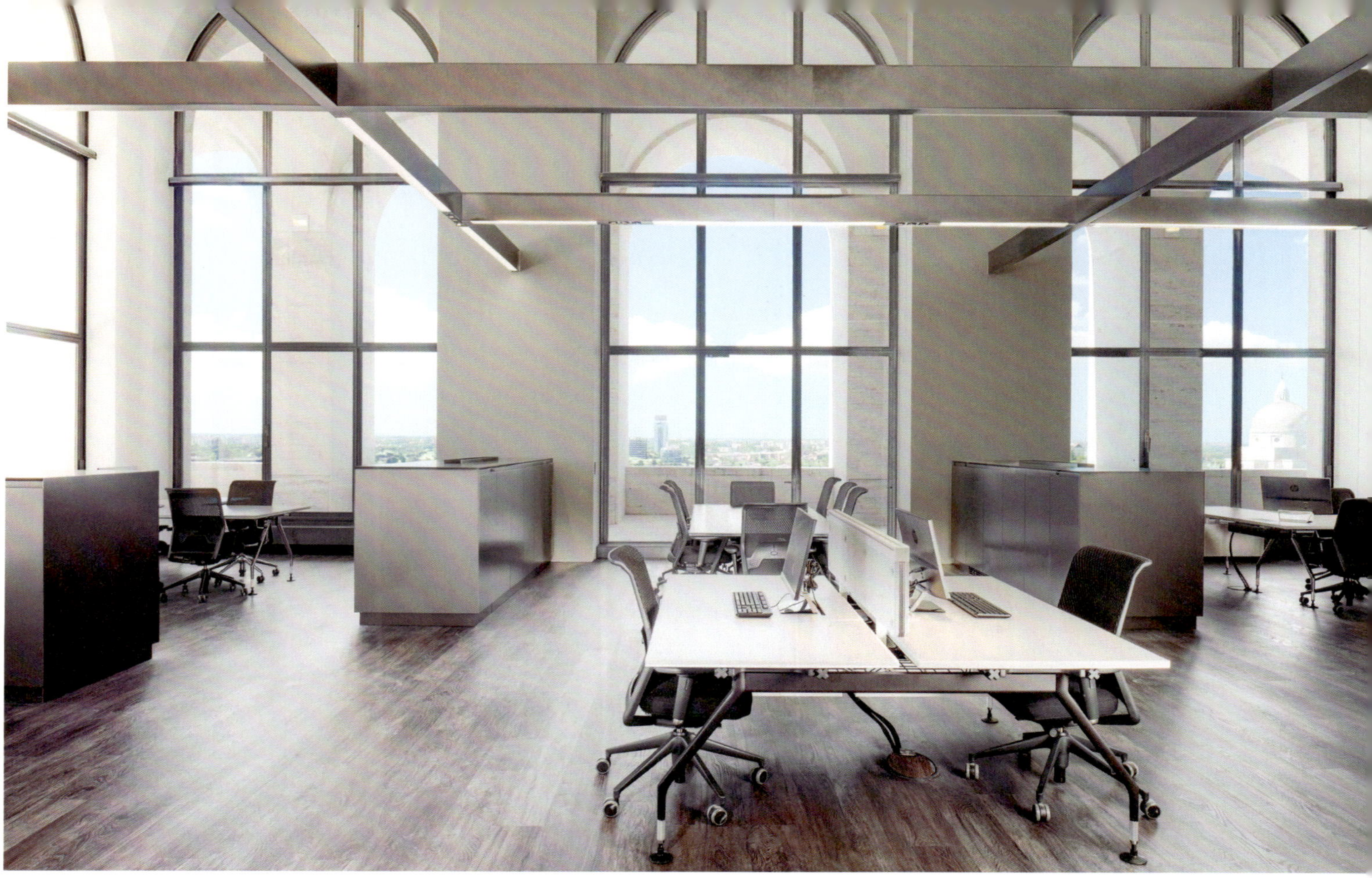

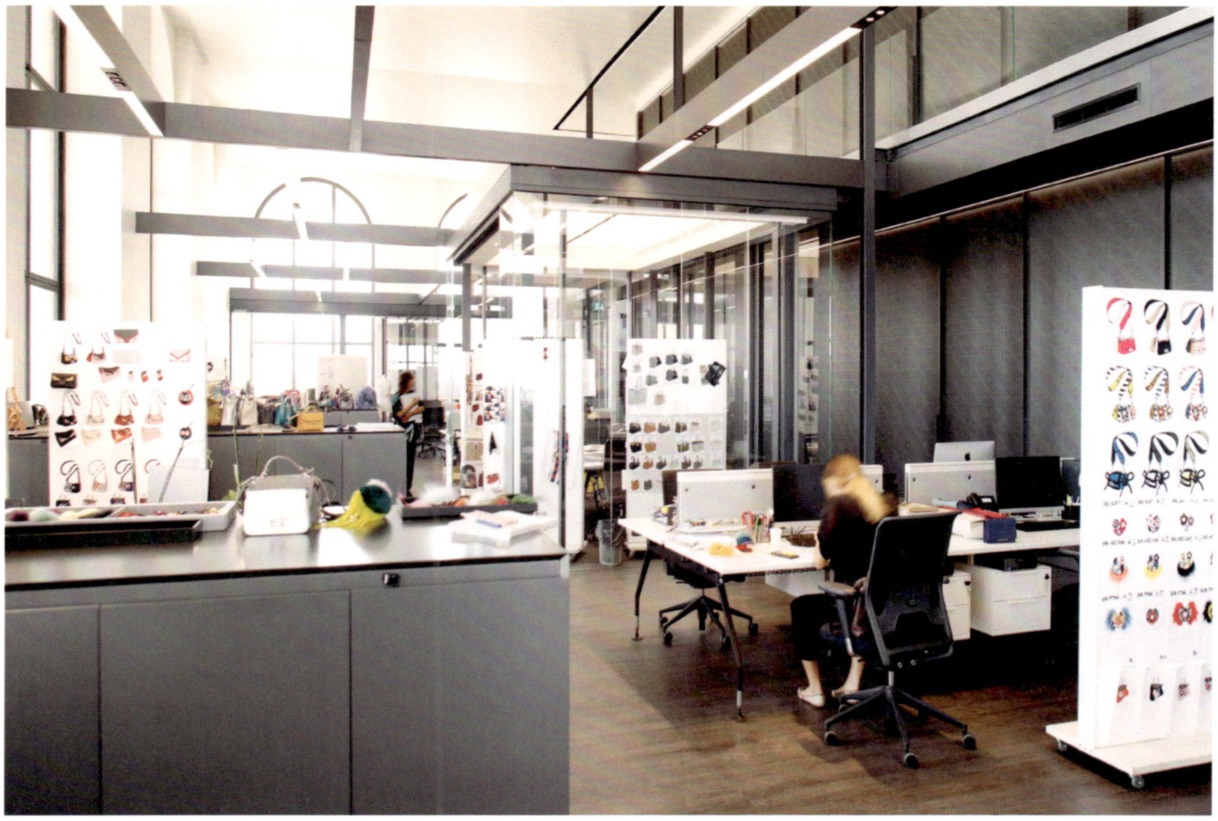

1941

Ruth Baumeister

AARHUS CITY HALL

Originally attacked for not being Danish enough, a city hall sustains itself for 80 years thanks to the consistency of its owner and user (hint: they're the same)

When talking about eternity in architecture, no one would consider the 20th-century office building. And with good reason: the office building typology is an invention of the modern period, with an intrinsic need to continuously adapt to the demands of the market and its constantly changing modes of work. And yet, Aarhus City Hall, designed by Arne Jacobsen and Eric Møller, is a rare exception to the office building's mutability, having sustained more or less in its original state for almost a century.

Landmarked in 1994, the building was subsequently listed as one of 12 architectural gems in the "Danish Cultural Canon."[1] Initially though, it was contentious at best, despised at worst: "I do not know of any building that has divided the public in Denmark as much as ... Aarhus City Hall,"[2] art historian Leo K. Jensen wrote, 54 years

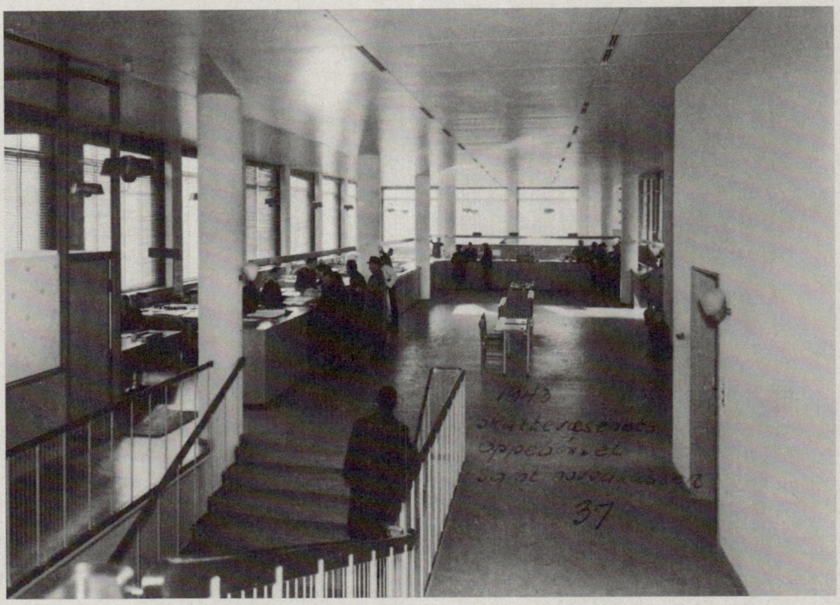
37

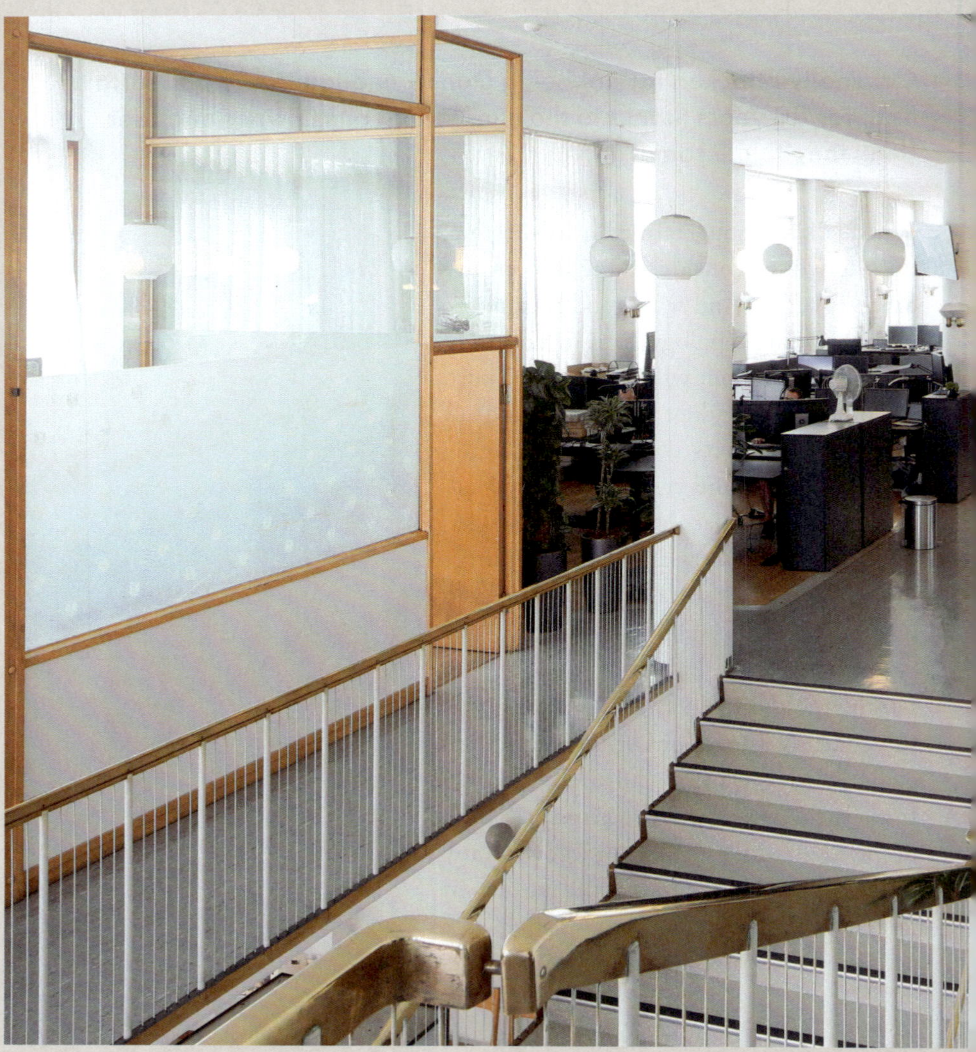

after a jury declared Jacobsen and Møller's scheme the winner in the competition for the building. The jury's report, penned in 1937, raved, "The building's exterior has a beautiful, monumental, and festive character which expresses its function in a natural way. The entry's design reflects exceptional talent and is an attractive and dignified solution to the assignment presented."[3] But the local press described the design as "[t]he ordinary style of the time, which here expresses itself as a slightly mitigated and sad form of functionalism."[4] The building was described as a "cement or glass box," or an "administration building in the style of an aquarium."[5] This critique triggered a heated discussion among politicians and the public. How is it that a building can divide a nation — especially one renowned for its aspirations for unity and its capacity to achieve consensus?

When the design competition was announced for Aarhus's new city hall, there had not been a public commission of this scale and prestige in Denmark since Copenhagen City Hall, inaugurated in 1905. During the last quarter of the 19th century, Aarhus's population had tripled and in the 1930s the city was still booming. Now the second-largest city of the kingdom, Aarhus was eager to compete with the capital. A civic reinvention was called for.

The new city hall was part of a larger urban extension that was started at the beginning of the 20th century, and its site was previously used as a cemetery. Jacobsen and Møller's winning scheme consisted of three orthogonal buildings of different lengths, depths, and heights, aligned along Søndergade and Park Allée in an L-shape composition, its configuration and formal language echoing Walter Gropius' Bauhaus buildings in Dessau. Both the main building, parallel to Søndergade, and the tall administration wing along Park Allée were accessible from a large atrium lit from above. The main building contains the entrance hall; hovering over it on the level above is the city council assembly and a large multifunctional space with offices on either side. The administration wing contains offices connected by bridges and galleries from the atrium. The lowest of the three volumes – with open office space for public services – distinguishes itself through larger windows and a gridded concrete façade.

Jacobsen and Møller's sober scheme was a provocation for some: such a restrained, undecorated design could not promote the image of the rising city of Aarhus. During the mid-1930s, Denmark was threatened by Nazism in neighboring Germany: Hitler designated Danes part of the Aryan "race" and culture, and absorption into Germany was the goal. Danes fought Hitler's ethnic characterization and asserted Danish culture and values as independent of Germany. Free of references to national symbolism or building tradition, for its critics Jacobsen and Møller's scheme was not Danish enough. The architects' principles of function and utility engendered an anonymity that triggered politicians and the public who demanded a monumental and symbolic architectural language for a civic project of this scale. Povl Drachmann, a conservative, waxed lyrical:, when he stated, "For many years, Aarhus was in need of and has worked on getting a new city hall as a new heart for the city, an icon, a unifying symbol for the effort in Jutland to find a powerful center point. Imagine, if a town hall had come to be monumental, really jutlandish in its lines and power, shaped by the mainland's strong soil, dignified, self-conscious and rising partner in the face of Copenhagen's city hall… Oh, are you the house of the capital, then I am the house of the mainland. Let us together lift our towers and peaks towards Denmark's sky, together we are equals. Each one of us with roots in its own soil, but nevertheless both Danish!"[6]

Such sentiments forced Jacobsen and Møller to unwillingly incorporate, a clock tower with a viewing platform into their scheme, in order to boost the building's iconicity. The fact that the clock is placed on the lower end of the tower, which makes it difficult to read both from afar and from up close ridicules its purpose and points to the architect's reluctance to incorporate it. Furthermore, they had to replace the white plastered façade they proposed with one of distinguished Norwegian Porsgrunn marble.

Aarhus City Hall incorporates what modern architecture became famous for: functionality, flexibility, and technology. The exterior walls and floors of the two large volumes are loadbearing, solid cast, reinforced concrete. Inside, the large atrium is lit from above and by huge windows. Walls of reinforced concrete with bear space for hot-air channels, closets, doors, etc. The building is divided into bays of 3.15 meters along the longitudinal axis and all intersecting walls can be moved without any structural changes. The smaller volume, on Park Allée, is constructed of a reinforced concrete frame, to allow the larger windows, which give light to the deep open-plan office space inside. The same concrete construction is used for the 60-meter bell tower.

The entire building, from the urban scale to the smallest detail, is characterised by soft contours: the ramp leading up to the main entrance is rounded and the open space in front of the entrance on Park Allée is curved. Inside the building, loadbearing concrete is rounded with smooth plaster; softened edges are also found on the building's doors, stairs, and balustrades. Exquisite parquet floors, brass fixtures, and curving spiral stairs lend a generous, elegant atmosphere inside. Comfort, enabled by technology, was critical: every office was equipped with radiators running from a district heating system, and those offices were accessed by elevators. Underfloor heating warmed the circulation spaces, balconies, and bridges; additional convection heating was provided in the main hall.

During the Nazi occupation of Denmark during the war, the new city hall was secretly used by the resistance. In the large basement, flyers were printed, weapons were stored and the long, narrow space under the administration wing was used as a firing range. The basement hideout was discovered a few months before the end of the war, and in an act of revenge, the Nazis bombed the building, in February and March 1945. It was severely damaged but quickly rebuilt after the war without any major alterations.

The design of Aarhus City Hall, which initially divided the nation, today is considered one of the highlights of Scandinavian Modernism. The building became considered a *Gesamtkunstwerk*: everything – from the urban scale of the building to the interiors, the uniforms and briefcases of some of the personnel, as well as the lamps, ashtrays, coat hangers, and stamps – was subject to design. For the furniture design, Jacobsen and Møller hired the young cabinet maker and then recent design graduate Hans Wegner, who became one of the most successful Danish furniture designers worldwide. Due to their comfort, timeless aesthetics, and the quality of the craftsmanship, much of the furniture is still in use, almost 80 years after the building's inauguration (an impressive sustainability credential). A glance at the mayor's office today speaks for itself: "The cigar box has been removed and the bitters hidden from sight, if they are there at all,"[7] is how an architect recently described the almost untouched spatial setup of the room.

Besides the repairs due to the war damage, there have been no major large-scale renovation since the building's inauguration in 1941. Some office partition walls have been removed or added, changes that were easily metabolised thanks to the building's structure. Apart from renovation of the glass roof on the main building and the large window in the multi-purpose space to improve thermal performance, the renewal of some toilet facilities, and the restoration of the bell tower, no significant alterations have been made. Contemporary additions such as accessibility ramps, a smoke detection system, CCTV, and coffee kiosks, have had minimal impact. Occasionally, single office windows and worn-out pieces of linoleum or wooden flooring or stairs are replaced. When it comes to additions, adaptions, and repairs, invisibility is the goal.

The building's ability *to sustain* has been enabled by factors beyond architecture though: the owner – who also happens to be the user – has not changed since 1937. Moreover, the owner and user also maintains the building. Craftspeople and facility management are in-house and a committee of representatives from all departments of City Hall collectively agree on changes or adaptations, which are then forwarded to the architect-in-charge. Those who complain about the draft in their office are reminded that they inhabit a landmarked building and are advised to bring an additional sweater.

Plan af Stue

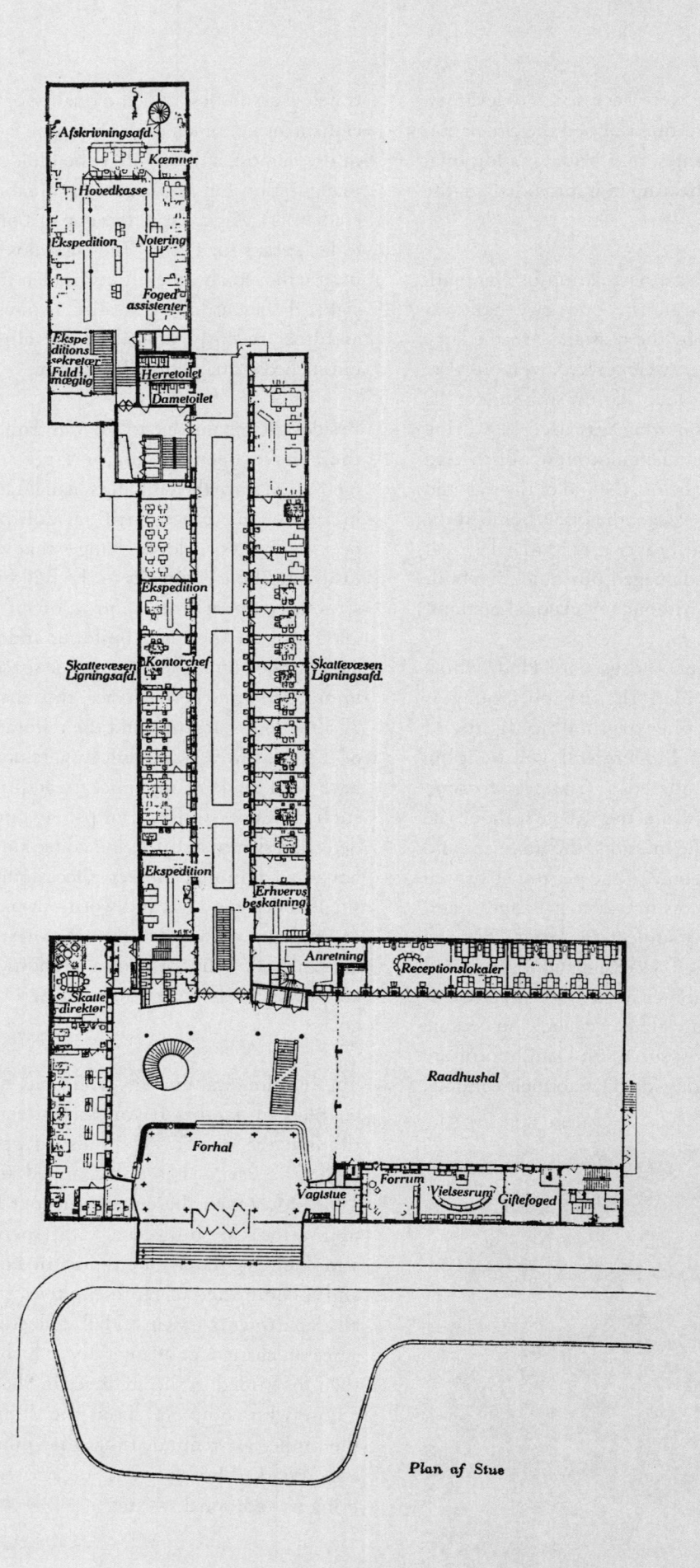

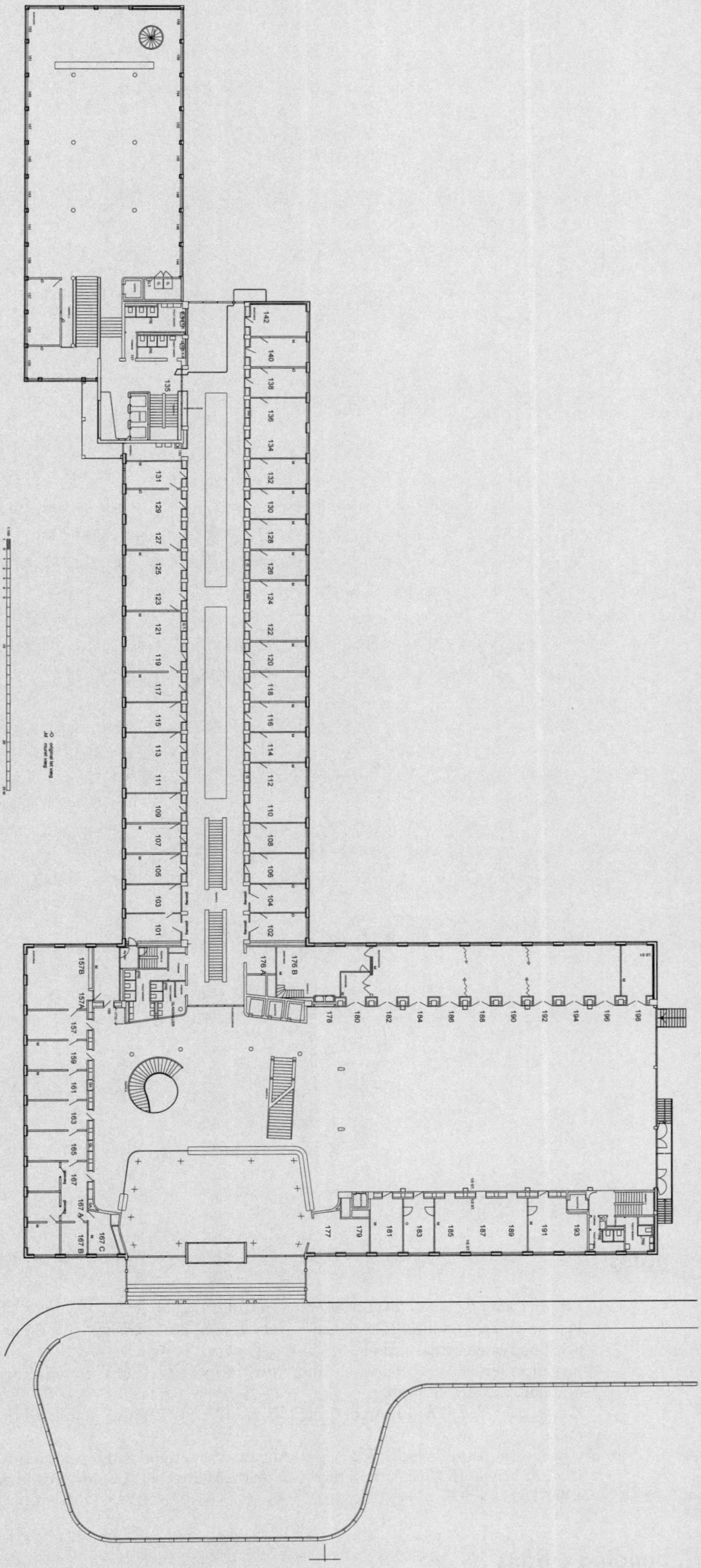

notes

1   *Danish Cultural Canon*, (Danish Ministry of Culture, 2006.)
2   Leo K. Jensen, "Rådhusdiskussionen" in: *Århus byhistoriske udvalg*, (ed.) Byens Hus (Aarhus, 1991), p.13, translated by the author.
3   Jury members' recommendation, from: *Aarhus City Hall*, (Danish Architectural Press, 1991/2017), p.9, translated by the author.
4   *Aarhus City Hall*, (Danish Architectural Press, 1991/2017), p.16, translated by the author.
5   ibid
6   Povl Drachmann, *Berlinske Tiderne*, 19 August, 1937, translated by the author.
7   Claus P. Navntoft, "*The Past 25 Years*", in: Aarhus City Hall (Danish Architectural Press, Skive, 1991/2017), p.97.

building credits

client: Municipality of Aarhus
architect: Arne Jacobsen and Eric Møller
furniture designer: Hans Wegner

photo credits

p.92, 94, 97, 102, 104, 106 (above): unknown
p.94-95, 101, 103 (all), 105 (all), 107(all): Jens Frederiksen
p.106 (below): Unknown Copyright Manager: VISDA

2017
RÅDHUSPLADSEN 2
AARHUS, DENMARK

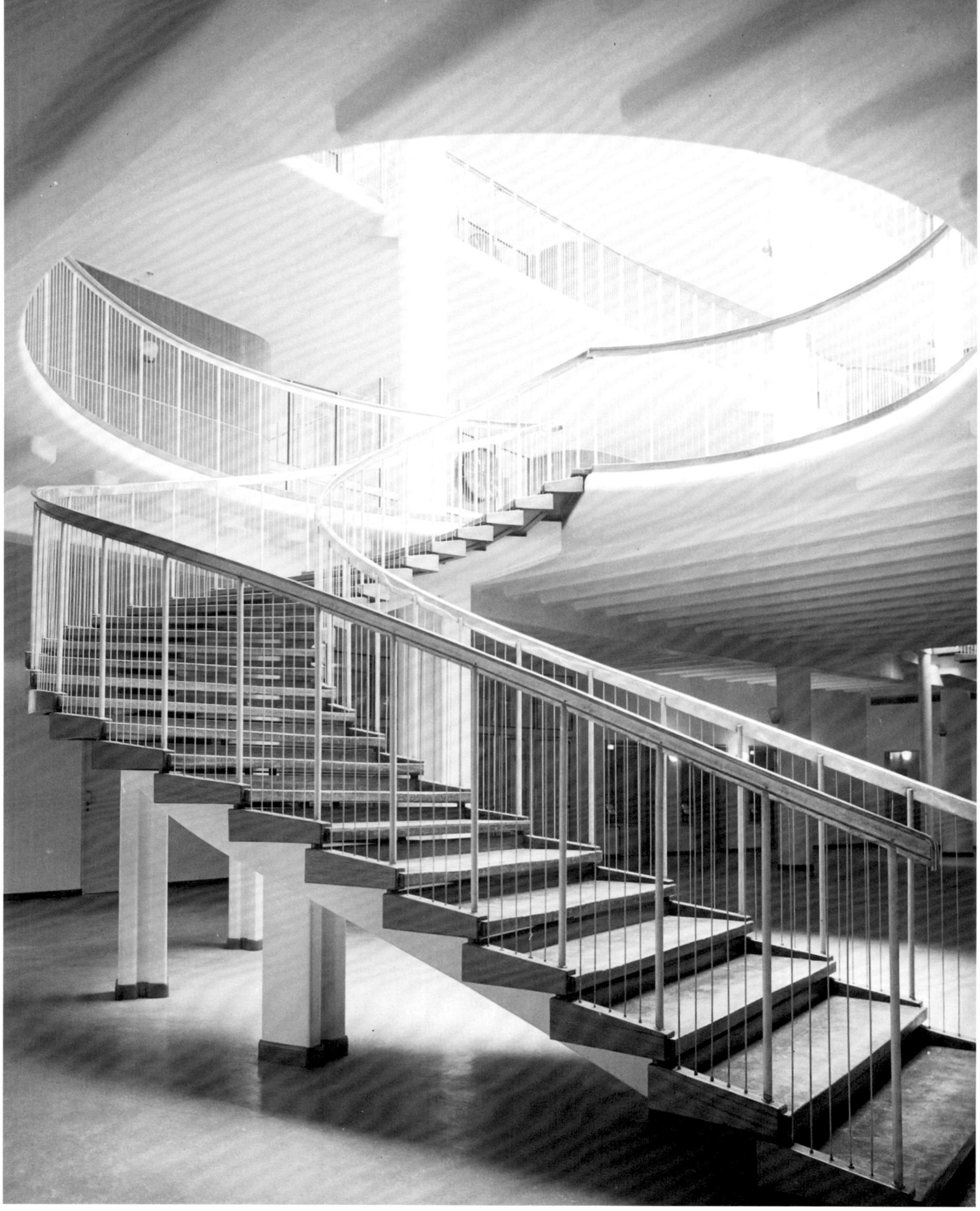

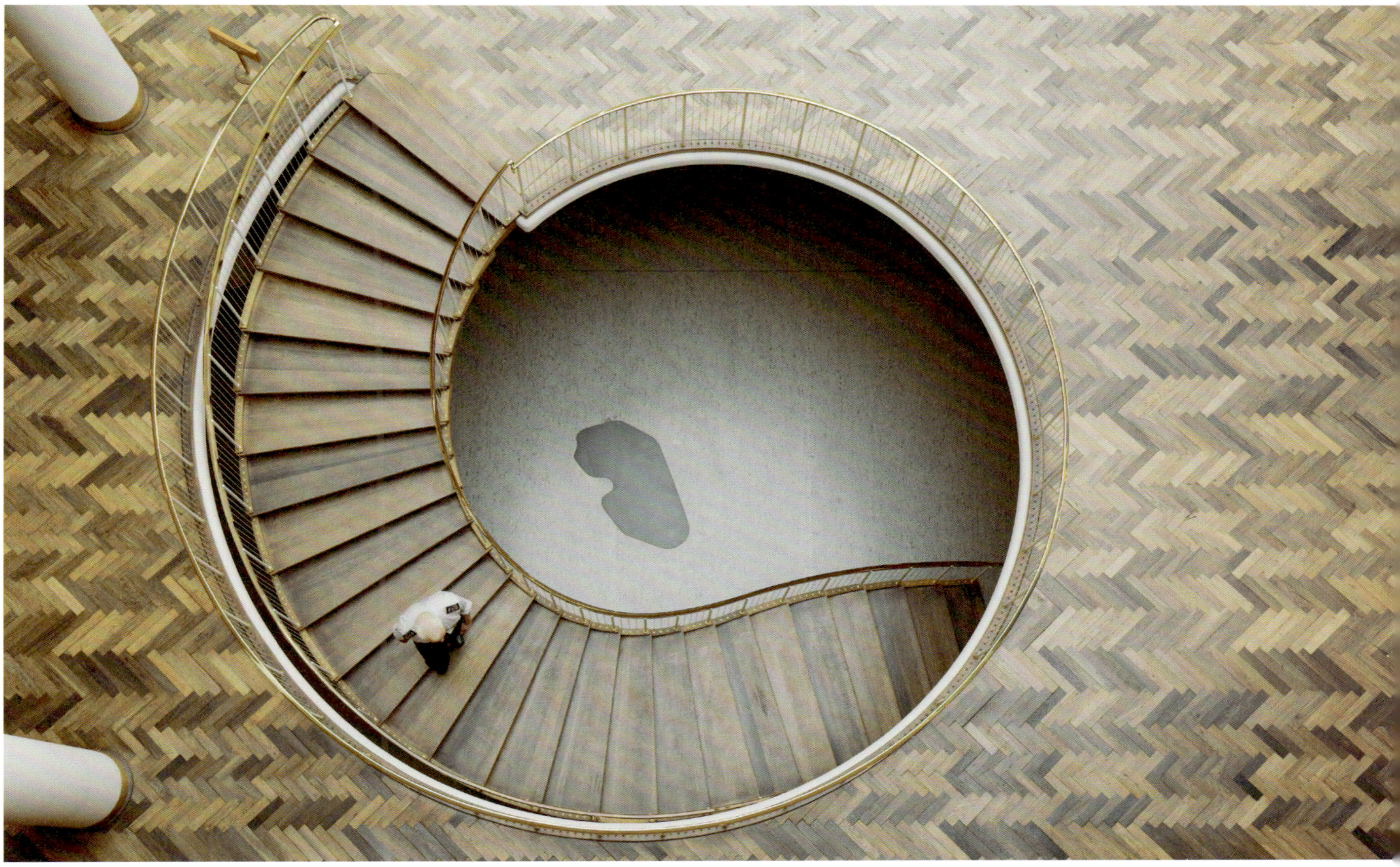

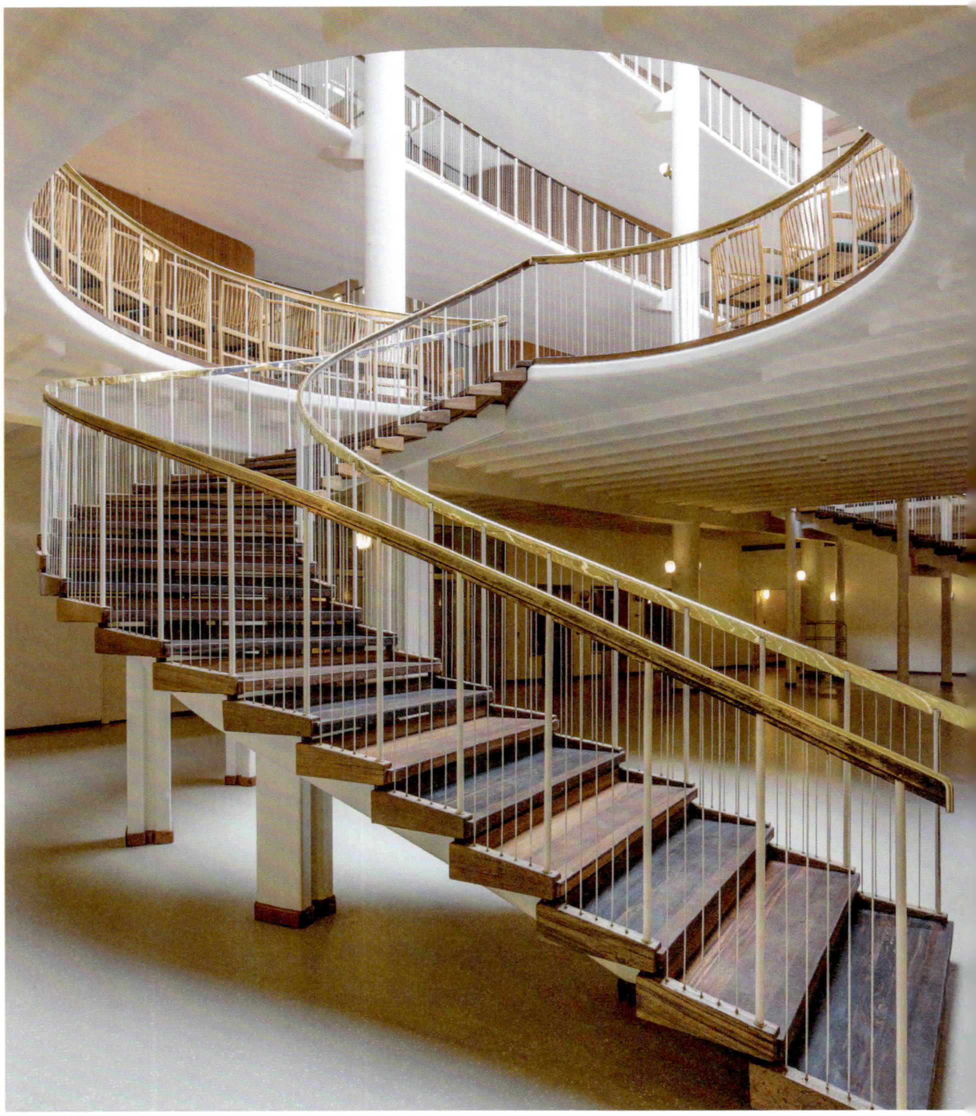

104

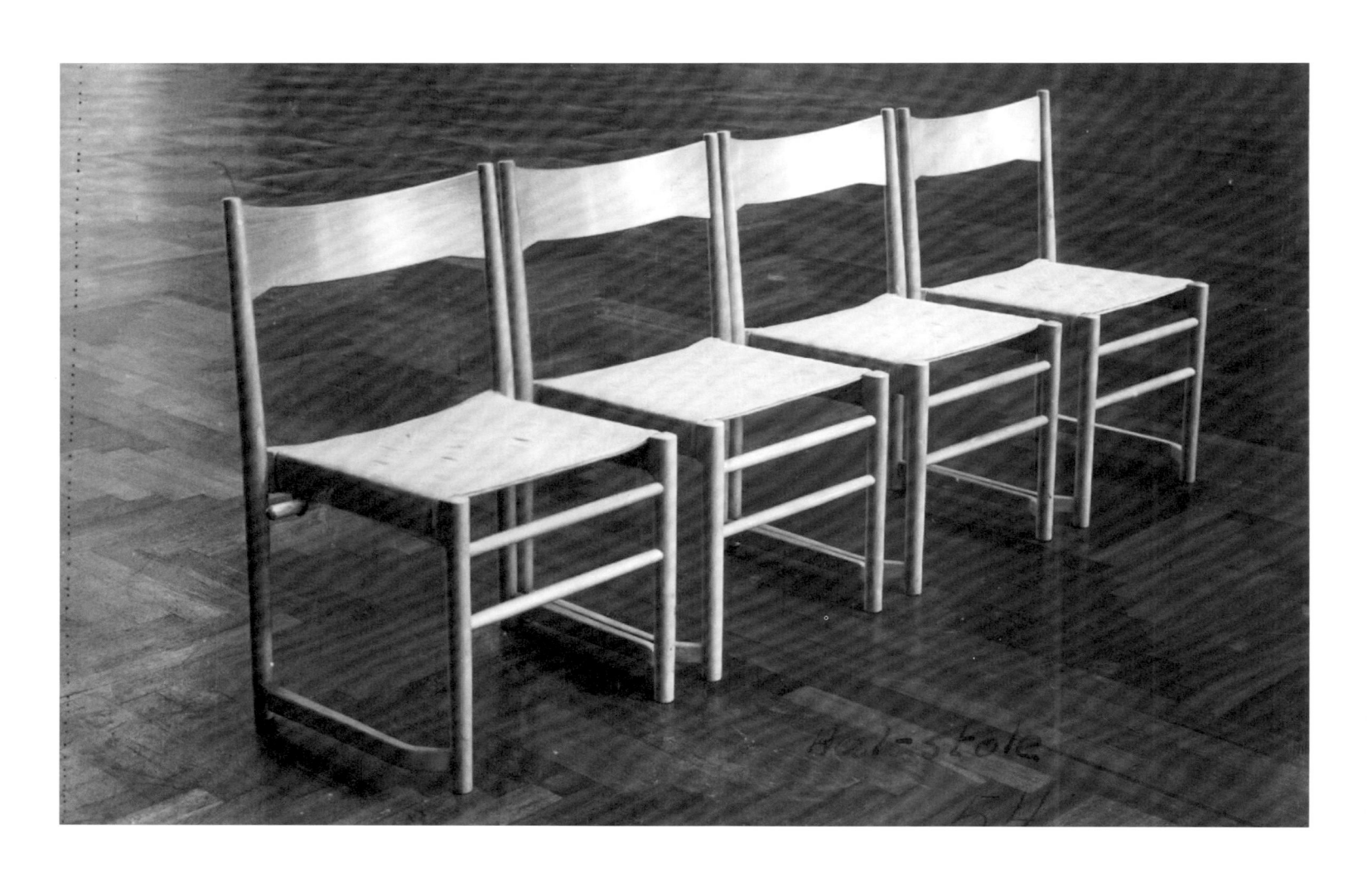

105

Skrivebord Ad2 o 4-Ad
Jalousirealer:
    Ad1 a 5-9J - D5-9J.
Kontorstol Ac2a1-Ba
Bordforlænger Ad1a1-D1.

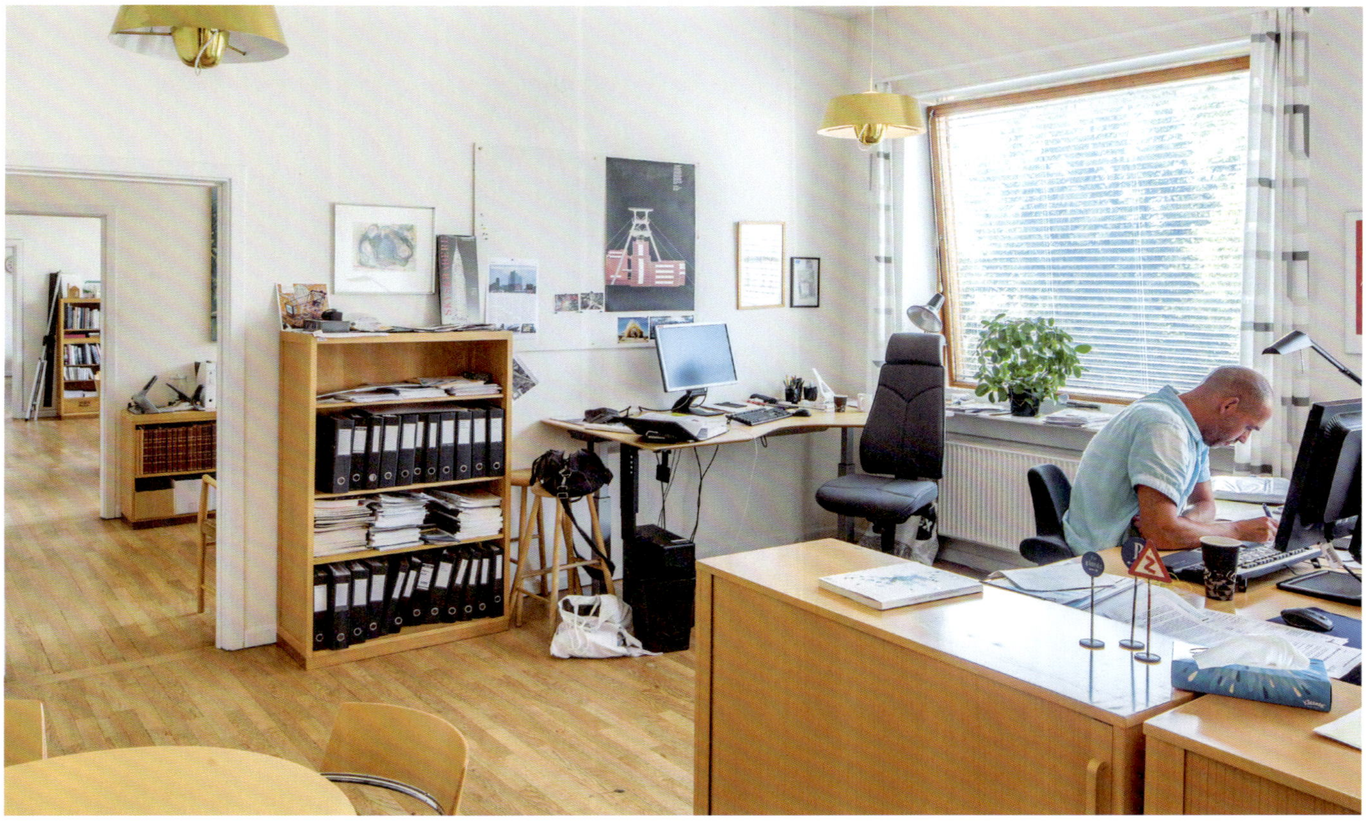

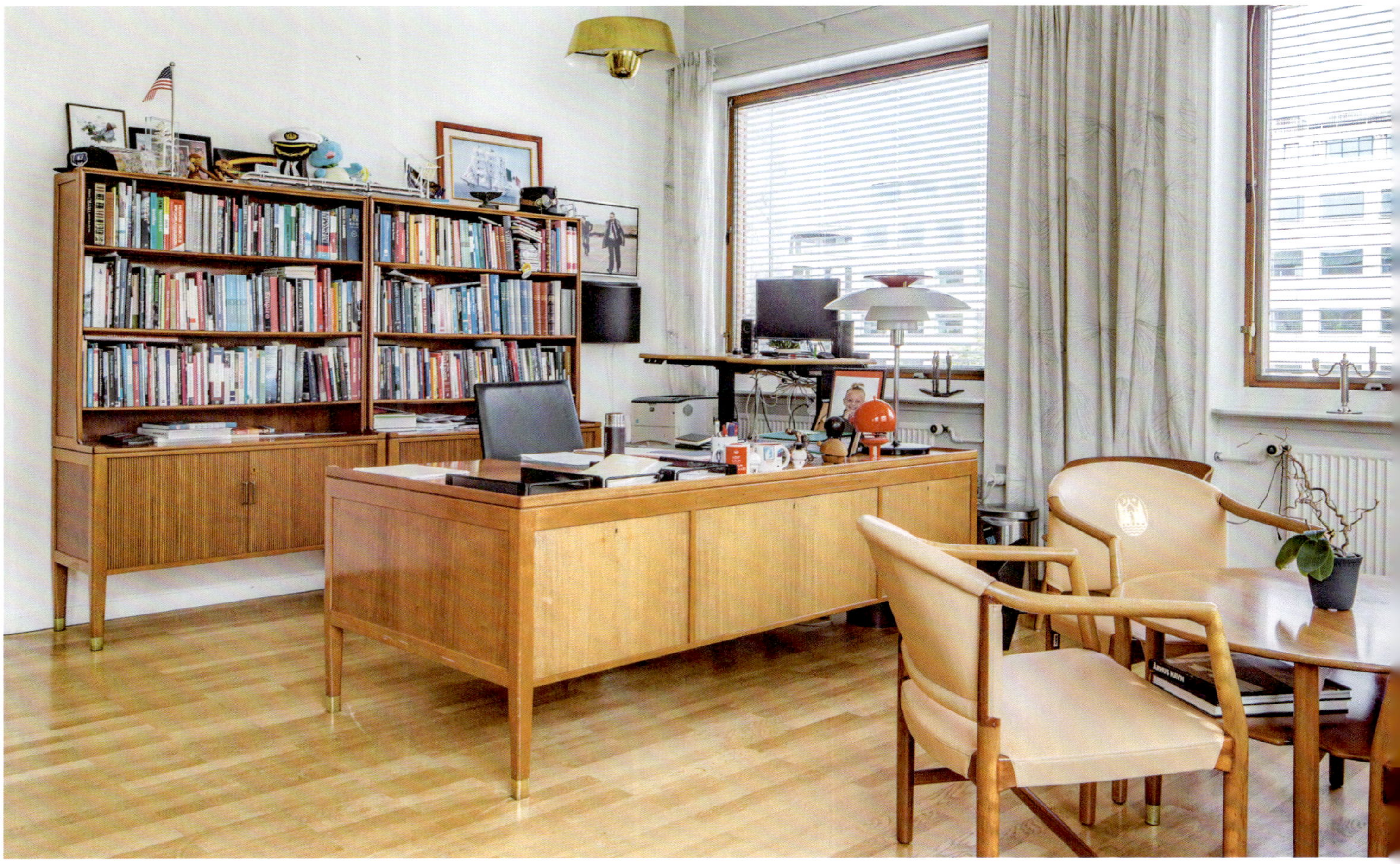

1953

Shaun Fynn

SECRETARIAT BUILDING

A monument of architectural and political history, utterly unburdened by its monumental status

The Chandigarh Capitol Complex remains fascinating not only for the ambitions and magnificence of Le Corbusier's works but also for how the patina of time has changed that work in ways he could never have foreseen. The Capitol Complex has remained somewhat veiled in secrecy ever since its construction in the 1950s: a military presence and barbed wire fences have always separated buildings from citizens, contributing to the enigma Chandigarh has become.

The Secretariat, home to approximately 5,000 workers, is the largest of the Capitol Complex buildings and is their visual anchor, with its massive, ocean liner-like appearance. Originally envisioned by Le Corbusier as a vertical edifice, he turned the idea on its side, creating a groundscraper 240 meters long, 24 meters deep and 50 meters tall, all in concrete. The exterior is a breathtaking, gradated composition of brise-soleil and balconies. The interior is composed of a double-loaded corridor, offices on either side, with upper floors accessed by ramp and elevator. Sculptural counterpoints adorn the roof and the area around the ministries, while the double height allocation for these rooms clearly indicates an administrative hierarchy.

The interior of today's Secretariat is a somewhat crowded experience as workers move between floors on primary-colored access ramps, peaking in a rooftop café where Le Corbusier's signature window details and the pervasive aroma of the lunchtime thali are equally striking.

The legacy of Indian culture has imposed its own visual codes on the adaptation and decoration of Chandigarh's buildings over the decades. These alterations are apparent across the Secretariat's office landscapes, which exhibit a comfort with visual anarchy and a disregard for typical notions of workplace order. The principles and forces of 'jugaad'[1] are at work everywhere. Occupants alter the facade at will, while security personal reside in tents and sheds that casually disrupt Le Corbusier's compositions.

To enter the secretariat today is to enter a past age, defined by Nehru's nation state in pursuit of a modernity unfettered by the past, while, paradoxically, scaffolded by a bureaucracy inherited from the era of British rule. With mountains of paper filed in a manner surely only understood by the filer, hand-painted signage, patinaed walls, and air conditioners freely mounted on the sacred brise-soleil, we are led to question if the original design utterly failed to take into account daily use and climatic considerations, or whether it was merely discarded by the current occupants, oblivious to the monumental status of the building in architectural history.

Le Corbusier's historic Capitol complex and sector 17 government centres have been somewhat eclipsed by the ubiquity of more recent developments on Chandigarh's periphery. New office and residential complexes proliferate and air-conditioned shopping malls provide safe harbour for global brands. Chandigarh presents a story where the visions of a master and his associates met the political ambitions and intricacies of the post-colonial era.

In 2016, the Capitol Complex – comprising the Assembly, the High Court and the Secretariat – was listed as a UNESCO World Heritage site. It seems likely that this designation will always be challenged by the day-to-day in Chandigarh and by the constant push for development. In its 2020 annual report "state of conservation" to UNESCO, the Chandigarh administration detailed its plans to build a 5,000-car basement parking, with ramps that would emerge within the protected zone, an extension to the High Court and a chiller plant near the Punjab secretariat.[2]

notes

1 The cultural practice of the work-around, a frugal, improvised quick fix that will probably become long-term.
2 "Capitol Complex: Contentious multilevel parking on list of upcoming projects shared with Unesco," *Hindustan Times*, November 22, 2020.

building credits

architect: Pierre Jeanneret and Le Corbusier

photo credits

p.108 (above): Pietinen / Helsingin kaupunginmuseo
p.108 (below): Norma Evenson
p.110-111, 115 (below): Shaun Fynn
p.113 (above), 115 (above): Iwan Baan
p.113 (below): Christian Richters
p.114: Canadian Centre for Architecture, Pierre Jeanneret Collection

2019
PUNJAB CIVIL SECRETARIAT
CAPITOL COMPLEX
CHANDIGARH, INDIA

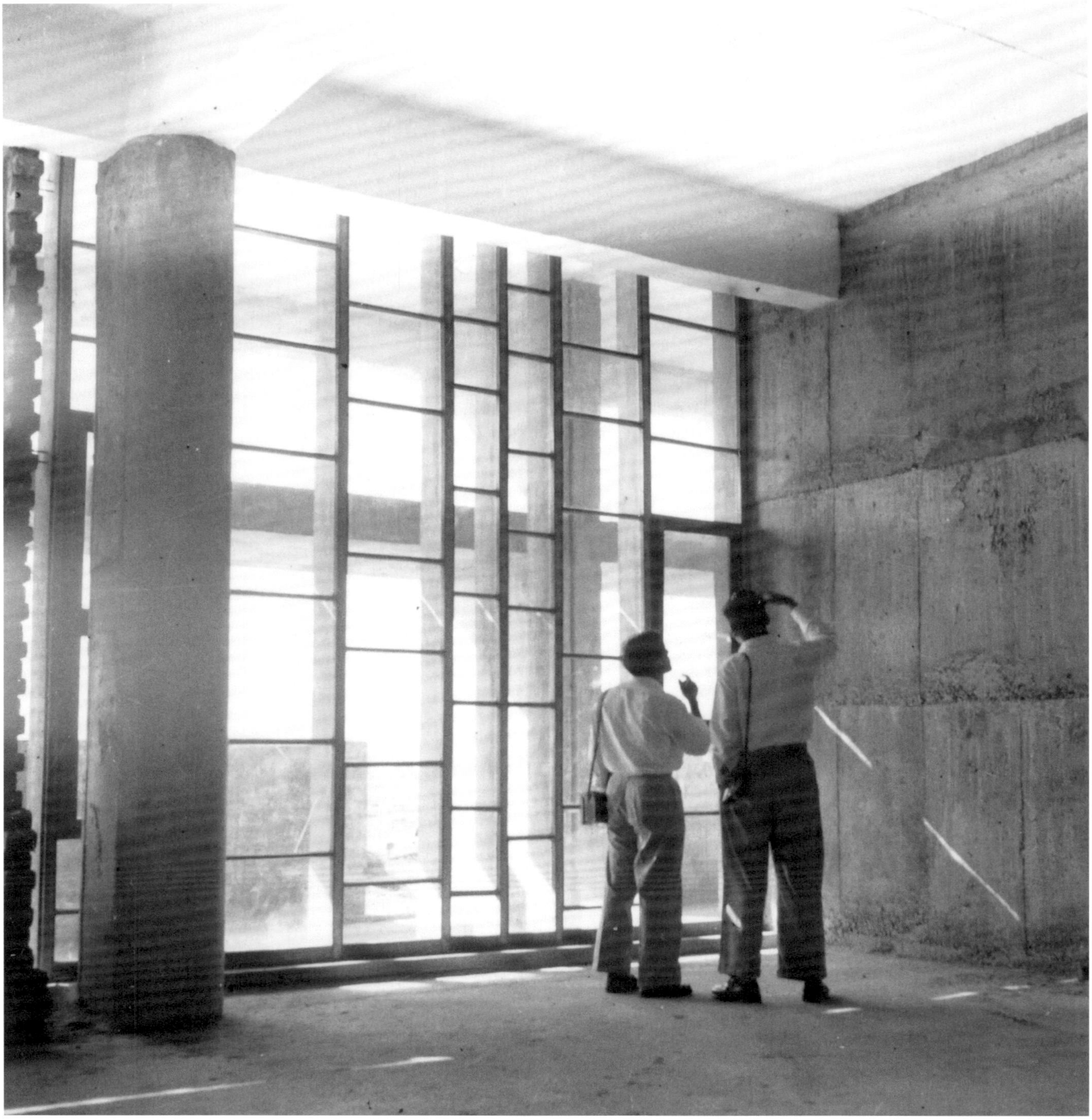

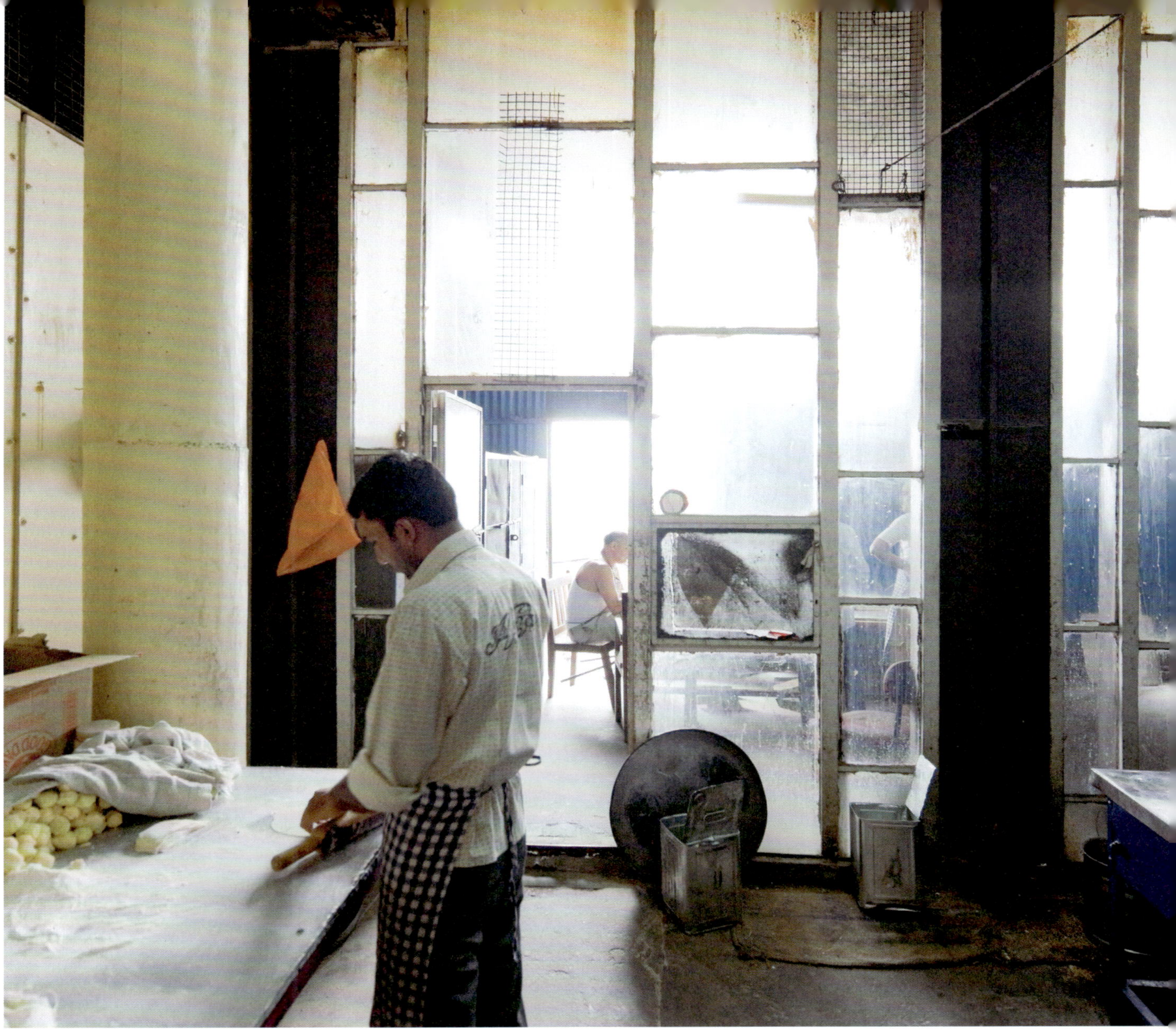

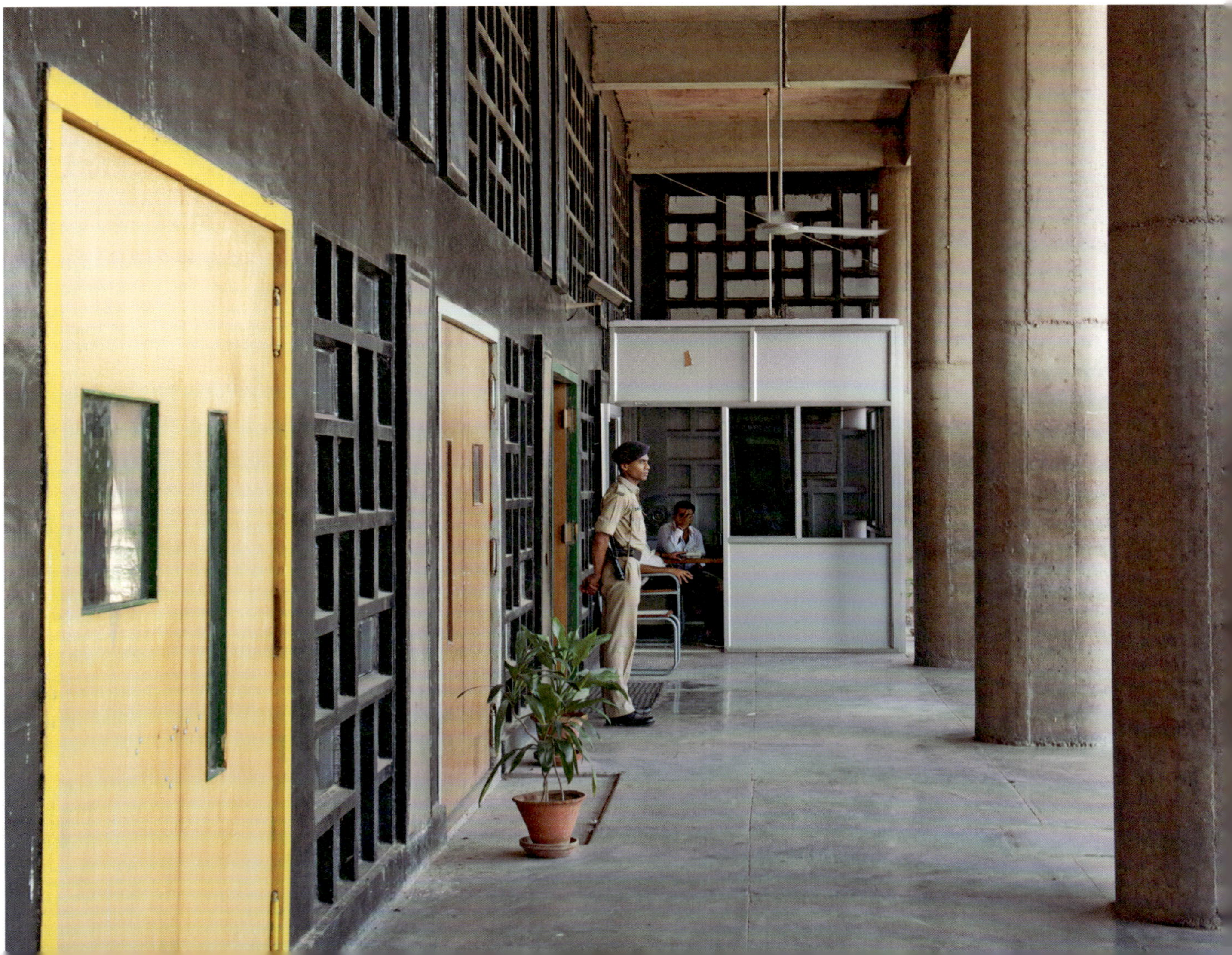

1955

Ruth Baumeister

RAUTATALO

Aalto places a cuckoo's egg in an office building, quickly taking over the nest

When commissioned to design purely commercial projects, Alvar Aalto always had reservations, and typically tried to mitigate what he considered a boring typology by providing something public. Rautatalo (meaning Iron House), an office building for the Finish Hardware Dealers' Federation, is a case in point.

Aalto received the commission after winning the competition in 1951. The brief called for office space, between five and seven two-story retail spaces, and special consideration for fitting the building into the urban context at the heart of Helsinki. The building was located on Helsinki's most prominent street, Keskuskatu (meaning "central street"), designed by Eliel Saarinen in his 1921 urban plan. Saarinen had also designed the red brick office building next door to Rautatalo.

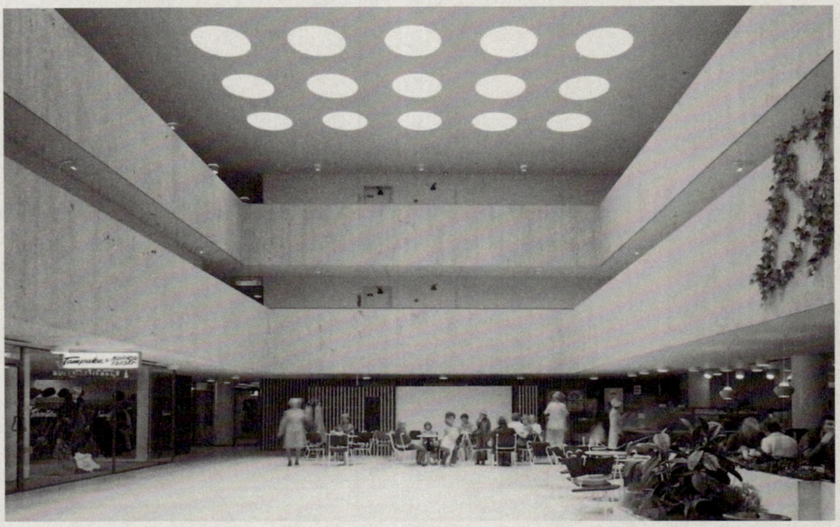

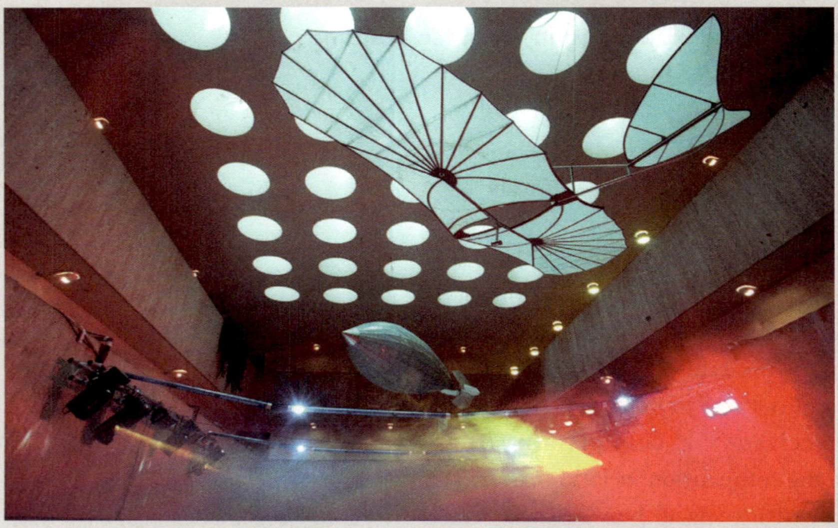

Aalto's competition-winning design, titled *Casa*, consisted of two large, interconnected volumes, one parallel and the other one perpendicular to the street. To promote his client's corporate identity, Aalto distinguished his building from the brick buildings surrounding it by using copper cladding. (Aalto also mediated the surrounding context by using brick for one side wall connecting to the neighboring buildings, including the one by Saarinen.) The elegant details of the façade belie the anonymity of the office space within, while large windows on the ground floor and on the piano nobile attract the interest of passersby. Artek, the interior design and furniture company co-founded by Aino and Alvar Aalto in 1935 to promote modern culture, was supposed to have its retail spaces on the street level, showrooms on the first floor, and design department and offices inside the building.

But what proved decisive for Rautatalo in the long run was the *Marmoripiha* (meaning 'marble yard'), an interior piazza several-stories high, with white marble floor and travertine on the surrounding balustrades. This was Aalto's gift to the city. Aalto aimed at transplanting the spatial and atmospheric qualities of an Italian piazza, an open public space which he was fascinated by, to cold, rainy Finland. Like a cuckoo's egg, he deposited this bold semi-public square into the scheme of a private building without having been asked for it by the client. However, the competition jury's report pointed to the potential of this interior piazza for future adaptation: the building could easily be converted into a department store, for example. Perfectly concealed behind the minimalist copper façade, accessible from the busy street through the main entrance and an elegant stair, visitors enter into what might now be called a 'slow space.' A water fountain creates a pleasant soundscape, a grid of circular lights above simulate daylight and skylights allow the experience of different weather conditions while being protected inside at the same time. Inside the Marmoripiha,

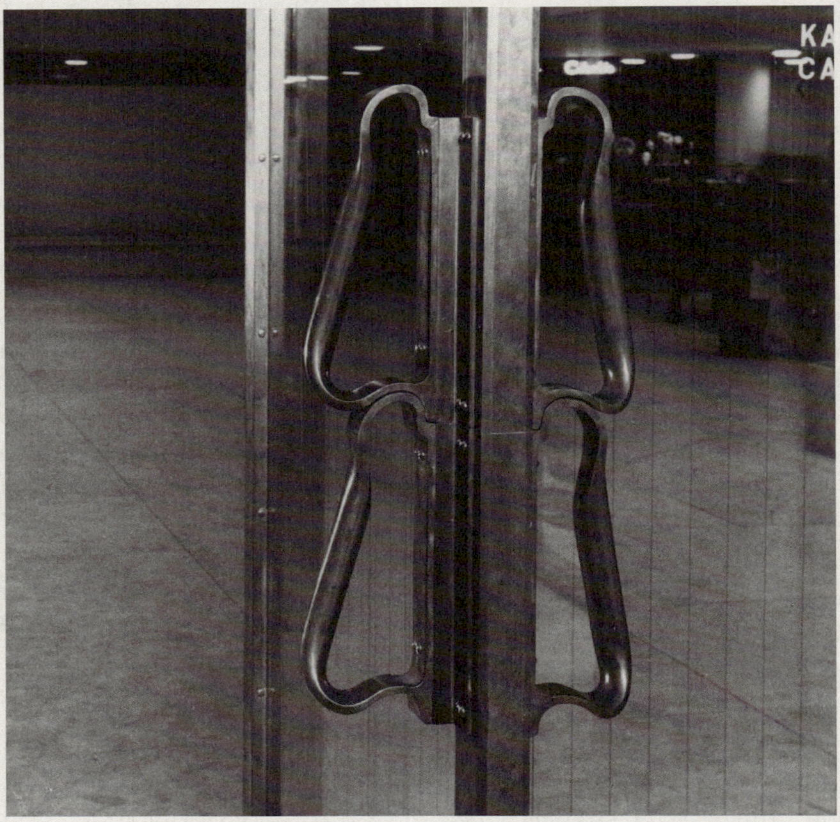

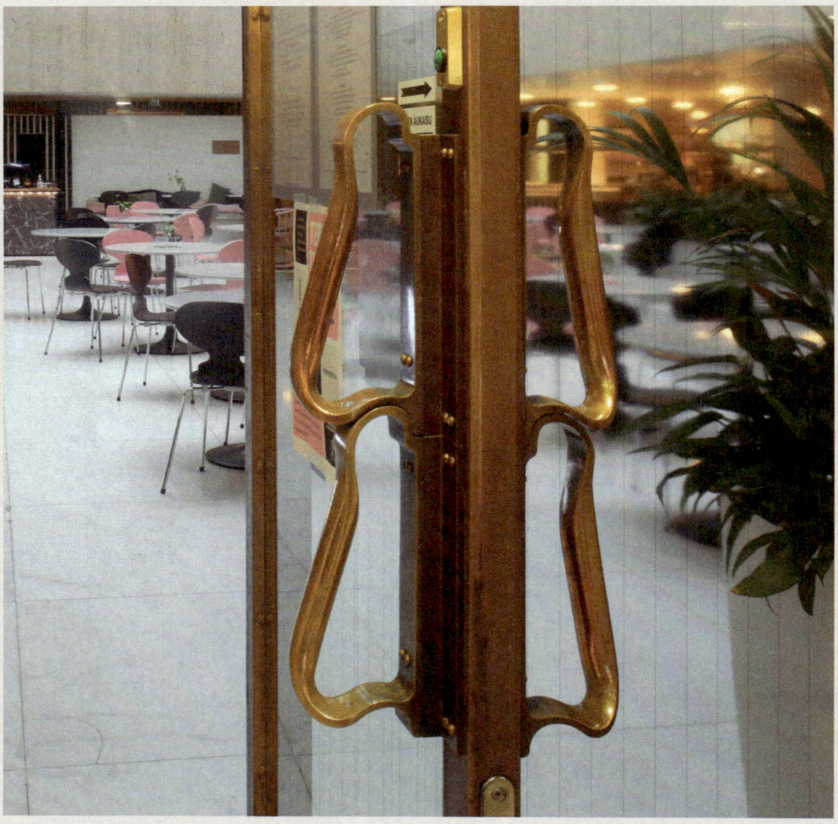

Café Columbia, with all its details designed by Aalto, it was said to be precisely the right size to hold all the intellectuals of Helsinki. At the party on the occasion of the building's inauguration, the Finnish prime minister, actors, and celebrities turned out alongside Aalto.

After the inauguration, the discourse centered around the piazza and not the building's ostensible purpose, the offices. That is not unusual, as those who commission and build, and those who write about, office buildings tend to concentrate on the representational spaces and features – entrance, lobby, atrium, façade, and maybe the structure – while the workplaces themselves are of lesser (or zero) interest. From the beginning, Rautatalo was conceived as a multi-tenant office building, with offices of various sizes and configurations. Apart from a few exceptions, tenants would decide the design of their workplace and either ask the architect to realize their ideas or put up partition walls themselves. Aalto provided a structure, partly prescribed by the load-bearing columns, but then filled it in with partition walls to create various office spaces according to the client's demand. Windows in the partition walls allowed a visual connection between the offices and provided a more open atmosphere. Corner offices were equipped with a reception area, a counter, and a large window to welcome customers.

The Aalto archive in Jyväskylä holds very few photographs of his office interiors, and most of them depict the executive offices at Rautatalo. Strangely enough, even though Aalto gave great consideration to the interiors, furniture and light fixtures in his buildings, he never designed any office furniture. At Rautatalo, only fixed furniture such as kitchens, cabinets, cash registers, and service counters were designed by the architect. Movable furniture, like that used by the women in the photograph here, was made by Billnäs, a large manufacturer that supplied many Aalto buildings during the 1950s.

Since its completion in 1955, Rautatalo has undergone several alterations. Only three years after construction was completed, the north wing was changed when an increase in building height was allowed. The corrugated aluminum on the courtyard elevation was replaced with plastic-covered metal sheets in 1970 (and again in 2013). During the 1970s, the wooden-batten cladding of the café and the suspended ceilings on the undersides of the Marmoripiha balconies were removed, and the first alterations were made to the office spaces. In 1985, Café Columbia closed and soon after, a fish restaurant opened in its place. As the new owner did not like the furniture designed by Aalto, all the remaining loose pieces were moved to the new *Café Aalto* at the Academic Bookstore building nearby.
(A decade or two earlier, Arne Jacobsen's iconic plywood chairs, a popular indicator for any kind of Nordic design, had entered the space.) In 1986, the building received an interim protection order and five years later, parts of the building were landmarked, but this did not apply to the furniture, since under Finnish law, movable parts of buildings cannot be protected.

Most controversial though was the transformation of the Marmoripiha into a nightclub. Supposedly, Aalto's phone booth was repurposed by couples seeking a quiet place for kissing: "What was a life-enhancing harmony in Aalto's hands is now ugliness. It is clear that this has profound implications for our values, both aesthetic and ethical. Your soul will be injured when you visit the current Rautatalo," psychoanalyst Veikko Vainio wrote in a local newspaper after a shocking visit to the building in 1997. The tide turned with a comprehensive renovation between 2000–2002. The café was restored towards its original appearance and the furniture and lamps were re-installed, the fountain was also restored and the space was replanted with vines and other plants according to the original design. In the offices, new partitions were installed; brick walls in the corridors and door frame

/ Eino M

ducts were removed. Suspended ceilings in the corridors were altered to allow a new ventilation system. The linoleum floor was renewed according to the original design. From 2002–16, Nordea bank was the major tenant and Marmoripiha served as a banking hall, but was also frequently used as an exhibition space, for example during the Helsinki design week.

Between 2007–14, the offices as well as the main stair to Marmoripiha were redone. Due to an amendment of the city plan, which allowed the upper basement floor to be converted to commercial use, interior connections to the department store across the street and the neighboring Academic Bookstore were created. In 2017, ground floor metal windows were redone, and wooden windows at street level were restored. The rusted ground floor main doors were redone in 2021. The tenants of the retail spaces changed several times during the years. The most prominent move though was when Artek left Rautatalo in 1991. Fourteen years later it moved back to Keskuskatu, but not in Rautatalo – in Saarinen's building next door.

Judging by the press response after the inauguration and the discourse around the building in the following years, the offices never played an important role for the building despite the fact that they were the main part of its program. They were renovated and reconfigured again and again during the multiple renovations, becoming an appendix to the building's history and status. The main attraction for tenants has always been the building's name, its location, and the exquisite design of the Marmoripiha.

building credits

client: Rautakonttori Oy, Rautakauppojen Oy and Turkiskauppiatten Oy
architect: Alvar Aalto

photo credits

p.116, 126 (below): Aalto Foundation
p.118 (above), 120 (above), 122 (above): unknown
p.118 (below): Juhani Niiranen
p.119, 120 (below), 122 (below), 123, 125, 127 (all): Jens Frederiksen
p.126 (above): Pietinen/Helsingin kaupunginmuseo

2021
KESKUSKATU 3
HELSINKI, FINLAND

126

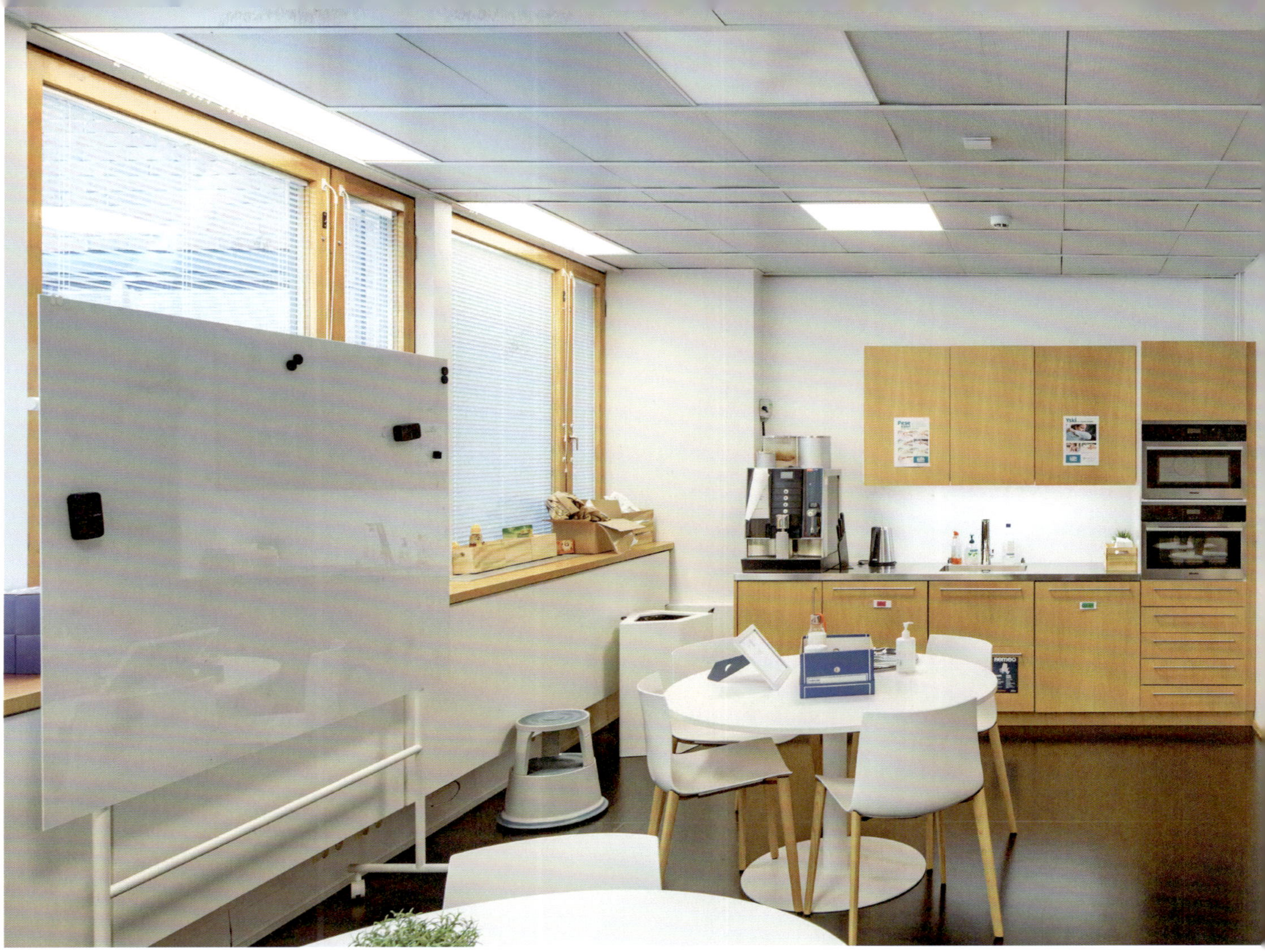

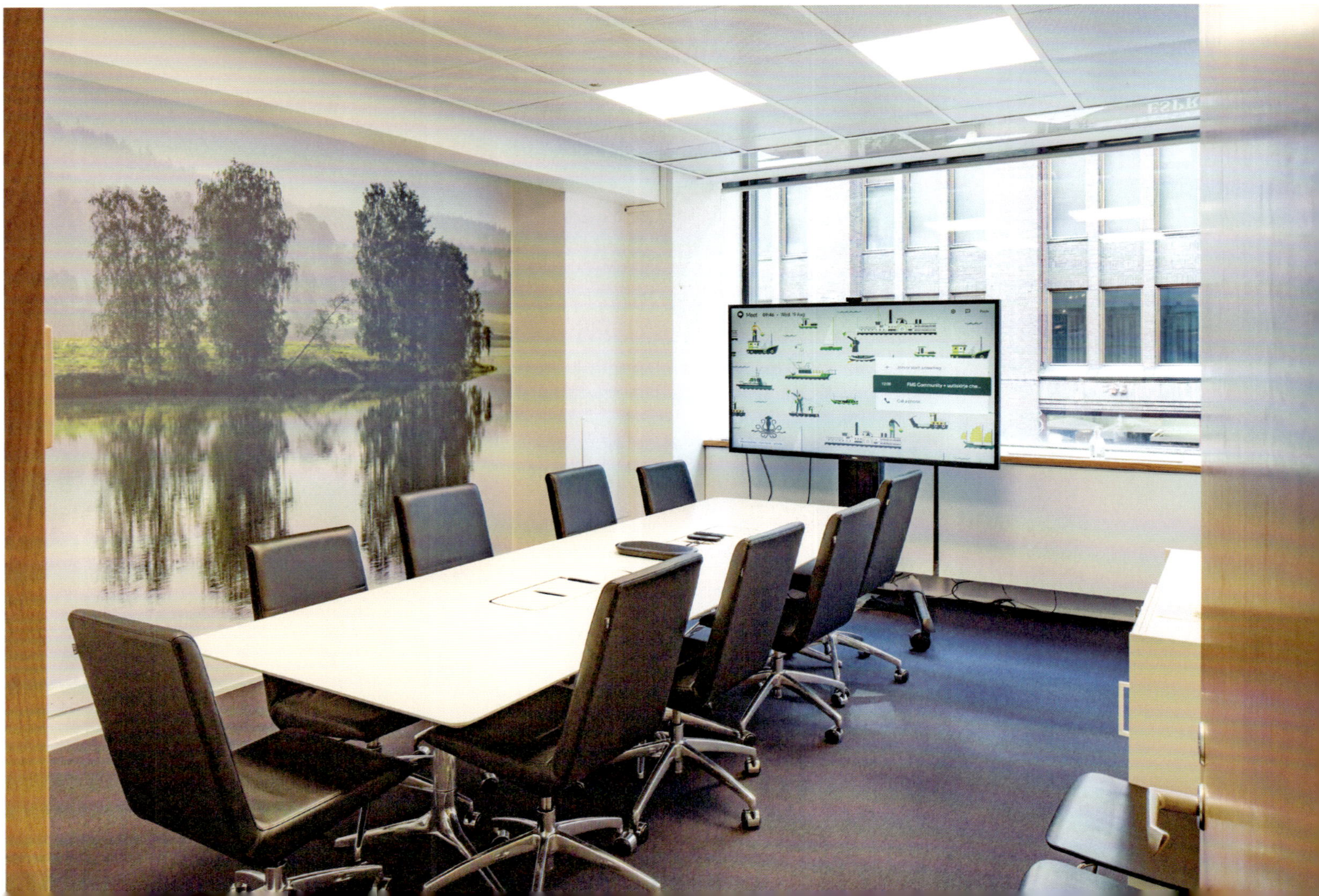

PRICE TOWER 1956

A live/work tower in a small oil town on the prairie fails to endure as an office, finds new life as a museum/hotel – the contemporary thing to do in an old booster town

The Price Tower is a programmatic and a-contextual marvel: the first multi-use tower ever built in a rural landscape. Conceived to introduce urban life in an "upended street" within the small town of Bartlesville, Oklahoma (pop. 36,000 in 2019), all the needs of the H.C. Price Company, including doctors, dentists, and optometrists, were housed in the building. The tower defied the conventional orthogonal grid too, employing a 30-60-90° parallelogram module. Wright designed furniture for all the tenants who requested it, which was almost a necessity because of the unusual shape of the rooms. The first changes to the tower were made by Wright's team in 1960, a year after his death, with unused apartments transformed into additional office space for the Price Company. The Price Company relocated to Dallas and the tower was sold to Phillips Petroleum in 1981. The new owner had difficulties using the building. The plans were too tight. The lack of a service elevator meant that furniture had to be built on-site by the staff carpenter. Philips Petroleum transformed the tower into a storage facility. The 1987 oil and gas market crash forced cutbacks at Phillips Petroleum and the Price Tower was left vacant for over a decade. In the late 90s, the Bartlesville Museum persuaded Philips Petroleum to pay $4 million for the renovation of the empty tower, and then donate it to them. Bartlesville Museum reinvented itself as the Price Tower Arts Center. Echoing Price's entrepreneurial spirit, and Wright's original multi-purpose dream for the tower, the Arts Center created a new hotel for the other vacant floors. Robbie A. Morris, vice chairwoman of the Arts Center board, later said, "We were afraid the tower would be cannibalized, because it was worth more in parts than the whole. We could have been left with a concrete rusting shell."[1]

1. Patricia Leigh Brown, "Built on Oil, Banking on Design," *New York Times*, October 16, 2003.

2017
510 DEWEY AVE
BARTLESVILLE, OKLAHOMA, US

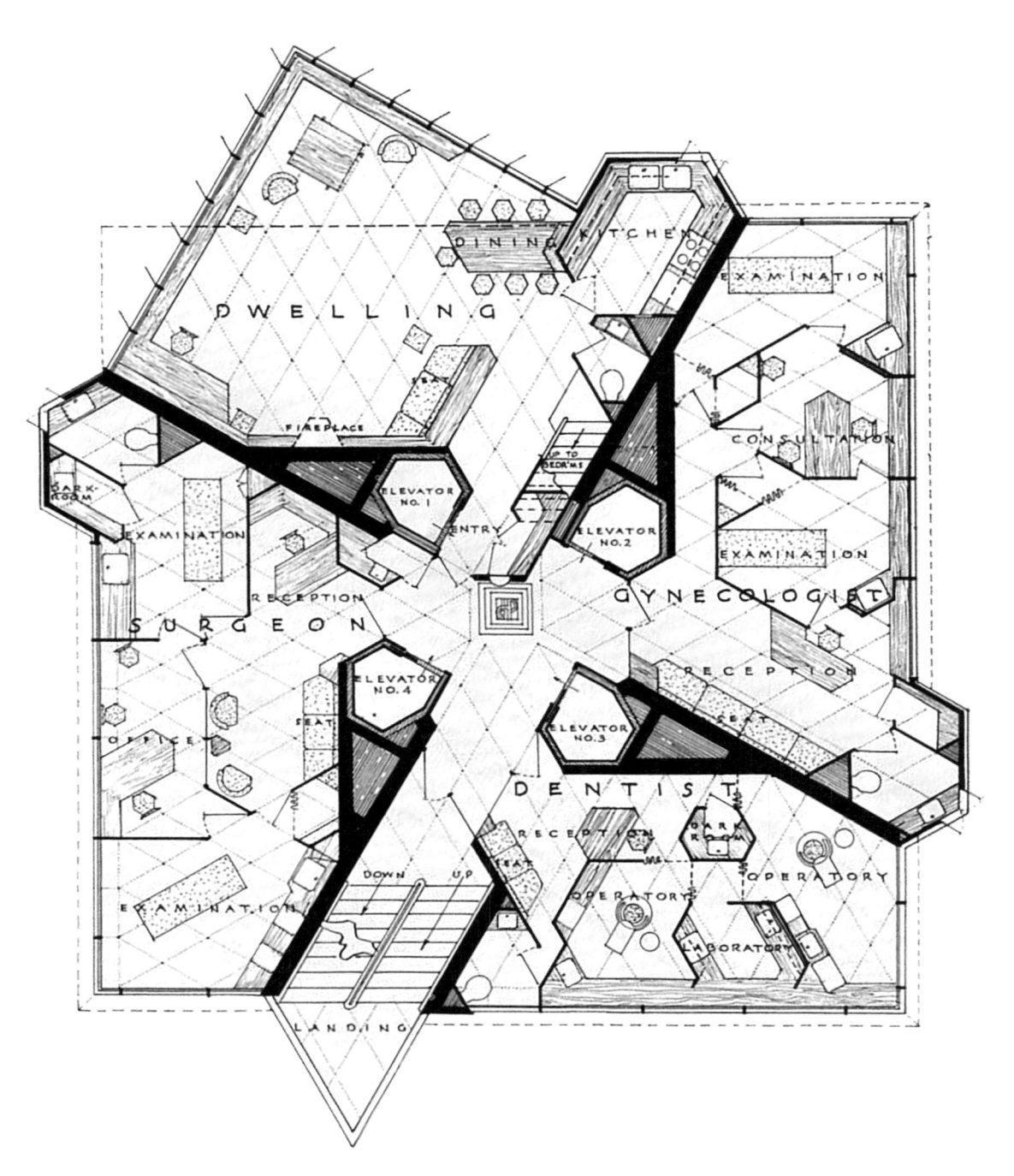

building credits

client: Harold C. Price
architect: Frank Lloyd Wright

photo credits

p.128: nomination form for Price Tower, in the National Register of Historic Plaxes, Sept. 13th 1974
p.129, 131: Christian Korab
p.130: unknown

HOTEL SUITE 7D
LOWER LEVEL

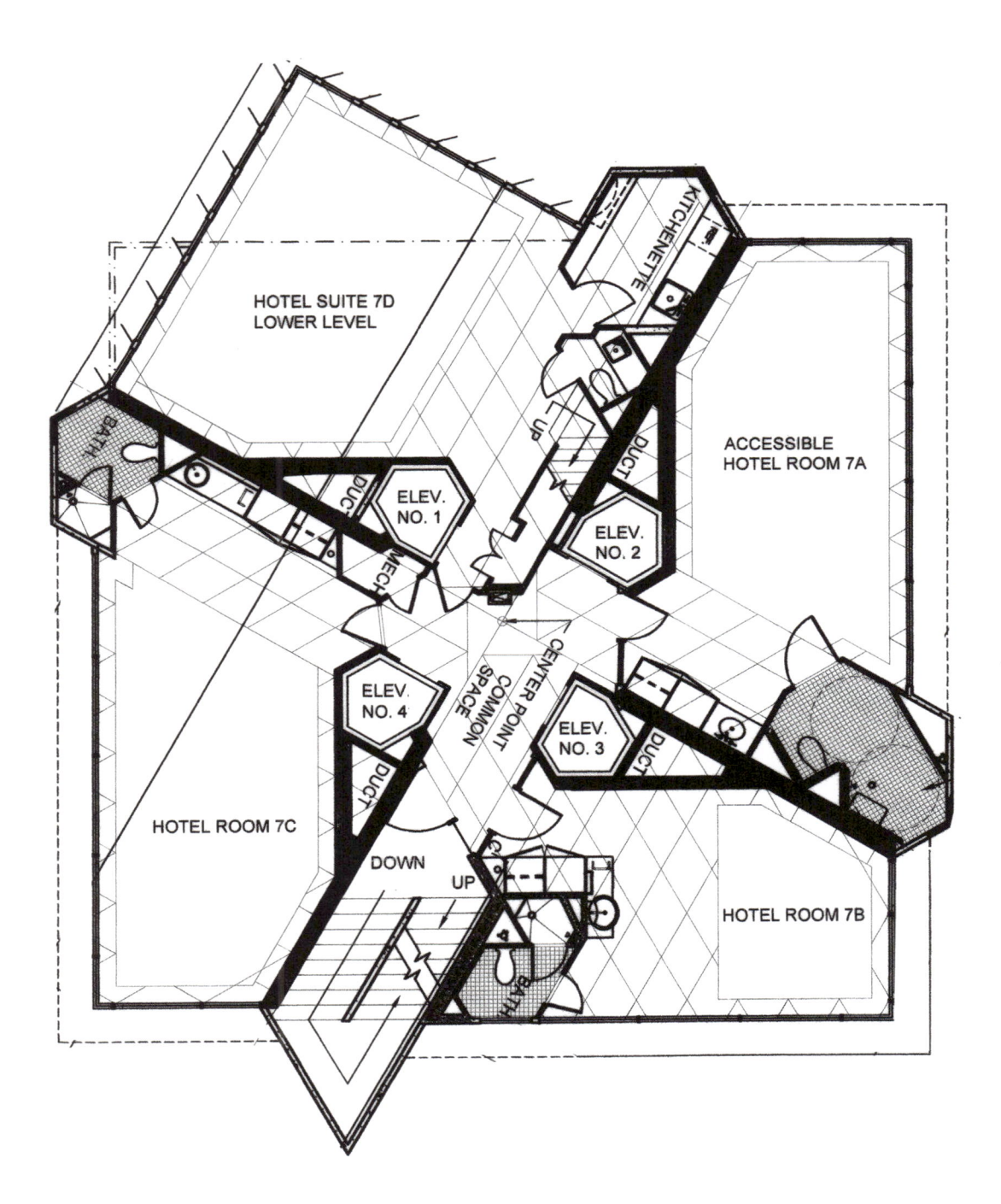

KITCHENETTE

BATH

ELEV. NO. 1

DUCT

MECH

ELEV. NO. 2

ACCESSIBLE HOTEL ROOM 7A

ELEV. NO. 4

DUCT

CENTER POINT COMMON SPACE

ELEV. NO. 3

DUCT

HOTEL ROOM 7C

DOWN

UP

BATH

HOTEL ROOM 7B

1956

Ruth Baumeister

NATIONAL PENSIONS INSTITUTE

Aalto prefigures the cubicle in a Helsinki people's palace;
two decades later, a cybernetics enthusiast in the US designs the version that
becomes ubiquitous; both versions cultivate the dignity of the office worker,
a possibility of the cubicle quickly forgotten…

Dear Friend,
To complement our negotiations, the content and spirit of which I accept con amore, I would like to submit to you the schedule of fees for interior design. You proposed that these matters be taken up in a few weeks' time. However, I believe that in such an important project THE AIR MUST BE CRYSTAL CLEAR FROM THE START. Therefore, I desire that you and through you the Board should be aware of the overall magnitude of the project so that there can be no confusion between us in such an important undertaking… One important factor is that I cannot keep negotiations open and create a building for the Social Insurance Institutions at the same time. As Wallenius puts it, "You cannot go fishing for whale and herring at the same time."[1]
– Alvar Aalto, letter to Kaarlo Hillilä, director of Finland's National Pension Institute (Kela)[2]

The whale Alvar Aalto was referring to in his letter was the new headquarters for Kela, a commission he received in 1948 after winning a competition together with his wife, Aino. Given the fact that Finland was still suffering from a shortage of food and building materials in the aftermath of the Second World War, the Aaltos' winning design seemed out of proportion both with the context and the means available: they called for a building more than five times the size of the Finnish parliament. Characteristically, Alvar demanded equal attention and resources directed to the interiors of this huge office building as were made available for its exterior.

In the end, the architects had to scale down their design when the project was moved to another, less prominent site. And yet, the Kela headquarters, built over a period of eight years, became the Aaltos' first major office complex and a testing ground for their ideas for a modern working environment. Many stories have been written about this extraordinary office building. Some praise the building for its superb detailing and exquisite interiors as a postwar Gesamtkunstwerk; others understand it as the inauguration of the rising Finish welfare state. Even those not so familiar with the building know the lamps and furniture that were designed for it, and which have subsequently become classics, many of them still in production today. Maybe because of the fact that the regular office workspace at Kela was conceived of conventional cell offices, nobody would possibly think of Aalto's building as the birthplace of that over-burdened symbol of modern work, the office cubicle? This invention is always accredited to Robert Propst (1921–2000), a free-spirited American designer, about a generation after Aalto.

But the differences between these possible origin points are highly instructive and tell us about roads not taken – roads blocked by industrialized progress. Both must be viewed within the context of the development of post-war office buildings. On either side of the Atlantic, from the mid-1950s onwards, many companies commissioned new office buildings, because trade, production and with it the scale of office-based business was growing rapidly. Moreover, the rising service sector demanded more and more clerical workers. Existing organizational systems, building typologies, and furniture seemed outdated, not fit for the demands of a fast-changing working environment. Especially in the US after the war, scientific management ushered in new ideas regarding office design, not least to protect office workers' health – e.g. by improving and controlling indoor climate and investigating ergonomics to reduce workers' fatigue and discomfort – to guarantee continuous productivity.

In 1958, Propst, who was a Jack of all trades, holding patents of playground equipment, heart valves, timber-harvesting machines, and airplane parts – was hired as a chief designer at Herman Miller Inc., a leading American furniture manufacturer. He set up his own interdisciplinary research lab in Ann Arbor, Michigan– distant from the firm's main location and in close vicinity to the University which would furnish him with talented researchers of all different kind. With his interdisciplinary research team, including furniture designer George Nelson, Propst created the Action Office series: a system of movable office furniture to be installed in any given environment. Its various standard components, e.g. movable desks, shelves, etc. could be combined and recombined according to the changing needs of the clerk and the surrounding workplace. What they added up to though was essentially the cubicle as we know it: cellularized spaces for individual workers in an otherwise open-plan office.

AO I, released in 1964, featured desks and workspaces of various heights, allowing the clerk to select the best possible working position for a given task. As the system was expensive and difficult to assemble, its sales were far below expectations. Undaunted, four years later Herman Miller released AO II: less costly, easier to assemble, and so successful it would change the office landscape forever. Evaluating office design in the era of Propst and the AO, Nikil Saval, in his book *Cubed: A Secret History of the Workplace*, writes, "By and large … Europe hadn't provided design ideas for workspaces in generations. American offices had been the dominant form of design, with European offices at best furnishing smaller versions of the gargantuan American bullpens and skyscrapers. Indeed, the bullpen office itself became known in Europe as the 'American Plan,' one that Europeans used sparingly, if at all."[3]

Did Saval overlook the fact with 'Kela Hall' – a monumental triple-height interior, naturally lit from above – Aalto designed not only provided one of Finland's first open office spaces, but also a prescient solution for modern workplace design? Aalto installed a grid of 28 four-meter-square wooden boxes for customer service, creating private areas within the monumental space – and in doing so, he prefigured the cubicle-as-we-know-it by almost two decades

There is no evidence that Aalto and Propst knew each other personally or that Propst, who was significantly younger than Aalto, was aware of the cubicles in Kela Hall when he developed the AO system. Nor does the geographical distance between both cases suggest a relation. During Aalto's professorship at MIT (1946–48), Gyorgy Kepes, an artist and expert in visual communication, and Norbert Wiener, the founder of cybernetics, were also teaching there. Kepes experimented with various technical devices such as microscopes, x-ray machines, etc. to capture images that are otherwise invisible for the eye. Their theories formed a new attitude toward human's relationship with the environment. Visual science and cybernetics infused the research by Propst and his team at Herman Miller, Inc. Aalto and Kepes participated in a conference at Princeton in March 1947[4], where Kepes lectured on the relationship between image, form, function, and human needs. He called for an integration of organism, environment, and "plastic truth" by focusing on order and structural unity, a mandate echoed in Aalto's design for Kela Hall, where even the wooden door handles of the boxes seem crafted to perfectly match the human hand.

"Today's office is a wasteland… It saps vitality, blocks talent, frustrates accomplishment. It is the daily scene of unfulfilled intentions and failed effort,"[5] Propst wrote in 1960. Indirectly, he was referring to the predominant Taylorist organising principle of the office, designed to maximize efficiency, generating factory floor-like open-plan spaces into which workers were crammed, while bosses could observe them from generous private offices. Even though there were about 20 years between Kela Hall and AO, conceptually, the point of departure was the same for Aalto and Propst: how to design individual workplaces in relation to the human scale which could provide intimacy and dignity in a large open space? How to create workstations that were not only efficient for production but also served the well-being, the spatial needs, and the ergonomics of the clerk?

Aalto was no doubt aware of the scientific management principle that workplace design had a profound impact on productivity. His architecture was minutely designed for the activity performed in it, but, more importantly, to fit the needs of the clerks who execute and are subject to it. Compared to the size of Kela, which filled an entire city block and provided offices for several hundred clerks, the three entrance doors from the street seemed rather modest. This was Aalto's opening gesture in an architecture tailored to the human body. Upon entering the building, customers were greeted by the receptionist and admitted to the adjacent waiting room, with cloakroom and seating space, with details exquisitely designed by Aalto. The conventional spatial set-up of customer services before the invention of hotlines and online chats with avatars consisted of long rows of desks with clerks behind them, forming a barrier in front of which (increasingly aggravated) customers would line up. At Kela, no space was needed for such queues: once customers were admitted to the hall, they received a number from an usher for the cubicle they would go to. The clerk did not have to get up from their chair in order to fetch the customer; technology took care of this: small lights on the outside of the cubicle were operated from the inside by the clerk, signaling their availability.

Just like in the AO, Aalto worked with prefabricated elements installed on site. All boxes had the same equipment: a desk with telephone, a filing cabinet, a wooden shelf, an office chair and a more comfortable chair for the visitor, and a light fixture attached to the box. Everything except the telephone was designed by the architect. No great, sweeping movements had to be made to file the documents; everything needed to perform the job could be reached within arm's length.

Most importantly, the proto-cubicles at Kela provided qualities that had been sacrificed by scientific management in the early 20th century in the name of increasing efficiency. The desk had become the focus of optimization: "The desk is the most used piece of furniture in the office. The office employee is at it constantly. The highest type of working efficiency in a desk is obtained when the desk itself is so constructed and so arranged that it doesn't in the slightest degree interfere with the progress of a person's work, but ... aids it in every possible way."[6] Looking back at standard office equipment in the 19th century reveals that the desk constituted a small, private domain, as it enabled the clerk to oversee the paperwork in front of them and get a glimpse around the sides of their desk. This desk had a high back with pigeonholes in it and was equipped with lots of drawers where the clerk could store papers as well as personal belongings. At the same time, they could not be easily surveilled from a distance; the superior would have to come up close to see what they were working on. Typically, the desk had a roll-top that could be locked, which gave the clerk control over its content. Scientific management argued that clerks would store and forget about important documents in such a desk. Gradually, the high back was removed, the filing space was eliminated and pedestal bases with drawers were replaced by simple legs. The clerk was left with a flat-top desk, and a maximum of six drawers. The desk was no longer a storage place or a place to feel sheltered, but an instrument for the quickest possible turnover of business papers, with surveillance always possible. It was argued that the change was made to facilitate cleaning, in the interest of the clerk's health.

With both the AO II series and the cubicles at Kela, Propst and Aalto attempted to reintroduce the privacy and intimacy that were characteristic of the 19th-century desk, lost under scientific management.[7] In Kela Hall, clerks sat in cubicles that were only open at the top; there were doors and glass windows at eye level, so the clerk could oversee the surroundings and have control over who accessed the space. To guarantee a certain amount of privacy, AO II, unlike its predecessor, was conceived around mobile patrician walls. The latter demarked the workspace but as it did not have a door, the clerk did not have control over it.

While Propst and his team developed the AO system to empower office workers, its effects soon spun out of the creator's control, and served different agendas. In 1970, two years after the release of AO-II, Nelson distanced himself from the system in a letter to Herman Miller, Inc.'s vice president, Robert Blaich, stating, "One does not have to be an especially perceptive critic to realize that AO-II is definitely not a system which produces an environment gratifying for people in general. But it is admirable for planners looking for ways of cramming in a maximum number of bodies, for 'employees' (as opposed to individuals), for 'personnel,' corporate zombies, the walking dead, the silent majority. A large market."[8]

There is hardly any better critique of the cubicle as workspace than Jacques Tati's 1967 movie *Playtime*. Monsieur Hulot, the protagonist, travels to Paris and finds himself on an odyssey through the modern city, ruled by technology. He is continuously misdirected, seemingly desperate and lost in a futuristic high-tech architecture, which is completely alien to him. In one scene, Hulot wanders around a double-height office containing a perfect grid of cubicles, with head-height walls, each one isolated like islands. The apparent rationality of the layout quickly leads to absurd inefficiencies in communication between "departments", or cubicles. All of them are identical, with no possibility for the clerk to appropriate and personalize it. The message is clear: Western civilization has created individuals and alienated them simultaneously. The cubicle becomes the symbol par excellence of the dull, inhumane office job.

But the spread of the cubicle and the inversion of its original intentions were not necessarily due to anything inherent in the design. Cubicle farms, enabled by mass production, were a cheap alternative to redesigning the floorplan and facilitated quicker cycles of obsolescence. In conjunction with new tax rules in the 1960s for depreciating assets, shorter lives for office furniture and equipment became the norm. Faster cycles of refurbishment and disposal made sense on investors' spreadsheets, but not for those who worked in these spaces, and even less for the world outside the office. Later on, Propst and Herman Miller distanced themselves from the unfortunate turns their invention took, but by that time, AO-II had already set the blueprint for the office cubicle, which proliferated in offices around the world.

How about Aalto though? The Finnish architect was known for using individual buildings as a field of experimentation where he developed details or elements, which were then used for other projects. The system of round skylights at Kela's library, for example, had been developed in Viipuri library in the mid-1930s, then used at the Rautatalo and finally implemented at Enso Gutzeit office building. But Aalto never used the cubicle again after Kela. During the 1920s and early 30s, Aalto was fascinated by the potential standardization and mass production of architectural systems, but by the end of the 1930s he had turned skeptic. Reflecting on his experience in the US after the Second World War, he wrote in 1947, "The freedom required by human nature has come into conflict with industrial mass production in America. … Standardization means industrial violence against individual use."[9] He lamented, "the tyranny exercised by industrial mass production over small man."[10] At an event at Princeton titled "Planning methods for man's physical environment," Aalto urged not to take calculations of everything since "man's attitude to life is the ultimate yardstick."[11] On first sight, Aalto's cubicles, just like the later AO system, seem to be composed of standardized elements, easy to assemble and extend. And yet, a closer look reveals that this is not the case. Even though the boxes were made off-site at the Boman factory, the exquisite timber work – with finishes of mahogany outside and ash wood inside – made them difficult to assemble. The fixtures in the wall elements were made of brass, and parts were not interchangeable.

Even though both the Kela cubicles and the AO series started out with a similar premise – providing privacy within a large open office, imbuing the clerk's workspace with dignity, and facilitating ease of use depending on a clerk's task – the solution each came up with was radically different. While Kela integrated the cubicles into the larger whole of the building and the processes performed in it, the AO enabled constant change, not only for the elements in space, but also for the clerk. The AO system was independent of the surrounding architecture and could be installed in any given open space.

According to business journalist Julie Schlosser, the cubicle, as the core element of the AO, has outlived all subsequent office systems, as it still generates $3 billion dollars annually in sales.[12] Aalto's cubicle structure at Kela did not sustain. The first change it saw was the removal of the client's chair and the installation of a bigger desk around 1973, when customer service was moved out of Kela Hall and the cubicles were converted to single workspaces. In 1987, the cubicles were finally removed and the hall was transformed into an exhibition and event space. The only component from Aalto's cubicles still commercially available is the drawer cabinet, which could be found in one of the earliest Artek catalogs[13] from 1936 and has been in production with more or less the same drawer sizes now for about 85 years.

notes

1   Erkki Sarkkinen, *Elevating the Everyday*, (The Social Insurance Institution Fund, Helsinki, 2007), p.47
2   Undated letter.
3   Nikil Saval, *Cubed: A Secret History of the Workplace* (New York, Doubleday, 2014), p.200
4   Documented in *Planning Man's Physical Environment Planning Man's Physical Environment* (Princeton: Princeton University Press, 1947).
5   https://www.hermanmiller.com/products/workspaces/workstations/action-office-system/design-story/
6   J. W. Schulze, *The American Office*, (New York, 1913), p.62
7   "Would you have your daughter work in an open office?" asks the *Observer magazine* on November 3, 1968, hinting at the fact that women's legs are exposed at such a desk and that there was no privacy in an open office.
8   Stanley Abercrombie: George Nelson: *The Design of Modern Design*, (MIT Press, Cambridge, Massachusetts, 1995)
9   Alvar Aalto, "Kultuuri ja teknikka" [Culture and Technology], in: *Suomi/Finland* – USA, 1947, quoted from: Göran Schildt, (ed.), *Aalvar Aalto in his own words* (New York: Rizzoli, 1997), p136–137
10 Ibid
11 Ibid
12 Julie Schlosser, "Cubicles: The great mistake, *CNN Money*, March 22, 2006
13 Finmar limited cataloque made for the UK.

building credits

client: Social Insurance Institution of Finland
architect: Alvar Aalto

photo credits

p.132, 142 (all): Aalto Foundation
p.134-135, 136: unkown
p.139: Herman Miller
p.141, 143 (all): Jens Frederiksen

2021
NORDENSKIÖLDINKATU 12
HELSINKI, FINLAND

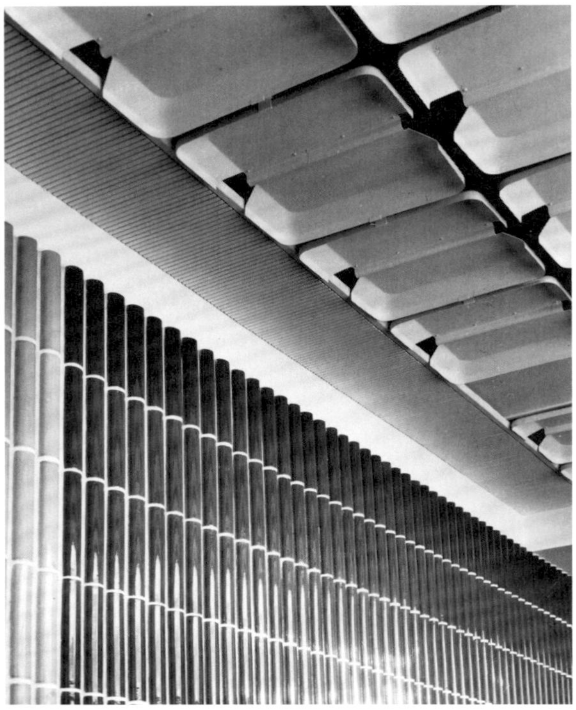

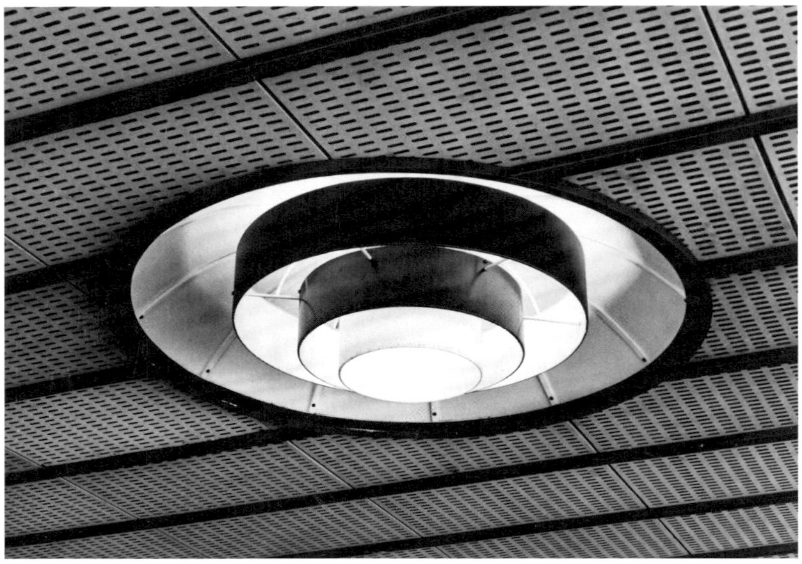

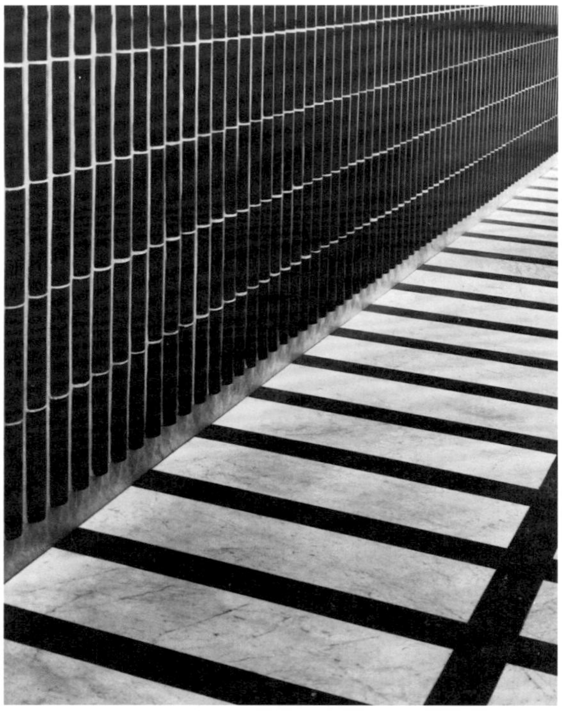

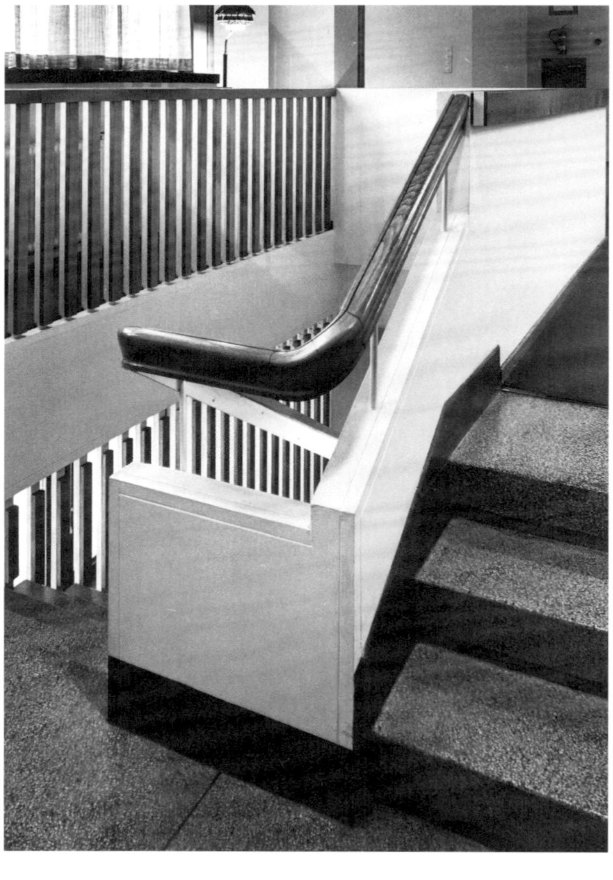

143

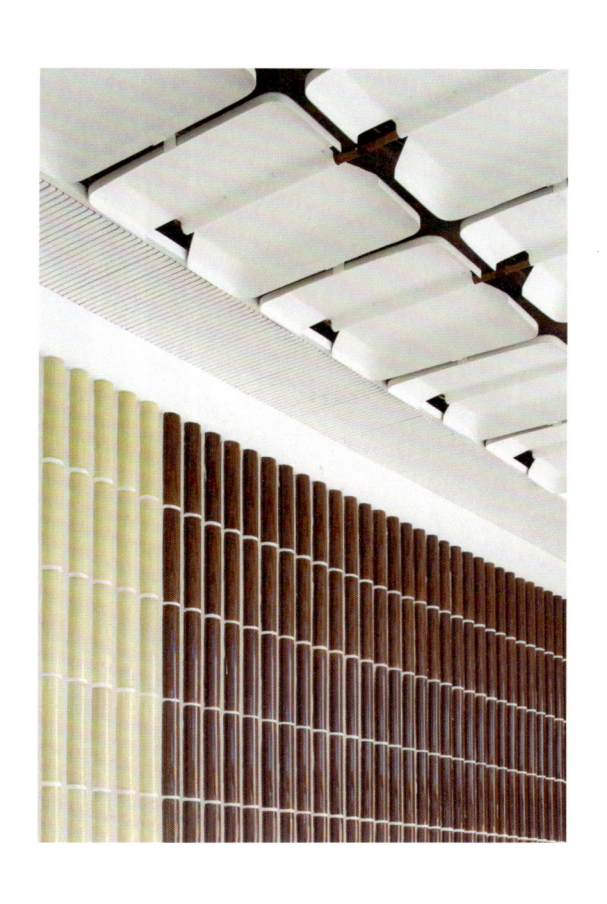

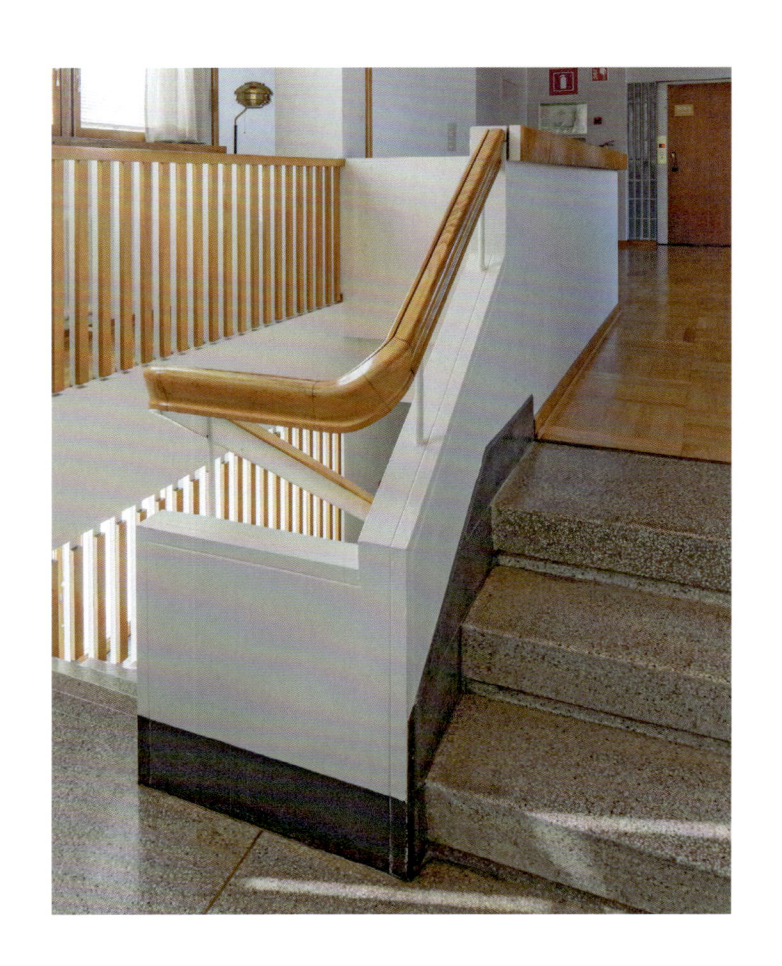

1958

Stephan Petermann

VAN LEER HEADQUARTERS

A Breuer classic, lacking stable ownership, gets made over again and again

On December 10, 1985, the Dutch newspaper *Financieel Dagblad* published a short article on the sale of the Marcel Breuer-designed headquarters of the Dutch industrial packaging giant Van Leer. Built in 1958 and located in the suburban polders outside Amsterdam, it was the third building by the American-Hungarian architect in the Netherlands, after the Bijenkorf department store in Rotterdam (1957) and the American Embassy in The Hague (also 1958). Van Leer's HQ was one of the first American-style pastoral corporate office landscapes in the Netherlands. *Financieel Dagblad* remarked that the building's new owners, the engineering and consulting group Grontmij, would drastically renovate the building: "The now inefficient building will … become easier to partition."

The original Van Leer project was incredibly generous. The local council, Amstelveen, demanded an eight-hectare park surrounding the 6,000-square meter office building. with several small lakes be created. Visitors accessed the Van Leer HQ through the park, driving up a hotel-like ramp as they approached the low-slung, two-winged, glass-fronted building. At the door, a large concrete canopy led to an impressive foyer with elegant exposed concrete structure, only touching the floor with tiny steel column heads. The large hall doubled as sales area, with the offices serving as theatrical backdrop. Above the entrance lobby, a suspended steel bridge connected the upper floors of the two office wings, with visitor and employee circulation strictly separated. Flanking this space on the right and left were double-height open-plan office wings with floor-to-ceiling windows. They were probably the highest office ceilings in Europe at the time.

Everything in the old photos breathes elegance, light, and modernity. According to one source, the climatic conditions in the building weren't great.[1] Apart from that, criticism of the building remains unregistered. Grontmij's 1985 renovation was the first crack in the building's pristine elegance. A floor was added in the office wings, lowering the 5.5-meter ceiling height to less than three meters. The new level canceled the simplicity of the floor division and required a more elaborate core which obstructed the original transparency. Floor plans from the 1990s reveal the conversion of open floors to double-loaded corridors serving cellular offices. The building's modern steel structure made this relatively easy to do, another report happily remarked.[2]

In 1995, *Parool* reported the acquisition of the now-vacant building by KLM's retirement fund. Van Leer had moved to a "more practical" 2,000-square meter new building realized on the same, vast, plot of land. A 1999 renovation further occluded the original qualities of the building. The next owner demolished the air bridge over the lobby and added a new staircase. According to the architect on duty, Dutch firm ZZOP, the air bridge "couldn't be saved." A large hole in the lobby's floor created a new visual connection to the basement/ground level. The original triangle-shaped floor tiles were replaced by a generic motif in light natural stone. In ZZOP's judgment, this new owner restored the building "to its former glory."

In 2017, the Indian-owned educational organization Amity opened an international school in the building to serve the growing ex-pat migrant community in Amsterdam. Large blue signage in front recalls the previous phases of the building's life, with a patina of removed business names like M2M, Fuse, BrandScience, and Omnicom.

The park surrounding the building is still beautiful and perfectly maintained. In the approach to the building, you see large stainless steel air conditioning units and ducts placed seemingly randomly on the roof. The grand entrance is now less grand. The canopy is still in good shape, but the steel balustrades have turned from round to clunky, a new corridor underneath diminishes the original lightness of the staircase, and new entrance panels and revolving doors bring further distraction. The lobby, without the air bridge, and with obstructed views and the hole in the floor nevertheless remains impressive thanks to the concrete structure, now painted white. The office wings have been refurbished with colorful furniture and optimistic posters made by the school kids. The school clearly invested in high-grade new furniture and takes advantage of the canteen, which, for Dutch education standards, looks very luxurious.

The Van Leer office building was listed as a national monument in 2010. In the local pre-listing advice, the city's preservation commission raised the fact that this is the most complete Breuer in the Netherlands. But besides the travertine façade panels and the concrete structure, there is really nothing original left. The immense growth and splendor of the surrounding park since 1958 exposes the comparative weakness of architecture over the march of the decades.

Grontmij's 1985 assertion that through their work they would increase the efficiency of the building seems dubious at best. While technically the building's functioning might have improved, its spatial quality suffered, which didn't go unnoticed. The temptation of adding more square meters through the insertion of the extra floor was impossible to resist and likely impossible to undo. It's a pity that, as in all other cases, n=1. There is only one Van Leer building. You wish you could see what would have happened to the building if in a parallel world the "inefficiencies" noted in 1985 would have been solved with more care or ingenuity over the ensuing decades. The current version of the building mainly reveals the compound damage that can be done by successive renovations by architects, clients, and property consultants who are guided by "rational" engineering and economics rather than by an understanding of the original qualities of the building – which, in the long run, would have generated more value, had they been preserved, than the heavily-adapted building currently generates. More SQM doesn't always lead to more money.

notes

1   Comment appears in "Hoofdkantoor van de Koninklijke Emballage Industrie Van Leer B.V. - 2004", amstelveenweb.com, no date.
2   N. Mens, *ZZDP Architect-Ondernemer* (010, 2010), p.20. The renovation of the building was designed by Van den Broek en Bakema.

building credits

client: Van Leer's Vatenfabriek: Bernard van Leer
architect: Marcel Breuer

photo credits

p.144, 150, 152, 154 : Jan Versnel
p.146, 149, 151 (below), 153, 155: Ossip van Duivenbode
p.151 (above): Arno Hagemans

2019
AMSTERDAMSEWEG 204
AMSTELVEEN, NETHERLANDS

150

151

152

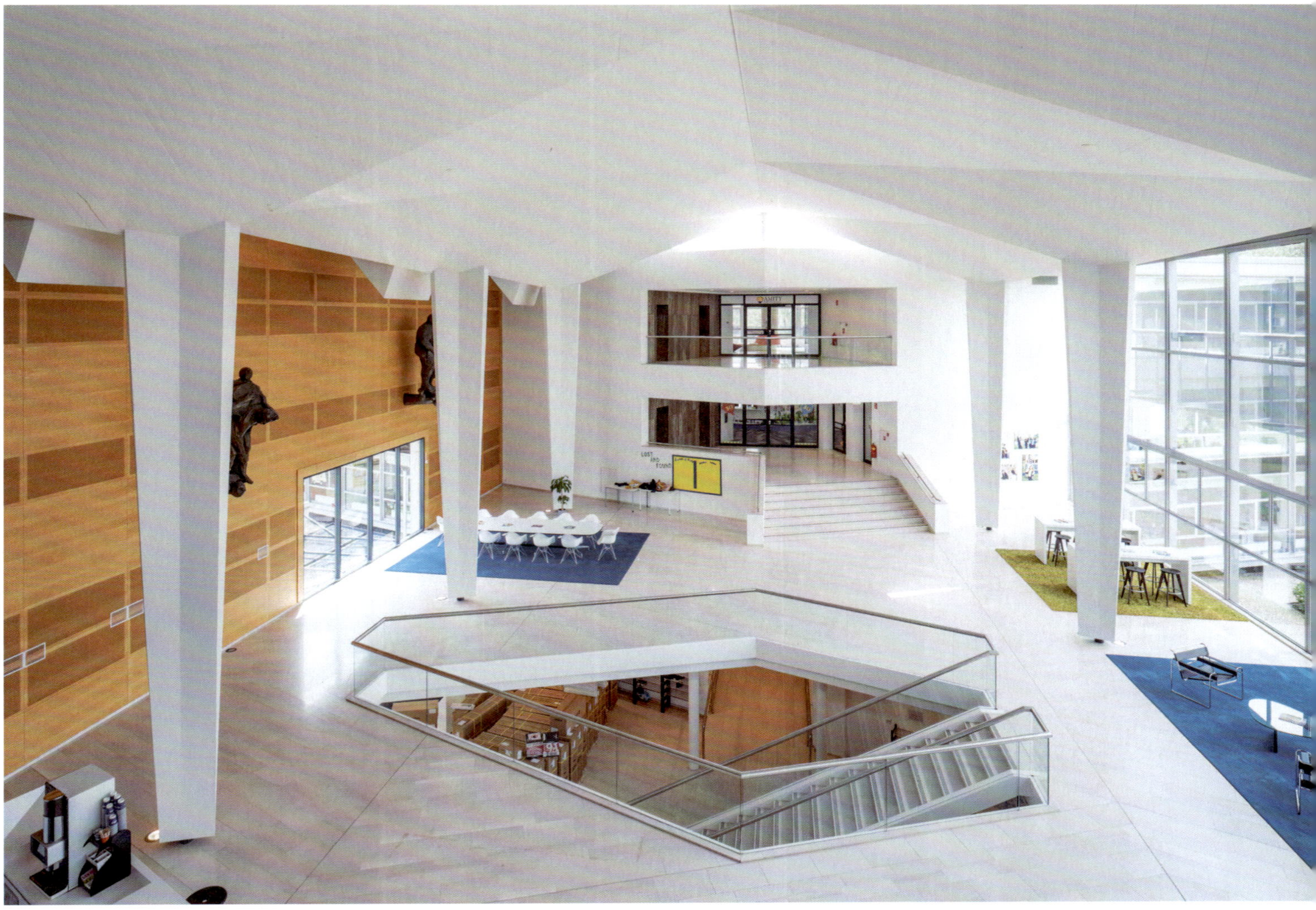

154

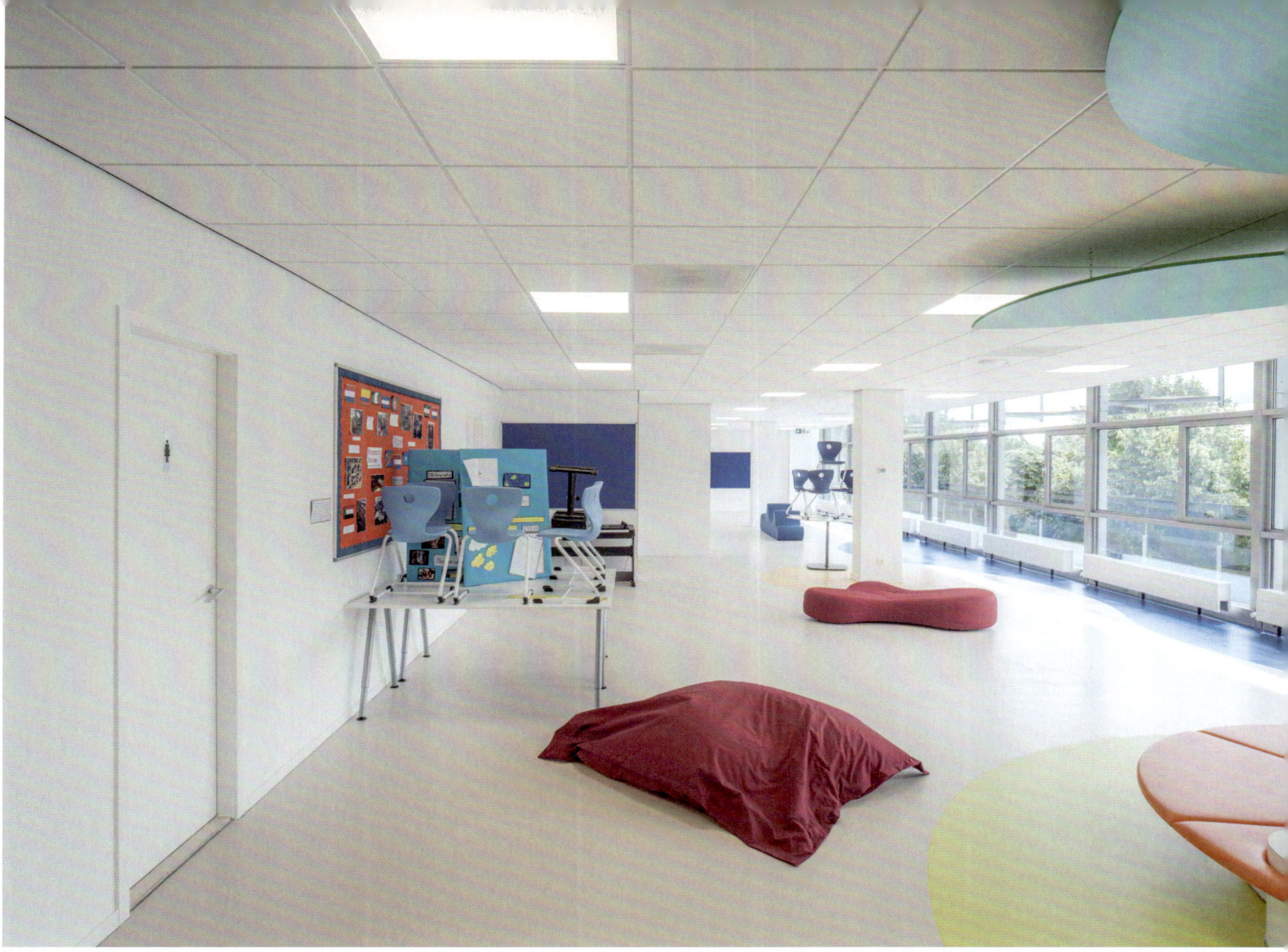

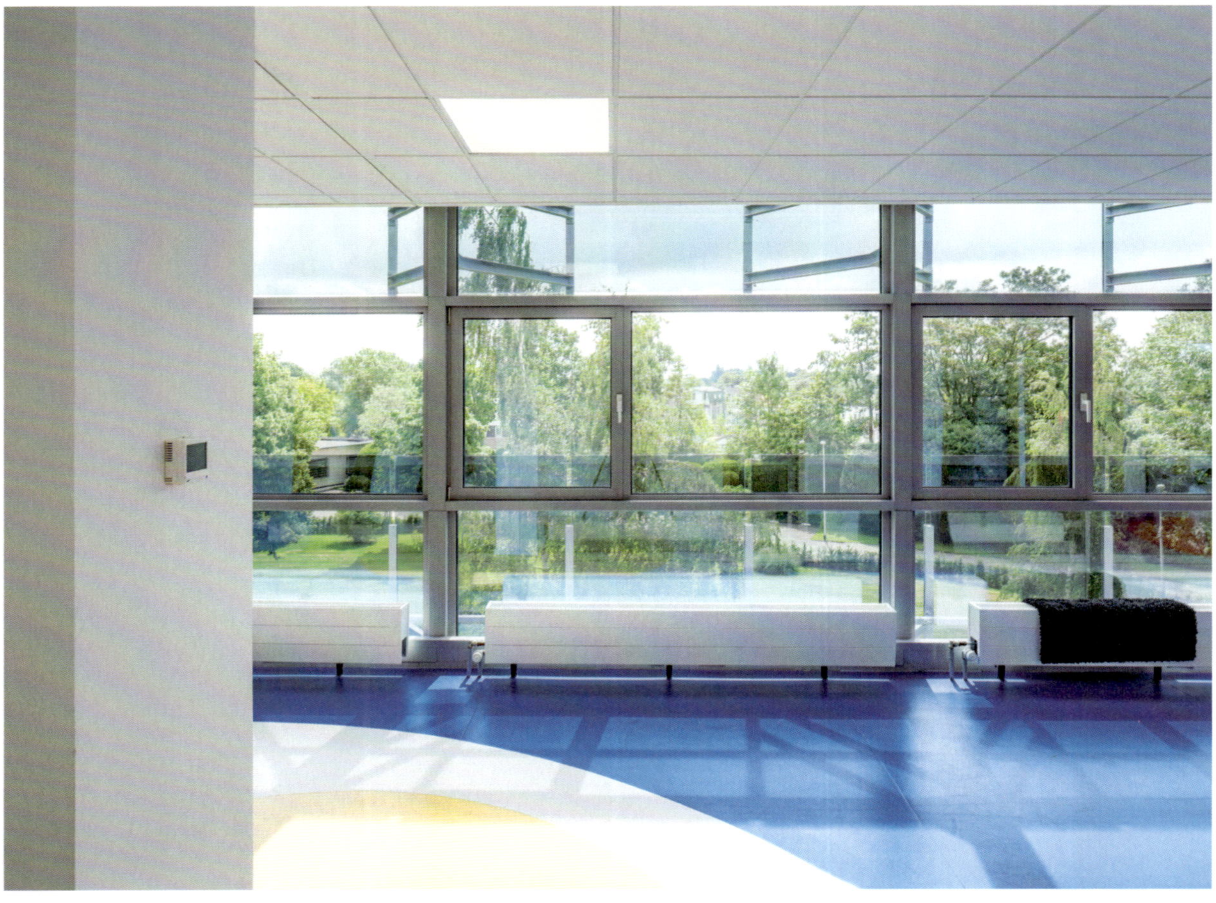

1958

INLAND STEEL BUILDING

An office building for a steel magnate and designed to evoke a man of immaculate tailoring, sticks to its omnipresent grid dimensions and still looks sharp

The Inland Steel Building, designed by Walter Netsch and Bruce Graham of SOM and the first tower to be built in Chicago's Loop after the Great Depression, is yet another 'zero hour' moment in (office) floor plan history. Following the early innovations that accelerated office development – artificial light, elevator, air conditioning – the introduction of the fully load-bearing exterior steel frame in the 19th century had technically allowed for an entirely free floorplan without obstructions. Despite this new freedom, the development of centralized cores and staircases in office towers remained a staple. The Inland Steel building was the first office building where literally everything needed for support (mechanics, restrooms, elevators (seven of them), stairs, etc.) was finally cleared from the office floors – in this case to a separate, connected tower,

"In its implacable precision it represents not only a noble continuation of the Chicago school of steel frame building but also a strong example of where SOM stands on total design."
— *Interior Contract Series*, 1958

"Ideally, the architect would like columnless space and wafer-thin walls for an office building. Essentially this is what has happened in the Inland Steel Building, because all the columns are outside the skin, and the stainless steel sheathed walls are only two inches thick."
— Skidmore Owens Merril, 1958

"With the unobstructed rectangular work area the modular principal of construction was employed to its maximum. Complete freedom of dividing the offices into the size of any multiple of the 5-foot 2-inch module is permitted."
— R.C. Hamm, 1958

"The new building sets a number of architectural 'firsts.' It is the first major structure to be erected on steel piling and with its steel 'ribs' showing on the outside, and the first large Loop building with 100 percent air conditioning 'built in.'"
— *Chicago Tribune*, 1958

which is windowless and clad entirely in stainless steel. The office tower is 19 stories: the service tower 25.

This so-called freedom manifests in the building via a strict modular grid. Following the request of Inland Steel chairman Clarence Randall that the new office should be designed "like a man of immaculate tailoring," the building evokes the notion of a universal order, in which a 5'2" x 5'2" module is implemented throughout. The building's exterior and interior seek a language of absolute coherence: every interior wall, ceiling tile, light, vent, etc. aligns within the grid. SOM was involved in every aspect of the design: from picking the silverware in the cafeteria and designing its trays, to commissioning artworks including Alexander Calder wall hangings and 20 paintings made for the building – mostly relating to steel.

The architects also became tenants, renting three floors. On one of them, Ezra Stoller captured the iconic image of the American architecture office: men wearing white shirts and ties calmly and confidently designing the built expression of America's post-war boom. SOM moved out in 1980. Inland Steel (only the eighth-biggest steel manufacturer in the US when they commissioned the building, which speaks to the might of their industry) occupied the top eight floors until 1998, when the company was acquired by Ispat International, later ArcelorMittal. (also that year, the building became a Chicago Landmark)

In 2005, Frank Gehry, an admirer of the building, convinced his friend, Perry Herst Jr., a retired real estate developer, to put together a group of investors to buy it and save it from disrepair. They did, for $44.5 million, and gifted Gehry a 2.5 percent stake as a finder's fee. Refurbishment began on the lobby and some restrooms, but SOM wasn't involved, and works halted when the market dipped. Gehry was reportedly furious, but when the group put the building on the market he persuaded his friend Richard Cohen, the Manhattan real estate developer, to purchase it and this time do the renovation properly. Cohen likened the building to owning an old Porsche, and wanted it restored to its former glory. Gehry's stake increased to five percent and SOM was hired.

The 2008 financial crisis delayed the project, but when it restarted, Michael Jividen and the SOM team started a precise renovation using original materials. The renovation builds on the legacy of the tightly gridded approach while adding green ambitions to reduce the energy usage with motorized shading and active cooling in its new ceiling panels. Further ergonomic adjustments in the furnishing reflect how its new workspace radically changed and yet simultaneously also stayed the same. The $18.7 million rehabilitation included a $5 million tax credit. The occupancy rate shot up from 50 to 98 percent. In 2021, 84 percent was leased – slightly lower than the 87 percent average for downtown office buildings at the end of the first quarter, according to brokerage CBRE – with 16 tenants averaging 1,155 square meters, according to a Cushman marketing flyer. The building is currently up for sale.

It is striking to see how throughout its lifespan, the freedom Inland Steel promised always looks like it is still yet to come. Looking at Stoller's photo of the open plan, 60 years of progress have delivered an additional fire exit sign, added surveillance, a glass partition, slightly more color, some vegetation, and height-adjustable desks with dual screens. And finally, perhaps most significantly, female presence.

notes

1   Oak Street Health, a network of primary care physicians for Medicare patients, is the largest tenant with a little less than 26,000 square feet, according to real estate information company CoStar Group.
2   See: Fred A. Bernstein, "Frank Gehry (a Part Owner) Helps Develop a Landmark," *New York Times*, November 16, 2010.
3   Oak Street Health, a network of primary care physicians for Medicare patients, is the largest tenant with a little less than 26,000 square feet, according to real estate information company CoStar Group.

building credits

client: Inland Steel Company/Joseph L. Block
architect: Skidmore, Owings, & Merrill (SOM)
schematic design: Walter Netsch
lead architect: Bruce Graham
lead structural engineer: Fazlur Khan
interior designer: Davis Allen
contractor: Turner Construction Company

photo credits

p.156: Hedrich Blessing
p.158 (above): unknown
p.158 (below), 162: Ezra Stoller/ESTO
p.159, 161, 163: Brent Hall and Patrick Small

2017
30 W. MONROE STREET
CHICAGO, ILLINOIS, US

162

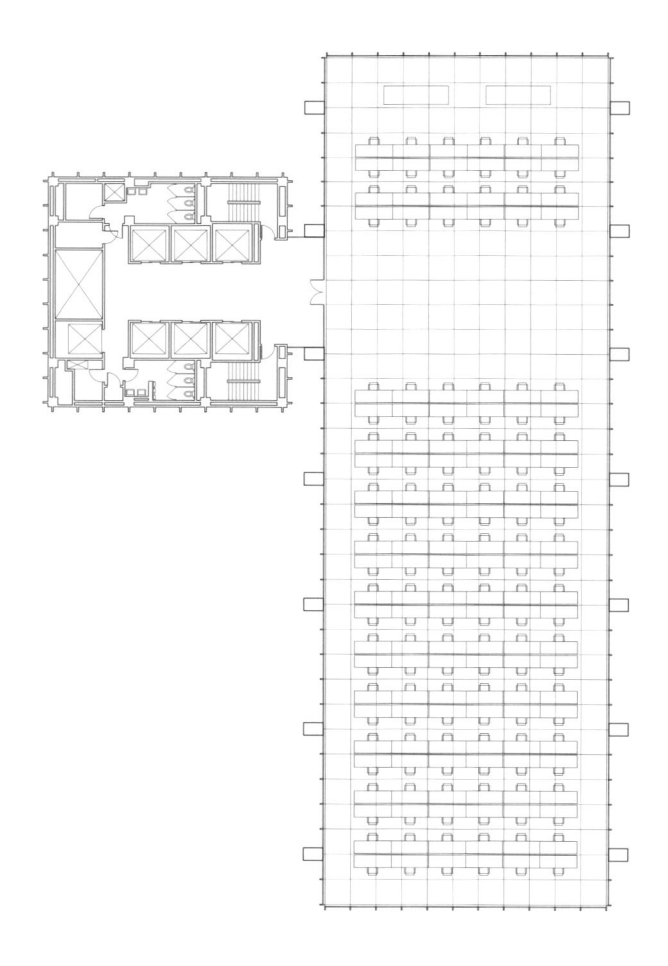

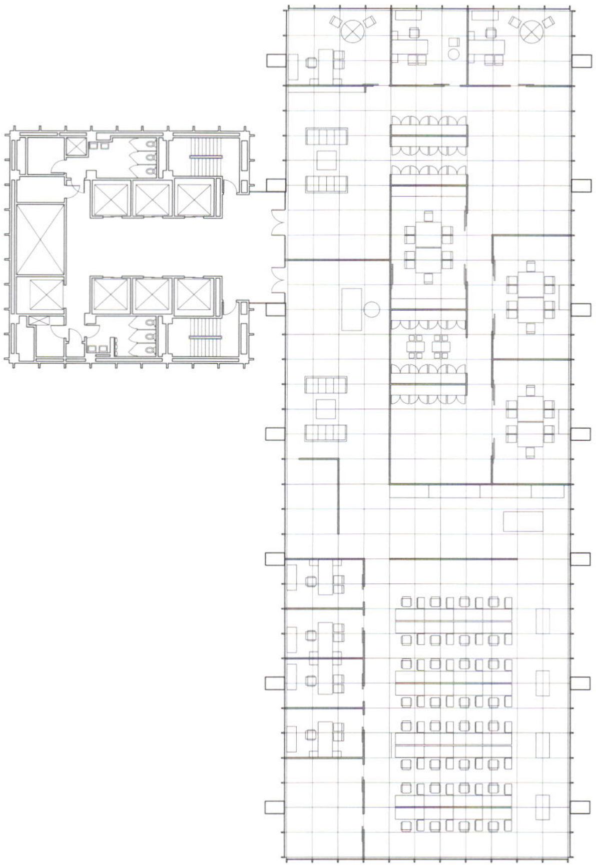

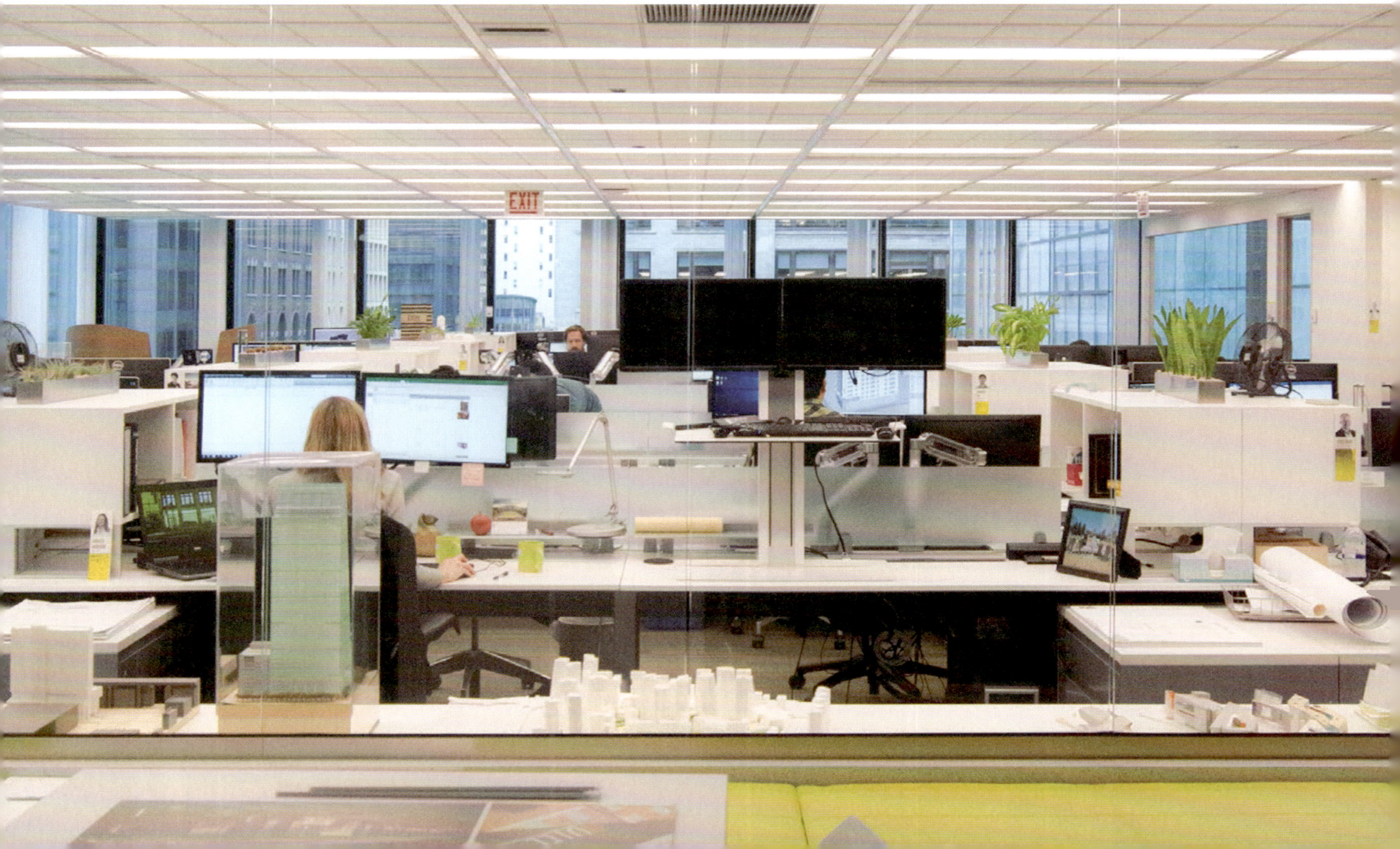
EXIT

1958

Rem Koolhaas, AMO, Nicholas Potts
Elements of Architecture

SEAGRAM BUILDING

WALL

SEAGRAM: METABOLISM OF A MONUMENT

1 INTERIOR VS. EXTERIOR

Solid on the outside, the Seagram building is designed for constant manipulation on the inside. The enabler of the large multi-tenant building type – of which Seagram is a pioneer – and a solution to the increasingly bespoke workspaces demanded by 20th-century corporations is the partition wall, offering both guaranteed fireproofing and the promise of endless flexibility. This new breed of wall, liberated from its former load bearing burdens, is also a symptom of a new partitioning of architectural practice into core and shell – a division manifest in Seagram between Mies, responsible for the exterior – the monumental, structural, and aesthetic calculations – and Philip Johnson, responsible for key enclaves within the interior, and an overall palette that would be later manipulated by a parade of tenants over the decades.

The role of the partition wall in catalysing Seagram's interior metabolism intensifies after the rewriting of tax codes in the 1960s, giving businesses tax breaks on the cost of replacing interior walls after 10 years, whereas costs associated with maintaining the exterior envelope of their building could only be written off over a period of 40 years.

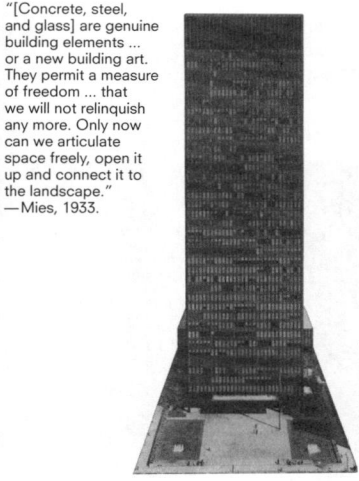

"[Concrete, steel, and glass] are genuine building elements ... or a new building art. They permit a measure of freedom ... that we will not relinquish any more. Only now can we articulate space freely, open it up and connect it to the landscape."
—Mies, 1933.

Changeable interiors: in the upper left, an open plan; upper right, a semi-partitioned office/meeting space; down in the lobby: total transparency. Illustrated for Helmut Jacoby's "Special Report on 375 Park Avenue," *New York Times*, April 7, 1957.

Peter Smithson spots the internal/external divide of Seagram:
"What faults it has seem to start behind the external skin. One is worried by an arbitrariness in the relationship between the supporting columns and the mullions seen from the outside, and in the inside they are clumsy in the office spaces. The inside spaces are fine when they are simple and one can see the outside, but none of the suites of rooms which have been specially designed seem to have any relationship with the fundamental organization of the building, or to utilize the potential relationship between the outside space and the views. It may be that a Mies building can only really have one sort of internal space."
—*Progressive Architecture*, June 1959

WALL

2 INTERIOR PALETTE
For the July 1958 issue, *Architectural Forum* creates a users manual to the Seagram Building, describing in intricate detail the palette of interior design, along with the measures taken to preserve tidiness on the outside. Seagram is "a half-million-square-foot laboratory in which new and special office designs are being tested in actual use."

Rigorous control of the facade extends to shading options.

INTERIOR PALETTE:

Seamlessness: doors as tall as walls.

Washable wall panels, with space for wires.

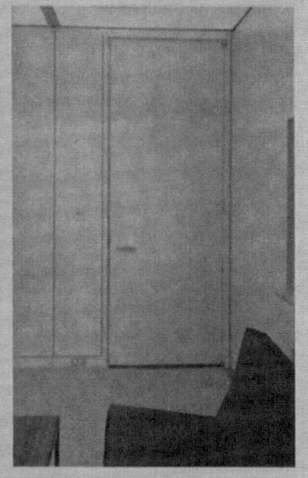

Travertine-clad partition walls modules in the toilets line up with illuminated ceiling modules.

PHOTOS: (ABOVE) © EZRA STOLLER; (OTHERS) GEORGE CSERNA

2. Controlled Venetian blinds were specially designed to stop in only three positions: all the way up, all the way down, and at half mast. The angle of the slats is fixed at 45 degrees to let pedestrians get full impact of lit-up building at night. These controls produce façade patterns that always look neat.

3. *Floor-to-ceiling doors* (far left) added nothing to the cost of each opening, made doors look like integral part of paneling, hence gave interiors greater unity. This corridor is part of Seagram's executive suite.

4. *Floor-to-ceiling partitions* (near left) are stock units reworked for Seagram by the architects. Greatly simplified in detail, partitions have reveals at panel joints, recessed wiring chases behind baseboards, specially designed doorknobs and hinges, and continuous tubular rubber stops around door frames. Panels were finished with many different materials, all washable. The system is now standard with its manufacturer.

5. *Floor-to-ceiling travertine* slabs (far left) divide washroom on Seagram's special executive floor. Orderly appearance was achieved in part by use of ceiling grid as module for partitions. All fixtures in all washrooms were specially designed, including pipe-connections at lavatories and toilets.

6. *Floor-to-ceiling elevator* doors reveal interior of cab lined with panels of stainless steel and bronze mesh designed for Seagram in a cartridge-belt pattern. These metal panels are removable, easily maintained (because they do not show scratches), reflect light from luminous ceiling above. Elevators are of the electronic brain type, which adjusts to changing loads at different times of day, eliminates need for elevator operators.

WALL

3 ADJUSTMENTS

The stark modernity of the interior palette – wood, travertine, plaster – is immediately augmented in executive encalves, and it only takes 15 years for Seagram's entire offices to undergo a refit, stripping away some of the wood-clad luxury…

DISTINCTION—Traditional décor may be found at the summit of Executive Row even when the rest of the office is "contemporary."
Drawings by Ajay.

"In New York's Seagram Building, a contemporary architectural showplace, the offices of Seagram clerks and lower- and middle-echelon executives are starkly modern. But the hierarchy at the top is housed in offices with Chippendale, Eighteenth-century satinwood desks and an Irish hunt table, all purchased through antique dealers in London."
— "Office Decor," *New York Times*, May 24, 1959.

1958 Meeting room: wood panneled wall, curtain wall.

White wall, curtain wall.

Multiple partitions creating small single occupancy offices; illuminated ceiling replaced with generic ceiling closer inside.

1958 Seagram offices: warm wood pannelled walls, ab-ex, leather chairs, ash tray.

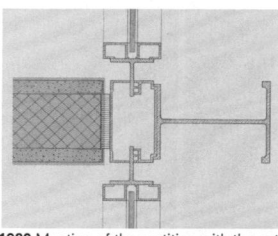

1980 Meeting of the partition with the exterior wall: must be behind the mullion. Article 26 is one of the most finnicky preservation orders in the lease agreement activated when the Teachers Insurance and Annuity Association of America becomes the owner of the Seagram building: "Article 26… applied to the inside face of the exterior wall: No changes could be made to the bronze frame, the air distribution enclosure, the venetian blinds, or **the way partitions meet the outside wall: they can only be located on the module line at the back of the mullions and are limited to a width of three and one half inches.**"
—Phyllis Lambert, *Building Seagram* (Yale, 2013), 216. While preserving the appearance of the building from the outside, the partition walls within shift constantly…

1974 Seagram offices: white walls, Pop art, red fabric couch, exit sign.

95

WALL

4 FOR RENT
Floors available for rent through the Seagram building's owners, RFR real estate, over the course of 2013. Axos show the variability of wall configurations on the different levels. While the exterior of Seagram must remain frozen in time, the interior is deeply unstable, susceptible to fluctuations in the market and in taste.

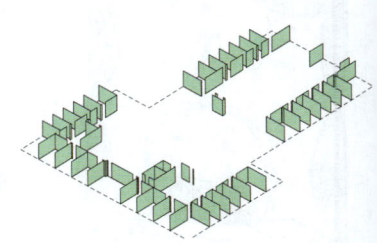

8th: private offices on perimeter, open in the middle.

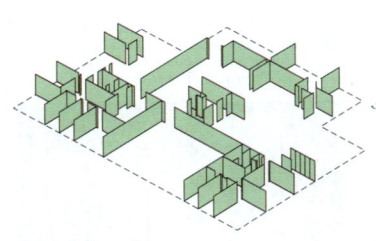

15th: hybrid conditions.

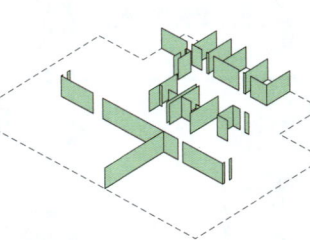

16th: near total open plan.

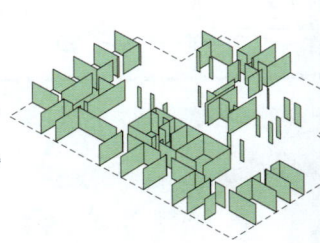

21st: smallest cells.

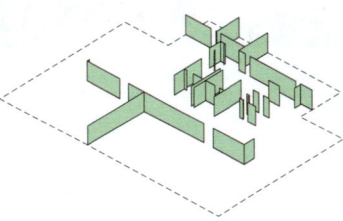

22nd: almost wall-less.

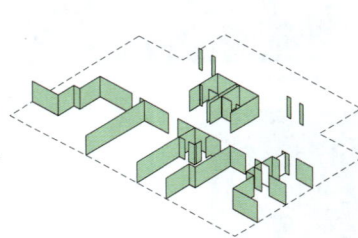

25th: a jog in the partition.

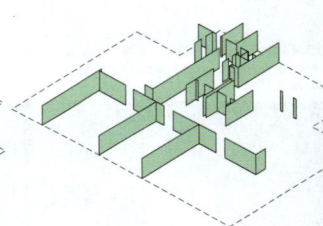

26th: large open spaces.

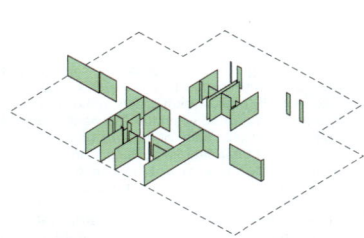

27th: density between two large open spaces.

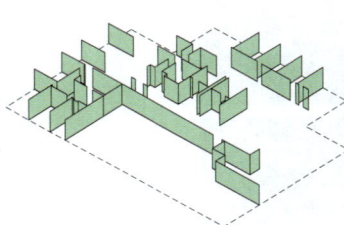

36th: huge open space + smaller offices.

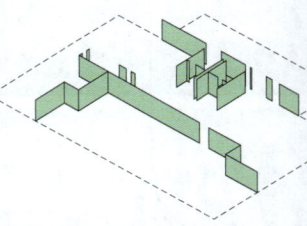

38th: largest open spaces.

WALL

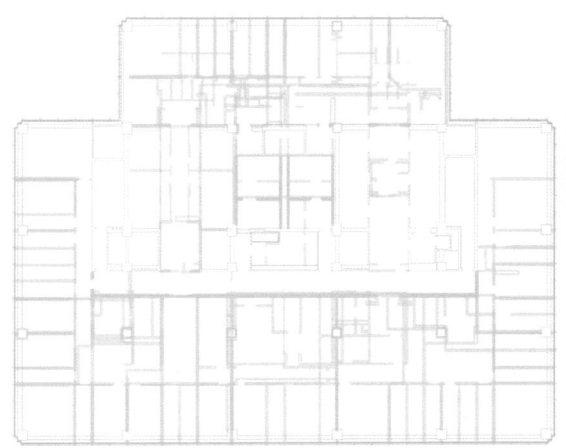

Palimpsest of floors shown on facing page. Thicker lines indicate the most popular location of walls: a corridor near the elevator bank, a tangle of walls in the projecting area to the west, and smaller cubicles in the middle strip.

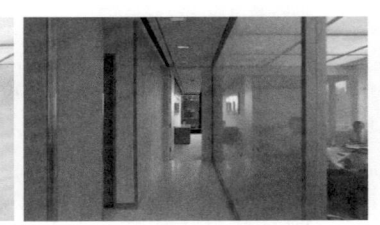

FOR RENT: generic spaces of Seagram, with varying wall configurations, the result of recent vacancies, strip-outs, and fit-outs…

97

WALL

5 GYPSUM PALACE

1990–2013 Over 467 interior rebuilding projects in the space of 23 years, the partition wall is the most powerful and inexpensive medium of the Seagram building's frantic internal metabolism, compared to the static, unmolested elements of the core and shell. Data on the cost, frequency, and location of interior refits, gleaned from the New York Department of Building's Information System, is applied here to a cost estimating formula (assuming a standard interior partition assembly of 3-5/8" studs covered in one layer of 5/8" gypsum board), in order to project the length of new walls added or reconstructed on every floor of the Seagram building between 1990 and 2013 (the DOB could not share earlier data). The data reveals a flimsy gypsum palace hidden inside a dignified, seemingly eternal container. From the calculations we can conclude:

1. In accumulated waves of refurbishment*, many floors have changed or added the equivalent of the height of the building itself in new walls.
2. The total surface area of all new walls far exceeds that of the current facades of the building, enough to build a tower of gypsum containing a larger volume than the real Seagram.
3. With a thickness of 12mm for each gypsum panel used for the new walls, if you stacked all those panels, the pile would reach higher (169m) than the top of Seagram (156m).

*In 2005, costs for internal refurbishment projects reach 20 percent of the total construction cost for the entire building.

ALTERATIONS AS % OF ORIGINAL BUILDING CONSTRUCTION COST

Color code indicates projects started in same year, to compare new wall length between floors. Colors recur each five years.

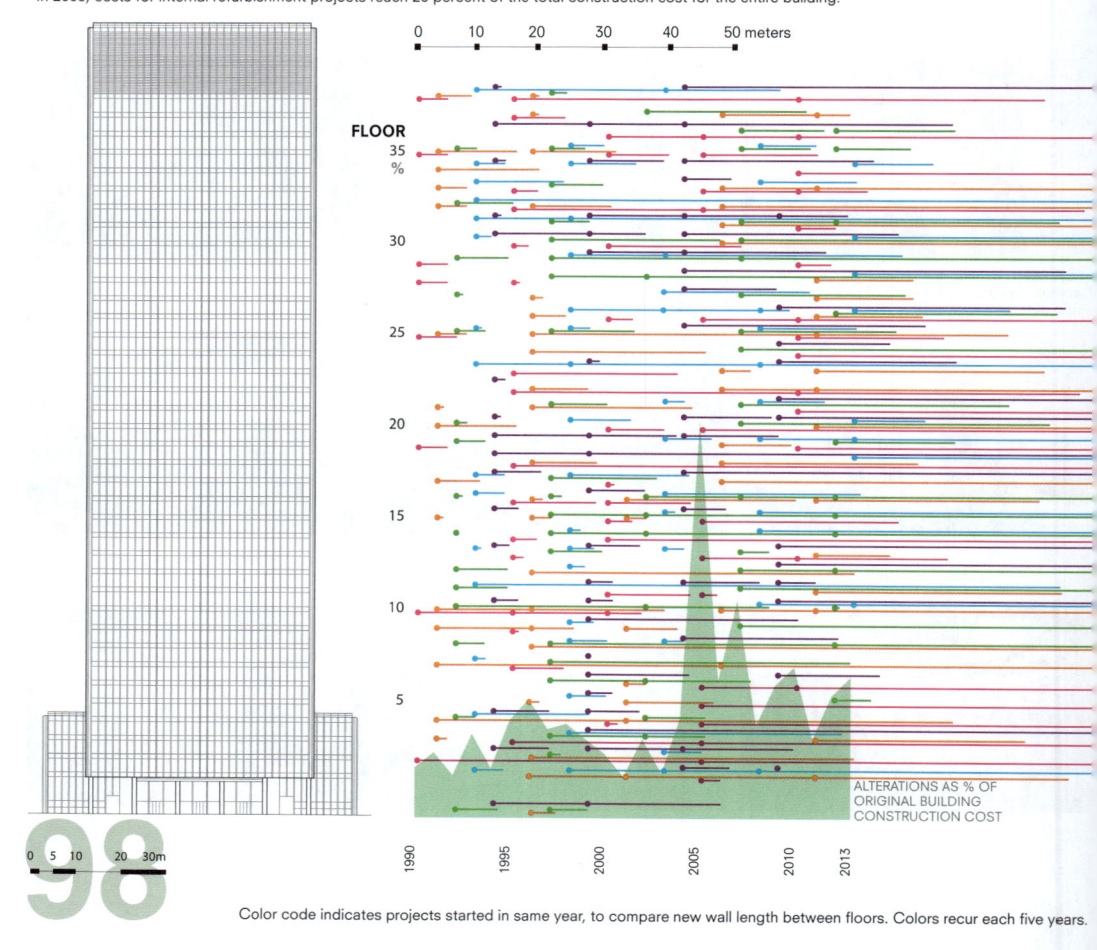

WALL

...the irony of the Seagram is that, since
the building is a crucial part of Manhattan's
heritage, it is particularly onerous to change
its internal configurations, to rearrange
its partitions. The flimsy is ennobled by
the aura of the solid...

**New or replacement
wall construction
in meters, 1990–2013:**

Total	16,925.7 m
Penthouse	3.4 m
38	219.8 m
37	53.0 m
36	236.4 m
35	110.4 m
34	341.8 m
33	263.1 m
32	377.9 m
31	363.6 m
30	372.5 m
29	603.2 m
28	227.0 m
27	86.7 m
26	405.3 m
25	260.2 m
24	322.9 m
23	253.4 m
22	239.8 m
21	711.1 m
20	362.1 m
19	744.2 m
18	768.8 m
17	420.8 m
16	503.0 m
15	274.3 m
14	494.9 m
13	408.1 m
12	388.5 m
11	219.6 m
10	683.6 m
9	614.2 m
8	725.0 m
7	278.2 m
6	782.9 m
5	112.0 m
4	906.5 m
3	1013.3 m
2	889.0 m
1	411.1 m
0	85.1 m
-1	85.0 m

Magenta: 1990, 1995, 2000, 2005, 2010
Orange: 1991, 1996, 2001, 2006, 2011
Green: 1992, 1997, 2002, 2007, 2012
Cyan: 1993, 1998, 2003, 2008, 2013
Violet: 1994, 1999, 2004, 2009

99

WALL

6 POSTSCRIPT: WALL VS. WEAVING

In 2014, in a Semperian farce, Aby Rosen, the owner of the Seagram building, attempts to remove, possibly forever, Picasso's 1919 tapestry, *Le Tricorne* – originally a scenographic backdrop for the Ballets Russes – from the corridor leading to the Four Seasons restaurant.

In *Building Seagram* (2013), Phyllis Lambert, daughter of Samuel Bronfman, Mies's client for the building, and director of the building project, describes how the tapestry is integral to its environment. Installing it in 1958, "It seemed a miracle to find a work whose size, muted tonality, and classical repose would fit Mies's building so perfectly," she recalls. At nearly six meters, it is the exact height of the wall, and "marks the summit of the plaza entry sequence: designed to be seen from afar, its magisterial presence is the focal point of the long vista of successive spaces leading from the building to the restaurant entrance, making it wholly and intimately connected to both the Seagram building and the restaurant."

Rosen claims a steam leak, plus dangerous sagging of the travertine-clad walls around the tapestry, as the reason to urgently remove it, so repairs can be carried out, and the tapestry saved from harm.

Le Tricorne (The Three-Cornered Hat) has been hanging there so long, more than 50 years, that it has ossified into a solid but very brittle wall. Removing it could cause it to "crack like a potato chip," according to Rosen's own team of movers.

The *New York Times* reports on February 3 that Rosen, a collector of contemporary art, had called the tapestry a "schmatte" (Yiddish for rag) and "has told people that he wants to showcase highlights of his vast trove in the space now occupied by *Le Tricorne*."

The Landmarks Conservancy, the owners of the tapestry, has limited power since wall coverings are exempt from the protected status of the Four Season's interiors – softness is deemed temporary, even expendable, by preservation rules.*

Belmont Freeman, an architect who worked on earlier restoration of the Four Seasons, alerts the Conservancy that there is in fact no travertine cladding behind the tapestry – Philip Johnson apparently deliberately didn't put it there, where it wouldn't be seen and wasn't needed.

A judge rules in favor of the Conservancy, restraining Rosen from removing the tapestry, which remains in place for now, acting like a curtain, covering the nudity of the unclad wall behind it. Both wall and weaving – both forms of decoration in this case – remain, according to the protagonists, on the brink of collapse; only preservation of the status quo can save them both…

"The space was designed so precisely for the permanent installation of *Le Tricorne* that Johnson omitted the travertine finish. Thus, the terrible prospect of a slab of travertine delaminating from the wall and ripping through the curtain, as RFR claims, is utterly specious. Likewise, the building plans indicate no steam pipe or anything else in that wall that could be leaking and thus requiring invasive repair."
—Belmont Freeman, FAIA
"Commentary: Needless Destruction," *Architectural Record*, February 6, 2014.

*Article 29 of the lease agreement provides that "Under New York law, *Le Tricorne* ... [is] not [a] fixture appurtenant [attached] to the Seagram Building and, thus, cannot and should not be designated as interior architectural features of the Building."

A wall in itself: the time-hardened tapestry *Le Tricorne*, by Picasso, crowns the entry sequence to the Four Seasons but is now under threat from maintenance and changing tastes: monopolizing the wall, no other artwork can be hung there…

100

client: Phyllis Lambert
architect: Ludwig Mies van der Rohe

photo credits

p.164: Ezra Stoller / Esto
p.165-172: Taschen
p.173, 175 (below): Richard Pare
p.174 (all), 175 (above): unkown

2020
375 PARK AVENUE
NEW YORK, NY, US

174

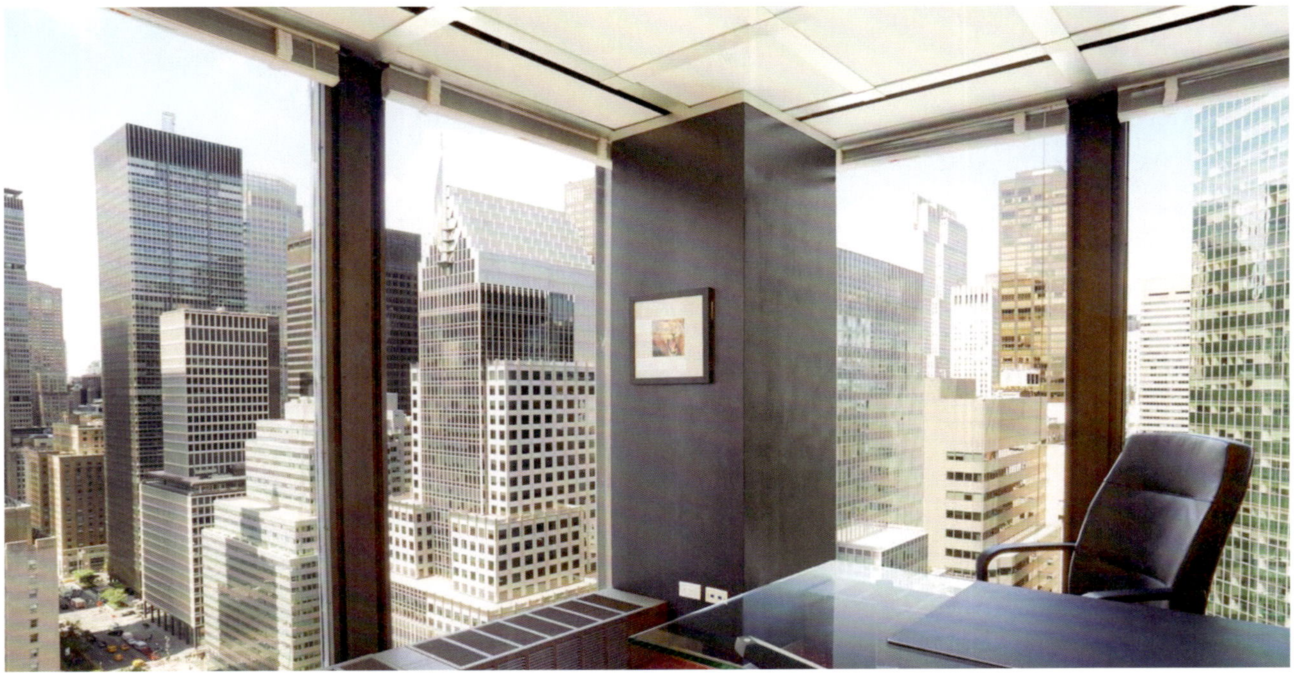

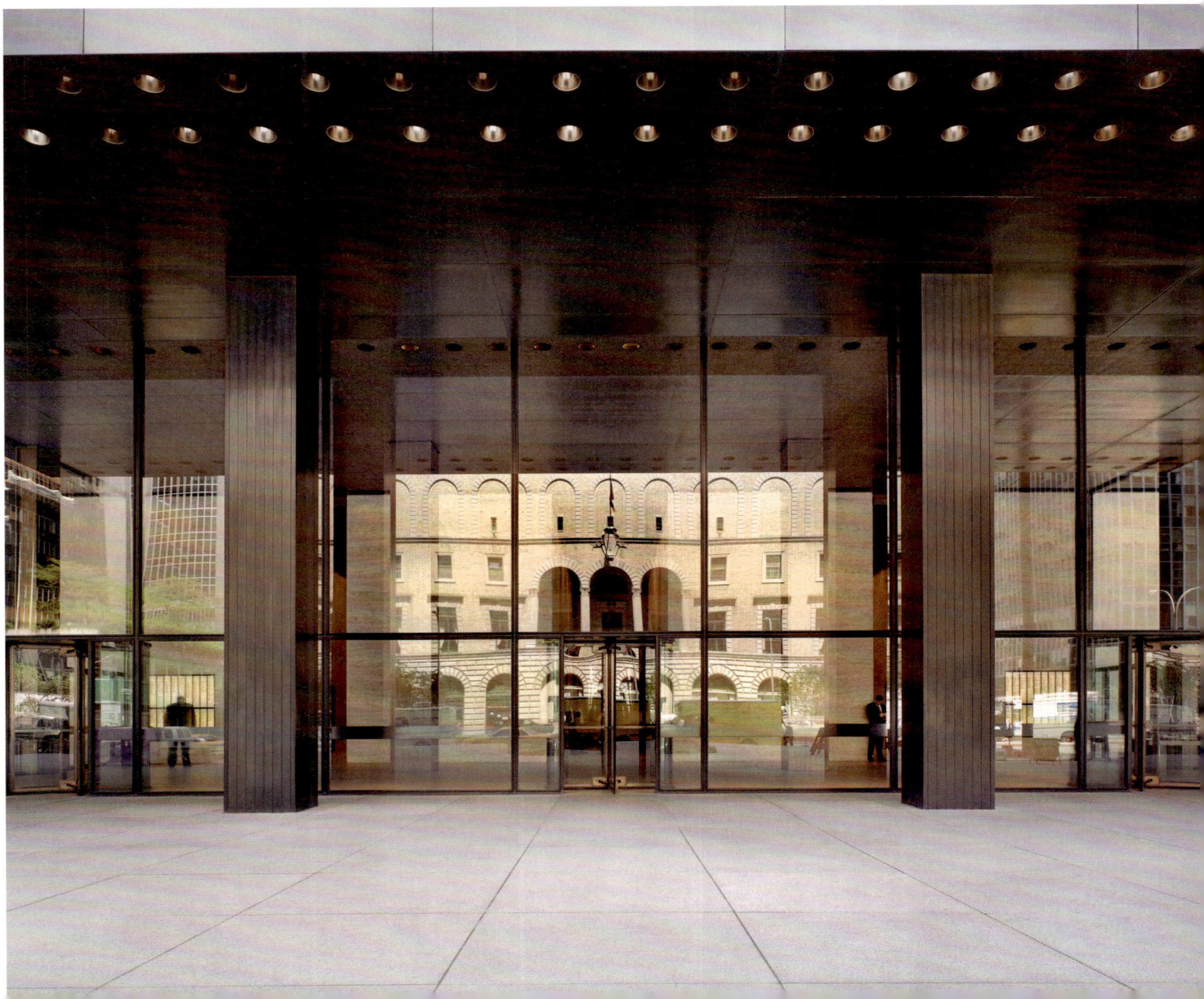

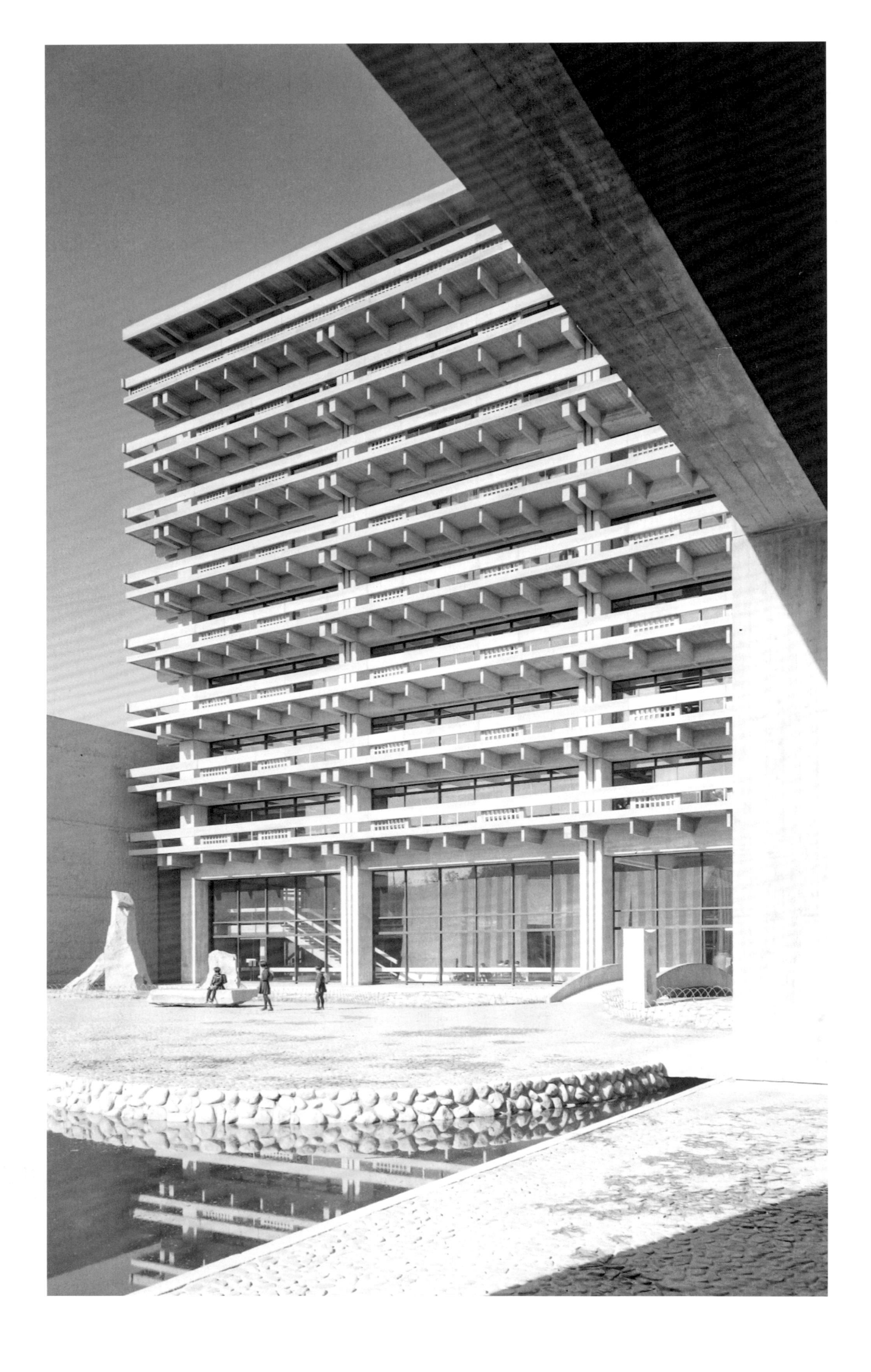

1958

Hiroki Senda, Yae Faye, Abudjana Babiker
Keigo Kobayashi Laboratory, Waseda University

KAGAWA PREFECTURAL OFFICE

A group dedicated to cleaning and maintenance, providing jobs for families bereaved by the war, helps give a governmental building five decades of life

Designing democracy
The Kagawa Prefectural office building, designed by Kenzo Tange, has been continuously in service since its completion in 1958. With its design anchored in a modular system and supported by a special team of janitors, the building has maintained both its function and its appearance. At its inception, in 1955, the governor of Kagawa Prefecture, Masanori Kaneko, commissioned the building with the following criteria:

1. Be considerate of the climate of Kagawa and the environment of Takamatsu (the prefectural capital).
2. Be appropriate as the symbolic building for Kagawa Prefectural Office.
3. Be a positive factor in the urban planning of Takamatsu.

4. Be reflective of the prefectural government in the age of democracy.
5. Be respectful of the existing government buildings and do not be wasteful.
6. Be mindful of sourcing local materials as much as possible.
7. Be careful to keep the construction cost within the budget.

As Governor Kaneko searched for an architect capable of realizing his precise vision, he ran into his old high school acquaintance, Genichiro Inokuma, who had become a famous painter. Inokuma encouraged Kaneko to create a building that matched the beauty of Kagawa and arranged a meeting with Kenzo Tange, Japan's leading architect, who was working on the design of the Yoyogi National Gymnasium for the 1964 Tokyo Olympics.

Tange sympathized with Kaneko's vision for the new prefectural government building that would symbolize the new age of democracy and rejuvenate a city destroyed by the war. Tange responded with a scheme for a large entrance hall opening up to the city under pilotis. Tange believed it was the role of urban planning to juxtapose private functions inside buildings with public functions outside, and it was necessary to consider architecture on the urban scale. Now into its seventh decade of life, the entrance hall and its pilotis are still enjoyed by locals as a place to relax, connecting the interior governing functions with the outside city.

Grid
The metric system was officially introduced in Japan in 1951 as part of its postwar modernization, replacing the traditional Shakkan-hou measuring system. The design of Kagawa prefectural office started soon after the implementation of this new law, meaning the transition between the two measuring systems had to be confronted.

Tange proposed using a minimum module of 30 centimeters – almost the same as one Syaku-unit in the old Shakkan-ho system. This module dictated the unfolding of all aspects of the building. In addition, Tange designed the office floor to be a single large space without any fixed walls, and the modular system allowed partitions and fittings to be installed using a grid with multiples of 30 centimeters.

Seiji Kagawa, assistant manager of the Construction and Repair Department of Kagawa prefectural office, explained to us the advantages of Tange's modular system: "In the prefectural office, new sections are frequently created, and the number of personnel changes from time to time. In such cases, the layout of the offices can be freely changed using the small beams within a 180-centimeter ceiling grid as the guide. Also, since the pillars are positioned to avoid the modular grid, readymade partitions and fittings can be applied without any alteration, making it highly convenient. Because of these factors, this system has been in use for more than 60 years."

In 2008, at the 50th-anniversary lecture celebrating the Kagawa Prefectural office, Masamitsu Nagashima, an architect and one of Tange's students, explained: "The organization of the Kagawa (Prefectural office building) grid was perfect. I think it is wonderful that Kagawa was able to establish a single logical system that connects and organizes everything all the way to the facade. However, thick columns made of reinforced concrete have a different life span and scale from the partitions and sashes. Therefore, it's better to place these big columns within the squares of the grid, like the pieces within the shogi [Japanese Chess] grid."

Sweeping, wiping and polishing
In May 1958, governor Kaneko established the Kagawa Seiwa-kai as an organization to clean and maintain prefectural office buildings, in the process securing employments for families bereaved after the war. Never forgetting its motto of "sweeping, wiping, and polishing," the organization cleaned the building every day since its opening, contributing to its longevity without compromising its original appearance. Tadashi Yamamoto, working in the architecture department of the Kagawa office since its completion, played a major role in supporting and coordinating with members of Seiwa-kai in their efforts to maintain the building. (Yamamoto's relationships with artists and architects facilitated interaction between public office and creative sectors. He later left public office to become an architect and helped set up the Setouchi Triennale, where architects and artists create works in the Setouchi islands.)

On March 31, 2008, Seiwa-kai ended its 50 years of service, replaced by another building maintenance company. The consequences of their work can still be seen throughout the building: original furniture and fittings remain in use, retaining original colors and materials, thanks to the dedicated team of the cleaners.

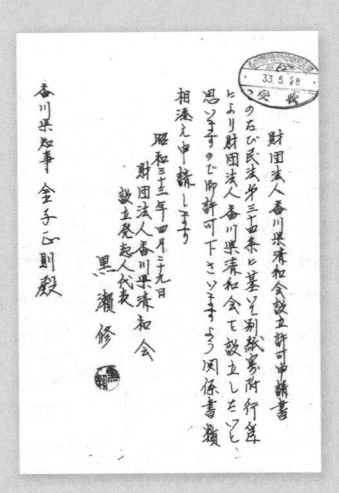

Permission for the Establishment of the Kagawa Prefecture Seiwa-kai Foundation (Kagawa Prefectural Archives)

Application for Permission to Establish the Kagawa Seiwa-kai Foundation:
In accordance with Article 34 of the Civil Code, I hereby apply for permission to establish the Kagawa Seiwa-kai Foundation in accordance with the attached Articles of Endowment, together with the relevant documents.

April 29, 1958: Representative of the founders of the Kagawa Seiwa-kai Foundation, Shuichi Kurose with Masanori Kaneko, governor of Kagawa Prefecture.

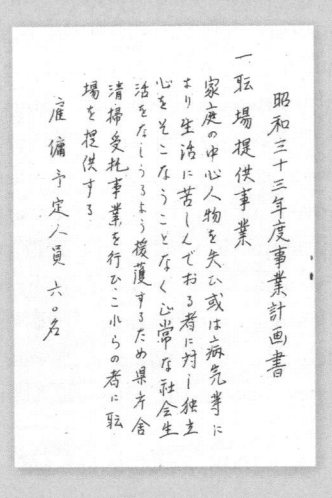

Business Plan for Fiscal 1958 (for Seiwa-kai)
Workplace Provision Project:
In order to assist those who have lost the central figure in their families or are suffering from illness, etc., so that they can lead a normal social life without losing their independence, we will provide workplaces for these people by undertaking the cleaning of prefectural office buildings.
Expected number of employees: 60.

building credits

client: Masanori Kaneko
architect: Kenzo Tange

photo credits

p.176, 178: Toshio Taira
p.179: Seiji Izumi
p.181, 183 (all), 185 (all), 187: Hiroki Senda
p.182, 184 (all): Fumio Murasawa
p.186: Construction and Repair Department, Kagawa Prefecture

2021
4-CHOME-1-10 BANCHO
TAKAMATSU, KAGAWA, JAPAN

182

183

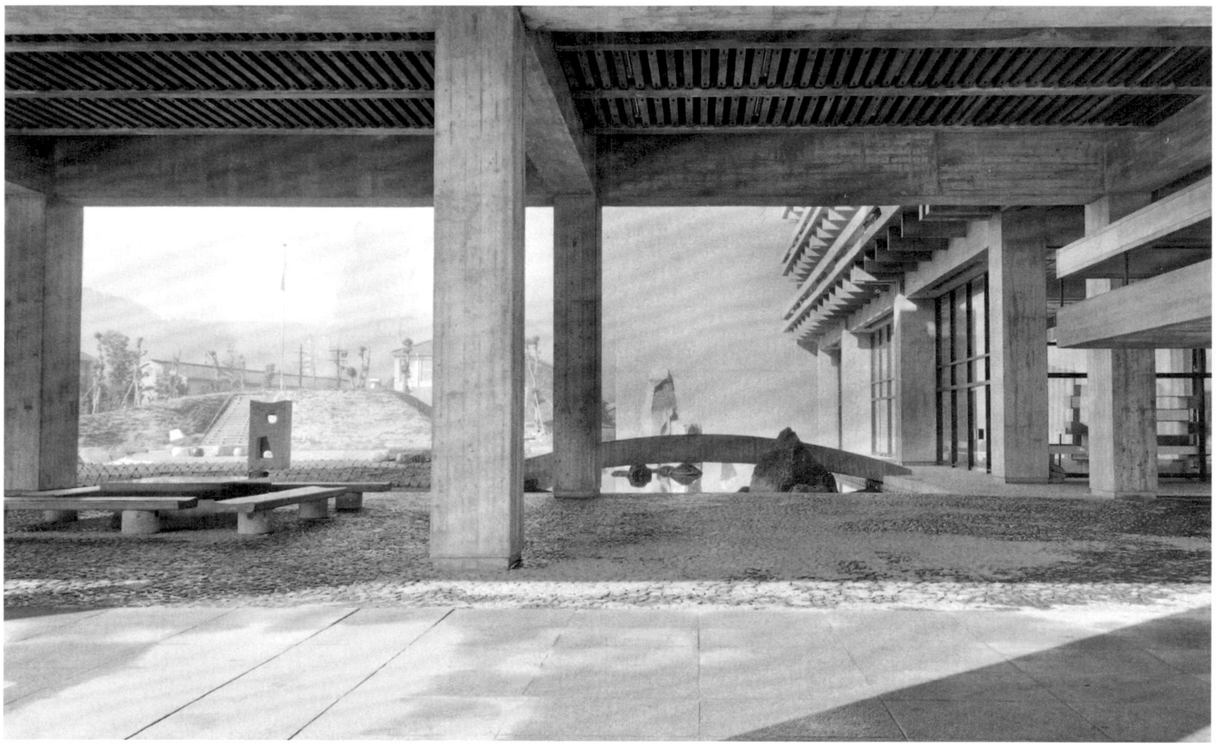

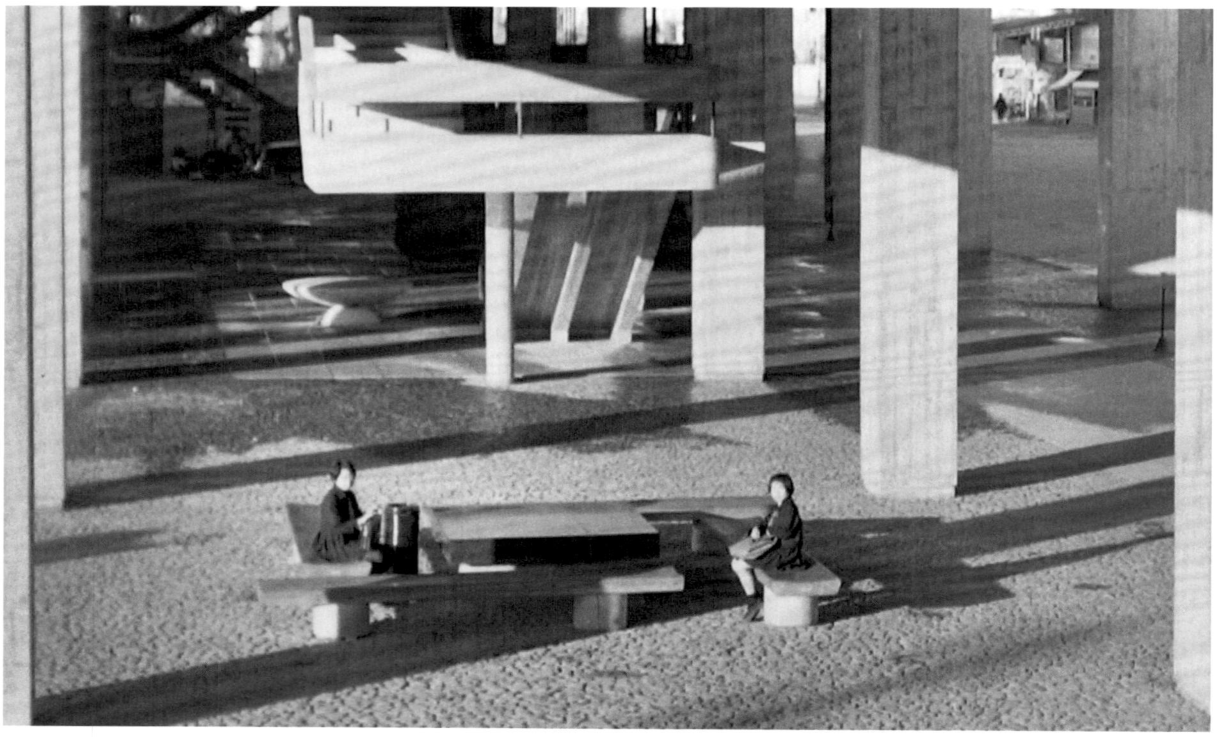

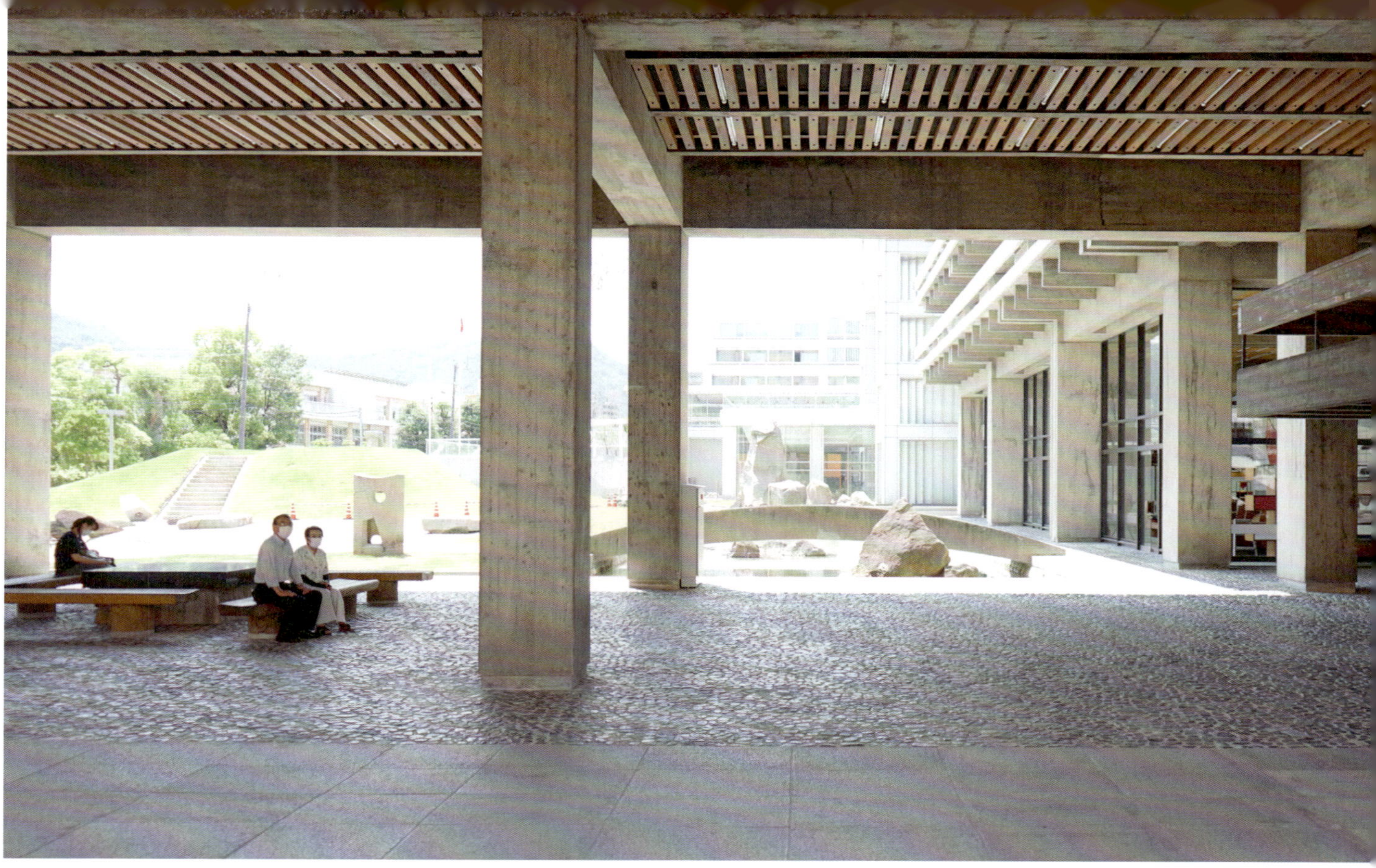

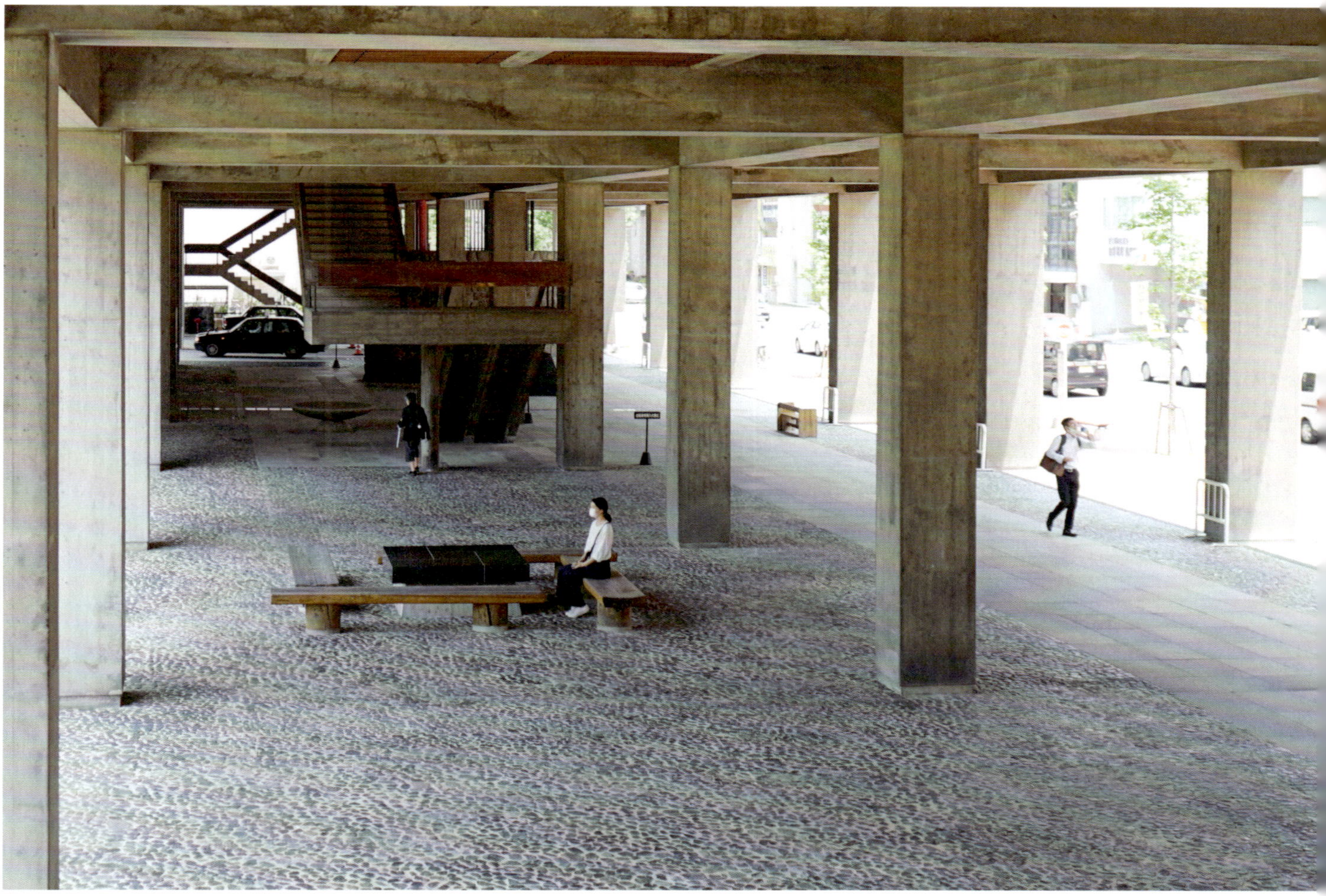

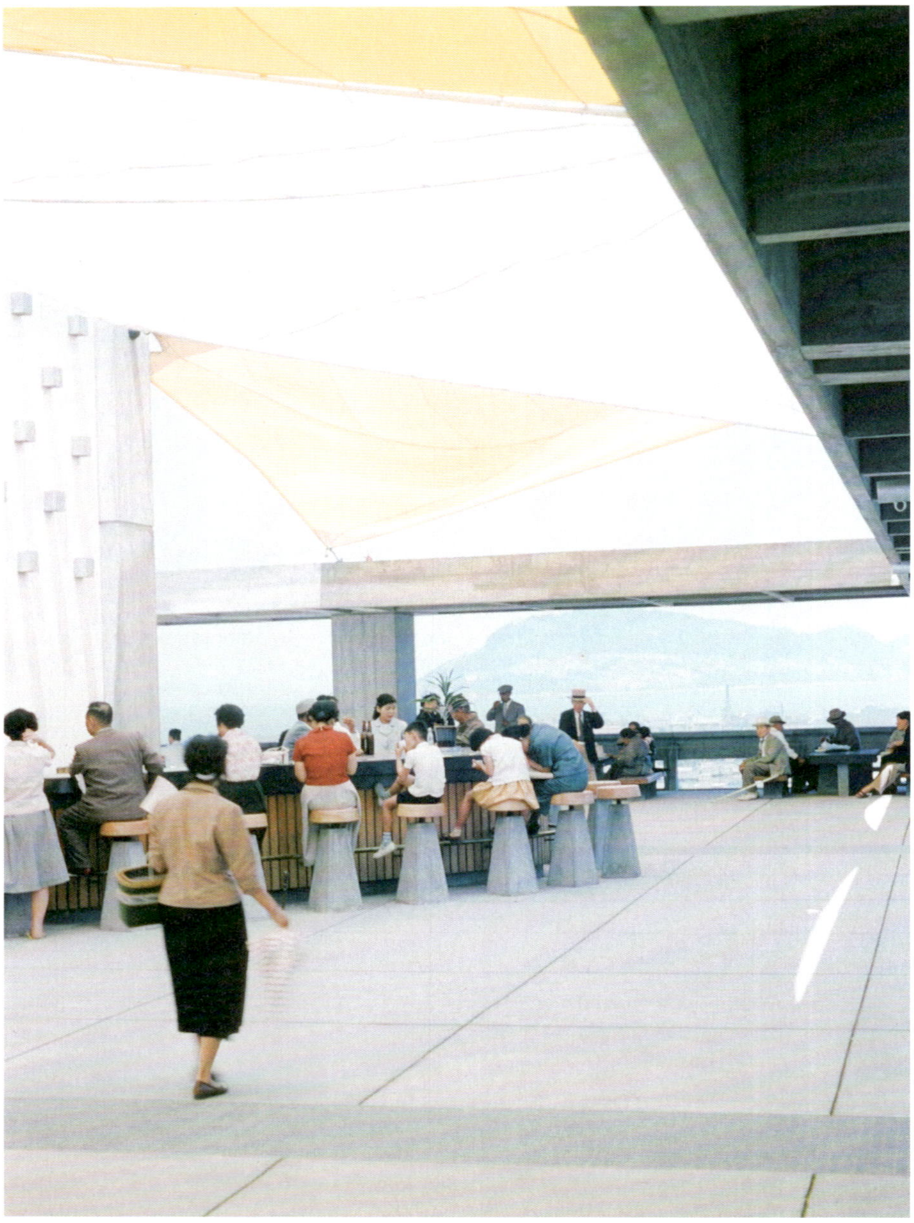

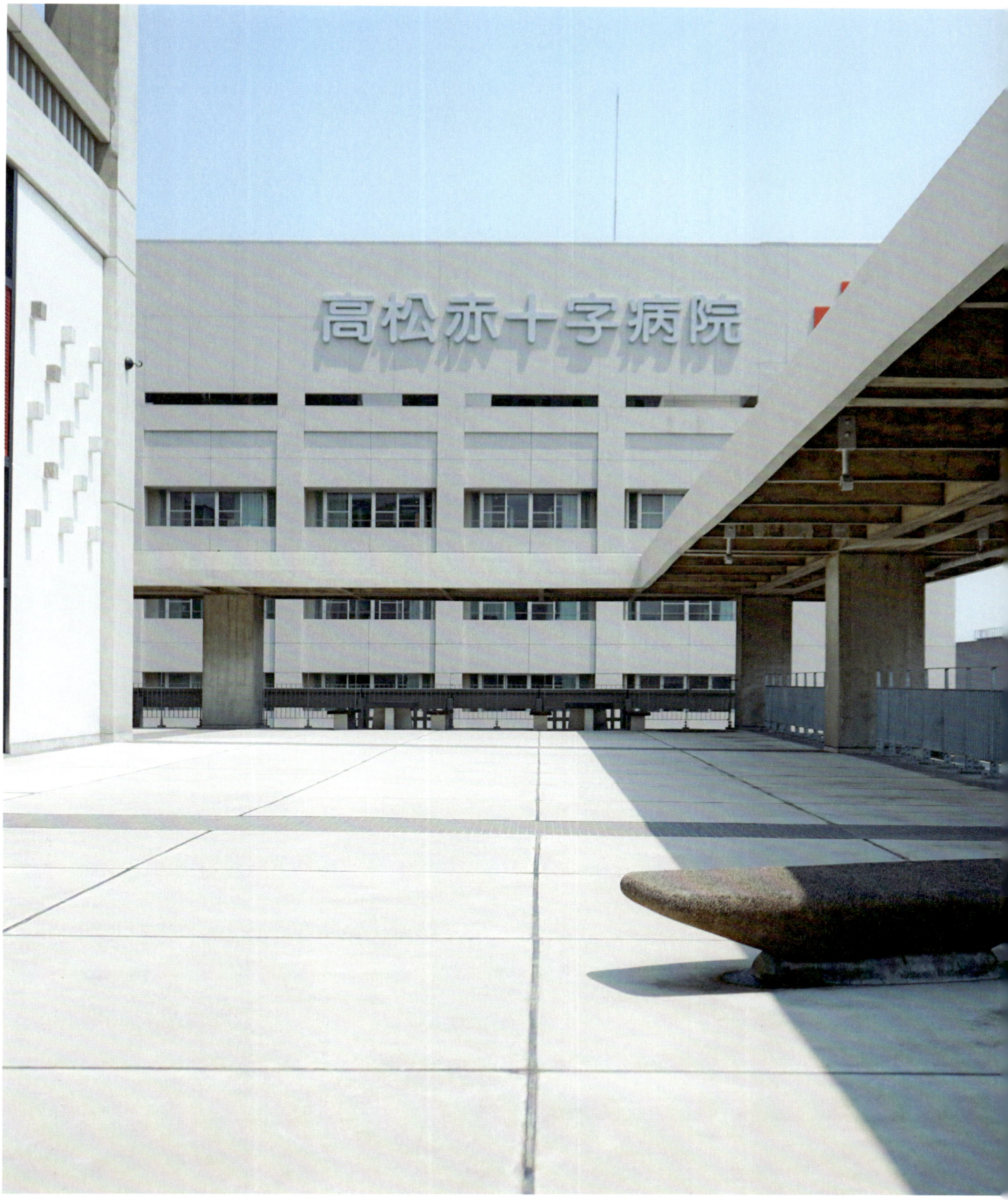
高松赤十字病院

1960

Ruth Baumeister

PIRELLI TOWER

A beloved tower, designed as "finished form", symbolizing Italy's 1960s economic boom, is renovated after a bizarre accident

Plane Crash
Shortly before 6 p.m. on April 18, 2002, a small plane crashed into the 26th floor of the Pirelli tower, one of Milan's most prominent buildings. The plane, coming from Switzerland and destined for Milan Linate, had a problem with its landing gear, and an emergency landing was prepared. The control tower instructed the pilot to turn west, but he turned north – possibly trying to take a shortcut to the airport across the city – and struck the building. The pilot and two people working in the building were killed. The incident caused significant damage to the tower. Apart from the gash in the façade as a result of the crash itself, the water used to extinguish the fire caused by the fuel explosion damaged the floor and the slabs at levels 26 and 27.

Renovation
Questions were raised over the tower's structural viability, and whether it was possible to repair the damage. *Not* saving the Pirellone[1] – how the Milanesi affectionately nickname the building – was never an option. "Pirelli is Milan," said Laura Riboldi of the Pirelli foundation. "And the Pirelli tower is one of the strong symbols that define the identity of a metropolis and a region, its economic dynamism, innovation and the architectural quality of its working and living environments."[2] Shortly before the plane crash, two architecture firms – ISA, Grassi & Crespi and Marcora – had been appointed for a partial renovation – ceramic tiles were falling from the facade and windows were no longer airtight (the rubber gaskets were worn out). Now the architects found themselves charged with a completely different task. Over the next two years, apart from fixing the damage from the plane crash, the entire façade was renewed to meet contemporary demands of climate performance and security; it was also equipped for media projections. While the craft knowledge that produced the original ceramic tiles for the cladding did not exist in Italy anymore, the job could be done in China. During the course of the renovation, the layout of the offices was changed from a large open plan to a mix of single offices and smaller open spaces. The auditorium in the basement was restructured and the belvedere on the roof was redesigned. A recent photo of the 26th floor shows the space empty. In the foreground, the yellow-blueish black linoleum floor resembles the beach, the windows creating the horizon line, and the belvedere an entre to the sea of buildings in Milan.

Advertising architecture

In 1956, the brothers Alberto and Piero Pirelli, patrons of the world's leading tire manufacturer, commissioned Gio Ponti (1891–1979) to build their new headquarters on the site of their former production facilities, which had been destroyed in the Second World War. They called not only for a new office building but for an emblematic corporate architecture. They got what they were asking for. British architecture critic Reyner Banham wrote, "The Pirelli tower is certainly the most impressive, probably the best, building put up in Milan since the War. The visitor is seized by its quality the moment he steps out of the Central Station and sees it rising dramatically on the right-hand side of Piazza Duca d'Aosta."[3] But Banham noted, "Pirelli must be discussed as a piece of advertising architecture; the questions it raises, even in matters of function and structure, are nearly all questions about what advertising does to architecture, and how far architecture is a fit medium for advertising."[4]

Ponti promoted the Pirelli skyscraper as the materialization of his concept *la forma finita* (finished form), based on a structural framework produced by a variation of forces, rather than a conventional rectangular mass. Finished form was meant to be simple, and did not allow for any additions. Those parts of the program that would not fit into the slender, elegant tower – auditorium, conference rooms, lecture theatre, cafeteria, parking, and service rooms – were placed by Ponti in a partially-subterranean wedge-like volume at the foot of the skyscraper.

By suppressing all the functions that would not fit into the tower itself, Ponti achieved clarity in the total image of the building, so that the outside form almost becomes diagrammatic. In collaboration with Ponti, engineers Pier Luigi Nervi and Alberto Danuso developed an elegant, slender new tower type that became a model for office buildings around the world, including the Pan Am Building in New York by Walter Gropius and Pietro Belluschi, the Telefunken Highrise in Berlin by Bernhard Hermkes, and the Alpha Tower in Birmingham by Richard Seifert & Partners.

Materials, structure, and interior
Ponti – sometimes called the architect of lightness – was the first in the world to use a 25-meter span frame, employing concrete piers that gradually become thinner as they rise, shrinking from 200 cm at the bottom to 50 cm near the top. This response to the structural load not only saved material, but also increased the rentable floor space. The façade was composed of anodized aluminum mullions holding the windows and the tiled panels onto the balustrade, which together produced crystalline reflections. The concrete pillars in the façade and the butterfly-shaped concrete load-bearing structures at the extremities made the surface look like a curtain. The lightness reinforced by the roof, which is supported by a secondary structure and appears to hover like a thin metal sheet over the building. Inside, the Pirellone provided office space for about 2,000 people, 1,200 of them employed by Pirelli and the rest by associated firms. The façade structure allowed for column-less open plan office space within; dividing walls could be put up at will to create offices and meeting spaces to match the work performed in them.

Ponti on Pirelli
The legend goes that when the Pirelli tower was finished, the 63-year-old Ponti, at the peak of his career, told his two daughters, "She is so beautiful that I would like to marry her." Referring to his buildings as female was not only an instance of gendering, but a means to express his affective and sensual relationship to his buildings. On TV, Ponti explained his idea of creating landscape with the Pirelli tower: "There are cities like Paris, Rome, Florence, Turin. These cities have a larger river, then there are cities that have hills, like Rome, Florence, Turin, or that have the sea, like Genoa, or Naples, which has the sea, islands, Vesuvius and lots more. God helped them a lot in this, he helped make them beautiful. But for us in Milan, God did nothing, nothing at all. So it is up to us to make Milan a beautiful city. It is a question of creation." In the absence of God, he put the architect – himself – in the position of creating the Milanese landscape. The bar he set for himself was high: the building had to be something of divine quality that would redefine the city. Knowing what happens to those who challenge the gods in mythology, Ponti showed some humility by installing a copy of the Madonna from the Duomo on the tower's rooftop, and the archbishop of Milan blessed the first bucket of concrete when the foundations were poured on July 12, 1956.

The Myth
The Pirelli tower was inaugurated in 1960, a pivotal year for Italy. The *Financial Times* called the Lira the world's most stable currency, Federico Fellini's *La Dolce Vita* won the Palme D'Or at Cannes, and Italy finished third in the medal table at the Rome Olympics. Pirelli, founded in 1872 as a producer of rubber goods, played a part in Italy's economic, cultural, and social success, focusing on tires in synch with the motorization of the country in the postwar years, and growing exponentially. Ponti's selection of a skyscraper – the most modern typology – for the company's headquarters, not only identified Pirelli as a multinational business, but it also identified Milan as Italy's powerhouse, deprovincializing the city.

Pirelli's corporate PR helped establish a myth for the new building that built on this context. The best photographers and graphic designers were hired to document the years of construction. Countless images of the skyscraper under construction as well as completed were used in Pirelli's catalogs and advertising campaigns. *The Pirelli Magazine*, produced between 1948–1972, went beyond being an advertising organ, presenting exhibitions, concerts, and book reviews with prominent contributors like Milan Kundera and Umberto Eco.

Out of a vast array of imagery, the following is a selection of those that best explain how this particular piece of architecture was instrumentalized to create this myth.

Pirelli's Raincoats[5]
This photograph by Ugo Malas (1928–73) was published the year before inauguration and pictures a scene from a construction site, with the façade of the Pirelli tower in the background. In the foreground, which is elevated, a woman is casually leaning against a wooden balustrade. The saturated blue of the woman's Pirelli raincoat, her nylon stockings, red lipstick, clean brown leather shoes with golden decorative clasp, and leather gloves reveal that she is not working, but posing. Two construction workers nearby provide a contrast in class. She remains disconnected from what is going on the construction site. And yet, the Cary Grant-like figure to her right is looking up to her from the lower level and the smile on his face shows his interest. The scene encapsulates not only class divisions, but also the ambition of social advancement. And it is no coincidence that this scene plays out in front of the rising Pirelli skyscraper.

Il Sardo
Another photograph – not intended as an advertisement but captured by the photographer Uliano Lucas – features

'59
'60

a man crossing the tramlines outside Milan Central Station right in front of the now finished Pirelli tower. He is a migrant from Sardinia, holding a suitcase in one hand and balancing a taped cardboard box on his shoulder. His expression is puzzled, his clothes are worn, and his appearance not as stylish as the businessman in the background, who had probably just exited his office in the Pirellone and is about to leave in his Fiat, parked on the right-hand side. Lucas sought to capture the contradictions and conflicts in the growing city, and again, Pirellone symbolizes the growth, aspiration, and division in the city.

Workspaces
What distinguishes the publications of the Pirelli skyscraper from those of other office buildings at the time is that they celebrate the workspaces themselves. Interior photos show exquisite modern materials such as anodized aluminum, as well as rubber and glass on the walls; the extravagantly patterned linoleum floor; the stylish furniture (Arflex chairs, tables made by Rima with linoleum tops for the clerks, and wooden tops for the directors). In the tradition of 19th century *Gesamtkunstwerk*, everything was designed by the architect. Among the peculiarities of this building are the unisex toilets, which must have felt outlandish in Catholic Italy during the 1960s.

Happy Pirelli Family
Pirelli's employees feature prominently in the documentation of the building. This is no accident. Working for Pirelli meant being part of a bigger family and with it the feeling of belonging, had to be communicated. Pirelli promoted this sense of belonging for this new class of white collar workers – men as well as women: "People step in and out of the lifts on the different floors, with office workers and other employees, officials, engineers, and senior managers, occasionally exchanging greetings. They are all part of this little vertical city, this famous little city, all rather proud of being citizens of the famous Skyscraper."[6] Social mobility is meant to become a reality right here, inside the Pirelli building. This vertical city also provided space for leisure. In the auditorium at the base of the tower, cultural events were taking place. The company not only provided a forum but also promoted a new, progressive culture, with the skyscraper acting as its symbol.

1978: Lombardi takes over
The golden years of Italian Capitalism, the 1960s, which the Pirelli tower symbolized, did not last long. Towards the end of the decade, student demonstrations, social unrest, and worker protests revealed the reality of Italian 'Family Capitalism.' Only a handful of families owned the country's industries and controlled the political system. Pirelli was part of this. New car production systems impacted the tire business, and Pirelli struggled to adapt to the global market.

In 1978 Pirelli sold the Pirellone for 52 billion Lira to the Region of Lombardi, which moved in two years later after, happily associating itself with the dynamism the building conveyed. This led to the transformation of the public entrance (reconstructed again in 2002), the conversion of the auditorium, and the council chamber moving into the former data processing space. The Dutch-born Italian designer Bob Noorda, who previously worked for Pirelli, together with Egidio Dell'Orto followed by Vico Magistretti did the interior design. They renewed the presidential and vice-presidential suites and the offices and service spaces. Many of the open spaces were converted to cellular spaces; colors were changed and original furniture replaced, partially by new system furniture. All movable walls and vinyl cladding were replaced by marble and carpeting featuring the Camunian Rose, the region's new symbol. The most spectacular change was the transformation of the upper service room into an event space and terrace. In 1995, the building won protection under copyright law but was not yet listed as a monument.

notes

1. In Italian, the suffix -one is used to make things extraordinary big; the Pirelli tower far exceeds the Duomo and the Torre Velasca.
2. Laura Riboldi: "The Future of Memory to Strengthen Business Culture" in: *Skyscraper Stories*, (Marsilio, 2020), p.75
3. Reyner Banham, "Pirelli Building Milan", in: Architects. Ponti, Nervi & Associates, *AR* 129, March 1961, p.195
4. Ibid
5. There was even an entire catalogue featuring the clothes in relation to the skyscraper, entitled *La moda e il Grattacielo* (Fashion and the Skyscraper), 1959, with photos by Ugo Mulas and graphic design by Bob Noorda.
6. Pirelli Magazine by Dino Buzzati in Piccole storie del grattacielo, (1970), quoted in: Laura Riboldi: "The Future of Memory to Strengthen Business Culture" in: *Skyscraper Stories*, (Marsilio, 2020), p.77

building credits

architect: Gio Ponti
structural engineer: Pier Luigi Nervi, Alberto Rosselli, Arturo Danusso

photo credits

p.188, 191, 192, 194 (right), 198, 200 (all), 202: Fondazione Pirelli Milan
p.190: Mario Carieri, Pietro Carieri
p.194 (left): Uliano Lucas
p.197, 199, 201 (all), 203: Jens Frederiksen

2021
PIAZZA DUCA D´AOSTA
VIA FABIO FILZI, 22
MILAN, ITALY

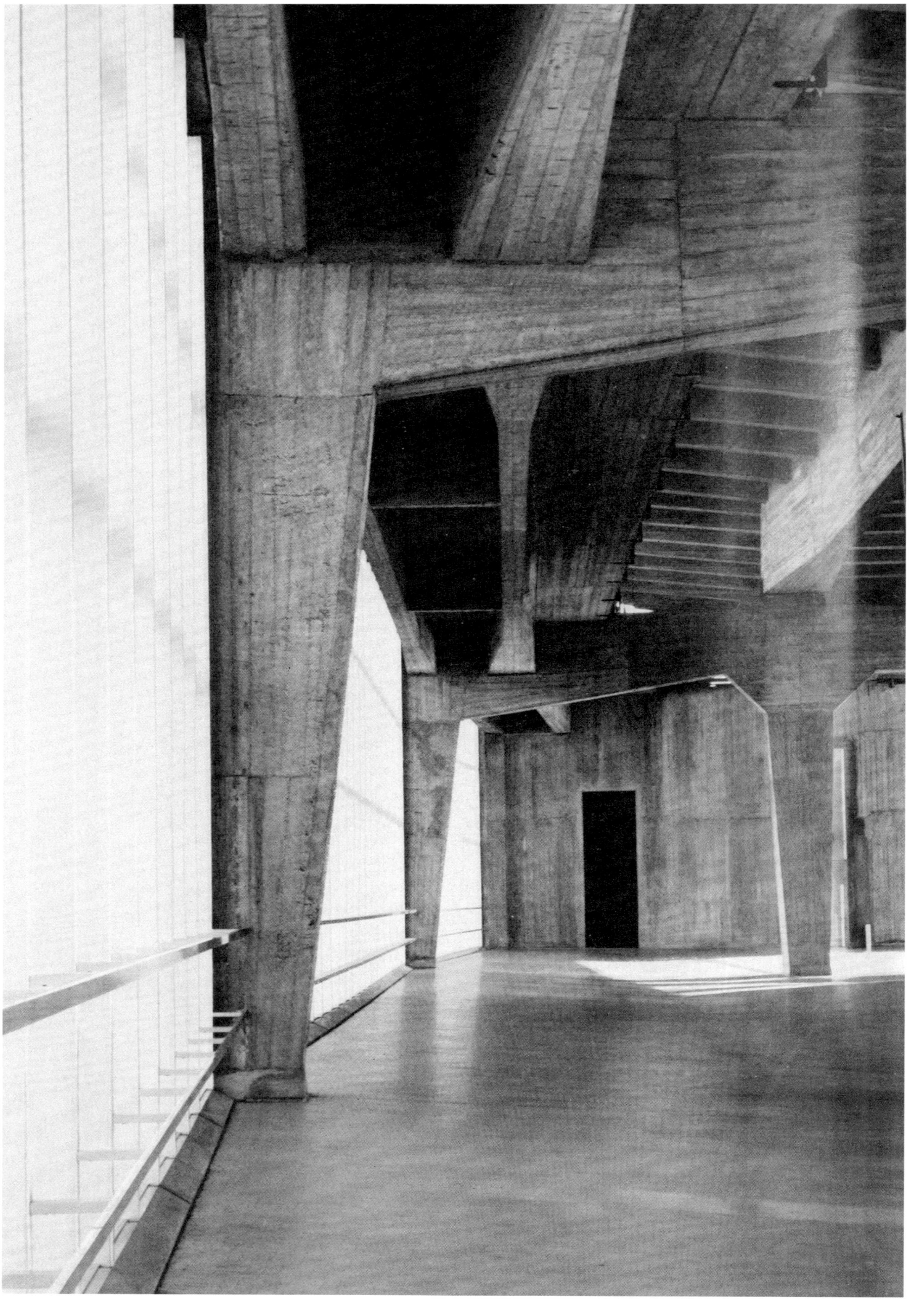

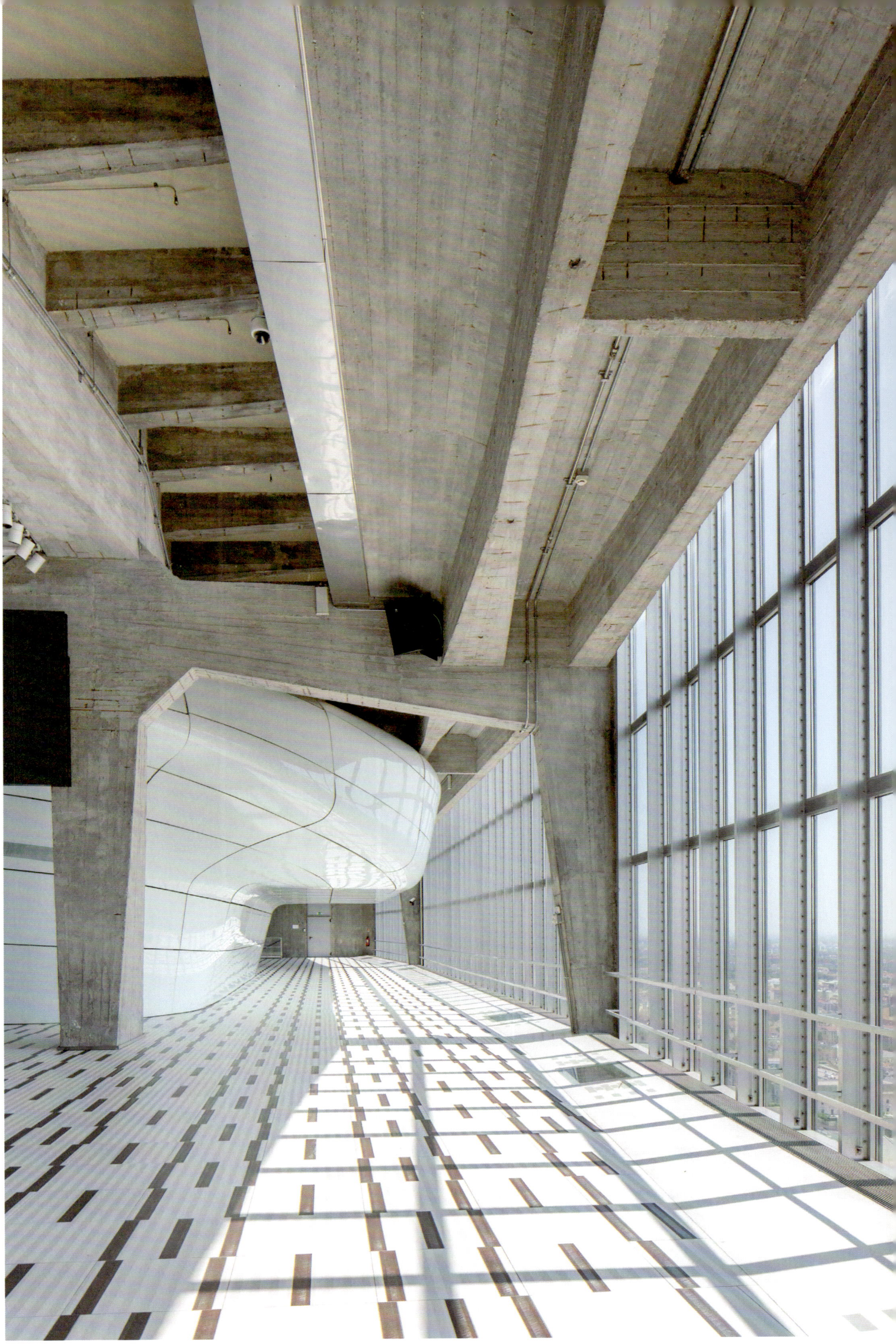

200

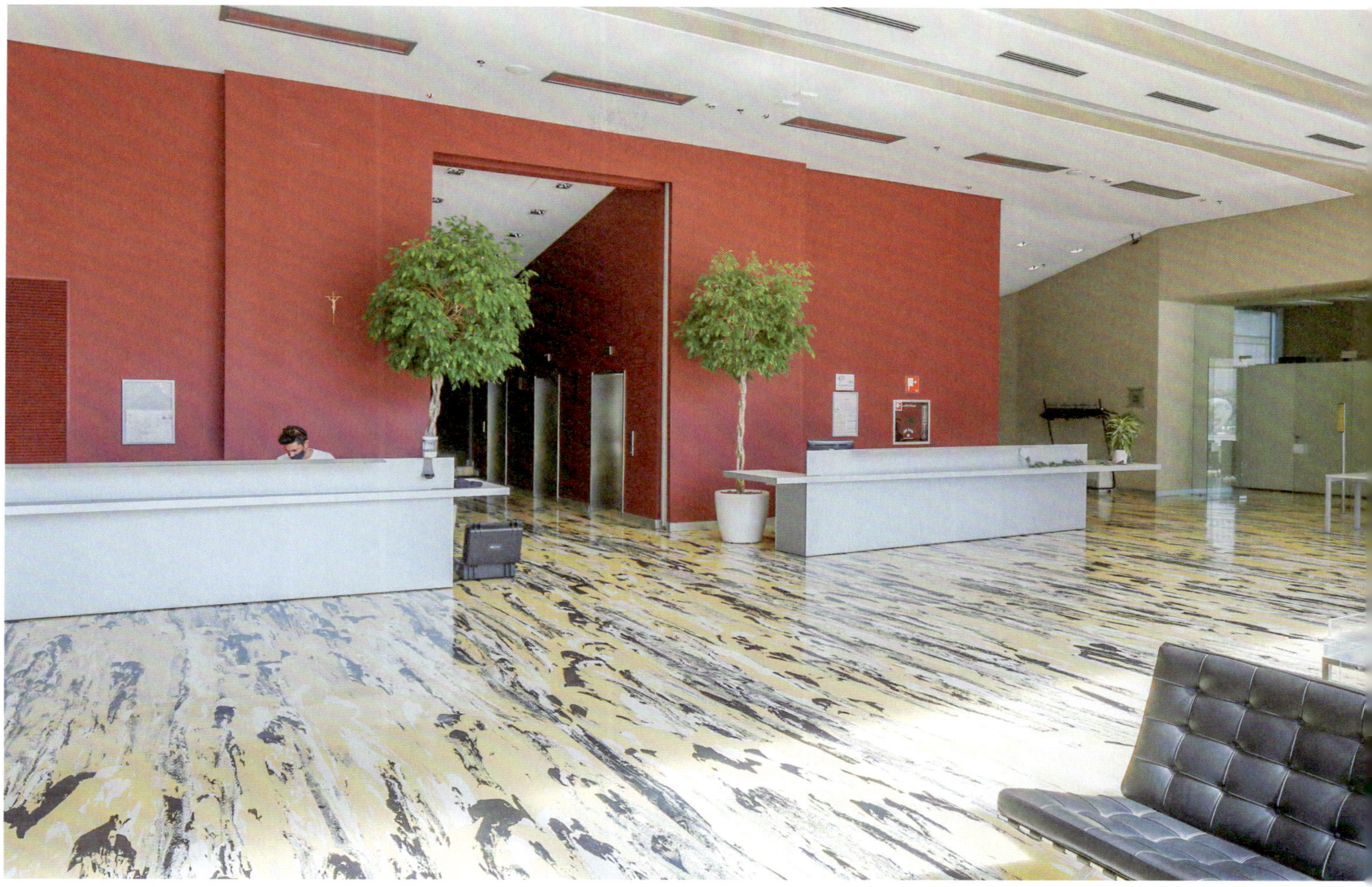

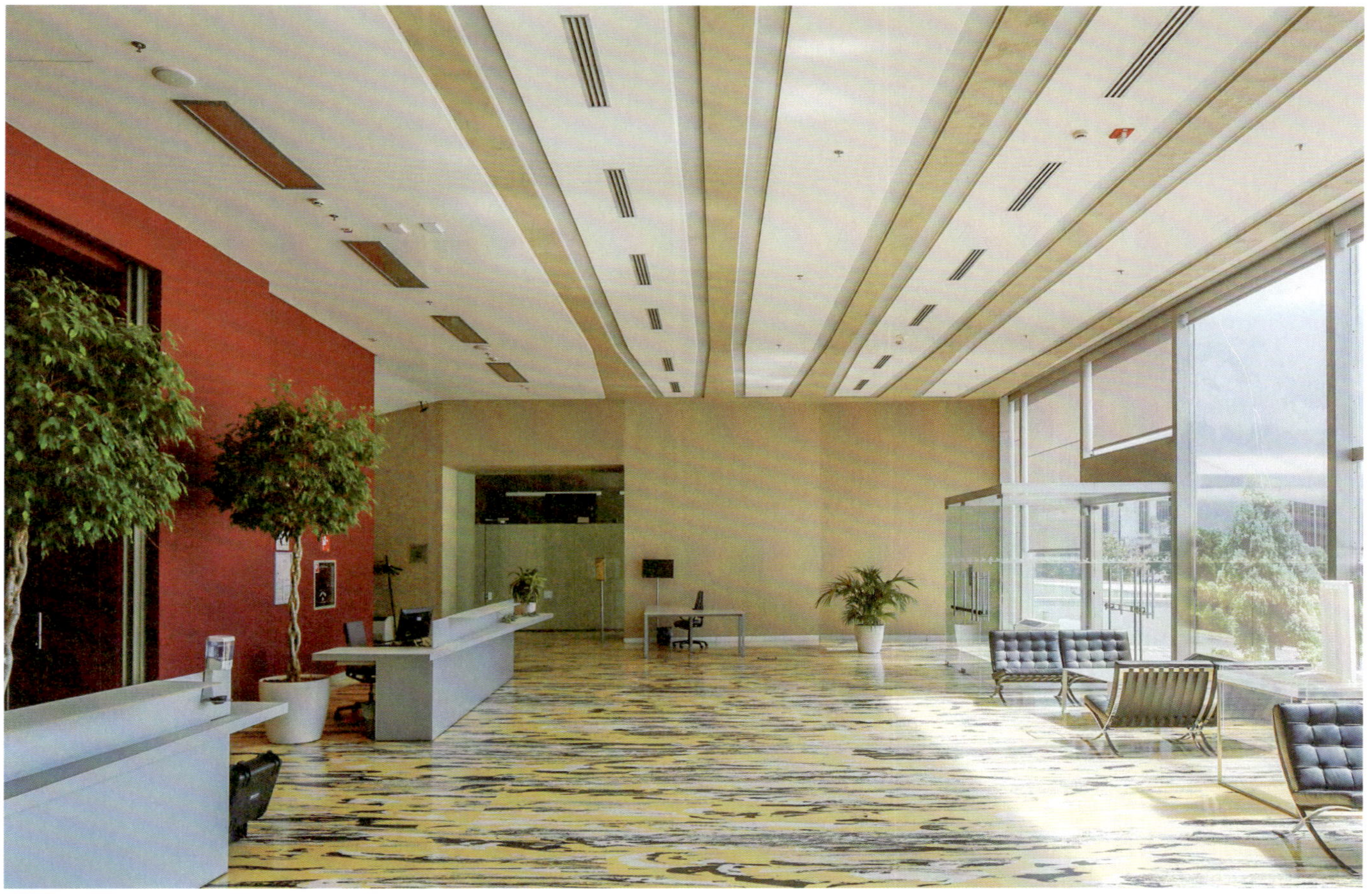

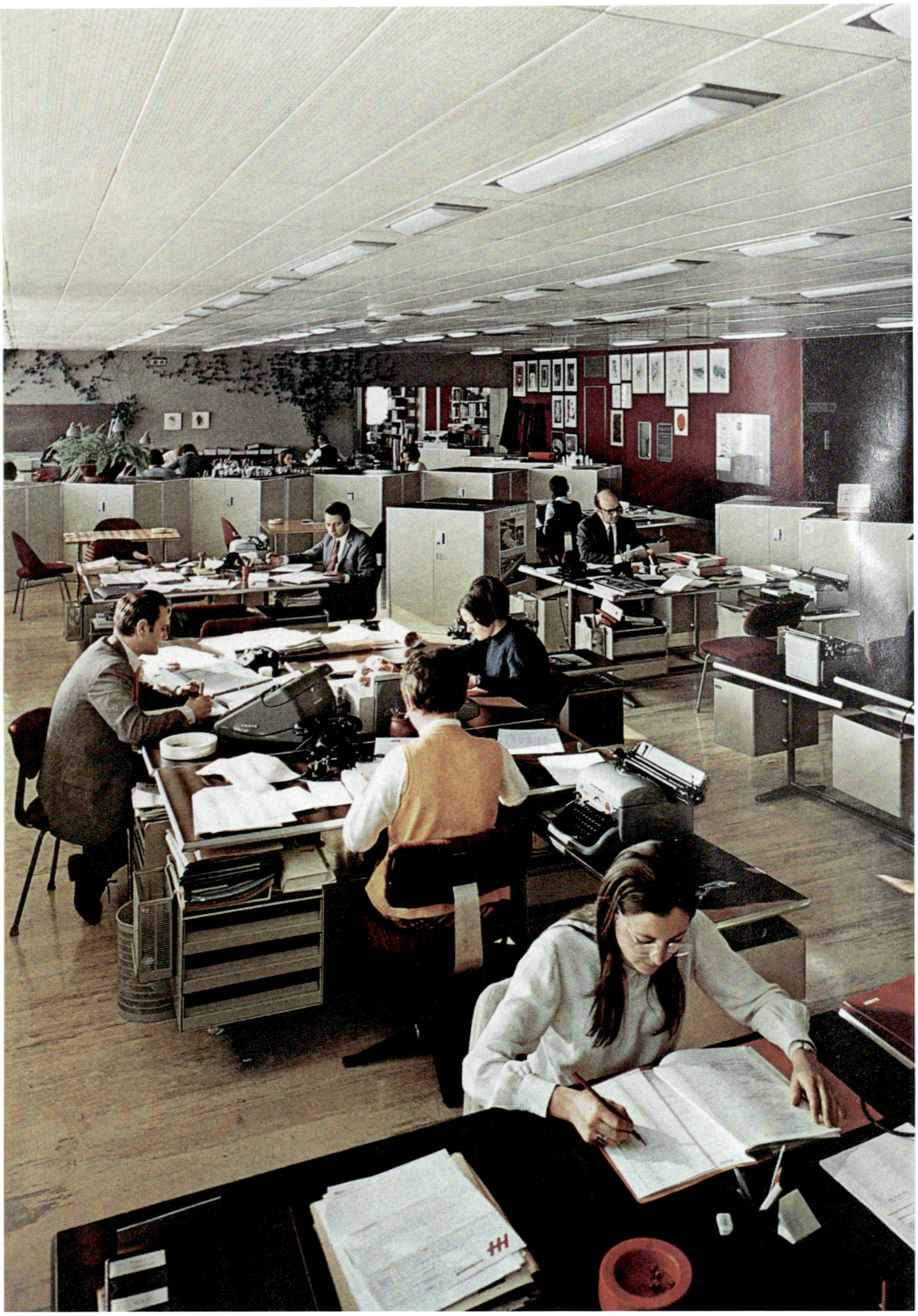

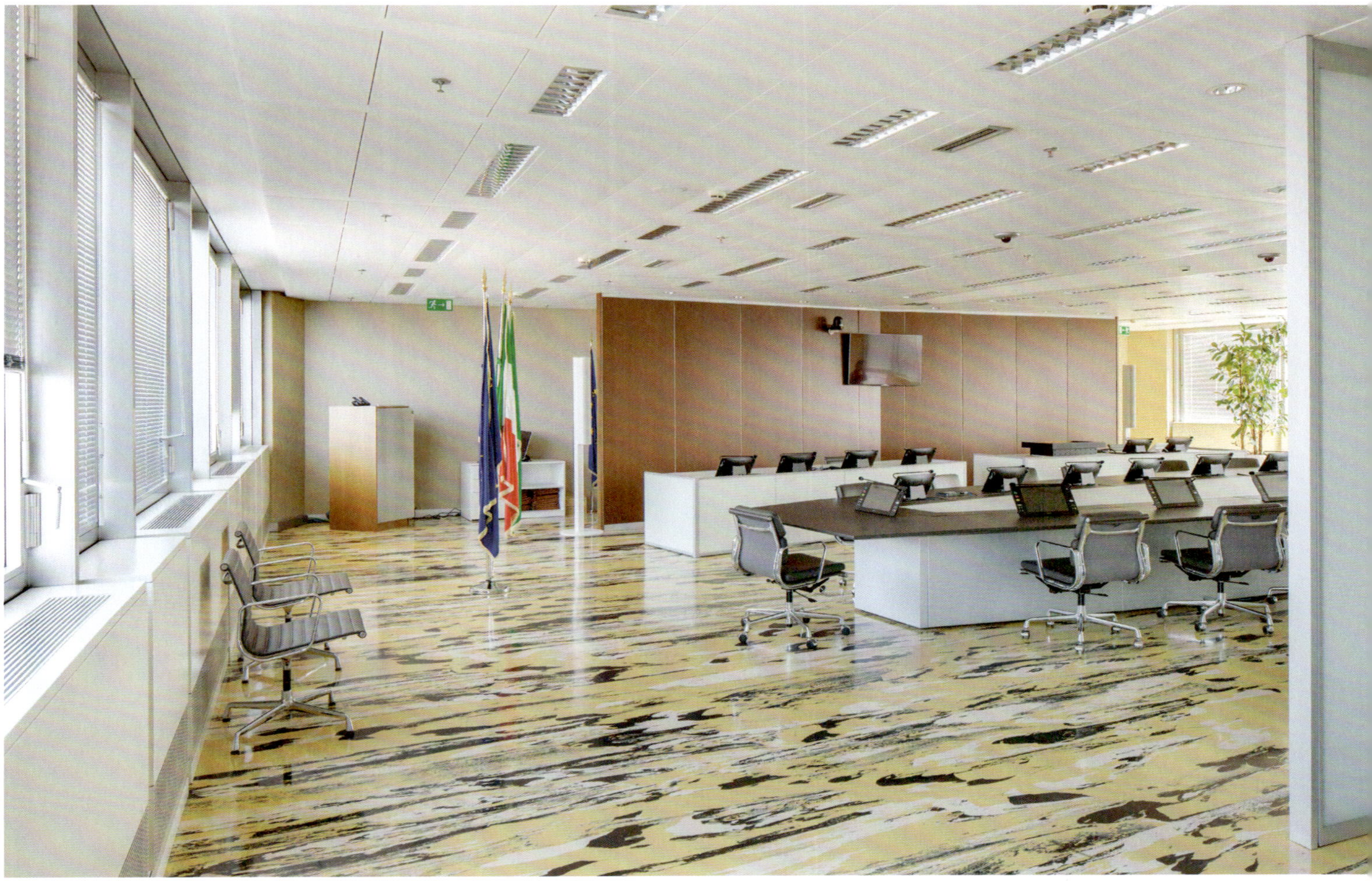

1960

Stephan Petermann

NESTLÉ HEADQUARTERS

The 90s renovation of a Swiss modern masterpiece cost more than a new building would have — and history, corporation, building, architect, and client all reap the benefits

In conversation with Kenneth Ross
In 1997, Kenneth Ross was a 30-year-old architect at Richter Dahl Rocha when he was appointed to lead a team of architects and consultants working on the large-scale renovation of Jean Tschumi's massive (60,000m^2), revered, but already much-changed-since-1960 Nestlé headquarters in Vevey, Switzerland.

Stephan Petermann [SP]: How did Richter Dahl Rocha get this huge commission for renovating the Nestlé HQ?
Kenneth Ross [KR]: An external consulting committee was appointed to select the architects. Around 10 offices were interviewed, including the office of Jean Tschumi's son Bernard, who was already well-known by then.

SP: He might have been the obvious choice, perhaps?
KR: I think Bernard might have undermined his own chances. Word was that in the interview he suggested that he wanted to radically break with his fathers' building. It's my understanding that the client was more interested in looking to build on the history and reputation of the building.

SP: And they weren't interested in the oedipal dimension Bernard's project may have created…
KR: Perhaps. Our office was small, and the partners Richter and Dahl Rocha were both in their early 40s. Apparently they made a strong impression. They have complementary characters, they are a pre-formed mini-team, and that quality allowed the client to envisage a constructive collaboration.

SP: On the client side, who was there?
KR: The CEO of Nestlé at that point, Helmut Maucher, and the heir-apparent, Peter Brabeck-Letmathe, were closely engaged with the renovation. In particular, Brabeck was keen to have real conversations on architecture and art. After we were selected as architects, a series of discussions were organized in which we developed potential schemes incorporating the built heritage and the ideological choices the renovation implied. The client realized that the renovation could also be representative of the company's values: "building on their foundations." Maucher and Brabeck stayed on board all the way down to the furniture design. In the late 1950s, Jean Tschumi's original Nestlé clients, Jean Corthésy and Enrico Bignami, of the same generation as Tschumi, had been equally engaged: they traveled to the US with him to visit all kinds of buildings during the design process.

SP: What was the brief like? What was the incentive for the company to renovate the building?

KR: Actually, there was no brief. They brought us in together with various consultants and we were first tasked with making a technical assessment of the building's condition. By that time a lot of things had been modified from the original. In 1975, the HQ doubled in size, and some functions were rearranged and some new ones were inserted. The original floor plans had become muffled by the introduction of testing kitchens, coffee roasting and tasting areas and such. In the early 90s Jean-Michel Wilmotte had redesigned the management floor, on level three. This building was technically advanced for its time of construction: it used water from Lake Geneva for thermal cooling and employed a special aluminum alloy in a triple-glazed façade incorporating solar shading, just to name a couple of examples. Nevertheless, this technology needed updating: it no longer functioned correctly or was not adapted to the end of the century's new requirements.

SP: So there was no brief. Was there a budget?

KR: Our discussions with the client were intense and constructive. They were always in search of the ideal solution and did not limit their thinking with budgetary constraints. This allowed us to seek out the best options for the renewed workspaces for the next generation of Nestlé's top management. We all shared the view that this was more than just a building, it was a part of the company's history, and as such the way it was treated was emblematic of its relationship with its past while looking towards the future. It would probably have been cheaper to replace the building, but it was clear this was not what they were aiming for.

SP: It was also already listed as one of the earliest modern buildings of its kind in Switzerland. Did that bring any tax credit for instance?

KR: No, but it did provoke very enriching exchanges with the Cantonal services and obliged us to question the meaning of maintaining or replacing elements of varying sentimental, architectural, or historical value. We developed several scenarios for the project, and we worked from there. In the end, we gutted the building down to the structure while leaving the most iconic parts in place: the double helix staircase, the entry canopy, and several other features. The process went in a straight line up to the CEO, who wanted to find the right balance between the existing Tschumi building and the new embodiment of the company at the dawn of the 21st century. In replacing elements, we worked like archaeologists, going into the details to get as close to the original as possible. Quarries were reopened to mine the exact same stone. A member of Nestlé's board persuaded Alusuisse to recreate the same aluminum alloy used in the original façade. Certain features were a source of inspiration, the original masonry walls separating the offices from the corridors were replaced by glazed elements, but the door frames were designed in a similar form as the originals, albeit in extruded aluminum and integrated into the partition system.

SP: It's so impressive, because we see a lot of buildings accommodating changes that quite quickly end up as downgrades, and then downgrades of downgrades…
KR: We like to think we avoided this, and that we may have even added value, respecting the spirit of Tschumi's oeuvre, while taking it onto the next stage of its hopefully long life. For example, we found a sketch from the archives where he had originally conceived a large skylight above the double helix staircase, which apparently got scrapped because they needed space for the ventilation systems. We were able to move those to the basement and in a way realized a part of Tschumi's original ambition.

1960

2000

2019

SP: When did the relationship with Nestlé end?
KR: We did several other, smaller-scale projects on the building after this[1], and then managerial changes caused the relationship to end, at least for the moment. New updates to the building have been designed by Brönnimann & Gottreux architects, based in Vevey. For instance, introducing activity-based working; their website suggests a responsible design – they check the boxes of accepted globalized international taste: adding not-too-intense colors, Aeron-like chairs, more homely. The façade and structural steel look like an oddity in this constellation, like a faint memory of a once starker identity. As far as we are aware, this latest renovation seems to be aimed at further densification of the floor plans and seems less connected to the building's original qualities than the work we were able to do.

SP: Is that something you see more and more?
KR: This project was foundational for our office; it was an incredible learning experience. Occasionally we might get a client as engaged in a project as Maucher and Brabeck were, but in general, this form of involvement is less common. Like so many others, we are often constrained by purely financial considerations, and little or no debate is possible with the client about the way their project can be enhanced by collaboration rather than simply efficiently solved.

SP: Is there any advice you give in hindsight to Tschumi?
KR: I never thought about that, it would be totally presumptuous.

notes

1   Including a concept for the company store façade (2001), interior design for the WelNes center (2008), and a culinarium (2013).

building credits

client: Jean Corthésy and Enrico Bignami, Nestlé
architect: Jean Tschumi
renovation architect: Kenneth Ross and Richter Dahl Rocha

photo credits

p.204, 206, 208, 214: Nestlé Historical Archives, Vevey
p.207, 209, 210, 211 (all), 216, 217: Richter Dahl Rocha
p.213: Yves André
p.215: unknown

2000

55 AVENUE NESTLÉ
VEVEY, SWITZERLAND

214

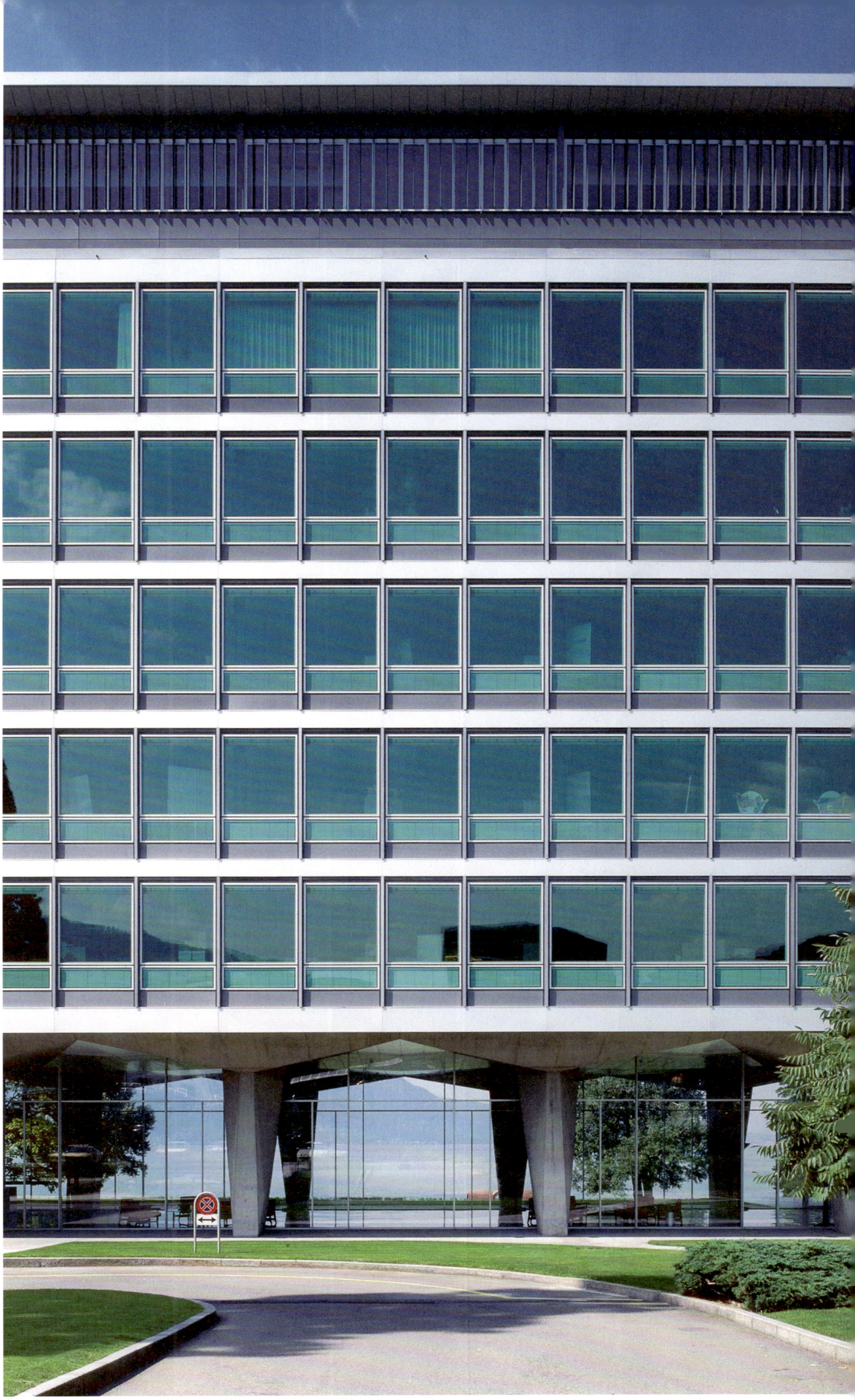

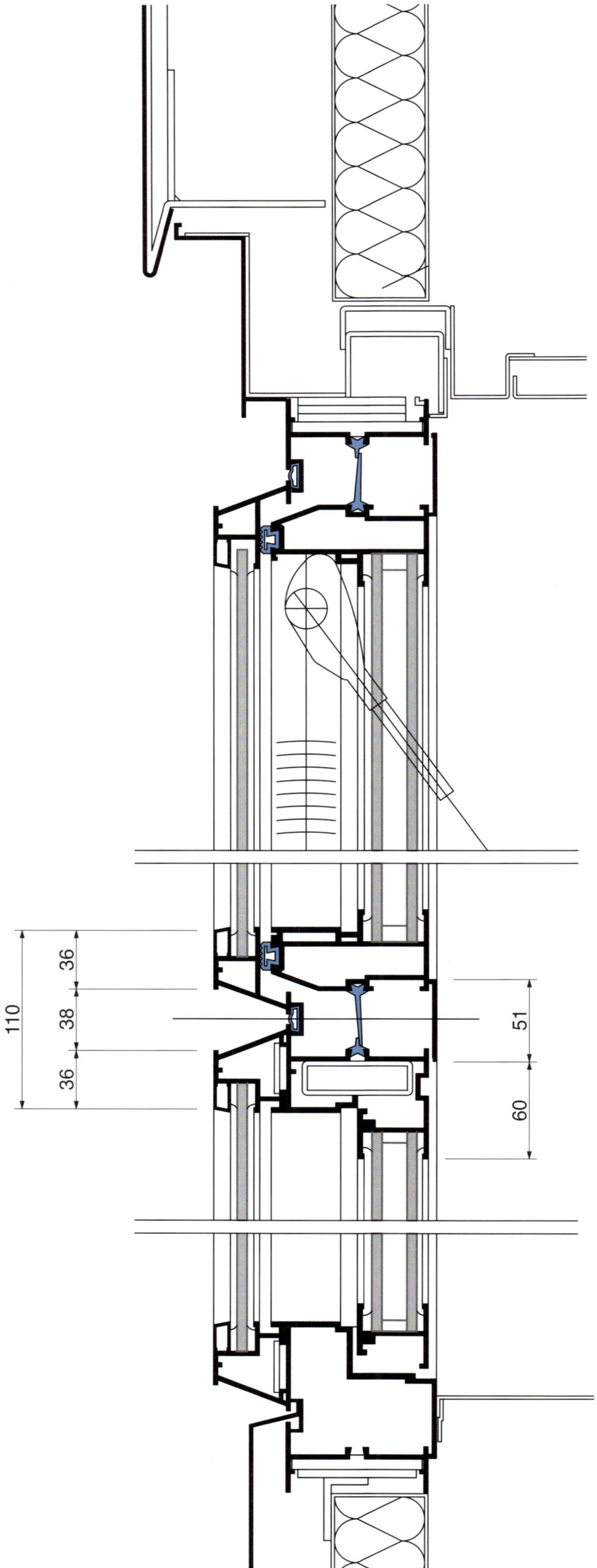
36
110
38
36
51
60

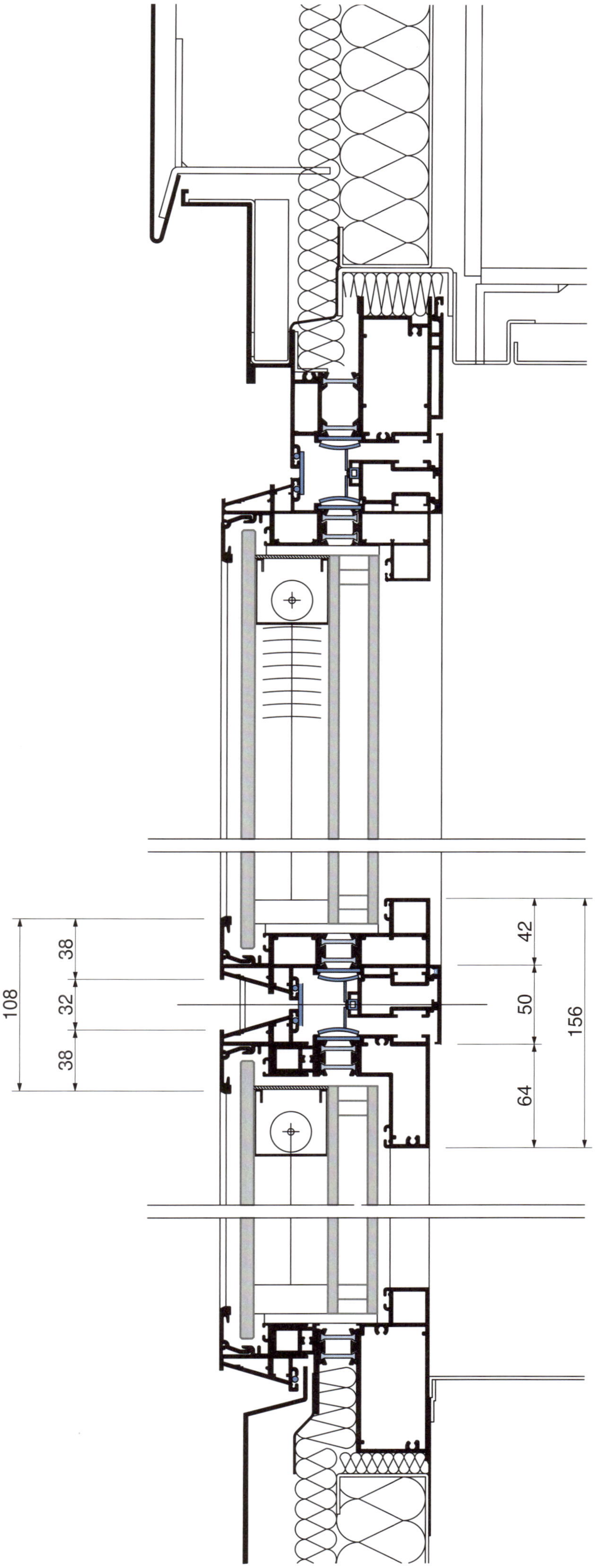
108
38
32
38
42
50
64
156

PEPSI-COLA HEADQUARTERS   1960

"The small, silvery building at 500 Park Avenue, on the southwest corner of 59th Street, is at the top of the list, with Seagram and Lever House, of the city's few modern landmarks. Built in 1960 as the headquarters of the Pepsi-Cola Corporation and later bought, and then sold, by Olivetti, its fate has been hanging in the balance for some time. This is one of the superb "skin" buildings produced by Gordon Bunshaft for the architectural firm of Skidmore, Owings and Merrill; only 11 stories high, it is designed with the precise and beautiful refinement of an expensive Swiss watch. The taut delicacy of its sleek glass and aluminium facade and its perfectly adjusted proportions make it an elegant miniature among the city's large commercial structures - a kind of Pazzi Chapel of corporate design."

— **Ada Louise Huxtable**, "Architecture View; 500 Park – A Skillful Solution" in *New York Times*, May 3 1981

building credits

client: Alfred Steele
architect: Skidmore, Owings & Merril

photo credits

p.218: Ezra Stoller/ESTO
p.219: Ossip van Duivenbode

2019
500 PARK AVENUE
NEW YORK, NY, US

219

1961

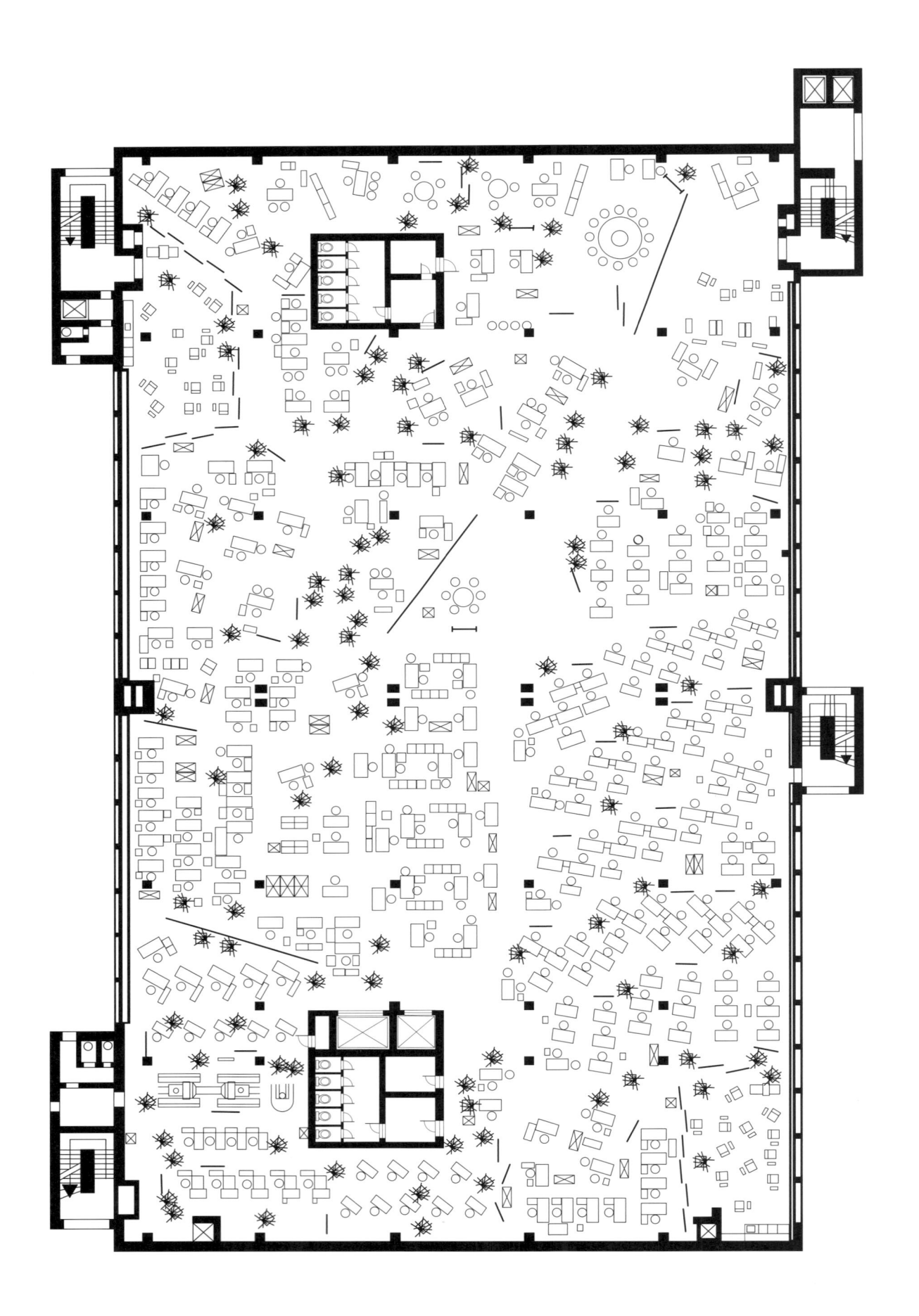

Stephan Petermann

BUCH UND TON

The rise and fall of the Bürolandschaft, a scientifically-generated rambling office landscape

In photos of this key moment in office design from the 1960s, we typically see a woman at a typewriter, surrounded by plants, with a jungle of desks seemingly randomly placed across a vast open-plan office. This was the Bürolandschaft – the office landscape – and it was first realized in Gütersloh, Germany. It was on the top floor of a storage facility and housed the sales and distribution department of Buch und Ton, a mail-order division of the Bertelsmann Media Group for books and records. Think of it as the Netflix of its time.

Bertelsmann's CEO Reinhard Mohn had been to the United States as a POW in WW II and was inspired by American offices with their deep open plans. (see p. 492 for more background on Mohn) Mohn hired architect Walter Henn to design an experimental space based on the fundamentals of the offices he'd visited. For the interior planning, Mohn commissioned the Hamburg-based Quickborner Team, run by the Schnelle brothers, Eberhard and Wolfgang. They were also inspired by American offices and philosophies of work, specifically Frederick Taylor's "Scientific Management."[1]

With the assistance of Bertelsmann's management, Henn and his architects spent 10 days sifting through the minutest details of the company's internal workings. They tracked every letter delivered to the office, down to which hands it passed through, the departments and decision makers who received it, how they actioned it, and how it was ultimately filed. Their research was synthesized by Quickborner into flow charts and connected to tables of data with standardized basic units for physical requirements. Then, by some form of alchemy, this was translated into office planning: desks –and clusters of desks– were arranged according to required proximities and sightlines, so each employee in the larger machinery would have a natural connection to the most relevant colleagues. The layout that may have looked like a freeform, jazz-like array of desks, it was in fact – to them and their clients – a rational, optimized office environment.

The Schnelle brothers also designed the mechanical and aesthetic performance of the space. Absent natural light and fresh air, they determined the optimal synthetic replacements: 1,900 light tubes to introduce three different light conditions; 50,000 cubic meters of mechanically purified air pumped in per hour; a modicum of acoustic dampening delivered via cognac-colored velour carpet; an acoustic ceiling with drop tiles; small pastel-colored movable partitions (the colors strategically chosen); and high-quality custom-made modern wooden furniture, identical for all.

The Bürolandschaft was about half the size of a soccer pitch and offered space for 250 employees. Four external cores containing elevators and stairs, one internal elevator, and a regular column grid anchored the space. Visitors entered in the southeast corner at the reception. A diagonal axis, loosely defined by pot plants, formed the main circulation artery, from which a few branches delineated smaller working clusters. Management sat behind the reception to ensure a sense of overview. To its right: human resources; behind and to the left were two fields of typists and distribution employees. The far corners contained a novelty on the office floor: a small pantry providing hot and cold beverages at a heavily subsidized price, and some lounge chairs on which to enjoy them.

In November 1961, Bertelsmann's internal newspaper ran a glowing review of the project, highlighting the technical advances made in the new space.[2] Two months later, another report spoke highly of the experimental office layout: "The move of the sales departments of the commission house into the transformed sixth floor was the most important achievement of 1961. Six months after completion you could say that the experiment is a success and has brought significant improvements to the workflow."[3] Echoing a similar sentiment, an article in Baumeister by architect Henn explained how the design in Gütersloh – and several other offices – improved on the American deep-floor predecessors. Where the US floor plans were still based on a typical uniform gridded alignment of desks and closed-off workstations, the more fluid organization model developed by Quickborner made it into a real landscape.[4]

In March 1962, the first jokes about the space started to appear. Bertelsmann's internal newspaper published the review "How to behave in the open-plan."[5] It discussed the difficulty of giving people directions to reach your desk, the new pauzenzones (informal break areas), the too-bright artificial lighting systems, the occasional cacophony of typewriter sounds, and the carpeting.

In 1963, Frank Duffy, a student at the Architectural Association in London, later to become the world's most influential workspace consultant, paid Buch und Ton a visit. In his report for The Architectural Review, Duffy signaled some technical and organizational problems but was convinced of the Bürolandschaft's potential, "In general the impact of this development lies more in its broad human implications than in its detailed technical achievements." In the years following the initial construction, the Bürolandschaft idea spread from Buch und Ton to other Bertelsman offices in Gutersloh (which was the company's main seat).

In November 1964, CEO Mohn spent fourteen days working in the Bürolandschaft and experienced shortcomings in acoustics, lighting, and climate, and he judged that, due to the need for secrecy, the Bürolandschaft environment was not suitable for the location of top management. Mohn wrote a five-page memo on the issues but remained convinced of the space's principles, noting the number of visitors who were drawn to the office, and encouraged management to do more research: "The criticism against the open plan was made by people with only superficial knowledge of the workplace conditions. It would be great if, through your personal experience, our discussions could be further developed into a more deeply founded knowledge so we can determine what the true problems are."[6] It is not clear whether management accepted his offer.

In 1966, Ottomar Gottschalk reviewed Quickborner's work in a book by the Schnelle brothers about flexible office buildings: "Despite significant oversights in construction (climate, blinds, power supply) [the space is] in good shape. Excellent acoustical conditions. The space has ... facilitated many organizational improvements." Quickborner began consulting for major industrial firms like Goodyear, Ford, and Osram and in 1967 opened a branch office in the US and, not long afterward, another in Caracas.

Ten years later though, a survey across all of Bertelsmann in 1977 indicated that support for the Bürolandschaft was dwindling: more than 30 percent described themselves as unhappy with their working conditions. Many were adding partitions. In 1981, Mohn retired as CEO. In 1982, another survey by Quickborner showed that the workspaces had become unacceptable to the majority of the staff. An annex was added to the main building to facilitate the return of single-cell offices. In 1985, a competition was launched to refurbish Bertlesmann's headquarters. Although the Bürolandschaft experiments were spoken of fondly, their failure was assumed. The Quickborner Team was not involved in the new competition; four German architects participated and most of the plans featured larger partitioned spaces.

Our request to visit the space in 2014 was met with skepticism. Buch and Ton had been rebranded as Arvato decades before. It was unclear to the building managers which part of the building we were actually referring to when we talked about the Bürolandschaft. The company archivists, who worked at Bertelsmann for decades, were unaware of the office's iconic status in the architectural community. And even though the facilities manager had been taking care of the Gütersloh buildings since 1986, the images we showed him were completely unfamiliar.

Taking a staircase from the fifth floor, we approached what used to be the entrance to the Bürolandschaft. Within seconds the doubts of the facilities manager became clear to us: we were confronted by partitions – lots of them. Behind an abandoned reception desk, we faced two angular corridors, one short and another long. We walked into the long corridor, where an exit plan revealed that the entire space has a new infill of small and large rooms and, toward the center, two unexpected open-air patios.

The majority of spaces were recently abandoned, awaiting refurbishment to comply with new fire regulations. A standard drop-ceiling hid an equally standard plethora of mechanical systems. Everything was generic. The 80cm-wide office partitions had plastic seams. Sockets in the 40 x 40cm raised floor tiles provided power and network access. New operable windows had been added as an alternative to the forced-air cooling system. The only original parts of Walter Henn's building or Quickborner's Bürolandschaft we could find were the concrete column grid and the elevator. Although, we were not able to determine the exact date of the massive transformation and cellularization of the Bürolandschaft, by appearance it seems to have occurred in the early 1980s, around the time of other refurbishments, perhaps shortly after Mohn's departure as CEO.

The mood in the occupied rooms was bureaucratic but good. It was quiet on the floors, and the temperature was agreeable. A middle-aged team with a large amount of personal space, occupied by prism-shaped desks, was designing calendars. Almost everything seemed to be done without any strong agenda for how an office should be, yet it all seemed to be functioning well enough. A lounge area with a small coffee bar, a couch, and some comfortable chairs in bright colors may be the only trace of the revolutionary past.

Visiting the spaces makes you think about the prospect of a tidal wave of creative, entrepreneurial, and motivational efforts washing over them at some point in the near future, changing everything yet again. Will anyone ever care again so much about this office environment as Mohn and Quickborner did? It seems unlikely. There is only one certainty: the concrete will remain solid until it is demolished or left behind to decay.

notes

1 Frederick Taylor (1856–1915) was an American engineer. Central to his approach of scientific management was breaking industrial production into smaller specialized elements that were allotted a specific amount of time considered necessary for completing a task. He published his findings in his 1911 book *The Principles of Scientific Management*.
2 "Großraum im Kommissionshaus," *Bertelsmann Illustrierte*, November 1961, p.8.
3 The original German: "Der Umzug der kaufmännischen Abteilungen des Kommissionshauses in die zum Büro umgebaute Ebene 6 dürfte wohl das wichtigste Ereignis im Jahre 1961 gewesen sein. Ein halbes Jahr nach Inbetriebnahme kann man sagen, das Experiment ist gelungen und hat in der gesamten Arbeitsabwicklung erhebliche Vorteile gebracht." *Bertelsmann Illustrierte*, January 1962, p.10.
4 Walter Henn, "Bürogrossraum und Architekt," *Baumeister*, July 1962, p.655–66, p.659.
5 Sein Arbeitstag im Großraum," *Bertelsmann Illustrierte*, March 1962, p.15.
6 From the Bertelsmann company archive, accession number Akte 0041_76_Erfahrungsbericht Grossraum: "Bisher ist es häufig so gewesen, daß Argumente gegen den Grossraum vorgebracht wurden von Personen, die sich nur oberflächlich oder überhaupt nicht mit den Arbeitsverhältnissen vertraut gemacht hatten. Entsprechend würde ich es begrüßen, wenn durch eine persönliche Erfahrung unsere Diskussionen versachlicht werden könnten, bzw. wir durch fundierteres Wissen schneller zu den eigentlichen Problemen gelangen könnten."

building credits

client: Reinhard Mohn
architect: Eberhard Schnelle and Wolfgang Schnelle

photo credits

p.220, 225: Maximilian Kürten
p.226 (all): Bertelsmann Corporate Archive
p.227 (all): Stephan Petermann

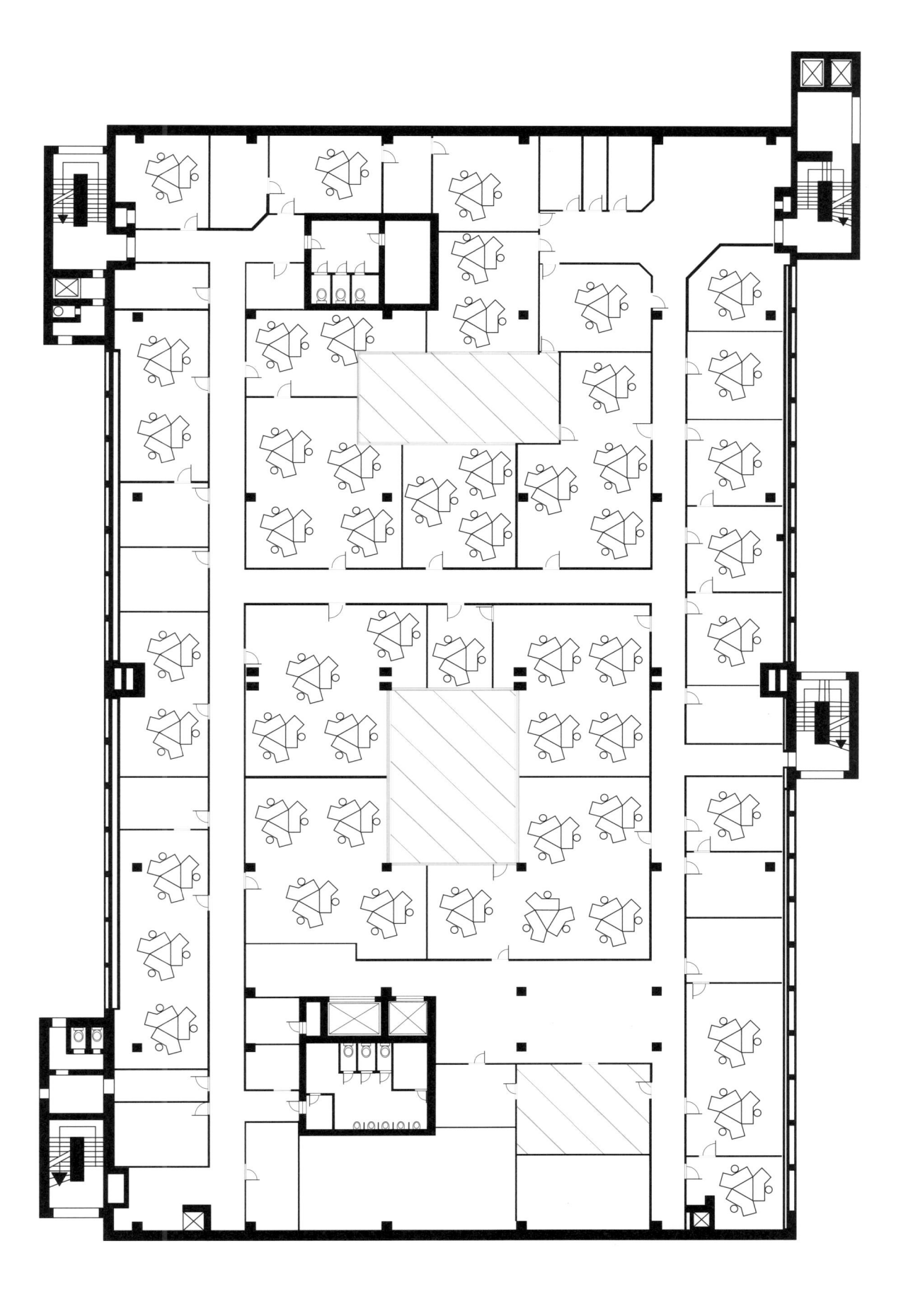

2015
CARL-BERTELSMANN-STRASSE
GÜTERSLOH, GERMANY

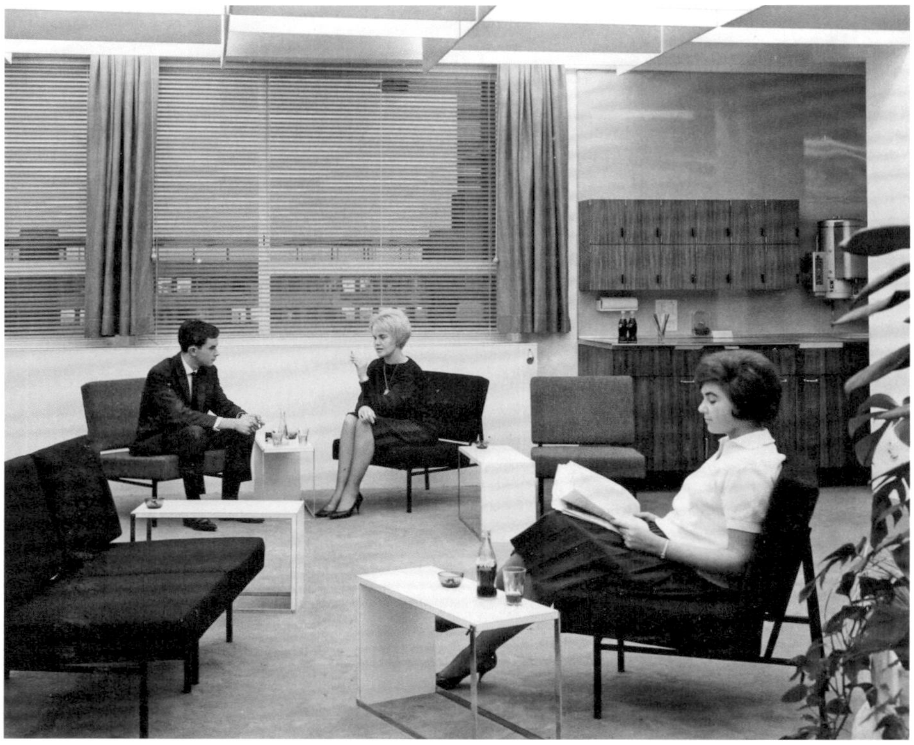

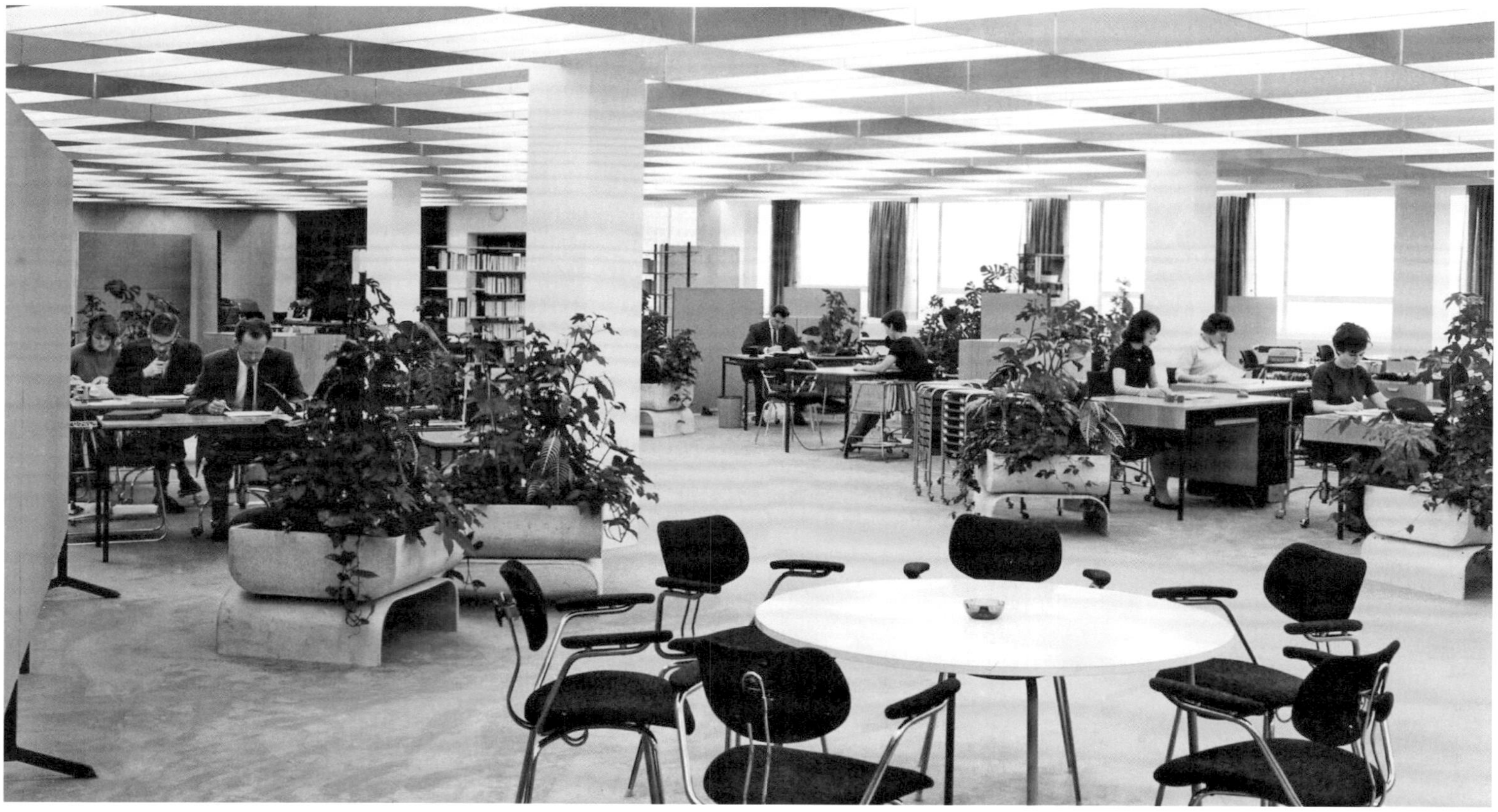

227

1962

Stephan Petermann

BELL LABS HOLMDEL COMPLEX

Saarinen's rural behemoth for Bell Labs, too big for a new single-tenant and falling into disrepair, is rehabilitated and rebranded as a slice of the city in the suburbs

Interview with:
Ralph Zucker, Somerset Development
Alexander Gorlin, architect
Paola Zamudio, interior designer

The Architectural Record's cover for the October 1962 issue is a daunting single-point perspective photo, by Ezra Stoller, of a curtain-wall groundscraper that stretches almost as far as the eye can see. The building, by Eero Saarinen, is probably the most austere and abstract pastoral office of its time. He designed a similar one for IBM, but that was curved. For Bell Labs, in Holmdel, New Jersey, Saarinen went for orthogonal geometry to create the starkest opposition to the bucolic surroundings imaginable. Behind the glass façade are four large steel enclosed volumes wrapped with walkways that connect to a long spine atrium. The plans suggest that the 6,000 engineers and researchers working inside the volumes wouldn't need daylight for their lab work. Exposure to the landscape is reserved for smoking breaks in the corridors and lunchtime walks. Moreover, the plans leave little doubt about how to understand this building: the shape and configuration is almost indistinguishable from that of a transistor, where every minute element mechanically plays its part within the larger orchestration of scientific progress.

It reminded me of a 2015 visit to the Google HQ in Menlo Park and Facebook's Mountain View offices (not the Frank Gehry behemoth). I was struck by the fact that the workers had windows, but most of them had the shutters down, and were sitting in dark insular cubicles. In the relentless expansion of the company, most of the spaces we visited featured no attention to detail – the real estate departments were just happy to fulfill management's half-yearly requests for more desks. A groundscraper on the outskirts of New York could have been a perfect headquarters for a large Silicon Valley HQ.

After the decision by the next tenant after Bell, Alcatel-Lucent, to sell the Holmdell campus in 2006, the destiny of the once-famous hub for tech and radio innovation was uncertain – until Ralph Zucker came along with his firm Somerset Development. Zucker started Somerset as a suburban residential developer, inspired by the Jane Jacobs-informed New Urbanism, with its human-scale masterplans designed for people, not for their cars and trucks. Zucker redeveloped several large-scale projects where underutilized, vacant, or soon-to-be-vacant factories, and in doing so learned to engage with communities in the often difficult repositioning of assets. In a first visit to Holmdel, he felt he was struck by lightning. He persuaded architects Alexander Gorlin and interior designer Paola Zamudio to give new life to a 185,000 square meter rusting giant in the New Jersey countryside…

Stephan Petermann [SP]: Did the Bell Labs building appear on your radar through your redevelopment experience in the area?
Ralph Zucker [RZ]: I walked into Bell Labs in 2007, when it was vacant, but with great bones in the design.

SP: Great bones?
RZ: You could tell immediately. The building was zoned into obsolescence and also practically obsolete. Everything leaked, nothing worked. The offices were really laboratories, all behind closed sheetrock and steel walls, you couldn't even see the outsides of this beautiful glass box. It was cluttered, it looked tired. But that concrete structure, the Corten steel, the glass skylit atriums, and the great walkway down the middle – intuitively, I realized that if we could clean all this out, we could have a great building flanking this internal pedestrian street…
Alexander Gorlin [AG]: Part of the bones, I think, are the dimensions of the atrium. It's 100 feet wide. I found this dimension in many great historic buildings and places. There are many boulevards with this dimension, but also the Crystal Palace in London. Even St. Peter's Basilica is 100 feet wide. So there's something about that dimension: it's grand, but also human-scaled. You can always see people, and you can see faces from that distance. It's monumental but intimate at the same time.
RZ: The atrium just hit me like a thunderbolt, an inspirational moment. With my years of development and new urbanist interest, I felt that it could be a great pedestrian street. If we could reposition it with retail and shops and offices above, it could really work. I don't know how much you're interested in the deal structure, but to me almost more interesting than the practical aspects of it and how we went about zoning.

SP: Absolutely we're interested.
RZ: It was 2008, the last limo was leaving Lehman Brothers and we went to contract for buying the property, which was originally at $40 million. We realized we would need a major repositioning of the area's zoning. It was zoned for research, single-tenant, single-use, with no residential – and it's 185,000 square meters with 472 acres around it. It's in North Jersey. There isn't a big office market around this beautiful countryside. The municipality did not greet us with open arms initially, and we spent five years struggling. We finally closed the deal in 2013 on the 14th amendment to the second contract for $22.5 million dollars.

SP: Off to the races…
RZ: Yes, and along the way, we earned the trust of the people. We had a lot of conversations with the senior communities in a town hall meeting. That brought the political echelon along. Finally, this enabled changing the zoning to mixed-use for residential, retail, health, wellness, fitness, hospitality, almost anything. But when we had to find equity for a $250-million redevelopment, the financial markets still didn't believe in what we wanted to do. We sold the entitlement for the residential area to Toll Brothers, a luxury home developer. For the building itself, we started by trying to land a 40,000-square meter medical office. That did not pan out. By and by, we realized our plan to find a large tenant to activate the space wasn't going to happen. So, we started very small. Our first tenant signed a five-year lease for about 110 square meters.

SP: Only 184,890 square meters to go.
RZ: With Alex, we laid out the broad plans for renovation. We got the building on the National Register of Historic Places, and that opened a can of worms. Once we were in the National Register, they wanted us to keep everything exactly the way it was. We branded it as Bell Works. We started to understand the attraction of the building because of the architectural history, and the research that happened here. I wanted to create a living room-type atmosphere. And this is where Paola was crucial.

Paola Zamudio [PZ]: Like Ralph, I was also very intimidated the first time I visited. It was Ralph's enthusiasm that convinced me. As a trend forecaster, I did a lot of research, but in the end for me, designing is about people. You're bringing people together, creating a cozy space in this huge building. We created a cafe and it was like magic: people started coming in and sitting on the couch. Then I saw the brokers giving tours to people but there was nothing to see really. So we decided to create seven different prêt-à-porter offices and that changed things. Potential clients saw these offices and they were like, this is the look, when can we move in?

SP: Sounds like smooth sailing from then onwards?
RZ: There were some issues. One of our earliest tenants put cubicles up against the glass walls. We learned from that to put in some basic guidelines to keep some of the clarity.
PZ: Luckily Rob is very design-oriented with attention to detail.
RZ: I haven't said the word, Metroburb.

SP: Sorry?
RZ: Metroburb. That's a word that I'm proud of creating. And it means a metropolis in suburbia. We actually have a definition. The idea is that even people in suburbia want an urban vibe and urban cool, comfort, and convenience. And that's what we've done. There's a great quote that Paula brought to the office one day…
PZ: It's from *What If…?* by David Rockwell[1]. It was in my first presentation to Ralph for Bell Works: "What if the office became a place to live, create, play, research, entertain, connect, dine, incubate, broadcast, mentor, muse, learn, party, invent?" We took this quote. And we made 19 signs outside the building with this mile-long drive coming.
RZ: It captured everything we're doing. I had a hard time early in the process of

selling our spaces. We would sometimes tour people and we could spend three hours, four hours explaining our intentions. And when they would leave, they would say, "Oh, so you're building a mall."

SP: We have been looking at more headquarters buildings around the world, and they all struggle when the original tenant leaves. You're basically stuck with an enormous, aged volume that somehow needs to be reformatted.
RZ: The biggest difference between this and other buildings is maybe that when it was Bell Labs, it also had a restaurant, a bank, and other service functions. It was closed to the public, but still, our most important move was to make the central atrium publicly accessible. Now the building is open from 6 am to 12 pm and anyone can walk in and relax, use the WiFi, buy a coffee. There are concierges who greet you, no security, which also makes a great difference. We train them to be inviting, having the right posture and hospitality. It's not just a space, it's also how you manage the space.

SP: How do you understand the original intentions of Saarinen?
RZ: Saarinen was hired by Western Electric and Bell Labs. They wanted a space that would create serendipitous encounters or bring people together. It's actually your standard trendy office building, but inside out. You typically have offices up against the window and against the central hallway. Our building instead has these four large volumes wrapped by walkways on the perimeter. We resisted the urge to grab the extra real estate of the walkways. This was crucial, as it provides energy and a sense of community. And in-between the volumes we created retail space, with things like a dentist, a manicure place, etc. You can drop your kids off at the daycare, there's ice cream, golf, the bar, the gym…

SP: We have looked at some offices that went for maximizing net office area and it never pans out. There is a value in this 'extra' space, on your bottom line as well. And the pandemic means that if we are going to have offices, they have to provide high-quality and spatially-attractive experiences.
RZ: When the pandemic hit, we wanted to keep our vendors alive at all costs, because they provide the reason for people to come here. And today more than ever, you need a reason to go to an office. You have to remain an inspirational space. And the perimeter walkways that give us unbelievable flexibility: we can give you 30,000 square meters or three square meters. And we are still over 90 percent leased. We have tenants from when we started leasing space at $250 per square meter, but we also gave away free space and offered all kinds of incentives. And today we're doing leases up to $500 per square meter. That's because we have a space that people want to be in.

SP: If you could jump back in time, what are the things that you would ask Saarinen to reconsider or adapt?
RZ: I don't really have any. Maybe I wish he would have done double insulated glass on the perimeter.

SP: How about the steel partitions?
RZ: We heard there was an original drawing that had glass partitions, but for some reason, they were changed into the steel ones, which we removed.
PZ: They wanted to keep things private – a lot of things were done here…

SP: Was there no interest from Silicon Valley in your project? I have been there, and could imagine this would be perfect, even with all their secrecy…

RZ: Adam Lutz, who's head of real estate for Google, flew out here together with a large architecture firm and provided early encouragement, because of the floor plates. They're very deep, around 126 feet from side to side, plus the eight-foot walkways on each side. But they were taking a space in the Meatpacking District. Adam encouraged us to open up the space because Saarinen built with columns every 4.2 meters, which sort of divided the space into sections. In between those columns was ductwork, power, and everything, and it created a wall, even after we took off the sheetrock and everything. So we made a big and expensive decision to rip out the entire heating and cooling system and put in a modern one. This enabled open spaces of up to 6,700 square meters. Even the bare columns are great.

SP: Could we get back to this concept of the good bones?
AG: There's this three-foot module that governs the entire building. Saarinen, but also people like Mies van der Rohe, would decide on a module when they started planning any office building. They usually range from three feet to five, or even to six feet. I convinced the National Park Service, the keepers of the heritage status of the building, that as long as we maintain this module, the interior facades opening towards the walkways and the atrium could be glass, and did not have to be opaque. And they accepted that argument. That allowed the entire interior to become offices that could be rented out in a modern way with daylight.
The bones of the building are also conducive to having multiple activities. The building accommodates this better now than it did before. When we found the building, the main atrium was clogged with a weird geometric series of enormous 10-by-10-foot-high concrete planters, like a labyrinth. Ralph said, let's take them out, which I wasn't sure about because they were part of the original plan. But that allowed all these activities to take place on a blank slate. And now each of the atriums has a different sensibility.

PZ: The building has so many special details that I want to celebrate rather than change. There was a plan to change the lobby walls to marble, which was nuts from my end. We ripped up the tile that was there and now it's just exposed concrete, very rough and it's just beautiful. Why would we want to change this into a Midtown office?
RZ: We're going to bring up Italian Carrara marble…
PZ: There were also original New Jersey Bell phone booths in the elevator lobbies. I managed to change them into wellness rooms, for example, for women who are breastfeeding and need privacy, and it's the perfect fit.

SP: Saarinen's other buildings, from John Deere to General Motors, to the renovated TWA terminal in New York are in perfect shape. Their workspace in a physical sense is unchanged, an antithesis to innovation. Do you have an idea what the genius is that he put in? What's the thing to learn from this design?
RZ: I think it's the human scale. To me, there's something magical about the space and the dimensions. The other thing is the ability to create a space within a space without a wall, like the sunken conversation pit. We tried to continue that in the living room spaces, where Paula and Alex were inspired by people like Josef Albers.
AG: My favorite detail is the way the granite curves at the entry of the sunken waiting areas, which become the base of the tables and the wall.

SP: Saarinen does very little, but what he does, it's just rock solid and smart. The sunken plaza with these massive granite blocks… I read that he didn't allow any art to be on the wall because he felt that the people were the art.
RZ: They are! And looking at the post-pandemic condition: why are people going to come back to the office? Are they going to come back to work or to ideate and collaborate and get inspired to go back home and work? A lot of people will come to the office to talk and to meet and inspire

and then I get my work done at my kitchen table. Companies are fearful, uncertain about the office at this point. Do I need a 10-year lease? What is the office going to look like? So we've created a new campus plan. We took one floorplate in the building and allowed tenants to slice it like a loaf of bread with 600-square meter slices separated by a zipper-like wall system. And again, because of Saarinen's simplistic genius, he gave us such a clean, easy, platform, that we were able to do this.

SP: Before COVID-19, the location was a disadvantage, but now it seems the location actually becomes a strength. There may be a renaissance of the pastoral workplace, with balanced, affordable suburban lifestyles less dependent on cities. What do you take from these experiences to other projects?
RZ: We're taking the lessons that we learned here to a site in Chicago. It's a building that was designed in the early 1990s by Dirk Lohan, a grandson of Mies van der Rohe. The work we have to do there is harder because he had these walkways but also a lot of complicated early 90s architecture. But the rezoning was much easier: what took us five years in New Jersey took us five minutes, because we had a proof of concept to show. We're looking to create Metroburbs all across the United States. It's a brand. But now it's evolved into a methodology, all thanks to Saarinen.
PZ: But it's not just the architecture or interior design. It's also designing events, designing the graphics, the messages that we put out there on every platform. We curated the playlist and what the building smells like. It's also about bringing people together: The bar at Bell Works, Barbella, is key and the tenants love it. It's not just a boring building to go to work, there's life there too…

SP: Would it even lead you to build a new Metroburb?
RZ: Here's the problem: finance. We bought 472 acres with 185,000 square meters. To build what we inherited from Eero Saarinen before the enhancements would cost $500 million. It would work if we started with a large anchor tenant like Google. But they would have to change their philosophy and open up their campus to others, which is unlikely.

SP: Though it would be healthier for these companies too. That would be an outside world visible, to counteract the entrapment model that Dave Eggers wrote about in *The Circle*…
RZ: Maybe you can't do better than what Saarinen did. Even in a city, the numbers would be hard to work. It's just not a metro building: it's a Metroburb.

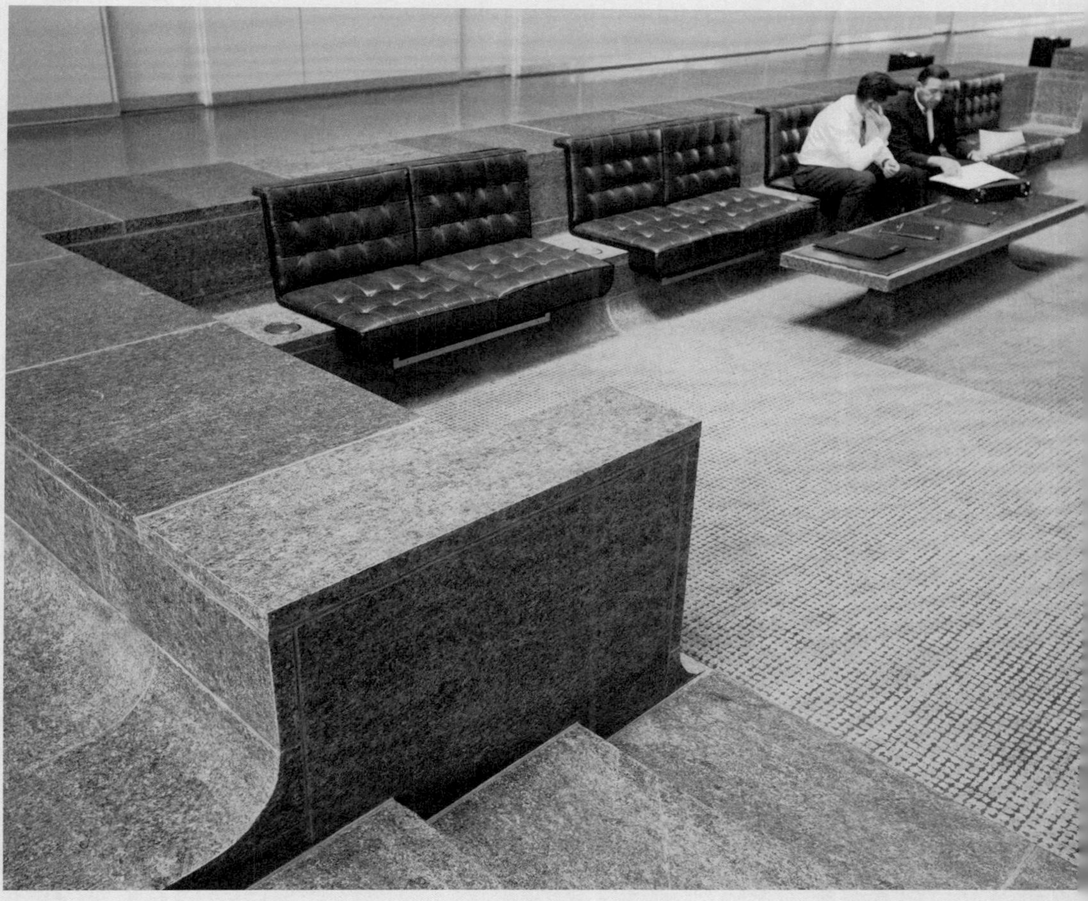

notes

1	Metropolis Books, 2014

building credits

architect: Eero Saarinen and Kevin Roche, John Dinkeloo

photo credits

p.228, 235, 238 (all): Ezra Stoller / ESTO
p.237: Evergreen Media
p.239 (all): Brooke Petrany

2021
101 CRAWFORDS CORNER RD.
HOLMDEL, NEW JERSEY, US

237

238

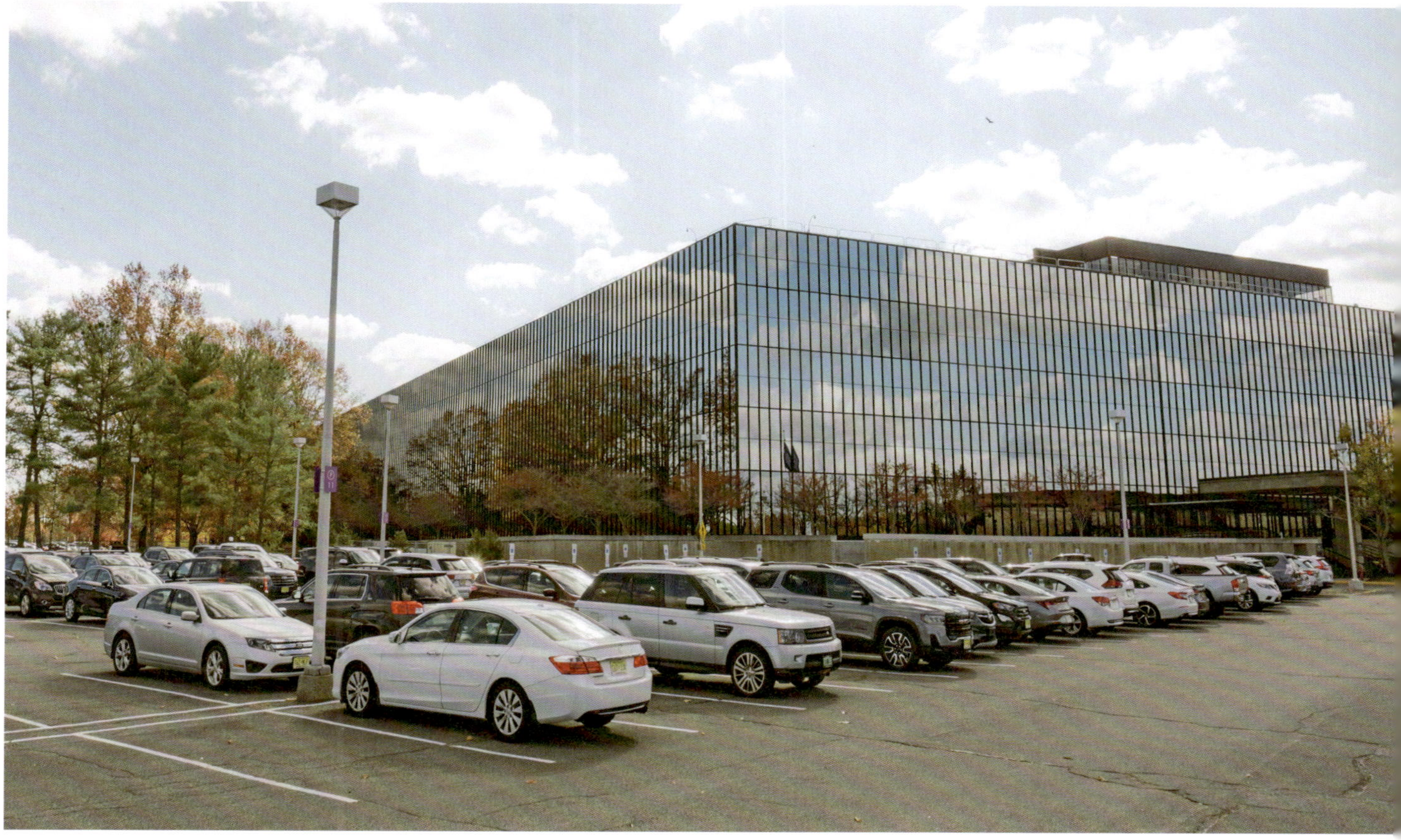

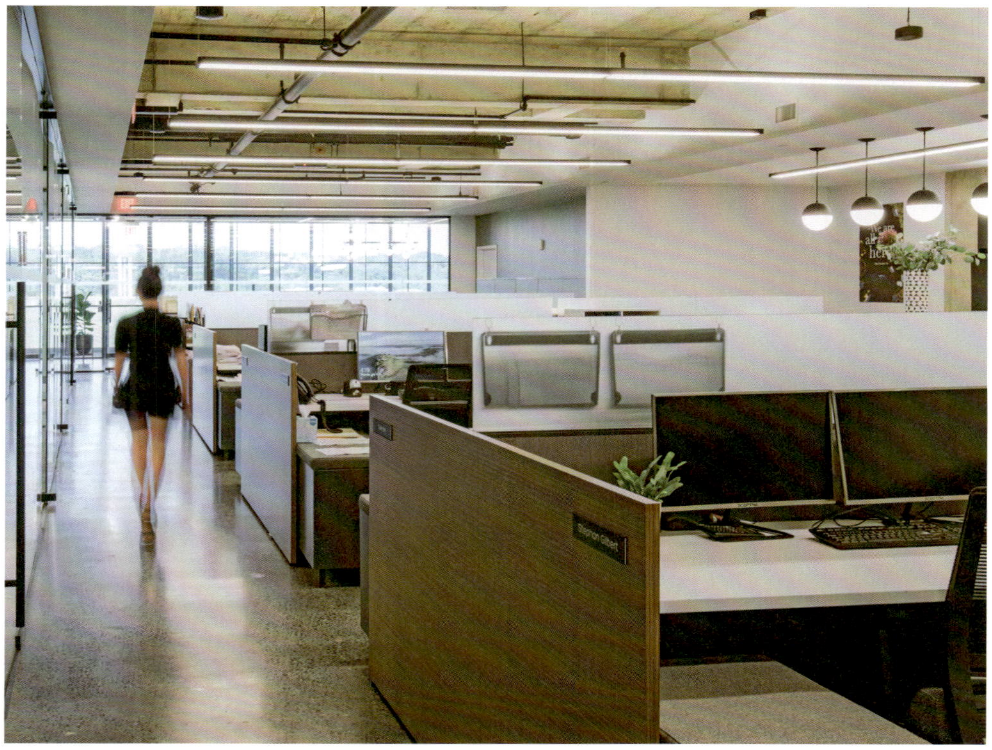

1962

Stephan Petermann

TOMADO HOUSE

"There's always something happening when I'm doing the dishes": a modern office icon, decades after losing its owner-occupant and housing multiple tenants, is converted into apartments

The following is a translation of "Tijdens de afwas gebeurt er altijd wat" ("There's always something happening when I'm doing the dishes") by Salwa van der Gaag in *Algemeen Dagblad*, July 7, 2016.

What's it like to live in the famous Tomado House in Dordrecht? Right across from the train station, with a terrace on your doorstep. First inhabitants Freek Valster (26) and Doren Berecz (23) share their experiences.
"The view is amazing", Freek Valster enthusiastically reports. He is pointing towards the train station which looks very impressive from the window of the loft. Two weeks ago he moved into the finished apartment with his girlfriend Doren Berecz. He moved to Dordrecht from Alblasserdam. She is from Hungary. They are the first inhabitants of the lofts in the Tomado House.

notes

1   Upon its completion in 1962, the Tomado House was one of the most sophisticated office buildings in the Netherlands, incorporating a unique construction with the latest building technology: escalators with movement sensors, advanced heating and air conditioning systems, automated pneumatic post systems, phone and telex services throughout the building, auxiliary power units, electrically controlled integrated Venetian blinds, a state of the art archiving system, and electrically cooled drinking water. The unique construction system was described by Maaskant as a self-supporting car chassis: besides a central concrete core, it consists of a load-bearing structure of concrete facade panels which liberated the floor plan of columns. The building had an un-Dutch elegance in its interiors, using expensive walnut and wengé wood, carrara marble, colorful Italian-made mosaic walls, and furniture by famed designers like Mies van der Rohe and Arne Jacobsen.

2   Tomado was founded as a furniture company in 1923 by the Van der Togt brothers in Dordrecht. Shortly after the Second World War, the company grew rapidly thanks to its innovative shelving systems. The company also made kitchen storage items and became a Dutch equivalent of Tupperware. Jan van der Togt was Maaskant's client. A self-made man, infatuated with US corporate offices, he also asked Maaskant to design two factories for Tomado, and the two became close friends. Maaskant considered van der Togt an ideal client, one who shared his vision of the importance of architecture and design and gave him maximum design freedom. The Tomado House helped establish Maaskant's as an 'industrial' architect. For more on Maaskant' and van der Togt's relationship, see Chapter 9, "Faith in Technology" in Michelle Provoost monograph, Hugh Maaskant: Architect of Progress (Nai010, 2012).

3   After the success of its Household products in the 1950s, Tomado gradually lost market share due to its competitors using cheaper labor in other countries. In 1971, Tomado was forced to merge with Bekaert, Belgian makers of steel products. But their decline continued. Money was no longer available for continued investment in its expensive office buildings. Part of Tomado House was leased to an insurance company. In the 80s, a multitude of tenants colonized the building, including a kitchen vendor, a blood bank, and the offices of the province of Zuid Holland. This led to a new interior organisation and renovations: the staff entrance was closed, and the bike shed and house of the building supervisor were transformed into additional office space. The elegant paving surrounding the building was removed and transformed from public space into parking lot. In 1987, the building was listed by the city of Dordrecht as a regional preservation object.
(Monumenten Adviesbureau, Bouwhistoriche Verkenning Tomadohuis, 2014. Unpublished.)

4   "Maaskant described the curtain wall — although he would later sporadically apply the principle — as something unnatural in the Netherlands: 'With our modern glass palaces, however fascinating and compelling they may be, we suggest a contact with nature that actually does not exist at all. To make these buildings liveable requires massive air-conditioning installations and keeping the windows shut. In our climate what we want is not to sit in nature, but to be protected from it, and to have a good visual contact with the outside world.'" Provoost (2012), p.242

5   "An inventory of equipment in any office building today would probably produce an even longer list, but at the time the level of technological perfection displayed by the building created quite a sensation. Some reacted with wary bewilderment, like the Goed Wonen journalist who compared the doorman on the first floor with Orwell's Big Brother: 'Via a barely noticeable television eye, he keeps watch from there on the gigantic lobby downstairs, where an automatic sensor concealed immediately beyond the entrance alerts him to every visitor. 'Good afternoon, sir,' says the eye with a lady's voice, when you've barely walked in and are vainly looking around for a doorman. 'Would you please proceed to the first floor?' I was disoriented by this greeting that seemed to come from no one, and I went off in the wrong direction, but the eye immediately said, 'the other way, sir.' And if that were not enough, the lift doors opened by themselves, and the conveyance started moving when I had merely pointed my right index finger at the button bearing the number one. A light immediately went on behind it to let me know that touching the button was entirely superfluous.'" This commentary rings with the same mix of disapproval and amusement we see in Jacques Tati's Mon Oncle (1958) and Playtime (1967), where hilarious situations are created by the alienating effect of excessively perfect technology. ... Van der Togt said he could not understand what all the fuss was about: "In America, where I spent a long time touring countless offices, this is completely normal. Nothing, nothing in this building is a new invention — it's all been around for a long time; it just hadn't really made it to Europe until now." Provoost (2012,) p.244.

6   "Maaskant, however, was quite aware of how much the building's technology would lead to controversy: 'We are conscious that this building, while it may not contain any revolutionary ideas, does present a problem. In the Randstad Holland [the urban conglomeration in the west of the Netherlands], which has the highest population concentration in the world, culture is going to displace nature. We cannot accommodate our growing population by filling up all the small towns and villages. If we are to ensure that our country is not riddled with all sorts of small buildings, we will have to concentrate the vast majority of the population increase in our cities. The people who live there will adopt the typical culture of the urban dweller to a significant degree. Our grandchildren will likely distinguish two kinds of neon light as easily as two kinds of trees. This is the price we have to pay to technology — the same technology we need in order not to starve.' He added that the Tomado House was not just about technology, and certainly not about a domination of humanity by technology, but about 'putting the people who work in it in an environment that will convince them of the opportunities presented by our generation's technological potential' ... Furthermore, the Tomado House in fact represents an elaboration of ideas about human relations and psychotechnics. The care devoted to the interior and the collective spaces, and the attention paid to personal work settings demonstrates an unusual concern for the staff. The generous amount of square metres per person (only 145 people worked in the Tomado House) was another expression of the emerging policy towards personnel and management. A good work environment and working conditions were decisive factors in the recruitment of personnel in the tight labor market (around 1960, the Netherlands had virtually full employment). Van der Togt was able to make the following statement: 'I believe that beauty and perfection in joie de vivre and stimulation definitely earn back what they cost in investment.' And Maaskant: 'An actual rise in work performance can only be achieved through ideal working conditions.'" Provoost (2012), p.248.

7   Two years later, in 2018, the fine-dining restaurant Copenhagen, in the former display and reception area of the Tomado House, closed its doors and was replaced by the more informal cafe-restaurant Buddingh. At the start of the second COVID-19 lockdown in the Netherlands in the spring of 2021, Buddingh was redeveloped into Macho Mamma by the same owner: Mexican inspired cuisine, a first for Dordrecht.

"I was really one of the first to register to get one of these lofts," Valster shares. "The location is excellent and the space very beautiful." You reach the fourth floor through the staircases which are still under construction. Only the top floors are inhabitable at the moment. Construction workers are rushing to finish the other apartments. In six weeks everything should be finished, explains Tessa Kuiten from iResidence. The corridor recalls a luxury hotel with black carpeting. But as soon as you enter the loft, the space is bright.

"The windows are really nice. They actually aren't that big, but they manage to make it feel more spacious," says Valter. Berecz was mainly responsible for the furnishing. And that was quite the struggle, due to the plan of the apartment. "The bed is in the same space [as the living space] and the space for the table is rather small. You have to be creative to find good practical use," she explains.

On June 18, national day for architecture, the Tomado House was opened to the public and they took their chance. With a tape measure they were walking into their new House still occupied with a lot of strangers. The Hungarian still needs to get used to her new city. "But I really didn't want to live in Alblasserdam. I really like Dordrecht," she says smiling. "The view is the best part of living here," says Valster. "There's always something happening when you're doing the dishes. It seems like there is somebody being arrested daily at the station. Just observing the people is fun."

They haven't been to the terrace of Copenhagen, but they are definitely planning to go.

building credits

client: Jan van der Togt
architect: Huig Maaskant

photo credits

p.240, 248, 250: Fotocollectie Rijksvoorlichtingsdienst
p.245, 247 (all), 249 (all): Ossip van Duivenbode
p.246 (above): unknown
p.246 (below): J.L. du Parant
p.251 (all): Victor van Breukelen

2019
STATIONSWEG 4
DORDRECHT, NETHERLANDS

246

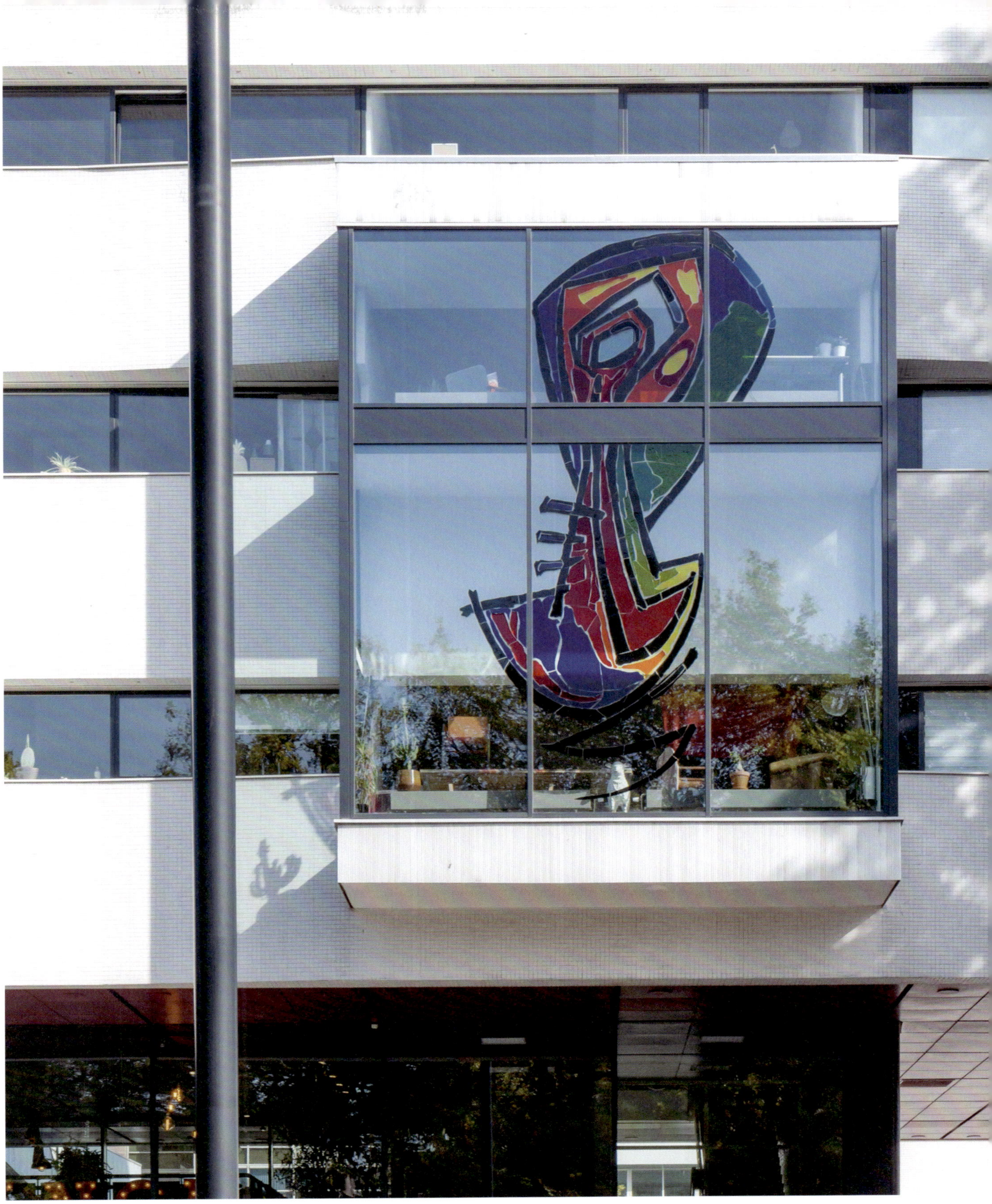

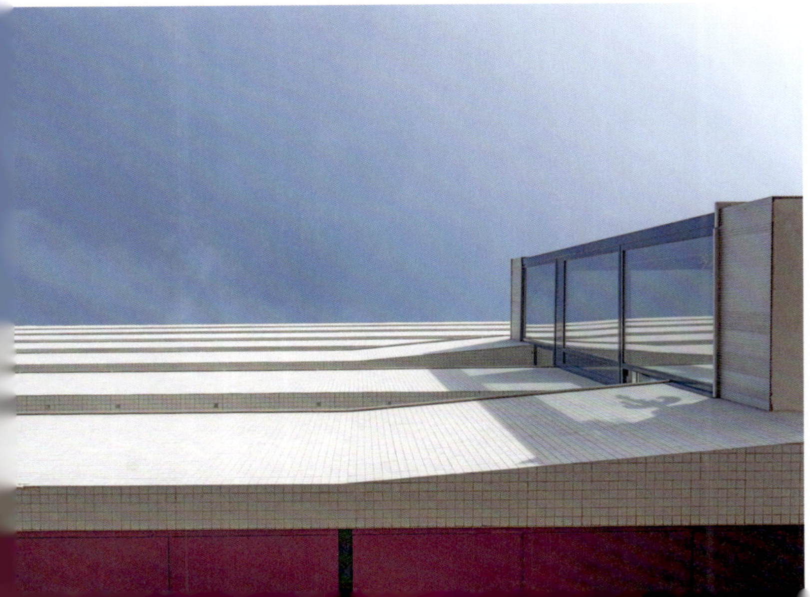

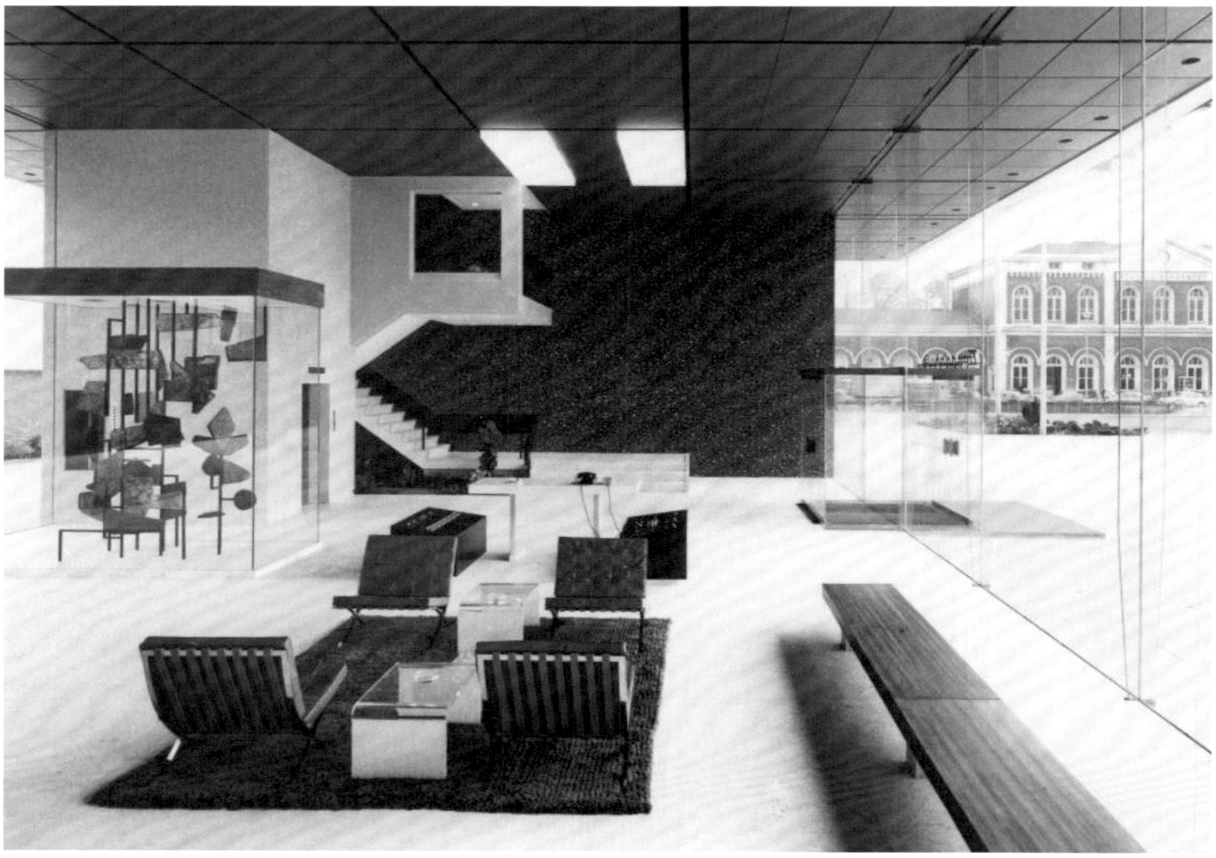

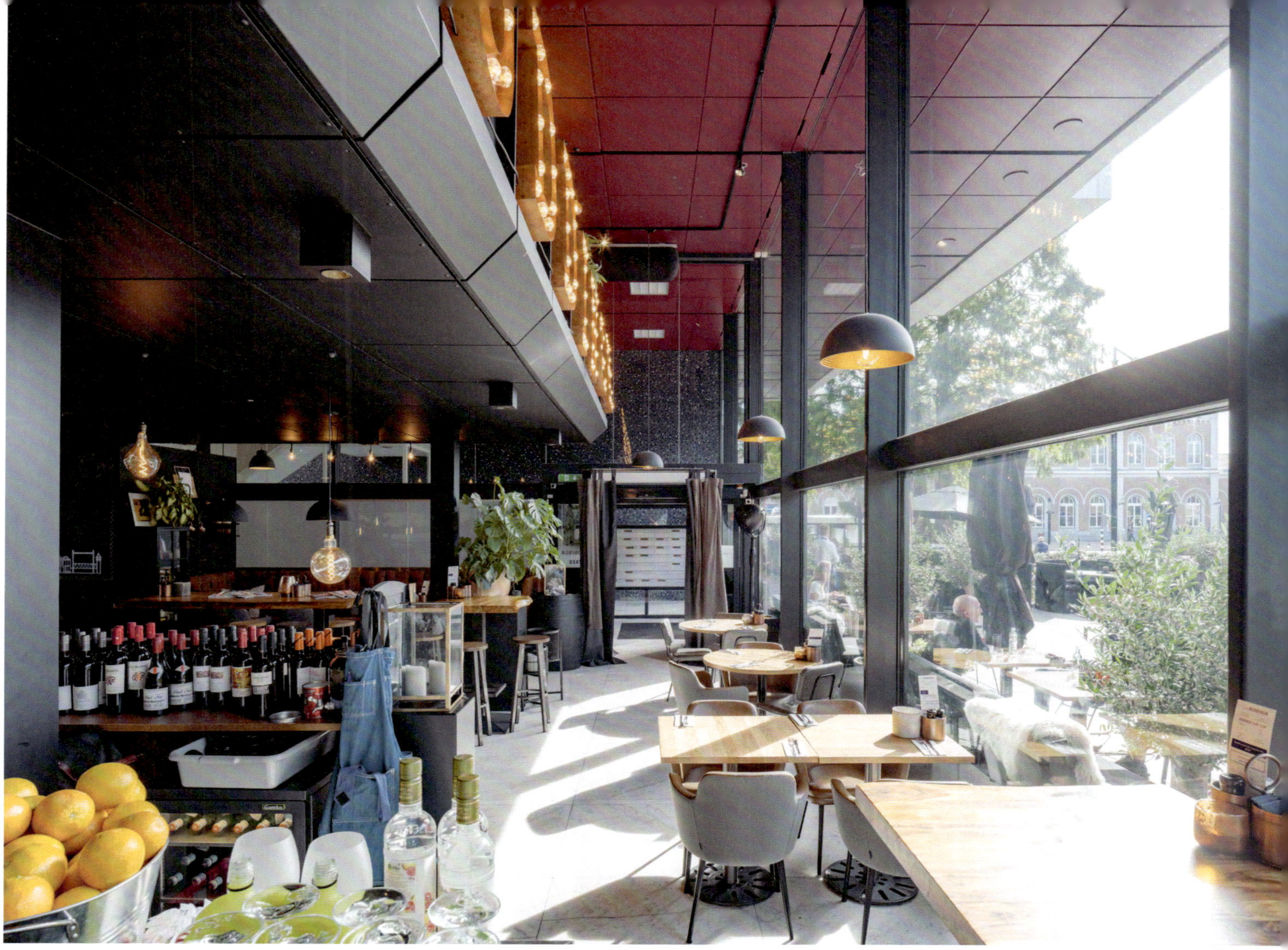

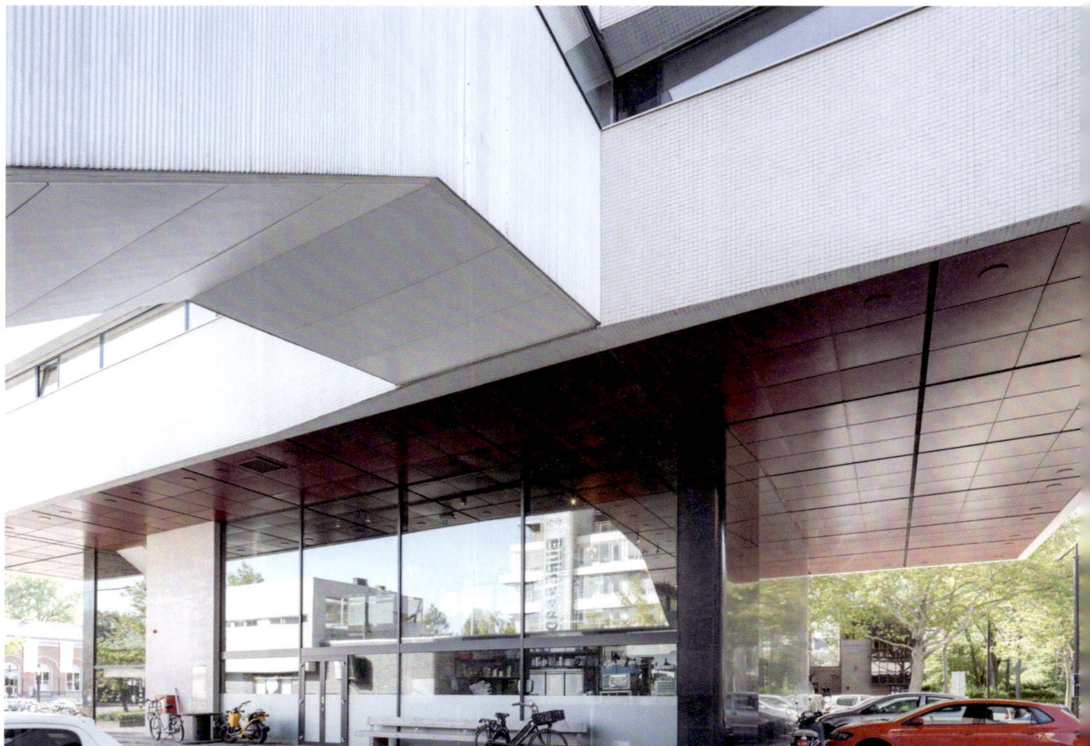

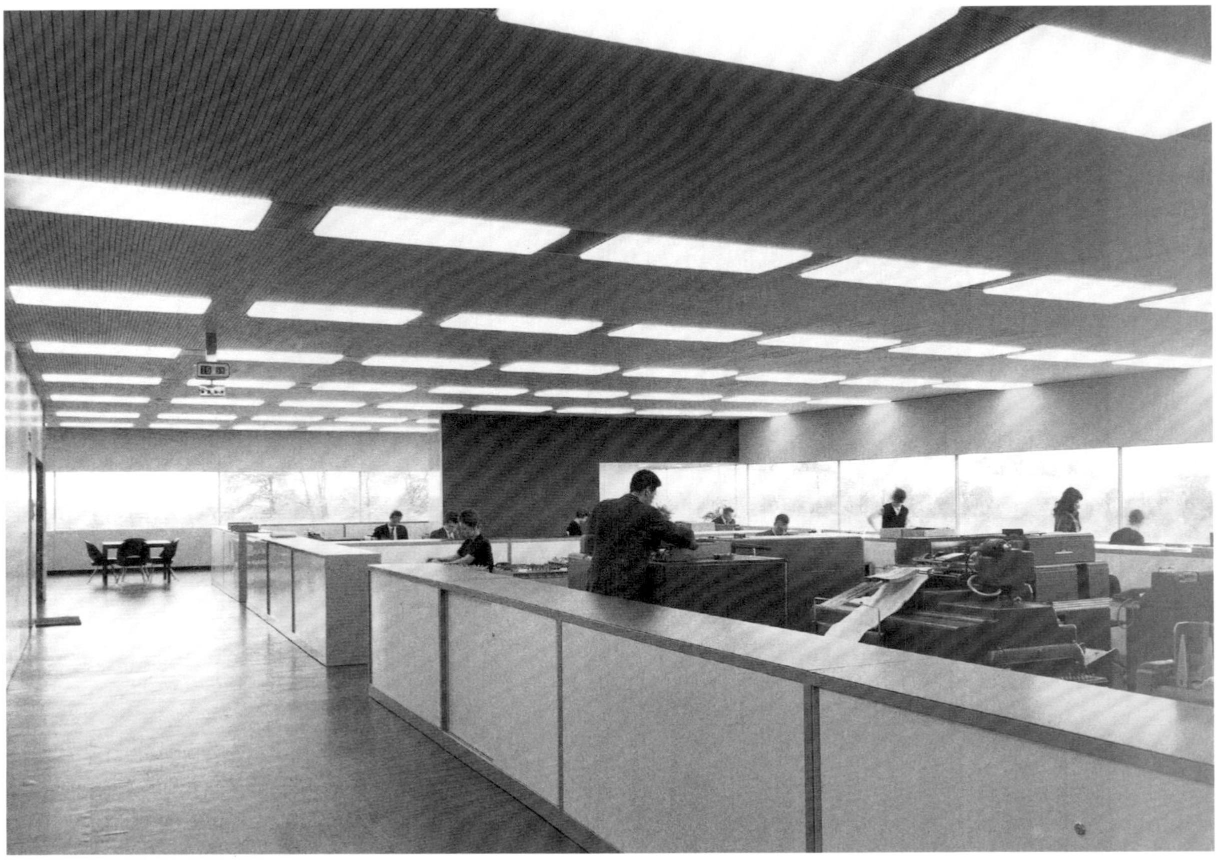

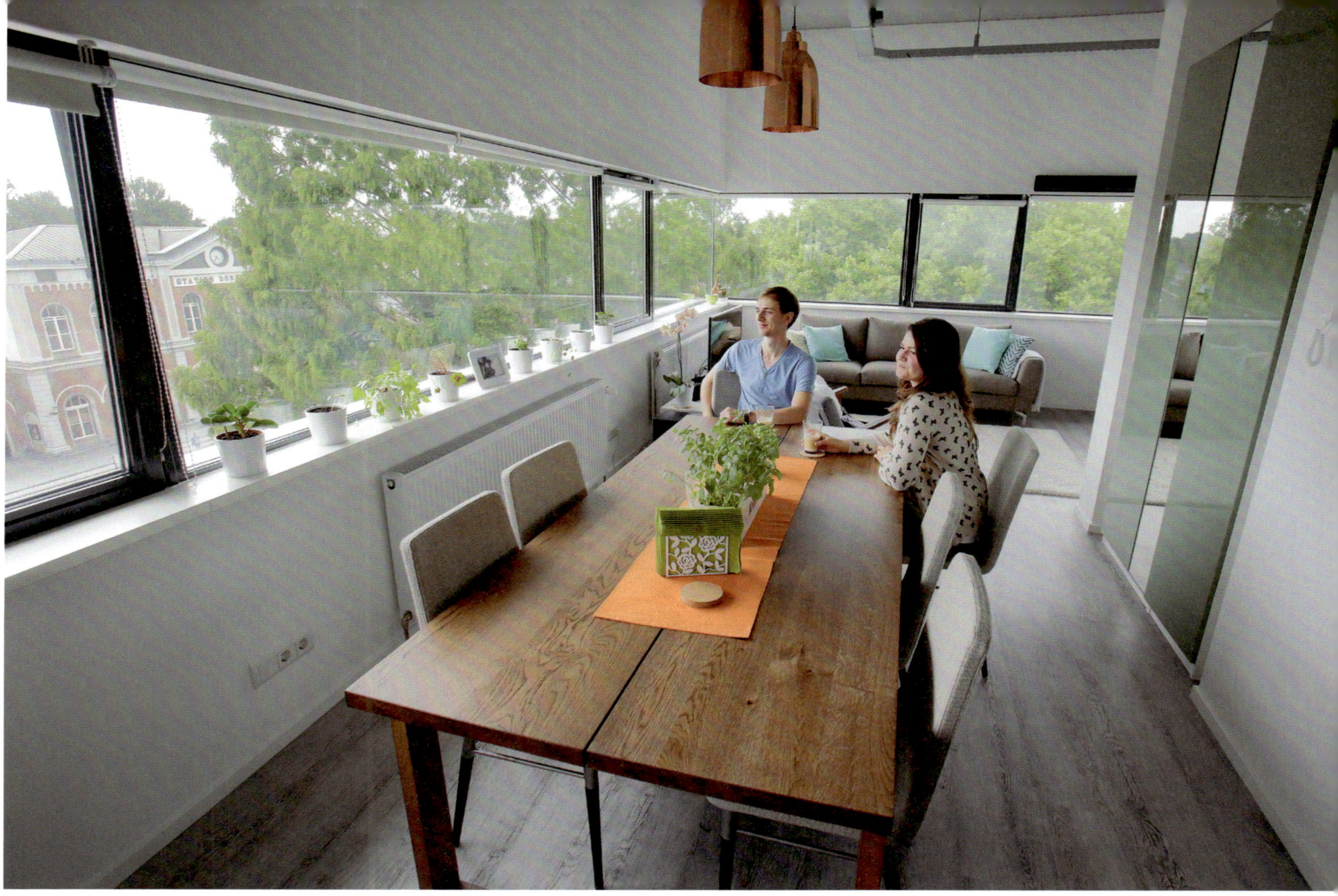

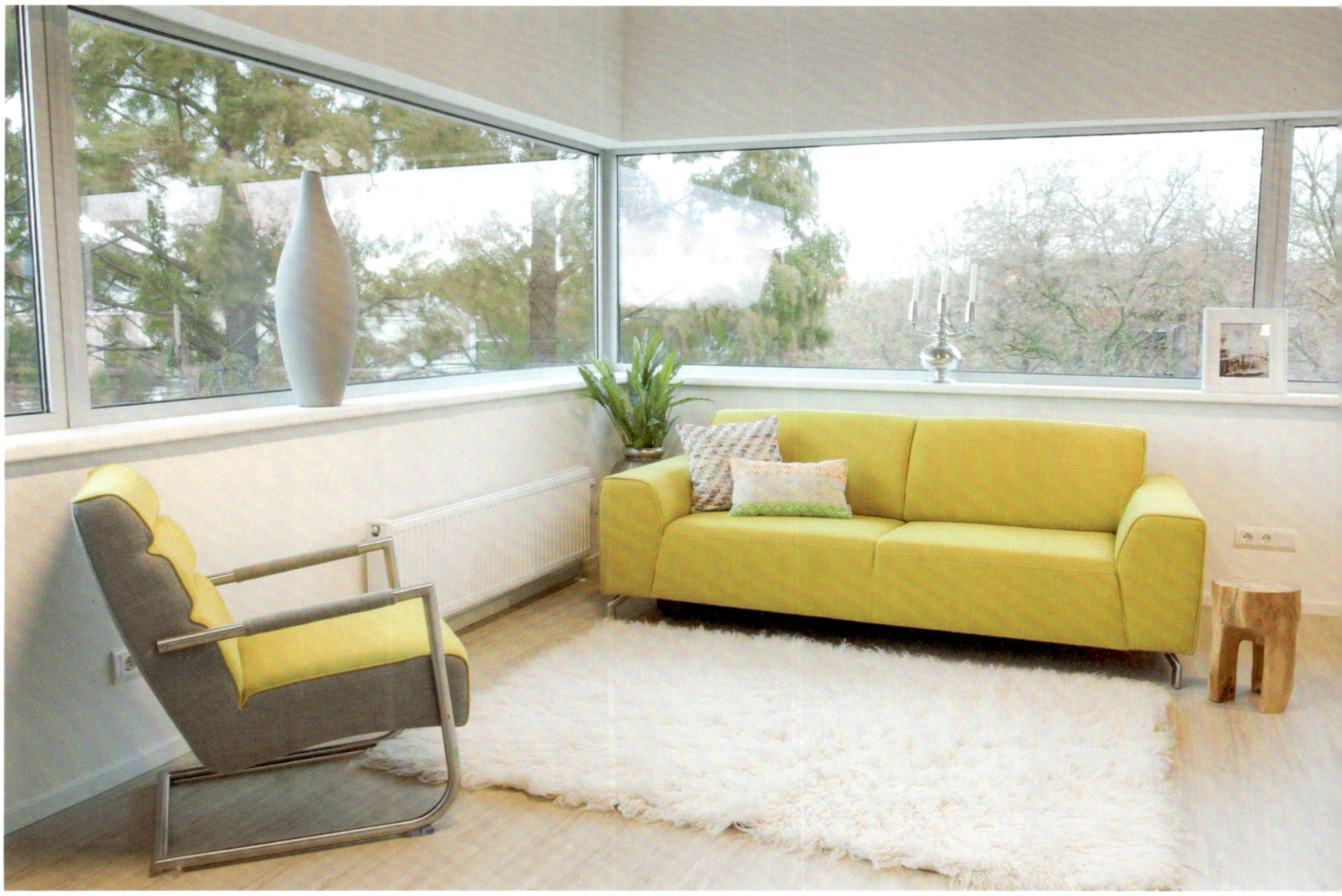

1962

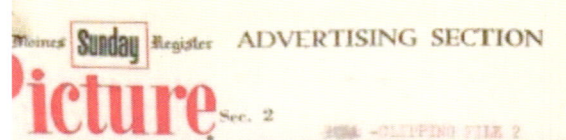

Stephan Petermann

HOME FEDERAL SAVINGS AND LOAN

God is in the details

The former Federal Savings and Loans bank by Ludwig Mies van der Rohe, in Des Moines, Iowa, is now the administrative seat of Bishop Richard Pates of the Diocese of Des Moines. Every morning, the bishop crosses the street from his residence – a 19th-century rectory – to enter Mies's building. The landscape surrounding the building looks remarkably unchanged from photos taken in 1962. But a modest sign above the building's entrance – a steel crucifix with curves on the outer ends – and new lettering in the Miesian typeface on the travertine cladding reveal the new religious function of the building.

Federal Savings and Loan shut down in February 1990 after a government bailout guaranteed local savings. Being prime real estate in downtown Des Moines, there was a strong interest in this particular branch, mainly in replacing it. Threats of demolition triggered international attention and a plea to preserve it, which moved the city administration to landmark the building. A wealthy philanthropist bought the building and gave it to the diocese.

The Bishop holds the corner office on the upper floor, overlooking the splendor of the 19th-century Romanesque cathedral across the street. His office is sparsely decorated with dark wooden furniture and a light carpet, in contrast to the tiled-carpet areas in the rest of the building.

When Federal Savings and Loan went bust, Mies's furniture was auctioned off, and it's apparently still used in architecture practices across the city. The diocese property manager Norm Bormann thinks much of the interior at the time was original: "New tenants in the building had added walls on the second floor … but apart from that it looked pretty much the same."

Bormann oversaw an initial renovation in 2004, which replaced the roofing, upgraded mechanical systems, and re-painted the interior. Life in the building was halfway reasonable: "The pneumatic systems weren't the best, and the boiler was old. But we got by with it." In 2014 the diocese realized the façade was rusting: "We understood this wasn't going to be like painting a house, more like painting a car."

A campaign raised $10 million for the overhaul, including a $2 million tax rebate after rigorous scrutiny into the impact of the preservation effort. The funds allowed Bormann, with BBS Architects| Engineers and Harboe Architects, to hew close to Mies's original design.

The entrance is sparser now. The tellers sitting behind their desks in the Kubrickesque photo of the central ground floor area are gone and so are their desks. During the reconstruction, it was discovered that the columns were even more rusted than expected. Paint colors were checked to make sure the building was the correct shade of black.

The windows were the biggest change. "After completion of the building we think a layer of film was added on the inside of the windows which gave it a smoky look. The new glass is a fully double-sheet glass with a film on the inside. According to the grandson of Mies, Dirk Lohan, that was closer to the original," explained Bormann.

The Bishop has a staff of around 80 people occupying the 4,000-square meter building, a generous spatial distribution. Individual offices remain in their original locations. The partitions, built just after completion, are unchanged. The only patina visible is in the dramatic square lighting fixtures in the ceiling, which seem to have turned slightly yellow.

Asked what advice he would give Mies, Bormann chuckles, "The heating and the cooling remains difficult. Energy efficiency of the building remains an issue, it's a pretty expensive building to run. With the renovation we improved it, but still less than expected. We have nine months of either heating or colling – sometimes even heating one side of the building, and cooling the other side. The concrete is tough to work with. But we like it a lot, we all admire and adore it."

There seems to be a natural fit between the newfound humility of the Catholic church and this building. Even the less elegant furniture and generic carpet tiles seem to be in keeping with Pope Francis's attempts to steer the religious community to more public service, for example, by introducing showers for the homeless in the Bernini colonnade in Saint Peters square. Asked for the religious connotation and the presence of God in Mies' building, Bormann turns shy, just as Mies would have liked it.

building credits

client: Jonathan Fletcher
architect: Ludwig Mies van der Rohe

photo credits

p.252: Des Moines Sunday Register
p.255 (all), 257 (all), 259 (all): Cameron Campbell
p.258 (all): Hedrich-Blessing

2017
601 GRAND AVENUE
DES MOINES, IOWA, US

258

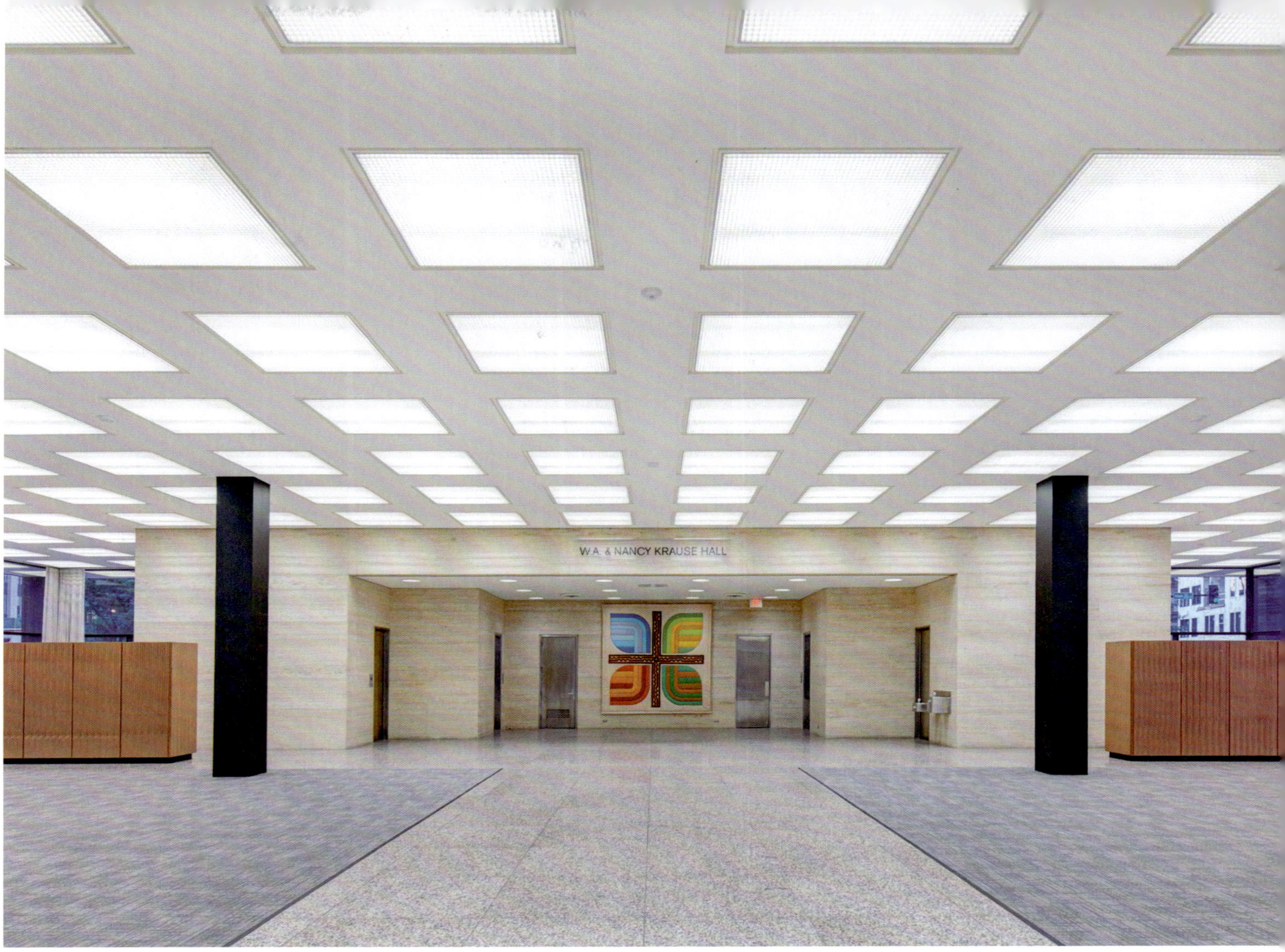
W.A. & NANCY KRAUSE HALL

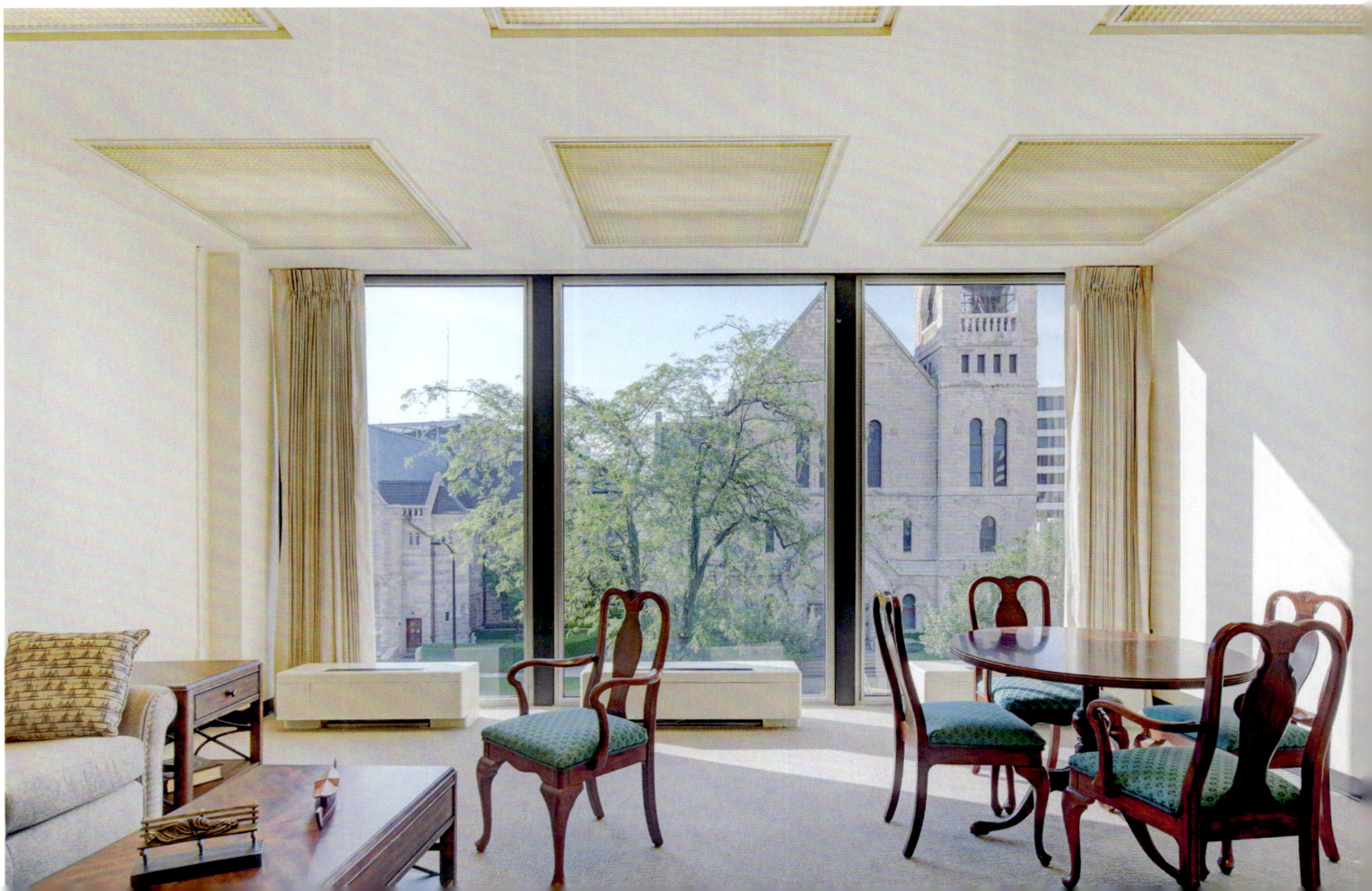

1962

Ruth Baumeister

ENSO-GUTZEIT HEADQUARTERS

A forestry company prepares to move out of its modern marble-clad HQ, which has sustained for 60 years, and build anew in the name of sustainability

The client-architect relationship between Alvar Aalto and Enso-Gutzeit, the Finnish timber giant, began in the 1930s. While growing steadily the company commissioned Aalto to design several projects throughout Finland, including masterplans for mill-based communities, a mill with service buildings, housing for management and workers, and a country club. It did not come as a surprise, when Aalto received the commission to build the company's headquarters in 1962, because director William Lehtinen, art collector and the person in charge of the company's building projects, was a close friend of Aalto. The new HQ was to be located in Katananokka, Helsinki's passenger ship harbor.

Enso-Gutzeit turned out to be one of Aalto's most controversial buildings, positioning him between modernists and traditionalists.

The site was historically charged, surrounded by neo-classical public buildings, among them the Presidential Palace across the street and the Russian church behind, hinting at Finland's painful history of occupation. Supposedly, Aalto expressed concerns about building at such an exposed location but stated that if anyone should build something there, it should be him.

Aalto left his mark in the heart of the Finnish civitas with a six-story cubic volume, with a white, gridded façade. Locals call it the sugar cube, though it's recessed on the backside towards the church and its main entrance faces the city via a portico. The sixth floor, housing the executive offices and the café, features a mundane terrace with breathtaking views over the city and its waterfront. The floor plan organizes meeting rooms and offices of various sizes and configurations around a service and circulation core, with a reception area on one side.

To make space for the new building, Norrmén House, a 19th-century neo-renaissance housing block, was torn down. This act of destruction raised a public controversy in which Aalto positioned himself as an architect who wants to create rather than only preserve: "I, for my part, have not signed a single one of these petitions… against the demolition of old buildings, because the totality of the capital cannot live in a museum stage. But it is obvious that there are cases where the city of Helsinki towards the sea, and to this the Katajanokka canal belongs, is, in my opinion, a more important part of… [the city] that we have … a task to protect [more] than the façade of any private building." Aalto prioritized the urban scale over any single building, and he was dreaming of his beloved Italy when conceiving of this new urban waterfront. He wanted to develop the harbor along the lines of the Riva degli Schiavoni in Venice, used the term "palazzo" when referring to the new Enso HQ, and decided to clad its façade in Italian Carrara marble, even though it was questionable for Finland's cold, wet climate.

According to Göran Schildt, author of the four-volume Aalto biography, the architect referred to his office buildings for banks and corporations as "palaces for the Medicis of today." His approach drew criticism, especially from those who resisted ostentation and the appropriation of important public spaces in urban centers by private businesses. On the one hand, the blank orthogonal, flat-roofed building neutralized the power of the Russian church behind it, disappointing those who defended tradition in Katananokka. His choice of marble cladding upset both traditionalists – who thought it amounted to the emperor's new clothes hiding the cheap mass-produced structure behind it – and the avantgarde, who resented the classical references this exquisite material evoked. Moreover, they criticized the architect's conception of the building as a *Gesamtkunstwerk* –carefully designed from the urban scale all the way down to the furniture and light fixtures – which they considered to be part of a bygone era.

Stora Enso, as the company is called today, still continued to occupy the building 50 years after it was inaugurated. The fact that the offices proved inefficient in terms of usable square meters per workplace, combined with the fact that the building lacked an open and communicative environment triggered a massive interior reconfiguration in 2011–13, increasing the number of workstations significantly. Nevertheless, Stora Enso sold the building less than a decade later and launched a competition for a new headquarters a stone's throw away.

We spoke to Timo Heikka, who has worked for 25 years at Stora Enso, most recently as Vice President of Stakeholder Relations and R&D in Finland. Heikka reflects on why the company decided to put an end to its relationship with Aalto's architecture, which had sustained for almost a century on various mill sites and 60 years at the head office at Kanavaranta 1 in Helsinki.

Ruth Baumeister: Why is Enso leaving the building?
Timo Heikka: First of all, because the building is too small for collective activities. Over the years, we have had to rent additional offices throughout the city, but it's also because we are now producing contemporary wooden building elements ourselves, which are beautiful. We can deliver material for a very nice office building, especially from the point of sustainability and architecture. When these materials are skillfully used by good architects, even a massive wooden building can be placed close to this historic center. We have to showcase our office by working with the best architects we can find.

RB: Already about 10 years ago, the interior was changed drastically. Why was that and what kind of changes were made?

TH: There was not enough space. We had 1950s-style workspaces, with reception spaces in the middle that you had to pass to get to the leader's office. There was a lot of storage, a safe for money deposits, etc. which you don't need anymore. All this could provide us with extra square meters to fit more people in. So we tore down some chipboard partition walls. It's very much an open office space now. It was quite a dramatic change. The Alvar Aalto Foundation was part of it and they wanted us to preserve even more. How do you keep up a building in a good condition and make it fit for all the future generations? You use it! They understood that you have to adapt and many details turned out nicely. New lamps were made, new handles and handrails and so forth were made according to old sketches. The combination of old and new looks quite nice. The best-preserved part is the sixth floor where the guest areas are located. All in all, it's a combination of radical renovation and preservation.

RB: You said the major reason to move out was the lack of space. Has the pandemic changed the parameters?
TH: Yes. There will be a revolution in the way businesses work. Hybrid is the new catchphrase, often when describing the future of office work. For the coming autumn/winter season, it looks as if many companies will have one-to-three office days and the rest as remote days working from home. But fully remote is very difficult in my experience. When you start something new, you need to have some days on site. And when you meet new people, you need the office; you can't just meet in a café, for example. Team spirit does not work if you aren't ever physically present with your closest working colleagues. Human communication needs that. People are fed up with Microsoft Teams and quite a few of them now want to go back to the office. There's also a danger if a person is an introvert because isolating alone at home might contribute to mental health problems. In Helsinki, unfortunately many people live in rather small flats, and spending

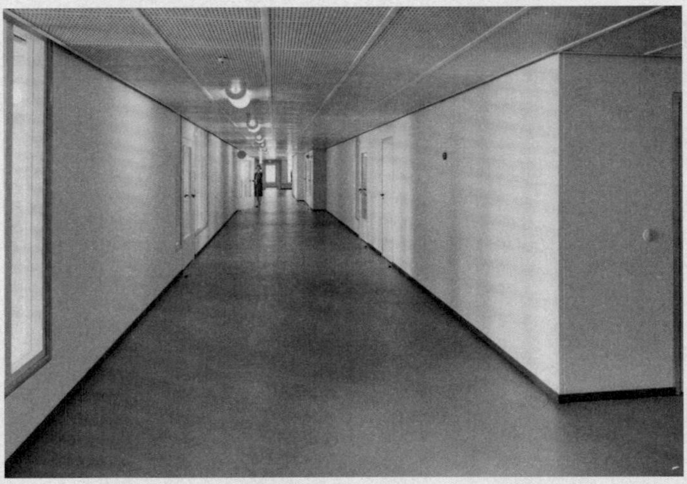
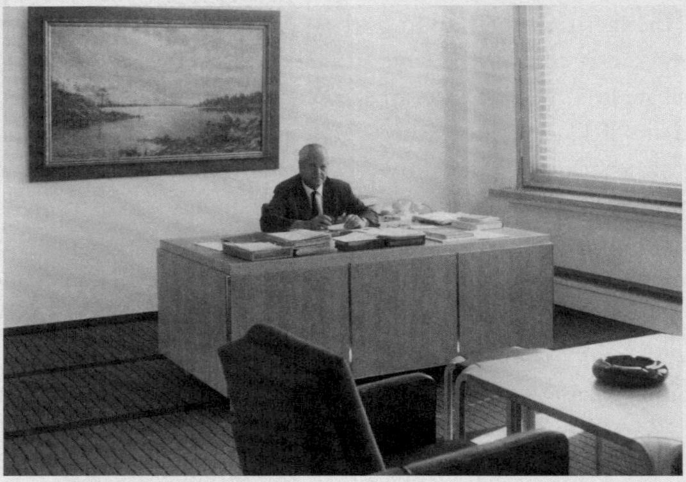
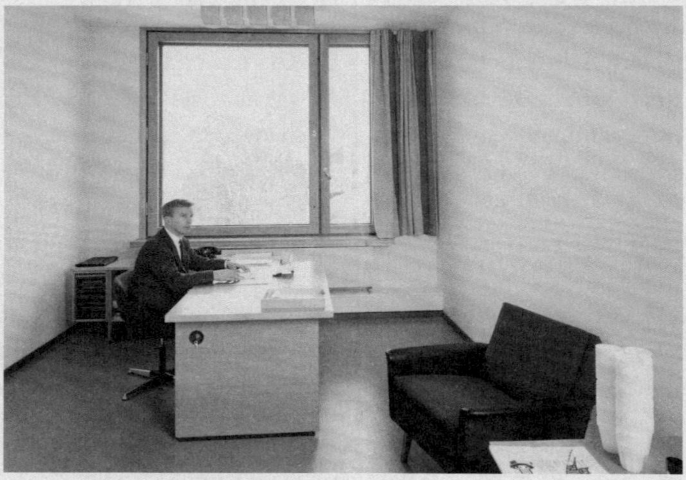
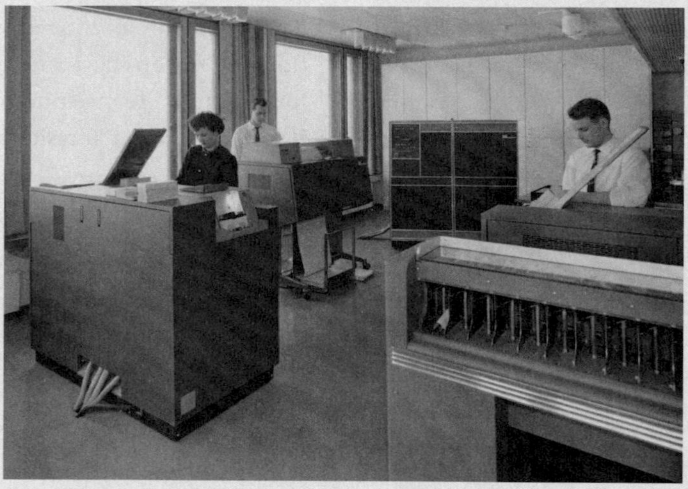

the whole day in a five-meter radius is a challenge. I don't believe the solely remote version of working envisioned by many companies will succeed.

RB: What kind of offices will we see in the future?
TH: It will depend on the activities that need to be performed. Personally, I don't like it when you don't know which desk you'll have in the morning, but that will be the case. We need flexibility, and different technical solutions were created for that: silent, small meeting rooms, sliding walls, sliding doors, and so on. And a funny thing is that you install telephone booths inside an open-plan office.

RB: Could you imagine this kind of flexibility in the Aalto building?
TH: We tried to make the building fit for such a use through the renovation in 2013. But still, the number of people is – or was, before the pandemic – too big. But then, there is also the aspect of showcasing, which companies like Supercell in Helsinki do.

RB: Where will the new headquarters be?
TH: One hundred and fifty meters from here. There's an old storage house, which has been empty for a long time. Inside it's already been emptied, and they will recycle the materials, up to 98 percent. That is now a prerequisite for tearing down such a building. The materials are already nicely sorted. Also, the loadbearing structures, the walls, etc. will be dismantled in such a way that they can be reused.

What is the message the company wants to send out with this new building?
TH: That we are modern, strongly export-oriented, and international. And that we walk the talk with sustainability.

RB: One could say this building has become more of a museum: it's a piece of cultural heritage. And now you want to move out of the museum and build yourself a new showcase better tailored to the firm's needs. Is that right?
TH: Partly, but not fully. After the renovation, it was adapted for modern use, so it's not a museum. It's too small and we need a showcase building for our own products. It will be in a prime location by the Baltic Sea.

RB: Does location matter for you?
TH: Yes, now we will not be somewhere by the Ring III road, which circulates the greater Helsinki area, but at a prime location and that gives us the possibility to showcase our new projects, which are again based on wood.

This industry is renewing, transforming and the source is still the forest. In Finland, the forest is the only large-scale resource we have. Forestry has an important meaning for the national economy and therefore the company's activities and value creation are also very important for the country. The building and its location underline that fact. Despite the decrease in the consumption of paper for printing and writing, we come up with new products all the time, like building with new wooden components and other materials. For instance, we extract lignin, the material that keeps wood fibers together, from sulphate cooking liquor. In the mill site of Sunila, 130 kilometers east from Helsinki, by the Gulf of Finland, we now have a pilot mill that makes so-called 'hard carbon' for anodes of lithium batteries.

RB: In the new building, you will only have open offices, correct?
TH: Yes, but let's see how the planning proceeds. As I mentioned previously, when it comes to the configuration of office space, they are trying to adapt towards a new hybrid. Glass will be used and the space must have good sound insulation. If there is a lot of noise, you cannot concentrate. It will be interesting to see how the architects in collaboration with the company will tackle this problem in the new building.

RB: Aalto had a very close relationship to the CEO when he built the headquarters. Is there a similar constellation now?
TH: No, it was an anonymous architectural competition, and now the procedure is based on cooperation. Before the competition, we collected ideas from people, and we are involving our employees through questionnaires. It's not just the CEO and his closest advisors who discuss the project with the architect; it's a participatory process where they work with all of our people.

RB: Does Enso own the new building?
TH: No. The pension insurance company Varma will own it and we will rent space inside it. There will be many other activities in it as well.

RB: That's very different from the set-up in Aalto's time. What percentage of the building will Stora Enso rent?
TH: Somewhere between 25 and 30 percent. It's a big building and there's a big lobby, with exhibitions, a restaurant, and other activities, which will be open to the public. Because this is a special area in the heart of the city, close to the presidential palace on one side and ocean liners on the other, it needs to be a multi-purpose building, open to people. There needs to be life in the building outside of office hours. Otherwise, you would block one of the most beautiful parts of Helsinki with just another private office building.

RB: What kind of response did you get from the public about the new building?
TH: The response was mostly positive, and the request for building permission didn't get any major conditions.

RB: And it will be made completely out of wood?
TH: It's a hybrid building – like Supercell or Google in Helsinki – in the sense that the foundations, and possibly even elevator towers, etc. are of steel and concrete, and everything else around is massive wood. So far, the highest building in Finland made using our products is a 14-storey student residence. Even the elevator tower is made of laminated veneer lumber LVL, with veneer layers glued together to become very thick, strong, and stable.

RB: And how about fire regulations?
TH: You would think that timber would burn quickly, but it will not. Try to burn a heavy log. It's the same. In the event of a fire that could be extinguished, it would only get a rather thin layer of blackening, which could be sanded away. And the building would not collapse. A steel balk or column will, after some 15 minutes, be 800 degrees inside and close to collapse. But what really burns explosively is furniture, textiles, etc., not the structure. There is another advantage to timber construction: they are resilient in earthquakes. The first Finnish success in wooden houses was in Kobe, when there was a powerful earthquake about 30 years ago. Then there are the climate benefits of building with wood. That is a big reason for the demand we have from clients and architects.

RB: When you mentioned that location is important, is it because it shows the importance of the company? Or is it also because you attract different personnel?

TH: The location is important for attracting employees. Many of our people come from other countries. So yes, I think the new building will also be some sort of business card.

RB: Is it only about representation or is well-being higher in a place that's well designed?
TH: For me, every morning when I come to work and grab Alvar Aalto's door handle it's a bit uplifting. And the view you have in summer with the sailboats, the Baltic, etc. is marvelous. It affects you.

RB: You get a lot of input through physical encounters with objects or with people, which doesn't happen if you work from home.
TH: I also notice a shift in attitude: I see a positive and productive attitude when I come here. I've heard similar comments from my colleagues. It affects: a good capitalist understands that your people are more productive when it's like this.

building credits

client: William Lehtinen
architect: Alvar Aalto

photo credits

p.260, 264 (all), 270 (all): Helsingin Kaupunginmuseo
p.262, 265, 267, 269, 271 (all): Jens Frederiksen

2021
KANAVARANTA 1
HELSINKI, FINLAND

269

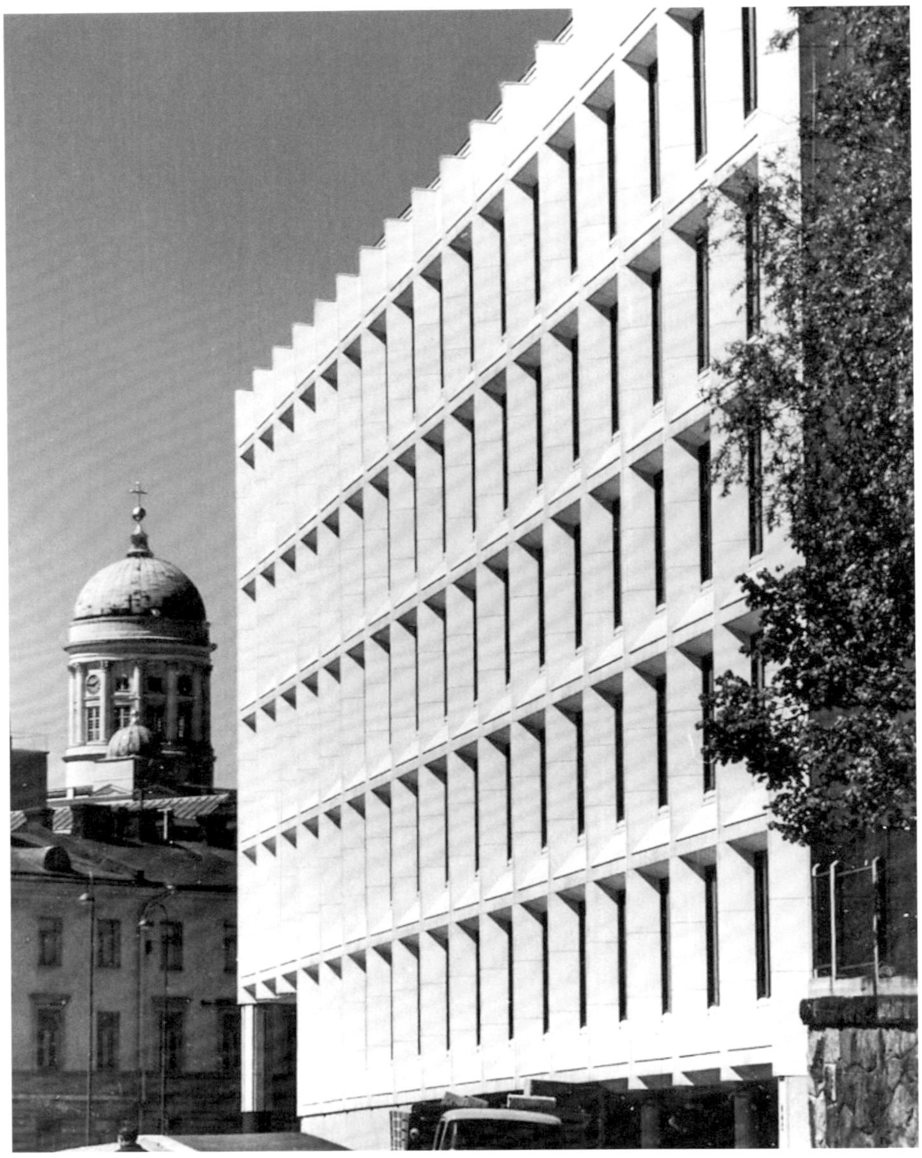

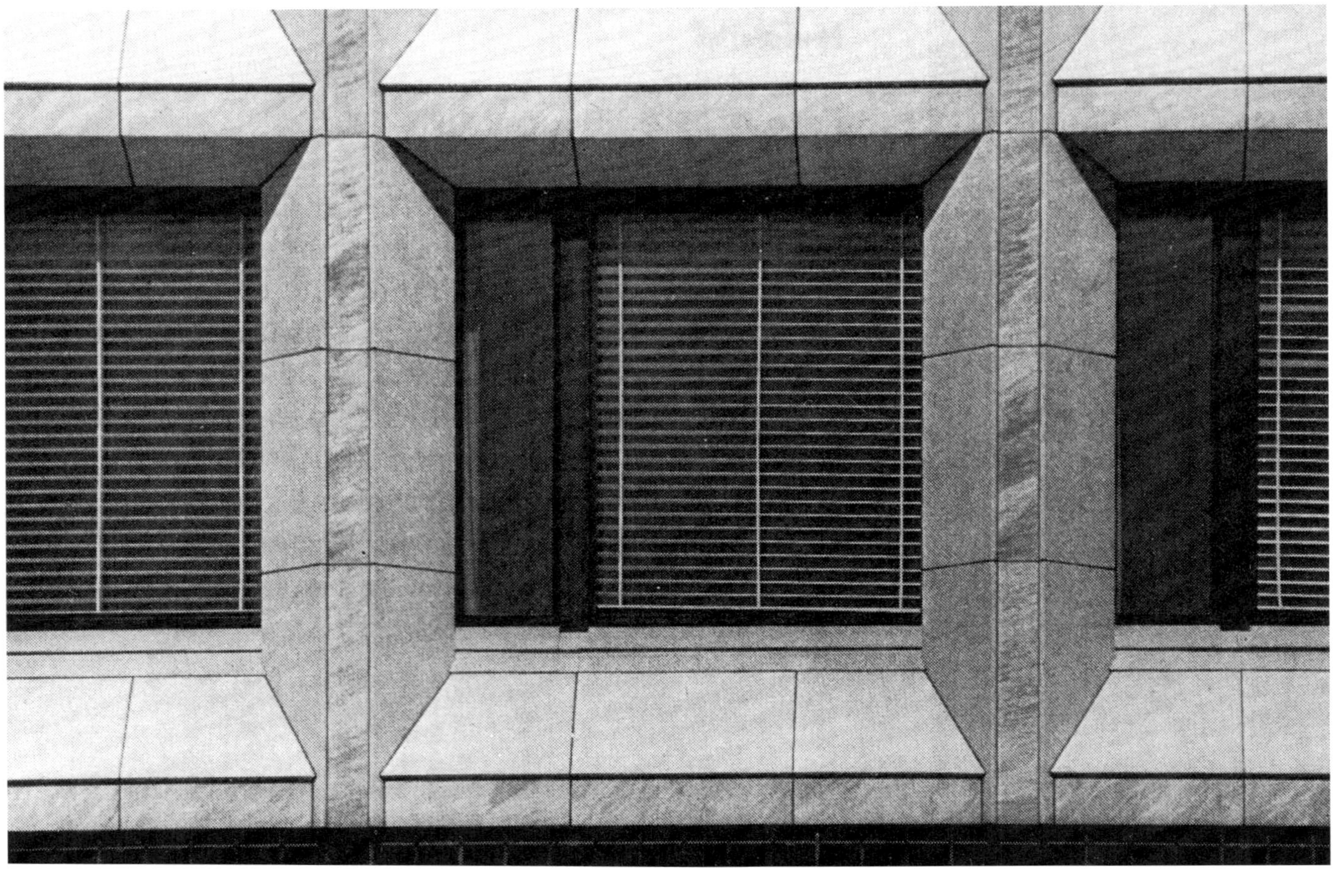

271

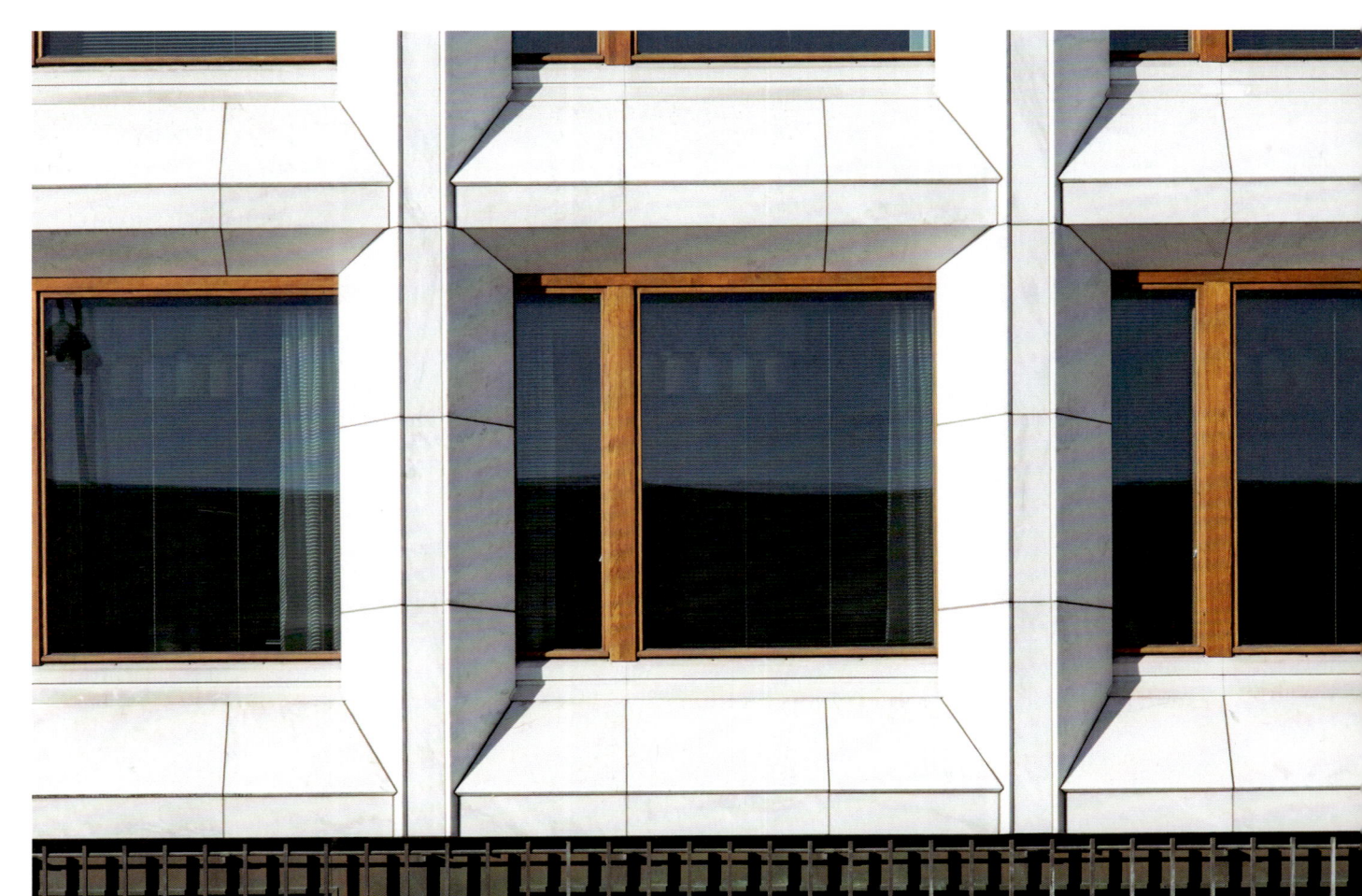

1962

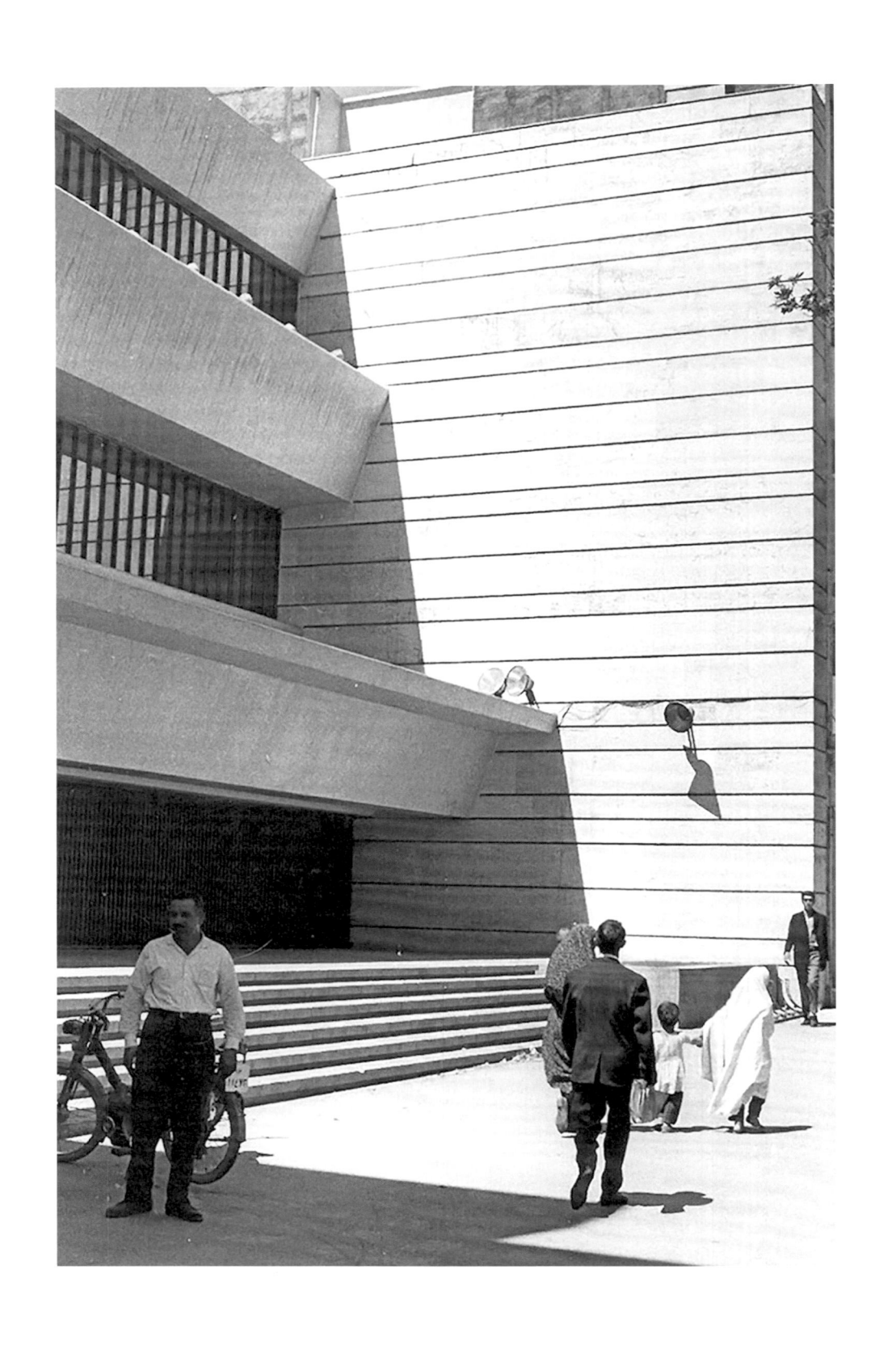

Solmaz Sadeghi and Ali T. Dinani (Inter-Esse Studio)

BANK MELLI UNIVERSITY BRANCH

Scene and Scenario: Jørn Utzon's rapprochement with the workplace in postwar Iran

In conversation with Henrik Sten Møller in 2004, Jørn Utzon summarized his foremost intention throughout his career: "The most important thing is to build for people... Being an architect is, for me, being a humanist."[1] Utzon's Bank Melli exemplifies this approach, acting as a backdrop for urban scenes from quotidian life to epochal struggles. However, the ideological foundations of each phase brought many difficulties in following the architect's disegno.

For Iran, the 20th century was the century of nationalization, for both the banking system (1928) and later the oil industry (1951). Postwar Iran pursued rapid urban growth during the reign of Shah Pahlavi II. The oil boom, as much as the social and geopolitical reconfiguration, provided an international stage to explore historical influences and engineering solutions which are reflected in national projects like Utzon's Bank Melli.[2]

In February 1959, en route to Sydney for the groundbreaking of the Opera House, Utzon stopped in Iran to begin designing the 'University Branch' of the Bank Melli (National Bank) in Tehran. The invitation came from Jorgen Saxild, co-founder of the Kampsax engineering company, involved in many of Iran's construction projects from the 1930s until the 70s. Project architect Hans Munk Hansen noted Utzon's desire to experience the cultural context before starting his design. "We didn't discuss the Bank Melli until coming back from Isfahan, where Utzon dealt with Persian architecture and tradition." Kampsax's report concurred, stating: "Utzon's great interest in dome and shell construction led him to Isfahan quite naturally."

As a work of Iranian modernism, Bank Melli represents an anti-monumentalism, which nevertheless endures in the modern city. Rather than conceiving it as a national symbol, Utzon planned a generous, flexible building embedded in city life: Bank Melli was an analog to a bazaar, dedicated to people who traditionally would gather under narrow slits of light. A key reason for Bank Melli's success lies in its capacity to evoke architectural memory. Together with the light and spatial hierarchy within the bank's platform[3], the Utzonian wall, the threshold, and the space's flexibility are memorable architectonic elements for Persians. The wall serves as a historically significant element in this particular context, a matter of living in a harsh climate and within the culture of veiling; the wall becomes a generator of external simplicity and internal complexity, working with the protagonist element, namely the roof. The threshold, which coexists with the wall, is the traditional nexus of domesticity and city life.

Bank Melli is Utzon's single public building designed within an urban fabric, but it has not become an icon for contemporary Tehran. Its muted façade is set back from the street to emphasize horizontality rather than verticality. The vast threshold is slightly elevated from street traffic by a ribbon of steps running across the façade, making a scene open to small street vendors or for public congregation. The building has an articulated roof placed on three parallel walls over a platform. Post-tensioned concrete beams expressed the roof lighting in the banking hall where the staircase led to the first and second floors above the entrance.

Inside, Utzon emphasized flexibility: "[W]e have succeeded in accomplishing a complete flexibility in the bank fittings. It is, in fact, possible to change indefinitely the disposition of rooms, since there does not exist any structure that may hinder the components of the building."[4] For Utzon, flexibility was a strategy of "spatial redundancy," a creation of excess capacity, which resembles an Iranian room, yet as a complete work rather than an unfinished disposition of architecture, which Adrian Forty elucidates in his description of the word within architectural criticism of the 1950s.[5]

Utzon's vision went beyond political notions of Iran's National Bank offering a narrative of modern Iranian architecture. The architect was not consumed by concepts like nationality and identity, or superficial interpretations of national and international. The bank authority, however, neglected some of Utzon's ideas during the construction stage. Munk Hansen dredges up details of Utzon's furniture proposals that received a flat refusal. He also remembers rejecting the proposal to partially clad interior side walls "with rough perforated brick." The client preferred luxurious-looking American acoustic panels.

Utzon's involvement ended with the inauguration of the building in 1962. Early modifications of the building began in the late 1960s: in the façade, travertine cladding was added on exposed parts of concrete walls and later on the beams. The layout of the 'dispatching hall' changed too: the counter moved, and the southern wall was opened towards the backyard by a row of windows.

In the 1970s, the client required a circular counter to provide a wider reception for customers, apparently the legacy of Mohsen Foroughi, the Iranian architect of Bank Melli's main branches.[6] Artificial lighting was installed between the V-shaped beams by 14 projectors of 2,000W, though Utzon's original lighting scheme had been sufficient.

At the end of 1978, the building bore witness to popular protests. Enghelab (Revolution) Avenue, where the bank is located together with Tehran University, bookstores, and publishers' offices, was a key muster point during the 1979 revolution. Demonstrators entered some offices, banks, cabarets, and cinemas, throwing documents and furniture out in the middle of the street, where they were set ablaze. On November 4, photographers captured broken signage on the façade and a huge fire in the street between the bank and cinema Diana opposite. In the chaos, protestors entered the heart of the banking hall.

In the 1980s, following the revolution, Bank Melli's technical office of the occasionally made alterations to the building. Spread out in the banking hall are all the services, including the accounting department and guardroom on the ground floor, and administrative departments on the first and second floors. This resulted in a mixture of hierarchical positions, all able to look upon the hall. The upper floors were occupied by the meeting room, prayer room, and a ping-pong room.

A major renovation in 2010 extended the area for workstations partitioned by ready-to-assemble elements in the hall, re-paved the floors, installed LED lighting under the V-shaped beams, added a glass partition wall on the first-floor balcony, to separate the space from the atrium, replaced the frequent mullions on the façade with a lesser number of aluminum double-glazed windows, filled in openings between three beams above the entrance, and added steel handrails to the steps.

In 2015, aluminum composite panels covered the façade, as part of an effort by the bank to rebrand itself as more upmarket. Alerted by social media, architects and students protested on the bank's steps, leading to the removal of the cladding and later, in 2019, to the listing of Bank Melli as a National Heritage Monument. Yet, following protests of November 2019 against the petrol crisis, the bank intensified its security in 2021 by solidifying half of the entrance next to ATMs with metal panels.

Private interests associated with state dogmas have adversely affected what the bank is. In addition to symbolization and capitalization as the political underpinnings of Pahlavi national projects like Bank Melli, after the revolution, there was a tendency towards the privatization of the public domain. In the bank, privatization serves as a sort of dictated setting: the silent ideology that shrinks public space, invisible but impacting everything. The building has lost dignity as a result. The initial changes to Utzon's design during construction and the many subsequent changes over the decades demonstrate the contrast between the architect's original vision and the interests of the bank's directors. This division has turned into a conflict between the bank and the public over the authenticity of the renovations.

notes

1 H.S. Møller and V. Udsen, *Jørn Utzon Houses*, (Living Architecture, 2004), p.23
2 Sadeghi, S and Dinani, A., "Between Red and Yellow: Utzon's Melli Bank in Tehran 1959–1962," *International Utzon100 Symposium, Utzon centre*, Aalburgh, 2018
3 See: Richard Weston, *Utzon: inspiration, vision, architecture* (Blodal, 2002) and Michael Asgaard Andersen, *Jørn Utzon: drawings and buildings* (Princeton Architectural Press, 2013)
4 Jorn Utzon, "The Bank Melli Tehran, Iran," *Zodiac*, Vol. 5, 1959, p.94–95
5 Adrian Forty, *Words and buildings: A vocabulary of modern architecture*, Vol. 268. (Thames & Hudson, London, 2000)
6 Mohsen Foroughi (1907–1983) developed his proposals mainly by Bank Melli: Bandar Anzali (1939), Tehran (1948), Rasht (1951), and Bank Rahni (1956)

building credits

architect: Jørn Utzon

photo credits

p.272, 278 (all), 280 (all), 282 (all): Hans Munk Hansen
p.275: Michel Setboun
p.277, 279 (all): Parasto Nowruzi
p.281 (all), 283 (all): Milad Panahifar

2019
1186 ENGHELAB STREET
TEHRAN, IRAN

278

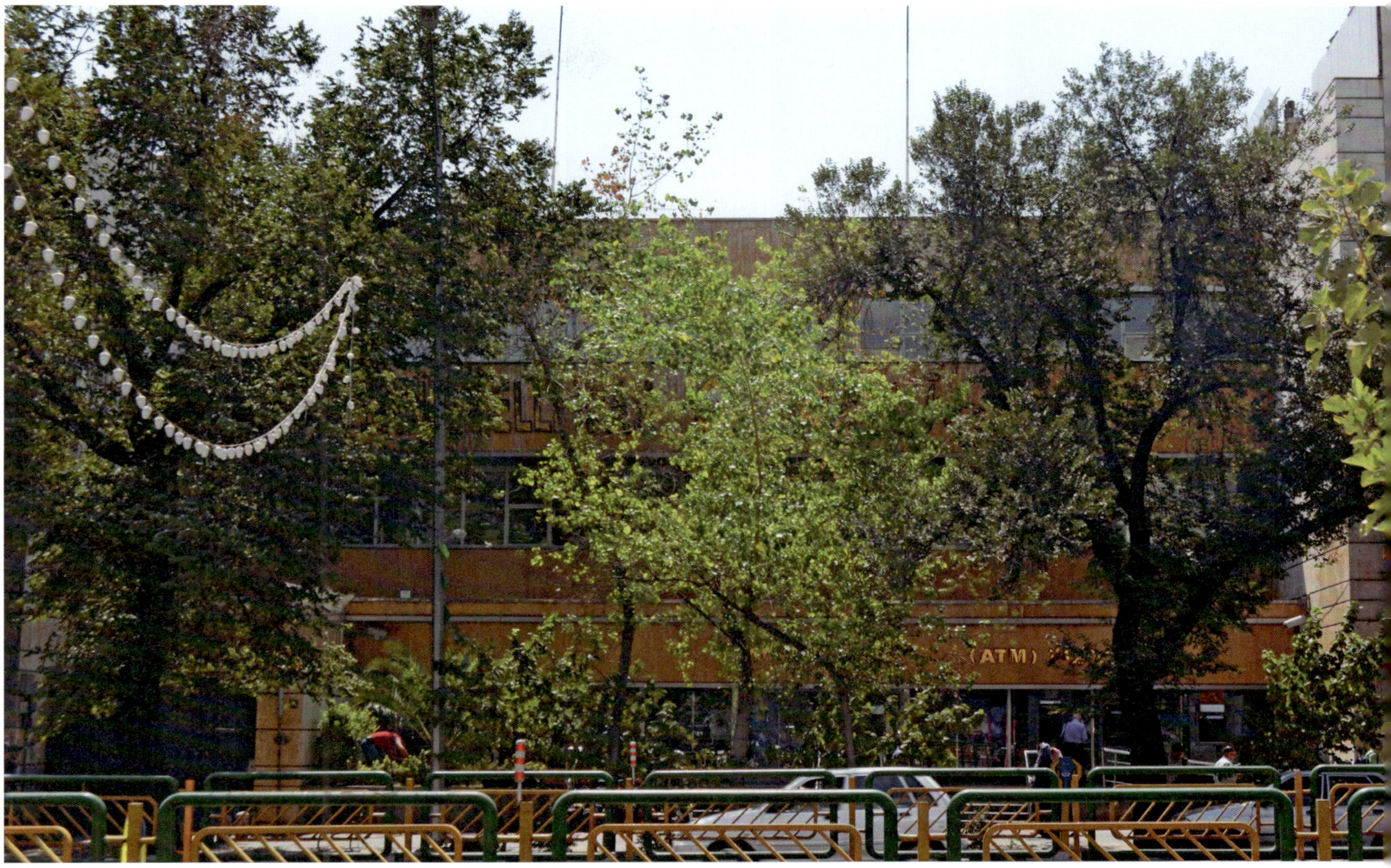
(ATM)

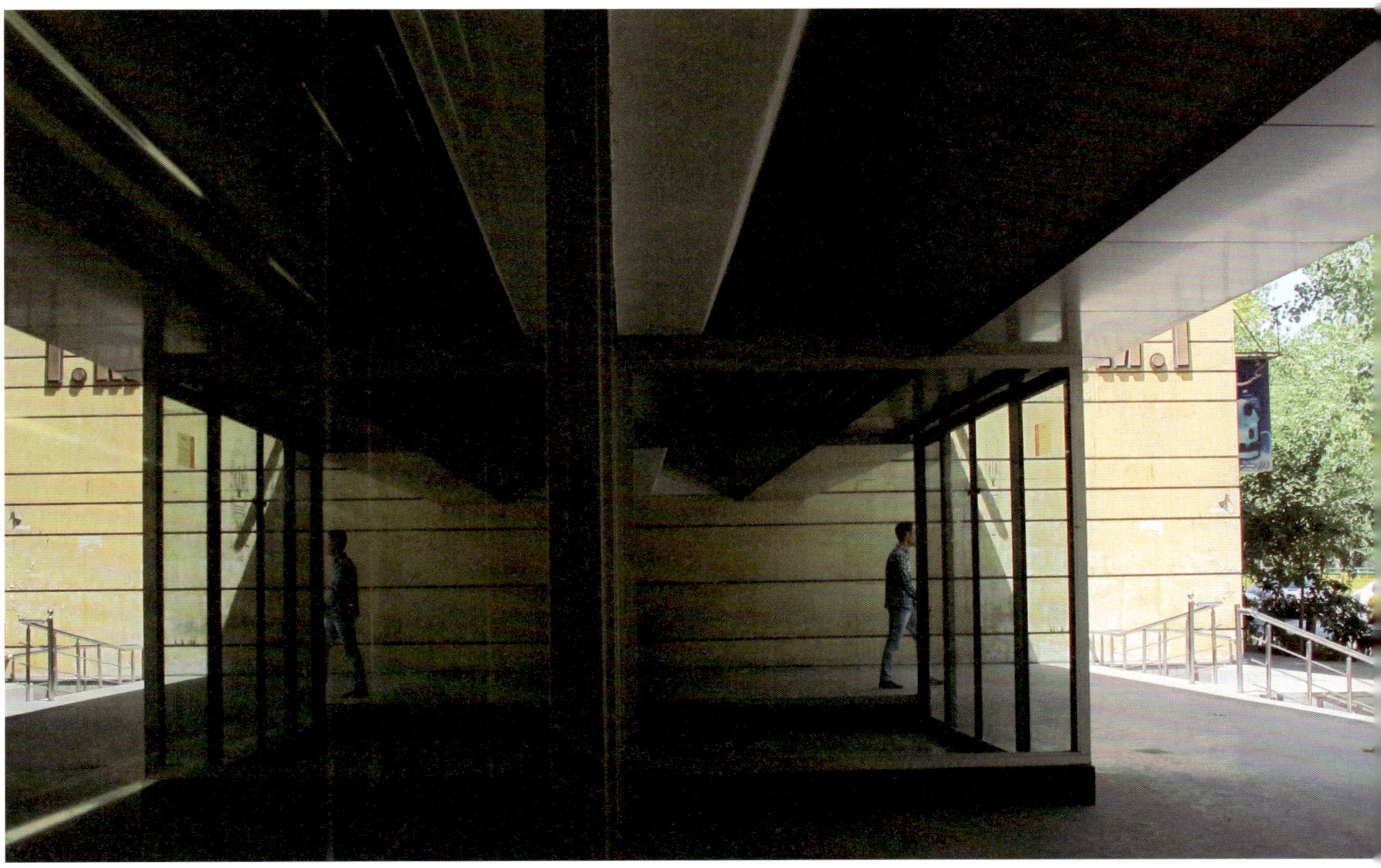

280

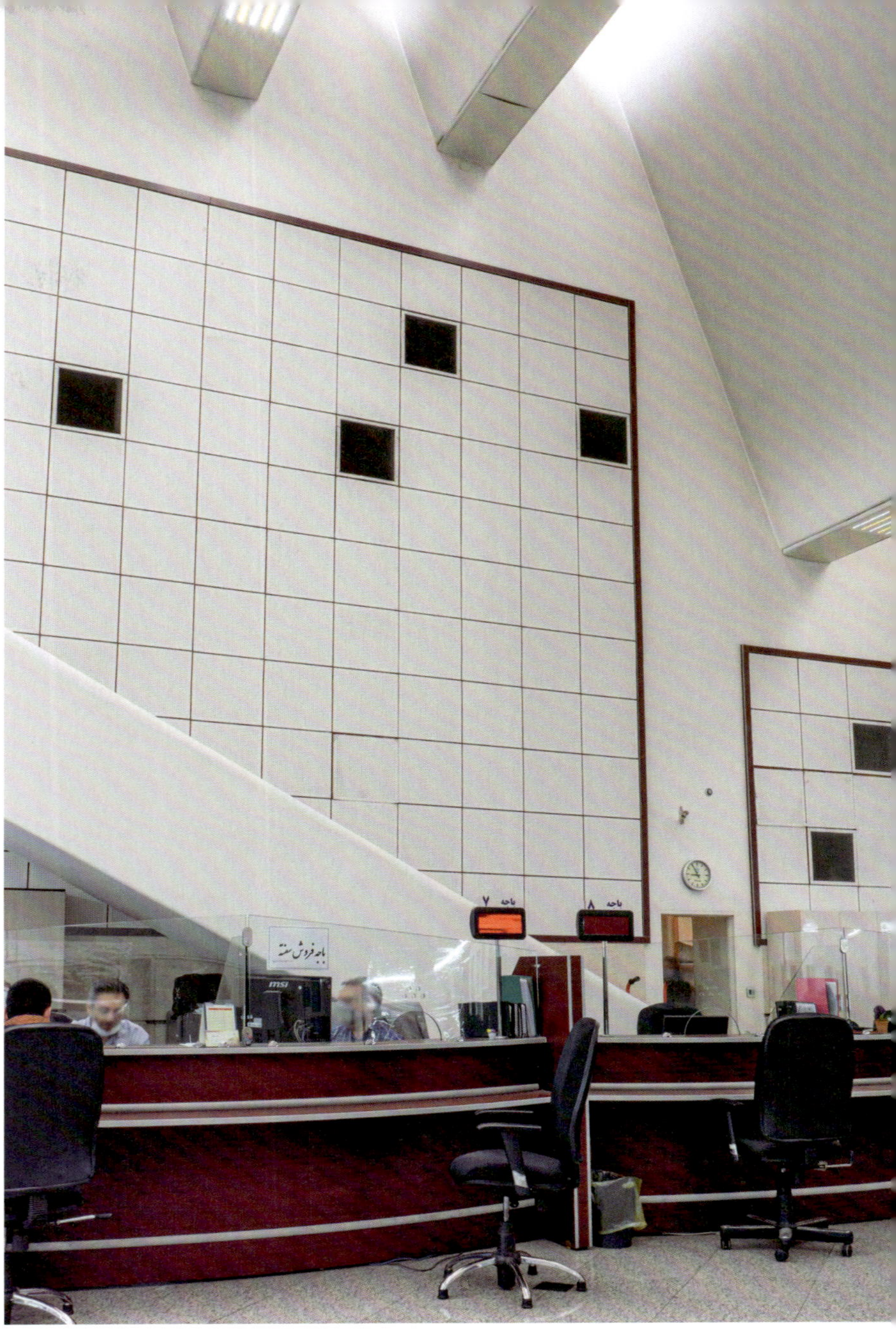

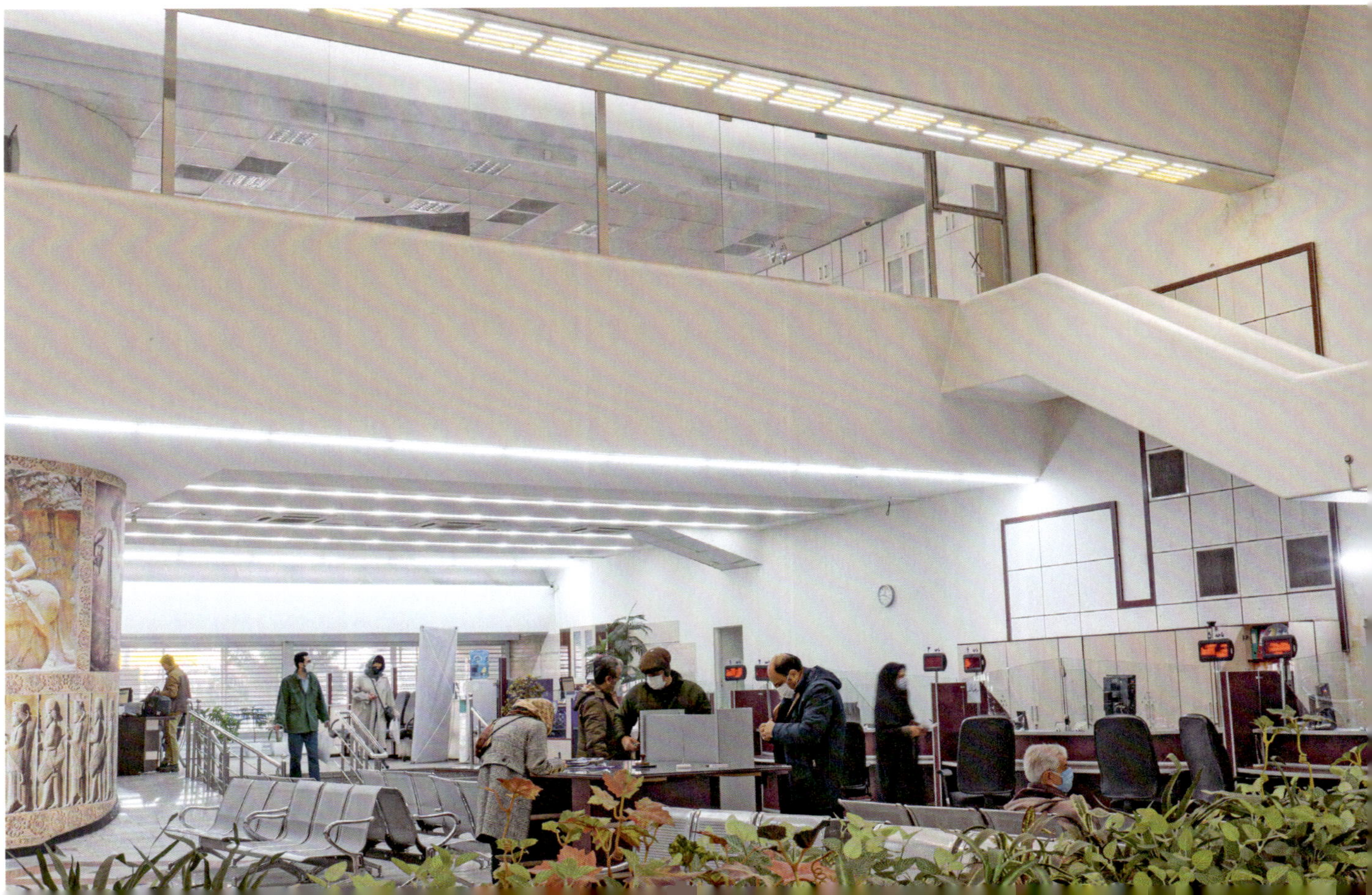

282

283

1962

Ashley Schafer

BACARDI HEADQUARTERS

How 60 years of occupying Mies' black bat base camp yields minimally increased partitions and a new soda machine...

Situated on a tropical garden site adjacent to the northern edge of Mexico City in the municipality of Tultitlan, the Bacardi Headquarters stands as Mies' sole built project in Latin America. Commissioned in the late 1958 and opened in 1961, publications of the building in the architectural press and in books has largely been overshadowed by Mies's first Bacardi headquarters project in Cuba (scuttled by the revolution) and its northern liquor headquarters rival, the Seagrams Tower in New York. When it openend a few of the major contemporary periodicals (Architectural Forum, Architectural Design Architectural Record and Bauen und Wohnen) covered it minimally in two to three pages, with an accompanying project description, usually alongside other Mies office buildings. *Bauen Und Wohnen*'s article offered a bit more detail, describing

Mies' use of material (steel, travertine, and Yucatan mahogany), the gridded modularity, and the environmental controls (extoling the virtues of the heat-absorbing glass and natural ventilation achieved by combining roof mounted fans with dampened openings at the bottom of the perimeter). Also noted in the short text was that the office included forward leaning electric technology: "Each desk is equipped with a power point."[1]

The building's greatest champion, Sigfried Giedion, thought highly enough of the newly built headquarters to include it in *Space, Time, and Architecture*, published just a year later, in 1962. He lavished praise on the modestly sized structure, as "possess[ing] the most sublime architectonic instrumentation" having "arrived at perfection through the smallest alterations of position and proportion." Although Giedion's assessment provides the most extensive documentation of the building, his text echoes the dominant narrative about the project focusing on its material and tectonic qualities and the company's intent to align its brand with a refined international corporate modernism. The focus on patronage and the failed Cuban commission circumscribe the building's position as corporate icon – a means to occupy the black bat.

Little has been written about the open offices themselves, designed as "one continuous space".[2] According to a Bacardi in-house publication, this was an "ideal office…where there are no partitions, where everybody, officers and employees, can see one another."[3] Ideal for whom?

One intention of the entire project may have been to promote loyalty among employees in the context of a family-owned business, yet as designed, the four corners, shielded behind the wood partition walls were designated for single executives with specific titles such as lawyer and manager, with the open are in the middle labelled "general office and sales area."

While the plan remains open today, a second level of hierarchy has been introduced with head-height wooden partitions surrounding the desks along the exterior walls, diminishing the status of the desks in the center of the space, which only have low partitions. Air conditioning has been added to the landscape of recessed canned lights on the ceiling to compensate for the heat gain and the curtains seem to be drawn more often than not.

As designed, the inset diminutive footprint of the glass-enclosed first floor –and its minimal function and furnishing as reception– allowed the second floor to float over the travertine ground plane that extends from the exterior to interior. In the intervening years, the open volume has suffered from horror vacui and corporate branding in extenso. The two Barcelona chairs and daybed have replaced with Bacardi memorabilia display cases, an open bar and glass conference rooms, the exterior walls of which are occluded by large promotional posters. The new bright red fire alarm pulls and signage favor Bacardi's corporate colors rather than Mies's original scheme of black, white, beige and wood.

Outside, the breezeway and lawn immediately adjacent has been filled with benches and chairs (in red). The most jarring disruption is a tall red box pushed against the travertine core –a soda vending machine with the iconic logo "Coca-Cola"– the traditional mixer for the classic "cuba libre" cocktail that catapulted Bacardi's rise to prominence in the 1960s.

notes

1 Mies van der Rohe,"Verwaltungsgebäude Ron Bacardi bei Mexico-City." in: *Bauen Und Wohnen*, 16(10), p.407-411 (1962)
2 Mies van der Rohe, Bacardi building, Mexico City in: *Architectural Design*, 32(10), p.470 (1962)
3 Samuel Gallo, *Bacardi 1862–1962* (1962), n.p.

building credits

client: Jose "Pepín" Bosch
architect: Ludwig Mies van der Rohe

photo credits

p.284, 290 (all): Balthazar Korab
p.286–287, 289, 291 (all): Arturo Arrieta

2019
AUTOPISTA QUERÉTARO-MÉXICO
TULTITLÁN, MEXICO

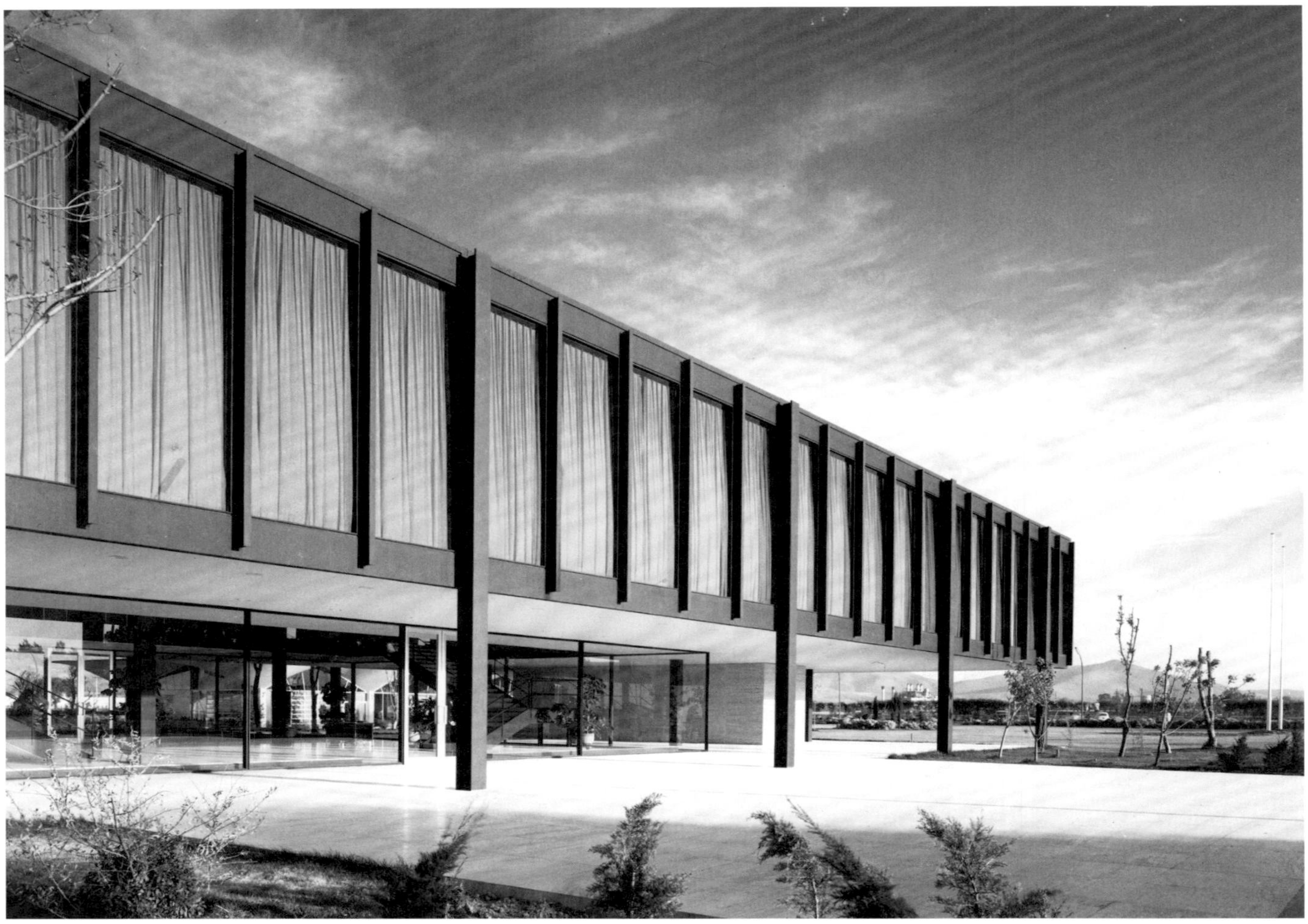

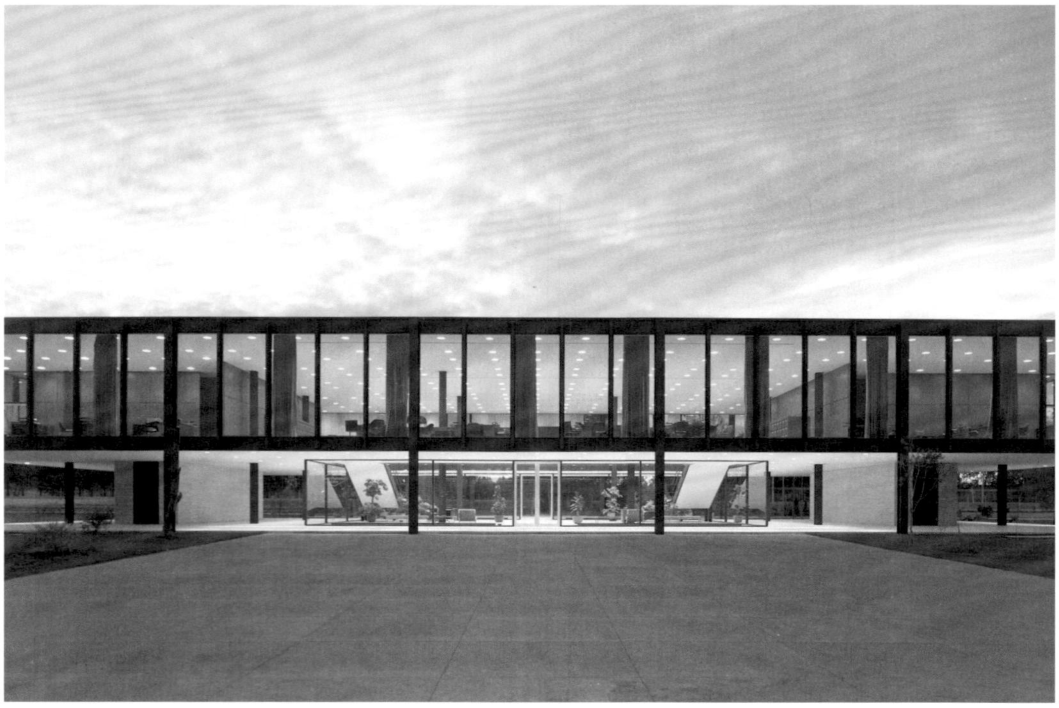

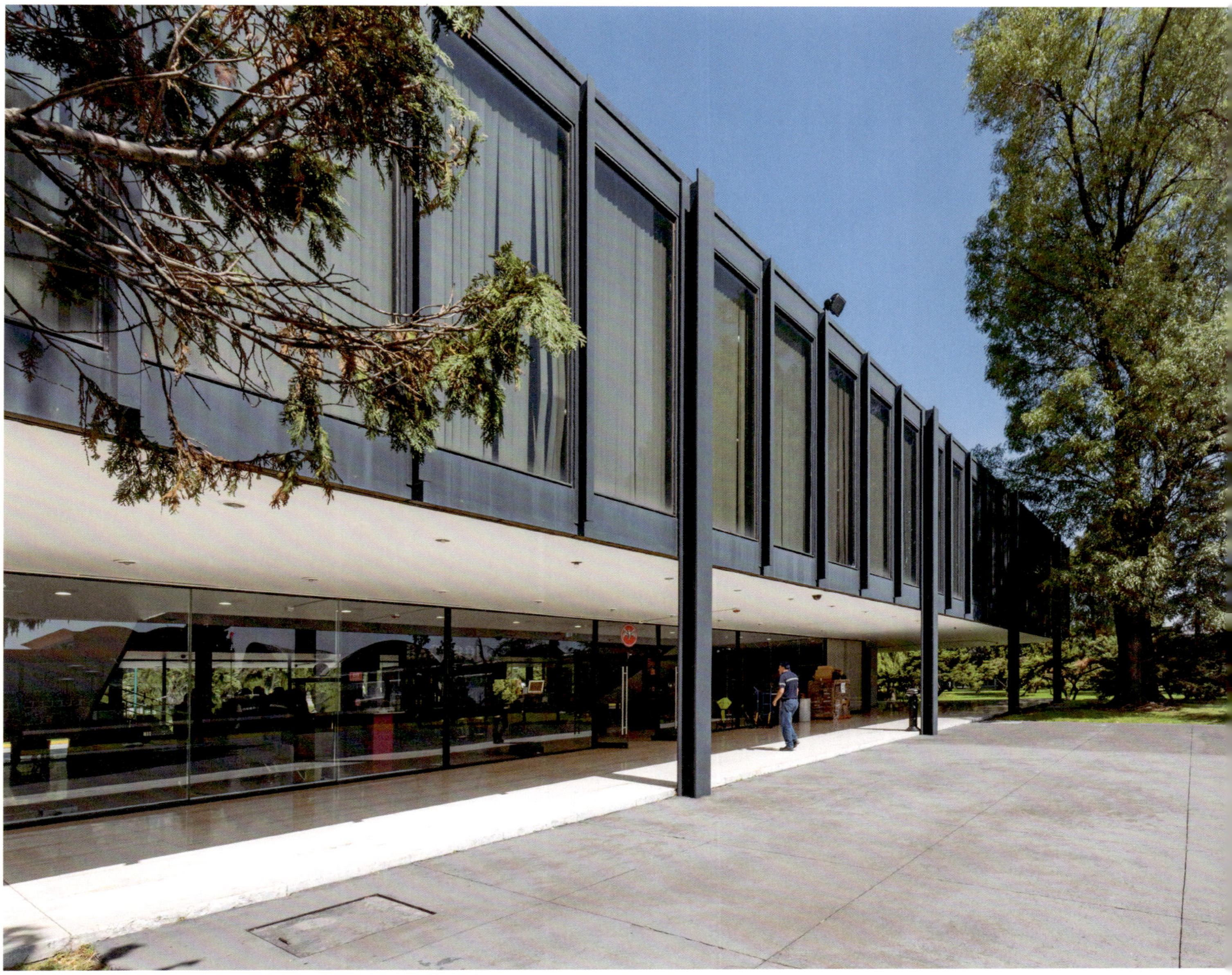

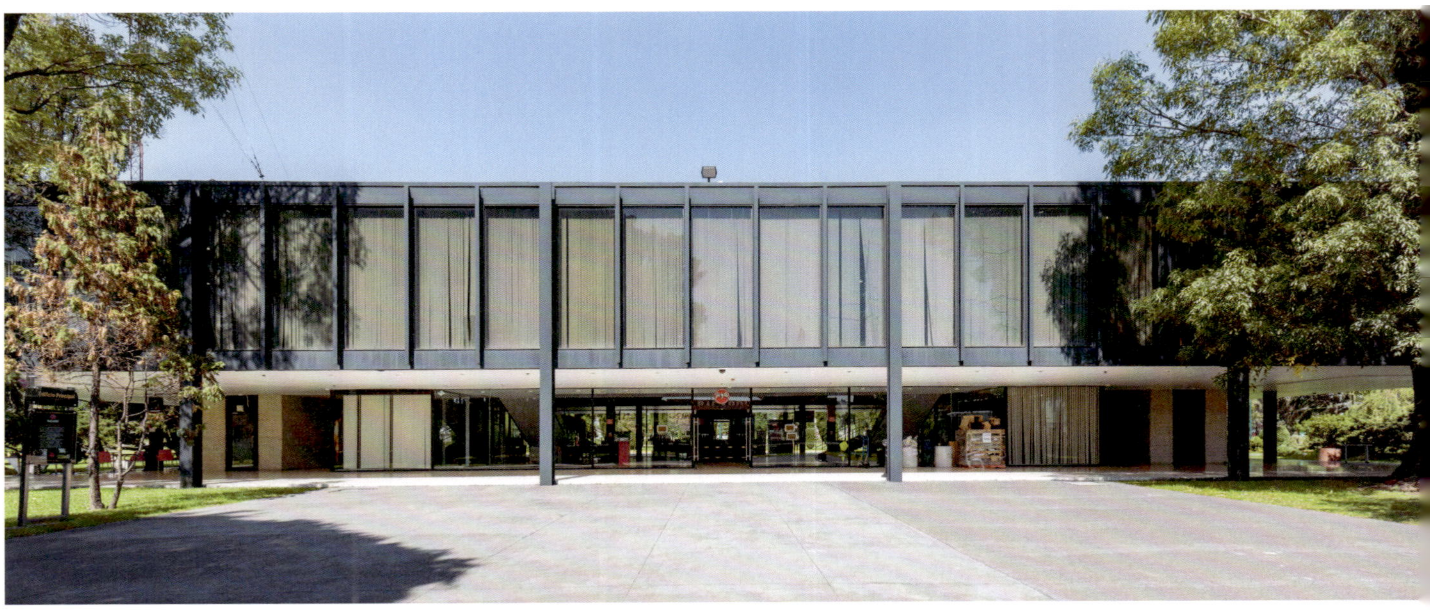

1964

Ruth Baumeister

UNILEVER HEADQUARTERS

A building twice blessed by municipal concessions, before it was even completed, and again as it was transformed...

On September 19, 1958, when a group of internationally acclaimed architects was invited to board a hot air balloon for a tour over Hamburg, it was not for pleasure: the aim was to study the city. The goal was to envision how a high-rise they were about to design for a competition would affect the city's skyline in the future. After many years of tiresome negotiation with the city, Unilever, which had moved its headquarters to Hamburg in 1948, had threatened to leave town unless they were allowed to build a representative building in the very center. This led to one of the largest and most debated demolition acts in the history of the city: 1,500 people and 100 businesses were displaced for it. What was saved from the bombings of the Second World War had to finally make way for a new myth. As the local press put it, "Citizens of Hamburg should no longer have to bow

BLATT 10

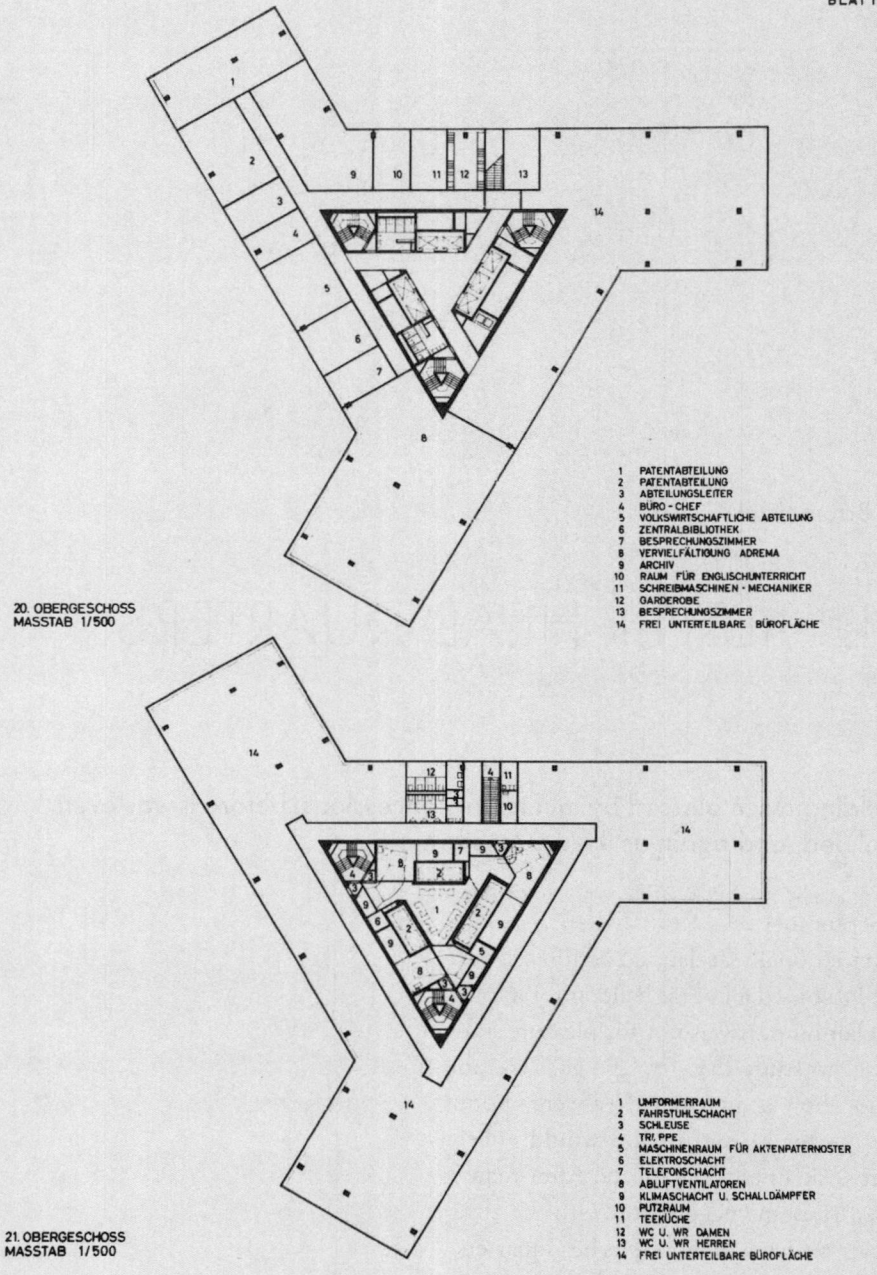

**20. OBERGESCHOSS
MASSTAB 1/500**

1 PATENTABTEILUNG
2 PATENTABTEILUNG
3 ABTEILUNGSLEITER
4 BÜRO - CHEF
5 VOLKSWIRTSCHAFTLICHE ABTEILUNG
6 ZENTRALBIBLIOTHEK
7 BESPRECHUNGSZIMMER
8 VERVIELFÄLTIGUNG ADREMA
9 ARCHIV
10 RAUM FÜR ENGLISCHUNTERRICHT
11 SCHREIBMASCHINEN - MECHANIKER
12 GARDEROBE
13 BESPRECHUNGSZIMMER
14 FREI UNTERTEILBARE BÜROFLÄCHE

**21. OBERGESCHOSS
MASSTAB 1/500**

1 UMFORMERRAUM
2 FAHRSTUHLSCHACHT
3 SCHLEUSE
4 TRI, PPE
5 MASCHINENRAUM FÜR AKTENPATERNOSTER
6 ELEKTROSCHACHT
7 TELEFONSCHACHT
8 ABLUFTVENTILATOREN
9 KLIMASCHACHT U. SCHALLDÄMPFER
10 PUTZRAUM
11 TEEKÜCHE
12 WC U. WR DAMEN
13 WC U. WR HERREN
14 FREI UNTERTEILBARE BÜROFLÄCHE

their heads trying to take a look through the crack in the hoarding. With their heads raised they should, instead, look down at the swarm at their feet. This is where a proud administration building is going up, at a place which was formerly home to a foul smell and where sin was dwelling in seemingly cozy timbered houses."[1]

Surprisingly, none of the competing designs came into being. Otto Jungnickel, head of Unilever's building department, developed an entirely new scheme which was realized in cooperation with HPP architects (Hentrich, Petschnigg and Partners), who were runners-up in the competition. They envisioned the project as an urban landscape dominated by a high-rise solitaire, surrounded by a generous, open green space nevertheless to be perceived from and accessed by car. The high-rise had the shape of a windwheel, with a triangular core for services. It contained office space, a large cafeteria, an auditorium, and a three-level underground parking garage, among other facilities. From a gigantic ramp leading to the underground parking garage, visitors would get a heroic view of the building. Inside, open-plan office spaces, flooded with light, provided a breath-taking panorama of the city. It was the highest building in Hamburg, crowning the skyline. Illuminated at night, it appeared crystal-like, like a cross-breed of Mies' Berlin Friedrichstrasse skyscraper design (1922) and Lake Shore Drive in Chicago (1951). Unilever, like no other building in Hamburg, embodied the Wirtschaftswunder era and stood as a harbinger of a better future in post-war West Germany.

Was it a trick that led to the building's first major modification between 1961–63 – which took place even before its inauguration in 1964? The building department had approved a height of 20 stories. However, during construction criticism arose because of an ugly concrete stump sticking out of the otherwise elegant crystalline building. The discussion was heated, as it was feared that allowing a private company to build beyond what was allowed by law would set a precedent. Finally, because of its importance for the city's economic growth, Unilever received permission to add another two stories to the tower, thus hiding the stump. Was the argument about aesthetics simply a means of finally obtaining permission to build higher? The mystery remains unsolved. Undoubtedly, though, it made the building an icon in Hamburg's skyline.

Unilever remained the one and only tenant for about five decades, until it finally decided to move, into a new, smaller building in Hamburg's new HafenCity development. Long before that, in 1989, they had sold their building to Union Investment, who – after Unilever moved out in 2009 – once again hired HPP for the renovation of the building, which had been landmarked in the meantime.

During the renovation, between 2009–13, the architects faced three major challenges: The new owners tasked HPP with increasing the rental space and turning the tower into a multi-tenant building. Meanwhile, the building department demanded urban densification and mixed-use, leading to the transformation of the Unilever building into what is today called the Emporio Quarter. To allow that transformation, the city – as in the beginning of the tower's life – had to make concessions. The building's landmark status would apply mainly only to the façade, artworks, and parts of the interior, like the entrance lobby, and the auditorium in the basement.

On the urban level, an eight-story complex, including a hotel, bar, restaurant, and apartments, was erected where Unilever's underground garage used to be. Along Dammtorwall, Dragonerstall, and Valentinskamp, this new block changed completely the landmarked design of the site along with the views of the tower.

On the building level, additions were facilitated through a process of extension and optimization: the existing tower was stripped to its bare structure, two (more)

Neubau UNILEVER-HAUS
SCHAU-TRIBÜNE

UNILEVER-HAUS
Geschätzter
BETON
ALUMINIUM
GLAS
ERDBEWEGUNG
3600 t
25400 cbm
170 t
35280 qm
80000 cbm

floors were added on top, and mechanical services that were originally housed in two upper levels were relocated to the basement. At the same time, the building was freed from toxic material and equipped with a sprinkler system. Due to light pollution regulations, the building may no longer be illuminated. It has lost its crystal appearance at night.

The owner's demand for a multi-tenant building with flexible units of various sizes required a modification of the ground plans, mainly in the service core: additional individual toilets, an extra elevator, an increase of elevator capacity. The Unilever building was based on a grid of 3.14 meters, making difficult an economical organization of different office sizes, especially single offices. A new grid was introduced, allowing

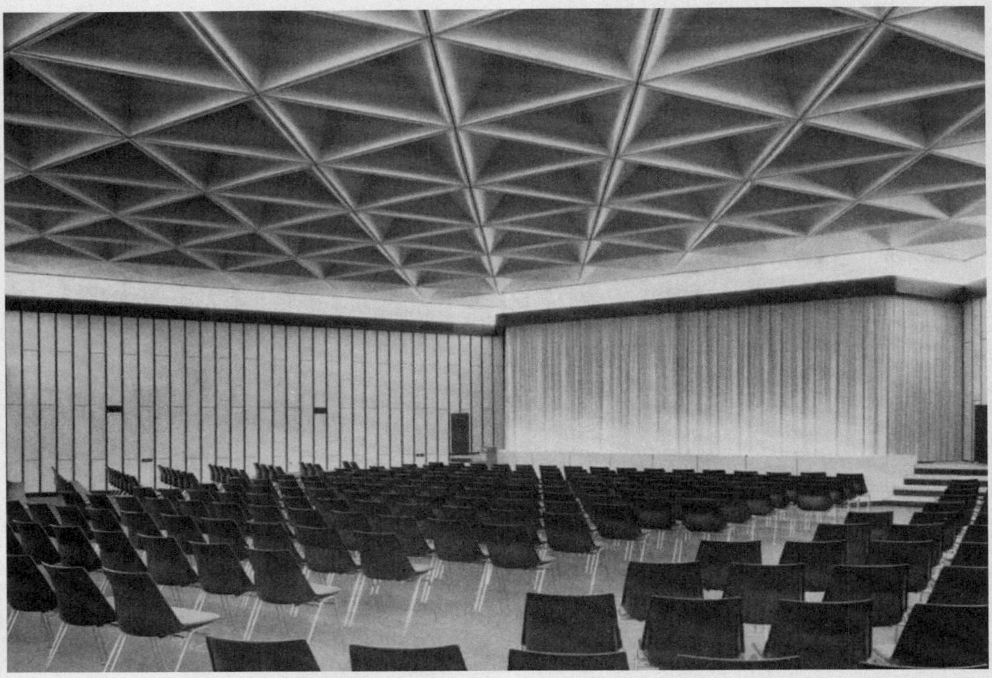

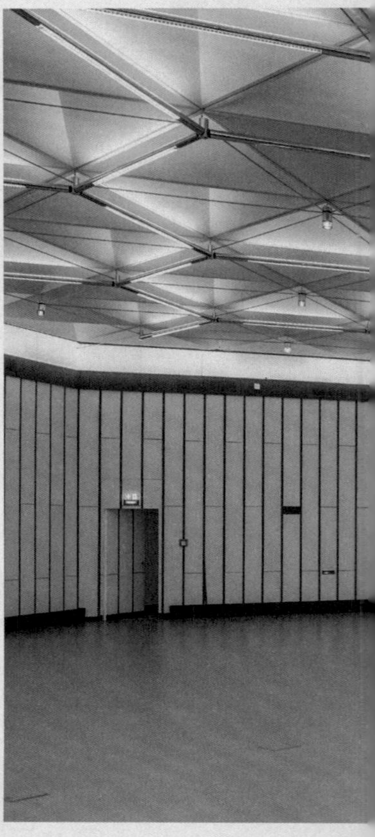

for a more flexible distribution of the ground floor area, which also had an effect on the design of the façade. Originally, the building had a single-layer glass façade and windows were not operable. It was equipped with the JETTAIR 3 pipe-high-pressure induction system for heating and ventilation. What was high-tech in 1964 performed poorly in terms of contemporary standards for interior climate and sustainability. A new double-skin façade in box construction, with an exterior skin resembling the original façade and an interior climate-proof skin with operable windows was installed. Removal of the convectors along the façade and the installation of a heating and cooling ceiling system further increased rentable space. While the original structural system of the floor slabs was exploited to an absolute minimum (10 cm concrete + 3 cm screed), the rather generous ceiling heights allowed for the installation of the new ceiling system and a raised floor.

When asked about the contradiction, in the fact that the slabs were structurally absolutely optimized, while the loadbearing columns and trusses were dimensioned in such a way that they finally allowed for the addition of further floors, Rainer Kaiser, HPP project architect in charge of the renovation, answered with a smile, "That is a good question! I could not tell for sure, but there is a good chance that our guys back then already envisioned the possibility of adding a couple of floors more in the future!"[2]

notes

1   Edith Oppens, *Die Welt*, September 23, 1961.
2   Interview with the author, September 2, 2019.

building credits

client: Unilever
architect: HPP architects (Hentrich, Petschnigg and Partners)

photo credits

p.292, 294, 296, 297, 298 (above): unknown
p.298–299, 301, 303: Jens Frederiksen
p.302: Hans Günther Suderow

2019
DAMMTORWALL 15
HAMBURG, GERMANY

302

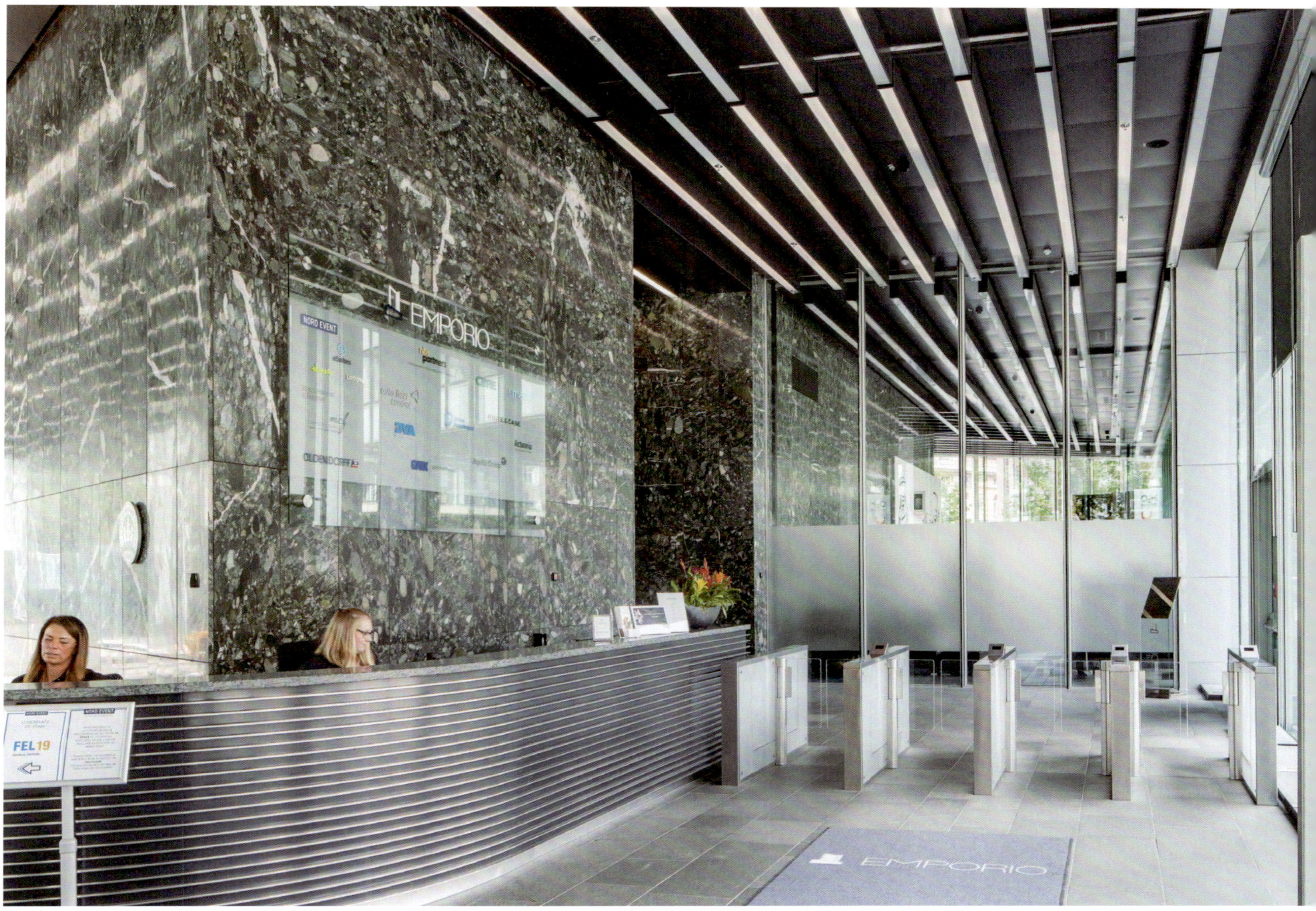
EMPORIO
NORD EVENT
FEL19
EMPORIO

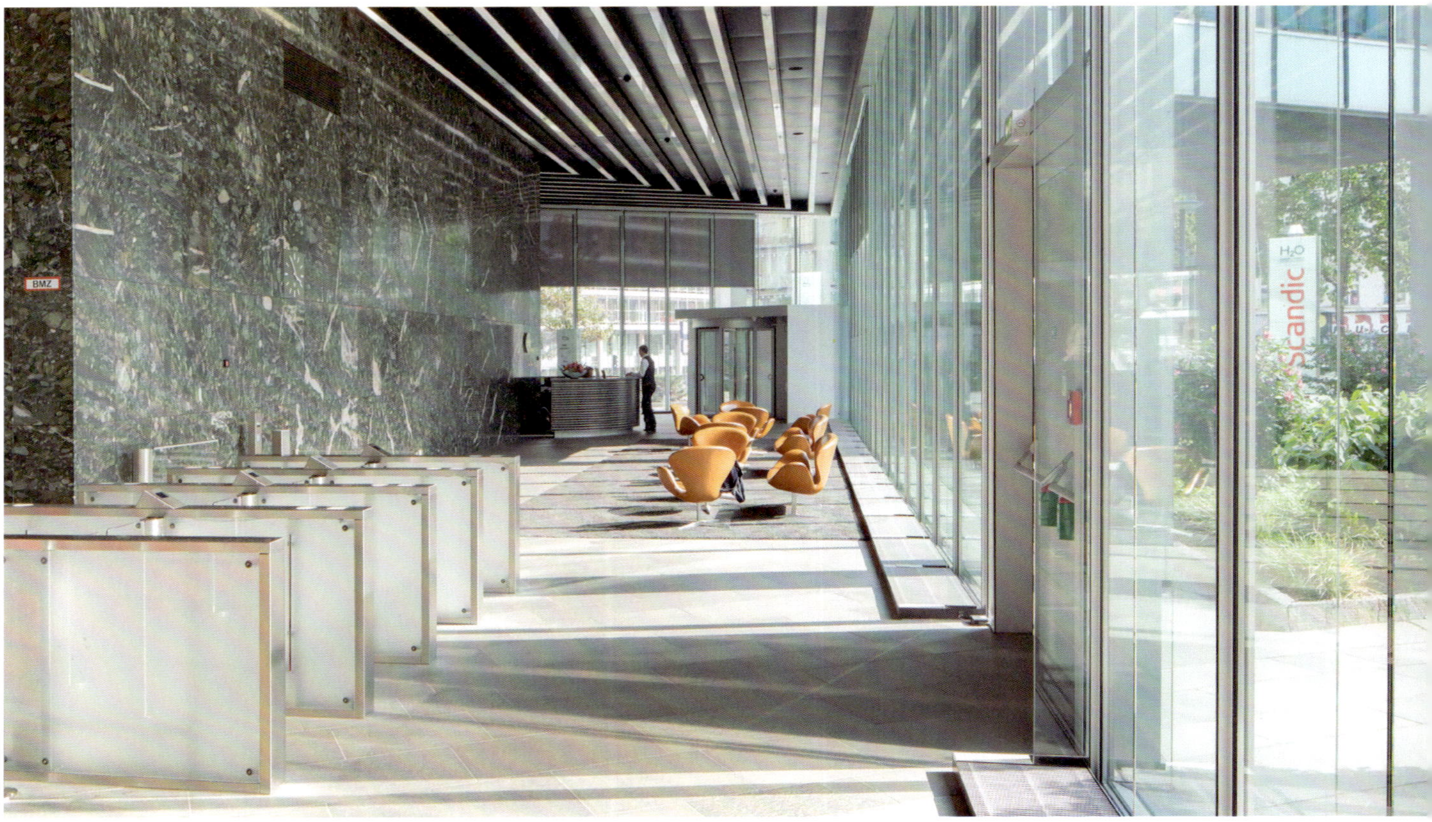
BMZ
Scandic

JOHNSON WAX HEADQUARTERS EUROPE

1964

"Mr. Johnson's relationship with architecture was very strong. He had commissioned Frank Lloyd Wright to design his headquarters in Racine, Wisconsin in 1936. Maaskant initially proposed quite a reserved sleek rectangular structure, more in line with his earlier works. In response Johnson Jr. delivered the message from his father, who he said he "doesn't like normal buildings." He wanted something more special, so Maaskant, versatile as he was, went for it. After the meeting, he instructed his team to design something more radical, while he figured a Y-shape with his arms. The team took it from there. Maaskant was a good listener, put his client first, delivered on time and on budget. He had the benefit that he was mostly speaking with the founders of the companies directly, mostly hands-on types, with organizations that might have also been less complicated than they are now. His architectural values also resonated with qualities found in the clients' companies: ideas of concentration, streamlining, flexibility, quality, iconicity, types of excess, abundance, etc. There was a clever trick he used when presenting, which other architects have also mastered. During the client meetings he mostly focused on extremely practical details, through which he avoided speaking about concepts. This preserved the space for him to define aesthetics and content. It was a way for him to keep control over the design process."

— **Interview with Michelle Provoost**, author of *Hugh Maaskant: Architect of Progress* (nai010, 2012).

building credits
architect: Huig Maaskant

photo credits
p.304: unknown, p.305: Iwan Baan

2013
N201, GROOT MIJDRECHTSTRAAT
MIJDRECHT, THE NETHERLANDS

305

ERIEVIEW TOWER 1964

The early 1980s presented the first real crisis for the building: according to the *Chicago Tribune*, the nickname, "Drearyview Tower", had surfaced. The generous central plaza in front of the tower had suffered as, the harsh climate left it uninhabited most of the year; its fountains broke and its paved surfaces cracked. Bell Ohio started leaving the tower in 1983, and in the same year the tower was sold to developer Richard Jacobs.

Jacobs commissioned Chicago-based Kober Belluschi Associates to regenerate the building. The plan was to build a shopping mall over the plaza, erasing the empty space and "softening the approach" to the tower. The mall was planned as a "crystal-domed structure" with 70 specialty shops, a food court, and bars. Ambitiously, it was named 'Galleria' after Galleria Vittorio Emanuele II, Milan's oldest shopping center. Bellushi said he wanted to capture its "strong urban vitality." Belluschi predicted that this "jewel-like project" could be the panacea for modern towers around the US that were similarly isolated in huge empty plazas. The regeneration project was a success. Occupancy rates in Erieview Tower increased from 50 percent in 1983 to more than 80 percent in 2009. But as the financial crisis unfolded, occupancy fell to less than 40 percent, with the Galleria standing largely vacant. In 2017 the tower was added to the National Register of Historic Places, making it eligible for tax credits. A year later, the building was sold once more to developer and local parking lot magnate James Kassouf. In the fall of 2021 Kassouf announced that besides 227 high-end apartments, a Marriot W hotel will take residence in the tower by 2024. The Galleria is set to undergo a transformation into a lifestyle center with a spa and gym, with heated parking garage underneath.

building credits

client: Anthony J. Celebrezze
architect: Wallace Harrison, Max Abramovitz

photo credits

p.306: Abramovitz Archives at Columbia University, p.307: Bethany Roman, Kayla Eland

2017

1301 E. 9TH STREET
CLEVELAND, OHIO, US

1964

Mildred Reed Hall, Edward T. Hall
The Fourth Dimension in Architecture

JOHN DEERE HEADQUARTERS

A scrupulous anthropology of John Deere's machine for working

In 1975, eleven years after the completion of Eero Saarinen's John Deere Headquarters in Moline, Illinois, the acclaimed anthropologist couple Mildred and Edward Hall published their study of the performance of the building over its lifespan so far. Edward Hall was an intellectual sparring partner of Marshall McLuhan and Buckminster Fuller and had an interest in contemporary design. During the 1950s, he worked for the State Department, at the Foreign Service Institute (FSI), teaching cross-cultural communications skills to foreign service personnel, and wrote popular books on intercultural communication. In the 1960s, Hall pioneered the theory of proxemics, a new field of research on personal and public space across different cultures.

The Halls' study on John Deere's administrative center was the results of five years of annual visits and interviews with employees at every level, starting before they moved to the new building. Deere's CEO Bill Hewitt gave the couple complete access and covered the Halls' travel and expenses. They published their report in 1975, and a year later the AIA journal picked it up, kick-starting a new section on learning from built buildings. That section endured for just two years.

The Halls celebrated a form of office working that is antithetical to our contemporary office thinking. They praise the office as a machine for working, acknowledging that the new John Deere HQ made everyone work harder. The Halls found that employees hardly seemed to miss any vestige of coziness, color, or "MickeyMouse" personal objects. Employees enjoyed the building's openness and generosity, its beautiful, landscaped surroundings, and its attention to detail. The new HQ even influenced what people wore to work. The Halls credit the close collaboration between the CEO and the architect for the transformation, and note that other office projects should learn from this model.

The Halls' survey questions – What would you like to change in the building? What do you think of your workplace? – reflect a pragmatism unburdened by the theories such as Marxism, non-western cultures, semiology, and language which were informing architecture discourse in Western Europe in the late 1960s, . The post-CIAM Forum movement was deeply involved in more Marxist social theory and borrowed from other famed anthropologists like Claude Lévi-Strauss, or an early Noam Chomsky, which led to linguistic inspired architectural theories on structuralism and influential works like Christopher Alexander's Pattern Language (1977). Without a political agenda the Halls celebrate an increase in productivity and worker efficiency for a corporation in an unfettered way.

The legacy of the Halls surveys lives on in contemporary human resources research like the Leesman Index and in different HRM platforms, used by large corporations to track employees' happiness through mostly short and more frequent online polls. Within the most commonly used online tools, most attention has turned towards immediate surroundings of workers like the quality of the furniture or physical well-being and other themes like social relationships within an organisation. The representational quality that the Halls found in the Deere building faded. Compared to the extensive in-person interview by the Halls, the quality of the data also shifted. The online survey tools now produce dashboard rankings with brightly colored gages showing performance in numbers. AI (artificial intelligence) is expected to be used to generate automated strategic organisational considerations stemming from the harvested data. The quality that makes the Halls study still impressive is their ability to tie deep qualitative, longitudinal survey data collected over time directly into reflections on how architecture and design direct organisational benefit. Few corporations in the 21st century would make a similar investment in anthropology to elucidate architecture and thereby improve employees' productivity and satisfaction at work.

A collection of excerpts from their report, The Fourth Dimension in Architecture, are shared here:

THE HALLS' INITIAL INTEREST IN STUDYING JOHN DEERE:
My first thought was: "What are the people of this unpretentious, folksy town going to say? How will they respond when working in such surroundings? What will they think? What will the farmers think? What will be the effect on the rest of the farm machinery industry and even other architects?" It would be impossible to catalog the thoughts flooding my brain. Clearly, the building must be studied, and in detail, over a period of years. The first reality I faced was that there was neither time nor money for such a study. Nevertheless, my partner, Mildred Reed Hall, and I decided the project was too important to abandon without consulting Deere. Broaching the subject with economist Dr. Lester Kellogg, I was told he would take up the matter with William Hewitt, Chairman of the Board and Chief Executive Officer. In less time than I could possibly imagine, word came back. 'Bill' Hewitt was enthusiastic and would even underwrite expenses while we were in Moline. We had carte blanche, could go anywhere, talk to anyone, and see him whenever we liked. ... The first interviews were conducted before the building had been occupied ... We returned each year for four more years, reinterviewing our original sample because we wanted to know everything about the building: the details of the design and how it functioned, employee morale, maintenance and performance. Did the building fit the people like a comfortable old shoe or did it pinch or even not fit at all? We heard comments from people before they moved in, such as, "Now we are going to have to work in 'Rust Palace.'"[4]

FIRST VISIT
During the early phase of our research in 1964, we first visited the headquarters of Deere & Co., producers of farm equipment and machinery, in Moline, Illinois. The building – then in the final stages of construction but still unoccupied – is situated off a highway some ten miles from the town of Moline. The visitor travels along the north side of a wide fertile valley hugging low rolling hills on the left. Abruptly and without forewarning the visitor rounds a bend and there it is, a breathtaking structure in COR-TEN steel and glass that looks as though some genie has transported it intact from the hidden valley of a Japanese emperor and, having selected just the right surroundings, set it down without disturbing a leaf. If this sounds romantic it is because we find it difficult to describe the impact of Saarinen's masterpiece. No photograph begins to do it justice because the camera works on very different principles from the eye and the brain.

FIRST INTERVIEWS: April 1964
During the first interviews, before the move, we wanted to know how much the employees knew about the building ... All but one person in our sample had seen the building at least once from the outside, and more than half of them had actually visited their own work area. The company had made a great effort to arrange tours of the building for each division and to acquaint employees with the building before the move. A majority of the 47 people in our sample liked the building. Most of them used very complimentary terms to describe it: beautiful, impressive, revolutionary, unique. Many said the building had "character and stature." Almost everyone commented on the beautiful setting – the grounds and landscaping. A few people had adverse comments and they use words like "crude, unpainted, disappointing." In thinking about how the building would affect them, most people cited the great advantage of having everyone in the company at one location. Most were preoccupied with their own workspace and therefore their responses were highly personal. Those who'd actually seen their workspace said it was well designed and equipped. There was a widespread feeling that the new building would have the effect of making people "sit up and work harder." Management-level personnel viewed this prospect with great favor. Some employees (especially lower-level employees) were less enthusiastic. A number of people feared the loss of informality they had enjoyed in their old offices and thought that they'd be "tied to their desks" more after the move.[5]

SECOND INTERVIEWS: October 1964

The second interviews, held four months after the move, gave people an opportunity to be quite specific in their comments about the building and their own workspace. Forty-one employees were interviewed. In describing the building, half the people mentioned its beautiful surroundings and all but one person used highly complementary words to describe the building itself. One person called it "our crystal palace." As to what they liked most about the building, they mentioned beauty of setting, their sense of pride in working for a modern, progressive company, and their sense of privacy in the rural location of the company. Changes they would make included none at all (most frequent response), improvement in the elevator service, and the addition of more color to the corridors. There were a few scattered comments about how hard it was to find the paper towel dispensers in the restrooms. As to their own workspace: over half were very pleased and most found it entirely satisfactory; only a small number felt they did not have adequate space and equipment. The arrangement of their workspace also drew favorable responses, a fact that Saarinen would have appreciated because he devoted a lot of time to the design of workspaces. Some people mentioned that adequate storage space encouraged them to be neat and some noted their improved performance and efficiency in the new building. Most people would not change anything in their work area. We included a question on the cafeteria and the work schedule because there had been some apprehension expressed about them at the time of our first interviews. They represented departures from the routine in their old offices before the move, but they had nothing to do with the building itself. The overwhelming majority thought the location of the building was great. A few said they missed being downtown where they could shop on their lunch hour.[6]

FINAL INTERVIEWS: April 1969

By the time of our final interviews in April 1969, our sample was reduced to 33 people. Some of our sample were on vacation or were ill, some had been transferred to another building, one or two had left the company. This attribution is to be expected over a five-year period ... The most striking thing about the general response to the building was the continued awareness and sensitivity to the beauty of the site. Again and again, we heard remarks about the building's beautiful surroundings and grounds. Most people mentioned this as the thing they liked most about the building. Appreciation for the beautiful pastoral setting more than offset the rare negative responses to the out-of-town location which we had heard in our interviews five years earlier. In addition to the beauty of its surroundings, most people mentioned the handsome character of the building itself — its modern, clean, comfortable appearance. There were three main changes that were suggested in redesigning of the building: 1. add color to the interiors — especially the corridors; 2. improve temperature-humidity control; 3. improve and relocate parking facility. A number of people said they found the low-key color schemes depressing and they wanted more color. Several people commented on the art (mostly paintings) which the company purchased and displayed near the elevators and along the walls in some corridors. People who appreciated the art wanted more. They felt it was a most welcome addition to the building itself and it added color and variety in the interiors. Most of the people commenting on the problem of temperature-humidity control were women. They noticed drafts in some locations and many of them observed that men didn't seem to feel these drafts but the women did. Women were also more aware of the lack of humidity in the building and complained of dryness in winter. The parking facility drew comments for the first time (by now they had been five winters in the building). Many people felt the parking facility was too far from the entrance, especially since there were no covered walkways. They said that in winter it was icy and difficult to walk from the parking facility to the building. Given the severe winters, several people suggested an underground parking area leading directly into the building. Also noted for the first time were some complaints about lack of privacy in their work areas. Many people felt that they were constantly "on display." Some of the secretaries in departments that had become overcrowded (due to unforeseen expansion) complained that the proximity of the desks made it impossible to work efficiently; they were constantly interrupted and felt they had to talk to people. Occasionally even men with private offices (with glass walls) observed that it was distracting to be peripherally involved with people in other offices. Employees from the Executive Floor (Second Floor) noted a lack of acoustical privacy. Sound travels office to office on this floor via heating and air conditioning ducts. To the question, "What do you think of your own workspace?", the majority expressed positive reactions ranging from "ideal" to "very adequate." The negative responses clustered around feelings of being crowded or dissatisfied with temperature control. Most felt that the arrangement of their workspace facilitated their work. There was very little clustering of responses to what changes they would make in their workspace. Most would change nothing at all. Other suggestions ranged from a desire to work near a window to redesigning the interior spaces of their desks. Most had made no change in their workspace since moving in but a few had been moved within their department as part of the reorganization. Almost everyone agreed that there was nothing in the design of the building that made it difficult for them to do their job. A few cited lack of privacy as a factor that hindered them. The effect of the building on work habits seemed generally very positive. Most thought the building had a decidedly positive effect on employee attitudes toward the company. They were grateful for the beauty and efficiency of their own work areas. A few noted that the new building was not as "cozy and friendly" as the older buildings. Most people noted a definite improvement in dress since the move to the new building. About 75 percent thought the building attracted better quality personnel and made recruiting easier. Most people did not think the building would become world-famous when they first moved in, although those people on the management and executive level did. About 90 percent said that it meant a great deal to them personally to work in a famous building. It was a source of pride and gave them prestige. 94 percent said the building was tremendously important to the company. They saw it as "improving the company image," increasing its prestige, giving the company international recognition, and helping the image of the entire farm industry. At the very end of the interview, we asked people if they had anything to add which we might not have touched on. Here are some replies: "I really look forward to going to work." (3 people said this) "People work better in this building." "It's as close to a perfect place to work as you'll find." "Everything about this building denotes quality." "Whenever I travel, I take pictures of the building to show my friends." "Everyone likes to work here, provided their boss is O.K." "The grounds are so immaculate you wouldn't think of throwing out a gum wrapper." "Salesmen really like to come out here." "Building and location are soothing."[7]

INTERPRETATION OF INTERVIEWS

Throughout the study, we were impressed by the strong positive reaction of most people toward this building. At the time of the second interviews (four months after the move into the building) many employees were rather like Cinderella in her new ball gown. They just didn't quite believe their newfound glory and they were just beginning to be aware of the tremendous impact the building was making on the outside world. Visitors were starting to appear from all over the world. By the time of the final interviews, they were quite used to the fact that the building was world-famous. The other thing that struck us most strongly was how hard people work. As we walked from one department to another, several days at a time we almost NEVER saw someone who was not hard at work. There's a minimum amount of "going to the water cooler." Many people originally commented on how efficiency had increased since the company moved into the building. Five years later we had this same strong feeling that an atmosphere of hard work prevails everywhere. Another thing we noticed right after the move and throughout our study was the great change in dress and appearance. Gone were the old sweaters and dowdy dresses that we'd seen in town. Everyone seemed to be dressed up to the building. Doubtless, this was reinforced by the fact that there is an army of visitors touring the building and employees are very much on display. Also gone was the old *atmosphere of easy-going informality in old buildings. We noted some complaints from earlier interviews had either disappeared or fallen off noticeably by the time of our final interview. These included: slow elevator service and short lunch hours. The slow elevator service was solved by resetting the elevators to "home" on the fourth floor and working out the usual bugs with elevator specialists. The new lunch hour had nothing to do with the building but people confused it with the building because it came about at the time of the move. When the company was located in town employees had an hour for lunch. After the move, the lunch hour was reduced to half an hour and the working day ended a half-hour earlier. This cut in lunch hour time required time for people to adjust and many of them resented it very much because it limited them in their contacts with friends. (Unless your friend has the same half-hour for lunch as you do, you cannot eat together as each department staggers its lunch hours.) The food in the cafeteria is another item we heard about which has nothing to do with the building — but again, people lump it all together. In our experience, people often feel strongly about food. It's a target for emotions that have nothing to do with food itself. Nonetheless, we listened to the complaints, which centered around high prices and poor food, and passed them along to the company. Neither complaint was justified, in our opinion. We ate in the cafeteria regularly and found the food less expensive and much better than most restaurant food. Perhaps the griping was due to the fact that people have to eat in the company cafeteria — with only a half-hour for lunch and no place nearby, where else can they go? The response to our final interviews was quite different from that to the earlier interviews. The last interview evoked more detailed data which convinced us anew of the value of a five-year study. When you come back and interview people three times (or more in the case of key personnel), they become more relaxed in their responses and the interviewer gets some perspective on the person and his or her problems.[8]*

THE BAD
In our interviews of Deere personnel, individual responses to the building varied widely. In contrast to some who felt inhibited by the building's design, there were several people (in product design, engineering and advertising) who mentioned that the building had actually changed their approach to their work. They felt freer to seek new solutions and to try things out. As one said, "This building changed my thinking and I'm not so much in a rut anymore." A few employees felt that their creativity as well as their own sense of individuality was hampered by the building. This was expressed as dissatisfaction with the fact that no one can personalize his or her own workspace. The design itself does not allow for "personal touches," and there are strict regulations preventing people from putting up pictures, photographs, maps, charts, etc. This is an effort on management's part to preserve the purity of design and keep out any 'Mickey Mouse' touches. Some people felt the building denied them privacy and they spoke of being "on display all the time." The large glass areas offer practically no visual privacy and most people are clearly visible to a number of others all day long. Even private offices have some glass walls. This imposes certain restrictions on people's behavior. You don't put your feet up on your desk or take off your necktie.

A few people mentioned to us that they found the building tiring. We began thinking about this and wondering what features contributed to this particular reaction. First, we thought of the work tempo in the building, which is very noticeable. You feel this when you walk into the building and as you go from one department to another. Everyone is working hard and pushing themselves. The building itself has a kind of "rapid beat" and is experienced by some as a little cold, a feeling that is contributed to by the florescent ceilings. Another factor that may be responsible for the feelings of fatigue is the fact that there are no areas where employees can gather informally — no lounges or meeting rooms. This means that on coffee breaks and at lunch hour people can only go to the cafeteria for socializing. There is no place other than one's workspace — and nobody socializes there! It is true, of course, that with a half-hour lunch nobody has much time to visit with friends anyway, but it strikes us that informal meeting places are needed.

This does impose definite restraints on individuality. As stated earlier, employees have virtually no way of personalizing their own space or their office. As one man put it: "When I leave my office at night, there is nothing left of me in it." The design of the building itself plus the company policy of not permitting anyone to decorate his or her own area does help preserve the integrity of interior design, but at a cost – the complete absence of the personal touch. As these comments indicate, this bothers people. "This building gives you the feeling that it's machine-made and mass-produced." "This building is monotonously functional." "We're inmates of the edifice." These complaints are common to many contemporary office buildings. One partial solution might be the establishment of a company art lending library where employees who so desire may borrow art and display it near their own desks and work areas.[9]

THE GOOD

In contrast to the employees working in windowless areas, most employees felt extremely enthusiastic about their environment and they felt that the furniture and equipment provided them with everything they need to function efficiently. Many of them also commented on their pleasure in being able to look out and see a lovely landscape filled with trees and wildlife. This tie with nature was something many people appreciated and took delight in sharing with us. ... Saarinen's [had] two objectives: "First, to provide functional, efficient space which would take care of future expansion in flexible ways." This he certainly achieved (only one department seriously underestimated its future growth). "Second, to create the kind of pleasant and appropriate environment which is part of Twentieth Century thinking." Here again, Saarinen succeeded admirably in most areas of the building.[10]

Perhaps the thing that most impressed us about the building on our last visit is the fact that after five years of occupancy it still looked brand new. For a building housing twelve hundred employees for five years this is no small achievement and reflects both the excellence of Saarinen's design and the superior maintenance provided by the company.

There are two kinds of communications received by employees about this building. First, employees respond to what the building does to them when they work in it ... Second, they respond to what the building tells them about the company. The most widely shared feeling about the building to emerge from our interviews was the tremendous pride in the company. Deere dealers from all over the Midwest bring their customers to visit on holidays and weekends. It's a major tourist attraction and emplhoyees love to show it off.[11]

On the management and executive level, the building symbolizes Deere's position in the industry. All the favorable publicity and awards have enhanced the company's image in the eyes of their own employees. On other levels of the company, employees seem very proud that the company thought enough of them to give them such a magnificent building. "They must really like us a lot to spend all this money on a building for us." This last reaction epitomizes our point that everyone looks at this building from his or her own point of view. The employee who works in the stock room or the typist may not care about the company's image in the industry, but he or she does see the building from his or her own point of view, and identifies with it strongly. One measure of the positive effect of the building in the company's public relations is the number of visitors who come to the building. Exact figures of visitors to the building are impossible to obtain, but since 1964 there have been over 366,000 registered visitors (through 1973). These figures do not include visitors who come to the building on weekends or after hours. Also not included are the many thousands who visited the building in June 1964 at the time of its dedication and open house, or the people who visit the building and do not register, or those attending community meetings held in the building. Our guess is that twice the number of the total figure would be more accurate.[12]

WHAT THE DEERE BUILDING CAN TEACH US

If the Deere Headquarters experience means anything at all, much more is required than just money and a cooperative client. A building, any building, is the result of many complex factors: personalities, talents, and skills of architect and client; availability of data about the company's exact requirements; interest in designing an environment that meets human needs – to name just a few. The Deere Headquarters was the result of an enormously complex and cooperative effort. Literally dozens of people worked on all phases of design and construction, and their combined efforts cannot be lightly brushed aside. But it is Saarinen who must receive the greatest credit. Some architects, without knowing it, build monuments to their own egos and have little concern for how their building will affect the people who use it. Saarinen was always aware of the individual who would occupy his spaces and of this person's needs. Saarinen was not interested in giving people "more of the same" – he wanted to give them the very best possible environment with the highest standards of quality. Today the American architectural scene is filled with buildings that don't work, laboratories that hinder research, university buildings that disregard student and faculty needs alike, libraries that satisfy the requirements of the custodial staff but ignore the needs of users and librarians, dormitories that offer totally inadequate facilities, even architecture departments where students are handicapped in their work. One might conclude that some architects don't care about satisfying human needs or they lack the know-how to design for people. Fortunately, such architects are in the minority. Most architects today, particularly the younger architects, are vitally interested in improving their knowledge of human needs and learning how to satisfy them. Saarinen has provided a very good model in his building-one we can all learn from.[13]

notes

1   See: Everett M. Rogers, "The Extensions of Men: The Correspondence of Marshall McLuhan and Edward T. Hall," *Mass Communication and Society*, November 17, 2009
2   Age 5 in the 1995 edition.
3   Donald Canty, "Evaluation: The Wonders and the Workings of Saarinen's Deere & Co. Headquarters," *AIA Journal 65*, August 1976, p.18–21
4   Canty, p. 5, 1995 edition
5   bid, p.55
6   p.56–57
7   p.58–61
8   p.61–62
9   p.26-31
10   p.34
11   p.26–27
12   p.39
13   p.48–49

building credits

client: William A. Hewitt
architect: Eero Saarinen and Kevin Roche, John Dinkeloo

photo credits

p.308 (all): Ezra Stoller / ESTO
p.317 (all), 319 (below): Pete Sieger
p.318 (all), 319 (above): unknown

2013
ONE JOHN DEERE PL
MOLINE, ILLINOIS, US

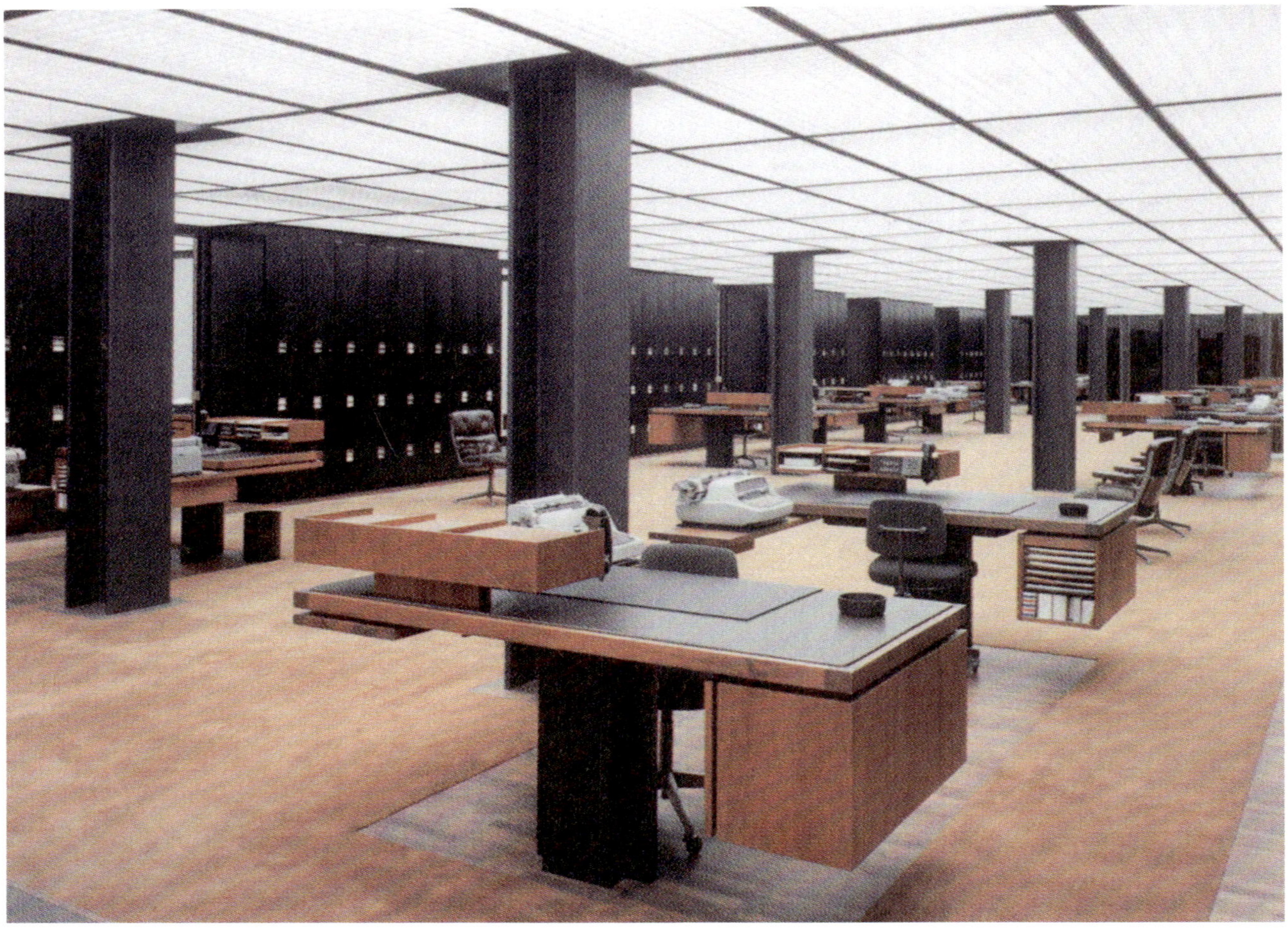

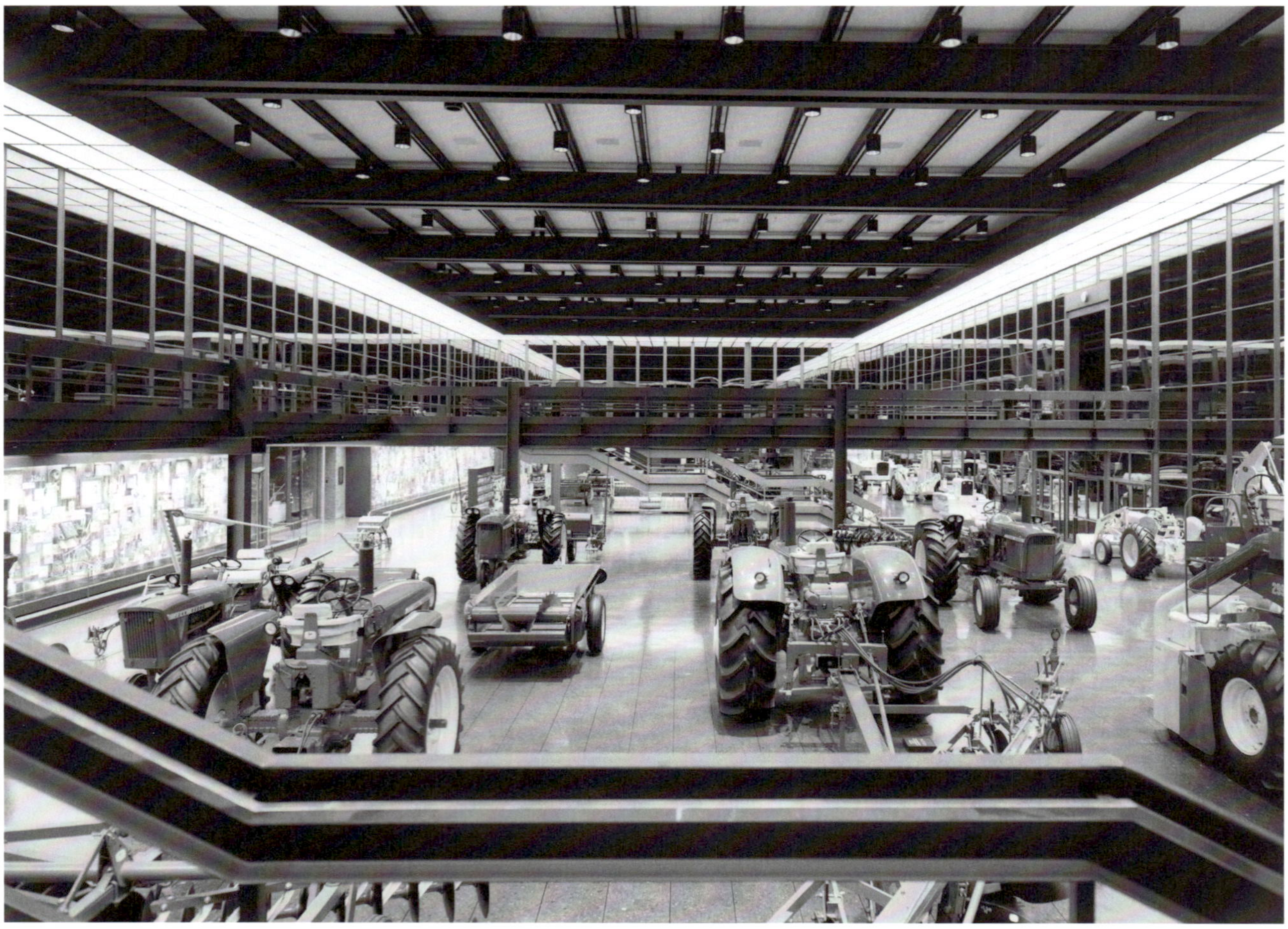

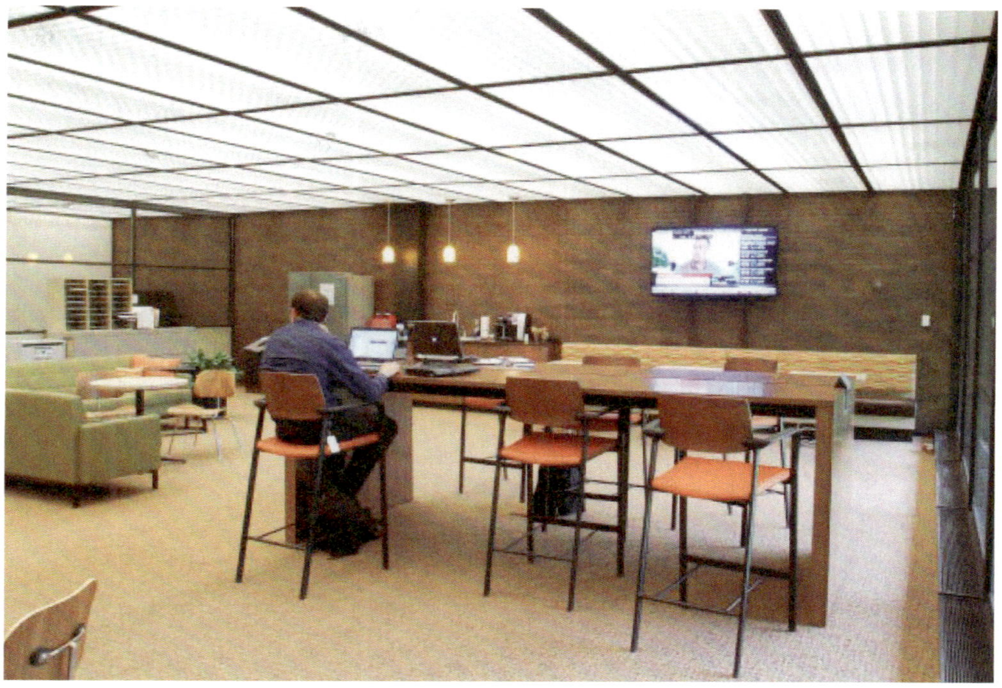

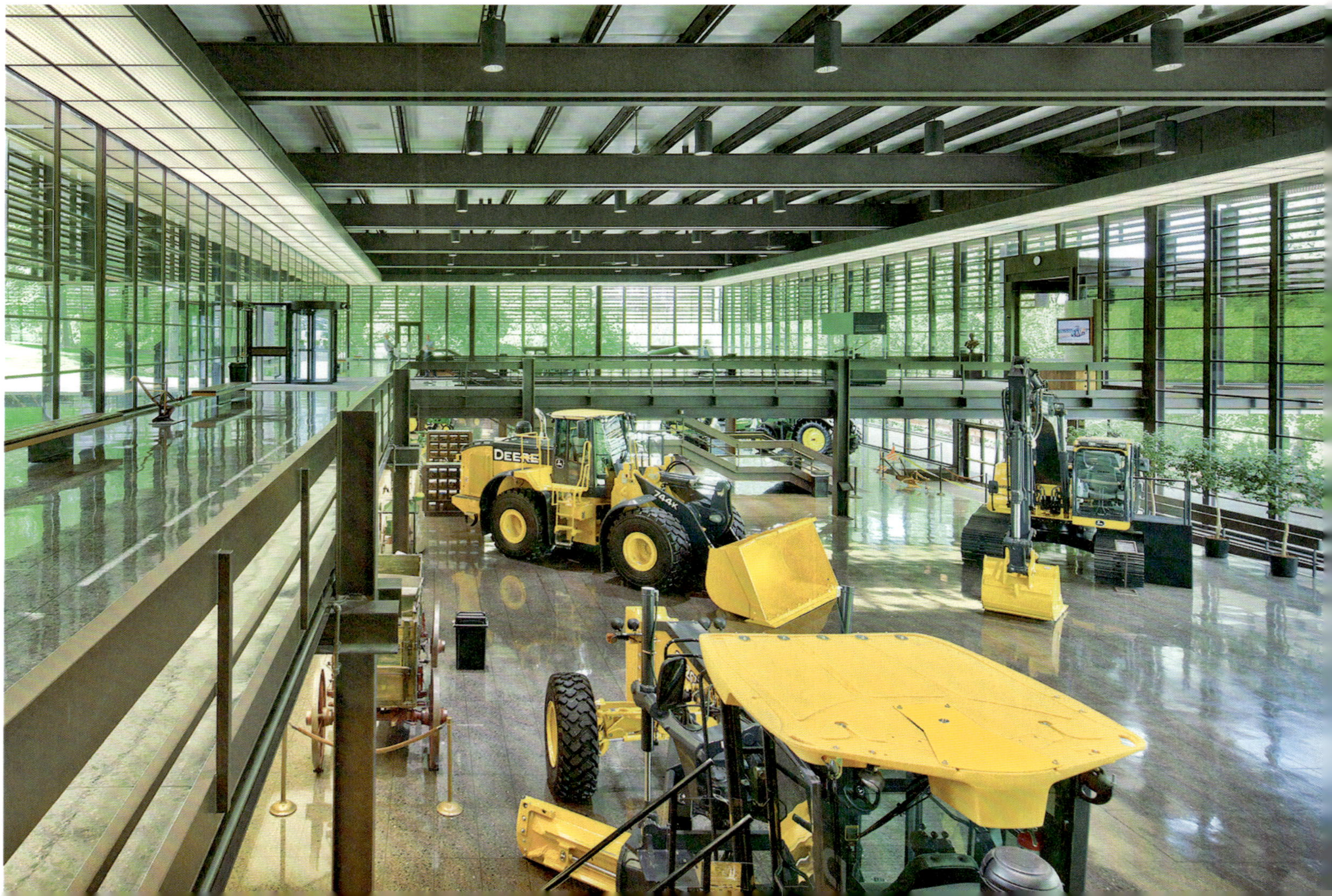
DEERE

1966

Hiroki Kotagiri, Tomomi Nakanishi
Keigo Kobayashi Laboratory, Waseda University

PALACESIDE BUILDING

Sustainable management: tenants unite to operate a massive Tokyo office building, fulfilling the architect's vision of phased design work

More than 50 years after its completion, the Palaceside building has remained largely unchanged. Constructed opposite the Imperial Palace in Tokyo, it was the last building to be affected by the city's height limit of 33 meters (100 shaku).[1] A long slab six stories high with two fluted white circular service cores (and with three stories below ground), the building is now a forum for shops, offices, restaurants, and clinics.

Previously the *Reader's Digest* office stood on the site as Tokyo's first postwar modernist building, designed by Antonin Raymond and completed in 1951. It only stood for 12 years before being demolished and replaced by the Palaceside building. Raymond was adamantly opposed to the destruction of his building and its garden, which included sculptures by Isamu Noguchi. Raymond told Nikken Sekkei, the architects of Palaceside: "It is our social responsibility as a business to ensure that the architecture built on the site inherits and exceeds the ideas of the lost architecture."[2]

Thus the Palaceside building, the new headquarters of Mainichi Shinbun newspaper among other tenants, was designed with the obligation of renewing history. Architect Shoji Hayashi believed any great architecture could be updated in the course of urban development and proceeded with the plan using the Staged Design Method (Dankai Sekkei-hou), which Hayashi explains as, "a method of giving buildings the possibility of adapting to future changes in the environment by dividing the contents of a large-scale building into stages according to the length of its life, and clearly phasing the design and construction according to this division."[3]

In accordance with this method, the framing and finishing work was done separately, and various decisions were made simultaneously. Many parts of the building are still open to the public, and the basement and first floor are currently occupied by more than 60 tenants, including restaurants. The distinctive design of the stairs, railings, and air conditioning units, as well as the funnel-shaped rain gutters on the facade and the louvers that block the morning and evening sun, have been recognized by the government as effective means for conserving energy.

Hayashi stated that he designed the building with the intention of it lasting 100 to 150 years – a form of sustainability ahead of its time. For example, expansion joints were used to separate the building into four parts, achieving earthquake resistance – a necessity after the Great Kanto Earthquake of 1923.

Upon its completion, the Palaceside building was equipped with the most advanced facilities of its time and was the first building in Japan to have an "automatic control system" and a central monitoring panel room. The system automatically adjusted the room temperature and the temperature of chilled and hot water on site.

Various organizations and alliances were formed for the completion and maintenance of the Palaceside building. At the time of construction, the Mainichi Newspapers, Reader's Digest, and Toyo Real Estate established Palaceside Building Co., Ltd. to operate the building, with NIKKEN SEKEI LTD. providing design supervision and a joint venture between Takenaka Corporation and Obayashi Corporation providing construction supervision. After the completion of construction, the building's facilities management, cleaning, security, and disaster prevention services were outsourced to Nippon Building Service Co. (now called the GLOBESHIP Corporation).

The first major renovation was the Five-Year Refresh Plan, launched in February 1990, which included the installation of showers and a complete reconstruction of the restrooms, as well as safety improvements, the installation of new boilers (a necessity ever since the Oil Crisis), and parabolic antennas.

In 1992, the building won the Building and Equipment Long Life Cycle Association (BELCA) award. The Palaceside Building Co, Ltd. was congratulated for unifying the tenants into a single management authority. BELCA praised the smooth collaboration between the organizations and the meticulous renovations required for modernization:

"The management system for maintenance and preservation is family-like, with a detailed human organization and division of work. There is good coordination with the tenants, and the various obstacles to use that have arisen over time have been overcome one by one through the establishment and implementation of systematic renovations. It can be said that an ideal relationship for maintenance and preservation in large-scale buildings has been established."[4]

With the passage of time, tenants and working styles have inevitably changed. But the maintenance and management regime has endured – the perfect legal instrument to execute Hayashi's original architectural vision of the Staged Design Method and allow the building to sustain.

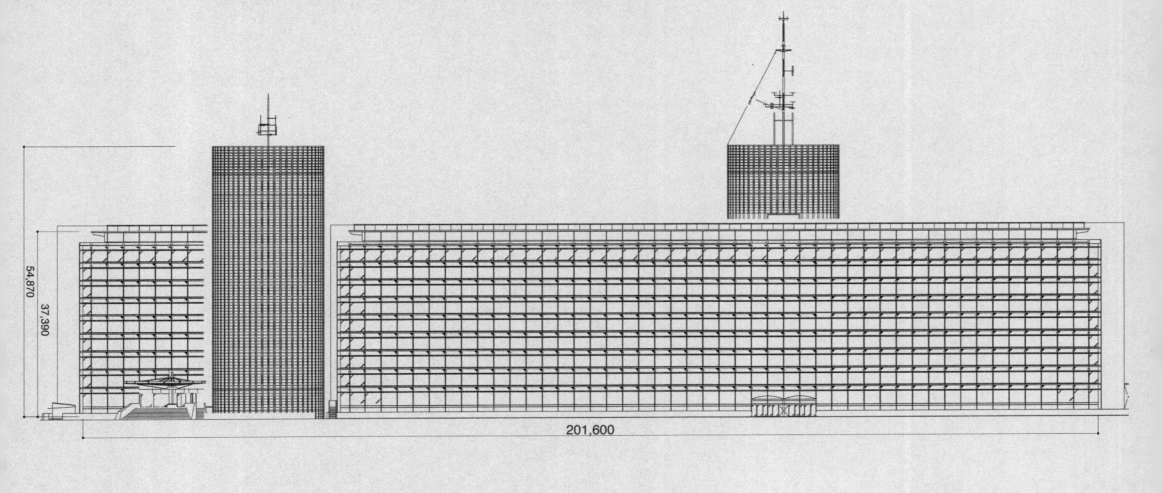

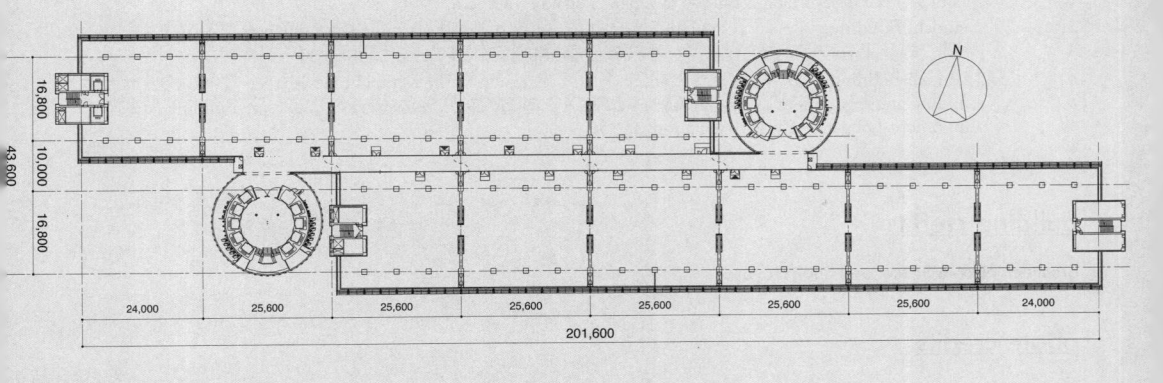

notes

1. Shaku(尺) is a unit of length unique to Japan. 1 shaku = 30.3cm.
2. Mainichi Building, パレスサイドビル物語―ビルに歴史あり (The Mainichi Newspapers, 2006), p.41
3. 林昌二の仕事」編集委員会(Eds.) 林昌二の仕事 (Shinkenchiku-sha, 2008) p.84
4. Mainichi Building, パレスサイドビル物語―ビルに歴史あり (The Mainichi Newspapers, 2006), p.91
5. Building and Equipment Long-Life Cycle *"BELCA NEWS" 10th Anniversary Special Issue* (Building and Equipment Long-Life Cycle Association, 1995)

building credits

architect: Nikken Sekkei and Shoji Hayashi

photo credits

p.320, 330 (all): The Mainichi Newspapers Co., Ltd.
p.325, 327 (all), 331 (all): Tomomi Nakanishi, Hiroki Kotagiri
p.326 (below): "Architect Shoji Hayashi Poison Book" Shinkenchika, p.105
p.326 (above), 328: Shinkenchiku-sha
p.329 (all): Vincent Hecht

2021
1-1-1 HITOTSUBASHI
CHIYODA-KU, TOKYO, JAPAN

326

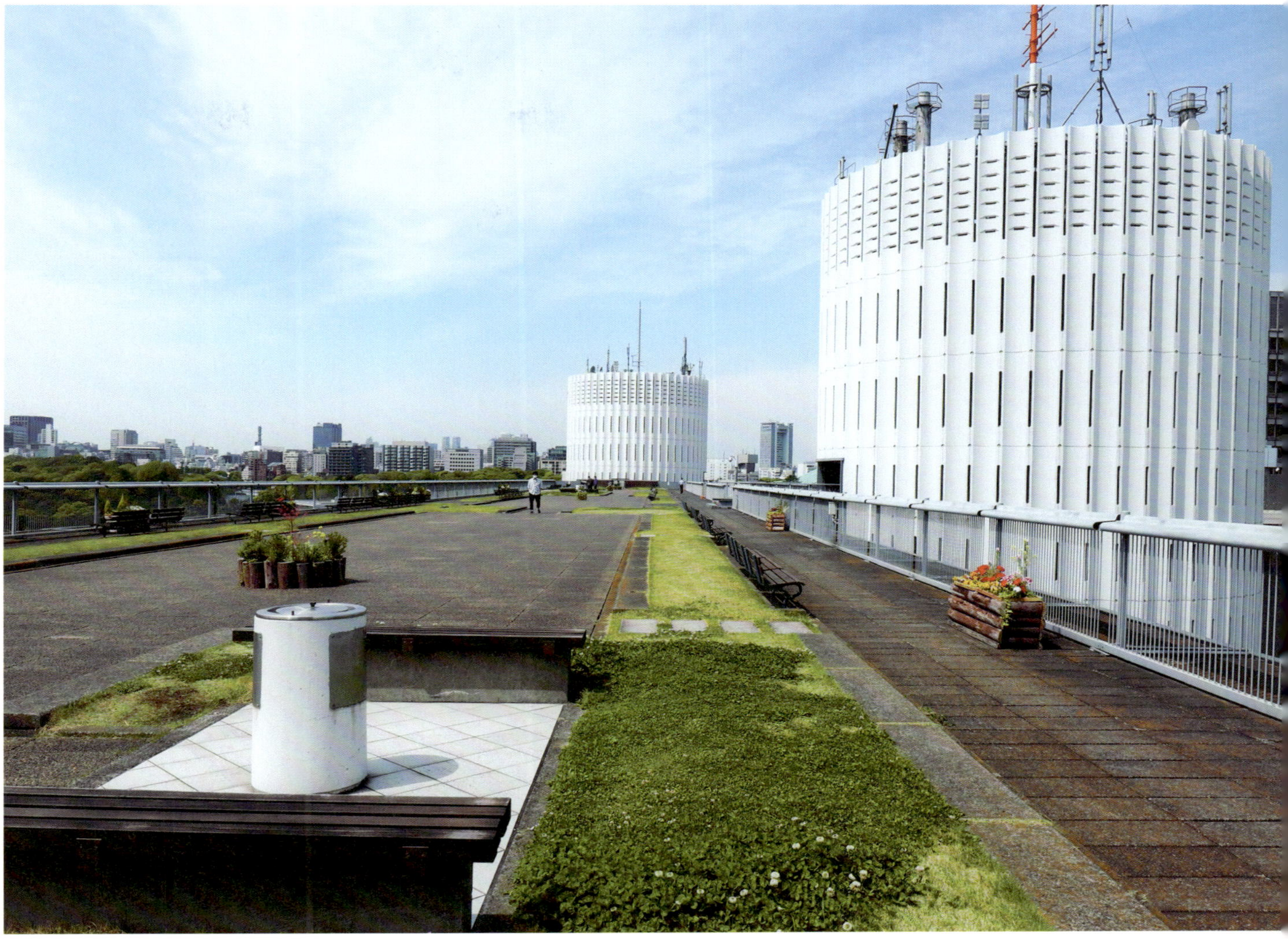

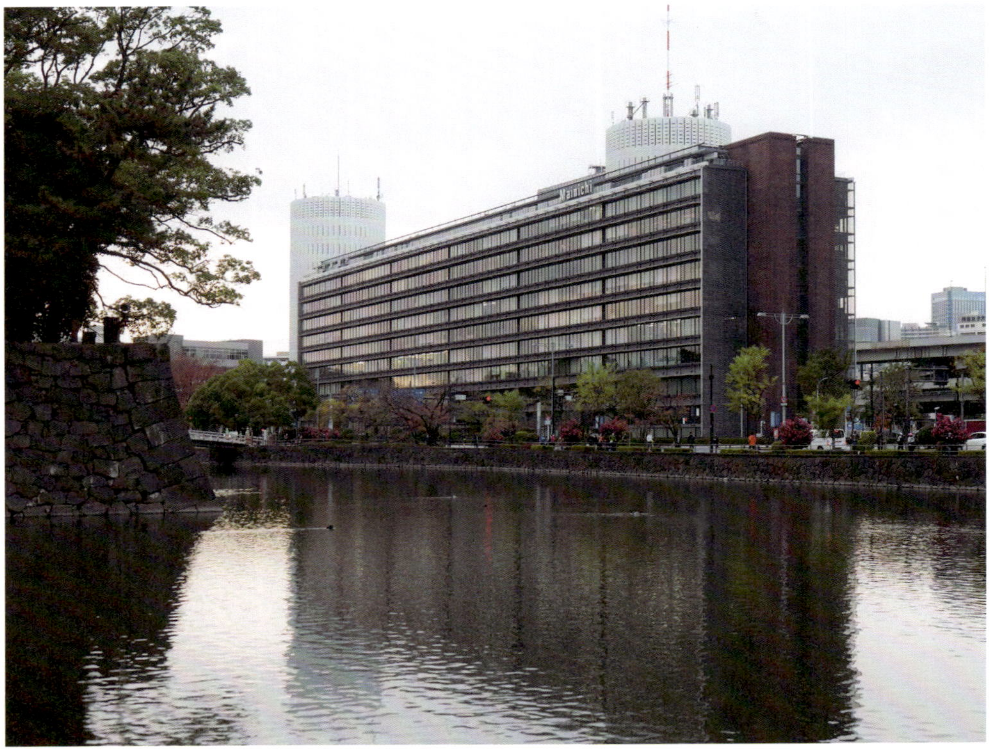

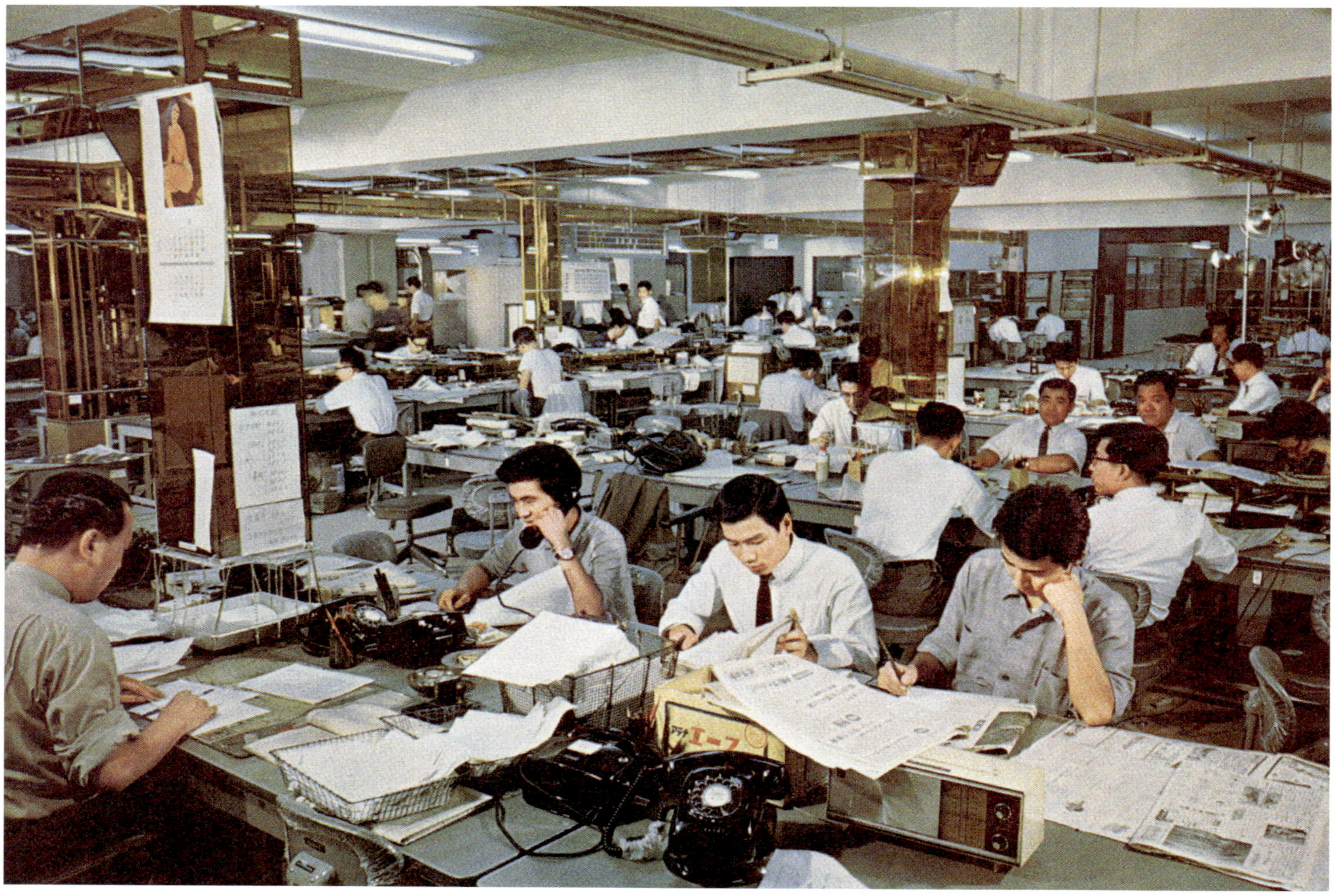

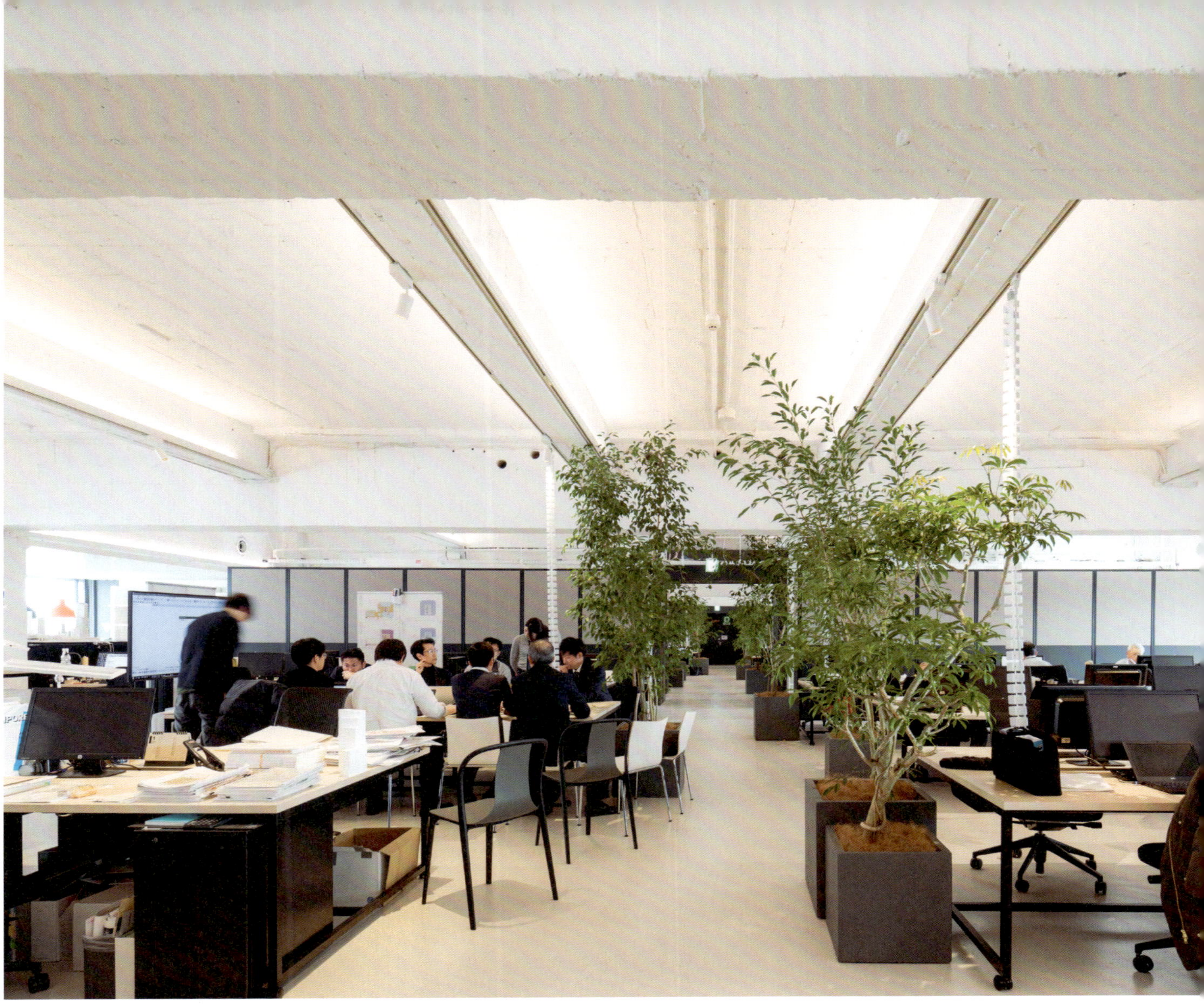

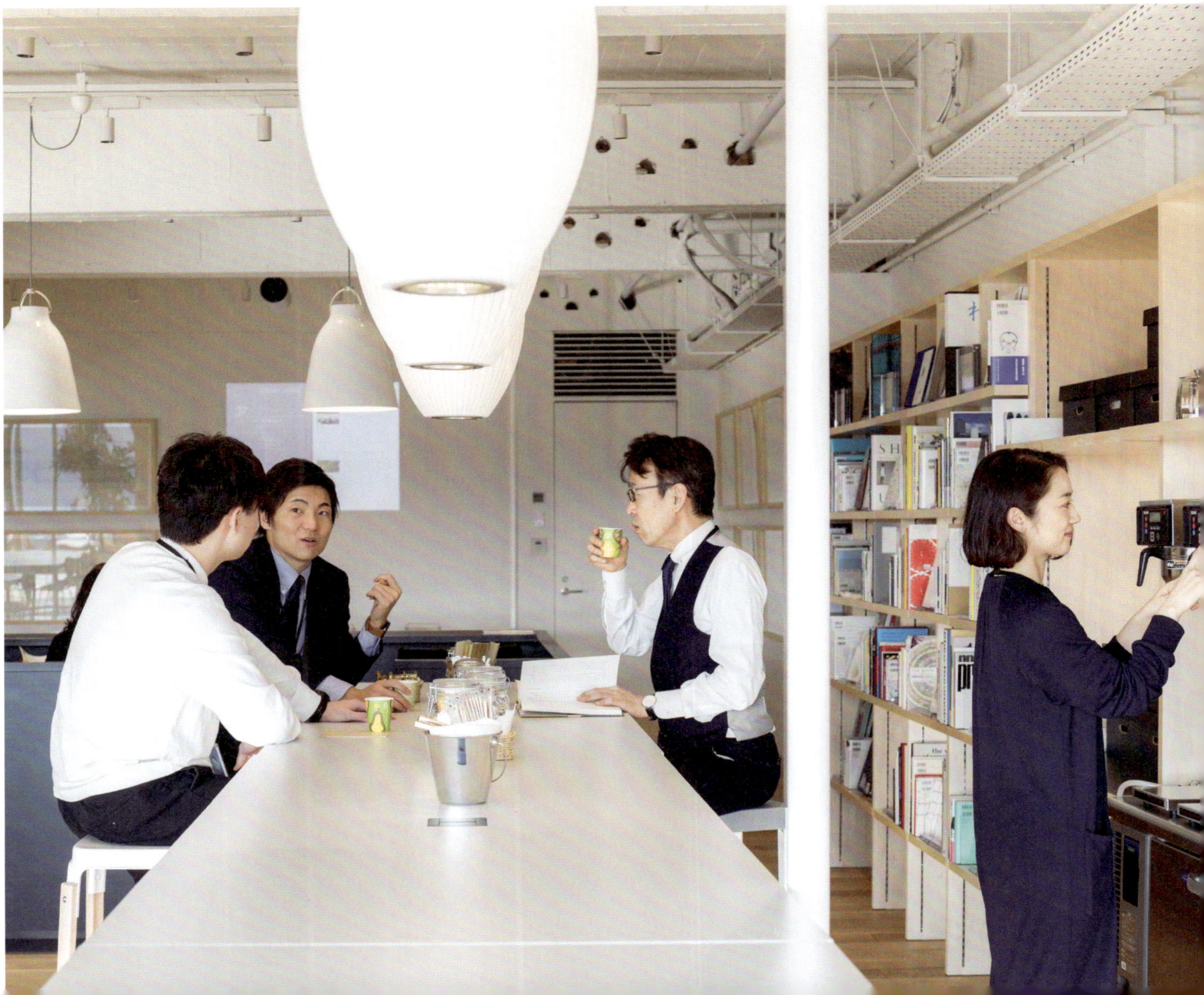

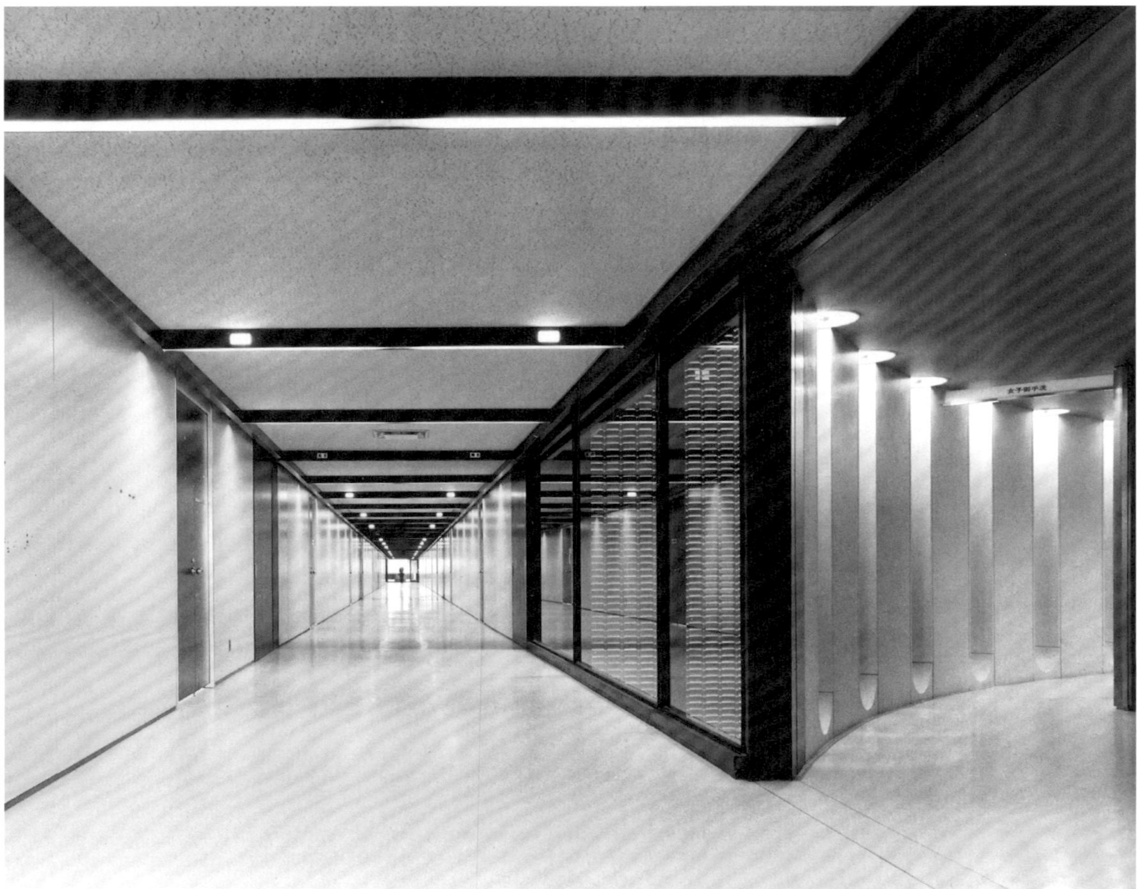

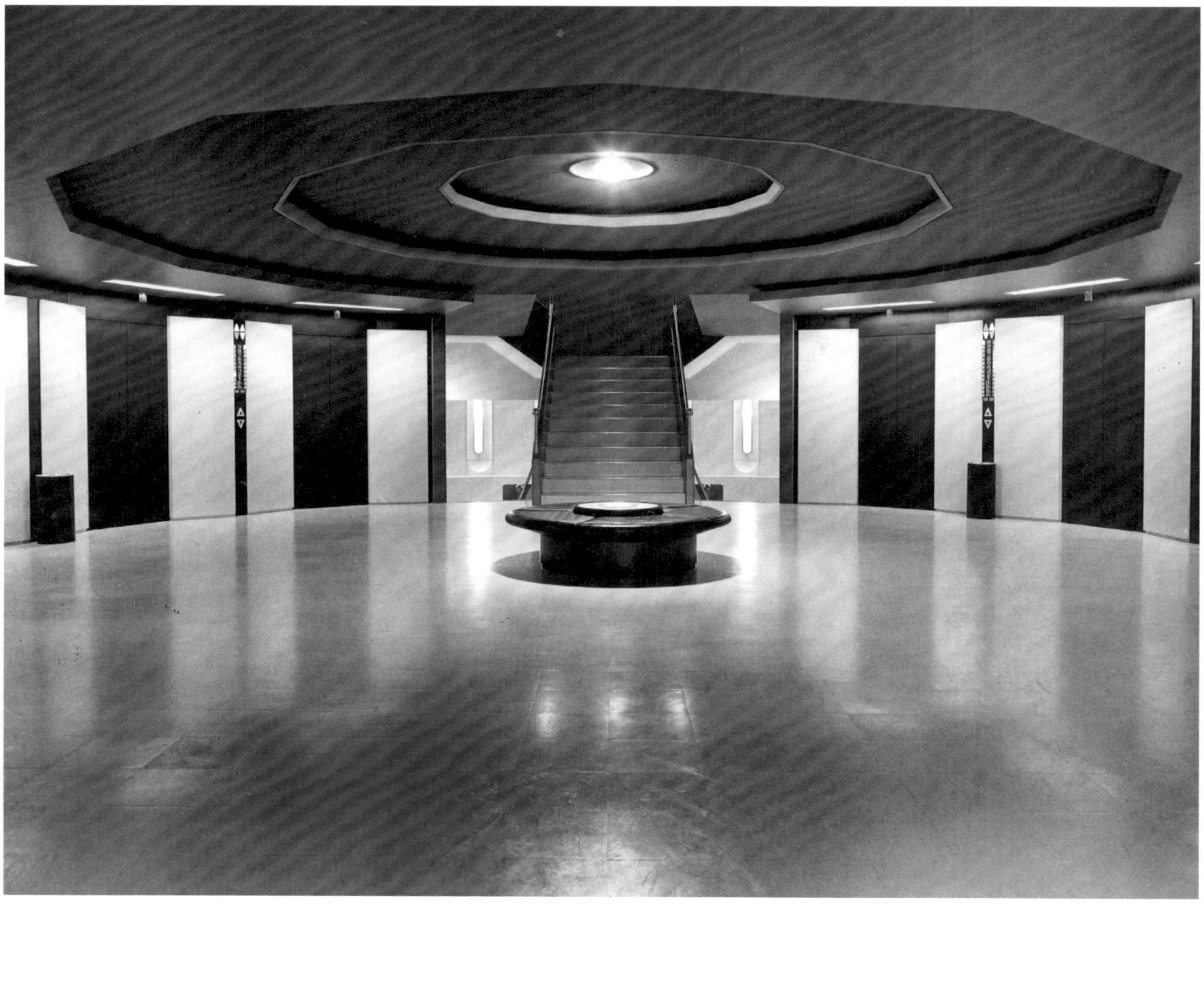

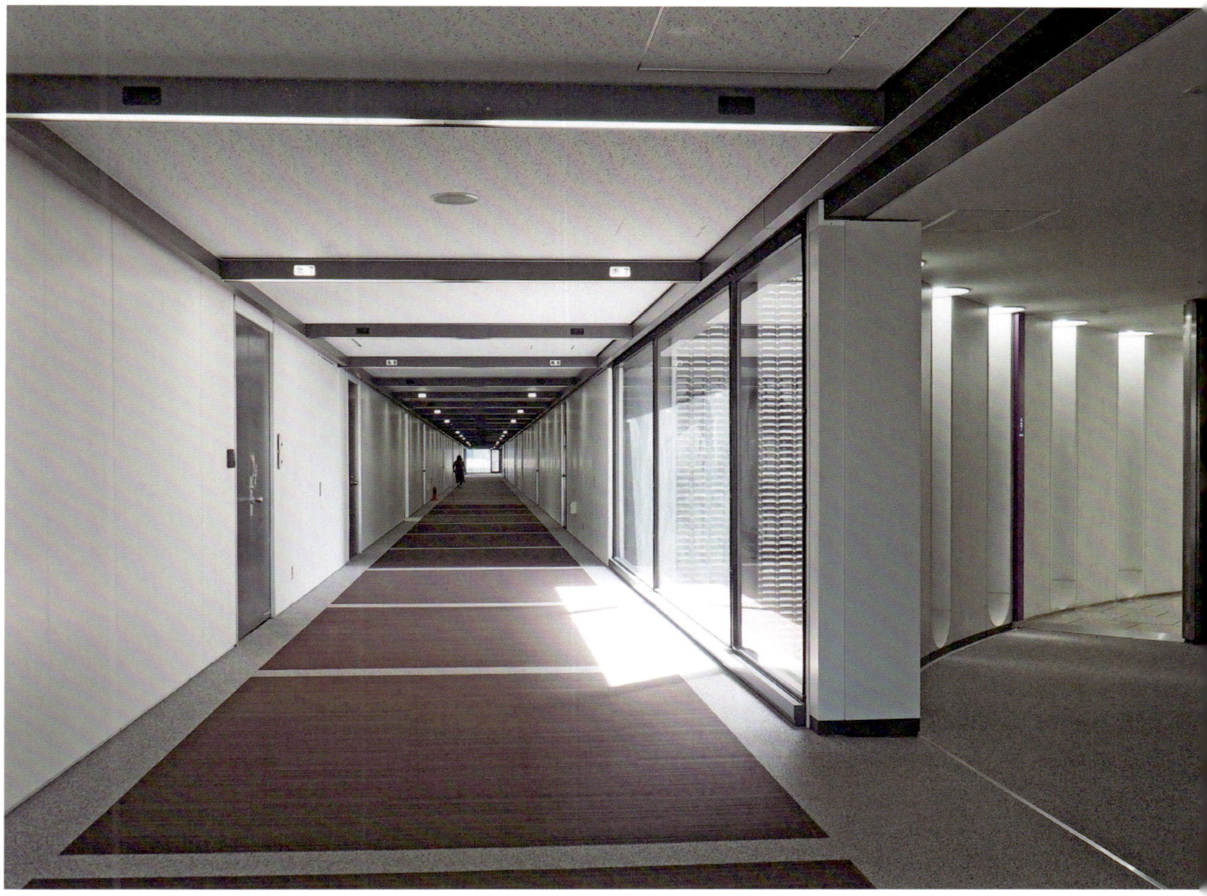

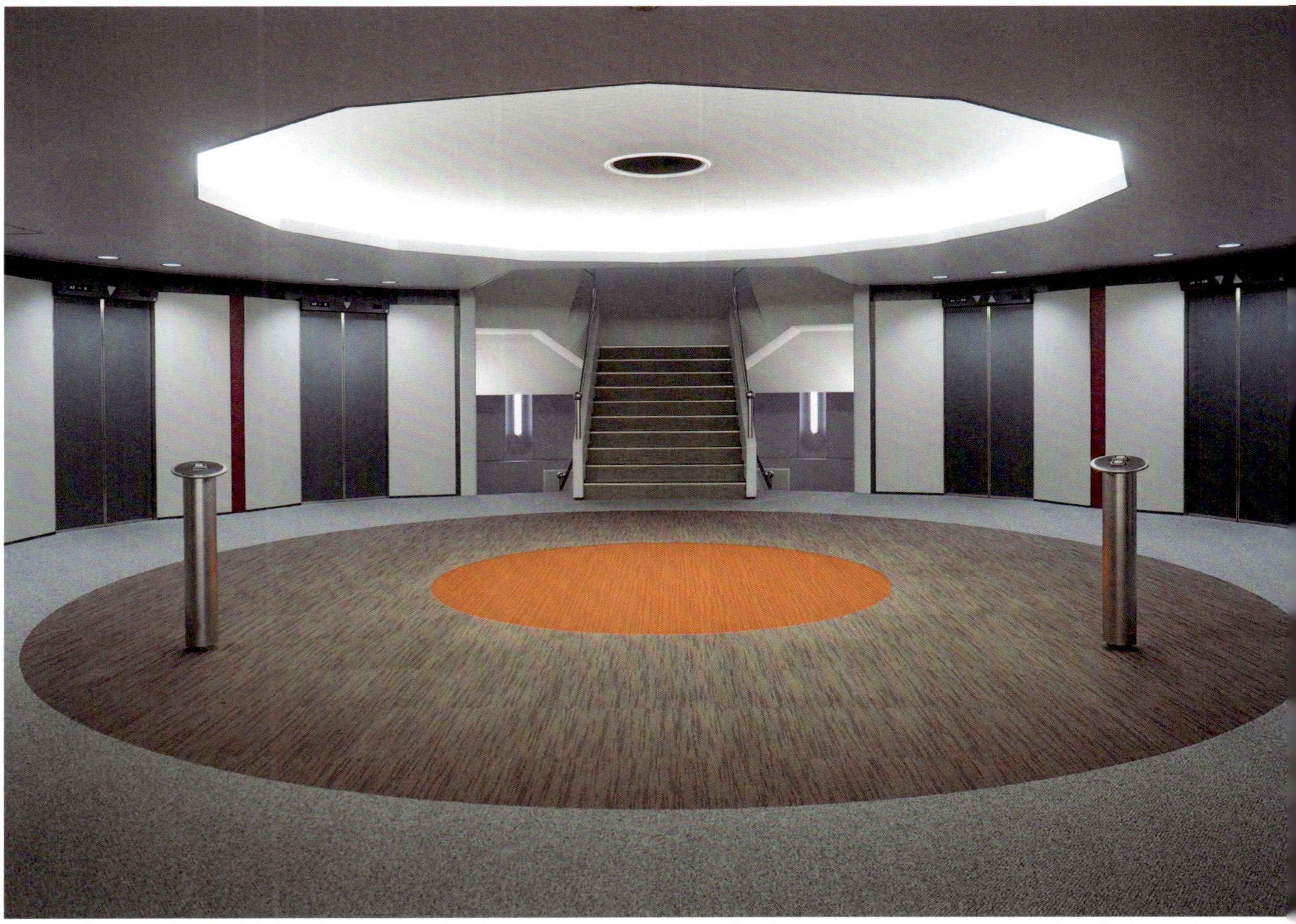

1966

Ruth Baumeister

FINNLANDHAUS

A *Baulöwe* uses the listed status of his office to clever effect

A tenant is asking: 'Where shall I place my bunker?'" reads a headline in the *Hamburger Abendblatt* on 21 July, 1967. The article describes the dilemma of Jürgen Z., who intends to build himself a subterranean nuclear shelter in Hamburg. But since he lives in an apartment building with no place for a bunker, he is asking the local authorities where to dig it in. One of the city's highest officials welcomes Jürgen Z.'s initiative and promises to help. A suggestion is made to rent an allotment garden. The article points out that the only public bunker built after World War II in Hamburg is located underneath the Finnlandhaus.

There are many stories to be told about Finnlandhaus, an office building constructed between 1961 and 1966 by HPP (Helmut Hentrich, Hubert Petschnigg & Partners), a large, Düsseldorf based architecture firm entering its corporate-modernist peak. The location is Esplanade, one of Hamburg's most prestigious addresses, close to the river Alster. The square-shaped, 14-story building, has a chunky central column and a 'void' on its first floor, making it appear to hover, mushroom-like, above the glass-fronted shopping arcade on the ground floor. An initiative of 16 Finnish companies – Finnlandhaus GmbH & Co – teaming up with property developers Robert & Anna Vogel, Finnlandhaus became an icon of the West German *Wirtschaftswunder* in the post-war period. The building is of austere Miesian elegance and the last thing one would guess is that it resides on a huge self-sufficient bunker, with its own 200-meter well, generator, air filtration system, etc., which should allow 2,000 Hamburg citizens to survive a nuclear attack for up to 30 days.

Finnlandhaus constituted an integral part of a new masterplan, Neustadt 5, which foresaw the demolition of the closed, neo-classicist street front of Esplanade's north side, which was to be substituted by three solitary mid-rises in an open, park-like environment. Esplanade was to become part of a larger ring of motorized circulation around the inner city and the new modernist buildings symbolized Hamburg's efforts to reinvent itself as a city of international commerce after the war.

Conceived as a multi-tenant building, Finnlandhaus accommodated retail space in a rectangular pavilion on the ground floor. Higher up the concrete stem was the Finnish Consulate General, several Finnish paper companies, Finnair, and on the top floor, a restaurant serving Finnish cuisine. The building, and the project of national cooperation that birthed it, conceived of Hamburg as a gateway to the North. The building itself acted as a kind of billboard for Finland: an enormous golden lion on red background – Finland's coat of arms – was positioned on the upper right corner of the four facades. This would become an important asset for the building as modernist building stock like this approached its expiration date.

Finnlandhaus's mushroom-like construction principle was revolutionary, used for the first time post-war West Germany. Supposedly, the investor, Robert Vogel, fell in love with this structural system during a trip to the US after World War II and hired HPP to construct a building with a similar one. The free-standing concrete core was erected first. Then a wooden platform for the concrete framework was hung from its top, upon which floor after floor was fabricated, starting at the top and working down. The reinforced concrete core not only provided space for infrastructure – elevators, stairs, MEP – but also served as its only loadbearing structure. This allowed maximal freedom in the configuration of the floorplans and a curtain wall façade. The innovative structural technology promised fast construction, and besides the eye-catching appearance of a 14-floor building balancing on a single central pole, it also allowed maximum use of the site, because it allowed transgression of the plot line above the ground floor.

The building underwent several renovations over the decades: in 1980, the windows and façade panels were insulated; in 1988, the elevators were renewed and four emergency slides installed on the eighth floor, to enable fast evacuation in case of emergency. In 1996, the Finnish restaurant was closed and executive office space installed, with views over the Binnenalster.

Finnlandhaus was landmarked in 2002. But the building was by this time run-down, and because of the particular construction method, the grid size was highly unusual, making a standard rehabilitation difficult. This, combined with its rather small size compared with newer office buildings made renovation of the building uneconomical and unappealing for most companies, for whom a more contemporary office space made more sense. Anyone taking on Finnlandhaus would have to do it as a labor of love.

In 2012, Finnlandhaus was bought by the developer Dieter Becken, one of Germany's biggest investors. After an expensive renovation in 2017, Becken's company moved into the upper five floors and rented out the rest. When asked by the author why he – as an educated mason, architect, engineer, and successful developer – chose to move his headquarters from a fairly recent office complex to the Finnlandhaus despite the high costs of renovation, he answered, "It is the architecture. I think the house and the location are very special, they both conceive a positive aura. As far as I'm concerned, this is Hamburg's best location for offices and I truly believe that I have the best office in Hamburg." Becken also cited the underground parking garage as a huge bonus – the space that could also be used as a bunker during the Cold War.[1]

In colloquial German, you also call an investor a *Baulöwe* (building lion). Around the same time *Baulöwe Becken* acquired Finnlandhaus, he was rebranding his business. He decided to hijack the golden lion in the landmarked Finnish coat of arms on the building he'd just bought and turned it into the logo of his own company. This move allowed him to circumvent the so-called *Alsterverordnung*, a law that forbids any kind of advertising on the facades of the buildings framing the river Alster. Since the landmarked coat of arms was now also his own logo, Becken's business is now the only one able to advertises itself at this prominent place: the lion is visible throughout the center of Hamburg.

notes

1   Dieter Becken in an interview with the author, February 18, 2020.

building credits

architect: Helmut Hentrich and Hubert Petschnigg

photo credits

p.332, 334: Robert Häusser
p.337, 339 (all): Jens Frederiksen
p.338 (all): unknown

2021
ESPLANADE 41
HAMBURG, GERMANY

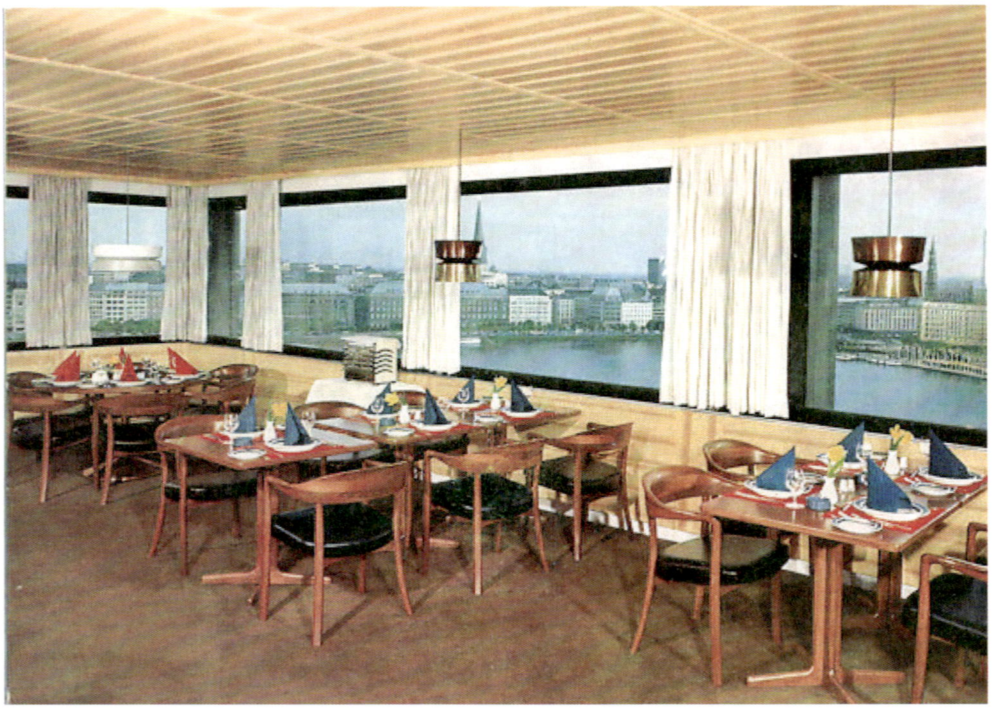

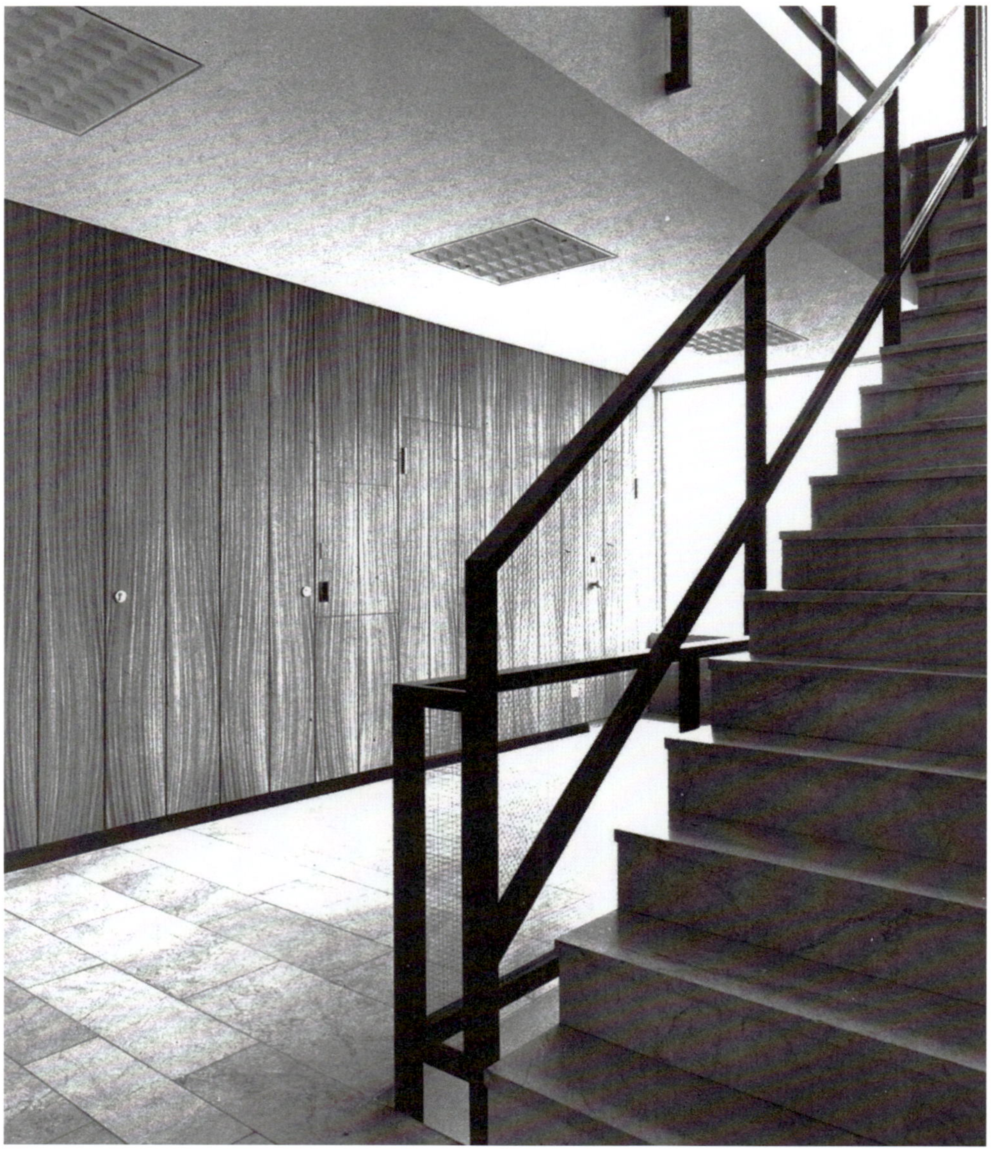

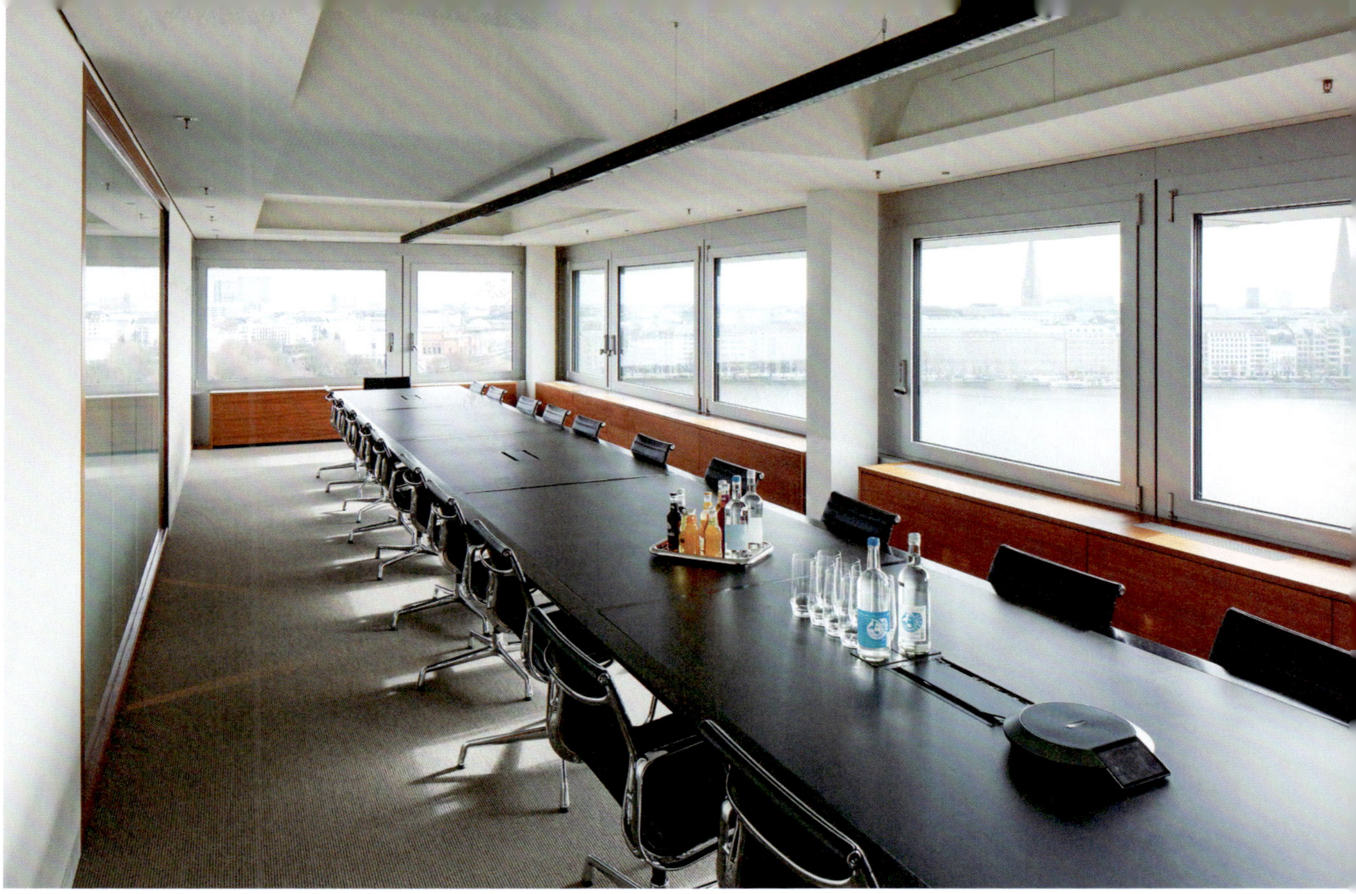

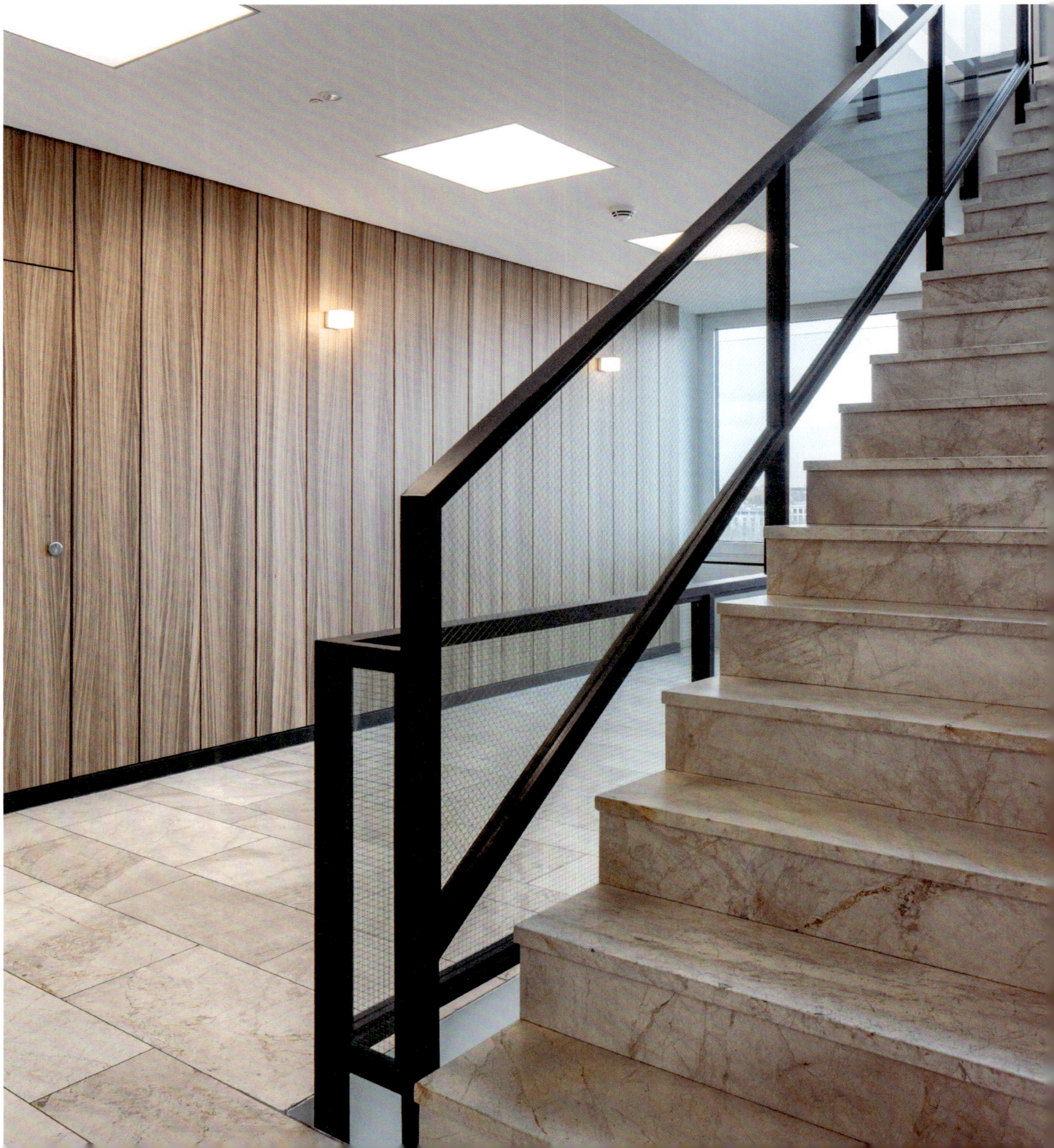

1966

Nadia Voynova, Stephan Petermann

OSRAM ADMINISTRATION BUILDING

Eulogies for the demolished

"Last December, at the end of an urban planning competition, two winning designs were selected, each of which provides for the construction of 400 new apartments. One design preserves the listed ruin [of the Osram building], one design does not. The jury recommended demolishing the Osram house for reasons of cost. City planning councilor Elisabeth Merk would have liked to have preserved the industrial ruin from the 1960s with its aluminum-glass curtain wall, as it is one of the few outstanding buildings of post-war modernism in Munich. But the costs would have been enormous. Because of the poor fabric of the building, two-thirds of the office building would have had to be demolished and reconstructed. The jury therefore opted for [complete] demolition, as did the planning committee on Wednesday."

—"Demolition of the Osram building is sealed" *Tz*, April 26, 2016[1]

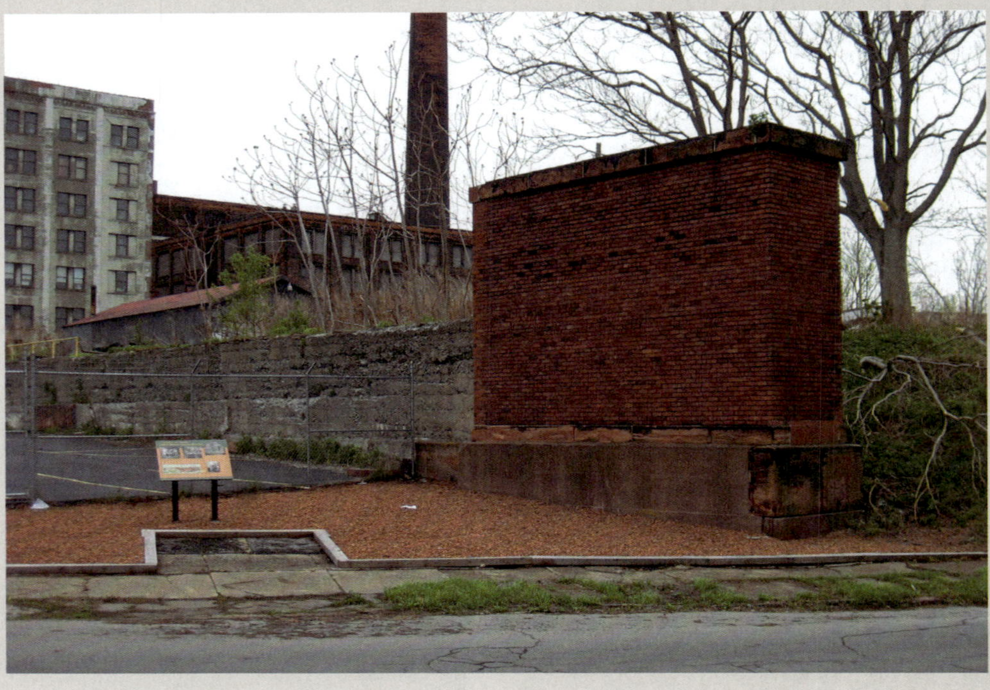

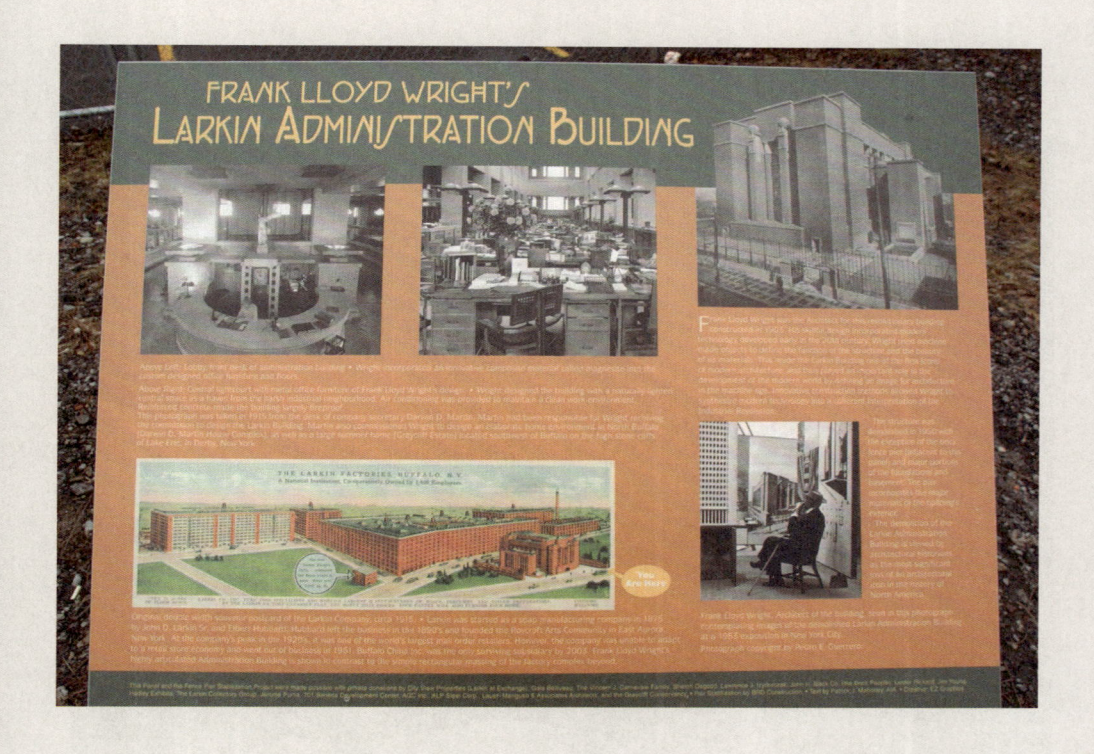

THE LARKIN BUILDING 1906–1950

Buffalo, New York
Frank Lloyd Wright

"The Larkin office building in Seneca Street, once the princely throne of a business dynasty that sold soap and household products in 48 states, has come to the end of its usefulness. Its steel girders will be used to shore up coal mines in West Virginia; its brick and concrete debris will help fill the Ohio Basin (now Father Conway Park on Louisiana St.). Wreckers who took the job on tearing down the 44-year-old building got more than they bargained for. It was built to stand forever.

"The floors of the seven-story structure are made of giant reinforced concrete slabs, 10 inches thick, 17 feet wide, and 34 feet long. They are so heavy that when they are cut into sections to be removed, they are apt to crash to the floor below. Structurally, the building is hardly without parallel. The floors are in tiers, around a deep well, and are supported by 24-inch steel girders, much larger in size than are generally used today.

"The wrecking contractors, Morris & Reimann, say the building designed by noted architect Frank Lloyd Wright, would cost $7,000,000 to $10,000,000 to duplicate at present prices. It was purchased from the city for $5,000 by the Western Trading Corporation, on the condition it would raze the building and erect a new structure to cost around $100,000. The new building planned would be a motor freight terminal.[2]

"The depredations that took place when the Larkin office building stood idle, while in the hands of the city, were not a pretty picture. Nearly every window had been broken, and thieves stripped the building of about 20 tons of copper, including the copper roof. When the Larkin clubs were popular, money from the customers poured into the Larkin building in such volume that it had to be tossed into baskets and barrels. The Larkin office staff performed its tasks while soft music was played on a famous pipe organ."

— Hilton Hornaday, **"Built to last Forever, Famed Larkin Building is Tough on Wreckers"** *Buffalo Evening News*, May 16, 1950.

"TREEHOUSE" FOR ENGINEERS...POISED ON A FOREST OF CONCRETE PILLARS

Atop the outreaching branches of 42 "trees" of reinforced concrete, the Emhart Manufacturing Company's unusual new research building sits 22 feet above its site.

For the large staff of engineers housed here, the building gives an impressive view of the countryside, as well as a feeling of spaciousness in the work areas. It also creates ample space for protected, out-of-sight parking, with the concrete providing the required fire-resistant barrier.

Color and textural interest are given the roof fascia, perimeter columns and slab edges through use of precast sections of white cement concrete, etched to expose the pale gray granite aggregate.

Concrete adds new dimensions to architecture...a freedom of form possible with no other material. (Write for a free copy of *Concrete Profiles for Industry.* U.S. and Canada only.)

PORTLAND CEMENT ASSOCIATION
Dept. 5-18, 33 W. Grand Ave., Chicago, Illinois 60610
An organization to improve and extend the uses of concrete

THE BEST IDEAS ARE MORE EXCITING IN CONCRETE

Emhart Manufacturing Company headquarters, Bloomfield, Conn. Architects: Skidmore, Owings & Merrill, N.Y. Engineers: Paul Weidlinger, N.Y., and Weiskopf & Pickworth, N.Y. (structural), and Syska & Hennessy, Inc., N.Y. (mechanical).

EMHART BUILDING 1963–2003

Bloomfield, Connecticut
Skidmore, Owings & Merrill

"The fate of the Emhart Building was probably cast at its conception. A peacock preening for corporate recognition, it was in some ways a silly building, trying to look so much bigger than it really was. It housed a hardware company making latches, locks, and doorknobs. Indeed, its reach may have exceeded its grasp. Its functional shortcomings were exacerbated when CIGNA bought it to use as an office building. In corporate parlance, the building failed to meet CIGNA's bottom line, and the company viewed it as an albatross. But this folly is so beautiful! And is not beauty, in and of itself, worth a saving effort? ... Early in 2000, when CIGNA first went public with its plan to redevelop and sell off most of its Bloomfield campus, little if any thought had been given to the architectural significance, historical importance, or stunning beauty of the Emhart Building. It was inefficient: That was condemnation enough, and with an air of good riddance, it was tagged for demolition.

... CIGNA would hear no more. This tunnel vision ... is what galled me most and motivated me to speak out in protest against CIGNA's redevelopment plan. To propose the demolition of a landmark building represented a failure of imagination and leadership.

The painful irony is that CIGNA could have made the Emhart Building into a functioning and economically contributing component of its development plan. In fact, it could have, along with the reuse of the nearby Wilde Building, lifted CIGNA's development plan from mediocre to unique. The corporate titans might have been heroes. Emhart was a lousy office building. But it could be a terrific clubhouse [for the golf course development] and conference center, with views of the Hartford skyline to the southwest and a pond to the west that can provide that seemingly essential water-hole finish to a championship golf course."

—"Beautiful Loser" *Hartford Courant*, June 22, 2003

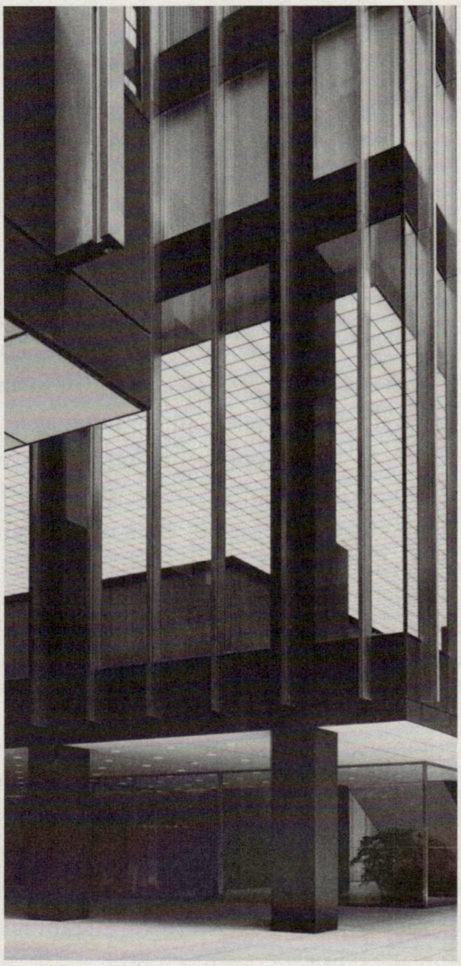

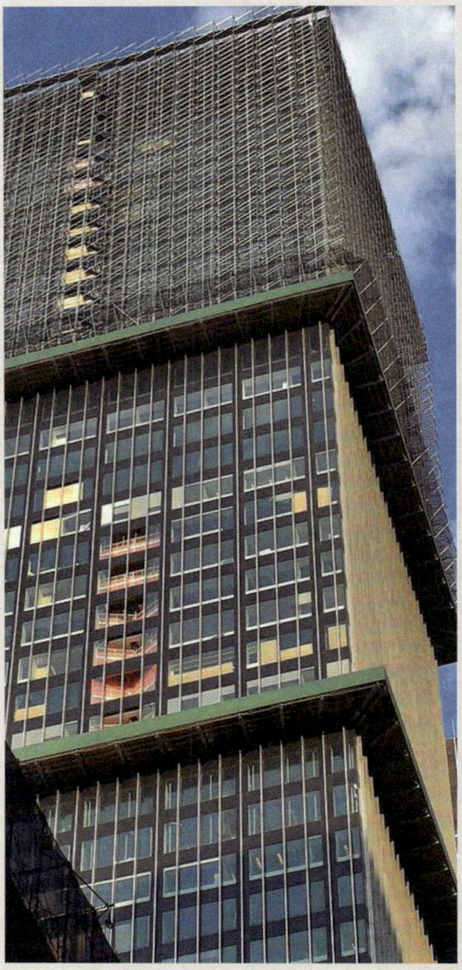

270 PARK AVENUE 1960–2019

New York City
Natalie de Blois

"270 Park Avenue[3] is being demolished as you read this. It's the tallest building ever demolished on purpose, the tallest building ever designed by a woman architect, and was completely rebuilt to LEED Platinum standards in 2011, where just about everything but the frame was replaced, so it is essentially eight years old. Much of it probably isn't out of warranty. According to a basic carbon calculator, its embodied carbon in the building amounts to 64,070 metric tonnes, equivalent to driving 13,900 cars for a year ... 270 Park Avenue is no Penn Station, but it is an important building that also marks the end of an era where architects can pretend that what they are doing is 'sustainable' and 'green' while vomiting out the carbon of fourteen thousand cars."

— Lloyd Alter **"Is it a new era, where architects should be held to account for the environmental impact of their work?"** *treehugger.com*, September 3, 2019

notes

1 Translation from the German by the author.
2 The building ended up being constructed on another site, with the Larkin site becoming a parking lot.
2 Originally the Union Carbide HQ, then JP Morgan Chase.

building credits (Osram Building)

architect: Walter Henn

photo credits

p.340, 350: H. Heidersberg
p.342, 344 (all): unknown
p.343: Buffalo News file photo
p.346 (left): Ezra Stoller / ESTO
p.346 (right): Adam E. Moreira
p.349, 351 (all): HGEsch

2019
HELLABRUNNER STRASSE 1
MUNICH, GERMANY

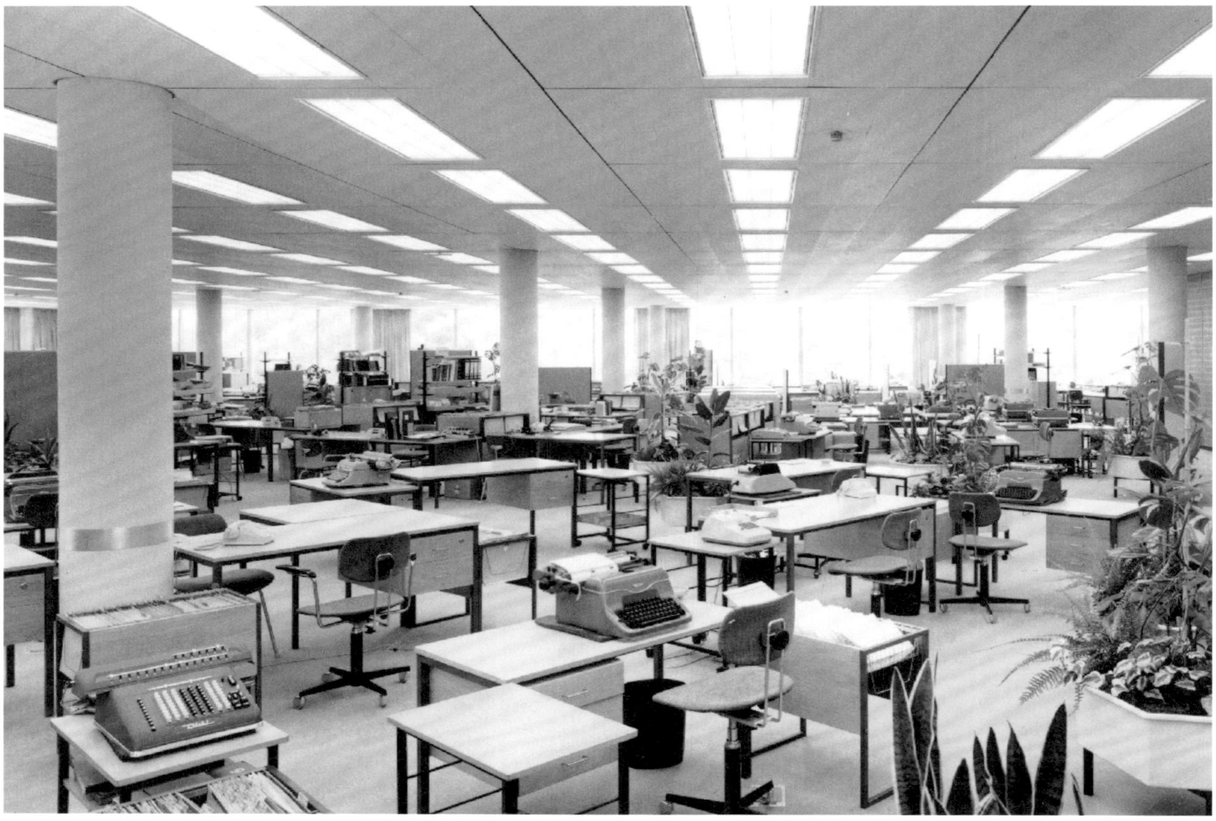

When Angela Merkel on August 31st 2015 in a press conference uttered the words "Wir schaffen das", the office workers of OSRAM in Munich had already been gone from their old Munich office campus for more than two years.
A few months later, 800 people found refuge in small living units, with improvised facilities in the OSRAM former headquarter building. Three years later the building was torn down and replaced by a new residential area.

1966

Konstancja Kusiak, Ruriko Ueda, Shoko Muranaka
Keigo Kobayashi Laboratory, Waseda University

MEGURO WARD OFFICE

From private to public: the conversion of an office building into a city hall guarantees its longevity

City Hall relocation
The current Meguro City Hall building, designed by Togo Murano, is widely known among architects as the former Chiyoda Life Insurance Company headquarters. Owing to their bankruptcy in 2000, the building was sold to Meguro Ward and transformed into the new Meguro City Hall in 2003.
The former Meguro City Hall was built in 1936. It was the oldest city hall building in Tokyo. An earthquake-resistance survey around the turn of the 21st century revealed that the building was in danger of collapsing, and the lack of space was so serious that office functions had to be spread out across six other locations. The city of Meguro considered renovating or reconstructing the building, but the cost was prohibitive and the challenge of continuing to operate office functions during the overhaul or construction was too great.

Taking over the Chiyoda Life Insurance building provided the city with a large amount of floor space in the center of the ward, at a fraction of the cost of renovating or reconstructing their home. The Chiyoda building had undergone a major renovation just three years prior to its bankruptcy, and surveys proved it would be durable for decades to come.[1]

Architectural values of Togo Murano
Around the time of the opening of the newly converted city hall, a conversation took place between the former mayor of Meguro Ward, Katsuichi Yakushiji, and Metabolist architect Kiyonori Kikutake, who used to work for Murano, architect of the city's new home. Kikutake noted the difficulty of establishing a new architectural prototype, but Murano was one of the few architects who managed to do so. These prototypes are known as 'Murano style' and Meguro City Hall was one of them. In fact, since it was completed near the end of his career, many Murano style elements condensed there.
Kikutake also mentioned that even as a private office building, Chiyoda allowed the local community to rent out the tea ceremony room and the other Japanese-style rooms, as well as opening up their plaza space for the yearly communal Bon dance event. If this building had been demolished, the relationship with its community would also have been broken. Now, as a municipal town hall, the building would be more public-facing than ever.[1]

Transforming private into public
Inheriting Murano's design, various efforts were made by Yasui Architects & Engineers, Inc. to transform a private company's building into publicly open architecture:

1. *Limiting Running Cost*
Since the public building needed to be maintained using taxpayers' money, anything considered excessive needed to be regulated. For example, the flame-shaped fountain in the pond in front of the building had to be shut down in order to save electricity and maintenance costs. The illumination of the acrylic ornaments and rails at the entrance hall were switched off for the same reasons.

2. *Additional security and safety measures*
The new public function of the building required that the management of security had to be adjusted. For example, the traditional rooms used for tea ceremonies, haiku reading, and other activities were renovated, but now included new gates to control access. Murano's Japanese-Sukiya-style rooms are regarded as one of the best Sukiya examples in Japan and because of this, the rooms in the city hall have been thoroughly maintained and protected.
With regards to safety, regulatory measures and general expectations are tighter in a public building. The best example of this is the symbolic staircase facing the entrance hall: the original height and design of the balustrades and the handrails did not meet requirements for public buildings; extra rails and acrylic panels had to be added, but with care taken not to violate the original design.

Another example can be seen in the parking area, which used to be the main plaza. Although the sculpture by Henry Moore is still located in one of the corners of the site, the stone bench has been removed and new metal fences have been installed to ensure that cars cannot crash into the pond below.

3. *Accommodating new functions*
Murano often wrote about the importance of staircases, and they are recognized by his critics as crucial elements within his architecture. The Chiyoda, now the Meguro City Hall staircase, is also one such example. It has now become the main backdrop for wedding photos after ceremonies at the city hall.

notes

1　　Conversation between Kikutake and the Mayor, Katsuichi Yakushiji, *Meguro Kuhou* (local newspaper), 1 January, 2003.

building credits

architect: Togo Murano

photo credits

p.352, 358 (all): Meguro City Hall
p.354-355, 357, 359 (all): Ruriko Ueda

2020
MEGORO-KU KAMIMEGURO 2-19-25
TOKYO, JAPAN

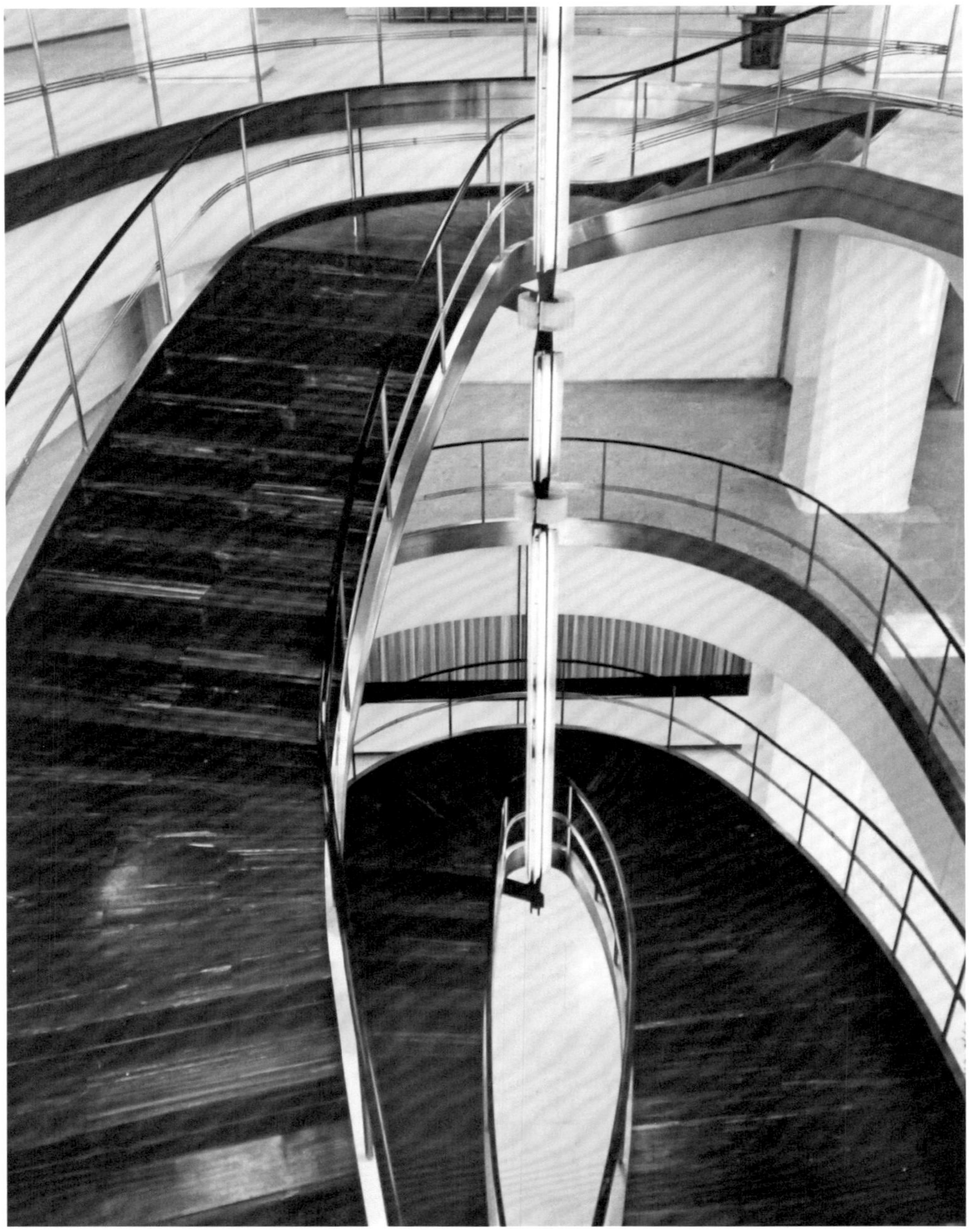

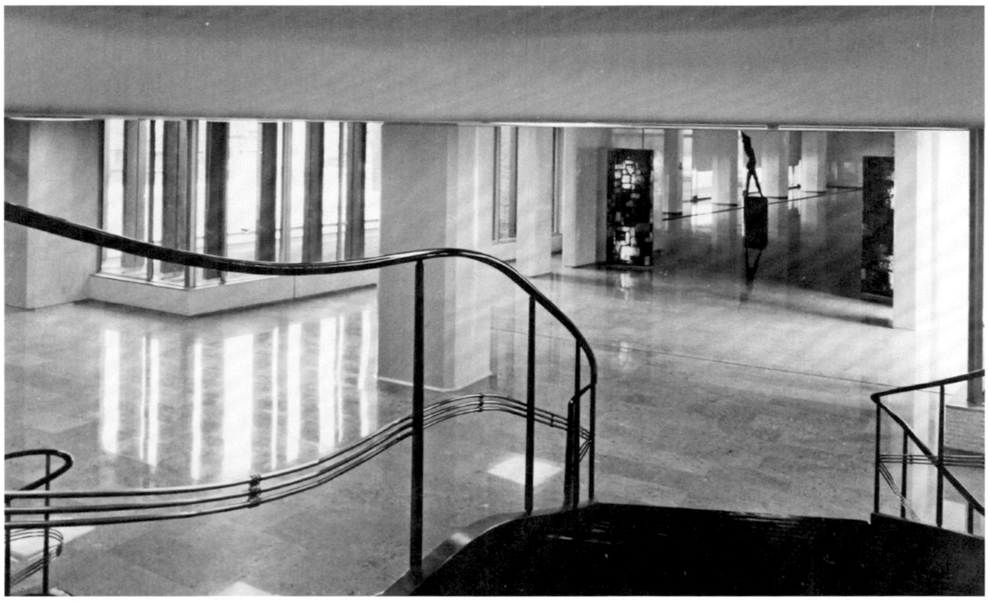

359

FORD FOUNDATION 1967

"A 21st Century Renaissance For Ford Foundation Landmark"

Some good news: Employees are moving back into the Ford Foundation headquarters, between 42nd and 43rd Streets, a stone's throw from the United Nations. A two-year, $205 million makeover is nearly done. ... After half a century, the building remained a gem but needed an upgrade. City officials gave the foundation until 2019 to remove asbestos, fix the sprinklers and make the site wheelchair accessible. The foundation's president, Darren Walker, saw the opportunity to nudge the headquarters, in other ways as well, into the 21st century. ...

The president's suite was the world's most spectacular tree house. Getting to it involved an ingenious architectural choreography of intimidation. Supplicants arriving for an audience with the president disembarked a leather-lined elevator at the building's 10th floor. Crossing a vertiginous balcony, levitated high above the garden, they negotiated the third of three separate reception areas, which in turn gave onto an enormous secretarial antechamber. If deemed worthy, they were finally admitted to the sanctum sanctorum, an office large enough to accommodate 40 people. Now the president's suite is chopped into that pair of conference rooms, named after Wilma Mankiller, the former Cherokee Nation chief, and Fannie Lou Hamer, the African-American civil rights and women's rights leader. This was Mr. Walker's larger goal. Another new conference room, dedicated to Nelson Mandela, features some of Mandela's own drawings along with a portrait of Mandela by Philip Kumah.

— Michael Kimmelman, *New York Times,* November 19, 2018

2018
320 EAST 43RD STREET
NEW YORK, NY, US

building credits

client: Henry Townley Heald
architect: Kevin Roche, John Dinkeloo

photo credits

p.360: Ezra Stoller / ESTO
p.361: Tefend and Dzierzak
p.362 (above): KRJDA
p.362 (left): Bruce Davidson
p.362 (right), 363: Iwan Baan

362

363

1967

Euridice Oliveira de Paiva, Erika Kakinoki, Kai Yoneyama, Yifu Zhang
Keigo Kobayashi Laboratory, Waseda University

SHIZUOKA PRESS AND BROADCASTING CENTER

Metabolizing Metabolism: Stable ownership, respect for history, and good maintenance ensure a building sustains for over five decades

While Kenzo Tange (1913–2005) was not a member of Metabolism, the architecture group founded in 1960 in Japan, he was their mentor and prefigured their work in several of his visionary projects, mostly unbuilt. One of these was the original design for the Dentsu headquarters, which featured a key structural motif of Metabolism: the 'joint core' (two of them in this case), often cylindrical, supporting column-less floors that cantilever from them – a "stem and leaves" formation. While Tange's design for Dentsu was never realized, he refined and realized this concept for the Shizuoka Press and Broadcasting Center building in 1967.

This building is one of the few with strong Metabolist features still in use, without any major changes, more than five decades

Comparison of duct lines
It can be read how the building was retrofitted from centralized temperature control system to an independent rent control system or the "multiple air conditioning system" with as little impact on the building's appearance as possible.

1967
5F

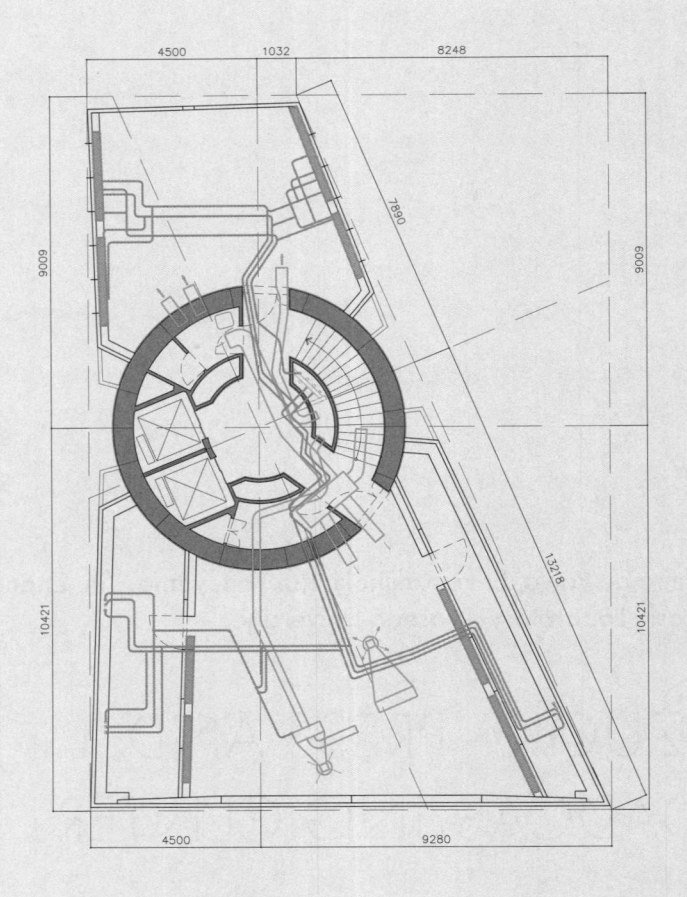

brown line: fan-coil system
blue line: air duct for ventilation

after its completion. The building's "stem" contains elevators, stairs, ducts, electric equipment, and other lifelines, while the "leaves" accommodate offices space and roof terraces.[1]

While longevity in the form of renewability is the heart of Metabolism's philosophy, the main reason for this building's remarkably long life is the care taken by its owners, the Shizuoka Press and Broadcasting company, which have inhabited the building since its completion. On several occasions, the company discussed replacing the building, but each time they ended up respecting the decisions made by their predecessors, as well as the building itself, which is considered heritage, designed by an architect who remains a national treasure.

Support from the owner is crucial to help sustain a building, but without sound structure, strong materials, healthy internal conditions, and a floor plan that works, a building can't survive for more than 50 years. Typically, the main structure of a building (i.e. reinforced concrete) lasts around 50 to 70 years, while MEP only lasts around 20 to 30 years. Although some Metabolist architecture was meant to be updated through the replacement of its capsules – as in Kisho Kurokawa's Nakagin Capsule Tower in Tokyo – Tange's Shizuoka building has metabolized through more conventional means: maintenance and renovation, applied

1998
5F

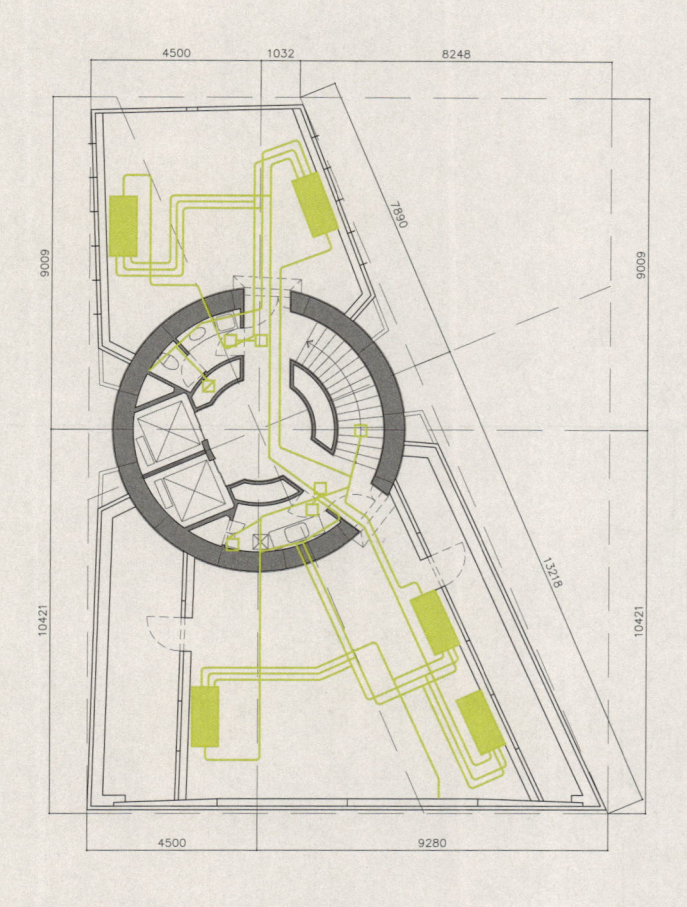

yellow line: water sourced heat pump system

cyclically with attention and dedication. Since its completion in 1967, the building has experienced two major overhauls, in 1998 and 2005, and was expecting another in 2021, which was postponed due to the COVID-19 pandemic.

The 1998 renovation focused on updating the building's mechanical systems: its outdated fan-coil system and fresh air supply ductworks were replaced by a new water-source heat pump system. The building no longer had to rely on collective boilers and chillers, with a single temperature control governing every space. But the chillers ,previously hidden at the top of the cores had to be replaced by numerous separate outdoor units, which ended up occupying all the roof terraces. Inside, the lighting system was completely replaced, but before and after photographs indicate that the use of space by the workers remained almost unchanged.

In the 2005 renovation, the cast aluminum façade panels – approaching the end of their 40-year life expectancy – were refreshed with new coatings and paints.

The third renovation, planned for 2021, coincided with the end of the second cycle of the MEP's lifespan, and comes close to the end of the lifespans of some of the metal, stone, and structural works. Accordingly, a new air circulation system will be installed together with new façade cladding and maintenance works on the existing structures.

1967

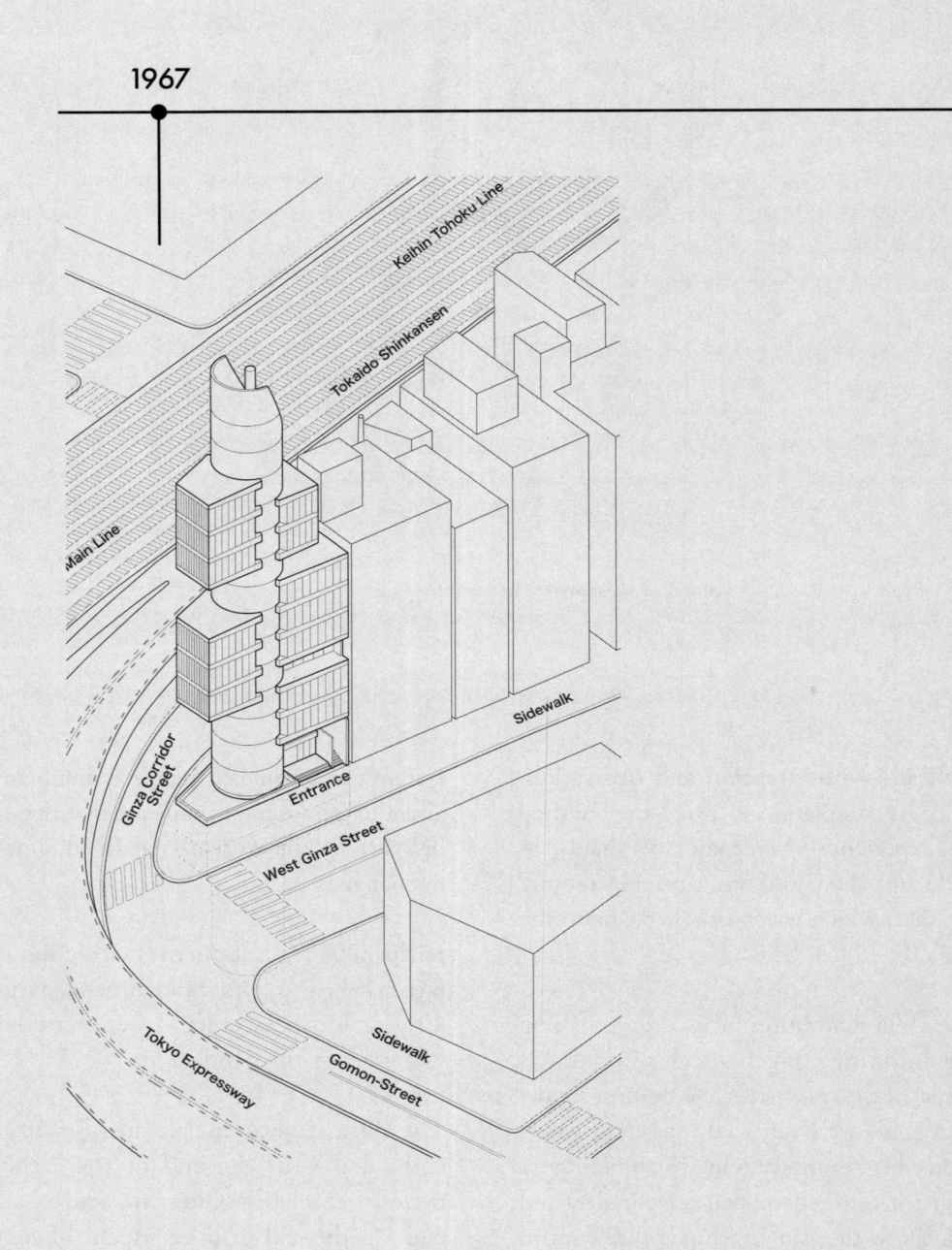

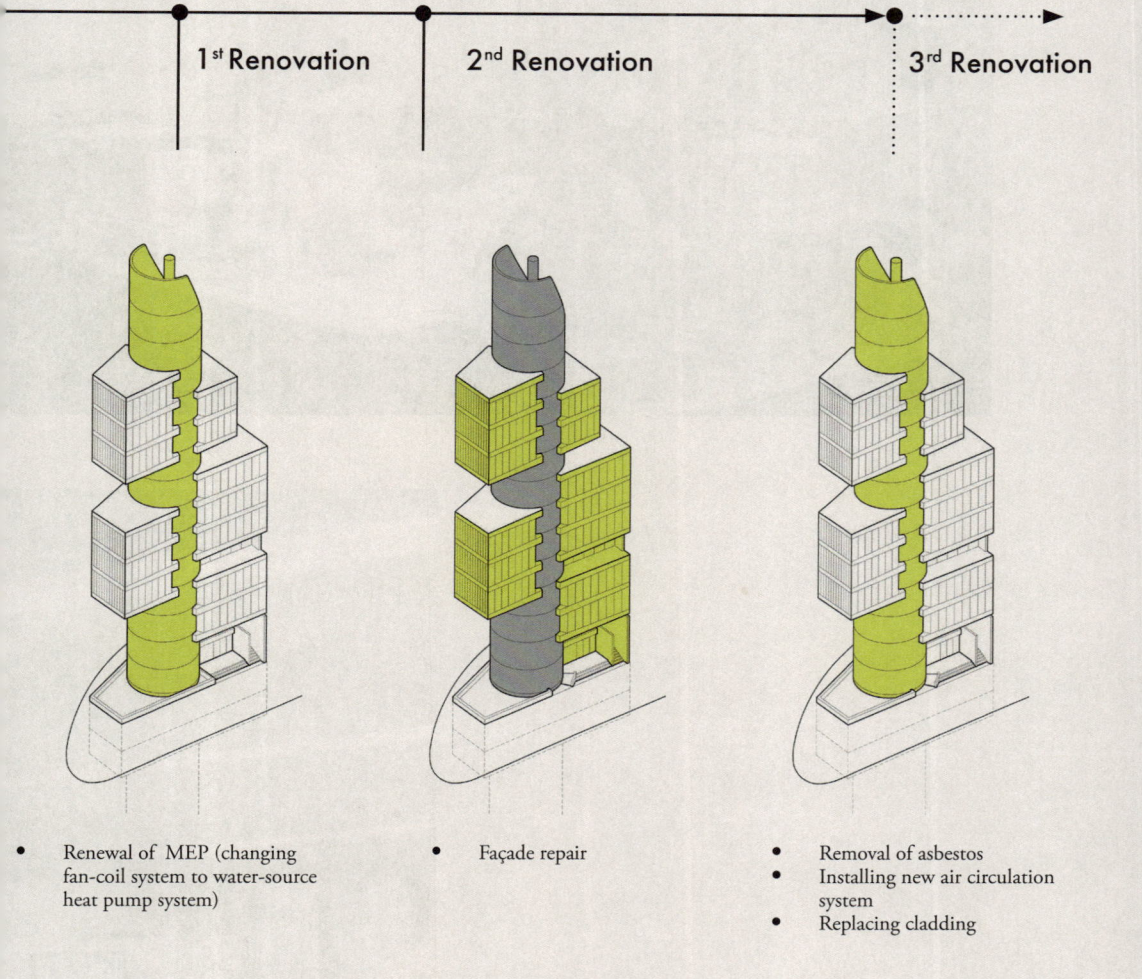

1998 to 1999 — 1st Renovation
2005 — 2nd Renovation
2021 — 3rd Renovation

- Renewal of MEP (changing fan-coil system to water-source heat pump system)

- Façade repair

- Removal of asbestos
- Installing new air circulation system
- Replacing cladding

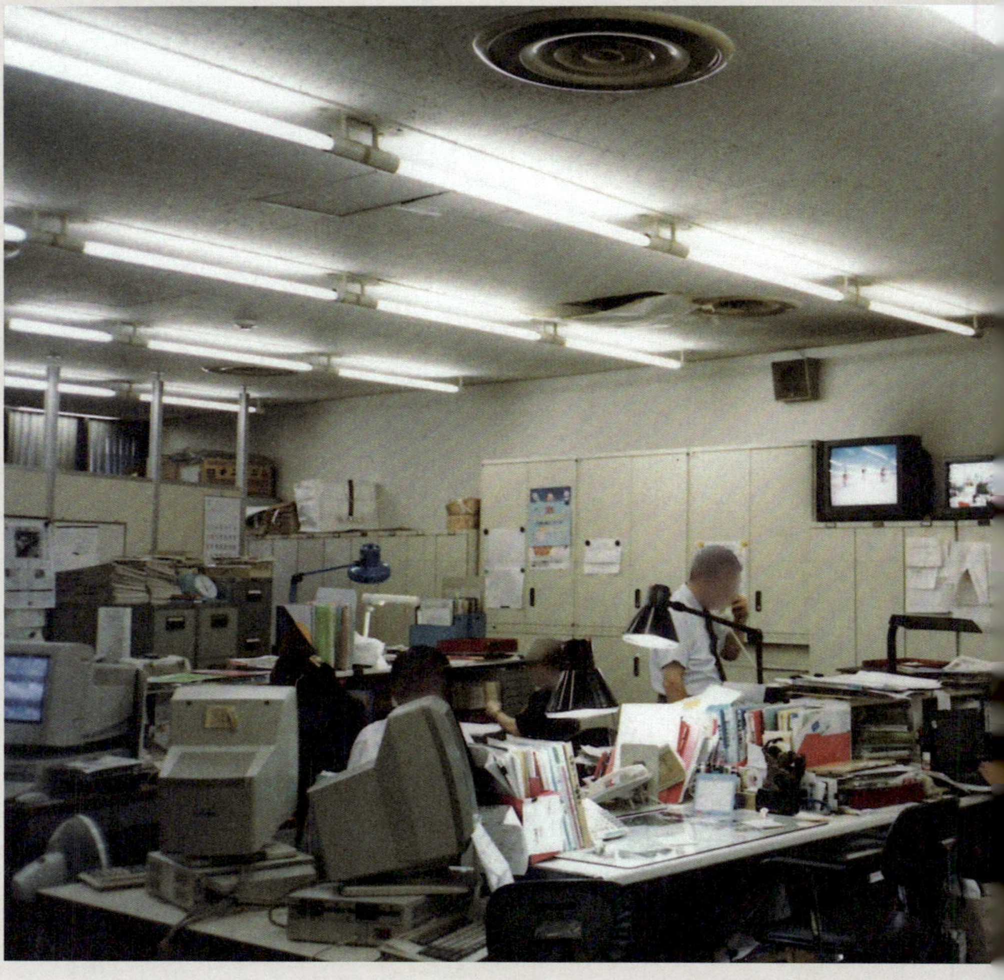

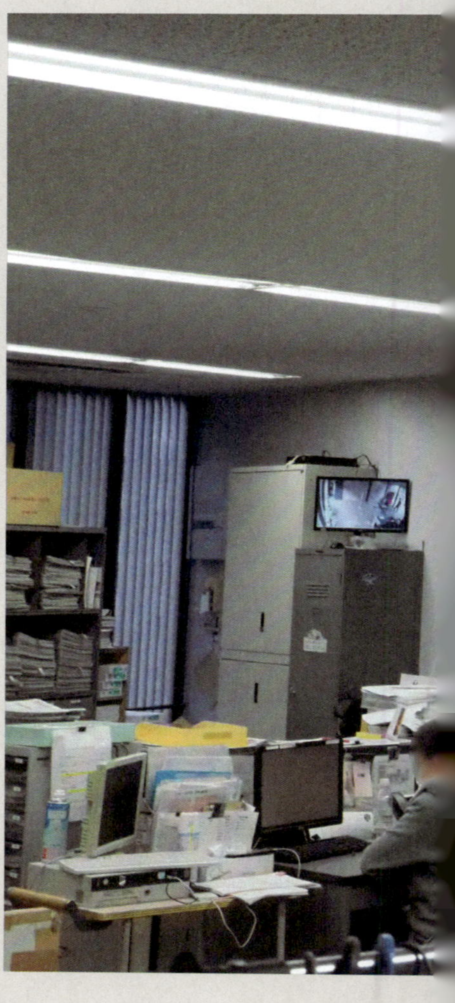

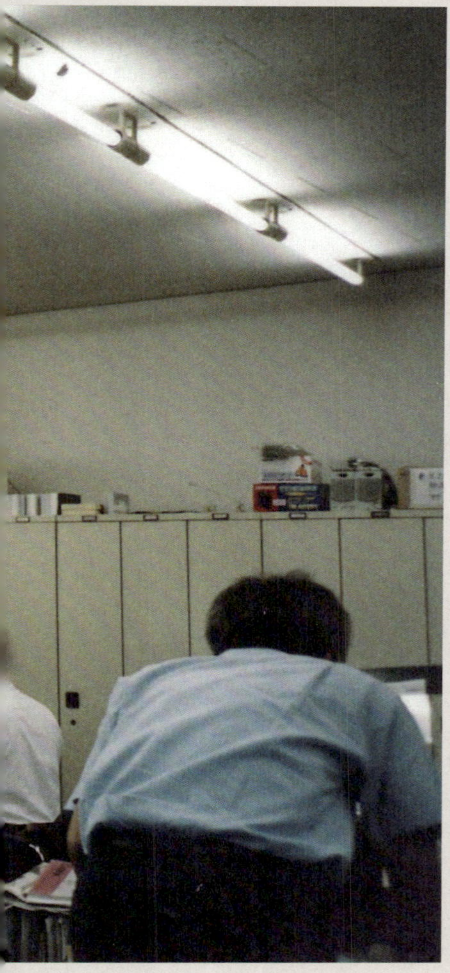

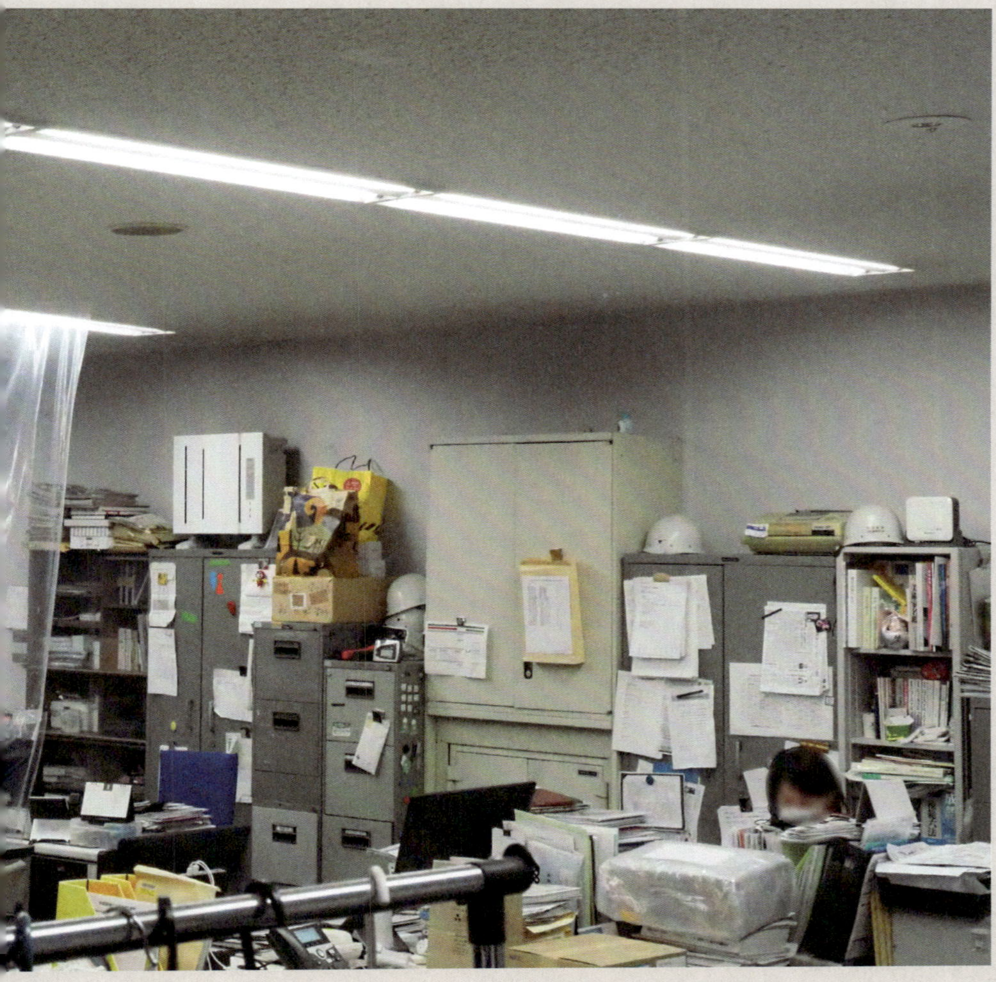

notes

1   The application of Metabolism is clearly found in what the stem is for the shaft and what tree leaves are for the rooms. The shaft contains elevators, steps, electric equipment, and lifelines, while the rooms offer office and guest spaces. The "stem" supports "leaves" by making the basic structure both physically and functionally. In "Yamagishi, K. 丹下健三+都市・建築設計研究所 . ""Shizuoka Press and Broadcasting Center " Shin-Kenchiku (Shinkenchiku-Sha Co., Ltd., 1968) p. 185-191

building credits

client: Ooishi Kounosuke, founder of Shizuoka Newspaper/Broadcasting System
architect: Kenzo Tange

photo credits

p.364: Copyright Osamu Murai
p.370–371 (above), 374 (above), 376, 378 (all): Shizuoka Shinbun
p.370–371 (below), 373, 375 (all), 377, 379 (all): Kai Yoneyama
p.374 (below): Taisei Corporation

2021

SHINBASHI, GINZA
TOKYO, JAPAN

374

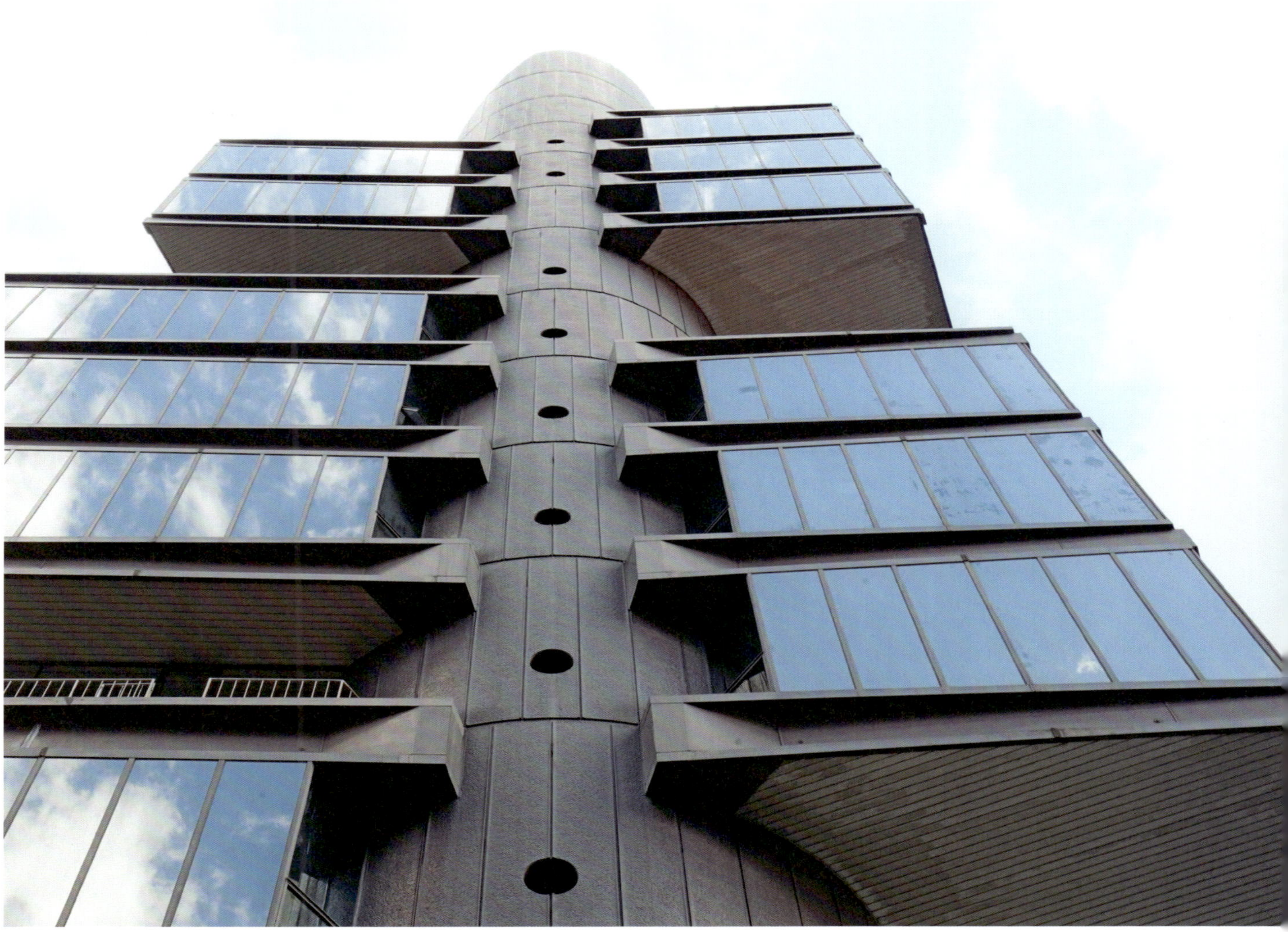

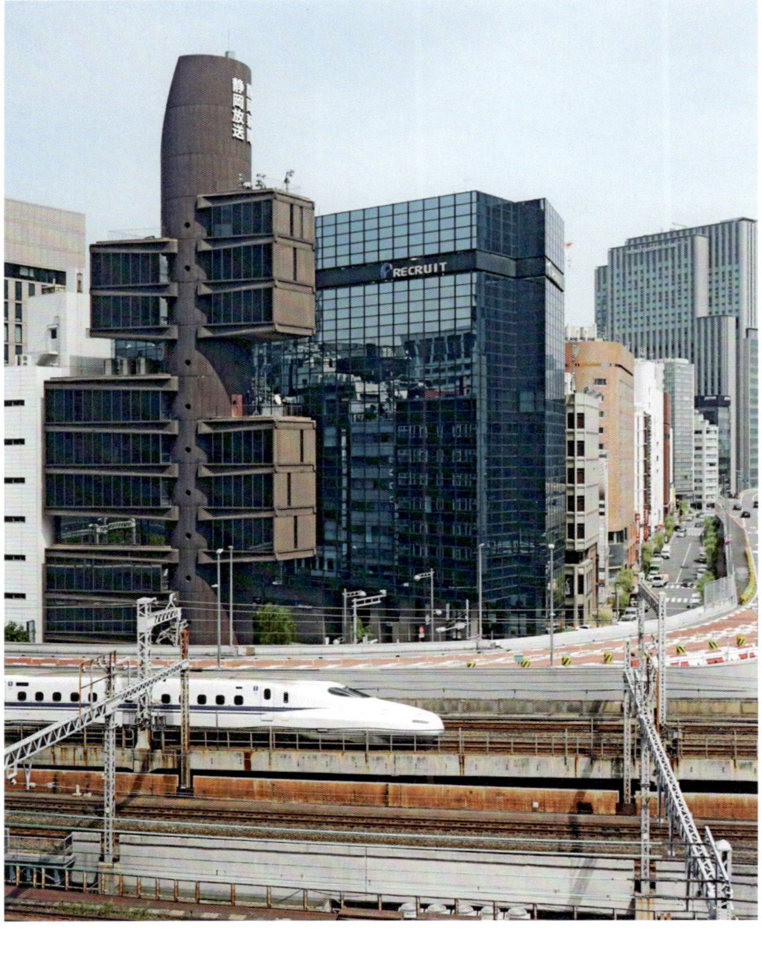
静岡放送
RECRUIT

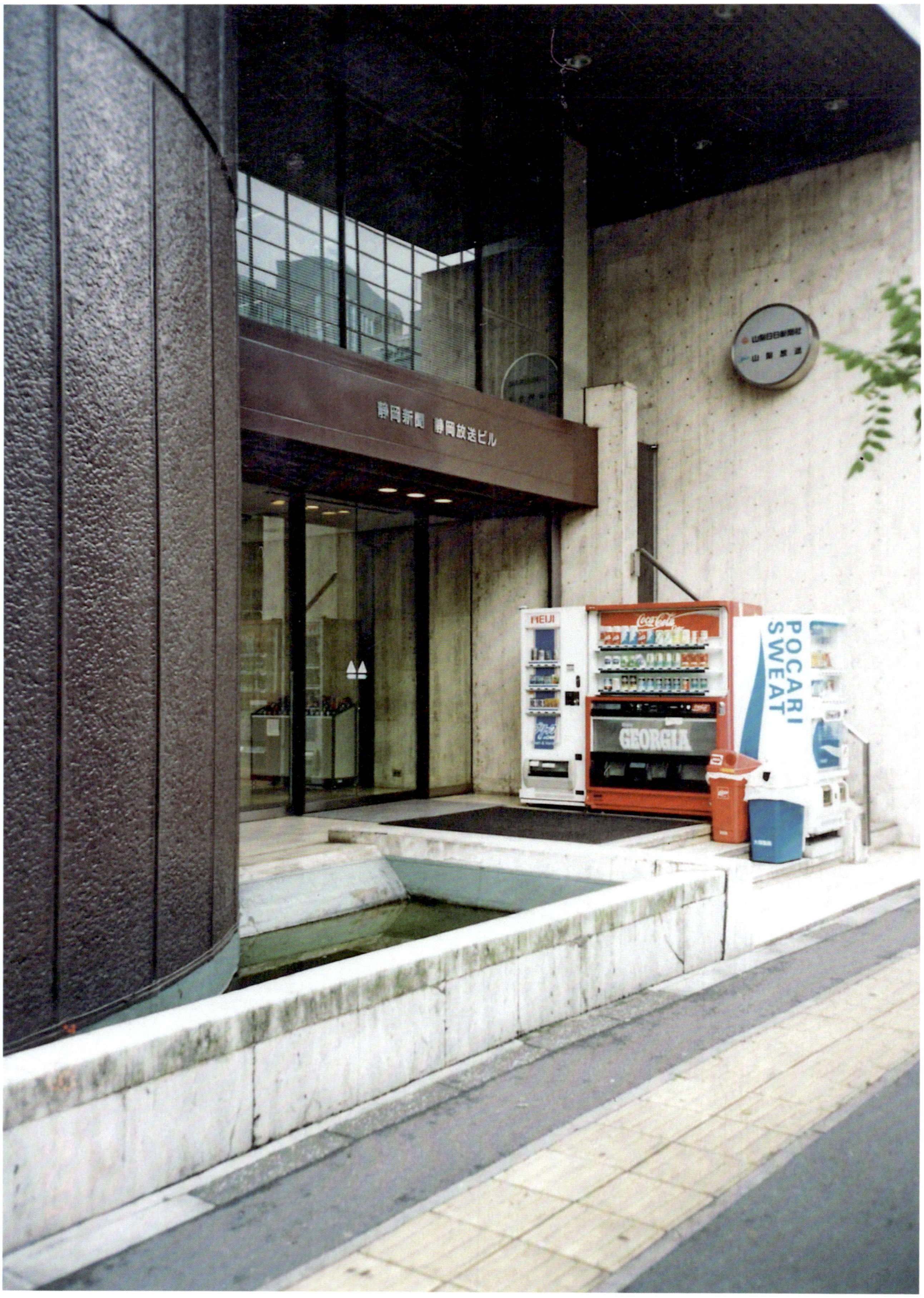
静岡新聞 静岡放送ビル
MEIJI
Coca-Cola
GEORGIA
POCARI SWEAT

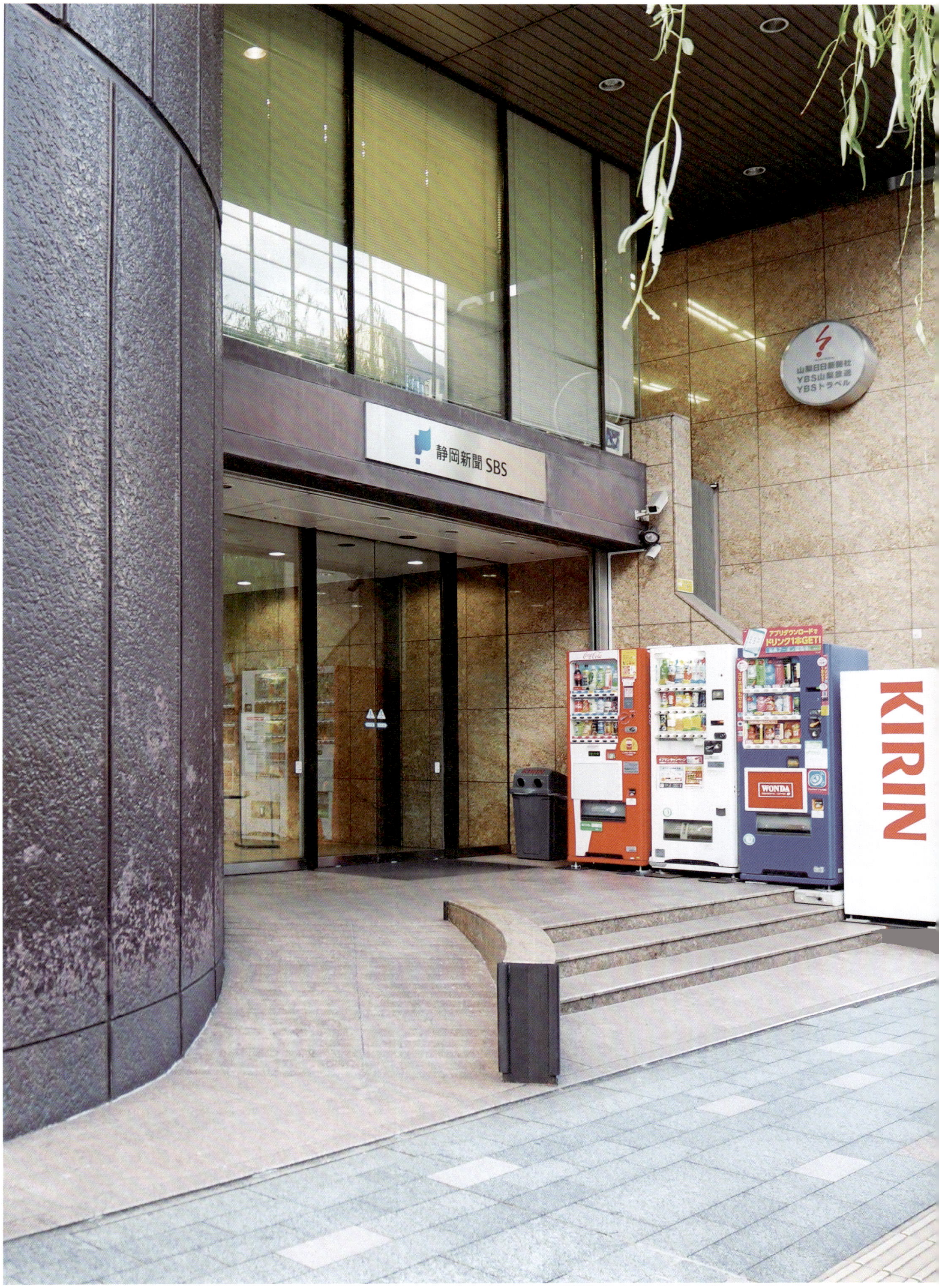
静岡新聞 SBS
山梨日日新聞社
YBS山梨放送
YBSトラベル
WONDA
KIRIN

378

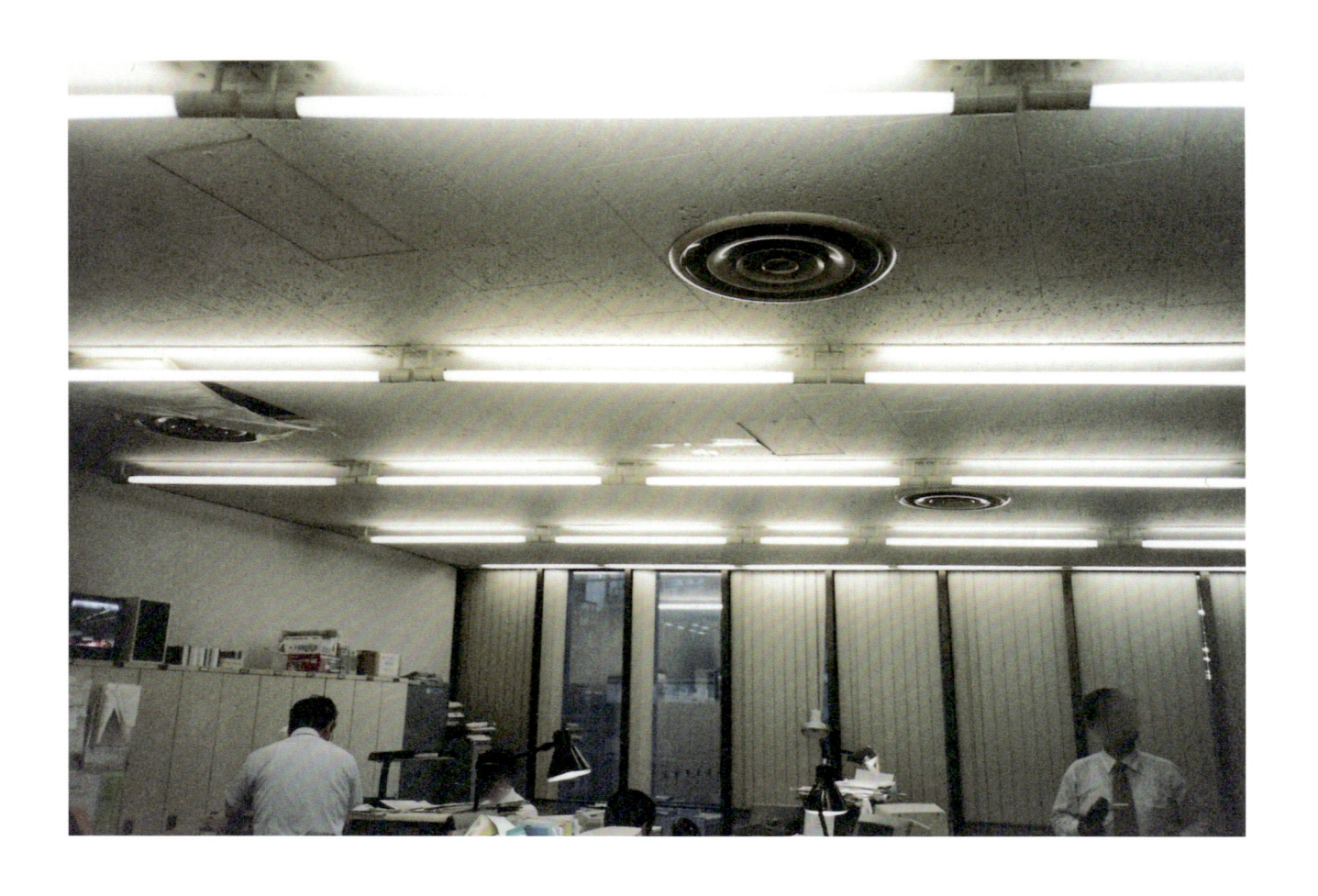

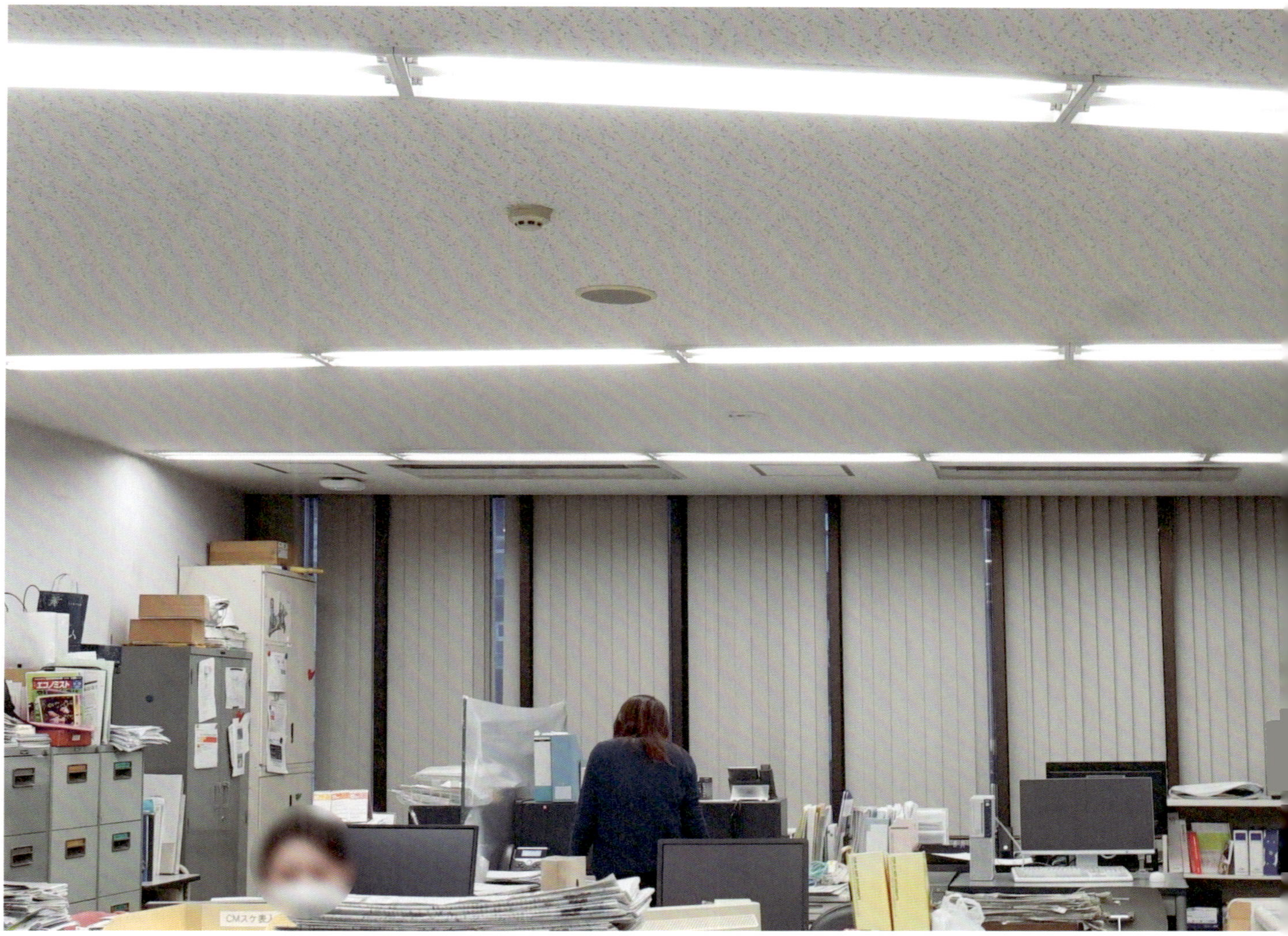

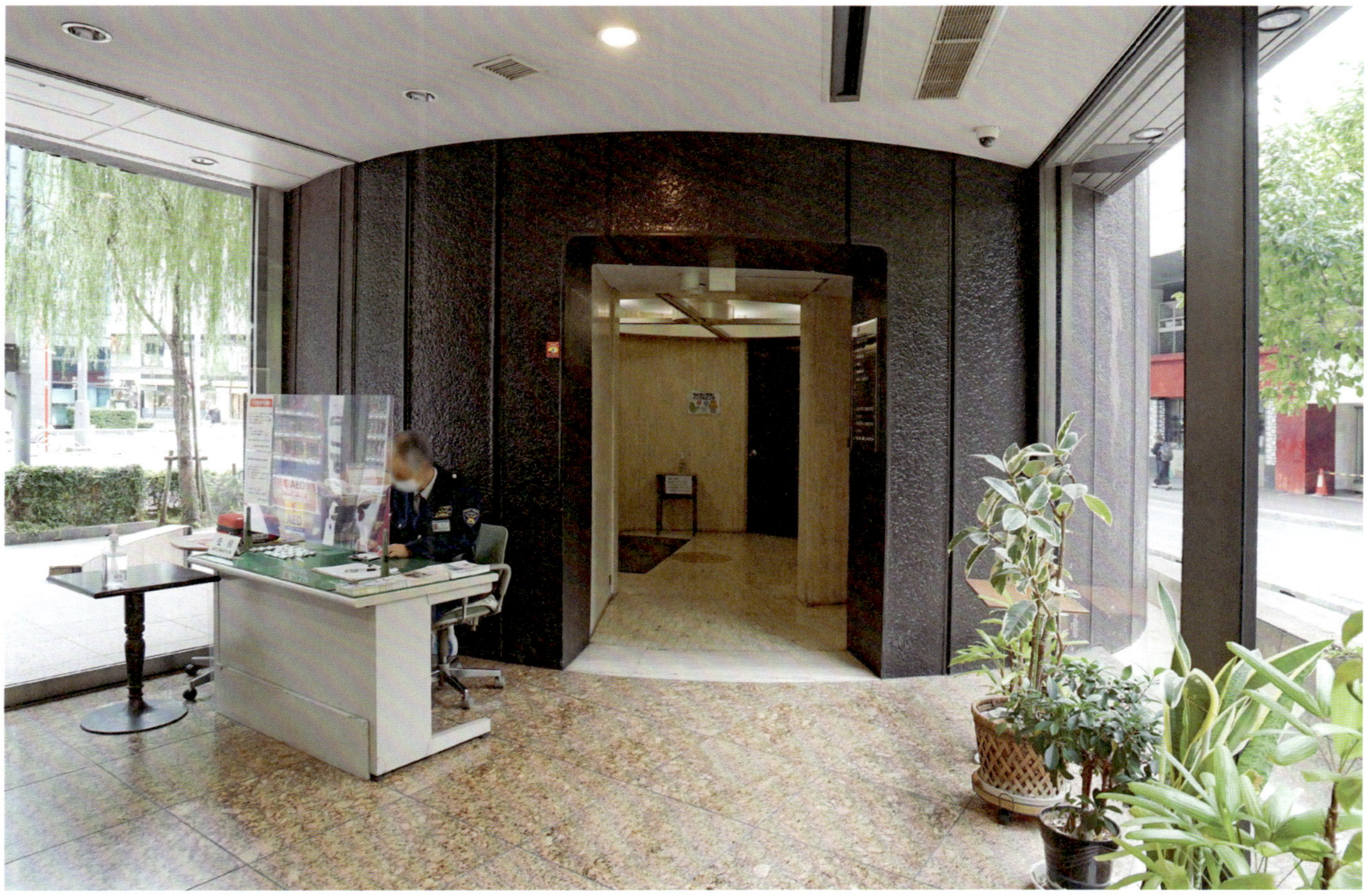

1971

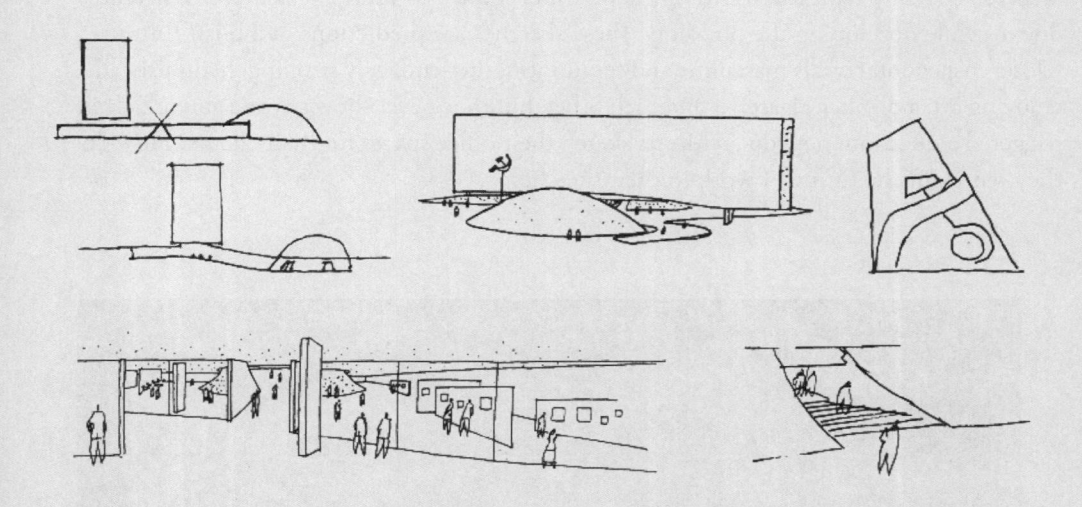

Stephan Petermann

COMMUNIST HEADQUARTERS

Sketching the future of work

While collecting images of the case studies for this book, we noticed how their representation gradually moves from the outside of office buildings to the inside. For earlier buildings, it was often a struggle to find any interior images, specifically of people at work. Whether this was due to the technical challenges of indoor photography, corporate branding and political opportunities offered by a focus on form – image – over content, privacy policies protecting workers, corporate IP, or because of a simple lack of interest in how office workers worked, remains unanswered. In more recent representations of office buildings, in publications like *Workplaces Today* or *The Other Office*, there is an inversion of attention, with an almost exclusive focus on office interiors.[1]

Oscar Niemeyer's work posed a particular challenge. His built work includes iconic public office buildings like the Ministry of Education and Health (1937–1943) in Rio de Janeiro and several governmental buildings in Brasilia, but exterior photography dominates the archive. The only representations of the interiors could be found in Niemeyer's sketches, drawn while developing the building. These sketches are predictions of a blissful future. Closer inspection reveals masculine and feminine figures endlessly strolling, hedonistically enjoying art, a drink, a cigarette, and each other, but they never show anyone at work. This triggered a question: how do architects sketch their office spaces for their clients? How do they represent the future of work in their sketches?

From his spacious private office, the Soviet bureaucrat reviews plans unfurled on a minimalist desk. A phone and a book are installed on a separate workstation (and a third remains unused). His comrade enjoys the view through a ribbon window revealing the landscape outside, while the adjacent wall shows a performance dashboard with graphs and diagrams, with a door opening to his secretariat. A built-in cupboard and shelves occupies the entirety of the other wall, nearly storing records and files.

— Centrosoyuz, Moscow, Le Corbusier, 1937

Besides lobbies, the executive office is a key sketch in office design. Always presented as well-lit in broad daylight but without occupation, with a significantly sized desk and executive chair positioned directly opposite the door as if it was an imperial throne. The executive office, not necessarily a corner office, always counterbalances the power-emitting heavy desk with an informal, softer lounge area. Plants are kept to a minimum and under tight control; carefully selected (art) objects express exclusivity and good taste. The office is in absolute control of itself, the company is not ruled by chaos or chance, but by design.

— Inland steel, Chicago, SOM 1958 (top)
— Nestle HQ, Jean Tschumi, Vevey, Switzerland, 1960 (below)

Two (friendly?) giants: architect Eero Saarinen (left) and client Bill Hewitt (right) broke through the partition walls of a large scale model of the John Deere HQ during design development. While sketches of the office spaces cannot be found in the CAA archive, a series of photos of models survive. Made by Saarinen's office, which had a reputation for working round the clock, these models are clearly used as a communication tool with the client (a mode under pressure today through increased digital modeling). The models show a striking level of detail ranging from the arrangement of interior panels, to precisely scaled ceiling elements and furniture – nothing is left to chance. The quality of the model ends up reflected in the quality of the spaces that were actually built.

— John Deere HQ, Moline, Illinois, Eero Saarinen, 1964

After the organized perfection presented in 1950s office illustrations, the *Grossraum* spaces (essentially the same theory and layout as the Bürolandschaft of Buch und Ton; see page 220) of the 1970s embrace chaos and informality: plants grow free, desks can be cluttered and positioned haphazardly with different heights and types of chairs; a flurry of magazines on a low coffee table surrounded by leisurely couches inviting workers for a smoke, and maybe even some casual flirtation at the office...

— Karl Schwanzer, BMW, Munich, 1973.

Chaos is limited at the offices of Pendorp and replaced by a delicate, informal, lively balance between inside and outside, between tiled pathways and carpeted (or is it grass?) areas with spacious workstations. The office is a combination of industrial – open steel structure – and soft, with an abundance of vegetation – biophilic design avant-la-lettre. Bonnema's vision suggests a multistoried peaceful integration of generations, genders, and disciplines underneath the pyramidal attic of the traditional Friesian farm, so important to Bonnema.

— Abe Bonnema, Pendorp, 1982

notes

1   Juriaan van Meel, *Workplaces Today* (Icop, 2015); Ana Martins, ed. The Other Office 3: *Creative Workspace Design* (Frame Publishers, 2019); Nicola Gillen, *Future Office: Next generation Workplace Design* (Routledge, 2019).

building credits

architect: Oscar Niemeyer

image credits

p.380 (all): Michel Moch
p.381: Oscar Niemeyer
p.382 (above): Fondation le Corbusier
p.382 (below): Eero Saarinen Collection (MS 593). Manuscripts and Archives, Yale University Library.
p.383 (above): SOM
p.383 (below): Jean Tschumi
p.384 (above): Karl Schanzer Archiv Wien Museum
p.384 (below): Abe Bonnema Archief
p.385 (above): Leonardo Finotti, The Tale of Tomorrow
p.385 (below), 387: Patrick Tourneboeuf
p.386: unknown

2020
2 PLACE DU COLONEL-FABIEN
PARIS, FRANCE

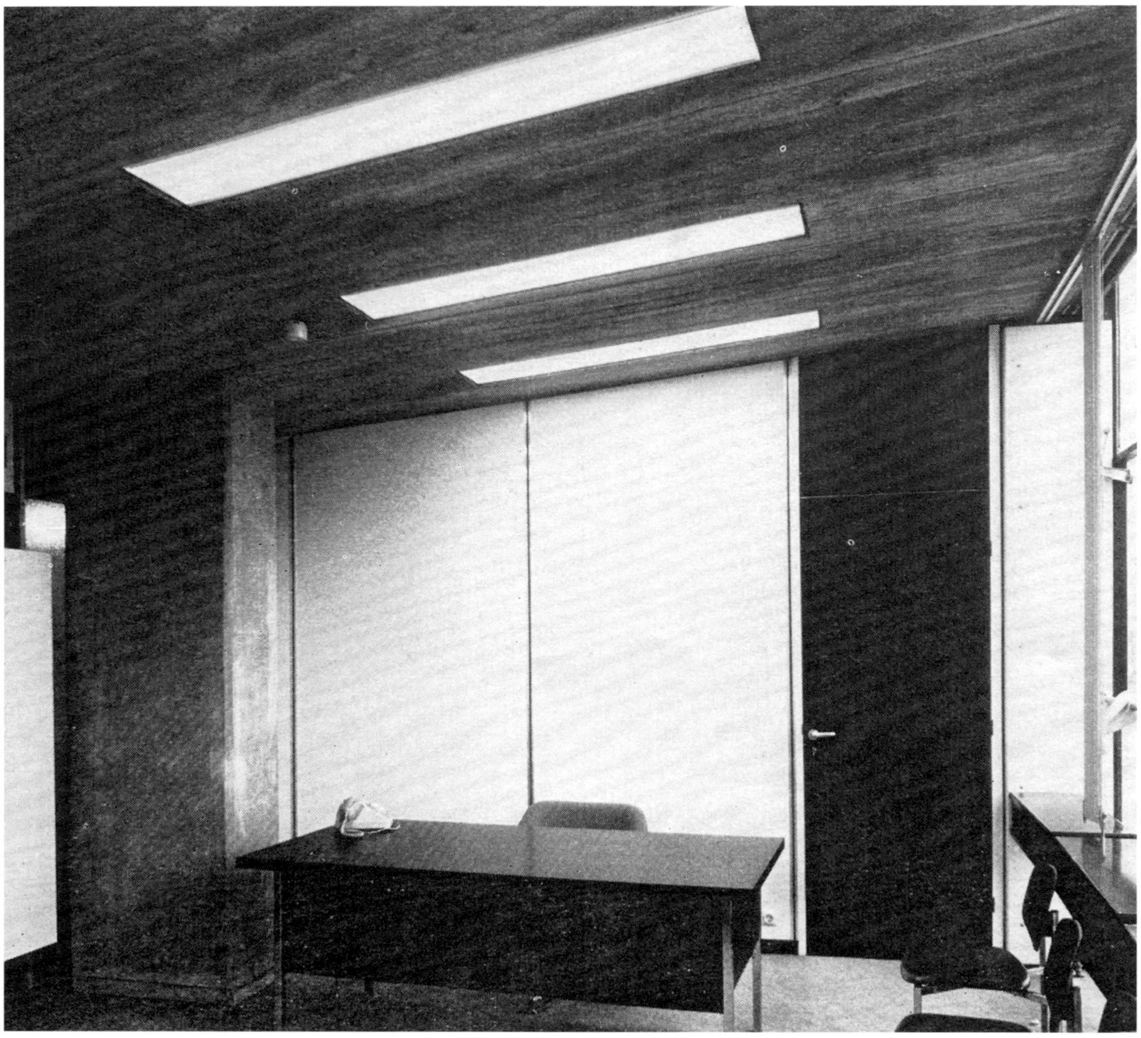

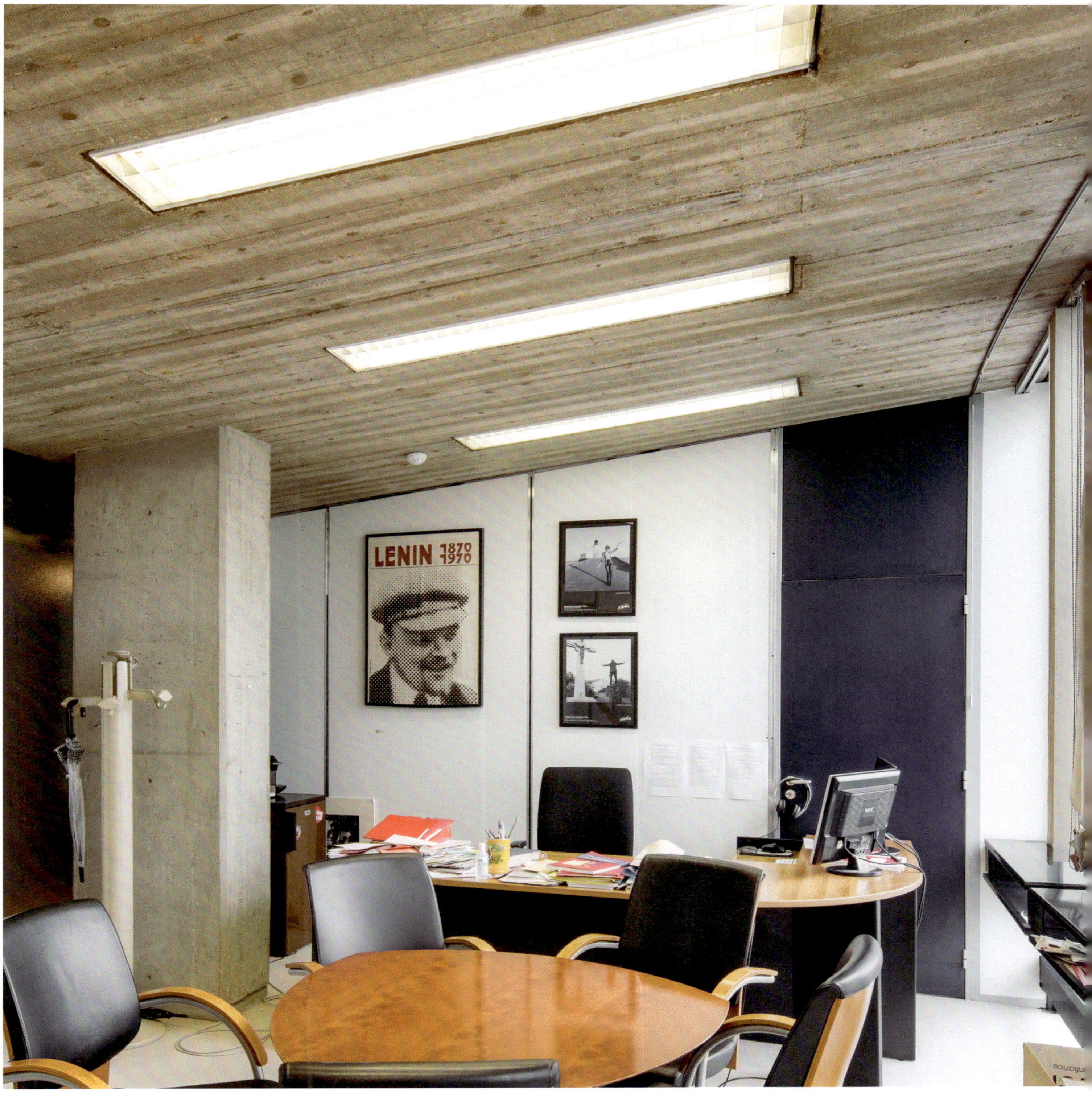
LENIN 1870 1970

1972

Stephan Petermann

CENTRAAL BEHEER

"They have no clue what they are destroying while they are trying to save everything."

The Designer:
Herman Hertzberger

The Rainmaker:
Barry Storm for Certitudo Capital

It's a hot afternoon during the summer of 2019 on the top floor of the 19th-century office building where Herman Hertzberger has his studio. I find him looking at a large screen processing emails, surrounded by around 20 fellow architects. Born in 1932, Hertzberger looks sharp wearing a grey suit with a pen pouch and phone in the left pocket of his dark grey shirt. Later, he will walk back and forth to his team members asking them for updates. The mood is good, focused, quiet. The week before, Hertzberger had been asked to unveil a statue of himself made by Certitudo Capital, with whom he is working on the future of the Centraal Beheer office building in Apeldoorn, which Hertzberger designed in the late '60s and was completed in '72.

The Centraal Beheer office building was sold in 2007 through a sale-and-lease-back deal between Centraal Beheer's parent company Achmea, SNS bank, and the real estate developer TCN. The idea was that the company would remain in the building for another 10 years or so. Three-quarters of the building was owned by the developer, and one quarter by the bank which financed the deal. In 2008, the building was listed as a municipal landmark. In 2011, Achmea announced it would leave the building by 2013 for a newly built campus. The owners announced a plan to develop the building into a business park. In 2012, the Dutch real-estate developers TCN went bust. In the fallout of the 2009 financial crisis and subsequent real-estate

Together with Hertzberger's biographer, Christien Brinkgreve, we try to reconstruct how the building was designed and what happened afterwards.

Stephan Petermann: Can you tell me about the client for the Centraal Beheer?
Herman Hertzberger: I was approached in '67 or '68 by the director of the Centraal Beheer insurance company, Mr. de Ruijter. At that point, Centraal Beheer was based in the GAK-building[1] in Amsterdam, and they had plans to build their own building somewhere. We always focused on the humanitarian reasons for the new building, but the fact that he couldn't find highly skilled workers in the area also weighed into the decision-making process. He was hoping that moving to a nice environment, with lots of nature and forests, would attract new people. I visited a lot of office buildings with him. He had also studied them himself, but he hated them all. Corridors with single cells. He knew that he could get something totally different with a new generation of architects. The German bürolandschaft, or office landscape, had just been tested and he was thinking in that direction. He coined a phrase that I believe I helped him with: "We want to build a workshop for 1,000 people." He would follow that with a story on the amount of time you spend in an office building. And anything but these corridors and cells.

Christien Brinkgreve: What was your starting point for the building?
HH: I had been toying around with the idea for office units. The year before I made a design for the Amsterdam city hall based on elements. They had been inspired by Aldo van Eyck and Louis Kahn. They were developing space-units. You would call them pixels nowadays. Such elements could be used in various ways. Van Eyck's orphanage showed that you could make standard space-units that could be used for different or specific purposes. This idea was based on the development in anthropology with Lévi-Strauss, who, to put it a bit bluntly, discovered that different peoples who didn't know of each other's existence lived using the same rhythms and structures. Noam Chomsky discovered that language functioned in a similar way. Even last week I read an article about a limited number of narratives in storytelling.

SP: And a similar system applies to building?
HH: That's structuralism.

SP: How did that translate in the design?
HH: The design is based on a nine-by-nine-meter modular grid, which can be used in different ways, with different amounts of desks, but also as restaurants, large meeting units, etc. The connecting middle zone, the crucifix grid, is the backbone. This is important because it creates extra space for expansion when needed. You keep a certain amount of flexibility to grow and shrink, a transitional zone between black and white. It also provides space for ducts, etc. It is very different from the [completely open plan] office landscape, which has been highly criticized because workers get distracted easily. This is an improved version of the office landscape, with in-between openings visually connecting it with other floors as well.

SP: And what about the client, Mr. de Ruijter? I also found a Mr. Mulder of Centraal Beheer who praises the design emphatically.
HH: They were both involved. They were very different characters. I proposed to create coffee bars, instead of having people serve coffee from carts. This was discussed at management level, but Mulder was afraid that the workers would be hanging around the bar all day. De Ruijter saw that as a benefit: "Great, that finally gives us the chance to find out who actually is working in this place…" I think I never had a client so willing to engage with my ideas.

SP: Can we talk about the life of the building? What do you consider the key moments after its completion, when did changes occur and why? And what can we learn from this?

crisis, SNS bank was on the verge of collapse until it was bailed out by the Dutch state. The Centraal Beheer building, valued at €38 million, was 'moved' to the now state bank's 'bad bank'. In 2013, Achmea moved to their new campus designed by Amsterdam-based ADP Architecten on the outskirts of Apeldoorn, leaving the more centrally located Central Beheer largely vacant. The building's heritage status created a legal obligation to maintain the building, which left a running cost of around one million euros a year. SNS bank offered the building to the municipality for free, but the city council declined. Due to an earlier crisis, also part of the financial crisis, the municipality of Apeldoorn was under legal restraint by the province. Developing housing is not allowed under the circumstances.

In 2015, the complex was put up for sale. Den Bosch-based real-estate developer Certitudo Capital bought it as the sole interested party for €2.5 million. Certitudo's leadership assessed that 2.5 hectares of prime land in the city center, close to the train station in a place like Apeldoorn, should never be a problem.

Enter Barry Storm, the 2019 rainmaker for the project for Certitudo. He agreed to meet at the building. From a construction portacabin on the building's premises, Storm explained his background in brokering hard-to-sell developments. In Eindhoven, he had been a key figure in redeveloping Phillips' research and production areas of Strijp-S. Phillips sold a group of large factories and development centers after the financial crisis, most of them still in pretty good condition. "Normally, we would do a more straightforward erase and replace scheme," Storm explained. "But there was no money in the market. So, we just started renting the existing places out. It was a move made more from despair than a clear vision," Storm added. A year-and-a-half later, the buildings in Strijp-S were full of young start-ups. Storm started to realize the potential of this model. The owners moved

HH: The key moment was some time after the completion. Due to a restructuring in the company, part of the building had been vacant and the idea emerged to house an art academy in it for a few months. We thought damn, you could actually make a very interesting museum here. Wouldn't be that difficult. The openness of the building is nice, but if you need more closed spaces that's okay too. It really gave me a boost to work on it in this way. After Centraal Beheer left the building, we also thought we could make it into a great school building, or student housing, but then you need students… You can turn it into anything! Now we are working on a scheme to turn it into housing. With fully openable façades and roof gardens. It's not that easy though due to strict regulations, which can drive you mad. But we will manage.

SP: We see that in a lot of the projects we are looking at.

HH: [Showing a floor-plan] Hot off the press. We are working on it constantly. The client keeps on changing his mind. It might be that we will add some office program again. One week they want larger apartments, the next week smaller. We received a call that they have been calculating and found a way to improve the value per square meter. We might need to add some staircases, but in general it works. I expect a phone call soon to add a supermarket or a hospital or so. So I want to build something that can face these changes. That's my proof of the pudding. It could be a remedy for all the buildings which after just a few years turn vacant.

SP: It is slightly ironic that an owner with Certitudo in its name is so uncertain of the future program of the building. When you pick a name, there might be a tendency to select the exact opposite of what you really are? What does it say about architecture?

HH: The story of functionalism has been slashed away by the times. You have to design something that can last forever. Housing is the final building type we can be certain of. We will always need somewhere to live. So I am happy that Centraal Beheer will turn into housing. I insist actually. I will not die until these apartments are in there! You have to be able to design something that can deal with change, while still having character. The building should have a personality which is able to change – but without becoming a flip-flopper.

SP: I found this note about Achmea's announcement of their departure from the building in 2011: "Achmea chose a new location over its current location at Prins Willem-Alexanderlaan. According to a spokesperson, there are new quality standards for offices and workplaces … and improvement of the current condition is not deemed adequate… We will be trying to find a new purpose for the building in the next five years. Demolition is not our preference." Did they ever discuss this with you?

HH: [waving it off, agitated] That's what they always say, with those nonsense arguments. They just tore down one of my retirement homes.[2] Exactly the same story. But the following day the media are full of stories about increased loneliness in society. I am really torn by it.

SP: I found all kinds of fantastic stories about Centraal Beheer at the opening in the early 70s. Employees who say they would be OK with making less money, as long as they can work in the building. It also makes me incredibly sad because that spirit was lost. Do you recognize that? Could you pinpoint a moment when that happened?

HH: Well, the employees used to be able to design their own workstation. You got a whole range of different outcomes: some took their pets with them, some brought in personal items. They could be themselves. And that stopped at some moment. They started wearing suits again, the ties returned… They don't feel like it anymore.

CB: This wasn't a management instruction?
HH: It was their own decision. With grey and striped suits.

from being classical real-estate developers to real-estate owners and hosts. He also claimed a significant economic trickle-down effect, boosting the city's overall economy.

When he started working on Centraal Beheer for Certitudo, the company was focused on the numbers: "They were less engaged with other factors like the broader picture of what you sell, the story. But with Eindhoven, we had found out that it really makes a difference."

The business case for the Centraal Beheer building remains difficult. "The gross-net rentable floor ratio in the building is in many ways dramatic, just completely off. At the same time, it's also what makes the building so unique and great."

The initial redevelopment scheme pointed to converting the complex solely into housing (Certitudo has a background in residential development). Storm was now trying to optimize the gross-net ratio by reintroducing office areas too: "The building can't be fully transformed to housing. One quarter will be housing, perhaps two, the other two for office spaces." What makes the redevelopment particularly difficult is how the pixelated structure of amassed cubes adds far more facade area than a regular building. And all these glass facades, designed before the oil crisis, will have to be replaced in order to reduce the building's energy consumption.

Storm was in the process of trying to get a loan for the first stage of redevelopment, which would total around €25 million. Updated fire regulations and financial limitations also pose challenges – literally cutting corners in the façade could dramatically lower costs in replacing the façade: "It will never be a high-profit development, but still we are fully convinced it will be able to generate enough ROI for investors and contributing to the larger ecosystem of the city."

SP: But when you look at the old photos it looks exactly like Facebook, Google, etc.
HH: Yes with pants with pre-made rips in them. That flows like waves.

SP: I also read about sustainability issues with the building, the energy usage.
HH: What could I do about that? It was designed when this was not an issue. The Club of Rome had just started. Always the same, like at De Drie Hove. They keep increasing regulations. They have no clue what they are destroying while they are trying to save everything.

P.S. Winter 2021: The ease with which Hertzberger can, in words, transform his beloved buildings remains in stark contrast with the reality of the building. The fate of the Centraal Beheer building is still unresolved. During a 2019 visit, the state of the building was poor, with signs of both burglary and vandalism. Since then, deterioration has accelerated, leading to calls from the architecture community to ensure the building's survival. Despite a housing crisis in the Netherlands and a booming residential market, the financial viability remained unsure. In October 2021 Certitudo capital announced that following a long-lasting court case concerning a neighboring building, a new plan for the entire complex is expected, without giving more details about its outlines. The plan will include additional buildings and also increase the maximum number of apartments to be inserted into the existing structure, to ease financial pressure. Certitudo has promised to make the building waterproof again over the winter period. A large office building that once housed the Dutch Ministry of Social Affairs in The Hague, designed by Hertzberger, is now also expected to be torn down and will be replaced by a new residential complex designed by Barcode architects, despite objections by Herztberger and local inhabitants.

"€25 million at the moment gets an easier and higher ROI with less risk than in the larger cities. But this building has a soul, you feel it can become something great again, which can mean so much for the city, so we have to really work outside of the box."

A lot of boxes actually.

notes

1   A large modernist office building designed by Ben Merkelbach, completed in 1960.
2   De Drie Hoven, Amsterdam.

building credits

client: Centraal Beheer
architect: Herman Hertzberger

photo credits

p.388 (above): Aerophoto
p.388 (below): Nationaal Archief, Rijksvoorlichtingsdienst
p.394, 395, 399: Stephan Petermann
p.397 (above), 398 (all): HHA
p.397 (below): Christian Richters

2019
PRINS WILLEM-ALEXANDERLAAN 651
APELDOORN, THE NETHERLANDS

397

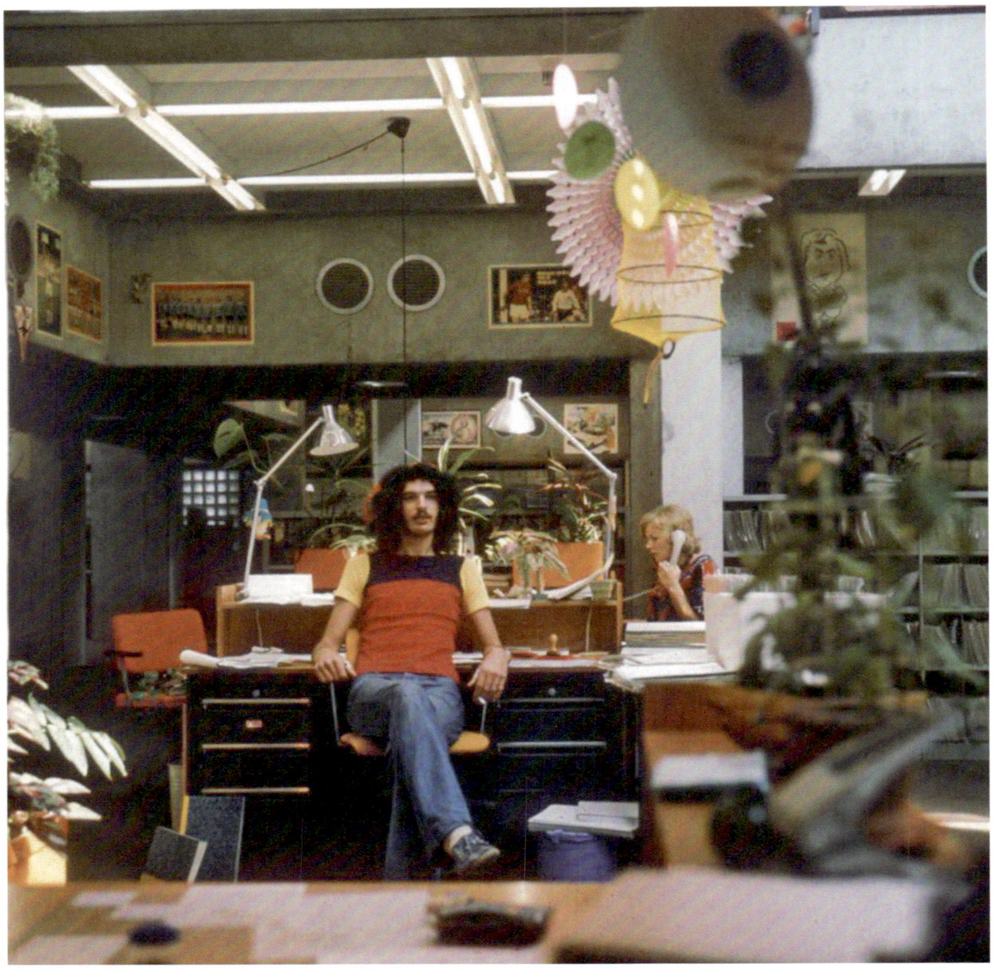

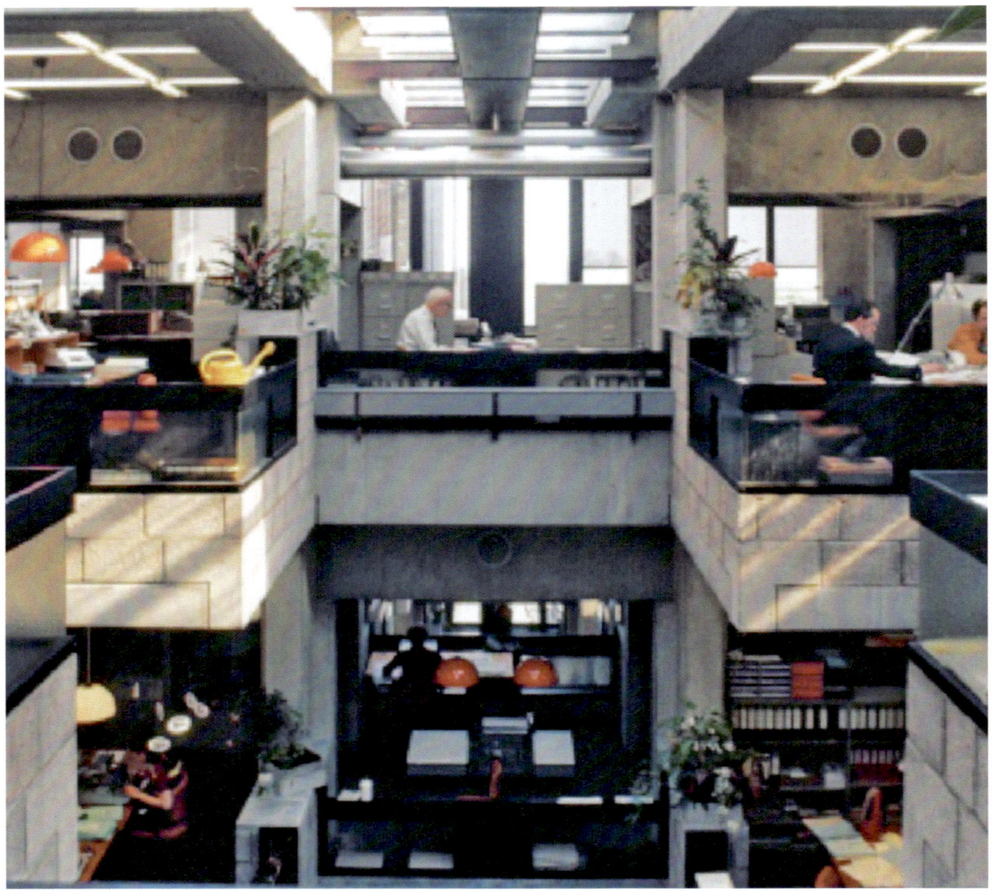

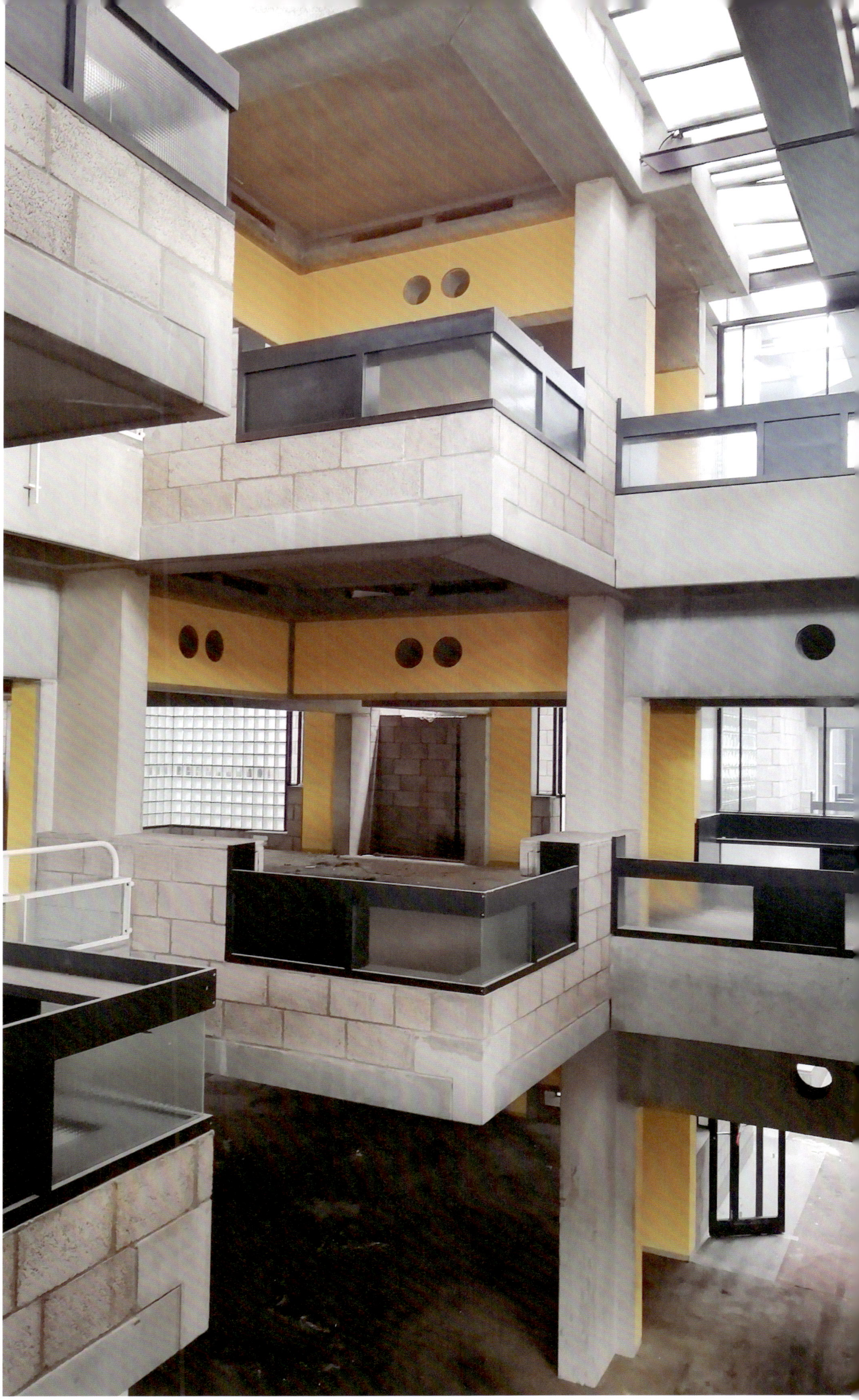

UNI-HOCHHAUS 1973

In 1968, Leipzig's Paulinerkirche – one of the few buildings to survive Second World War bombing – was dynamited by governmental degree. The 13th-century church, in the city's historical center, Augustusplatz (soon to be renamed Karl-Marx-Platz), had to make way for a large campus for Karl-Marx-Universität. The development would form a new cultural and political center of the city. Given the prominent location, the Politbüro agreed – surprisingly – to stage a design competition by invite. Hermann Henselmann (1905–95), teaming up with Bauakademie Berlin, only received third prize for his design, which included a 142-meter tower. Yet, he won the commission anyway due to the sympathies of party secretary, Walter Ulbricht. Henselmann's original idea to accommodate lecture halls in the tower proved unworkable; it was eventually used for university administration. For many of the locals today, the Weisheitszahn (wisdom tooth), as they sympathically call the tower, represents a myth. Its structure was erected at unprecedented speed – in time to mark the GDR's twentieth anniversary in 1969 – thanks to the innovative sliding construction principle. It was the highest building of both German states when completed in 1972 and its panoramic restaurant offered a breathtaking view over the GDR's commercial city. With its dynamic crown and facades curved like an open book, the building exemplified GDR's Bildzeichen Architektur, aimed at creating identity in the cities rebuilt after the war. With Germany's reunification, the political context transformed and so did the building. Henselmann's tower stood idle for years before the government sold it to a German investment company in 1999, which together with architect Peter Kulka initiated a $50 million renovation. The tower was reinvented as City-Hochhaus, with multi-tennant offices, in 2002. The interior was completely remodeled and the light aluminium cladding was replaced by grey granite. Paulinerkirche was partially reconstructed, materializing as a prayer room behind a huge postmodern façade mock-up by Erik van Egeraat. Karl-Marx-Platz became Augustusplatz again. These radical changes to the complex – delivered by the engine of the market economy – rendered one of the most remarkable postwar urban renewal in the GDR almost unrecognizable.

2021
AUGUSTUSPLATZ 9
LEIPZIG, GERMANY

building credits

architect: Hermann Henselmann

photo credits

p.400: Friedrich Gahlbeck, Federal Archives
p.401, 403 (all): Jens Frederiksen
p.402 (above): Sandra Schubert
p.402 (below): Sandra Schubert

402

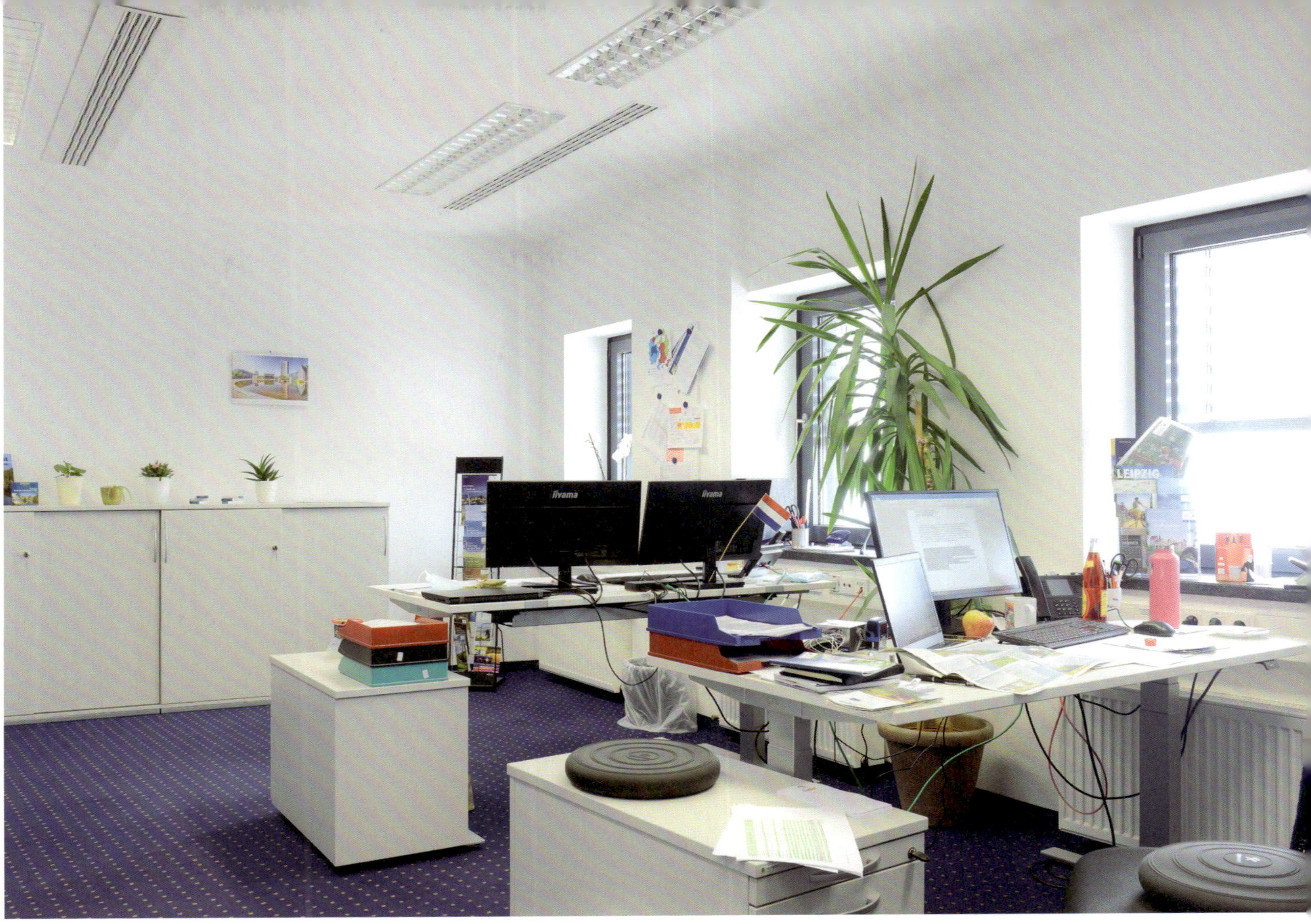
iiyama
iiyama
LEIPZIG

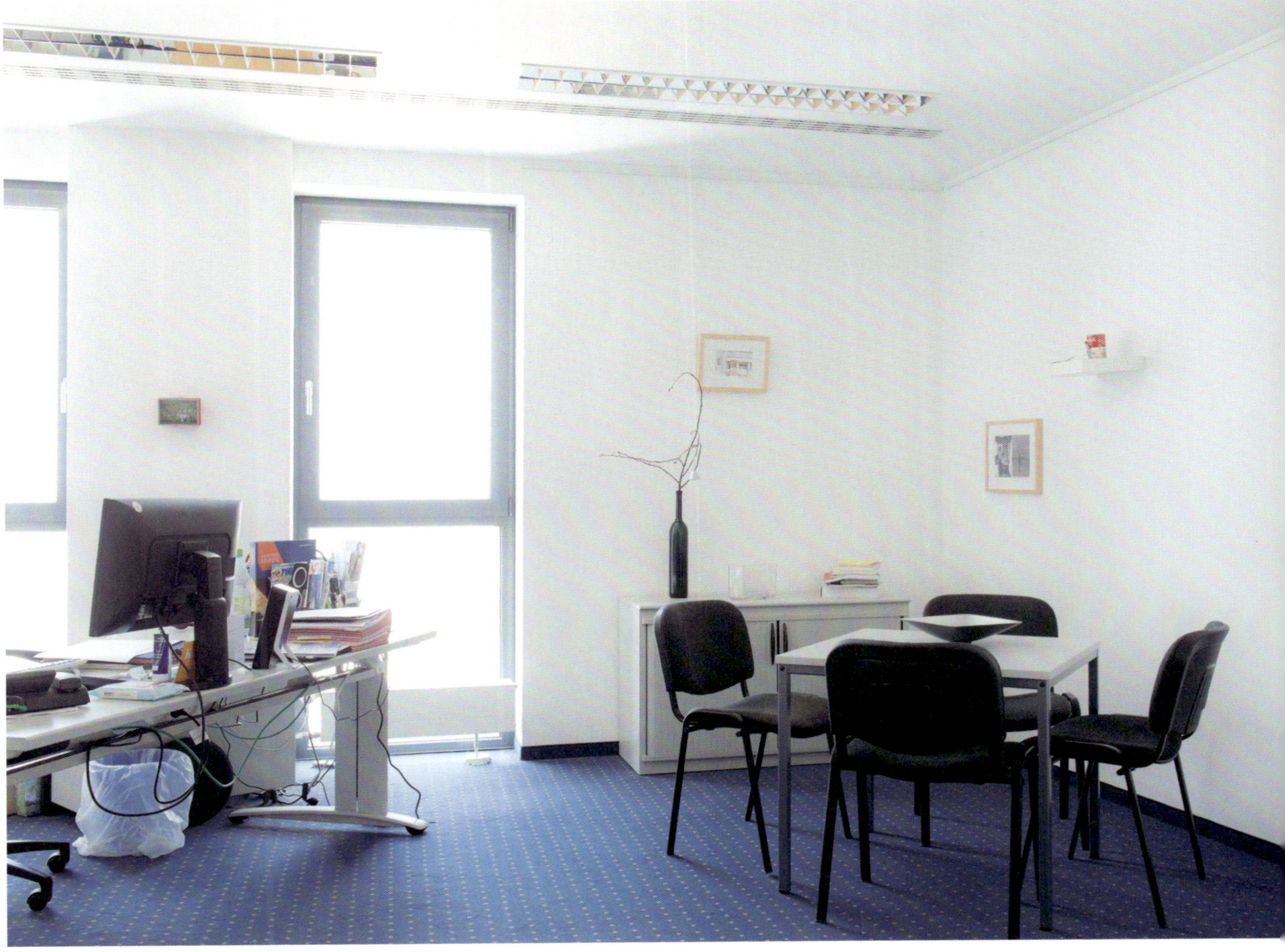

1973

CHICAGO FEDERAL CENTER

A federal building adds 50 bollards, 24 planters, and 28 courtrooms to cope with the impacts of late modernity

The Chicago Federal Center was a federal commission by the General Services Administration to Ludwig Mies van der Rohe in 1959 for two office buildings, the Kluczynski Federal Building (45 stories) and the Dirksen Federal Building (30 stories), as well as the Loop Station Post Office (1 story). Mies teamed up with three other architects to assist in the project delivery. The spiraling expenses of the Vietnam War caused a budgetary pinch, delayed the project's construction. The Dirksen building was completed in 1964, while the Kluczynski Federal Building and the post office were only finished ten years later.

BOLLARDS
In 1993, the World Trade Center bombing in New York City sparked an awareness of how vulnerable of buildings were to terrorism. Two years later, Timothy McVeigh

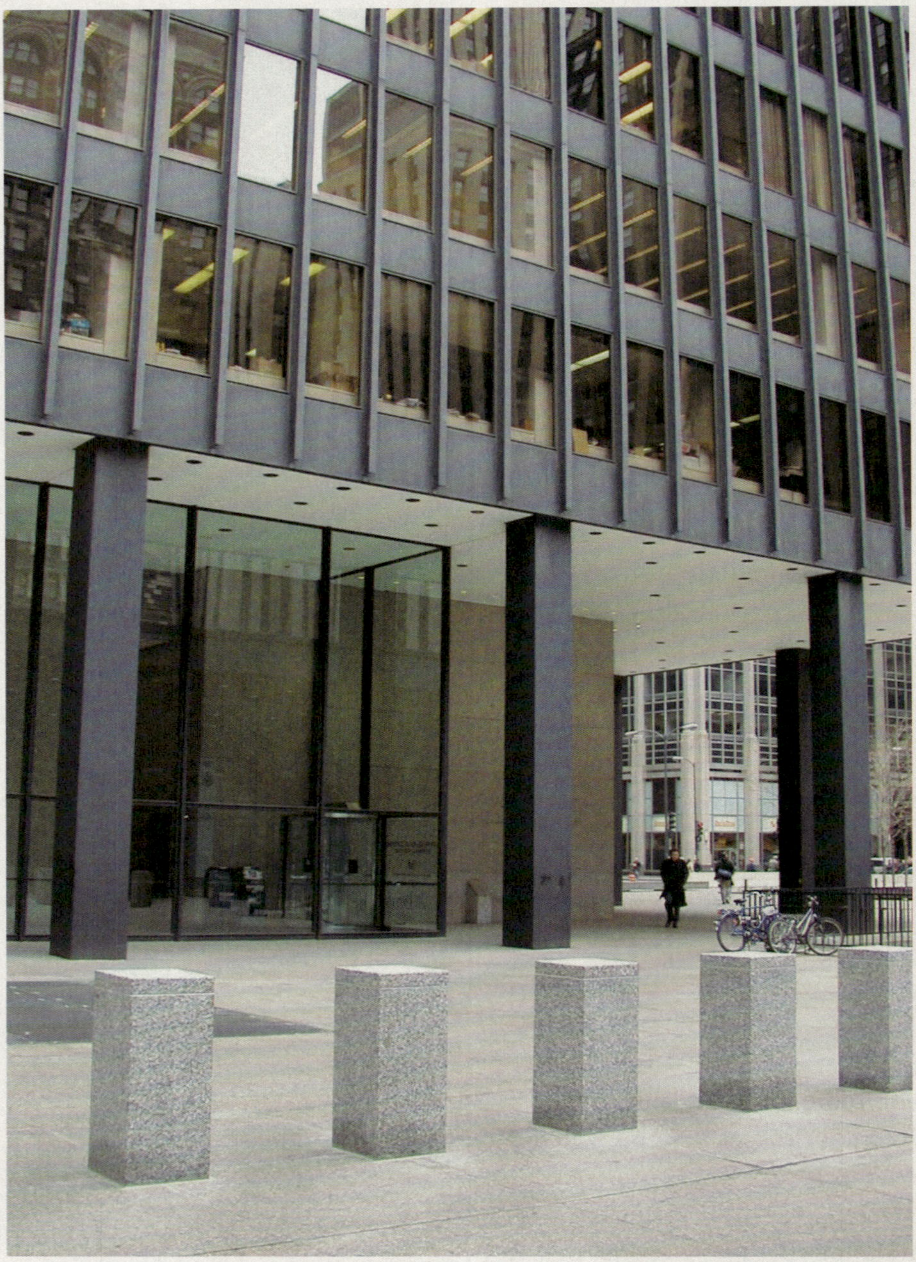

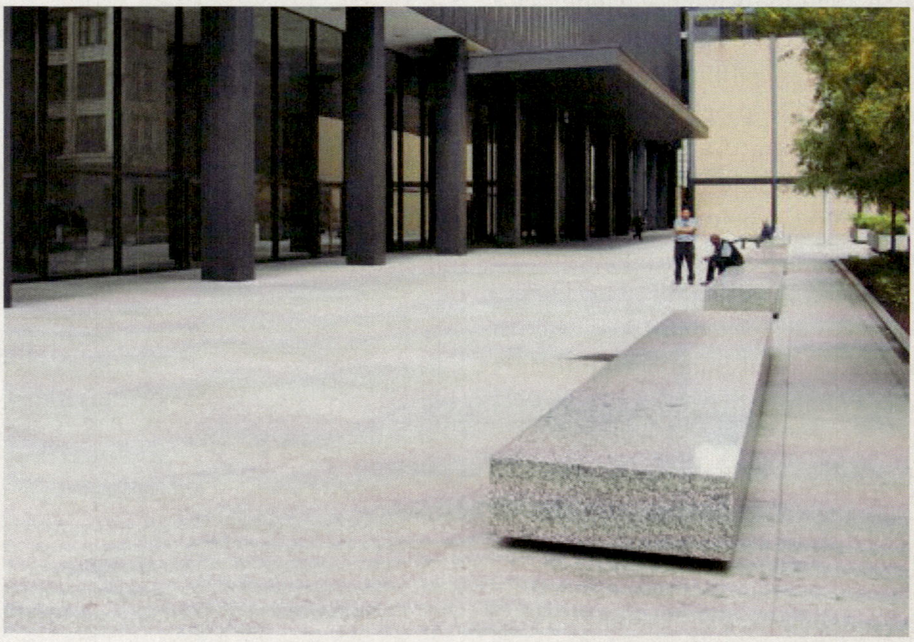

bombed the Alfred P. Murrah Federal Building in Oklahoma, killing 168 people. The event triggered an increase in security at US federal buildings. In 2007, FEMA (Federal Emergency Management Agency) published a design guide for defense against potential terrorist attacks, "Site and Urban Design for Security", which uses the Chicago Federal Center as a case study for how security measures should be designed in historically protected environments. FEMA proposed three layers of security should be added to the building's surroundings. The first layers aims at guarding the building from external calamities. Mies' embrace of granite is adopted by FEMA, adding massive planters and rectangular bollards of the material on the plaza's perimeter. The second layer added more barriers and planting on the plaza itself. The third layer aimed at the entrance area remained unspecified. More than 50 bollards, and 24 large heavy planters and benches were now fortifying the once open space. In addition to security, FEMA's design guide notes the added quality of an all year round planting scheme for the planters.

BADGES
A similar development occurred in the lobby. A glass balustrade cut the space in two, with a security scanner as the central gateway. The new divide created a need for exit signage, a white sign with black letters placed on the building's black columns. Badges are now given to visitors. At least six CCTV cameras monitor the immediate space outside, and an equal number observes the lobby. The original reception desk has an added (bulletproof?) glass barrier on the counter. A second reception desk has been added for additional security checks. A carpet has been added to the perhaps slippery granite floor. In the courtrooms, three seemingly randomly placed cameras break Mies' starkly gridded illuminated ceiling.

BENCHES

A dramatic increase of federal court cases – from around 50,000 cases nationwide in the late 1950s, to 200,000 cases a year in 2008 has had consequences for the floor usage in the Dirksen building. The original building included 21 courtrooms divided over six floors, which took-up around 17 percent of the total built area, 41 percent including supporting areas. The first addition came in the 1980s, when 20 mini-courtrooms were added, mostly in hallway-like sections. Mies' grandson Dirk Logan added four larger courtrooms in 1994. In 1998, Urban Design Group added another four. A full office renovation conducted in 2012 by SOM added yet another four. The building now has 49 courtrooms divided over 16 floors, using 90 percent of the office building (counting the support spaces).

The absolute symmetry of the original courtrooms had an intimidating austerity. All the later courtroom designs attempted to work with Mies' original design, but never achieved the same impact. While they all remain committed to the wood paneling and orthogonal motif, they lack the strict symmetrical design of the originals. In the 1990s, desk chairs with thicker padding were introduced. The single long perpendicular table in front of the judge was split into two separate tables, placed at a 90-degree angle. Single-toned velour-looking carpeting was replaced with dotted and striped carpet tiles. Also, in Logan's design, the judge sits slightly off-center, while the Urban Design Group reinstated the strict symmetry. The SOM design, while still referring to Mies, introduced more informality.

BEAUTY
Despite the success of the Federal center over time both in its recognized modern architectural prowess and the ability to adapt, the future for new federal buildings is not undisputed. In early 2020, the Trump administration released a draft executive order to prioritize classical architecture for new larger federal buildings. The draft *Making Federal Buildings Beautiful Again* proposes that "federal architecture should once again inspire respect instead of bewilderment or repugnance," and that "classical and traditional architecture styles have proven their ability to inspire such respect for our system of self-government" concluding that their use should be encouraged. The final executive order was issued in December 2020, a month before the transition to Joe Biden's Administration, and called for creating a committee to report to President Biden by September 2021. In late 2021, the link to the executive order became a 404 on the Whitehouse website. But for how long?

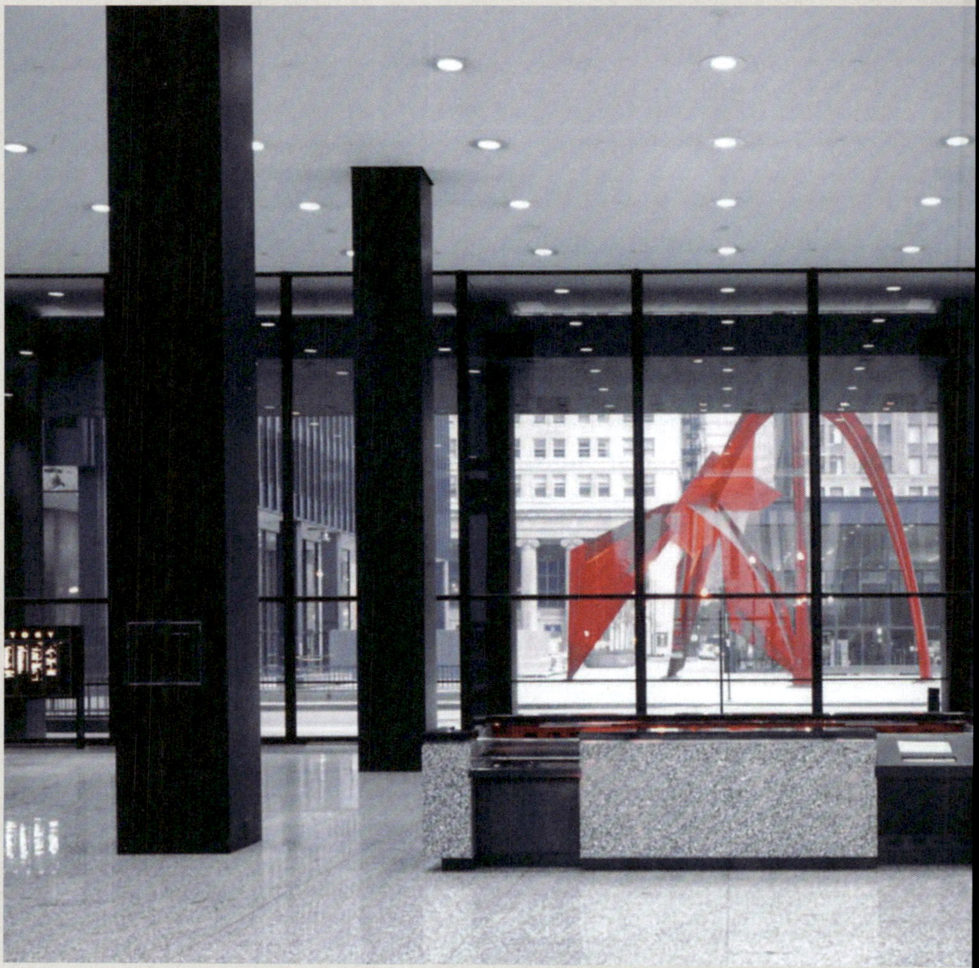

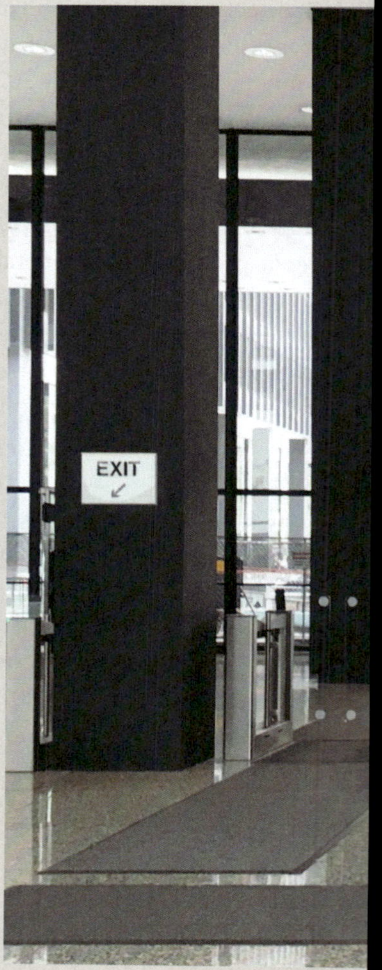
EXIT

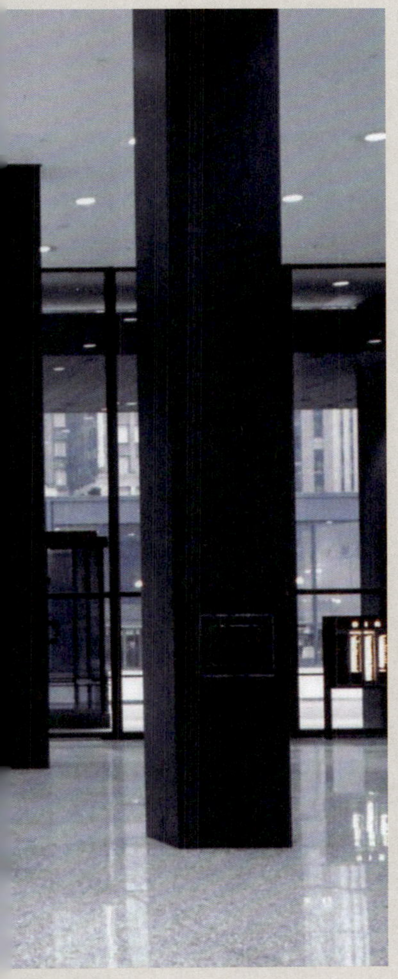

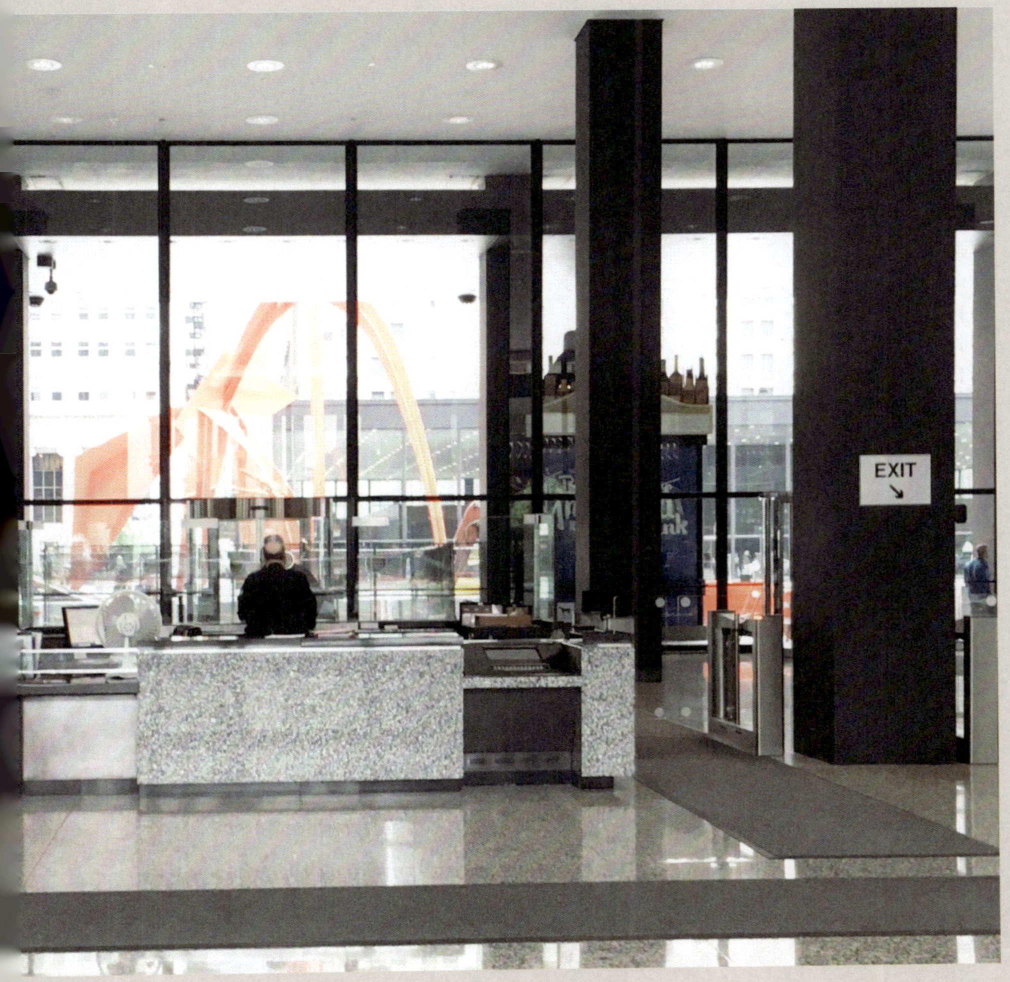
EXIT

photo credits

p.404: US General Services Administration
p.406 (above), 410-411 (above): unknown
p.406 (below): Jose Juan Barba
p.408 (all), 410-411 (below), 415: Stephen Angus, Danny Yontz
p.413: Carol M Highsmith, Library of Congress
p.414: Everett M. Dirksen U.S. Courthouse, Chicago

building credits

architect: Ludwig Mies van der Rohe

photo credits

p.404: US General Services Administration
p.406 (above), 410-411 (above): unknown
p.406 (below): Jose Juan Barba
p.408 (all), 410-411 (below), 415: Stephen Angus, Danny Yontz
p.413: Carol M Highsmith, Library of Congress
p.414: Everett M. Dirksen U.S. Courthouse, Chicago

2017
S. DEARBORN STREET
CHICAGO, ILLINOIS, US

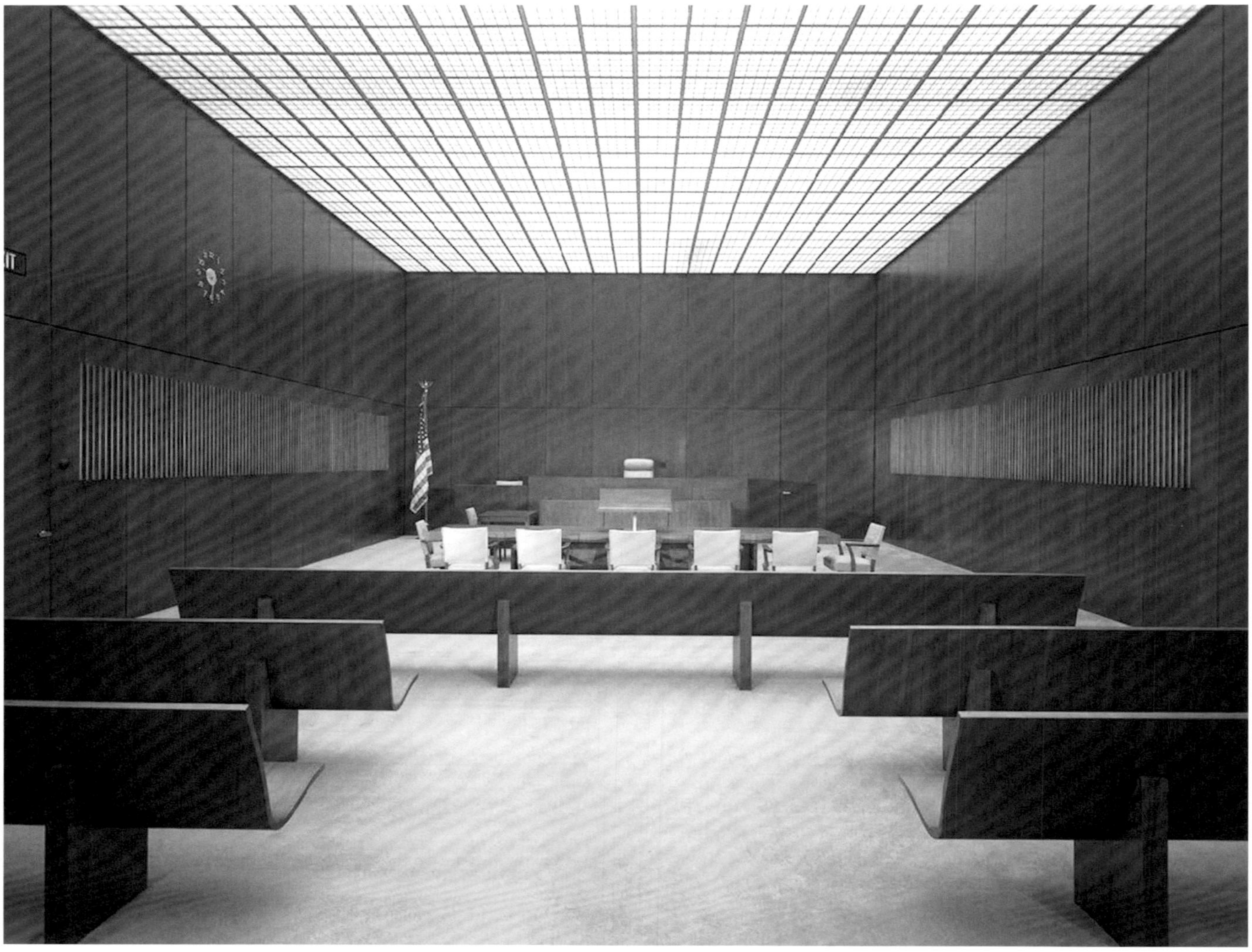

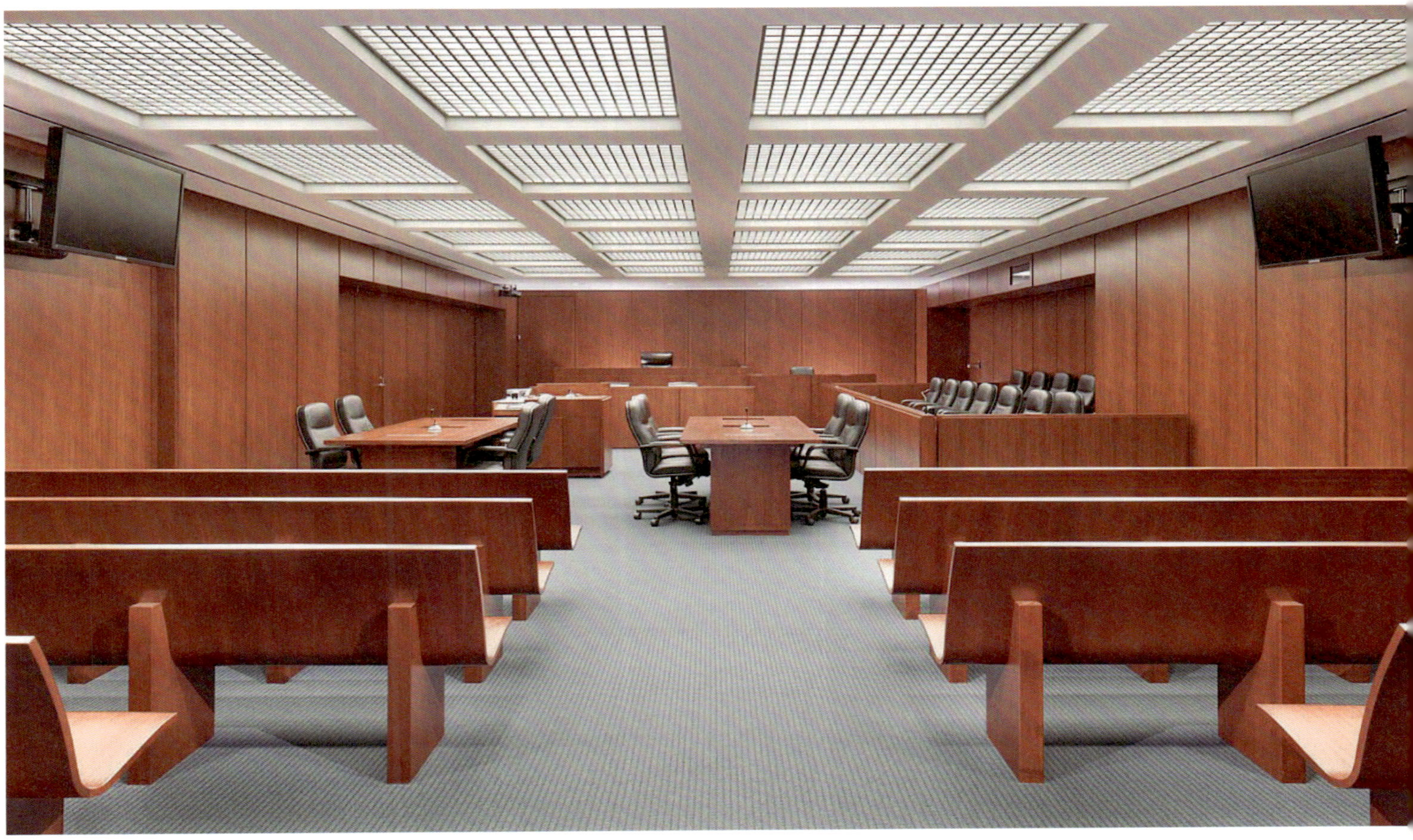

1973

Ruth Baumeister

BMW HEADQUARTERS

**A corporate HQ built for speed and branding
— sited next to Munich's Olympic Park —
is upgraded and still loved in the 21st century**

"What really interests me about Karl Schwanzer is this: he was a year or two behind the Mies tradition in the 1950s; in the 1960s, he got into systems building and massive pre-casting in so adventurous a way that most of his contemporaries must have been holding their breath; and now, in the 1970s, Karl Schwanzer is becoming the Supersculptor that the Archigram Kids and Cape Kennedy Freaks have long wanted to be – but he has really done it. What in God's name is going to be next?"[1]

It is no surprise that Peter Blake wrote this shortly after Schwanzer (1918–75) finished the BMW headquarters in Munich – an ensemble consisting of a four-core highrise tower, a bowl-shaped museum, and a modular parking garage. The composition still seems outlandish today.

During the 1960s – after almost being swallowed by its competitor Mercedes Benz – BMW experienced an unprecedented period of growth. German industrialist Herbert Quandt invested in the company, enabling the development of a new, extremely successful series of cars. Expanding from a small Bavarian car and motorcycle producer to a multinational corporate manufacturer of luxury vehicles, BMW saw a need to better represent itself. They launched a competition for a new headquarters adjacent to the Oberwiesenfeld, a former military area in the north of Munich. No first prize was awarded; instead, Schwanzer's ambitious design received one of the two second prizes. His extravagant scheme called for the most architecture not least because he proposed a museum to present BMW's legacy, which was not asked for in the first place. His 99.5-meter tower (just within the city's planning regulations) was composed of four cylinders of reinforced concrete, connected by a circulation and services core; on the roof, four beams cantilevered out, from which the cylinders were hung like a lampion. The tower does not touch the ground but hovers over a low-slung rectangular slab. Despite the jury pointing out some potentially severe functional problems – like curved walls in offices – they acknowledged that the tower's form would create a landmark for BMW in relation to the neighboring TV tower and Olympic park for the oncoming 1972 games. BMW sales executive Paul Hahnemann favored this audacious project and Schwanzer got the commission.

In BMW, Schwanzer – who used car terminology when referring to the tower as the "four-cylinder" – found an ideal client for his visions, driven by emotion in a time when most high architecture dwelled on function and efficiency. For Schwanzer's emotional architecture, the car was the ideal product to represent: a mobile fetish for the expression of social identity, driving a car had (and has) little to do with necessity or rationality; as a semantic object, it tells something about a person's status and political inclination.

What cannot be rationally explained needs to be propagated, and Schwanzer, who was nicknamed Austria's Foreign Minister of Architecture, was a brilliant communicator. Any potential problem in the scheme was overruled by the representation of innovation, style, and emotion – all made irresistible in Sigrid Neubert's photography. Supported by his sister in arms, Schwanzer produced films and published two sumptuous books – *Entscheidung zur Form* (A Commitment to Form) and *Architektur aus Leidenschaft* (Architecture of Passion) – in the year of the inauguration. A handbook – explaining the project's innovations and featuring its workers as well as local delicacies such as juicy schnitzel with Bavarian potato salad (available in the cafeteria) – was handed out to visitors upon arrival, to make sure they got the message.

What better theme could represent a car company than the notion of speed? With his *architecture parlante*, Schwanzer used the location as a stage to advertise BMW, and himself, locally and internationally. BMW filed an application to the local authorities to rededicate the official address of the site from Drostlerstrasse to Petuelring, the ring road for high-speed traffic that was still under construction. The fact that the new HQ was located right next to the 1972 Olympic stadium (which would also host the 1974 World Cup) offered a huge opportunity for advertising, but placed the project under enormous time pressure, with only 34 months to complete it. The tower's construction method was ambitious. It was a hanging structure of reinforced concrete with sliding formwork, and all floors were fabricated at ground level and raised hydraulically one by one. This sped up construction because scaffolding was not necessary, and work on the structural skeleton and shell could be done simultaneously. A construction crew of 150 worked overtime without weekends for six weeks to finish the concrete work.

Schwanzer requested to put up the BMW logo on top of the *Vierzylinder* before the Olympics started. CEO Eberhard von Kuehnheim[2] argued that the tubes emerging from the top of each cylinder were disproportionally high and disrupted the building's proportions; placing the logo on each side there at the top – like placing jewels in a crown – could fix the problem. Moreover, von Kuehnheim claimed that BMW is "not only an economic enterprise, but a factor in Munich and Bavaria – a company who managed to create a high reputation for itself in the world. I conceive it as rather shortsighted, if authorities in the city administration do not recognize that and therefore prevent us – also in the interest of the city of Munich and the free state of Bavaria – from showing our name in the world."[3] City authorities did not agree, and denied BMW permission to place their logo at the top of the tower in time for the Olympics. BMW found a workaround: for "experimental purposes," they fitted a huge canvas on the side facing the Olympic stadium instead. They were fined 100,000 DM for the stunt, but in the time it took the authorities to make them take down the sign, they had already benefited from TV broadcasts of the Olympics sending their logo out into the world without paying a cent for it. It took about another year of negotiations with politicians from all parties for BMW to finally receive permission to mount their logo on all four sides of the tower.

The notion of time and speed was inscribed in employees' everyday experience. A machine-readable card provided fast access to the building and highspeed elevators beamed them up from the ground floor to their workplace. A *Telelift* was installed to guarantee the fast in-house distribution of goods and information. The gentleman from the *Hauspost* took care of immediate delivery of office material, and the lady of the *Stockwerkdienst* was empowered to speed up communication through a telex service and innovative telephone system. AGIPLAN, a logistics consultancy, optimized working processes and people. Flextime, promoted by the regime of scientific management, granted staff authority – within a given framework – to manage their own working hours. Special consideration was given to the planning of the department for electronic data processing, located at the bottom of the tower. Those employees had to move into the building in 1972, before it was finished. Working in a building where construction was still going on was not frictionless; the union complained about security issues.

Finishing such an experimental piece of architecture in a short period of time came with a price. There were endless lists of deficiencies and demands for re-work. Client and architect argued over the choice of office furniture (Schwanzer lost his fight for green USM Haller furniture on BMW blue carpet; the client opted for beige furniture), inconsistencies in the façade, bad smells entering office floors via the central tubes, etc. Work took longer than expected, and costs exceeded 7.9 million DM.

From 2003–06 the entire complex underwent renovation, executed by architect Peter Schweger. The program in the plinth got reshuffled: the much-celebrated data processing department moved out; staff cafeteria transferred from the west to east side; a conference center and offices were inserted. Exterior green space, access, and circulation were rearranged; the reinforced concrete was rehabilitated. This posed a huge challenge, as the hanging construction and lightness of the concrete slabs already pushed performance to the limit. All of the material removed (around 40,000 tons) had to be weighed to make sure that what replaced it did not increase the load. A new climatic system was installed, fire regulations had to be met, and the renovated façade now enabled the opening of some windows. Open offices were refurbished with group zones and new furniture to support BMW's corporate identity. Executives remained in private offices. A new building, called BMW Experience World, was done in 2007 by Coop Himmelblau, Schwanzer's former students. The building serves as a brandmark for BMW and the *Vierzylinder*, which was landmarked in 1999 and appears on every skyline representation of Munich.

notes

1   Peter Blake, in: Karl Schwanzer. *Architecture of Passion: The Work of 25 Years* (Modulverlag, Wien-München, 1973).
2   V. Kuehnheim followed Wilcke as CEO on January 1, 1972.
3   Unpublished letter of CEO von Kuehnheim to politician Gerhard Wacher, 21 July, 1972 (bmwgroup archive, translation from German to English by the author).

building credits

client: BMW
architect: Karl Schwanzer

photo credits

p.416, 424 (below, all), 426 (all): unknown
p.421, 423, 425 (all), 427 (all): Jens Frederiksen
p.422, 424 (above): Sigrid Neubert

2020
PETUELRING 130
MUNICH, GERMANY

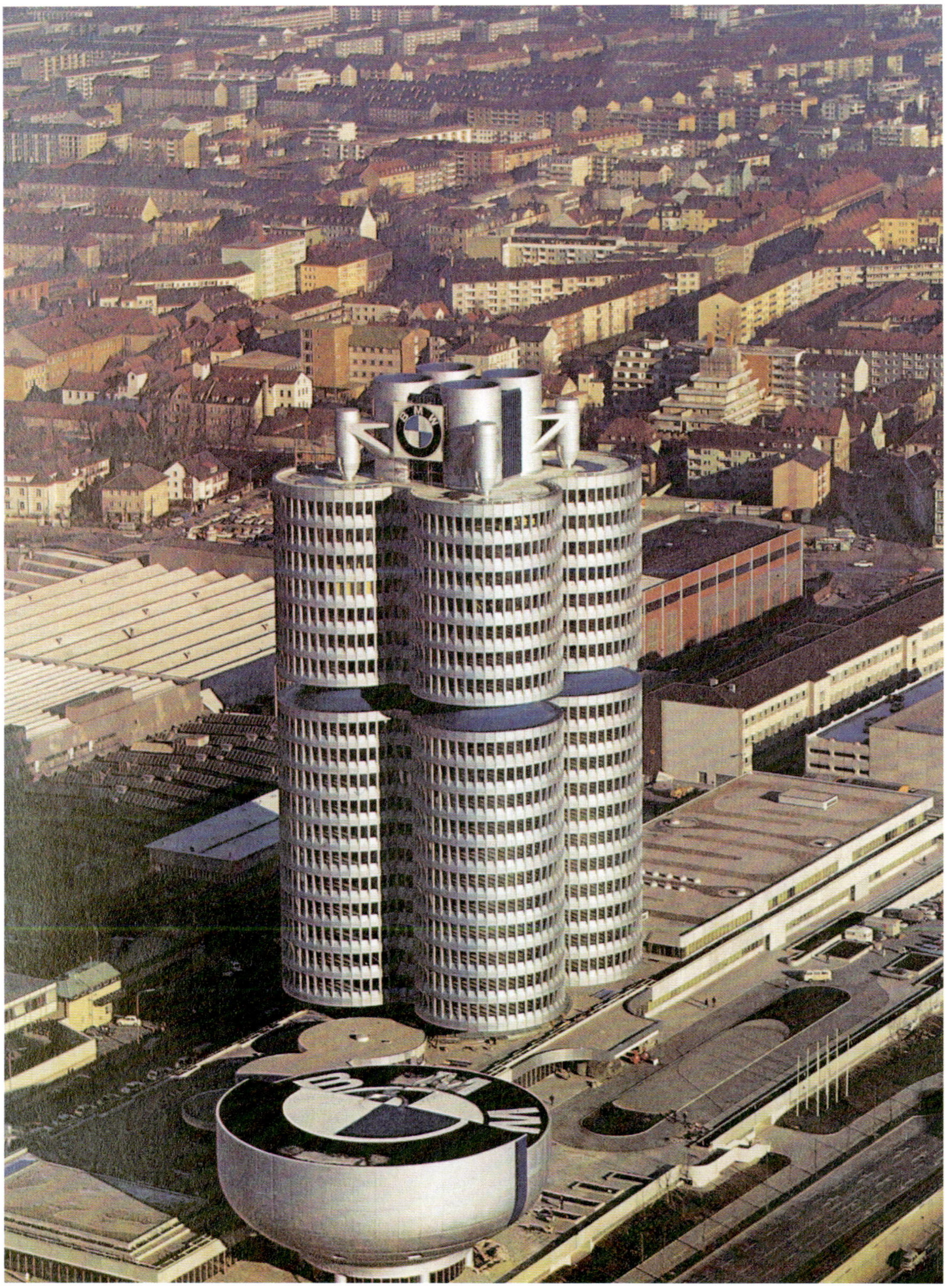

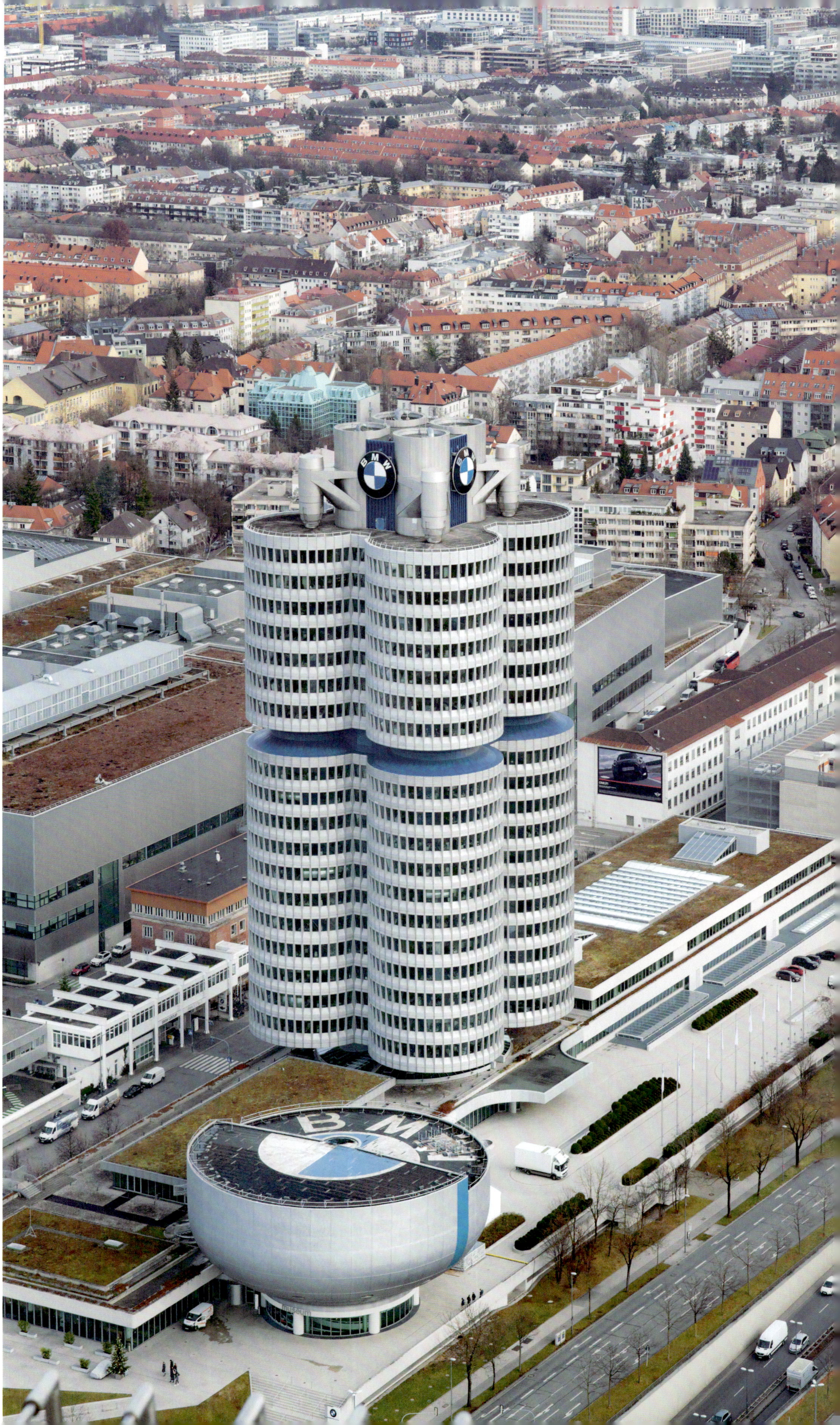
BMW

424

425

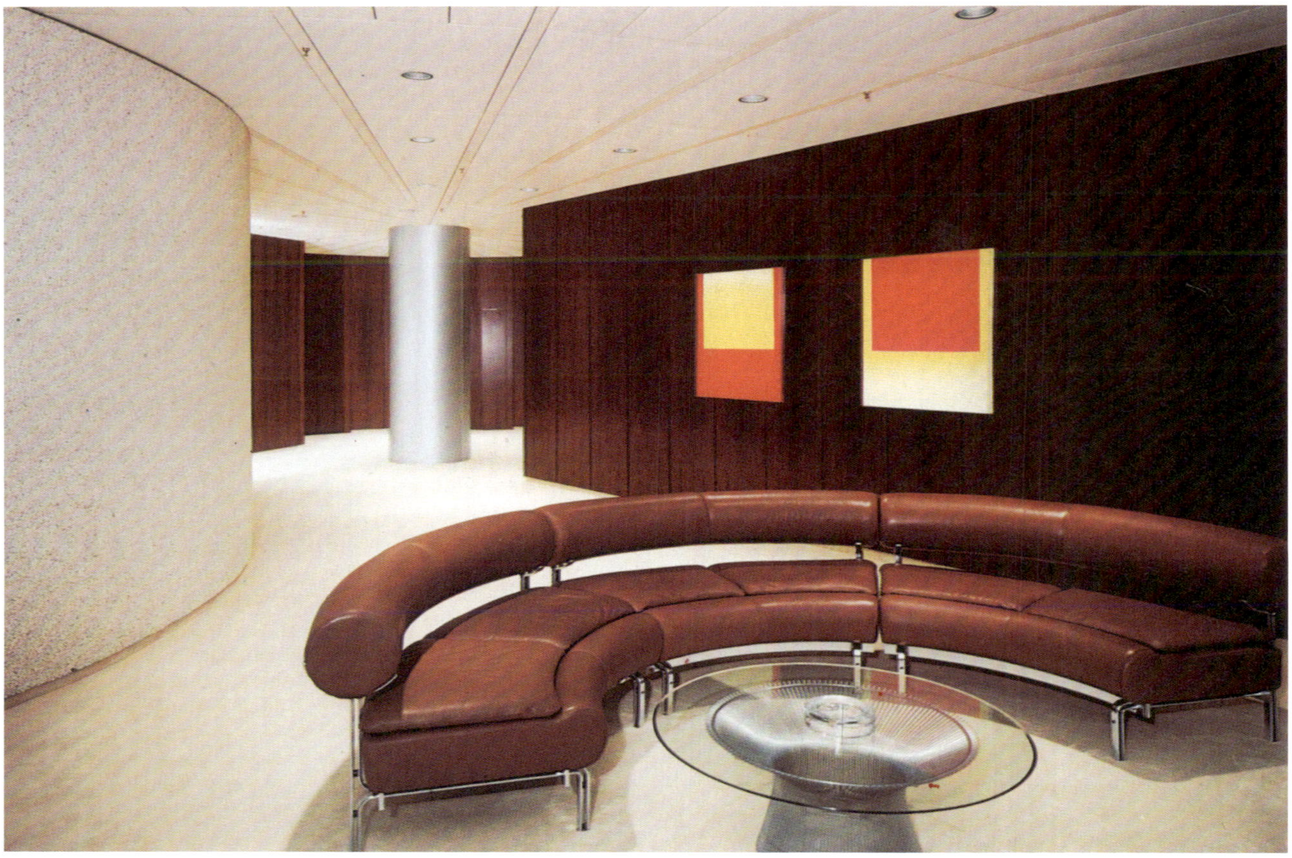

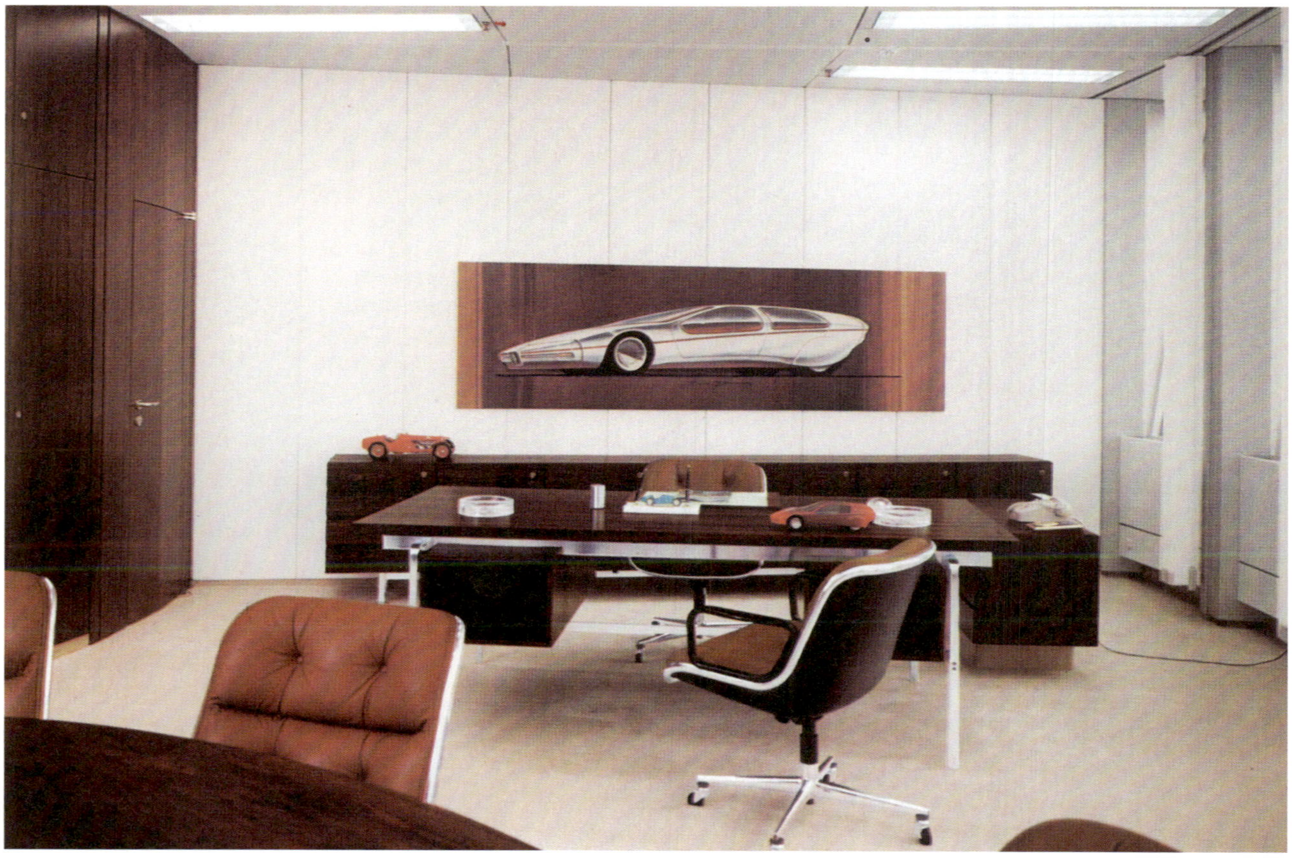

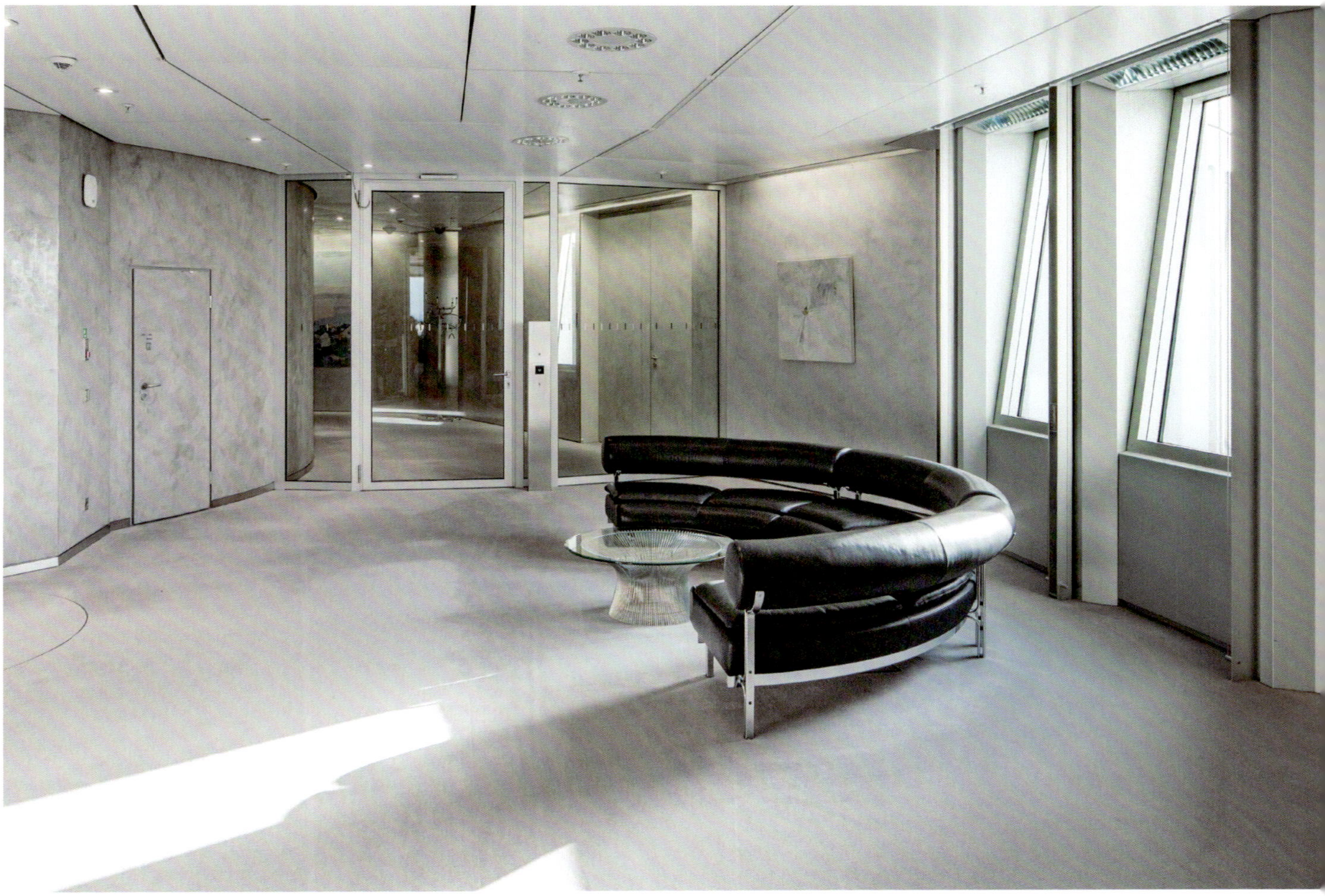

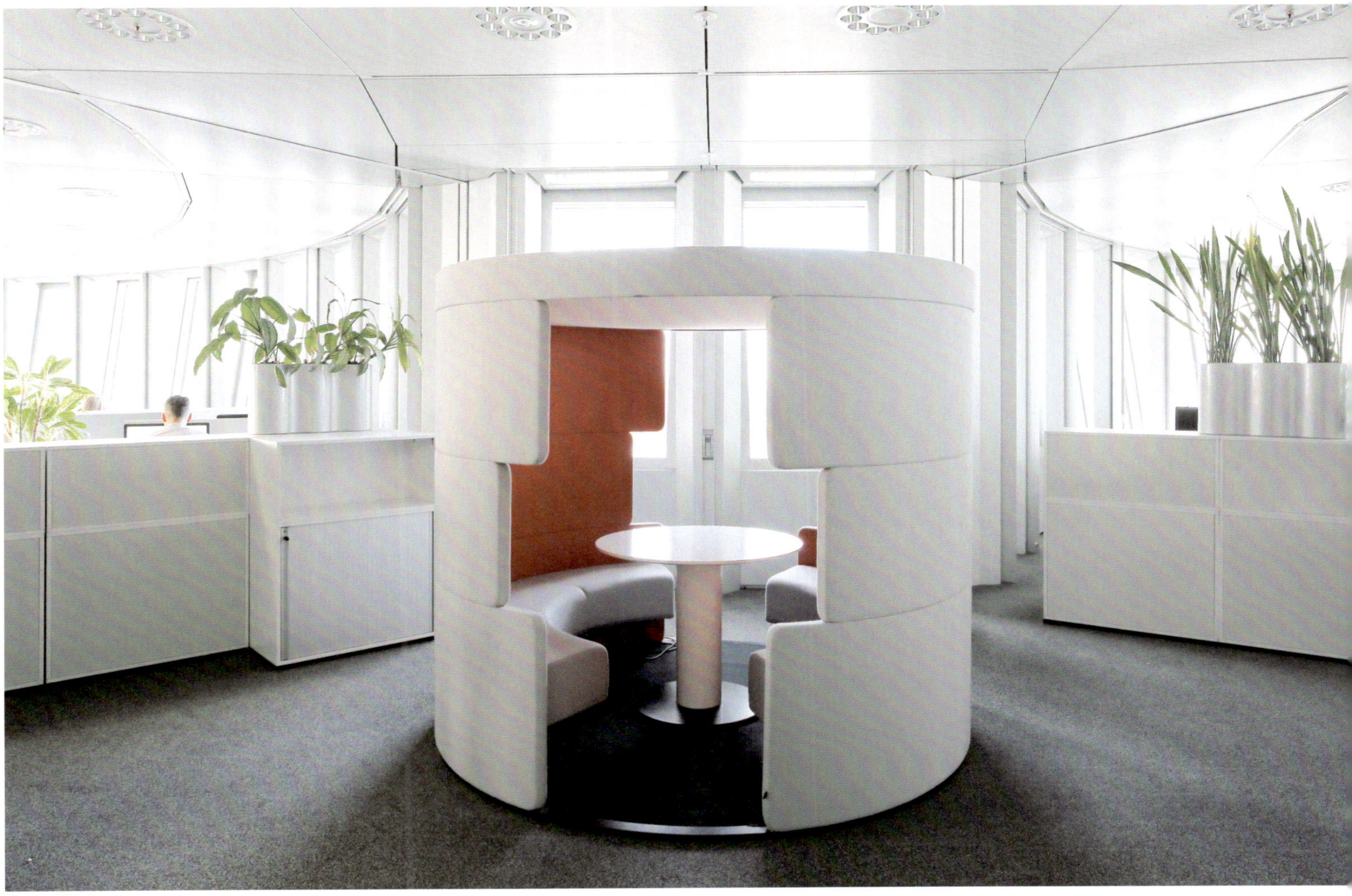

1978

Ruth Baumeister

DANMARKS NATIONALBANK

A monumental national financial center sustains thanks to its aesthetics and status

When Arne Jacobsen's Nationalbank in Copenhagen was landmarked in 2009, it was Denmark's youngest building ever to receive this status. The project was conceived in 1961, when Nationalbank, needing more space, launched a competition for a new HQ, to be realized at its current location in the center of the city: face to face with Christiansborg, the Danish parliament, the stock market and Holmen Church.

Jacobsen's scheme consisted of a five-story trapezoid-shaped building and two interior gardens, resting on a one-story wedge shaped volume which almost covers the entire site. The whole construction would be surrounded by a three-meter high marble perimeter wall running for several hundred meters, marking the border between the bank's facilities inside and the public space outside. The jury commended Jacobsen's scheme for its distinctive appearance in the cityscape, its spatial qualities, its use of materials and detailing, as well as the garden architecture.[1]

But it took another four years for construction to begin, as the scheme faced stern opposition from the press and the public. The power field which was symbolically created between the Nationalbank, the parliament, the stock market and the church was appalling for many Danish democrats. Worse still, the building was to be cladded with precious Norwegian marble, creating an enclave of monumental character. Critics argued that the colossal security wall, creating a hermetically sealed compound, meant the project would contribute nothing to public life in the heart of the city. In addition, an entire block of historical substance, including housing, would have to be demolished to make way for the massive scheme. Nationalbank agreed to offset the impact by building another residential block elsewhere in Copenhagen.

Jacobsen died in 1971, with the project still seven years from completion. Dissing & Weitling took over, finishing the building in 1978 and worked on its first renovation not long afterwards.

We talked to Hugo Frey, former director of Nationalbank, about the building's past, current state, and potential future.
Ruth Baumeister: You experienced the building at its inauguration, you witnessed its first modification, and you will play a decisive part in its upcoming transformation. There are few who know this building as well as you. How do you experience it?
Hugo Frey: I have been working in this building since 1984. I think the entrance hall is a unique space, one of the most beautiful in Danish architecture. If you visit the hall on certain days, at specific times, you see an absolutely amazing light display playing out on the wall.

RB: It would be difficult for an architect today to convince a client to spend a lot of money on an entrance hall like this. It's practically empty and the few things that are inside are designed for exclusivity.
HF: The carpets were manufactured for this place, and their colors are typical of the period. And the staircase – it's really a sculpture. A foundation called Nationalbankens Jubilæumsfond hosts its awards ceremony in the entrance hall every year, usually with one of Denmark's leading architects chairing the prize committee. Every year, they begin by saying, "Standing in this iconic piece of Danish architecture…"

PALACE
RB: How does this iconic piece of architecture perform as a home for the institution and a workplace for its employees?
HF: The building is located right next to Christiansborg, where the Nationalbank has been throughout its history: close to the political and financial center of Denmark. But the building is also very distinctive in itself, and we have used it in our communication in a very visual way.

RB: To help create the institution's identity?
HF: Yes, but that is one of the things we will have to reduce a little, now that the building is going to be renovated over several years and we will move to a temporary domicile.[2] We will need to work with the fact that the Nationalbank is more than this building. Our employees should be able to define themselves without it, and working in another building for several years does not mean we will be somehow amputated. Our task and who we are will remain unchanged.

RB: Do your employees thrive in the building?

HF: Whether they like it architecturally or not, I think all our employees are happy to be in this building because the conditions and the functions are very good. There is a lot of space, we have shower facilities, a basement car park, good views, a location in the city center. The most fitting thing I can say about this building is that if you were asked to build a palace in the 1960s, the result would resemble the Nationalbank. It is so expensive and the choice of materials so exquisite that it resembles Børsen and Rosenborg Castle.

GESAMKUNSTWERK

RB: How was that possible?

HF: Arne Jacobsen was given free rein, from the smallest details to the largest ones. I find it very impressive that when you stand here looking at the skylights, which are placed in a lattice structure, you can see it resembles all the door handles on the cupboards: a circle within a square, with the same proportions. The same goes for the window lintels in the gables – their patterns are also repeated. It's all consistent and accomplished. There are, for instance, no door frames, no door linings, just grooves all the way round, as there are outside on the facades. But you can't hang any pictures on the walls, because if they run across the grooves, it looks strange.

RB: Is this a *Gesamtkunstwerk* then?

HF: I think so. Many people are able to see how impressive it is, but they find it a bit boring. I think some of the colors used on the elevators and inside the spaces are incredibly beautiful, but they are also very much Arne Jacobsen colors – a lot of grey. If you don't have an eye for architecture, you would probably feel a bit like: Why can't I have this wall painted red? Or: Yes, but why can't the windows be opened? There are many things like that which make it a bit difficult to see the greatness of it. Some might find it relatively dull. But I like 'grey' architecture, I like to be in this room. It gives me peace and quiet.

TRANSFORMATIONS

RB: Can you describe what was changed during the 2002 renovation? Starting with, the reception desk. It was originally a small glass box sticking out of the huge marble wall visitors faced upon entrance into the hall. Why was that changed?

HF: That workplace was cold, so the decision was made to create a more practical and friendly reception area. We removed the glass cage at the entrance – we would no longer have a guard sitting there. There was also a desk on the left of the opposite wall upon entry and, actually, everyone went over to this desk with their requests. And this is where the reception desk is located today.

RB: How about the kitchen facilities and the canteen?

HF: The canteen was completely changed because the facilities were outdated. We also opened the roof opened up, and we constructed a roof terrace and installed a staircase leading up to there.

RB: Initially, the cafeteria was divided into smaller units with tables of only four, similar to a domestic setting. I was told that every employee even had his or her own fixed spot at a table. Is that true?

HF: Yes. It's also quite amusing to think that the staff had a smoking lounge. After eating lunch, you sat down to smoke and drink your coffee. And the bosses took their meals separately – they had their own canteen and their own smoking lounge. The culture back then was different. Today we are trying to make things more open: you mingle with more people.

SELF-SUFFICIENT

RB: Can you point out other changes?

HF: The bank used to have a library. There was a staircase leading down through it, which is now gone, and today there are workspaces in its place. The books that had any worth were given to the Royal Library and other collections. The books were intended as reference works for the bank's employees. Today most people use the internet.

RB: What else?
HF: There were two petrol pumps down in the garage, but not for the staff, only for the cars owned by the bank, which were used to deliver banknotes. Today, you would never design a building with its own petrol pump.

RB: Was this an unusual luxury to have in a building even back then?
HF: Not at all. I think it was a tradition that large companies were organised that way. If you look at the telephone companies, which were also publicly owned, they also had car repair workshops. So did we. Some of the green doors down there were car repair shops. Today, you would never employ a skilled worker such as a mechanic. You would drive your car to a repair shop. But when the building was in its early years, we were self-sufficient in many things. We employed craftsmen, including carpenters – there were once many workshops down in the basement. This was the case with many of the state monopolies.

RB: Do any of these functions remain here?
HF: There's still a car wash bay in the parking garage. Today, you wouldn't build such a thing for the staff, would you? And even back then, one would have asked why, if the Nationalbank needed its cars washed, didn't they just take them somewhere else? It reflect the mindset of people in the early 60s. Some of it is still here, other things have been shut down or changed. But we always made the changes in such a way that the overall expression of the building was retained.

BUZZING

RB: How about the banking hall? It was once the core workspace. Is it still like that today?
HF: When I started working here, the banking hall was buzzing with life. Stockbrokers carried in bonds, which were physical documents you could deposit here. There were big checks and suitcases with money going back and forth, and there was a desk that served customers. These days, this is all done electronically, so the banking hall no longer exists. We use the space for lectures, and one half of it is part of our cash supply. You can still enter the building, exchange a banknote and get a new one, but there are very few employees. It was certainly a more beautiful space then, but it would not work today. The physical framework of this building was designed for many things that are now completely gone.

RENOVATION

RB: Now, almost 50 years after the building's inauguration, Nationalbank is once again facing a major renovation. Did you have to change your renovation strategy when the building became a landmark?
HF: Even before the building was listed, we tried to stay true to Arne Jacobsen's design when we undertook renovations. We have often been in contact with his former design studio. Since the building has been listed, when anything needs to be changed, it goes through the Agency for Culture and Palaces. We have paid attention to preserving the building, and we try to make do with just the changes that are made necessary by our new styles of working.

RB: It seems that the programmatic challenge this time is not shortage of physical space, but abundance. De-materialization due to digital technology in the financial sector, and the obsolescence of the huge money printing facility in the basement, presents entirely new demands. How about issues of sustainability, energy requirements, and people's wellbeing in the building?
HF: I don't think Christiansborg or Børsen will ever receive an AAA+ energy label, and neither will we. You can't do that with a listed building, but we feel obliged to do what

we can within the existing architectural framework. It's easy to see that the building was constructed before the first oil crisis in the early 1970s: it is very energy-consuming and expensive to run. With the new renovation, we would like to implement energy improvements: we need a new air conditioning system, and we need to discuss whether something can be done about the windows to reduce the heating bills.

RB: What are the spatial problems you are facing at the level of the individual workspace?
HF: The building was designed like so many offices at the time: with very long corridors and cellular offices, and a lot of closet space. A modern workplace is based more on communities and large spaces and includes some more flexible ways of being together.

RB: Do you see any problems with the security standards of the bank, given its age?
HF: No. The building was built to accommodate both banknote printing and a banknote storage facility. We have now closed the printing facility: it was too costly and has been outsourced. This is why we are left with a large hall that we don't really know what to do with. It is huge and has no windows. Nowadays, security is about much more than banknotes and cash. Cyber risk has become much more important.

RB: What changes have been made in this respect?
HF: Now, at the staff entrance of the building, you have to go through speed-gates, which have been set up in our elevator lobby. We have permanently closed the entrance to the elevator, located next to our information desk. Because how could we come up with a solution for a speed-gate system in the entrance hall that looks good?

PROGNOSIS
RB: Consultancies recommend that office buildings today should be designed for a life expectancy of 15–20 years, for the floors, furniture etc., but also for the building itself. Many architects would claim that this is a rather short-sighted prognosis. If you use cheap materials, you are forced to change every 20 years. How do you see this in relation to Nationalbank's exquisite materials, furniture and detailing? Isn't it precisely because of this that we are still able to discuss the building today?
HF: If we say that this building has some of the characteristics of a palace, consider the fact that down in the former banknote production hall the floor is made of precious wood. Some things were built so as not to require maintenance, for instance all the panels for the cupboards. They don't need to be painted or otherwise maintained; they simply age gracefully.

RB: And what doesn't work, in terms of the fixtures and materials?
HF: Large-scale maintenance work is expensive due to the highly specialised solutions. Nothing is standardized. Even our tiles are slightly smaller than standard tiles. And this means it costs a lot of money. For instance, the pipes: some of them have been set in poured concrete, which means that when they have to be replaced, it is really a significant maintenance cost. So, I don't know just how sustainable, maintenance-free and long-lasting it actually is. We are also faced with having to replace the entire façade, which is made from Porsgrunn marble, as there is a risk it will start falling down sometime in the future.

NEXT GENERATION
RB: Do you know the reason for the facade damage?
HF: Down by the 'bastion,' close to the ground, some parts have been eroded by salt and water. And then there's something about the way the marble is held in place: water, sun and heat have made it expand and contract.

RB: What are you going to do about the risk to the facade?
HF: We have sufficient marble in storage to cover the facade one more time.

RB: Where does this marble come from?
HF: From a quarry in Porsgrunn, Norway, which has been closed for many years. But we had an option to buy up their remaining marble, and we did so. We have it in storage, and it has been cut.

RB: Replacing that amount of marble is not very sustainable.
HF: Indeed. Jacobsen used Porsgrunn marble in many places. We will replace ours, but it's the last of this marble left. I have no idea what the next generation will do when, in 50 years, the new marble facade will be worn away.

LAW OF JANTE
RB: How important is the location for you?
HF: We are an independent, economic and political authority pursuing monetary policy. We are also part of the center of power. We engage in close dialogue with the government and the ministries, which are next door. The bank consequently belongs here.

RB: But when you work digitally, you can work anywhere, in principle.
HF: I don't think you will ever be able to persuade the Danish parliament or the Ministry of Finance to move, nor any of the other ministries. I still remember the old series of books on architecture, one of which was entitled *Magtens Bolig* (The Abode of Power)[3]. It has a drawing of the Nationalbank on the front cover. This fits the impression you get when you enter the entrance hall – you are really put in your place. You cower a little.

RB: How did the architect express such power relations?
HF: The building is closed to the outside world and it is somewhat an abode of power. Most people who enter the building for the first time, standing there, think it's amazing. I remember when I came for my job interview here, arriving by train from Jutland. Just sitting for ten minutes down in the entrance hall, waiting for someone to come and take me to the interview. It was a bit *don't think you're anything special*. There is something of the Law of Jante[4] about it.

RB: I talked with one of your employees, and she had the same impression. At the same time, she said that the space gives her the feeling that here things are under control. Her words reminded me of large companies in the 19th century that wanted to demonstrate their power, but also wanted to show that they are there for people and take responsibility. Does Nationalbank want to communicate that to people?
HF: The building is probably a little too closed off for us to do that. It does not reach out to anyone. And this is actually the point: here is a monolith, where there is someone responsible for the Danish currency and for printing banknotes. And whatever else goes on in there, we don't know a great deal about. It is secret and mysterious.

MONK BRICK
RB: Consultancies claim that office buildings must be flexible. But our research shows that buildings that were extremely flexible still got torn down. And a lot of 1960s office buildings were built for one big company, but they gradually became smaller and didn't need so much space, so their HQ had to be turned into multi-tenant buildings. Others were located in the center of a city, and the development of surrounding real estate had a big impact on their life cycles. How can you approach such unforeseeable developments?
HF: I think designing something that could metabolize these changes would be very difficult. You can build from 'monk brick'[5] and make a building last for centuries. Some churches have lasted for 800 years. That's not the problem, though it's extremely

expensive. The problem is technological developments, the way we work, the functions we need, how society changes. In 50 years, a workspace will probably mean something completely different than it does today.

RB: Can you point at some of these kinds of changes?
HF: We had some of the original desks, but along came new considerations and the desks had to be height adjustable. So, we had to replace the old ones. At the same time, everyone was putting big computers on their desk, which had to grow into large L-shapes. Today, the computers are mostly laptops. So we got rid of that furniture because it took up too much space. This building was not built with computers in mind. But this is why we have to make sure offices are flexible if they are to retain their value. If you tie the function too much to something material that you cannot change, the office can no longer be used.

SILENCE
RB: Current discussions in office design center mainly around open plan versus singular spaces. What is your experience with this, given that you have almost exclusively cellular offices?
HF: There are big generational differences. Many young people who start working with us have only ever worked in open plan offices. This is how they prefer to work. The culture has changed a lot.

RB: Some people need more silence than others. Can you imagine a combination of the two typologies?
HF: We would like to have different possibilities. We make use of experts who know about space planning. They say the professions who are the hardest to get out of their single offices are lawyers and people doing research in various fields. I think when we return to this building after the restoration, the staff would protest if they just went back to the same offices. We need to introduce some workspace flexibility into the renovation.

RB: Jacobsen's office buildings have a long lifespan, even though by today's standards they would be considered 'unsustainable.' Do you think aesthetics plays a role in their longevity?
HF: Yes, they are icons. They are worthy of preservation, and it is our responsibility, as owners, to ensure they are still around in 300 years. But there's one thing that is difficult to get around: we want to preserve the place, but we also need to carry out the work we do as the Nationalbank. If we do not, we cannot remain here.

notes

1   Danmarks Nationalbank, (ed.), Nationalbankens Bygning (Danmarks Nationalbank, Seddeltrykkeriet, Copenhagen, 1983), p.19
2   The entire staff will move to another building during the four-year renovation.
3   Lisbeth Balslev Jørgensen, Hakon Lund and Hans Edvard Nørregård-Nielsen, *Magtens bolig* (Gyldendal, 1980). Published in the series *Danmarks arkitektur*, over six volumes between 1979 and 1981.
4   The Law of Jante is an unofficial codex of social behaviour in Scandinavia, regulating any individual ambition and expression that is not targeted towards a common goal. In short, you are not to think you are anyone special, or that you are better than anyone else.
5   A bricklaying system with two stretchers and a header in a basic repeating pattern.

building credits

client: Danmarks Nationalbank
architect: Arne Jacobsen

photo credits

p.428: Danmarks Nationalbank
p.437, 439, 441 (all), 443 (all): Jens Frederiksen
p.438, 440 (all), 442 (all): unknown

2020
HAVNEGADE 5
COPENHAGEN, DENMARK

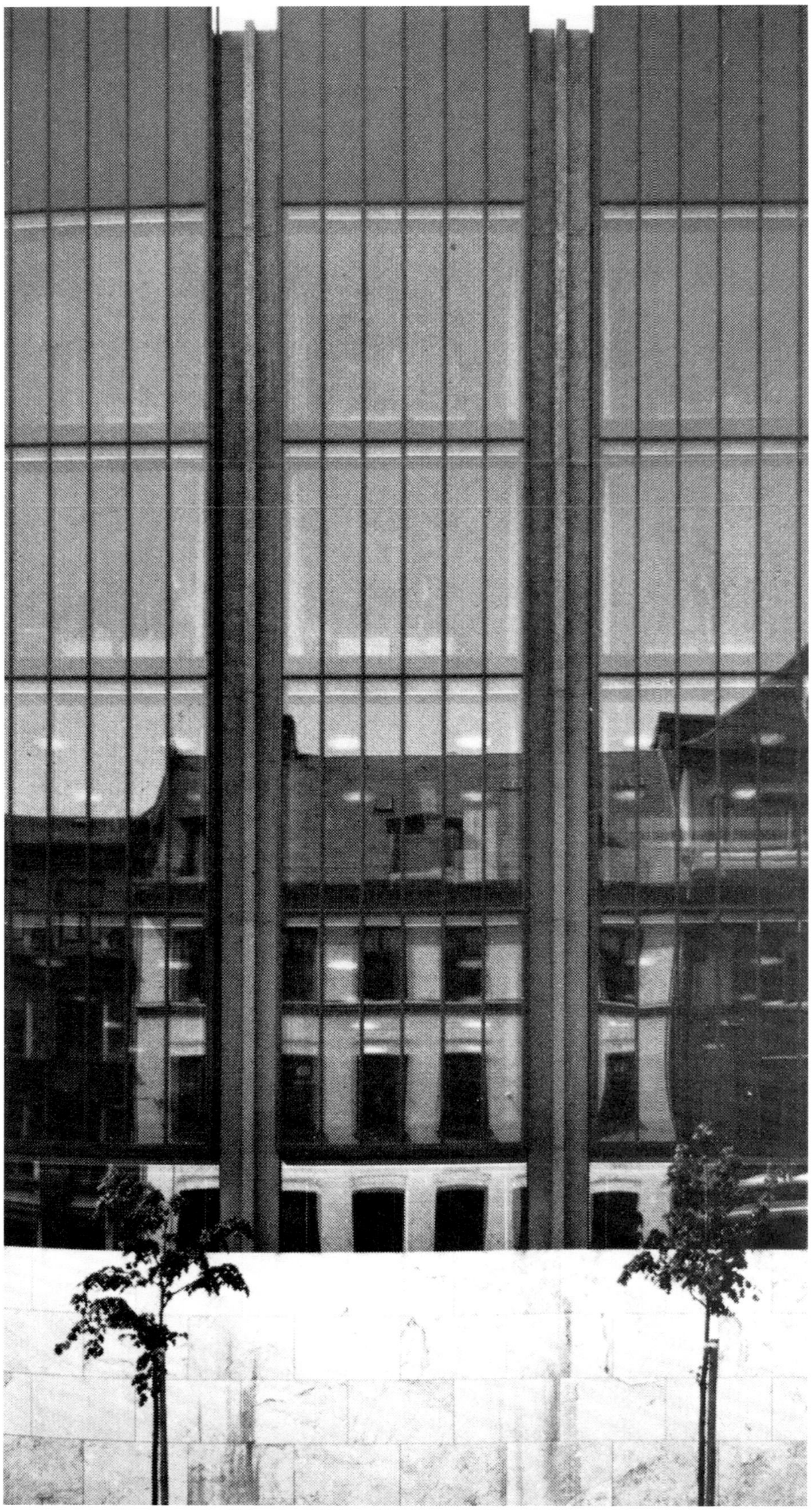

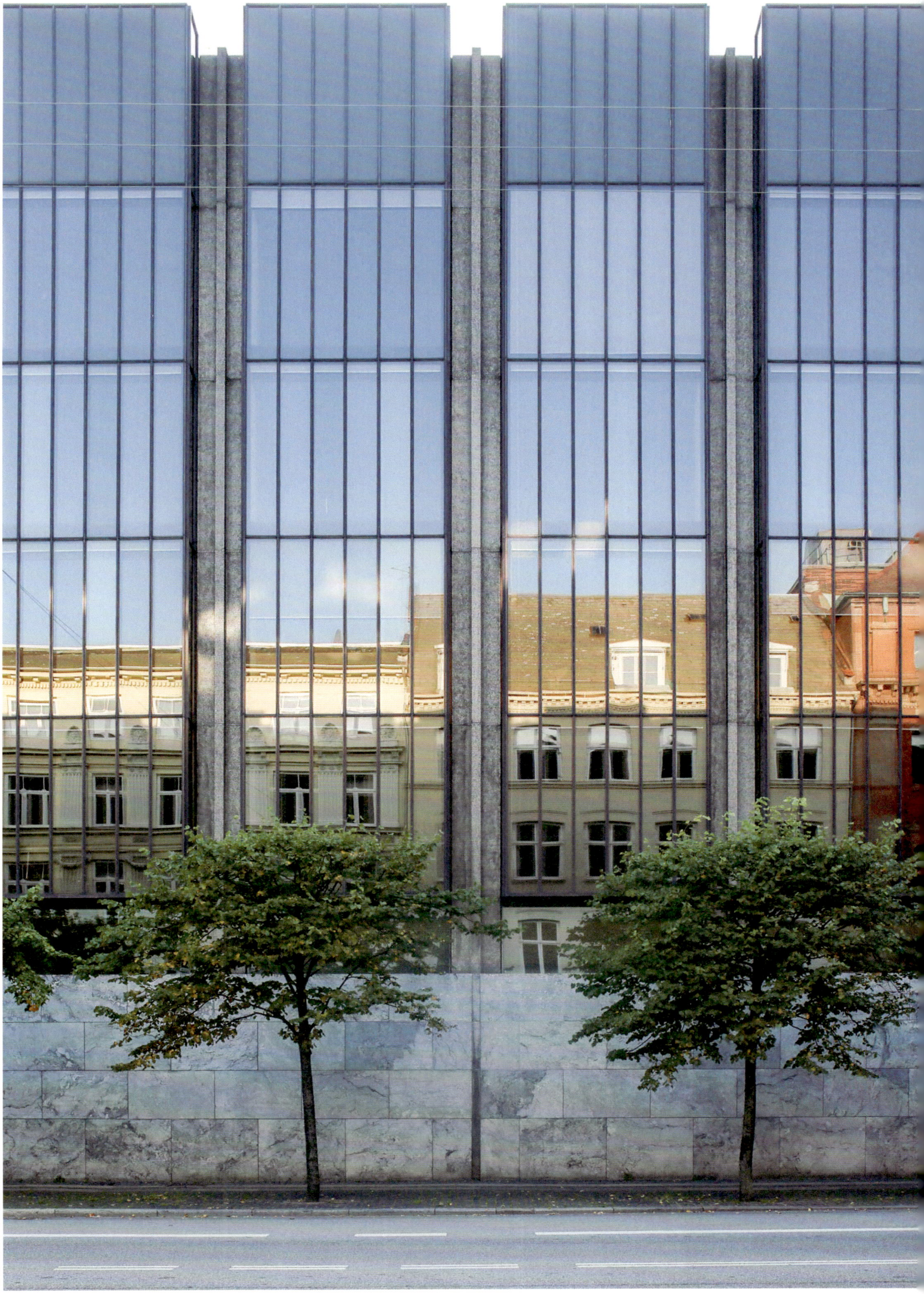

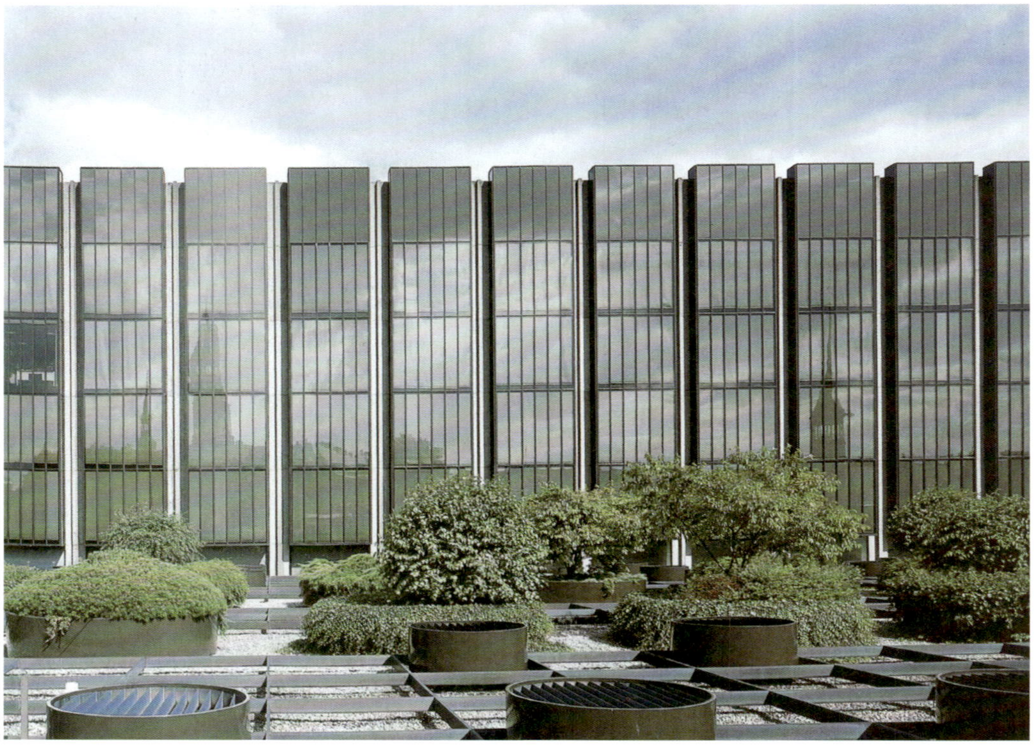

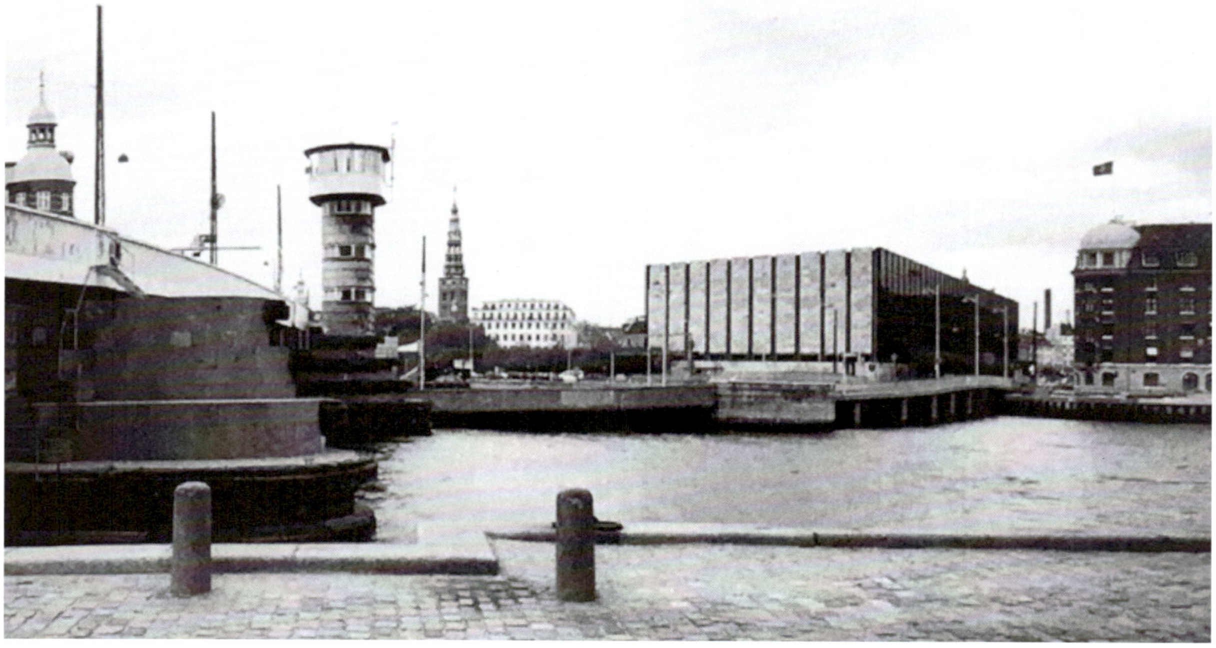

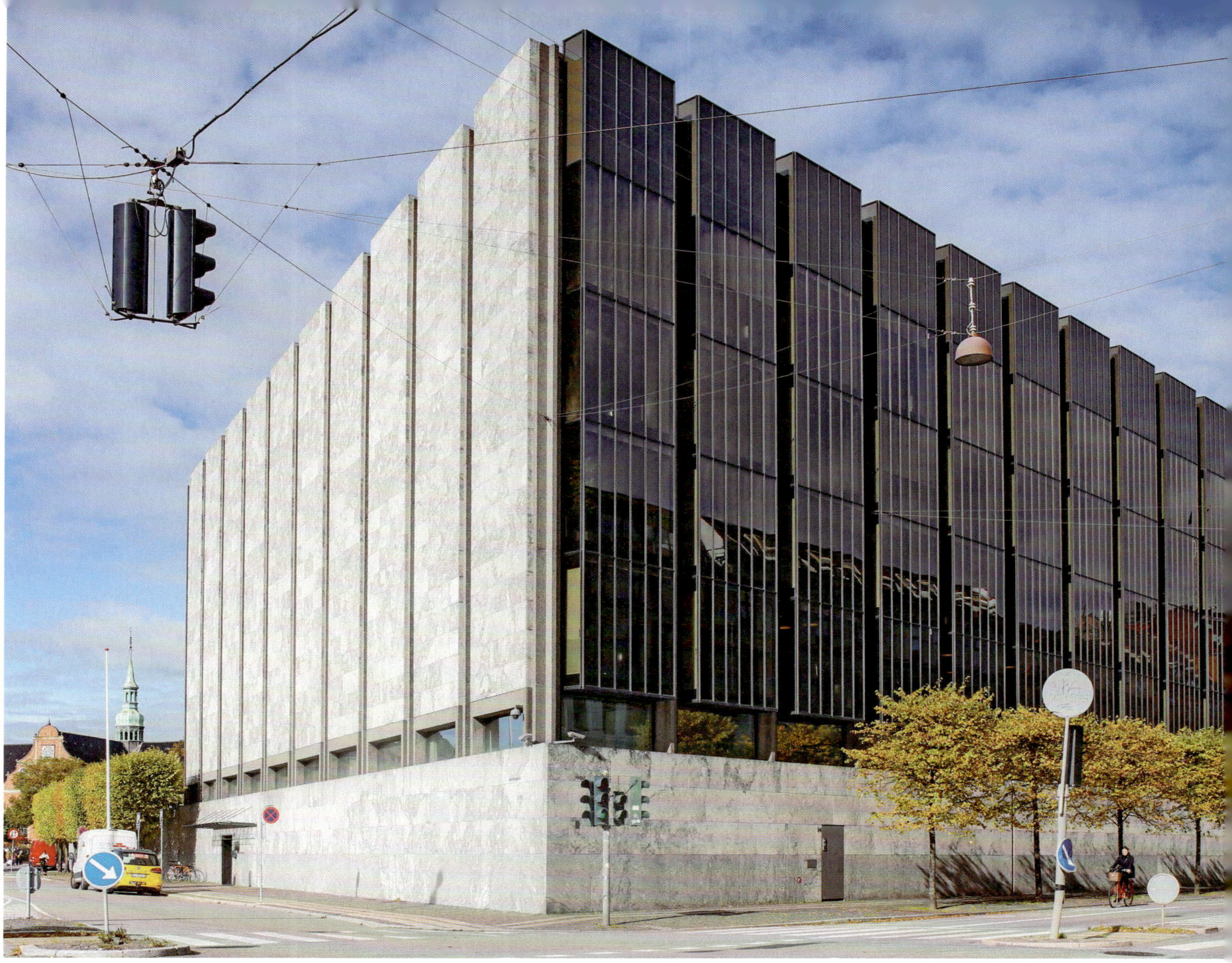

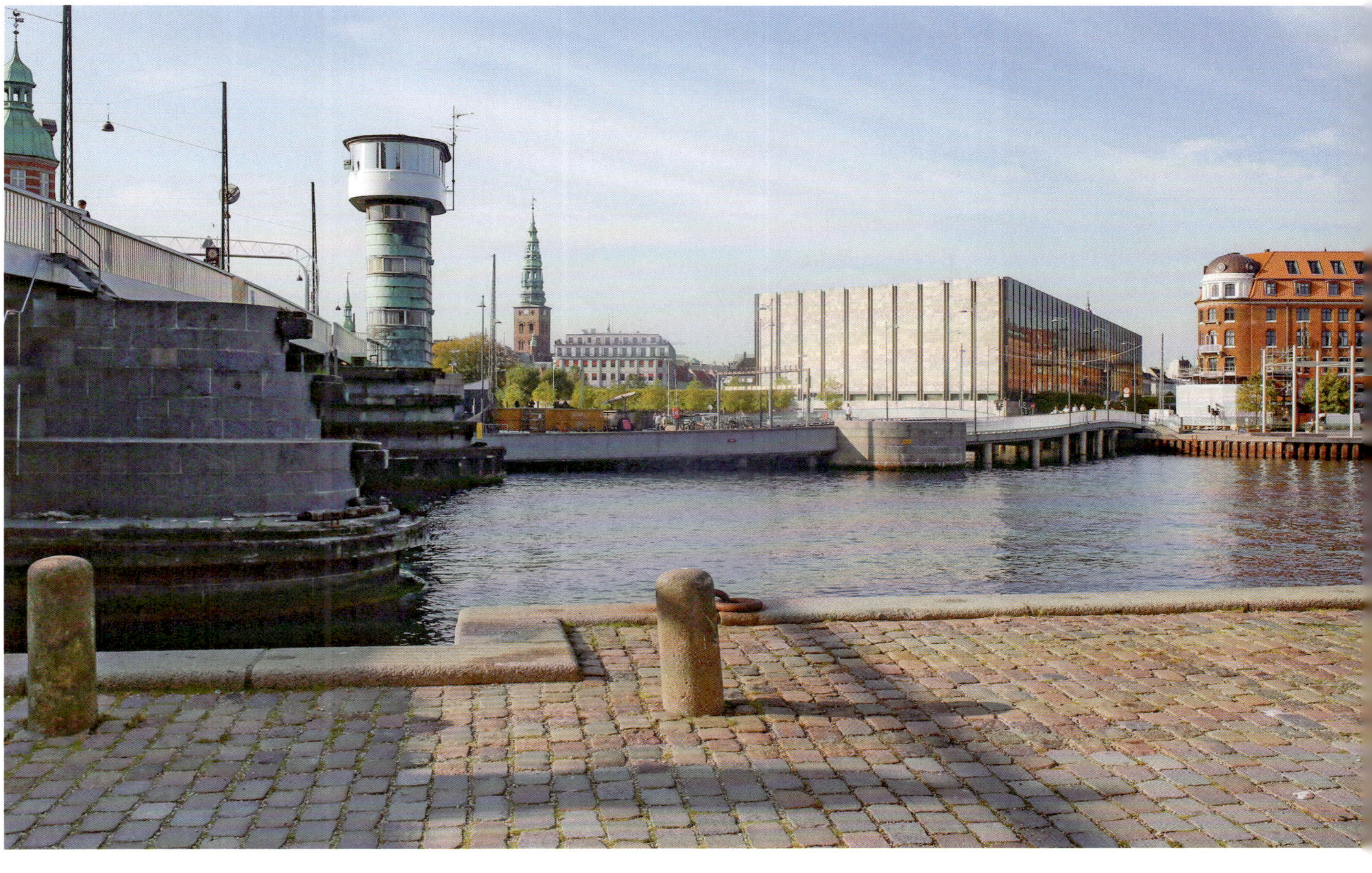

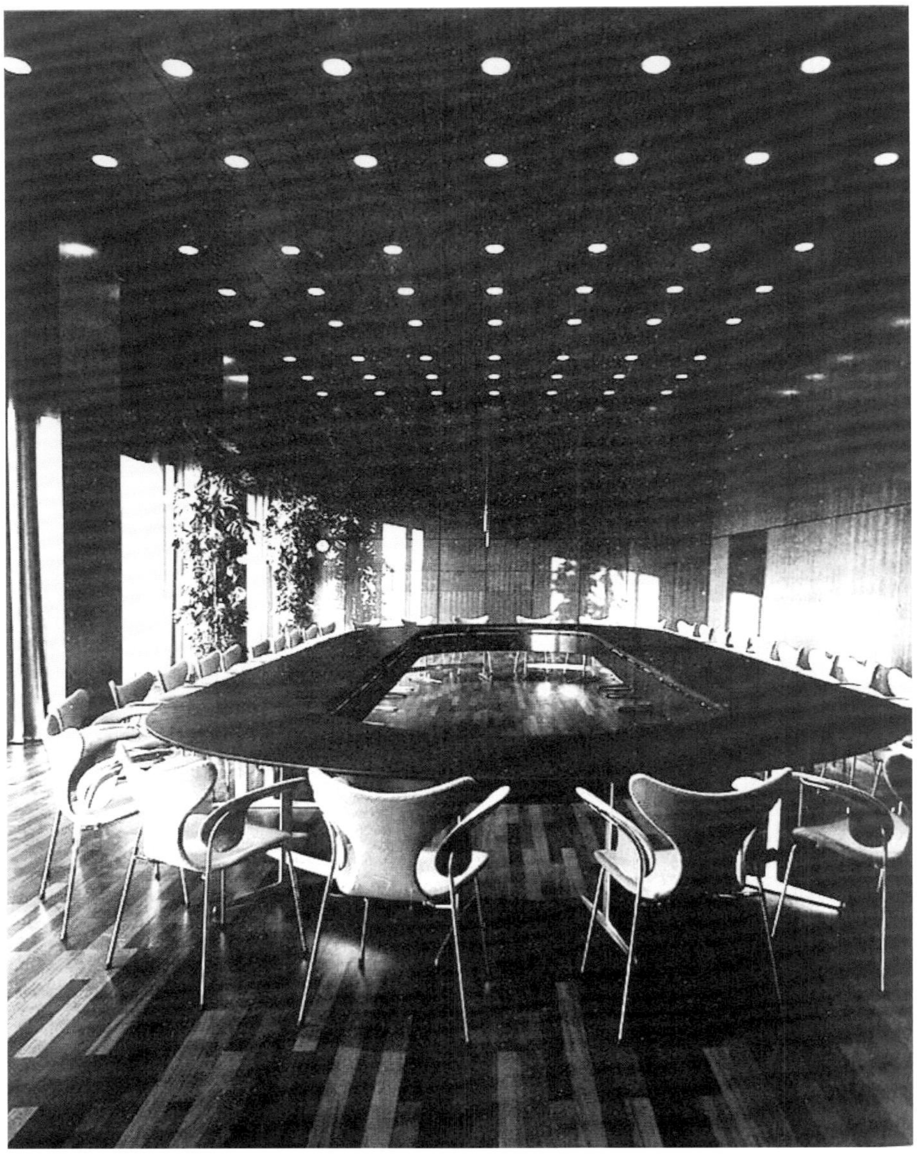

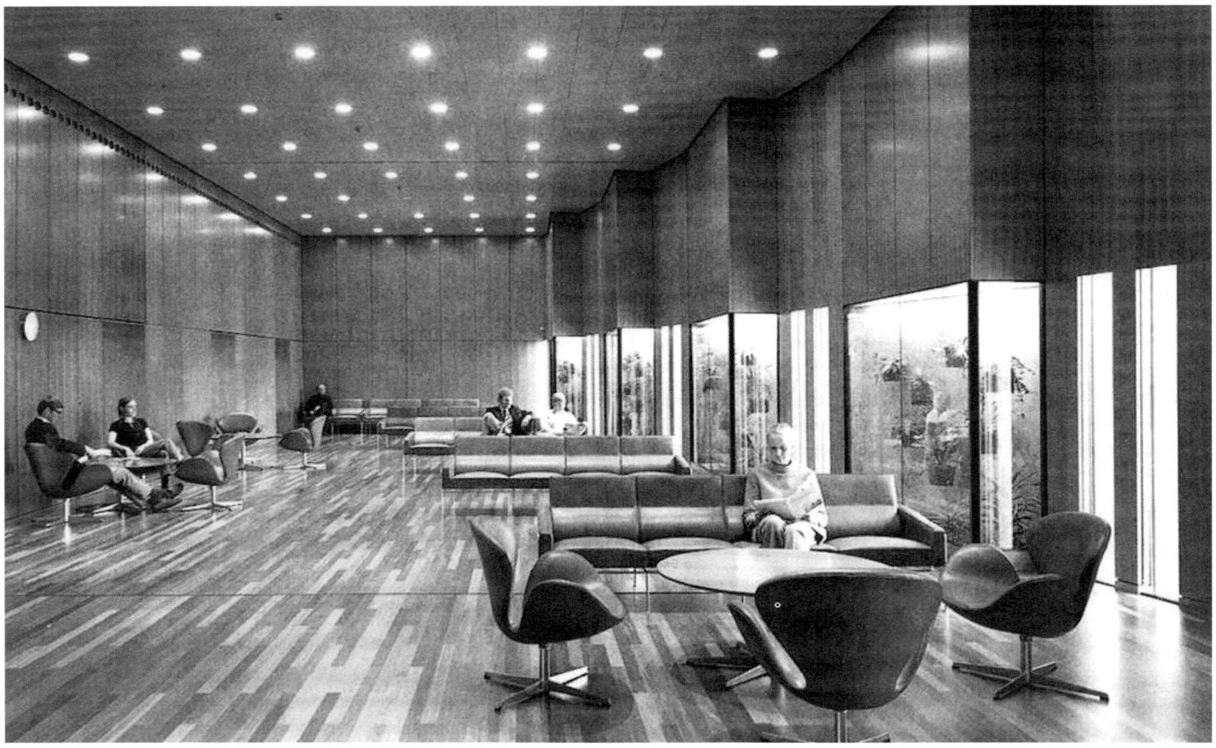

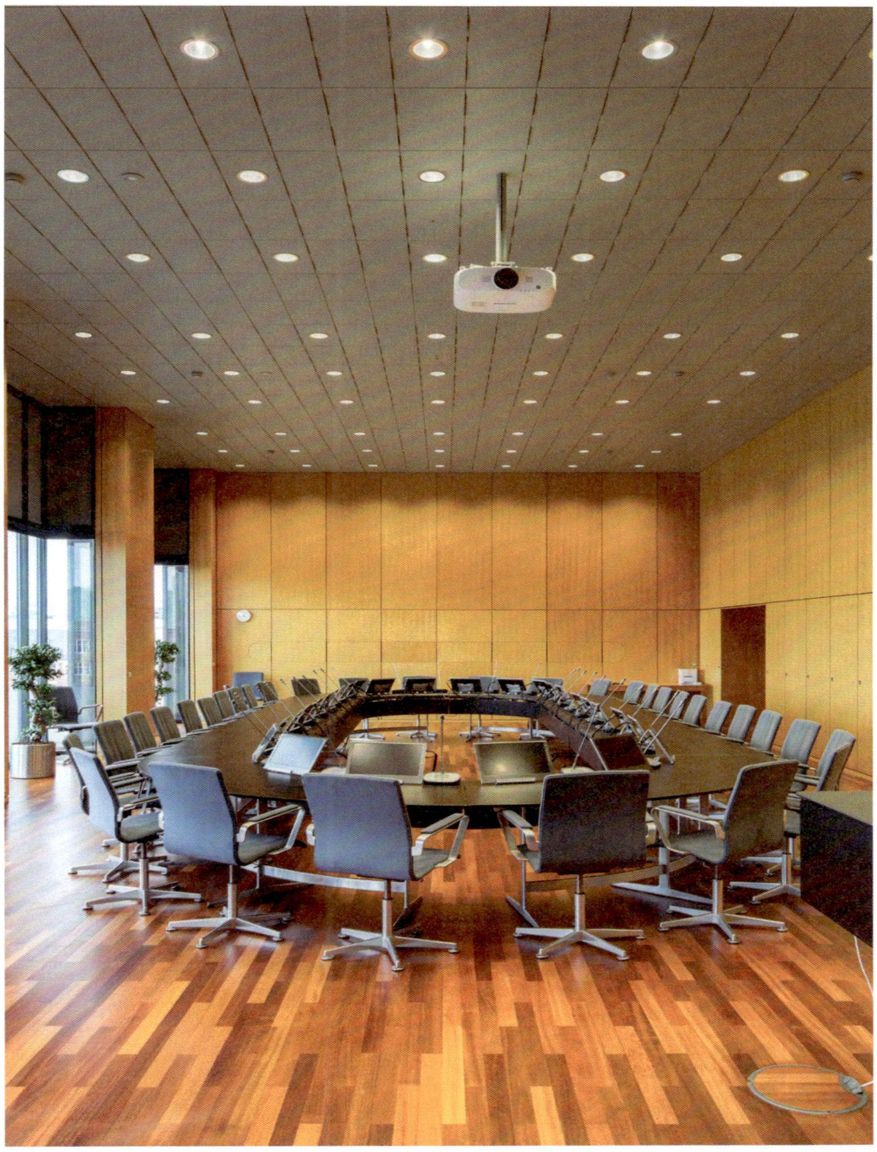

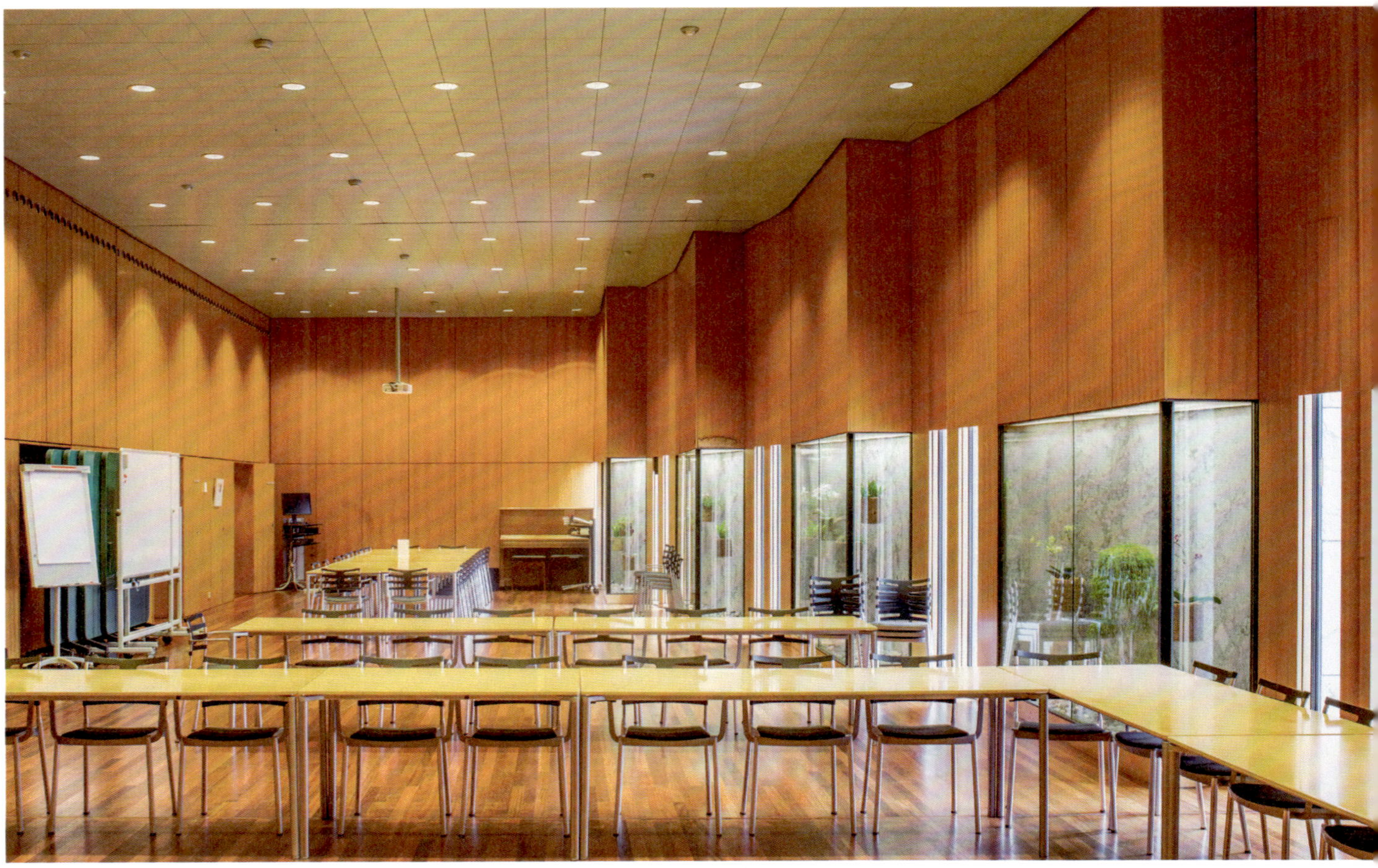

1982

Stephan Petermann

PENDORP

How to build a white elephant: a(nother) fine-grained, domestic-scale Dutch office campus, difficult to adapt, faces demolition

DRIVE
The drive from Amsterdam to Pendorp takes roughly 40 minutes. From the Amsterdam A10 ring road you turn north towards Zaandam and pass De Beemster polder. A sign along the road reminds you that this landscape is part of UNESCO world heritage – echt Dutch landscape. Pendorp is located on the outskirts of the provincial town of Alkmaar, famous for its traditional cheese market. Punching Pendorp into the navigation software brings up a different set of associations: streets named after inventors like James Watt and Alessandro Volta – a warning that you are heading into a disenfranchised industrial zone that peaked during the 1980 & 90s.

BRIEF
Cadastral maps from the early 1980s did not show any of the streets around Pendorp.

Instead, we see a pixelated block, in plan practically a QR code, set in a wide-open polder dotted only by a few historical windmills and farms. In 1982, Gerda ten Cate, writing for *Bouw*, wrote that she'd been alerted something weird was being built in this polder.[1] Something that defied typological description. A home for the elderly? A mental asylum? In fact, it was the new headquarters of a regional energy company called PEN. Because of its design, scale, and location in the open landscape, the complex is named Pendorp, Pen village.

In 1977, the advertising consultancy Twijnstra Gudde was hired to organize the relocation and redesign of the publicly owned energy company based in Bloemendaal, 30 kilometers south of Alkmaar. Joined by a representative group of 10 percent of the workers, Twijnstra Gudde toured offices throughout the Netherlands, both cellular and open plan. Their observations were distilled into a design brief composed of contradicting desires. The new office should not look like an office. It should not have air conditioning, should have high comfort standards, operable windows and low energy usage. The organization of office floors should be open but also closed, with most desks close to windows.
Based on this brief, six architects were invited to enter a design competition. Abe Bonnema (1926–2001) was on the list. Working from Hurdegaryp, in the northern Dutch province of Friesland, Bonnema had built housing projects and two large office buildings in and around Leeuwarden.[2] He outsmarted his rivals in the Pendorp competition in a brilliant stroke of opportunism. The evening before the jury made its decision – it must have been in early spring – Bonnema paid a visit to one of the jury members, architect Joop van Stigt, at his house. At the door, Bonnema took off his Friesian flat cap, revealing two lapwing eggs, which he offered to van Stigt. Friesland is known for its race to find the first eggs each spring, so the eggs were a significant gesture. Bonnema, teamed with celebrated landscape architect Mien Ruys, won the competition.

ARRIVAL
The initial design sketches by Ruys in 1977 show Pendorp in a pastoral polder setting with a few of the typical pyramid-shaped farm buildings in the background. Now, the canal is flanked with a mixture of housing and industrial barns, and the well-considered, almost mannerist plan of Pendorp is surrounded by generic office buildings: 1990s red brick office units rented out to an online marketing agency, a dentist, recruitment agency, administration office, and the likes. The traditional pyramidal farms that it drew on for its formal expression are hidden from view, which make Pendorp even more an oddity now than it originally was. From some distance, it is quite clear that Pendorp is not in use anymore. A few weeks earlier, a proposal for its demolition was accepted by the municipality. But even in a state of despair, the pixelated village-scape complex, with its signature pitched roofs, still trumps its surroundings.

BONNEMA
In 1978, Bonnema issues a *cri de coeur* in *De Architect*.[3] Like many architects of his time, he struggled between rejecting nostalgic historicism while looking for a more 'humane' modernism. He offered his own pre-cast concrete structural system, derived from traditional Friesian farm building craft, as a panacea. The system is based on 3D cruciform concrete columns set at 7.2-meter intervals. This serves as the base module at Pendorp.
The completion of the 1,000-worker offices of Pendorp in 1982 was celebrated with a small booklet produced by Twijnstra Gudde. Its title is somewhat ominous: "How to build a white elephant?". 'White elephant' is an expression for something rare but not a distinct subspecies; it also describes something so big that you wonder if it was worthwhile investing in. Twijnstra Gudde are specifically proud that, at a total of 91.7 million guilders,

the Pendorp project stayed within budget. For almost 23,000 square meters of gross floor area, an online calculator breaks this down to roughly €3,700 per square meter at 2021 prices, double the amount of a contemporary office building.
Bonnema's contribution to the booklet mainly speaks about the intensive finetuning of the project. Even the ceiling tiles were custom made. From the description you get the feeling a perfect-fitting glove had been built.

FUSIONS

In the early 90s, new market rules dictated that energy companies had to split generation and distribution into separate corporate entities. PEN's production side integrated with energy producers in Utrecht and Amsterdam was later bought by US based Reliant Energy. PEN's distribution side became part of Dutch Nuon. Nuon confusingly bought Reliant Energy and in doing so temporarily reunited PEN into one entity, until Nuon had to split off its distribution side once more, this time to Liander. Then Swedish state-owned Vattenfall took a 49 percent stake in Nuon and changed its name to Vattenfall the Netherlands. The latter currently supplies energy to more than two million households across the country. Amid this turbulent corporate reshuffling the offices at Pendorp, which were never used to full capacity, were inhabited until the mid-2010s, roughly 30 years.

ON SITE

I drive up closer to the fence. Signs show that three different parties are responsible for temporarily maintaining the complex, offering short-term anti-squatting residency. A new dark grey Mercedes pulls up behind me. A young woman gets out on the passenger side, loud dub-step pumping from the vehicle, and she opens the gate. When I ask if I can join them inside the driver gets out and acknowledges that visitors unfortunately aren't allowed. The couple lives in the building managers' residence on the north-east side of the plot, separate from other inhabitants now living in the office building. Even if they could let me in, they tell me I wouldn't be able to get out.
Later, I climb the fence anyway. Walking on the premises of Pendorp recalls the early 70s Dutch holiday resorts of Sporthuis Centrum. You expect a sign directing you to the subtropical swimming pool.
Still, the delicacy of the design is striking. The building document package shows at least 83 different window frames are used. Well considered details are apparent everywhere. The transition between inside and outside is finely interwoven. The quality of the landscape is harder to judge due to a lack of maintenance and the somber Dutch fall. But the spatial effect of an office both big and small remains impressive. Peeking through some of the windows, it's clear how well the interior is preserved. Normally after dereliction the speed at which decay sets in is mind-blowing. Here it seems work could resume any minute.
I stop at the southeast corner at one of the 3D cruciform columns and wonder if such a column will ever be built again. Two years earlier, in the interview with Herman Hertzberger about his Centraal Beheer building, his eyes lit up as he explained how flexible his grid system was. It seemed a moment of cognitive dissonance since he was, at the same time, struggling to save his revolutionary office – empty for years – from the bulldozers. Evidence that the system hadn't been that flexible. Both projects are great pieces of architecture made with devotion, while at the same time clearly failing in their original intentions.

FUTURE

A new future for Pendorp is currently in the hands of Rotterdam-based Zwarte Hond architects, who are also the custodians of Bonnema's legacy and archive. Two contractors bought Pendorp in 2018 with the initial intention of tearing it down completely and building a new residential quarter in its place. Pressured by the local architecture community they reconsider. Full renovation would have been too costly, partner-architect Bart van Kampen says in conversation, but in the end the landscape will be preserved in their new plan. Their latest sketch, published in 2021, shows an orthogonal modular structure for a new residential area that will be squeezed in to replace Bonnema's village. The new design is also pixelated yet with a higher density, and the characteristically sloped roofs are gone. Squares are cheaper and more practical. Zwarte Hond's desire to preserve Ruys's landscape will be difficult: Currently the gardens curve around the building in an intimate tango with moments reserved for artworks and smaller corners made for individual workers, which might prove hard to maintain in the transformation to housing.

DEPARTURE

I climb back over the fence and leave Pendorp, heading north. Just across the N9 provincial road a golf course breaks the strict geometry of the polder. Until it begins again, with historical windmills and West-Friesian farms stretching towards the dunes. I realize how much the building says about the office culture of the 1980s and our immediate future. About how a favorable addition of democratic voices in formulating the design brief led to a contradiction-littered program. How an architect managed to come up with a well-brokered workable solution. How he delicately weighed into the wrenching challenge posed of trying to connect to place and tradition, while remaining modern. How a system was implemented that opens up for future change and expansion, but never reaches its full potential, and now with less than 40 years of operation faces demolition. The situation seems to prove the risk of a single tenant building realizing vs. the opportunism of boring extruded multi-tenant offices. Which seems to point to us being stuck with that typology for much longer than Pendorp managed to live. Unless we beg to differ.

notes

1   Gerda ten Cate, "De paradox van neutraliteit in en door opmerkelijkheid," *Bouw No 22*, October 29, 1983. p.58–60
2   The offices were for the Postal bank (Giro, completed 1971) and the municipal social services (1975). See: abebonnema.nl.
3   Abe Bonnema, "Waar blijft de structuur in architectuur?" *De Architect*, year 9, issue 10, October 1978, p.109–116

building credits

client: PEN
architect: Abe Bonnema

photo credits

p.444 (all): Abe Bonnema Archief
p.449 (above): Stephan Petermann
p.449 (below): Regionaal Archief Alkmaar

2021
JAMES WATTSTRAAT
ALKMAAR, THE NETHERLANDS

1985

HSBC BUILDING

While banking has changed radically in the 21st century, the HSBC HQ in Hong Kong – the most expensive office building ever when it was completed in 1985 – looks remarkably impervious to time. Only paying attention to the details reveals its transformation. The sunlight 'catchers,' installed near the façade to ensure enough natural light filtered through into the atrium, have been turned into planters. New LED lighting fixtures cover the edges of the floor. While the tellers' desks and cubicles have remained largely untouched, overall transparency – echoing the actual banking sector – has decreased. New partition walls, more plants, higher guardrails, and ATMs with a huge digital screen above – where the reception desk used to be – obscure and break up its pristine airport-like cleanliness.

building credits

client: Hongkong and Shanghai Banking Corporation
architect: Foster and Partners

photo credits

p.450: Foster and Partners, p.451: Ian Dagnall

450

2018
1 QUEEN'S ROAD
CENTRAL, HONG KONG

1987

Ruth Baumeister

SAS FRÖSUNDAVIK OFFICE BUILDING

A Scandinavian groundscraper built to facilitate an "atmosphere of love" is still beloved... but too big for its anchor tenant

"SAS breaks every rule of Anglo-Saxon property development: it is specific to the requirements of a particular organization rather than providing generalized office space to meet generalized office requirements. It ignores the developer's goal of maximizing the value of the site. It is by developer's standards inefficient to the point of absurdity when measured against conventional real estate criteria such as the ratio of net lettable to gross area or usable to lettable or the ratio between length of perimeter and floor area. What is much more important than such supply side, efficiency-dominated criteria is that the entire SAS building is driven, energized and animated by a distinctive managerial agenda,"[1] writes Frank Duffy, founder of DEGW workplace consultancy, about the SAS headquarters, which was built by the Norwegian architect Niels Torp in a large park outside of Stockholm in 1986.

By the time the HQ was completed, SAS CEO Jan Carlzon had turned around the Scandinavian airline's troubled finances and transformed it into a flourishing international operation. Carlzon made a name for himself as (co-) author of managerial theory books: *Tear down the pyramids* (1985), and *Moments of truth* (1987). Torp had already collected experience designing offices when he won the competition for the SAS HQ. He was known for innovating the so-called combi-office, a floor plan where private cellular offices are organized around an open central space. Torp conceptualized the gigantic SAS HQ, designed for over 1,500 people, as a small city: five office pavilions are arranged along a central interior street that has shops, cafes, meeting, and sports facilities.
We spoke to former SAS CEO Carlzon and Torp himself together to look back on the ideas – managerial as well as architectural – which formed the basis of this building.
We also spoke to current SAS president and CEO Anko van der Werff on the future of Torp's building, SAS, and of office working generally. At the time of the interview, the young Dutchman had been in his position for just a couple of weeks.

Legacy: Jan Carlzon and Niels Torp
Ruth Baumeister [RB]: Conventional office buildings in the shape of a skyscraper, with executive offices on top and space for everyone else below reflect the hierarchies of the business world. In your management theory, you call for such hierarchies to be broken. How did your thinking influence the choice of architecture for the building?
Jan Carlzon [JC]: In the competition, I think we had seven architecture firms: three Swedish, two Danish, and two Norwegian. At that time, the Danish architect was number one in Scandinavia and he suggested a scheme where the president should be on the top floor and I should be able to see the aircraft come and go at the airport. So he was totally out.

RB: Can you explain in a nutshell what was innovative about your managerial approach at SAS?
JC: You have to define the difference between a manager and a leader. A manager stands in the middle of all people, pointing with one hand and giving instructions with the other. But with instructions, you limit people's responsibility. A leader is a person who listens to the people, and to the market. And when they are sure, they stand up bravely and say: this is the goal we are all heading for, and this is the way we should walk together to reach that goal, and on the way, you will have individual freedom and responsibility. I want to give people the freedom of a tight brief. That means they become more creative and surer of what they're doing. While if you say do whatever you want, they get lost. That's why the buildings here are quite narrow and the street is not that wide and it all ends with a beautiful pond at the end of the street. And then the bridges and small squares are there for distributing information. A person who is not informed properly cannot take responsibility, while people who have information cannot avoid taking responsibility. There are also trees and water flowing towards the pond. We had lunchtime concerts, a small choir singing, and artists making exhibitions here. Even poetry readings… It was there to create an atmosphere of love.

RB: What do you mean by "atmosphere of love"?
JC: Making people feel they are appreciated, that they are important. Taking away the fear and instead spreading the love. A person who works in an environment of love becomes creative because he or she can make decisions and be much more efficient than a person who is afraid of the consequences. All these ideas became manifest in this building.

RB: This kind of architecture costs money. Typically, office buildings are made cheaply and quickly, and given their depreciation, investors calculate for a short amount of time, even though the building itself lasts much longer. How do you argue against such short-sighted perspectives?

JC: I said we used to fly airplanes, now we have to learn how to fly people. Those who work close to the people in the market become the most important because they spread the good news, so to speak. The company is represented in every meeting between the employee and the consumer and that means that people in middle management should not give instructions to those in the front line. Instead, the customer should do that, and the top management should have nothing to do with it at all. The only thing they have to do is point out the philosophy of the business and the strategy that we all should comply with. The most important thing is to satisfy customers, nothing else. To answer your initial question: you have to make sure that every single decision, every action will reflect that strategy and you can visualize this kind of strategy in the building itself.

RB: Architecture is a powerful tool because it can interface between your ideas as a leader and the work environment. Most of the larger companies nowadays don't build their own buildings anymore. They rent because it's cheaper. Did companies give away the power to represent themselves through architecture?

Niels Torp [NT]: The people in the developer's corner do tend to think in different terms to those leading businesses. I didn't know Jan's philosophy when I did the competition entry, but I wanted to understand how you can accommodate 1,500 office workers in Scandinavia, in a beautiful setting. Many corporations at that time had a monumental HQ to demonstrate their power and wealth, and totally ignored the human aspect. My approach was to imagine 1,500 people coming to a place in the landscape. How do you treat them as individuals and not just a flock of people? A building like this was huge in Scandinavia, it was the size of a village. It's quite difficult to gather Scandinavians in a building like this, taking them away from the city ambiance and right into the wilderness. We dug out a mold and filled the building into the footprint and the height of the mold. So you could creep into the landscape and split the building into smaller entities, which were more common in Scandinavia at that time. Luckily there was no developer here and we worked under the culture of a client who wanted exactly what we wanted: to be friendly and give life and inspiration to lots of people.

RB: It was a perfect example of an office building of the welfare state. You looked at the single office worker, gave them amenities like a swimming pool, cultural events, etc. Why have you, Jan, been criticized for building something like this?

JC: If somebody starts to talk about worker as the most important resource, it was not immediately accepted as a bright idea. The general conviction was that the only way for a company to be successful was to cut costs. Cutting costs could be an excellent idea if you are in a monopolistic situation. But today, in a competitive market, the winner is the one who can cut costs and secure income.

NT: When a company or a person is very successful, the media wants to tear them down. That might be a Scandinavian way of acting.

RB: Talking about media, we looked into how CEOs talked about their headquarters and what kind of environment they envisioned for their employees. What they describe is exactly what both of you just talked about: the worker must feel comfortable because she or he is the most important resource in the company. CEOs all say they want to treat their personnel well in order to attract talent, etc. But we looked at their office buildings and discovered a big discrepancy: the working environments they provided did not meet their stories at all.

Do you have an explanation for why they cannot live up to their promises?
JC: Very few people really believe in what they say, but if you can create a feeling of love between people and the organization a lot can happen. For example, I had my office here and my secretary was right next door in a big room. When people came to present something for me, they had to wait in her office and I could hear through the door how they were laughing. By the time they got into my office, if they were nervous before, it was gone. They came in as strong people who have been surrounded by laughter and love.

RB: Atmospheres are very important for human beings and architecture plays an important role in creating them. The problem is that atmosphere is not measurable, especially in the planning phase. How can an architect argue in front of a client or investor for creating a building which nurtures love, trust, and respect within a given budget? How can you bring that into the Excel balance sheet?
NT: It's not a question of money, but of empathy and ideas. A building that caters for all the tender feelings you should have as a human being does not cost anything more than another one. You have the same elements, the same construction, the same ventilation system, the same glazing system. Everything similar – but it has to do with what you think a building should communicate. And it's quite easy to find an industrial construction with lots of empathy for what the people who will work in it will feel.

RB: When we walked through the building, Jan said everything is custom made here. And it's apparent that every single detail is made with love from the architect, which is costly. How can you argue that in opposition to a skyscraper, for example, where you design the lobby on the ground and the executive floor on top, and in between, you only have repetitive cookie-cutter design?
NT: Skyscrapers cost more per square meter. The construction, the number of lifts and vertical traffic areas are more expensive than a horizontal building. A horizontal office building is much more efficient than the skyscraper. Additionally you have more flexibility when you have a big floor plan. The SAS building is divided into different parts but connected with bridges – that's a very efficient composition without much vertical communication. All the time your staff uses for going from the ground floor up to the top can be very costly to build and to run it. Also, do not forget about what colors and materials can do. It's a question of the consideration the architect gives, like setting up a backdrop in a theatre.

RB: We have talked about breaking down hierarchies, and that means as a leader you shouldn't be on the top floor in the executive lounge. Jan, you were criticized because your office was slightly better located and had a better view. How do you look at it today?
JC: It could have been an issue back then: people might have accused me of not sticking to my philosophy. But I did everything I said as a leader. Therefore, at the time, the location of my office wasn't questioned. Maybe by the media, but not by the people I worked with.

RB: It's no secret that behind a good piece of architecture you will find a good client. How about the cooperation between the two of you? Niels, your idea was to build into the landscape, and almost by coincidence, it fit Jan's management ideas well. During the planning process, did you discuss how to materialize the company's philosophy?
JC and NT: [spontaneously in synch] No!
NT: It was natural for two Scandinavians to have the same view on many values. And on a site like this, it's absolutely forbidden to build a high-rise. You have a responsibility for the surrounding nature; the building should not disturb anything. It is a Scandinavian way of looking at life: you don't disturb, you don't destroy. You try to be decent and respectful

when you are talking about scale. It was a happy coincidence that our views of what a building like this were the same. The need for a good client to make a good building is definitely true. The problem with developers is that they put money before everything and their attitude results in the straightness of the building, the flat façade, the flat floor plan, and no round corners and things like that. It's too simple and it destroys architecture. Buildings from elsewhere in the world start to lose their local characteristics.

RB: Are you referring to architecture's capacity to create place?
NT: Yes. We need to have a regional view on everything we do. When you fly over Europe, you see that cities, high-rise buildings, and the square footprint is spreading everywhere. And when you come to Scandinavia, at least Sweden, Finland, and Norway, you have a landscape that doesn't take it that way. But when you look at Denmark you see square boxes everywhere now and they are spreading because the landscape is flat.

RB: Can you both point at anything in your collaboration that you would do differently, in retrospect?
JC: I don't think there's any special thing that I would change.
NT: I do not think I would change anything. You have to criticize what you've been doing, but it comes down to small details only. We really put our heart into the building and I think that's the most important thing.

Present and future: Anko van der Werff
RB: You recently moved to SAS from the South American airline Avianca, where you were CEO, to SAS. Can you describe how the workplaces differ between these companies?
Anko van der Werff: The fundamentals of society and also the concept of hierarchy are very different. The CEO at Avianca – and maybe all CEOs in Latin America – has a grand largely sized office. This includes a private bathroom, even a private shower. There are all kinds of amenities, like your own TV. I think these offices are a hindrance if you actually want to interact with people. They take up so much space that it's already a given that you have fewer people around you. On a typical floor, there is X number of people, but on your floor, there is half X. In my new office at SAS, it's all about a building where everyone is equal and we have about 12–15 people in the size of space where I was alone in Avianca. It feels great: you have far more interaction and develop a different sense of hierarchy.

RB: This Scandinavian notion of equality – do you really subscribe to it? You have different responsibilities and different privileges given your position, and that doesn't come with equality. I would say the major reason why the executive office is typically on the top floor is because it's a demonstration of power.
AvdW: I've never believed in that. I worked in a few buildings where I've tried to move down to another floor. Being with the team I work with is more important to me.

RB: Is there anything you miss from your former executive office?
AvdW: What is problematic about not having a private office anymore is that I always have to walk away when I call someone. And I call a lot, I don't like writing an email because it takes too long and you miss the personal interaction and people may misinterpret what you said. What was great about the office I had before was that I was alone, but you could easily ask people to come up and see you. You are with your team here, so you can immediately approach them. You can see when they're busy or not.

RB: How about space to retreat? Do you need that in your day-to-day work?
AvdW: I do, and that's a bit more complicated when you're the CEO. People know when and where you are, so it's very difficult to hide. And occasionally you need to hide because otherwise you're getting external stimuli all the time, which I don't believe is healthy. You want to have a bit of time to reflect, think, and read and I've tried to build that into my calendar.

RB: You're exposed because of your position and then you also have the spatial exposure here. Can you describe how you deal with that?
AvdW: Exactly, because everything is very open, very well lit, bright transparent spaces with windows. It was interesting to hear you say that there are a lot of privileges that come with the job. I'm actually not so sure in Scandinavia whether you are right. Wherever you go, people will always walk up to you and say, hey, how about this or that? Or could you please… or whatever… It is fantastic, I love it.

RB: At the moment, when walking through the building it seems rather empty. Are people free to choose to work from home?
AvdW: Right now, the rules are set by the government, which is encouraging people to work from home.

RB: So it's not for you to decide yet if people should work from home, at the office, or in a hybrid situation?
AvdW: Even if we wanted to make the decision, it's not a question yet and it's uncertain in what kind of configuration we will work in the future. Are employees allowed to choose if they want to work from home, at the company, or hybrid, who knows?

RB: Does everybody now have a fixed desk?
AvdW: No, that was already abandoned. The majority of the desks are actually flex-desks, but I think the staff who are here on a regular basis always choose the same desk.

RB: Does that also have an influence on how people care about their surroundings?
AvdW: I guess if you are here every day, you take better care of the environment because you're more conscious about that.

RB: It is often argued that this building is a product of the welfare state. Do you agree and how do you see that changing?
AvdW: Yes. Jan had this idea of flat hierarchies in business and the architecture of this building reflects that. Today, the structure of the business is more fluid. In my opinion, the building is timeless because if you look at the younger generations, they use those common spaces more than I would have done 20 years ago. It's much more about collaborative decision-making and brainstorming. The beauty of this building is that it provides the frame for collaborative working 30 years before that was even invented.

RB: Airlines or headquarters are always in the center of cities or at the airport. What do you think about the location of this one in a park?
AvdW: It comes with an enormous number of qualities, although I do like airports. Of course, it's also good for an airline to be at an airport because your mechanics and cabin crew, etc. are there and you can get together with them.

RB: If you had the possibility, would you call for a new building?
AvdW: I wouldn't. The vast majority of us are deeply fond of this building, and the surroundings are quite extraordinary. But how much space do we need? Will it make sense to stay here in the future?

RB: How many people work here at SAS?
AvdW: It's a tricky question because of Covid. A lot of people are not activated because we are an airline at the moment, but roughly we are an 8,000 to 10,000-person company. The majority of us are operational – pilots, cabin crew, mechanics, ground staff, who work

in airports. Initially, there were about 1,500 SAS people working in this office, and by now we're down to about 500. There are a lot of other companies now in this building, which creates a more dynamic atmosphere. You don't know them and they don't know you. I'm still trying, for instance, to set up a sports team. There's a beautiful sports hall downstairs and I wouldn't mind at all if we play sports there with another company.

RB: In the beginning, SAS used the entire building, but as you indicated, the space used by SAS has decreased enormously. And by necessity, a lot of people are now working from home. A lot of big companies are deciding to get rid of their office buildings. In London, for example, a lot of office space is empty. How do you see the future of SAS in this respect?

AvdW: I'm not sure whether this answer is specific to SAS, but I see two limitations of not being in the office. One is how do you train people? Typically, younger people always think they know everything anyway, right? When they're at home you have no way of training them and there are of course also other subtleties. I see that as a challenge. This idea that everyone can work everywhere, I don't think that's going to work. Secondly, physical presence is needed for true brainstorming, true creativity. You need a central place where you can come together. Whether there is a need for an office, I do not know. You could, for example, do some of that in a park or something like that. Our building here is timeless. If you look at it now, in the time of Covid, what is it people are looking for? They're looking for space. Well, it is beautiful here, we have a park. They're looking for stimuli, or other things to do well. You can kayak on the lake here, you can walk around the park, or you can go biking. There's a tennis court, a gym, and this whole concept of inside-outside and flowing between these places works well. I try and work from home now one day a week as well. To sum it up: I don't see SAS over the next few years abandoning the office. It won't work.

RB: Companies now hire offices and meeting rooms in a hotel or any other given space in a city on demand, to save costs. Would that be an option for SAS?

AvdW: When you have an employee base of 20-60 and you only have about eight or 10 of you that occasionally need to meet, I think such a solution could work – for example, if you're a small media company. I don't see it working for SAS or for airlines in general though. Airlines typically work together on the same product and the work process is less divided. In banking, for example, work is far more compartmentalized, but here you need a lot of people together in the same room to think or plan together. I could not see that kind of work being done on an on-and-off basis. I think we would be spending far too much time figuring out where we can go. We would then be compromised when discovering that the building we used last week is now full. I can see that we might reduce some office space, but to say as a general strategy that we're going to do without the office. No, that won't happen.

RB: Do you have any idea how much SAS may reduce by?

AvdW: No, I'm too new to the company and I don't have an overview. The difficulty of starting in the Covid period is that you actually don't even know how many are not in the building right now. There is one thing I observe, which is after a period of working from home because of the pandemic, a lot of people are starting come back to the office.

notes

1 Frank Duffy in: Niels Torp Arkitekter, *Art Consulting in Scandinavia* (Oslo, 1997), p.75

building credits

client: Jan Carlzon
architect: Niels Torp

photo credits

p.452, 462: unknown
p.461, 463 (all): Jens Frederiksen

2021
FRÖSUNDAVIKS ALLÉ 1
SOLNA, SWEDEN

462

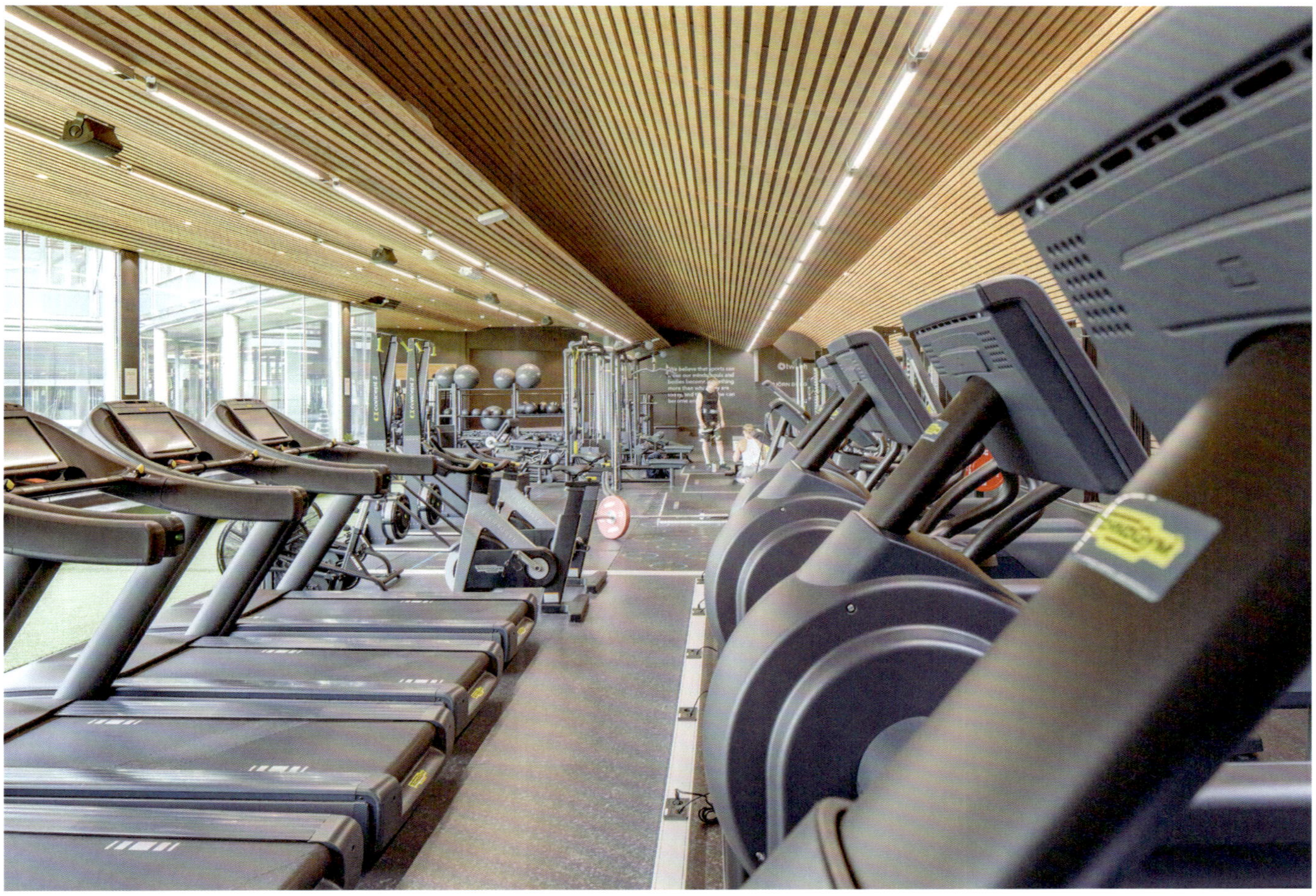

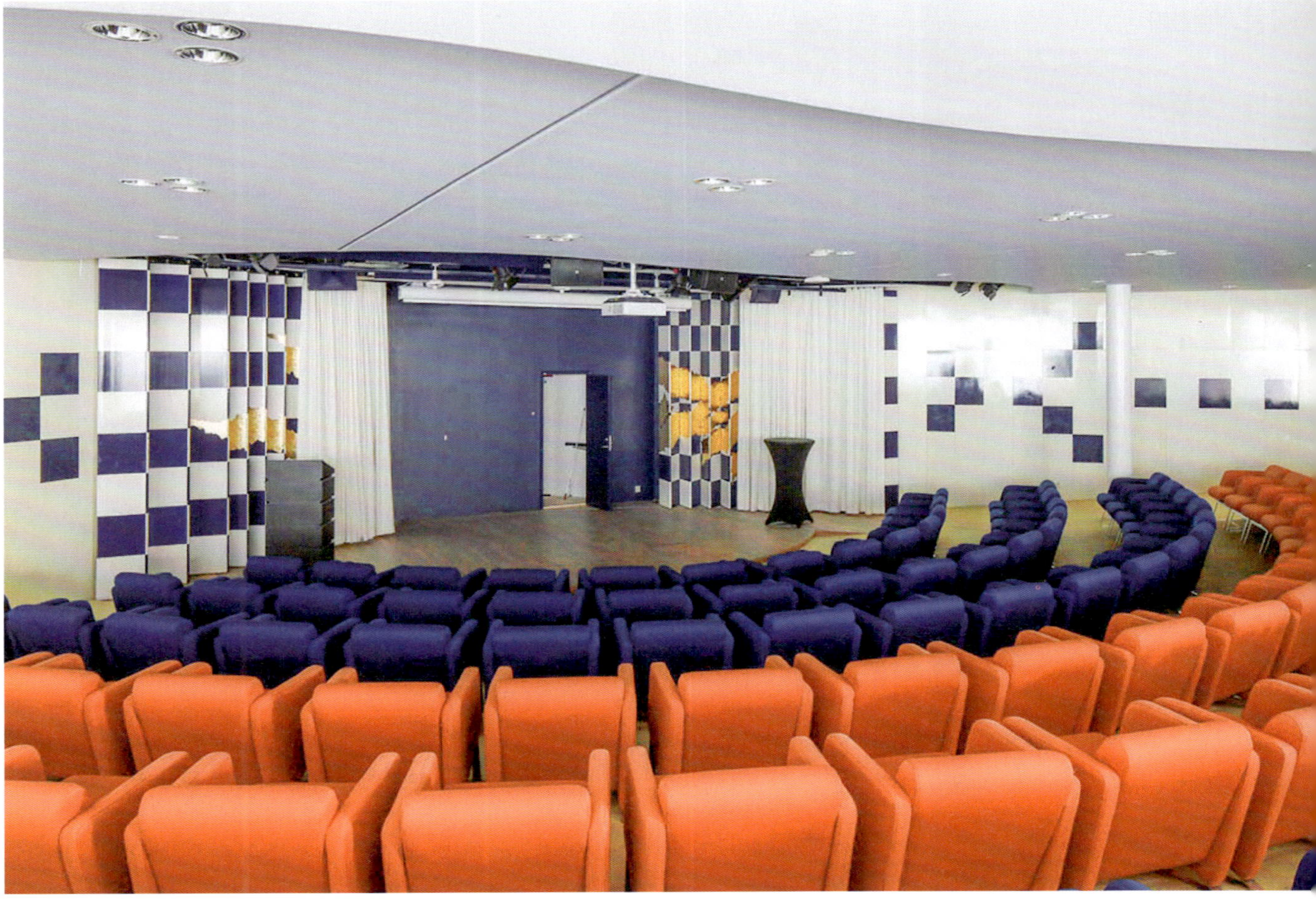

1989

LA GRANDE ARCHE

Less than 15 years after the completion of the modern equivalent of the Arc de Triomphe, the earth around the Le Grand Arche started to move. As part of a rejuvenation plan for La Defense, the government decided to move more of its bureaucratic apparatus into La Grande Arche, with various French ministries taking up space. The plan also triggers discussion over giving the Arche heritage status, which would make it one of the youngest monuments in France. In 2010, security concerns following an elevator accident (without injuries) shut down the popular panoramic elevator and scenic rooftop for visitors. Further safety studies in 2014 indicated that one in six of the porous Italian Carrara marble tiles that cover the building were susceptible to the weather and Paris's pollution, prompting a €200 million renovation, completed in 2017. The owners of the northern side of the building decided not to participate in the renovation, despite an appeal by a group of international architects, who were afraid that a partial renovation, resulting in two types of cladding on the facade, would ruin the overall quality of the building. The roof is reopened to the public featuring a restaurant and a new museum dedicated to photojournalism.

2021
1 PARVIS DE LA DÉFENSE
PUTEAUX, FRANCE

building credits

client: François Mitterrand (Grandes opérations d'architecture et d'urbanisme)
architect: Johan Otto von Spreckelsen and Paul Andreu

photo credits

p.464, 466: unknown,
p.465, 467: Jules Gorce

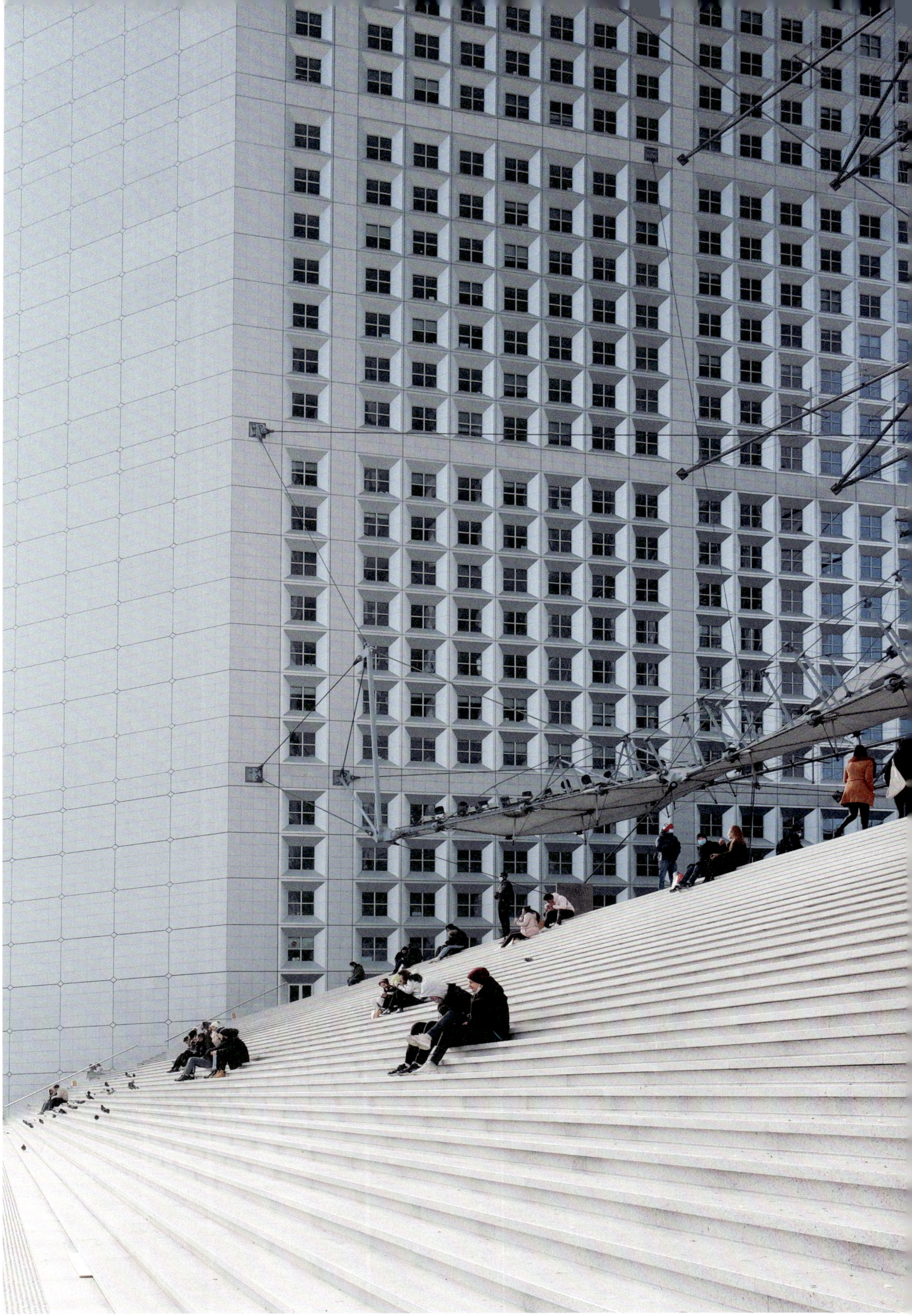

1991

Marieke van den Heuvel

DELFTSE POORT

Rethinking the office environment by creating an (almost) 100 percent circular interior

Commissioned in 1989 and completed in 1991, the Delftse Poort complex in Rotterdam was once the pride and emblem of Nationale-Nederlanden, one of the largest insurance and asset management companies in the Netherlands. Depending on the weather, the gridded glass tower shimmered bright blues or dark greys. On the one hand a typical 90s mirrored office building and on the other an icon of the Rotterdam skyline.
Until 2009, Delftse Poort was the tallest building in the Netherlands and for a decade hosted the Dutch run-up contest, it took the athletes 745 acidifying steps to reach the top. The building also served as a canvas for sponsorship campaigns, including a gigantic photo of soccer legend Edgar Davids, seemingly rushing out of the building's facade in 2010.

The whole complex comprises 106,000 square meters and is composed of three staggered planes connected by a three-story high plinth, thoughtfully combined by Dutch architect Abe Bonnema. Following a restructuring of the building's ownership in 2005, Nationale-Nederlanden reduced its footprint within the building and began sharing with parent company ING. By 2015, Nationale-Nederlanden was no longer the building's main tenant, resulting in the removal of the large orange logo that adorned the North Tower all those years. The building was bought by real estate magnate CBRE in 2009, and is now leased to several tenants, with Nationale-Nederlanden occupying 18,000 of the available 66,000 square meters of office space. This has not stopped them from investing in an ambitious 'circular' interior design for both the Delftse Poort and Haagse Poort, their head office in The Hague.

The shell and core of an office building can retain its value for decades or longer while the interior – within our current linear economy – loses its value the moment it is put into use. Office interiors are subject to an endless replacement of partition walls, flooring, fixtures, and furniture long before they are worn out. The vast majority of the material is not reused elsewhere but ends up being 'recycled' (which for the most part means incinerated in waste-to-energy plants) or in landfill. Nationale-Nederlanden opted to radically break with this habit for its Rotterdam refurbishment, aiming for the highest sustainability ambitions of a 100% circular design and Zero Waste.

This is easier said than done. It means making a painstaking inventory of every object and material in the office and finding a place for it in the new interior design or, where this is not feasible, a new destination has to be found elsewhere. What makes the Delftse Poort project remarkable is not the good intentions – green, sustainable, circular – which are widespread across the Netherlands by now, but the persistence of the client and architect in actually following the Zero Waste principle to the letter.

They also committed to scrupulously tracking their environmental impact in numbers. While architecture is increasingly subject to sustainable building standards laid down in building decrees and certificates, this has not been the case so much for interior design. The smaller size, shorter timelines, and lower budgets may explain the absence of credible certificates and systems for interior design. This limits the potential deeper analysis of 'impact' and leads to environmental strategies that are dependant largely on the designer's intuition and the client's appetite for greenwashing. In terms of size, interior re-fits are responsible for a considerable share of building waste because of the easy disposability of the material.

Speaking to different stakeholders involved in the renovation – the architects, client, consultants, and producers – reveals what is actually required of all parties in order to make their share of the work measurable. The starting point was the situation as it was, with everything already 'in there' as opposed to a (fictional) empty floor. From there the engineering firm LBP|SIGHT created, as a point of reference, an assessment framework by calculating the environmental impact of a regular project in which the old interior is discarded and replaced by a completely new interior. This assessment was paired up with definitions for waste leading to the decision to take "recycling to an equal raw material value" as the zero line. Re-use scored positively while incineration with energy recovery had the lowest negative score. It was not permitted to take anything to a landfill. By placing a great emphasis on reuse, but also through additional solutions such as packaging-free deliveries and the use of electric transport, a 70 percent environmental impact reduction could be achieved.[1]

In 2019, Delft-based Architects Fokkema & Partners were charged with this mission. Typically, they have to convince clients to take a more sustainable approach; with Nationale-Nederlanden it was the common shared starting point. Twan Steeghs, associate partner, and Dirk Zwaan, senior architect talked us through what it took to realize Zero Waste.

Marieke van den Heuvel [MvdH]: Can you describe the background of your practice and the inception of the National Nederlanden project?

Twan Steeghs [TS]: Following the financial crisis in 2008, many new construction projects were put on hold or got cancelled. Renovation and transformation of existing buildings therefore became an even greater part of our portfolio. Reuse plays a major part in this. There are currently millions of square meters of empty offices, even in prime locations, across the Netherlands. Due to new regulations[2], these buildings must be upgraded, which makes renovation an interesting exercise: to give the space a new life but not to throw away too much in the process. This is a particular challenge for interiors because they have a much shorter lifespan than a building. There is an entrenched culture of just tossing things out and producing waste. It's incredibly difficult to bring discarded materials back into the supply chain for building contractors because by definition they do not have intrinsic value – let alone added value – for a client. With Nationale-Nederlanden, the client was the initiator of sustainability, putting a full Zero Waste ambition on the table. It went as far as thinking about what to do with the discarded cigarette butts.

MvdH: Can you take me to the beginning of the project?

Dirk Zwaan [DZ]: We started in 2019, and the project was scheduled to be completed by the end of 2021. The design was executed in phases as they were still using parts of the building. The COVID-19 pandemic impacted our assignment: Nationale-Nederlanden divested several floors in the building and decided that more people will be sharing the office as most of the staff were only coming in part-time. Fortunately, our design already responded to hybrid and flexible work models, and we only had to make minor adjustments, in that regard the design was tuned into the zeitgeist quite well.

MvdH: How did the conversation with Nationale-Nederlanden about their circular ambitions begin?

TS: The client's goal was Zero Waste and a WELL certification.[3] Together with a consultancy and engineering firm called LBP|SIGHT, who joined the team, we've set up a conceptual framework using the 10-Rs model[4], with reuse as the main strategy, to reach those ambitions. LBP|SIGHT calculated all shadow costs[5] to provide insight into the reduction of the environmental impact compared with a classic renovation. This led to the choice of local manufacturing and using electric transport where possible. Throughout the development, all parties in this project were obliged to indicate where their products originated, which drove them crazy. The LBP|SIGHT entered all this data into an enormous and complex Excel sheet. In the design itself, we limited the use of new materials. For every existing element, we tried to find a function in the new design or a repurposing somewhere else. We were committed to doing this while maintaining quality. Only when there really was no other solution did materials get grounded into asphalt for road construction. That's the worst option, but at least nothing got burned.

MvdH: Do you know how old the existing interior was when you started?

DZ: Partly. The interior contractor had been working with the client for a long time. They knew that some of the pantries over in Haagse Poort were only one or two years old. Part of the bespoke furniture used in the Delftse Poort had also only recently been installed. We looked at what we could do with every single element. We re-used the existing pantries, but with added paneling because it had previously stood against a wall. We also brought back all the seating booths, but with new upholstery. We made acoustic panels from the old fabric.

MvdH: How did the circular strategies of 'harvesting' and collaborating with the building parties early on influence your design process?[6]
DZ: We started with a Preliminary Design as usual, although we didn't know whether certain materials would be available for use. A big difference with other projects is that we didn't make a Definitive Design, as is standard procedure in architecture; nor did we make a regular set of construction drawings, but rather we made a design manual. This manual described our vision, which we shared with the builders, and collaboratively we defined all materialization and details in workshops. For example, we showed visualizations of a pantry with a wooden finish and the contractors came with samples of 'harvested' wood. We also asked them to come up with alternatives for products such as ceramic tiles. One contractor proposed tiles made from construction waste and we ended up using that.

MvdH: Were you responsible for the complete inventory of the existing interior?
DZ: We had a real-time harvest map in which all collaborating parties such as the wall supplier, the interior builder, and the upholster kept track of their contribution. At the start, everything was divided into 'plots' that were assigned to the different parties, one encompassing all the carpets, one overseeing the partition walls, one for customized furniture, one for factory-made furniture, and so on. This way everyone knew what elements and materials were being used and what was available.

MvdH: You worked on two buildings at the same time – could you mix harvested materials from one site with the other?
DZ: Yes. There was a difference in ceiling heights, which made it harder to exchange the partition walls, though we managed it in the end. Shifting between the bespoke furniture was easier.
The idea was that all parties could use each other's materials, so if the interior builder had wood left over, it was used by the wall builder and vice versa. It sounds simple but it is a big challenge to keep the harvest file up to date: something changes every day, materials disappear, and new materials are added. At a certain point, the contractor started demolition and an older wall made of plasterboard appeared behind a retention wall. Because we didn't want any waste, we had to come up with a solution for that too.

MvdH: What was it like to work with so many used materials?
TS: A surprising experience was the carpet. Over time, many different types of carpets have been used in both Delftse Poort and Haagse Poort, all of varying quality. At first, I thought we would be re-using the newest carpets, but we ended up taking the oldest ones as they are fabricated in a way that the different materials cannot be separated anymore, making them impossible to recycle. However, they were easy to clean and very durable. The newer carpets have an eco-backing which makes them better suited to disassembly, so they were taken back by the manufacturer.
DZ: Then we were stuck with all the old bright green and orange carpets, a color palette that we would never have come up with. This meant we had to adapt our design mindset. There was no alternative, other than grinding them into asphalt. Then we looked each other in the eyes and said "OK, we're going to re-use it." The actua refitting of the carpets was not easy either. When we asked the upholsterer to harvest, clean and reinstall the old carpets they were not appreciative at all and initially rejected the task. We learned that it takes a lot of time and energy to get the implementing parties on board. You really need to get them

involved in the concept first. If we force this new way of working on these parties without convincing them of the reasoning behind it, the chances are the materials will end up in a dumpster.

TS: For example, an upholsterer is used to delivering a perfect project, that's the honor of their profession. When reusing the carpet tiles, colour differences arose, which they would normally not find acceptable. Also, some of the carpets were so damaged that they could no longer be cleaned. We chose to accentuate the colour differences by placing the carpets in a tone-on-tone checkerboard. It took several meetings to come up with a set of design rules for this, which finally convinced the upholsterer of the concept.

DZ: Initially, the upholsterer did a test where everything that could go wrong, went wrong: they broke tiles and bubbles were visible during installation due to the glue residues that were difficult to remove. The first estimate of what could be reused was only a small percentage, but eventually they got better at the new process, and it worked out well in the end.

MvdH: There's a lot of labor involved when reusing the carpet tiles. Is it realistic to do this in other projects, when you compare the labor costs to the price of new tiles?

TS: Good question. In a reuse project, there is a big shift from material costs to labour costs. I think we got lucky with this client and the budget was available to accommodate this shift. As far as Nationale-Nederlanden were concerned, this project was a business card, an exemplary project that they want to roll out as a standard for all of their offices.

MvdH: Is it more expensive to set up a project in a circular way than when you opt for more conventional solutions?

DZ: I don't have the most recent insight into the costs but it's definitely not cheaper. But we're also doing a few floors in the so-called "post-COVID-19 areas" where we focus on hybrid working with innovative and biobased materials such as fruit leather, chairs made with industrial hemp fibres, or a composite made of rice husks. These materials are exciting to work with but sometimes expensive and more difficult to use as some are still under development. This means they are only available in small quantities and their Life Cycle Analysis (LCA) has not been fully calculated. This was an extra complication because we were considering only materials with the lowest possible Environmental Cost Indicator (ECI). We decided to include these new materials because we believed that by using them, we were investing in the suppliers, hopefully leading to more interesting developments in the future.

MvdH: Have you made any new, surprising discoveries?
DZ: Yes. Even though I have also worked on other sustainably-driven projects, this one feels like– for the first time – genuinely circular. But a lot of research needs to be done, everything is still in its infancy. Companies say they have the most fantastic sustainable products, but there is still a lot of greenwashing out there. If you dig a bit deeper or have parties like LBP|SIGHT do the calculations, then there is a lot of hot air, or just very good solutions but just focussed on one specific area. In a sense, we are all pioneers.
TS: Sustainable and circular building is inevitable and will happen more and more. There is increased awareness with clients, who have stronger demand and I'm sure most designers are interested. It's the contractors that need to come on board.

MvdH: Another important circular strategy is that everything should be built for disassembly. Is that the case at Nationale-Nederlanden?
DZ: Yes, everything is screwed or made with a type of loose connection. Being transparent about how something is assembled creates a different aesthetic. But we still wanted to create seamless connections in the design. To achieve this, we used French cleat hangers. It remains a corporate environment and it cannot look homemade. The client accepted a lot of compromise, but there are limits to that.

MvdH: In which areas of the project did you gain the best results?
DZ: If you look at the diagram made by LBP|SIGHT you can see how the Nationale-Nederlanden project scores compared to a conventional office design: all categories considered, we achieved 70 percent less impact than a conventional office refit. It was

difficult to make a bigger improvement on a construction level because of the nature of the project, which was focused on the interior without large constructional interventions. The difference we made with individual pieces of furniture was significant. The challenge here was that we often could not trace the product specifications, so we had to find out by experiment if they would meet the current requirements. To do this, we created a specific room in which we put all the harvested furniture to assess whether it still contained any harmful substances.

MvdH: The client has already mentioned that they will continue changing the interiors. How do you ensure that this interior can be re-used again in the future?
TS: First, we have the harvest map we used during the development of the interior in which everything we used in the building is described and calculated. Additionally, Nationale-Nederlanden was considering the possibility of making agreements with other parties – the interior builder, the wall supplier, and so on – to maintain, repair, or take back products at the end of the office's lifespan. That is why it is so important to build demountable. That could not be done for the elements that belong to the building owner, such as the ceilings. But in the future, when the project is delivered to facility services, things will unavoidably shift or break. As designers, you pass on the baton, while the project ambitions require continued attention. Especially in this case – inherent to the concept of circularity – it never stops.

notes

1. Method of operation and scores were shared by Jeannette Levels-Vermeer, partner at LBP|Sight, in an interview with the author.
2. According to the Dutch National Building Code 2012, all office buildings must have an energy rating of C or above by 2023.
3. The WELL Building Standard is "a performance-based system for measuring, certifying, and monitoring features of the built environment that impact human health and wellbeing, through air, water, nourishment, light, fitness, comfort, and mind." (https://standard.wellcertified.com/well)
4. The R-ladder, widely used in the Netherlands, is a framework to define circularity strategies. The higher a strategy is on this list (ladder), the more circular the strategy is. R0, the highest rung, is "refuse": "make product redundant by abandoning its function. Followed by Reduce, Rethink, Re-use, Repair, Refurbish, Remanufacture, Repurpose, Recycle, Recover (meaning incineration to produce electricity). (Environmental Planning Office, 2017.)
   See also: Reike, Vermeulen, Witjes, "The circular economy: New or Refurbished as CE 3.0? Exploring Controversies in the Conceptualization of the Circular Economy through a Focus on History and Resource Value Retention Options," in *Resources, Conservation and Recycling*, August 2018, p.246-264.
5. The more common term might be 'environmental cost' or externalities: costs that are typically removed from accounting methodologies, hiding a project's broader impacts.
6. The collection and reuse of materials and objects.

building credits

client: Nationale Nederlanden
architect: Abe Bonnema
interior architect 2019-2022: Fokkema & Partners

photo credits

p.468: Jan Versnel
p.473: Marieke van den Heuvel
p.474-475, 479 (above): Lucas van der Wee
p.477, 479 (below, 2x), 481: Ossip van Duijvenbode
p.478 (all), 480: Sybolt Voeten

2021
WEENA 505
ROTTERDAM, THE NETHERLANDS

478

2018

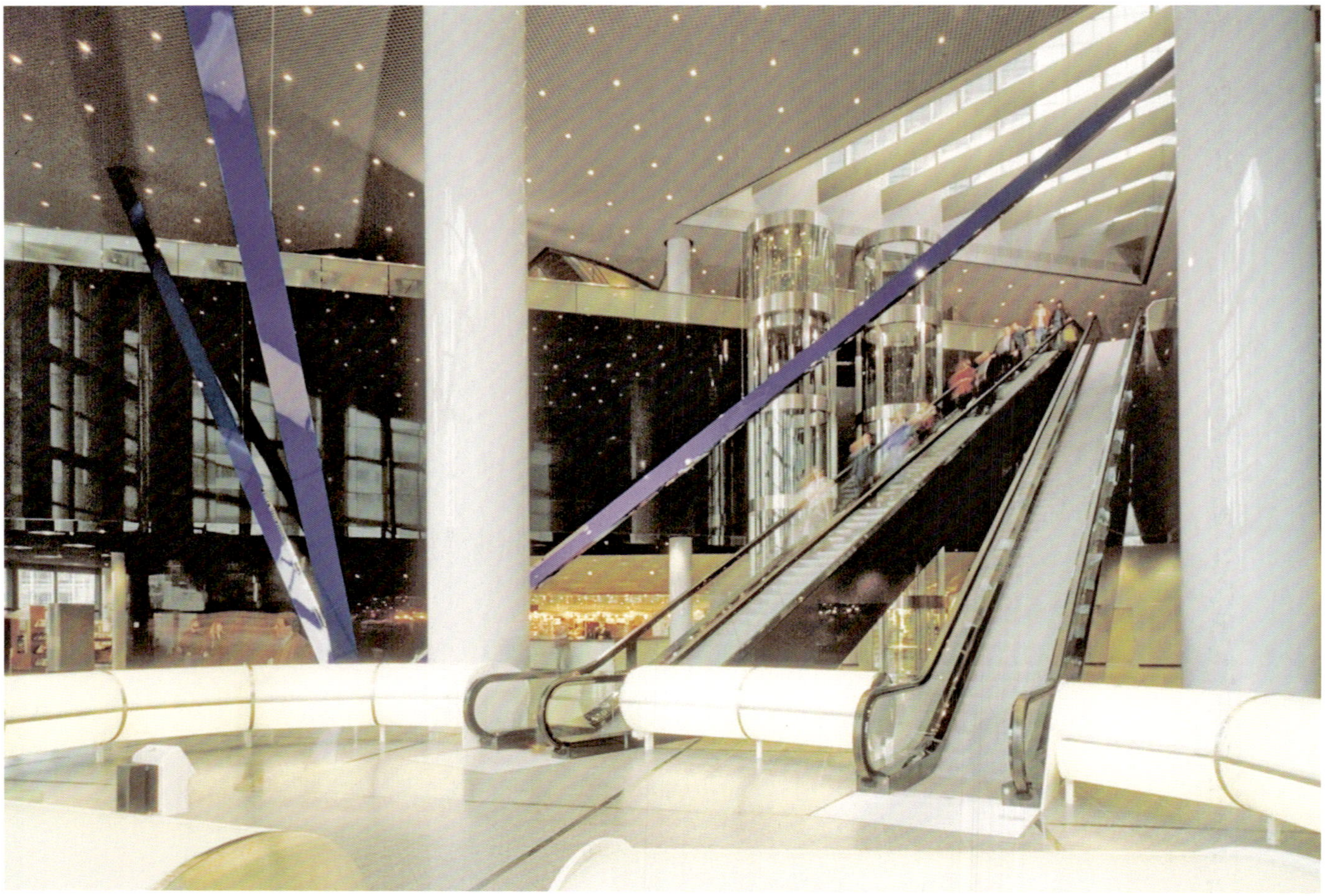

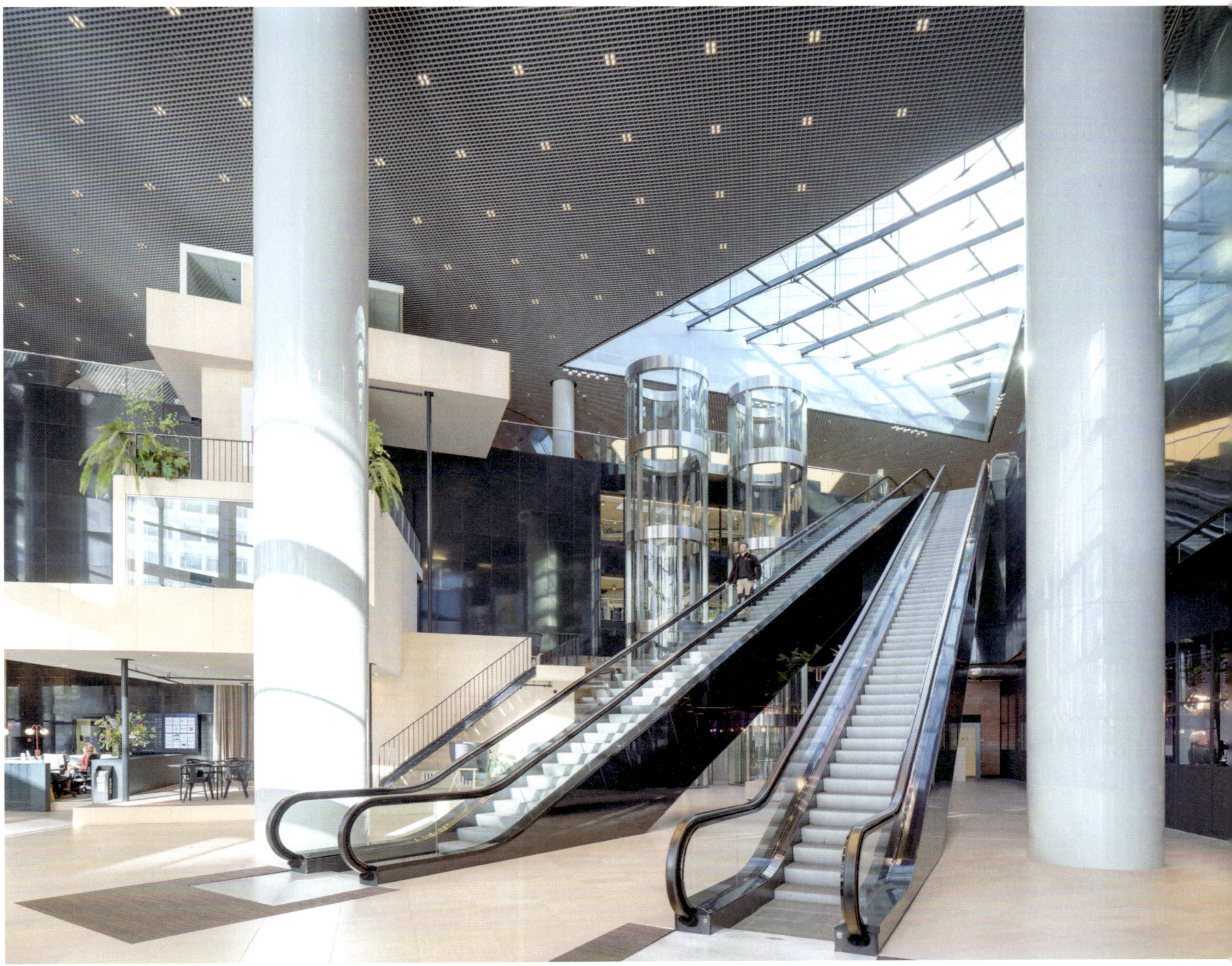

EXECUTIVE SUMMARY IN SIX POINTS

DEDICATED TO FUTURE COMMISSIONERS, ARCHITECTS, AND OFFICE CONSULTANTS

At the start of this book, three significant forces framed the way we think about office buildings throughout the 20th century: the development and promotion of its planning (represented by Frank Duffy), doubts about the usefulness of offices in the digital age (Jack Nilles), and the affirmation of the office as a stage for corporate culture (McKinsey's Tom Peters and Robert Waterman Jr.). It is clear that COVID-19 has significantly altered our perceptions, and the role of the office, though we are still grappling with the long-term ('blended'?) outcome. Perhaps the pandemic proved that all three historic figures were in essence right. We need more imaginative spatial planning for offices. We can work from home. We do (also) need a physical stage on which to work (and connect). The pandemic fades, but the whispering in the back of our minds, wondering what we are actually doing at the office, will not...

After several years of researching offices (and in the final phase being forbidden from entering even our own offices), there is one clear, simultaneously simple and complicated conclusion. It will not come as a surprise, but we do want to stress its importance.: It is the value of caring. On all levels, we see how devotion in all its different forms is essential to the sustainable and enduring life of any office building. From the moment office buildings are conceived, energy invested by commissioners and architects leads to more inspiring designs. Inspiring design in turn leads to pride within the workforce, including its cleaners and maintenance teams. Eventually, this leads to public recognition and finally financial value. Well executed, custom-made elements last longer than the quick and the dirty. If it looks good and works, you want to keep it looking good. That's the simple message.

Building on the experience of the 46 historic-and-present-day comparisons in this book, we offer the following six points as further insights towards workplaces that will *sustain* in the 21st century.

1__ HOW NOT EVERYTHING GOES ACCORDING TO PLAN...

When we started our research, the most important question for contemporary office design was whether to choose a single cell or open-plan office. (Frank Gehry's new Facebook HQ, where more than three thousand work in a space the size of eight football fields, seemed to be the apotheosis of the open plan, the final victory.) The development of the modern office building was first and foremost a development in the floor plan and it is no surprise that until this day companies, architects and their clients search for the most innovative, creativity-inducing plan. Technical innovations such as fluorescent light, air conditioning, system furniture, and digital communication massively expanded the range of possible floor plan configurations. Frank Lloyd Wright's Larkin building (completed 1906, see p.342), for example, was equipped with glass doors (so light could flood through), custom-made metal office furniture, air conditioning, radiant heating, and toilets that hang from the wall. The novelty in the plan was the arrangement around an inner void, naturally lit from above. In this arena, 1,800 clerks could work in a multi-tiered shared, contiguous space encompassing the massive lobby on the ground floor and the galleries from the second to the fourth floor. Despite the Larkin's obvious qualities, it was soon considered inappropriate for its user, sold, and by 1950 it was demolished.

Bertelsmann's Bürolandschaft (p.220), celebrated as a new organizational principle for large open-plan offices, was conceived to facilitate efficient communication and improved human interaction, rather than Taylorist principles of pure efficiency.

Despite its innovative quality this floor plan did not endure, and has now been transformed at Buch und Ton, where it was heralded in the late 60s, into a standardized cell-based plan.

Transforming from one floor-plan to another does not guarantee endurance for the building as a whole, as Jonas Malmberg, preservationist at the Aalto Foundation explained in the case of Helsinki's Enso-Gutzeit building (p.260). About 10 years ago, the foundation made far-reaching concessions to the owner, who was planning a major alteration of the building, by tearing down many of its partition walls in order to create "contemporary" open office spaces. But Enso decided to vacate the building anyway. Malmberg considered these transformations as fashions that come and go rather than a serious response to the needs of the people working in these spaces. What was really driving the change, Malmberg thinks, is the desire of CEOs to leave a personal legacy in the form of architectural transformation (and destruction).[1]

The never-ending, supposedly paradigmatic changes in the organization of office spaces (promulgated by the office consultancy industry) are actually difficult to track in

2015³   2017   2022   2021

↑   ↑   ↑   ↑

1961 Buch und Ton
Schnelle

1962 Tomado House
Maaskant

1895 Reliance Building
Burnham and Root

1962 Bank Melli University Branch
Utzon

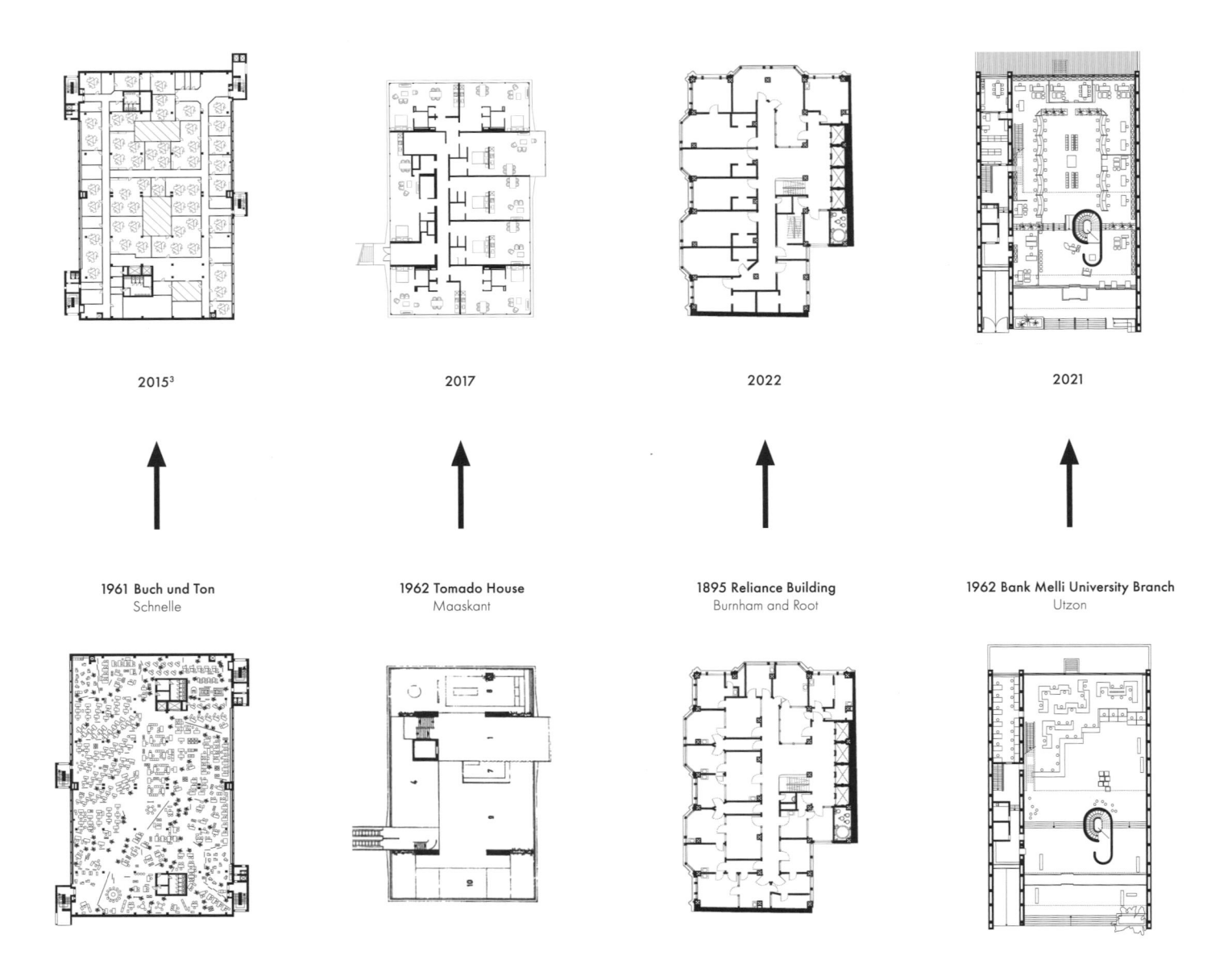

notes

1. Jonas Malmberg in a zoom conversation with the author, January 24, 2022.
2. Solid data on square meters per person is difficult hard to find as methodologies vary across different studies. A 2011 questionnaire by Knoll suggested that office space per person declined drastically from 21 square meters in 2001 to 19 square meters in 2006, 16.7 square meters in 2009, and 12.5 square meters in 2011. Planning guides like Ernst Neufert's *Bauentwurfslehre* (first published in 1936 and now its 43rd edition, 2021) sampled longitudinally also indicate a shrinkage in recommended square-meters per person, though the decline is more subtle. According to Frank Duffy in *Planning Office Space* (1970), the average office worker would require a minimum of four square meters for a workstation but suggests 10–20 square meters per worker as an overall guide for office space. In *Offices* (1990), Stephan Bailey suggests 5–25 square meters for staff, depending on their role. Van Meel in *Planning Office Spaces* (2014) suggests basic workstations of fcour square meters, regular desk areas of six square meters, and a total of nine square meters for a single office.
3. Floor plans are not shown to scale.

most of the offices we looked at. Against the grain of consultants' claims of dramatic change, we detected mostly minor adaptations in office floor plans over the years – the occasional moving of partition walls – rather than a radical overturning of the previous regime. Several plans designed for flexibility and expansion fell short, notably Centraal Beheer (p.388) and Pendorp (p.444), and some supposedly inflexible plans, like Aarhus City Hall (p. 92), Palais Nestlé (p.204) or Chilehaus (p.48), surprisingly endure.

Staff numbers are often increased and desks condensed, but these measures are often reconsidered over time.[2] Pre-COVID-19, and contrary to the data on the shrinkage of square meters-per-worker of office buildings, for many of our case studies we found floor density to be lower or at similar levels to when the building was inaugurated. We found no solid evidence for why. A possibility could be that increasing densities didn't lead to higher productivity (or happiness) per worker, or that 'our' classic modernist buildings were perceived as unfashionable or not contemporary enough for occupation by the most vibrant 21st-century companies.

Storage space for files and folders became largely obsolescent in the digital age. But in a few of our case studies, the original furniture, often 'designer' or custom-built, has

| 2019 | 2021 | 2000s | 2019 |

↑ ↑ ↑ ↑

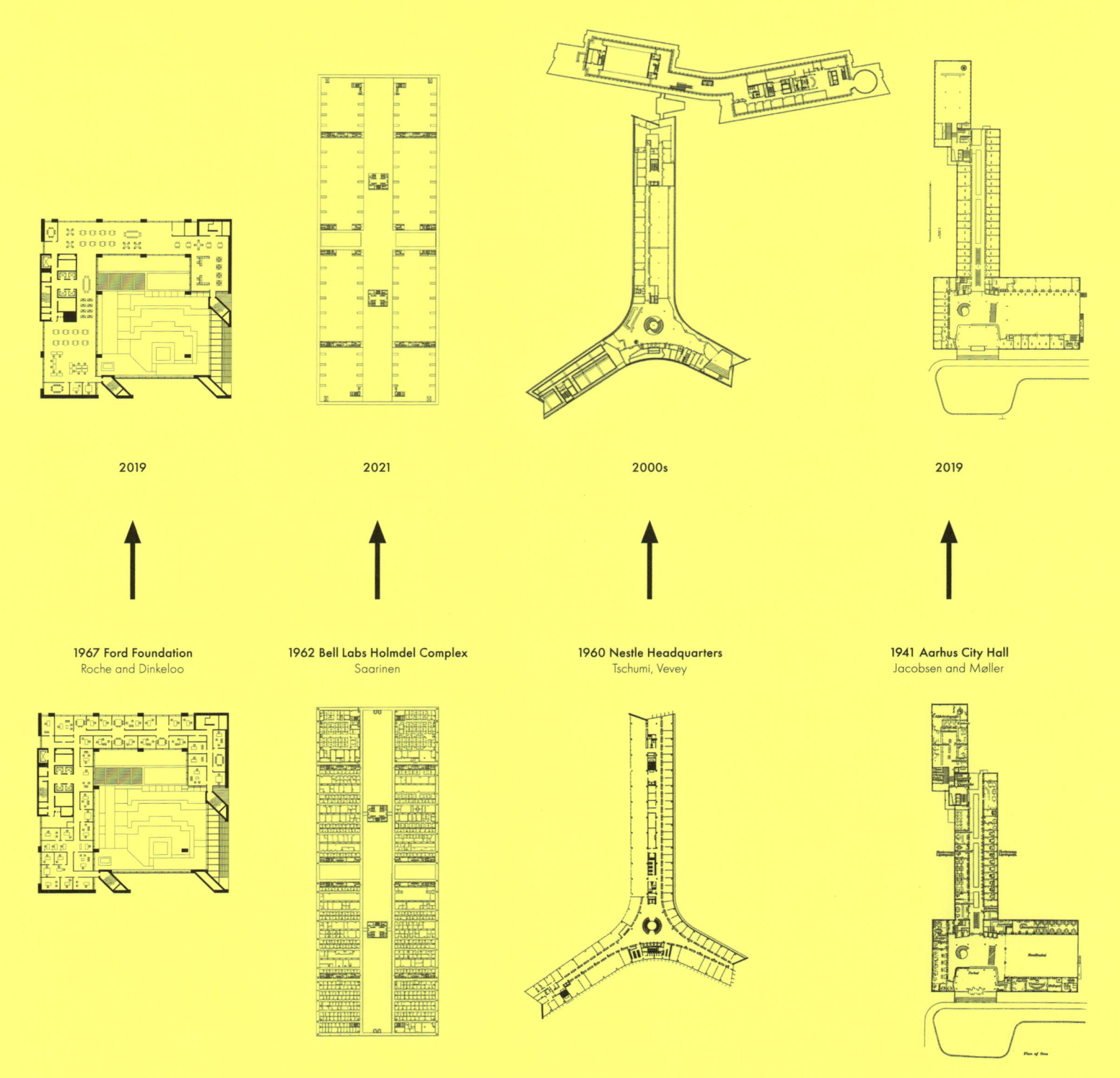

| 1967 Ford Foundation | 1962 Bell Labs Holmdel Complex | 1960 Nestle Headquarters | 1941 Aarhus City Hall |
| Roche and Dinkeloo | Saarinen | Tschumi, Vevey | Jacobsen and Møller |

been rejuvenated and is still in use – like Hans Wegner's custom-made furniture for Aarhus City Hall (p.92), now almost 80 years old and lovingly repaired. The majority of office furniture is replaced cyclically, but with much lower frequency than furniture makers and office consultants would like you to believe. A commitment to quality seems to outsmart constant newness over time. While floor plans often appear relatively unchanged at first glance, changes to office functions, and new fire and health codes have radically redrawn the HVAC and MEP landscapes that live in the office's ceilings, floors, and mechanical spaces, which only expand. Often this leads to improvised additions of mechanical equipment on rooftops, in ceilings or in new spaces which have a damaging effect on the overall appearance of a building. Only in rare cases did the architects foresee the need for this increase in technical spaces: Aarhus City Hall had empty ducts built in for future development. As post-Covid offices are poised to become meeting hubs, their physical needs for higher air quality, improved lighting, and more electricity will demand more technical space in the plans. Finally, we note how larger single-tenant buildings often struggle to find a new purpose when the original client relocates. Smart developers are able to repurpose the building (Bell Labs, p. 228), either with new office formulae or changes in program. Roughly 10 percent of the buildings in this book have been reprogrammed into hotels or a school, or redeveloped into residential and continue a successful economic life. With multi-tenant buildings, we generally see a replacement rate of both interiors and furniture that is alarmingly higher than in more specifically designed single-tenant buildings. The growth of investor-driven multi-tenant office construction will increase the ecological footprint of office design and has to be addressed.

1964 John Deere Headquarters
Saarinen

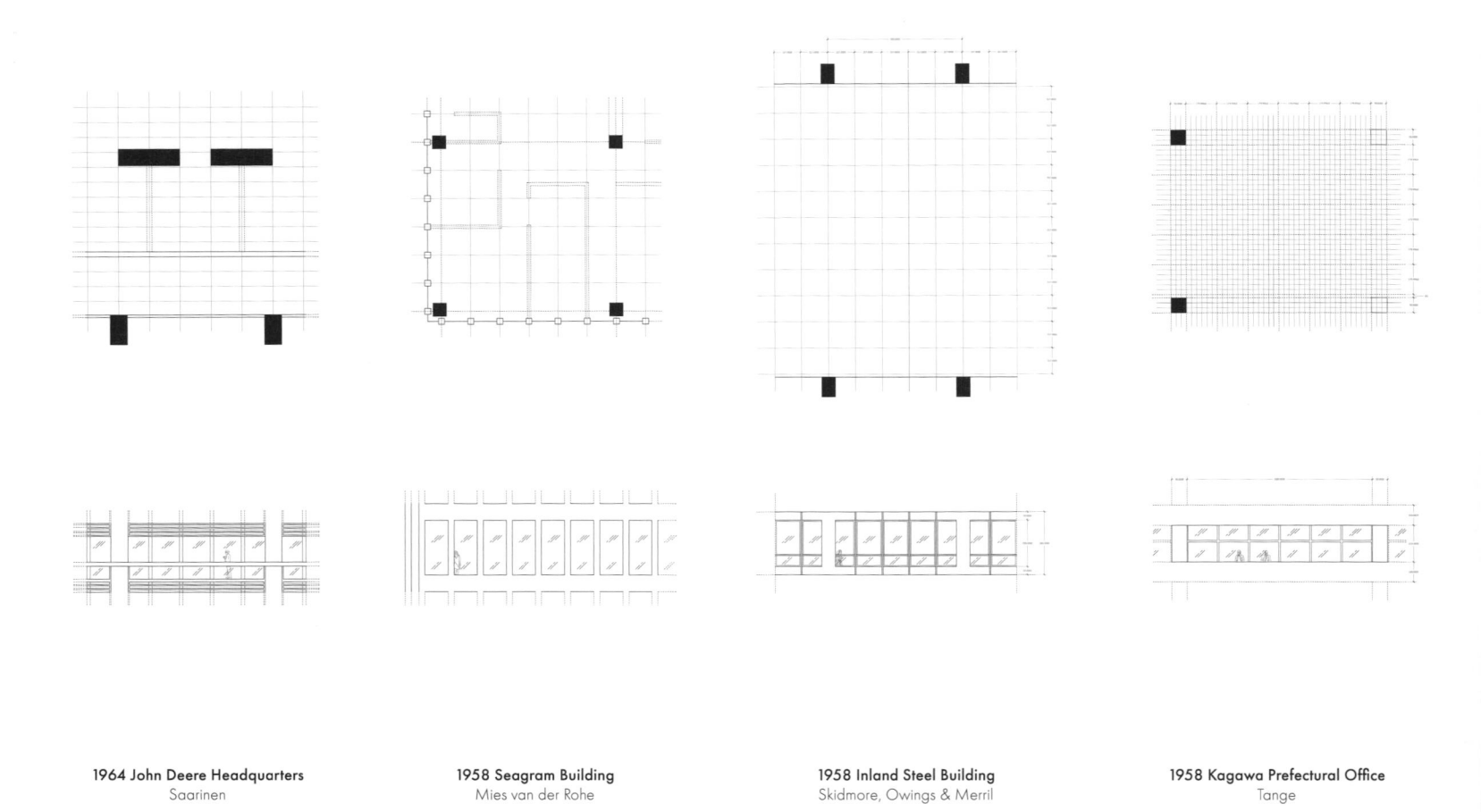

1958 Seagram Building
Mies van der Rohe

1958 Inland Steel Building
Skidmore, Owings & Merril

1958 Kagawa Prefectural Office
Tange

2__ GRIDS AND WINDOWS DIDN'T SAY MUCH, YET REMAIN ESSENTIAL...

Planning guides from the 1970s and 80s stress the importance of the grid (sometimes called the module) in the building's design and offer a templated way for defining it. The dimension of this grid should be generated by the minimum allowed width of a single-cell office, usually consisting of a 160 x 80-centimeter desk which, when circulation space is included, creates a minimum office width of 200–240cm. This width, via the grid, determines other aspects of the building's design, most notably its façade panels. These are typically 120–140 centimeters, in line with the offerings of industrial suppliers. The depth of office spaces is determined by minimum requirements of daylight penetration, which vary considerably across the globe.[1] These figures, after the corridor scheme is crunched into the equation, lead to the structural system for load-bearing, including the position of the elevator core in the plan. From there, smaller grids are developed for the placement of ceiling elements like HVAC.

We encountered a diverse range of grid definitions and dimensions. The scale of the grid, and the understanding of what should stick to it, varies: sometimes the grid very loosely

notes

1. Notably, US and Japanese building codes do not require workstations to have access to daylight, whereas in most European countries this is required.

1972 Centraal Beheer
Hertzberger

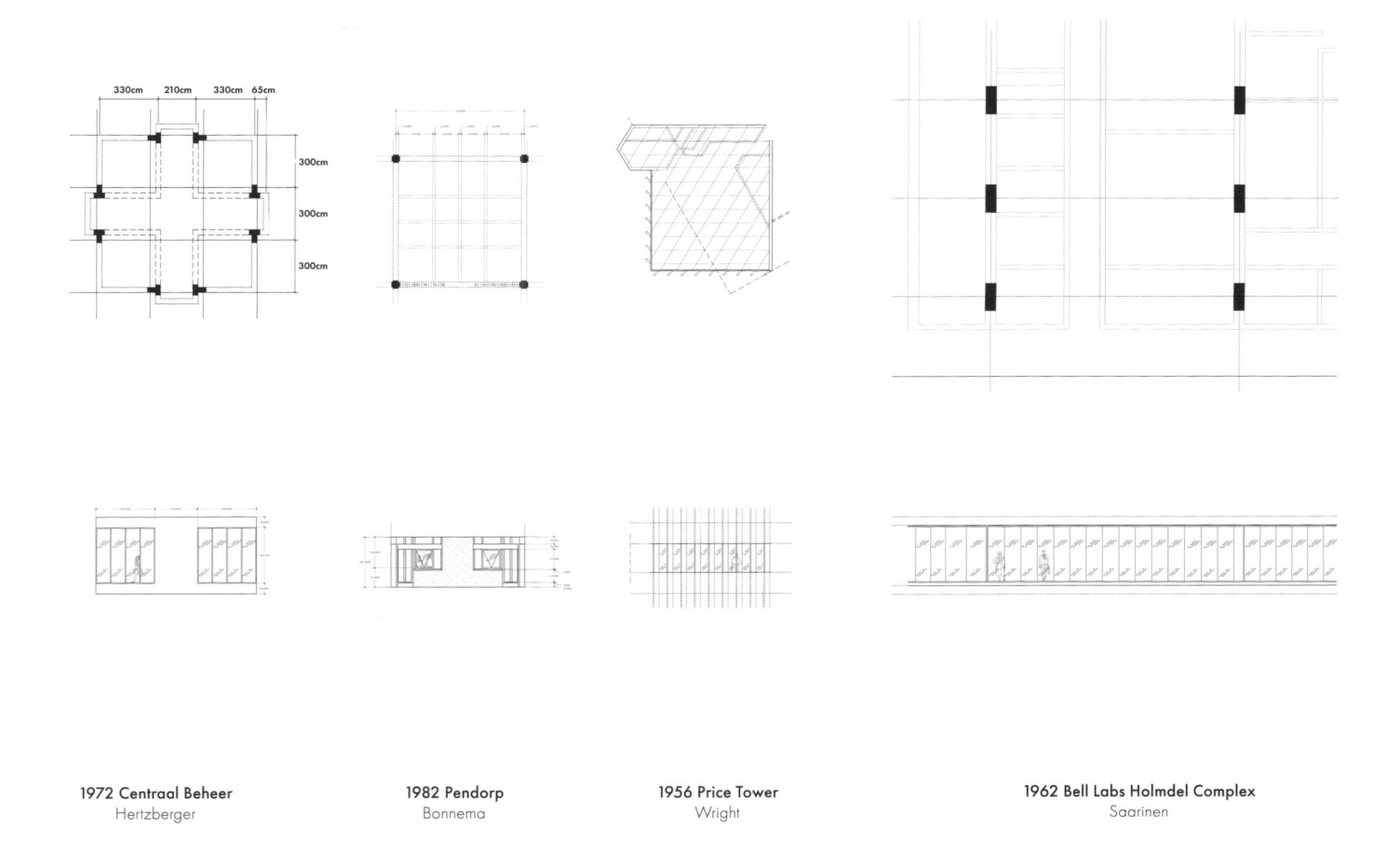

1982 Pendorp
Bonnema

1956 Price Tower
Wright

1962 Bell Labs Holmdel Complex
Saarinen

influences the positioning of larger building components, and none of the smaller ones; sometimes the grid defines all the fixtures in the building. While the grid determines the organization of floorplates and façade composition, in most cases, the size of the grid doesn't determine the building's performance over time.

Making office buildings deeper is more efficient for energy usage (since windows drain heat or coolness depending on the time of year), and can reduce the overall façade area in proportion to floorspace, thus reducing cost. Adding depth limits access to daylight for workers, which in turn affects the ratio between gross and net (usable) space. The Centraal Beheer building (p.400) plays with this conceptual dilemma: its pixelated grid creates a lot of façade area, which is great for workers, but the cost of façade replacement combined with a ratio that favor gross area – once useful as flexible spaces for adding desks – contributed to this supposedly adaptable building standing vacant for almost 20 years. It might be a coincidence, but the two buildings with the strictest adherence to their grid layout, Inland Steel (5'2" / 157 centimeters p.156)) and Kagawa Prefecture office (30 centimeters, p.176), which define anything from the width of façade elements to shelves and doors, have both remained fully intact with limited intervention.

While its use for office planning is seemingly limited, the grid remains essential since circular design benefits from standardization (or predictability). Post-COVID-19, with less demand for single-cell offices and more demand for meeting (and inspirational) spaces, suggests more deviations from the old grid. The new grid becomes the key instrument through which reuse can be effectively organised, while we explore less single-cell based layouts.

Stephan Petermann

3__ HOW ARCHITECT/CLIENT COMMITMENT ENABLES LONGEVITY...

A key invention of the early renaissance was branding individual artists and architects as the central figure responsible for a work of art. Their newfound public recognition was articulated in writing by others, and in the art itself through the addition of the signature, and it enabled new forms of mythification. Personal relationships and roles affected judgment and influenced attribution. Giorgio Vasari – considered the 'first' art historian in publishing his *Lives of the Most Excellent Painters, Sculptors, and Architects* (1550) – was himself an artist and architect, and tended to regard his home crowd in Florence as founders of the renaissance, ignoring significant contemporaries and significant places like Venice and even disqualifying some of them on the basis of gossip.[1]

The glorification of the architect, launched by Vasari, intensified with the centuries. Modern depiction of the architect as an ultimate creative mastermind, to name just two, include Ayn Rand's Howard Roak in *The Fountainhead* (1943) or The Architect character in *The Matrix Reloaded* (2003). The individual who actually triggers the architect, approaching them for their services and facilitating the whole process – *the client* – remains an uncelebrated, anonymous accomplice, barely even a Robin to a Batman.

This made it difficult to identify – and occasionally track down – the individuals responsible for commissioning the offices featured in this book. When we did find them, what could be retrieved of their role in the process was up to the archival competence and institutional transparency of the companies and public bodies they represented. For the most part, records were lost, tossed, or not made available. But where we were able to dig deeper, the intricate connections between architect and client became vivid. Despite unique circumstances in each case, there is an unignorable rhythm to the building process; success or failure can be directly linked to the relationships that developed. Some cases present a compound of personalities, each with a desire to engage with each other, combining hardship with friendship. These clients recognized that architecture is more than just a building, but a way to advance the company at large. The quality of the built work often correlates with a willingness to connect – to find trust, to be vulnerable, to solve problems, and most of all to love building. We see how most of these men – and hardly any women, regrettably – demonstrated a commitment for the new that went beyond a practical or financial interest but ended up serving both as a collateral benefit.

notes

1. There are various accounts; for an easily accessible one, see: Alina Cohen, "The Juiciest Gossip about the Renaissance Masters," artsy.net, May 31, 2019 (www.artsy.net/article/artsy-editorial-juiciest-gossip-renaissance-masters).
2. On Bacardi, see: Kathryn E. O'Rourke, "Mies and Bacardi," *Journal of Architectural Education*, 66:1, (2012), p.57–71. The relationship between Bill Hewitt and Eero Saarinen is documented in Mildred and Edward Hall, *The Fourth Dimension in Architecture* (Sunstone Press, 1975) and Wayne G. Broehl, *John Deere's Company* (Doubleday, 1984). On Tomado, see: Michelle Provoost, *Hugh Maaskant: Architect of Progress* (NAi010, 2013).

Some such clients:
- **Samuel Johnson Jr.** (Johnson Wax HQ Europe, p.304), **José M Bosch** (Bacardi, p.284), **Bill Hewitt** (John Deere, p.308), and **Jan van der Togt** (Tomado, p.240) explicitly used the design of the office, demanding non-standard building, to shape the identity of the company. They each had personal experience in sales and marketing, and most of them were founders of the company.[2]
- **Joseph L. Block** (Inland Steel, p.156) asked the architect to develop everything up to the trays in the cafeteria, most of it surviving to this day.
- **Mr. de Ruijter** (Centraal Beheer, p.388), appalled by boring office buildings, gave a young unrecognized architect carte blanche to rethink his office from the ground up.
- **Helmut Maucher and Peter Brabeck-Letmathe** (Nestlé HQ, p.204) decided against the cheaper option of demolition and new construction and instead used renovation to affirm the company's identity, legacy, and prospect, remaining involved to the last detail.
- **Phyllis Lambert** (Seagram Building, p.164) had a talent for moving her father, Samuel Bronfman, to recognize their societal, and artistic responsibility in designing a new office building for Seagram and didn't shy away from making it come to life.
- **Reinhard Mohn** (Buch und Ton, p.220) engaged with the perceived complications of his new office design three years after its completion, spending two weeks on the work floor reviewing the problems of his staff and developing solutions for them.
- **Oscar van Leer** (Van Leer HQ, p.144) convinced his father not to spare a dime, as he saw the construction of the Van Leer HQ as a once-in-a-lifetime opportunity to define the company for generations to come.

It is puzzling to see how the position of personalities in design has shifted in the 21st century. Both in public and private development, building culture has intentionally and unintentionally become depersonalized. The benefits of intimate engagement between client and architect are lesser known. On the public level, personal commitment is increasingly avoided as it may cause or reflect a conflict of interest. Tendering systems have been designed explicitly to defuse personal connections for the sake of the open competition and the avoidance of fraud. Crime is prevented, but so are the upsides of personal preference – the creativity and trust it engenders. The demand in the tendering process to demonstrate a track record of similar projects drastically limits access to the market – large, established architectural offices have a huge advantage. Inadvertently, a superior form of nepotism has been instituted, obstructing the flow of creativity and innovation. This could in part explain how the development of office architecture seems to have stagnated: when only the usual suspects are involved, you get the usual results.

Personal engagement is also under pressure in corporate architecture. Under the influence of markets, clients are more aware of their (limited) temporality. They are fixed by an umbilical cord to the real estate market through omnipresent financial lease-back constructs for instance. Office buildings increasingly function as a speculative object that never will be fully theirs. Economic logic dictates that the more personal or specific an object is, the more difficult it becomes to sell, creating the ultimate excuse for developing and designing the obvious: ever more curtain-walled glass towers with flexible interiors. The compulsion is not to add diversity or look for newness, but to create safe bets, to lower risk. Perhaps to counter the increasingly generic nature of contemporary office buildings, the aesthetic of the living room is introduced to parts of the interior. The uncertainty of the actual occupation of the space is mitigated by evoking the comfort and solidity of the home, an impression of fixed occupation, without having to commit to it.

Whereas historically, client teams dedicated to building were mostly in one place and focused on a relatively straightforward task, the complexity of contemporary corporate structures and the multitude of stakeholders and consultants involved in the development and design process is another factor making a close relationship with the architect difficult. If a new 'icon' is sought, the burden of personality is now put in the hands of the architect, buying into the myth of individual genius.

Despite all these systemic pressures eroding the client-architect relationship, in the end, the economic justification for building generically turns out to be false. When a building excels in its performance and contributes to the identity of the corporation, its valuation typically surpasses the cost of construction. The scarcely available data suggests that adding uniqueness or personality is not a trade-off but a win-win. It takes more effort, courage, and stress, specifically on the part of the client, but it does pay off.

It's a challenge to undo the current disconnect. To inspire new commissioners, we offer an homage to four brave clients engaged in their architecture we found in our research. Four documents collected here from clients' archives offer evidence of intimate relationships leading to successful buildings. Specific moments in the design process are identified here that make the difference between an ordinary and extraordinary building and shows how personality goes a long way…

A__ The scrupulous engineer in Reinhard Mohn sharing his observations following a two-week work experience stint on his experimental office floor

With the help of the Bertelsmann corporate archive, which kept meticulous records, we attempted to reconstruct each step that led to the commissioning, construction, and further life of the revolutionary Buch und Ton office floor. (see Buch und Ton, p.220–227) Amongst various articles hinting at the state of the floor from the company's in-house magazines the archive found a highly remarkable testing report of the Bürolandschaft by Bertelsmann CEO Reinhard Mohn (1921–2009).

In 1943, Mohn, who had ambitions to be an engineer, was captured by Allied forces in Tunisia, where he was serving with the Luftwaffe. He spent his three years as a POW in the US, enjoying an education and through it he became convinced of the new American way of working. After visiting more than 20 companies in the US, Mohn adopted the model of scientific management and US corporate thinking, bringing them back to his native Gutersloh in 1946 to restart the Bertelsmann publishing company run by his father. In 1959, the Kommissionshaus Buch und Ton was established to make newly developed production and service infrastructure available for other publishing and printing companies, for which the experimental Bürolandschaft office floors were developed. Their inauguration coincided with Bertelsmann publishing its corporate constitution, which articulated the role of freedom, rights, and democracy – values which the Bürolandschaft also tried to express.[1]

In a five-page report dated November 23, 1964, two years after the completion of the Bürolandschaft, we see how Mohn studied his new office floors extensively. It's not clear why the report had been necessary, or why it had become 'Chefsache' (a matter for the boss), nor who was on the receiving end, though he often addressed the company's executive board in it. Mohn's immersive reporting reveals his engineering mindset. He starts by dissecting the floor technically: acoustics, perspectives, and temperature – possibly the source of staff complaints. He carefully considers mending the unbalanced heating system, adding acoustical screens for the meeting spaces (though he finds that overall sound levels acceptable), and notes how everyone should have the same furniture. The only thing he finds lacking in the office landscape is privacy, which is especially needed for senior staff: "As my work is heavily focused on planning the future or taking larger decisions within the company structure, secrecy is often required. … In this way my workstation in the office landscape created considerable difficulties. … From the middle point of a conference table conversations could be overheard over eight to nine meters. This means its sound reached into areas where others were working ." The ideal of corporate transparency and democracy articulated through the space seemed to have a breaking point. It is the one thing Mohn did not offer a solution for.[2]

Taking the time to write the document demonstrates Mohn's deep engagement with architectural design and the physical welfare of his staff. The fact that Bertelsman allowed his study demonstrates a functional form of collectivity, a mode of leadership that connects pragmatism to egalitarianism. This is part of a larger Rhineland model of working whereby a corporation embraces responsibility beyond its bottom line; under the pressure of Anglo-American management such an approach came to be considered soft or socialist.

1. Joachim Scholtyseck, Reinhard Mohn Ein Jahrhundertunternehmer (C.Bertelsmann Verlag: Munich, 2021), p.68-69.
2. There is no record of whether or how Mohn's report was implemented. Two years later, Ottomar Gottschalk wrote that the office environment at Buch und Ton was upgraded, but it remains unclear whether this was the result of Mohn's report (see: Ottomar Gottschalk, *Flexible Verwaltungsbauten: Richtwerte, Lösungen, Kosten* (Hamburg: [publisher unknown], 1968), p.212. The original team that worked on the design continued working for other parts of the office buildings operated by Bertelsmann. A review of the offices by Bertelsmann in 1990 suggests that during the 1970s the Bürolandschaft concept was adopted at some of its other office buildings ("Umbau der Hauptverwaltung der Bertelsmann AG," *Deutsche Bauzeitung*, October 1990, p. 220.) Although a new headquarters building was designed by Fischer, Krüder, Rathai and completed in 1975 and was designed as a Bürolandschaft, by the time it was completed, the firm reconsidered the workspace concept.

Herrn Hennig/BS

Herrn Tilly z.Kts.

Erfahrungsbericht über die Arbeit eines Geschäftsführers im Großraum
_____

Um eine klarere Beurteilungsmöglichkeit über die Arbeitsverhältnisse eines Geschäftsführers innerhalb eines Großraumes zu bekommen, habe ich in den vergangenen 14 Tagen selbst im Großraum des Kommissionshauses Buch und Ton gearbeitet. Mein Arbeitsplatz war von den für diesen Bereich zuständigen Herren der Organisationsabteilung der Zentrale und des Kommissionshauses Buch und Ton unter Leitung von Herrn Schmidt, Revisionsabteilung, und unter Hinzuziehung von Herrn Alsleben durchgeführt worden. Den für die Einrichtung verantwortlichen Herren war die Auflage erteilt worden, keinerlei Neuanschaffungen durchzuführen, sondern mit dem vorhandenen Mobiliar auszukommen. Der Raumbedarf sollte demjenigen für eine solche Position vorgesehenen Bedarf entsprechen.

1. <u>Akustische Beeinflussung</u>

   Eine akustische Beeinflussung ergab sich störend nur in den ersten beiden Tagen der Eingewöhnung. In dieser Zeit bedurften manche Tätigkeiten, wie z. B. lesen oder der Entwurf von Plänen einer stärkeren Konzentration. Nicht störend wirkte auch in diesen beiden Tagen die akustische Beeinflussung bei Telefongesprächen und Besprechungen. Bereits am dritten Tage trat in dieser Hinsicht eine völlige Gewöhnung ein, so daß kein erhöhter Konzentrationsbedarf mehr erforderlich war. - Ich möchte vermuten, daß eine solche Eingewöhnung auch erforderlich gewesen wäre, wenn ich in einen anderen, geschlossenen Arbeitsraum umgezogen wäre.

   Bei Besprechungen in größerem Arbeitskreis von 10 oder 12 Teilnehmern störte der allgemeine Geräuschpegel im Saal. In solch einem Fall war es schwieriger, sich über den runden Tisch hin zu verständigen. Entweder hätten die Gesprächsteilnehmer sehr viel lauter sprechen müssen, oder man mußte sich sehr viel mehr beim Zuhören anstrengen bzw. konzentrieren. Entsprechend wird es sich empfehlen, eine solche Besprechungsrunde durch Aufstellen von Schallschluckwänden stärker abzuschirmen. - In diesem Zusammenhang sei vermerkt, daß mein Arbeitsplatz und insbesondere die große Besprechungsrunde überhaupt nicht durch schallhemmende Tafeln abgeschirmt war. Ich halte aber eine entsprechende Abschirmung sehr wohl für möglich.

B__ The cunning William A. Hewitt and how he turns the building of an office into the building of a company

In his 870-page *John Deere's Company* (1984), Wayne G. Broehl Jr. carefully reconstructs the momentum and importance of the company's headquarters project and describes how profoundly Eero Saarinen's design influenced the company at large. Broehl shows how in the early 1950s, Deere's newly-appointed CEO Bill Hewitt (1914–1998) went out on a limb with an ambitious plan for the tractor company, founded in 1837.

Hewitt was the son-in-law of Charles Deere Wiman, the great-grandson of the company's founder John Deere. Wiman was in charge of the company from 1928 until handing the baton to the 39-year-old Hewitt in 1955. Hewitt, after having worked in accounting at Standard Oil of California, had a career as an advertising copywriter. Early accounts of Hewitt at Deere in *Fortune* magazine suggest he brought an "unusual sense of style to the company."[1]

As a first step in his new role as CEO – and against the grain of the board – Hewitt commissioned the consultants Booz Allen Hamilton to review the company's organizational structure. In its 120-year existence as a company, John Deere had never thought much about architecture. It had relied on a collection of improvised workstations close to its production sites. Business had been easy in the early postwar years, but cracks in the surface were starting to appear. The company placed its emphasis on production rather than sales, figuring they would take care of themselves.

In his private outline for the future of the company, Hewitt noted how different departments were out of touch with each other and how he aimed to centralize the company's leadership. Hewitt's vision document includes the line "Build a new office building." This was part of an ambition to open up the company to outsiders. Hewitt thought the new building should be more of a campus, and secondly, that the architecture should not be dealt with by the company's own engineering department.[2] The delivery of the Booz Allen Hamilton report on Deere, which called for more coordination within the firm, galvanized Hewitt's building ambitions.[3]

For the question of who should design the new HQ, Hewitt called upon his close friend from Harvard, Robert McNamara, later defense secretary under John F. Kennedy and Lyndon B. Johnson. While part of senior management at Ford in the 1950s, McNamara had overseen the development of its administration center designed by SOM. McNamara sent Hewitt prospectuses of a dozen architects, including Saarinen. The decisive push towards Saarinen was given by Henry Dreyfuss, the celebrated product designer. Dreyfuss had been consulting for Deere on their tractor design and referred to Saarinen as "an architect's architect." He persuaded Hewitt to visit Saarinen's recently completed GM administration center near Chicago, where he met the architect.[4] In August 1956, Saarinen traveled to Moline with Hewitt to look at different sites for the Deere HQ. They found a 50-hectare wooded site with enough flat land that both were convinced of building on. Hewitt was aware of the radical changes he was proposing for Deere. The core of his vision was that the care and quality of their products should be expressed in something larger than

1. Wayne G. Broehl Jr. *John Deere's Company* (1984) Doubleday: NY, p.605
2. Ibid. p.617
3. Ibid. p.622
4. Ibid. p.638
5. Broehl. p.781

the product itself. After the site visit, Hewitt called a board meeting, from which Hewitt's verbatim notes survive. He made the case for Saarinen, showing some of his realized work. Then in a rhetorical move he asked the board, "Is he too fancy for us? No." Broehl acknowledges that this statement launched "this insular, Midwestern farm implement company into a new direction … as one of the world's best-known multinationals." Some older board members opposed Hewitt's plans for corporate centralization, thinking it would not fare well with the customer base, especially if it manifested in an exuberant office design. But the board grudgingly agreed to Saarinen. Over a seven-year intimate design process, Hewitt and Saarinen opted for a finely-articulated ruggedness using Corten steel for the HQ's façade cladding, while offering a slick and unified corporate campus. Saarinen died before the building was completed, when the board finally realized the impact of the building. Hewitt's boldness was recognized in Fortune magazine: "Hewitt recognized years ago what Deere needed most of all was an expanded vision of what was possible. His emphasis on perfection and style, symbolized by the Saarinen office buildings, puzzled many of the Company's older executives.". But one of the now-converted executives declared, "Bill made us realize just how good we were … We knew we could make it in Moline, but we didn't know that we could make it in New York. Bill showed us we could."[5]

DEERE & COMPANY
MOLINE ILLINOIS

WILLIAM A. HEWITT
PRESIDENT

Aug. 23, 1957

Mr. Eero Saarinen
Eero Saarinen & Associates, Architects
Bloomfield Hills, Mich.

Dear Eero:

Although you and I have discussed our building project in some detail on several occasions, I believe that it may be appropriate for me to set down on paper a few fundamental ideas that may be helpful to you in creating a new headquarters for Deere & Company.

First, let me say that I have no preconceived ideas as to the specific design of our new buildings. I believe creation of the forms and relationships of these buildings is basically your responsibility.

At the same time, I believe it is our responsibility at Deere & Company to do all we can to help you create building designs which will be in harmony with our functions and traditions, and also be indicative of the objectives and progress we envision for the future.

The men who created this company and caused it to grow and flourish were men of strength—rugged, honest, close to the soil. Since the company's early days, quality of product and integrity in relationships with farmers, dealers, suppliers, and the public in general have been Deere's guiding factors.

In thinking of our traditions and our future, and in thinking of the people who will work in or visit our new headquarters, I believe it should be thoroughly modern in concept, but at the same time, be down to earth and rugged.

Sincerely,
Bill

C_ The conviction of Oscar van Leer to build an everlasting office

Van Leer's founder, Bernard van Leer (1883–1958), was acclaimed as one of the richest men in the Netherlands before the Second World War. He made his fortune in the production of oil barrels and their caps. He sold his enterprise under duress during the war and fled to the US with his family. After the war, Bernard returned to the Netherlands to rebuild his company. His son Oscar (1914–1996) joined him in the firm, which grew to produce various kinds of industrial packaging. The project of building a headquarters had been on the boardroom table for several years, even before the war. In 1952, the board decided that something should, finally, be built.[1] Two years later, a list was drawn up featuring renowned Dutch architects, mostly modernists – J.J.P. Oud, Arthur Staal, Ben Merkelbach – who would be asked to make a proposal for a pastoral site outside of Amsterdam.[2]

The growth of the company, fueled by war-time internationalism, might have moved the board to seek an international high-profile candidate.[3] Le Corbusier declared his interest in a letter in the fall of 1955.[4] But he demanded full control of the project, only wanted to work with the construction firm (and not collaborate with the client), and asked for 10 percent of the building budget as a fee, significantly higher than the standard three percent prescribed by the Dutch Architects Union.[5] Two additional options were put on the table: Brazilian Oscar Niemeyer and American-Hungarian immigrant Marcel Breuer. Breuer had two major projects under construction – a Bijenkorf department store in Rotterdam (1955–1957) and the UNESCO building (1952–1955) in Paris[6] – and the board made arrangements to visit both.

From then on, Bernard put his son Oscar in charge of the new office design. Oscar, who had been educated as a physicist, was scrupulous and a perfectionist. He lived mostly in the US and corresponded with his father in English in moving letters. Oscar traveled to the UNESCO construction site at the end of 1955 to inspect Breuer's work. On February 11, 1957, a telegram from Oscar in the US to Van Leer's HQ in Amsterdam reports that he managed to meet Breuer in New York: "Had the most pleasant and extensive visit with Marcel Breuer who struck me as being most capable, understanding and thorough though not overly forceful." Oscar asked his Dutch staff to come to New York soonest to present the building program to Breuer. There is no record of the program, although there is an indication of a building consisting of "one huge hall with balconies on either side."[7] Oscar set up the memorandum of agreement with Breuer, with minute changes passing back and forth. In April 1957, design work began. On August 1, 1957, Oscar sent a 10-page report to his father saying that he'd spent considerable time with Breuer. He did not hide the fact that Breuer's initial design – "a troubling fish tank" – had failed to impress.[8] Oscar wrote that it was Van Leer's responsibility to "assist, induce, and cajole" Breuer further. Oscar acknowledged a feature of Breuer's original design – an umbrella type structure – and based on this he proposed a star-type building instead. Breuer accepted and developed a plan close to the H-shaped plan that would eventually be built.

Oscar pleaded with his father for more money for the project: "If we want to have an outstanding building which I believe Breuer to be capable of coming up with, then we

---

1. Van Leer meeting notes, 1952: "Het Hoofdkantoor in de Boardmeetings van het Van Leer Concern", included in folder 1621 of the Van Leer archive at the Amsterdam Municipal Archive.
2. Before the war, Merkelbach had proposed an office for Van Leer in the center of Amsterdam, which remained realized. In March 1954, Bernard van Leer invited Merkelbach to design the building, but he declined the offer due to limited capacity. Merkelbach proposed Mart Stam, but he was rejected by the board.
3. The archive includes a few articles on International Style and one on the recently completed Palazzo Olivetti factory. Palazzo Uffici, Olivetti Headquarters (1951-1954) by architects Gian Antonio Bernasconi, Annibale Fiocchi and Marcello Nizzoli, Milan. Undated included folder 1621 of the Van Leer archive at the Amsterdam Municipal Archive. Although the letter is undated- the position in the archive documents suggests it was received not too long from the follow-up discussions.
4. Although in his report to the board the Van Leer project manager left the door open for Le Corbusier, it's clear that the collaboration is unlikely to happen. Follow up note by G. Gelderman to Bernard van Leer, December 2, 1954, after a meeting where Le Corbusier's letter was discussed, casting doubt on his selection as architect.
5. Niemeyer had worked internationally, but had no experience in Europe, which might have troubled the pragmatic board.
6. Letter from Oscar van Leer to Bernard van Leer, August 14, 1957, in folder 1621, Van Leer archive, Amsterdam Municipal Archive. p1.
7. This is probably the initial design; an undated version can be found in the Marcel Breuer Archive at Syracuse University: Image ID T1449_011.
8. Letter from Oscar van Leer to Bernard van Leer, August 14, 1957, in folder 1621, Van Leer archive, Amsterdam Municipal Archive.
9. Instructions to the Staff, November 1958, included folder 1621.
10. Oscar remained friends with Breuer and after the project finished, the pair shared ideas on improvements and extensions.
11. Gert-Jan Johannes, De communicerende vaten van Oscar van Leer (Boom, 2009), p.253.

will have to spend more money than you have indicated … fact is that such a building would exceed our budget by about 1,000,000 Dutch guilders. [This is] a very serious matter but one which we should consider in the light and against the background of the fact that we are only once building a central office which will have to last us practically forever, and which should be a credit to our company for all that length of time."[9]

In a letter on August 14, Oscar asked Breuer for red bricks rather than natural stone. He is unnerved because the building is starting to look like the UNESCO HQ. Oscar called for something more unique. Breuer requested to talk in person about the matter and was apparently able to convince Oscar to stick to natural stone. A preliminary design was finished in early September 1957, called plan III. Construction started two months later, with the steel delivered by a Van Leer subsidiary. Bernard van Leer died on January 6, 1958, just as work began, and Oscar took over the company. The Van Leer building opened on December 23, 1958, costing a total of 3.5 million guilders (Euro 11.6 million, or Euro 1,506 per square meter in 2021). It took less than two years from start to finish.

A month prior to completion, instructions were issued by management, revealing concerns about the modern open plan: "The pros and contras … are beyond discussion at this point. The points of concern had been taken into account but research, mostly done in the US, points out that the benefits outweigh the disadvantages. The choice was made and we have to adapt."[10] Staff may have had reservations but critics were impressed by the open plan, the first in the Netherlands, and the project was hailed in the press. At night, the building was illuminated by 1,400 lightbulbs. Soon after completion, the building's plan itself – the H-shape – became the company logo.[11] The 10-page letter Oscar wrote in 1957 to his father, who he always refers to as "Boss," revealed his willingness to invest energy to make sure the building would become a crucial element for the company's identity for decades to come. But the building wouldn't last as long as Oscar proposed in his letter. In 1982, a year after Breuer's death, Oscar complained about the building for the first time: "What 25 years ago seemed the newest most efficient solution, now already appears to be an expensive and inefficient type of office building."[12] The company planned a new, smaller HQ on the premises with ZZOP architects, a Dutch firm known in the 80s for designing large scale commercial office buildings. The single-story structure was constructed on the site Breuer had suggested as an expansion zone. The move to the new building began in 1987, when Oscar stepped down as CEO.

D__ Phyllis Lambert, age 27, persuading her father to say no

After graduating from Vasser, Canadian-born Phyllis Lambert moved to Paris in 1952 and set up her own studio working as an artist. She also studied architecture and was fascinated by J.J.P. Oud and Willem Dudok, among other modernists. In the summer of 1954, Lambert, 27, received a plan from her father, Samuel Bonfman, concerning the construction of a new headquarters for his company, the Canadian Distillers Corporation-Seagram Limited. Lambert described her connection with her father at this time as "minimal," seeing herself as a "self-imposed outsider" in the family.[1]

Seagram's US headquarters had been located in the art deco Chrysler Building in Manhattan. It had made its name through innovative branding, creating a bespoke culture around drinking liquor, while promoting its consumption in moderation. To underline the company's sophistication, they adopted a Tudor-style office interior until the 1950s. The plan Lambert received from her father was for a new building for Seagram in New York designed by New York-based architects Pereira & Luckman. The design looked like a square wedding cake-shaped modernist high-rise. She knew her father had been planning a new building. Seagram had acquired a plot on Park Avenue opposite Lever House, the first International Style office building in Manhattan, built by SOM in 1950 (Pereira & Luckman had been involved in commissioning Lever House). Seagram executive Victor Fischel, who believed "architecture is a business not an art," appreciated the salesmanship of Pereira & Luckman and pushed them as the designers of Seagram's new HQ. In July, the New York Times reported on Seagram's new plans.

Lambert was horrified by the design, and wrote her father an eight-page typed letter with additional handwritten notes and sketches. She begins her appraisal with an emphatic "NO NO NO NO NO" and continues slightly more diplomatically, "you will forgive me if sometimes I use rather strong terms and sound angry but I am very disturbed and find nothing whatsoever commendable in this preliminary-as-it-may-be-plan for a Seagram building. … It certainly didn't aid my digestive processes and certainly raised my blood pressure."

She continued by lecturing her father on renaissance architecture, the sincerity of its goals, and the mindless copying of modernist styles evident in the Pereira plan. In her criticism of Peirera's plan she concludes, "There is not ONE REDEEMING FEATURE. It is a CHEAP product of a mind that has learnt to approach everything from the point of view of Sensationalism. It makes me too sick to go on but just as a last word to Messers Pereira and Luckman, I defy them to make a plausible grand plan out of this bit of vulgarity which they have dared to present to you."

She recommends Le Corbusier and Mies van der Rohe among others for the design. She recognized how she initially scoffed at the new UN building and Lever House but had learned how "new conceptions are put into the flesh and sometimes violently change our way of looking at things" and they needed to be considered over time. She stressed that a building should be "like a big family home", and "the people that work there must have a

1. For a full account of the Seagram Buildings conception see: Phyllis Lambert, *Building Seagram* (Yale University Press, 2013).

493

feeling of this being 'our' building and must be proud of it." She made proposals for humanizing the new structure, suggesting mosaics, glass patterns, and recreational facilities. She finally "takes it for granted that no other plans be forthcoming from Pereira and Luckman" and suggests to "PLEASE PLEASE PLEASE turn a deaf ear" to the building committee members. In her memoirs, Lambert suggested her father wasn't someone who heard "no" that often. His response to his daughter's letter was to invite her over to New York to select the marble for the ground floor. According to her family's account, Bronfman saw it as an opportunity to get closer to his daughter. He must have been impressed by her vigilant and energetic engagement, Lambert wrote, because he soon promoted her to become the de facto client. She engaged in a six-week research project in which she met with the most significant architects, writers, and curators. In a letter dated October 30, 1954, Lambert proposed Mies van der Rohe for the project. Lambert would become Director of Planning, working for four years in an office shared with Mies, on what would become one of the centerpieces of modern architecture, with herself as the inspiring client.

Her bold letter to her father is the perfect brief for any future office construction plan. It demonstrates the crucial qualities in a client that produce successful projects: character, attention to detail, social and societal commitment, and care.

Ruth Baumeister

4__ KEEP IT CLEAN

The first line of defense against obsolescence

In an interview in 1975, architect-artist Gordon Matta Clark defined architecture as a janitor to civilization. The difference between art and architecture, he said, is that architecture has plumbing. And that means architecture plays a role in cleaning – metabolizing, or interfacing between – humans and their societies. But what of the cleaning of architecture itself? Cleaners act as mediators between buildings and their users, monitoring the state of the building and gathering knowledge about how it performs. Their work has a critical impact on the endurance of buildings, which is underestimated in current sustainability discourse.

Another artist, Mierle Laderman Ukeles shed light on the importance of cleaning from a feminist perspective in her *Manifesto for Maintenance Art* (1969) and through a series of performances. In *Washing/Tracks/Maintenance: Outside*, (1973), she mopped the steps of the Wadsworth Atheneum museum in Hartford, Connecticut. In *Touch Sanitation* (1979–80), she shook hands with over 8,500 employees of the New York Sanitation Department over almost a year, thanking them for keeping the city alive. When she, as a white female artist, engaged in cleaning the museums she performed in, she did work typically done by people of color. In doing so, she called attention to the importance of those who clean. At the same time, Ukeles pointed out the social division between manual and mental labor in capitalist societies and elucidated their hidden interdependence, aiming to ennoble the labor and art of cleaning.

According to a Belgian study on health risks in the cleaning industry, the mortality rate among cleaners is considerably higher than other professions.[1] Cleaners – often migrants, people of color, or from an otherwise marginalized background, and mainly women – must work under precarious conditions: short term or no contracts, no benefits, informal arrangements, low pay, unattractive working hours, and high turnover. "I always say that if we did not exist, the rest of us would really have a problem. The fact that somebody has to get rid of all this shit is often forgotten," says Susanne Hotte, cleaner and author of the book *715 Euro: Wenn die Rente nicht zum Leben reicht* (When the pension is not enough to live.) Especially in office cleaning, it is not desirable to have people cleaning during regular

500

501

working hours. Head of Kela real estate group in Finland, Mervi Roiha-Muilu, welcomes robotic cleaning so staff are not distracted by human cleaners during regular office hours. In the West, as a cleaner, you are treated as a persona non grata by those you clean for.

The rate at which buildings decay when they are not cleaned can be staggering. Visiting the former Centraal Beheer offices in Apeldoorn, Netherlands, in 2014, just a few months after the insurance company left for new, less articulated offices on the other side of town, Herman Hertzberger's celebrated building was clearly worn from its years of use, but it still felt inhabitable. Visiting again two years later, the building, still awaiting a new future, looked like an apocalyptic scene straight out of a Christopher Nolan movie. Trespassers had left broken windows, floors filled with shattered glass, graffitied walls, ripped-out cabling and battered vents. It was unclear why the building deserved such punishment. Despite their solid appearance, the absence of cleaning, maintenance, and security reveals the actual vulnerability of buildings.

The impact of cleanliness on quality of life has been subject to extensive investigation by anthropologists and sociologists. In the discourse of landscape architecture, urbanism, material and building science, building codes, and insurance laws, the knowledge and practice of cleaning as a means to combat environmental pollution plays an important role. But topical investigations in the realm of architecture remain sporadic. Cleaning has hardly ever been thought of in terms of the social, creative, or ecological aspect of design, writes Hilary Sample in her book *Maintenance Architecture* (MIT Press, 2016). While architectural theorists have thoroughly critiqued modern architects' claim to promote hygiene and cleanliness in their fight against disease and chaos in urban design and housing,[2] the importance of cleaning as an activity that prolongs the endurance of buildings and that commitment that it requires from the user has long been underestimated. Only in building preservation does cleaning play a more important role, but it is considered from a technical point of view: choosing the appropriate tools, practices, and methodologies to conserve (or restore) historical monuments.

In 2008, filmmakers Ila Bêka and Louise Lemoine raised the issue of maintenance and decay in the documentary *Koolhaas HouseLife*, examining the tedious daily life of Guadalupe Acedo, the woman cleaning the acclaimed Maison à Bordeaux (1998) by Rem Koolhaas. Beka and Lemoine interrogate how the different parties involved in architecture – from the client who commissions it to the architect who conceives it, to the ones who inhabit it, all the way to those who maintain and clean it – experience the building. Most revealing is the monologue by Koolhaas himself, which comes as bonus material on the DVD. He does not pity Acedo for the tiresome work she performs, nor does he mind that his masterpiece gets dirty, or that it has decayed. Instead, he wonders why the cleaner uses old-fashioned technology like a conventional vacuum cleaner to clean something as exceptional as the spiral staircase in his architecture. Koolhaas says, "I can easily imagine if I were a cleaner – and maybe this is something we should have thought of – to devise some kind of protocol of what is convenient to be done by hand and what is convenient to be done with a machine."[3]

Even if he is obviously capable himself, it is not easy for the rest of us to imagine Koolhaas as a cleaner. It has to do with our conventional understanding of architecture design, which is associated with development, as the "pure individual creation," as described by Ukeles in her *Manifesto for Maintenance Art*. Architecture is conceived of as a heroic production that gives birth to and sets something new into the world. Cleaning, on the contrary, is understood as reproductive, as it assures an object's endurance in time. Ukeles argues that since cleaning is reproductive rather than productive, it is considered subordinate to the act of creation in most capitalist societies. At the same time, such a division ignores their interdependence (evident in the architect's confession of having overlooked the need for a cleaning protocol) and contributes to the lack of knowledge about how to treat a building once it is handed over to the user.

With the unravelling of the climate collapse and a growing awareness of the ecological and social impact of always employing new building materials, maintenance in the form of cleaning becomes increasingly important. Architects' responsibilities should no longer end with the inauguration of their buildings; they must provide a perspective on how they will impact at various scales and localities. While architecture schools focus on climate adaptive solutions, hi-tech energy efficiency measures, reusing, recycling, upcycling, circular economies, etc., cleaning is yet to be included to the curriculum.

The birth of maintenance-free

Many of the office buildings in this book – like Inland Steel, Seagram, John Deere, Pirelli, Unilever, among others – served or are still serving as headquarters of companies with a profound need to *represent*. Most of these HQs were built in the US and Europe from the mid-1950s to the mid-1970s. Hilary Sample discusses how only a handful of corporations influenced the aesthetic of a whole generation of postwar office buildings. These companies brought the idea of an iconic corporate headquarters into being. Cleaning played an important role in this process. "No epoch advanced the concept of being 'maintenance-free' more than the 1950s to 1980s in America," writes Sample.[4] Inland Steel chairman Clarence Randall told his architect that he wanted his HQ "to be like a man with immaculate English tailoring – his clothes are so good you are not aware of how well he is tailored."[5] These iconic buildings had to be immaculate to reflect the success and power of the corporations that commissioned and inhabited them. To assure this condition, the buildings needed to self-clean. Window cleaners hanging from a thin rope high up were replaced by machinery; Sears Towers (SOM, 1973) incorporated six robots mounted on the roof which were remotely operated by an engineer to frequently clean the building's surface. Being maintenance-free was also pursued on the material level: dark, reflective glass[6] made dirt less visible; Corten steel cultivated decay as a primary aspect of its aesthetic. These measures were paralleled by the introduction of automated operating systems like climate control and surveillance. Care of office buildings and their furniture was gradually taken over by machinery or outsourced, disconnecting users from the building.

Outsourced

For office buildings in general, outsourcing has its roots in flexibility, an indispensable feature of management theory in the West after the Second World War. In her essay 'The political economy of flexibility,'[7] Amy Thomas elucidates how from the 1970s, the instabilities caused by the adoption of the market-based system "were reinforced by financial deregulation and the rapid expansion of the service sector, meaning that organizations became increasingly volatile and susceptible to fluctuations in staff numbers, putting a premium on the flexible use of space and therefore requiring a reconceptualization of the office building that placed intrinsic adaptability at its core."[8] As a consequence, companies tried to reduce occupancy costs wherever possible: they sold their buildings to investors and subsequently rented from them; they outsourced maintenance services like repair and cleaning.

Perhaps more than any other buildings investigated in this book, Aarhus City Hall (1937–42) – both the building itself and the furniture – has sustained in its original condition. This was in part due to consistency and care in the cleaning and maintenance regime. "When I started here, the cleaning ladies were employed here and they were a part of everything," recalls Benny Holm Pedersen, chief of building management since the early 2000s. "They were allowed for example to move a paper on a desk and clean under it. Today, they will clean around it. Back then, they came every day and now they come only once a week, every Friday." Spending money on cleaning matters, Pedersen insists, "The building sustains longer if it is cleaned. For example, if you have a lot of dust and in the winter and sand on the floor, it harms the wooden surface."[9] Being part of the public sector, Pedersen must hire the cheapest firm in a tender process. Outsourcing has led to fierce competition among cleaning companies, increasing cleaners' workload while decreasing the time available for cleaning. Another dilemma is that if cleaning is outsourced, it is done according to a fixed procedure agreed upon in the contract, rather than on actual necessity, which is subject to change. "We don't tell the cleaners what to do," Pedersen says. Only if there's a big event is Pedersen allowed to say to the head cleaner instruct extra work on the floor. "Or, if the queen is coming, they do the toilets extra."

High turnover of cleaning staff typically results in a constant drain of knowledge. Even though they belong to an outside agency, the cleaning crew for Aarhus City Hall (nine women and one man, from Poland, Thailand, Togo, and Vietnam) has been the same since the early 2010s. This proves to be rewarding: "They are the same people every day, and they have the same area every day. If one of them has a holiday, they know exactly what to do." Eva, the leader, has been cleaning the building for 20 years.

"She knows a lot about the history in the rooms. She knows which chair is the cheap one and which is the expensive one. What special things to do with the carpets or the floor," Pedersen says. When it comes to window cleaning, the situation is less fortunate: cleaning the 500 double-windows is massively time-consuming. Two out of the four times they are cleaned every year, the 80-year-old windows need to be opened up so the two glass panes can be cleaned from the inside – a complicated process requiring two people to handle each window. Around every four years, the window cleaner contractor is changed though, Pedersen laments, "It takes years to teach them how to clean these windows and when they are good at it, they [the administration] say, 'Oh, now we change.'"[10] Pedersen suspects that firms underestimate what it takes to clean these windows, and therefore do not make as much profit as they hoped for when bidding for the job. Then they move on.

So is outsourcing actually cheaper than having their own cleaners on staff? "No!" Pedersen says, "But this is not something we decide, we need to follow EU rules."[11] Pedersen regrets the loss of knowledge that comes with delegating maintenance services such as repair and cleaning, but hopes for changes in the future. There are rumors that maintenance personnel might be hired again on a permanent basis.

Cleaning Cultures, or Cleaning as Culture
The Kagawa Prefectural office, a regional administrative building in Japan by Kenzo Tange, completed in 1958, shows the impact dedicated cleaning has on the endurance of a building. Over half a century, this building was cleaned on a daily basis by Kagawa Seiwa-kai, a small group brought into life by Governor Masanori Kaneko to manage the building. "Rain or shine, our staff have been working hard to keep it clean," Seiwa-kai wrote in a letter on the 50th anniversary of the building, in 2008. "The starting point of our cleaning work is 'sweeping, wiping and polishing.' It is no exaggeration to say that the success or failure of a cleaning project depends on the care with which we perform these tasks. Another essential requirement is to be 'considerate' of the building," the letter continues. Undoubtedly, considerate and professional care needs to be learned. A photograph shows the Kagawa Seiwa-kai attentively watching instructions for how to buff the linoleum floor.[12] *Seiwa-kai* is a composition of SEI (truth, honesty, sincerity), WA (peace, harmony), and KAI (organization). Kagawa Seiwa-kai offered employment to families who were bereaved during the war. To commit people who suffered such loss to a career of cleaning work might sound strange to Western ears, but cleaning has very different cultural connotations in Japan. At the soccer World Cup in Brazil (2014) and Russia (2018), for example, Japanese fans, as well as the team, were praised for picking up rubbish.[13] "We don't want others to think we are bad people who don't have enough education or upbringing to clean things up,"[14] commented Maiko Awane, assistant director of Hiroshima Prefectural Government's Tokyo office in a BBC interview. His remarks touch on two important aspects of Japanese cleaning culture: first, learning how to clean is part of a child's upbringing in the family as well as in school; second, cleaning is part of a person's morals.

While in the West, cleaning is often done with little or no education and training, in Japan it makes up part of children's education from early on. In the guidelines for elementary education, cleaning is discussed as a way to build collaboration and awareness of what is necessary to play a role as a member of society.[15] Cleaning of common areas, bathrooms, etc. is taken care of by janitors while students – boys and girls alike – clean their classrooms. "I vividly recall our disappointment when, in the middle of our elementary careers, our old schoolhouse in the suburbs of Tokyo was torn down and rebuilt with modern materials," recalls author Hiroko Yoda in *The Long History of Japan's Tidying up*, revealing the intimate experience of material qualities through the process of cleaning: "How boring the sterile concrete floors seemed in comparison to the rich wooden floorboards, their grain polished smooth by previous generations of students. It was like losing a friend."[16]

Cleaning goes back a long way in Japanese culture. It is about more than hygiene: it is treated as a practice creating the basis for mental well-being. For Shinto, the indigenous religion in Japan, cleanliness is godliness. "If an individual is afflicted by *kegare* [impurity/dirt], it can bring harm to the society as a whole… So it is vital to practice cleanliness. This purifies you and helps avoid bringing calamities to society," explains Noriaki Ikeda, an assistant Shinto priest.[17] As early as 927 AD, *Engishiki*, one of the earliest legal codes (a sort of government handbook) gave instructions about cleaning the Imperial Palace in Kyoto. In Zen Buddhism, which came to Japan from China in the 12th and 13th century, cleaning and cooking are considered spiritual tasks akin to meditation.[18] Washing off dirt, both physically and spiritually, is an important daily practice. It is common in Japan for cleaning to be formally embedded in a company's philosophy: around 8 a.m., office workers clean the streets around their place of work.

After 50 years of dedicated cleaning, in 2008 the Kagawa Seiwa-kai was replaced by a professional cleaning company, which was chosen by public tender. "I am proud to have been involved in the cleaning of the prefectural building and will pass on the baton to the next generation with satisfaction,"[19] their letter concludes.

notes

1. Laura Van den Borre, Patrick Deboosere, "Health risks in the cleaning industry: a Belgian census-linked mortality study (1991–2011)," *International archives of occupational and environmental health*, vol. 91,1 (2018).
2. Related to this, there is a lively discourse around how clean a building or a city has to be. See: "Dust," *Cabinet*, Fall 2009, Issue 35.
3. Transcription from video by the author.
4. Hilary Sample, *Maintenance Architecture* (MIT Press, 2016), p.49.
5. Inland Steel Building, National Park Service, National Register of Historic Places, August 2002: https://ia801608.us.archive.org/10/items/NationalRegisterNominationsForChicago/InlandSteelBuildingNrNom_djvu.txt, accessed January 24, 2022.
6. Inventions on the material level, such as self-cleaning glass, invented by Pilkington in 2001.
7. Amy Thomas, "The Political Economy of Flexibility: Deregulation and the transformation of corporate space in the postwar city of London," in: K. Cupers, H. Mattsson, C. Gabrielsson (eds.), *Neoliberalism on the Ground: Architecture and Transformations from 1960 to the Present* (University of Pittsburgh Press, 2020), p.127–150.
8. Thomas (2020), p.133
9. Benny Holm Pedersen, interview with the author, October 27, 2021.
10. Ibid
11. Ibid
12. Seiwa-kai, "Fifty years of polishing with the heart," in brochure published upon the 50th anniversary of Kagawa Prefectural Building. Translated with DeepL.com (free version).
13. Steve John Powell and Angeles Marin Cabello, "What Japan can teach us about cleanliness," BBC, October 7, 2019, (accessed January 30, 2022).
14. Ibid
15. See: Masatoshi Senoo, "Do you really need cleaning time at school?" Yahoo Japan, August 10, 2020 (accessed January 10, 2022): https://news.yahoo.co.jp/byline/senoomasatoshi/20200810-00192588.
16. Hiroko Yoda, "The Long history of Japan's Tidying Up," *The New Yorker*, January 25, 2021.
17. Ibid, p.3
18. "What Japan can teach us about cleanliness," BBC
19. Seiwa-kai, 2008.
20. Robotics companies boast that robots like Ella use less water and less cleaning chemicals than humans, and are therefore resource-efficient and sustainable. This of course does not take into account the resources consumed and waste generated by the march of generations of new robots that is now beginning.
21. Public spaces present an additional challenge to robotic cleaning: in private domestic spaces, a robot like Ella – bristling with sensors and cameras – would photograph whatever is impeding her – a sock, for example – and ask what to do with it. But that is not possible in public space because of data protection.
22. Jacob Rubæk Holm, interview with the author, March 2, 2022.
23. Rachel Hoffman, *Unf*ck your habitat – You're better than your mess* (Saint Martin's Griffin, 2016).
24. Menna Agha, "Cleaning is Architecture Work," lecture, Harvard GSD (via zoom), March 3, 2022.

How will the next generation approach cleaning? Can the close physical relation of the cleaner and the building become a model for maintenance in buildings in the future? What are the current developments in the global office cleaning industry, and how might they impact workplace design?

Robots

Ella's oval face, big round eyes, and stocky body recalls Spielberg's E.T. She is an office cleaning robot, the first in Denmark, and she has been specially programmed to clean the city hall of Silkeborg, a town of 60,000 inhabitants. Besides cleaning, Ella can tell jokes, sing birthday songs, greet you when you walk by, and warn you if you stand in her way. So far, Ella only communicates in English, but a Danish version is on its way from Singapore, where she was developed.

Reda Aleksandraviciene, who has been closely working with Ella for some time now, is content with her. With a tablet in hand, she shows her capabilities besides floor cleaning: during lunch breaks, the cleaning crew sometimes make fun of staff or visitors by having Ella talk to them. According to Aleksandraviciene, Ella has two major advantages: she is much faster than any human at cleaning the building's long corridors and open spaces, and after cleaning she leaves the floor almost dry. But she is programmed to leave a 20-centimeter uncleaned gap alongside walls. Theoretically, Aleksandraviciene could direct Ella with her joystick to clean these edges and corners, but it's faster if she just does it manually. Aleksandraviciene is not afraid of losing her job to Ella because Ella only does one thing: cleaning the floor. That leaves plenty of other work for humans.

Ella belongs to the species of *cobots* (collaborative robots), meaning she is only capable of supplementing, not substituting human cleaners. She carries a 40-liter water tank and a smaller one for cleaning chemicals, which need to be re-filled regularly by Aleksandraviciene and her colleagues.[20] She also needs to be charged every three or four hours. Apart from that, she is independent.

Like conventional cleaning machines (vacuum cleaners, polishers), cleaning robots are still bulky and are most effective in large open spaces without much furniture or other objects impeding them, like airports, train stations, hospitals, factories, and large shops.[21] Jacob Rubæk Holm, an economist and associate professor at Aalborg University who researches the effect of automation on the labor market, is aware of their limitations: "Automation has greater scope when there is a large number of standardized tasks to perform repeatedly, such as vacuuming a floor." Tidying is another matter altogether, states Holm, "It's much less standardized. The mess is different each time and putting everything in its right place, or in the trash, is different each time. Often something does not have a 'right place.'" Desks would need to be tidied by a human before a robot would be able to clean them. "As far as I know," says Holm, "a robot capable of tidying up a mess on a table before cleaning is not yet available."[22]

Ella costs about €30,000 to buy, but the municipality is only leasing her. Joel Engblad, head of cleaning for Silkeborg municipality has been in the cleaning business for almost 30 years and working at Silkeborg for 20. Engblad has found that not only are cleaners typically treated poorly, but as a business owner, he has been forced over the years to either cheat himself or ask his employers to do so in order to meet unrealistic contract obligations that resulted from bidding process. To ensure quality cleaning and to commit people to the job, Engblad encourages them to continue their education, but recruitment is still challenging. So in 2014, he began employing robots. It's not the architecture that determines whether automated cleaning is possible, he says. It's about finding the right robot for the specific task. Ella is mostly up to the task, but some of the features of Silkeborg city hall – a 60-year-old modernist building – present challenges. The elevator doors are part-electric and part-manual; here and at certain thresholds, corners, and uneven surfaces is where Ella's performance suffers. Robotic cleaning is highly standardized, meaning that it achieves the same quality every time. But it also means that inaccessible corners will be missed every time.

Robots will not replace human cleaners any time soon, but they will indirectly play a role in the spatial set-up of offices. Office buildings that aren't suitable for robot cleaners may become (even) less valuable as real estate. Larger open-plan offices will be selected because their cleaning can more easily be automated, saving money in the long run. "Everything will be flat; everything in its place. Workers have to tidy up before going home in order to let the robot clean overnight," Holm says. "Fewer people will be needed to clean, which will allow for higher wages for those that remain. Their jobs will change as they start using new technology. It's a managerial decision whether they will be further trained, or whether such competencies will be acquired from the labor market, for example, by hiring engineers." Which will be forced to adapt fastest – robots, architecture, or people?

Robotic or human cleaning – either way, the prospect for office workers who want to retreat to a cellular space, for those who need creative chaos, and for those who want to personalize their workspace is not very promising. Such deviations from standardized special conditions calls for nuanced, knowledge-driven cleaning regimes, which are more expensive. Should we revert to the Kagawa Seiwa-kai model? Undoubtedly, physical engagement in cleaning can be rewarding, as several cleaning guides for domestic environment promise.[23] But architects can learn from cleaning too, and change the way they conceive of their buildings. Architect and researcher Menna Agha[24] recalled a decisive moment from a design-and-build studio in Eugene, Oregon. The project was about the rehabilitation of an abandoned building. More than half the studio's time went into cleaning the building and its surrounding site. When she and her fellow students were finally ready for the design and fabrication phase, they realized their work had already been done. The pure act of cleaning made the building ready to be inhabited again. Cleaning work is thus not only reproductive maintenance, but productive – and transformative – architectural work.

Getting a sense of the economic life of office buildings is crucial for understanding their performance over time, but also maddeningly complicated and could easily fill a second volume of this book. We realize we are only scratching the surface of the economic mechanisms at play, but what we have found sheds light on the double or triple lives office buildings (can) have.

The logic of depreciation supposes that the aging of machines or buildings invested in by companies causes the value of those investments to decrease over time. If we leave larger investments throughout a building's lifespan out of the equation for a moment, this logic suggests the value of most properties we looked at would be close to zero, or simply zero. While financial data remains difficult to access, the available accounts of current property values suggest something more compelling. Property prices have gone up, rather than down, at rates seemingly disconnected from any investments made in them over time in the form of repair, upgrades, extensions, etc. Market forces and the imperative of economic growth means that when it comes to property – but not to the machinery or objects inside that property – appreciation trumps depreciation every time. Yet, companies are still allowed to claim depreciation in their property values when giving their accounts to tax authorities, creditors, shareholders etc. Understanding the interplay between appreciation and depreciation seems crucial to unlock long-term thinking about office development.

The concept of depreciation was conceived during the industrial revolution as investments by industrialists in machines and buildings increased dramatically. This led to fundamental questions regarding the reporting of asset value to creditors and tax authorities. Up until this time, it was customary to keep these investments on the books at their cost price. That value would only be removed from the books when the investment ceased to function. As investments accelerated and the wear and tear and turnover of machines and other items increased, this system created unrealistic readings of the assets companies owned. To bridge the gap between current value and cost at the time of purchase, the notion of a gradually declining value was introduced. Crucially, this required, at the time of purchase, the predicted lifespan of the machine/object/property being invested in. Obsolescence was now built-in to accountancy (long before it was built into production and marketing models in the 20th century). Whereas for machines this could be somewhat objectively quantified in terms of wear of components, buildings are more complex, as they consist of a multitude of components and materials with varying lifespans. Predicting or pronouncing the death of a building is more complex than it sounds – for instance, even after demolition of the building, the plot (and its value) would always remain. Determining lifespan became even more complex as the availability of new and more efficient machines started influencing the value of the older machine a company had bought. This draws unknown future events into the value equation, making the prediction of life expectancy and the rate of depreciation for office buildings and their contents a very imprecise science, left to accountants and property owners to play with, and undebated by the rest of us. There are no independent agencies actively researching or determining any of this.[1] These values are by no means innocent, as they frame further investment potential and decisions regarding the replacement of furniture, machinery, and other items, and ultimately the replacement of buildings themselves.

Large western nations still adhere to 19th-century models of linear depreciation for office buildings over time. In the US, the depreciation term (meaning when value drops to zero) is 39 years, France 25 years, Germany 50 years, UK 33 years. Dutch law leaves it

5__ FOLLOWING THE MONEY...

Is appreciation trumping depreciation?

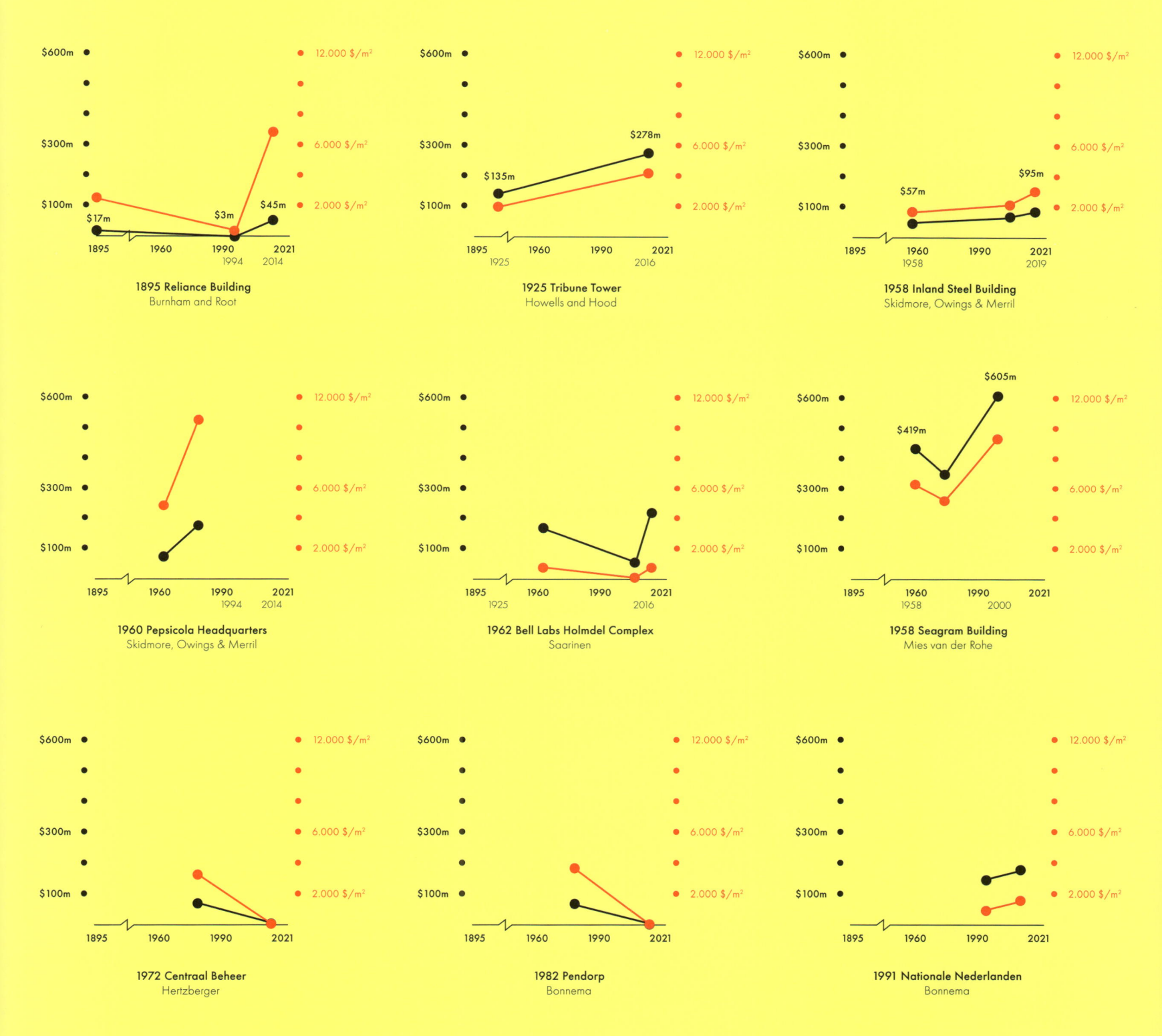

1895 Reliance Building
Burnham and Root
- $17m (1895), $3m (1994), $45m (2014)

1925 Tribune Tower
Howells and Hood
- $135m (1925), $278m (2016)

1958 Inland Steel Building
Skidmore, Owings & Merril
- $57m (1958), $95m (2019)

1960 Pepsicola Headquarters
Skidmore, Owings & Merril

1962 Bell Labs Holmdel Complex
Saarinen

1958 Seagram Building
Mies van der Rohe
- $419m, $605m (2000)

1972 Centraal Beheer
Hertzberger

1982 Pendorp
Bonnema

1991 Nationale Nederlanden
Bonnema

2021 corrected for inflation

509

to owners to determine the lifespan of the office building somewhere between 30 to 50 years, trusting the owners to act within a so-called "good merchants' practice" to self-assess value over time. The good merchants' practice is founded on the principle of reasonability; in case of a dispute between the company and the tax authorities or the creditors, the courts have final say. The Netherlands also has a slightly more advanced understanding of lifespan of buildings: different parts of the building – foundation, structure, installations – can be considered individually and included in or excluded from the calculation. The Dutch government and tax authorities introduced this system in the early 2000s, when the difference between valuation based on expected depreciation of property and actual sale value became too substantial. In addition, the government replaced straight-line depreciation with a building's so-called 'bottom value,' drawing from more ephemeral assessments of current market value. An institute, indirectly governmental, was launched to gauge what that market value is. This reflects how (office) real estate is an economy with a double-sided logic. On the one hand, office buildings are considered corporate investments subject to depreciation like any other piece of office equipment. On the other hand, the building is subject to a secondary form of valuation by the market.

An additional form of valuation is done by companies in their annual reporting to creditors and shareholders, which creates another alternate economic reality. Here the building's value and depreciation or appreciation is used as a lever to boost or degrade a company's balance sheet separate from tax filings. International guidelines for the valuation of office buildings in the *International Accounting Standard 16: Property, Plant and Equipment*, published by the International Accounting Standards Board, leaves considerable space for building owners to set their own terms when defining depreciation.

In market valuations we were able to find for our case studies confirmation of the traditional realtor logic: location and operating costs are the most important factors.[2]

A critical decline in occupancy and revenue seems to occur systematically 20-25 years into the life of a building. Our case studies revealed that this is connected to increased operational costs due to rising energy prices and the wearing of major elements like façades, MEP, and HVAC systems – the revenue drop is also associated with organizational changes (or bankruptcy) leading to prolonged vacancy.

In the US, reappreciation following this initial slump is often closely linked to municipal tax stimuli and heritage assessments offered to help the suffering real estate. As for the experimental nature of some office buildings and their iconic quality, different value assessors within real estate companies we spoke to recognize the existence of what they call an x-factor for additional value not found in 'normal' buildings. By definition, no clear outline for defining this x-factor exists. It's clear though how real estate 'projects' (when a classic building is bought up) use heritage in their branding and framing of the building. Here again things become murky in their actual definition and actual numbers.[3]

It is clear that a new assessment of how we think of value over time is long overdue. As we need to dramatically reduce our environmental footprint, one straightforward way to do so is by using less material, or reducing "material throughput," as ecological economists call it. Unchecked depreciation thinking has been a massive accelerant of such throughput in the domain of the office: refurbishments are unnecessarily frequent (and wasteful) because they are systemically encouraged – assets have to be valuable. If we are able to develop the dimension of time in real estate investment more precisely and connect it to the climate and ecological crisis, new possibilities for resource allocation should emerge. If we develop the tools to assess the actual lifespan of materials more critically – according to their performance rather than economic expedience – we can adapt our investment and taxation strategies to fundamentally challenge 19th-century depreciation logic.

notes

1. Prof. dr. T.M. Berkhout. *Fiscaal afschrijven op vastgoed* (2013) Kluwer, Deventer. On p.3 Berkhout suggests this topic is still subject to "Babylonian confusion" and quotes Mansfield and Pinder's "Economic" and "functional" obsolescence, their characteristics and impacts on valuation practice: "Much of the research to date has not satisfactorily distinguished the various forms of obsolescence, a term that now embraces a wide range of issues. This has led to confusion, with many aspects of the phenomenon being under-researched and ultimately poorly-understood by decision makers." (Property Management 26(3), 2008, p.202)
2. The limited data set available to us is due to economic and cultural differences, with US cases much easier to some extent to assess than i.e. German or Japan, or i.e. in the case of public buildings, or a lack of recent sales data.
3. Hilde Remøy's dissertation *Out of Office* (IOS Press, 2010) tried to connect spatial attributes of an office building to current vacancy by looking at the space ratio in height and size of office entrances, and floor height. Remøy found a correlation between lower ceiling heights and vacancy, though she found its effect to be limited within her experiment. (p.85)

6__ ...AND THE MURKY LIFE CYCLES OF OFFICE BUILDINGS DEMAND THAT WE RETHINK THE OFFICE OF THE 21ST CENTURY...

The Scandinavian Airlines (SAS) headquarters, by Niels Torp, housed about 1,500 employees when it was inaugurated in 1987. Frank Duffy considered it "the most brilliant example of the modern northern European tradition of 'street' office buildings" and praised it as a "superb example of the use of architecture to create an interactive environment."[1] But looking at the development of the building over time reveals a rather concerning history related to its capability to interact. Less than 20 years following the building's completion SAS sold all its buildings. According to Björn Frivold, SAS head of its facility management, the company did this to relieve itself from the obligations of property ownership, to gain immediate financial benefit, and to increase its ability to act more flexibly to developments on the market. The sale coincided with (or was promoted by) the rise of digital technologies, which enabled SAS to outsource administrative work to low-wage countries such as India and the Philippines. The headquarters became a playball for several investment companies: in 2003, it was sold to Nordisk Renting, a Swedish real estate company (owned by the Royal Bank of Scotland) specializing in financial lease-back constructs. In 2006, Nordisk Renting sold it to KLP, Norway's largest Pension Fund, who held onto it for another seven years before selling it to its current owner, a smaller real estate investment business called Mengus.[2] Upon the Nordisk Renting purchase, SAS signed a 20-year lease agreement and continued to use the building. In 2010 though, management decided they wanted to be closer to the airport itself and moved out of the building they commissioned and built, to offices in Arlanda.[3] Still bound to its 20-year lease agreement, SAS was forced to sublet the building, which proved difficult and occasionally resulted in SAS paying double rent. To save cost, SAS returned to the Torp building in 2014 and reconfigured the original single-cell offices into open-plan expanses (replacing ceilings and other fittings along the way). SAS now uses one-third of the 33,000-square meter building. The rest is rented to various smaller companies. According to Frivold, the consequence is that every time a new company moves in, almost everything in their space is gutted, disposed of, and rebuilt.[4]

What happened at SAS is emblematic of how values of ownership, responsibility for investments, and also subsequent irresponsibility over usage dictate the actual tempo (and quality) of change in office buildings over time. Office consultants have been complicit in these trends even while they try to mitigate them.[5] In 1989 Frank Duffy and his consultancy DEGW put out the book *The Changing City*, featuring several banks occupying buildings only about a decade old. The authors claim that the buildings were already outdated, unable to accommodate technical innovation or fluctuations in staff numbers.[6] Duffy's response was an act of dismantling. Rather than seeing buildings as an integral whole, he reconceived the office as a combination of several temporal layers: the shell, services, scenery, and sets. The main structure was understood as the shell, with a lifespan of about 50 years; services were infrastructural support systems such as plumbing, climate control, ducting, etc., lasting 15-20 years; sets formed the interior with partition walls, carpets, furniture, etc. lasting 5-7 years (embellished by accessories such as smaller furniture, plants, etc. changing more or less on a daily basis). The office was now defined as a process in constant flux, rather than a fixed form. Deconstructing – or delaminating – the various elements that constitute an office building, and defining them by a certain life expectancy, on the one hand introduced a metabolic rather than tabula rasa approach to the office; on the other hand it also facilitated the cult of 'flexibility,' a by-word for rampant refurbishing and its associated material throughput, all to accommodate the churn of capital.

Duffy's understanding of SAS office building as an interactive environment is precisely what the facility manager described in the building's change-of-ownership and tenants. Revisiting SAS HQ less than a decade after inauguration, Duffy admitted that the building was too "lavishly equipped to house effectively the number of people who were to occupy it." But he stated in the same paragraph that "[c]ontemporary business criteria would conclude that the building could, *without losing any of its quality*, be used more productively" (our emphasis).[7] In other words, he supports the building's potential to accommodate more tenants, and at a faster rate of turnover. This allowed for the quick renting of the shell combined with the potential of a constant update of the interior. It created endless cycles of waste, as the life span accounted for had nothing to do with the actual performance and state of the materials, installations, and objects.

notes

1. Frank Duffy, "SAS headquarters, Stockholm, Sweden, 1988," in: Francis Duffy, *The New Office*, (Conran Octopus Limited, 1997), p.38.
2. "KLP Sells SAS Headquarters," *Nordic Property News*, February 19, 2016.
3. See p.452 for a chronology of the ownership and inhabitation of the SAS building.
4. Interview with Björn Frivold by the author, April 29, 2021,"[…] Inside the building it looks like a modern office, the façade and everything outside is completely as it was in 1988 and in the interior street it is not exactly as it was originally. Today, the landlord has tried to create more activity in the street and therefore they have put additional furniture into the street."
5. By the time the SAS headquarters was complete, DEGW had become a world-leading space planning practice with offices in Europe, the US, and East Asia.
6. Francis Duffy, Alex Henney, *The changing city* (Bulstrode Press, 1989)
7. Frank Duffy, (1997): p.39
8. The book is full of (unacknowledged) tensions – between technological optimism and environmental concerns; between vernacular language and minimalism and modernism – weakening some of its fundamental points.
9. Duffy and Brand acknowledge a lack of data to support their model and suggest some variations. But many of the numbers used in the book are still mobilized by the office consultant industry. (Duffy is quoted in the book: "[T]here is a shocking lack of data about how buildings actually behave. We simply don't have the numbers. We measure what is easy to measure and ignore what is difficult," p.213). Brand also recognizes the shortcomings of his anecdotal approach and his lack of cultural attunement to areas other than California: "[T]o ever get beyond the anecdotal level – typified by this book – will take serious statistical analysis over a significant depth of time and an adventurous range of building types."
10. Brand hints at a prototype of the 'material passport' concept, through which companies and consultants can track the life of buildings and their components: "What if every commercial building had an on-site journal and maintenance log?" There seems to be an alternative layering that has more to do with material quality than with function. More generic interiors tend to have shorter lifespans than custom-made designs. Designs that have a 'story' or specific quality last longer, regardless of style.

Steward Brand's 1994 book *How Buildings Learn: What Happens After They're Built* echoes and elaborates on Duffy's deconstruction of the layers of the office. Brand was well-known as the founder of the *Whole Earth catalog* and an important member of the early Silicon Valley counterculture movement. In the tradition of Bernard Rudolfsky's Architecture without Architects (1966), the book celebrates the lo-tech, the undesigned, the vernacular, and the improvised over the planned, modern, and immaculate.[8] Office buildings play an important role in Brand's research and Duffy is his main interlocutor. Brand created a diagram of architecture titled "shearing layers" which extends the tiered conception of buildings proposed by Duffy. Brand added "site" and "skin" as extra layers; where Duffy refers to "sets", Brand uses "space plan." He assigns a greater life-expectancy to each layer of the building than Duffy did. He draws parallels between the functioning of ecosystems and the (capitalist) notion of change, flux, and constant growth. What remains uninterrogated is the assumption – or romantic notion – that change is always a force for good. But what if it isn't? What if – like activist shareholders realizing that pure profit-driven development doesn't work as it will eventually hurt society – we recognize the problematic elements that change entails, the waste it brings, not least to the accumulated architectural knowledge embedded in office buildings? Within the discourse of circular design, Brand's "shearing layers" diagram is an *ur*-text; Duffy's is almost unknown. When we tried to match our findings with their models, we discovered that assumptions about the lifespan of structures – 50 years – to be way off the mark.[9] Apart from two buildings, structures have easily lasted their 50 years; some managed double that stretch. Most will remain structurally viable for decades to come – or basically, indefinitely. If anything will bring them down, it will be developer speculation (demolish and rebuild) rather than the poor performance. The real lifespan of other layers is much harder to assess, too dependent on construction techniques and how they have been used to assert any universal rule. Some *skins* were minimally adapted over time, with only the windows replaced. In the most extreme case, a third replacement curtain-wall façade has been installed (Palais Nestle, p. 204), which still means a lifespan exceeding the 20 years estimated by Brand and Duffy. For *services*, the data is too hazy, but experts suggested to us that they too usually last longer than their supposed life expectancy, especially if they do not contain moving parts. For *spatial organization* much depends on the occupancy type. Multi-tenant buildings predictably show a high frequency of change compared to the HQs and public buildings we looked at. The *stuff* layer, lacking a clear definition of what stuff is, is impossible to track. But all in all, through our significant but simultaneously limited data, it is clear that iconic and revolutionary office buildings have easily outlasted Brand's and Duffy's assessments on all fronts. It seems necessary to either redevelop or rethink the layered approach to life-expectancy. Without market pressures for constant churn and change, what could materials really do? How could the sudden changes inflicted by COVID-19 be properly metabolized?

In his book, Brand acknowledged its shortcomings, how it should be a basis for deeper study, and how his research leaves him with more questions than answers.[10] We feel the same way. To kickstart a conversation on what this book reveals, and to underline the necessity of rethinking the environment we work in without resorting to short-lived trends forecasting agile or blended working – working X.0 and the like – we end with some questions.

STUFF (< 3 years)

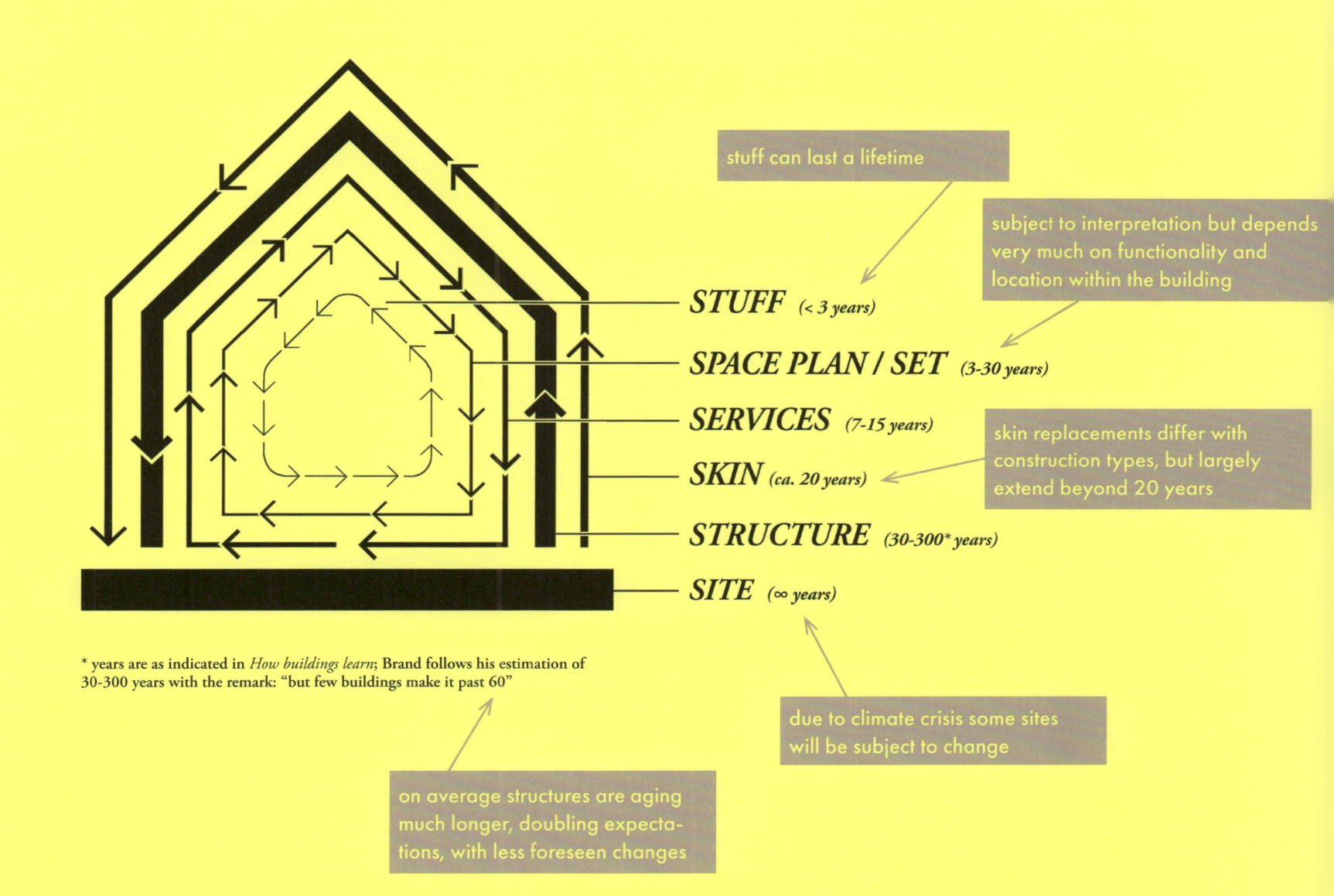

SPACE PLAN / SET (3-30 years)

SERVICES (7-15 years)

SKIN (ca. 20 years)

STRUCTURE (30-300* years)

SITE (∞ years)

* years are as indicated in *How buildings learn*; Brand follows his estimation of 30-300 years with the remark: "but few buildings make it past 60"

stuff can last a lifetime

subject to interpretation but depends very much on functionality and location within the building

skin replacements differ with construction types, but largely extend beyond 20 years

due to climate crisis some sites will be subject to change

on average structures are aging much longer, doubling expectations, with less foreseen changes

- Could we require each building plan to anticipate future events – like the growth of HVAC systems, energy usage, or change of function? Can we require a further heighten the minimal cleared ceiling height that encourages transformation over time? Should we differentiate – in real estate and tax codes – between multi-tenant and single-tenant office buildings, since multi-tenant buildings tend to wear faster? Is it possible and desirable to standardize building products and maintenance procedures, similar to IT or the food industry, in order to make them future-proof? Can we develop integrated solutions for re-use within the office industry or at least require more transparency on resource availability? A yearly increase in the requirement for material re-use?

- How can we make sure that innovation or perpetual change aren't the goals, but making progress is? How can we disconnect from office 'trends' while remaining open to future moves? Or how could 'trends' become sustainable? If this can't be achieved voluntarily, should we penalize companies for promoting unnecessary spatial changes (without changing anything else about the way they operate)? Build a surcharge system for useless interventions? Should every office building be zoned into elements that can and can't be changed? Or should we consider it within our immediate and cultural-defined behavior: how can we limit our yearning for change? Can we limit our ever-increasing standards of comfort, so that we can bear the insufficiencies of 100-year-old buildings, instead of demanding persistent upgrades? Or even bigger: how can we adapt our industries to build towards necessity rather than growth for its own sake?

- How can we rethink the office through adjustments to taxation and markets? How can we untangle the complexities and contradictions of economic deprecation and market valuation and instead build a system that incentivizes long-term commitment to what works? Should we consider valuing real estate using satellite data and actual usage? Or something more simple: a reinvented version of the window tax? Can we ask the UN to develop a charter for sustainable office use and heighten the accounting depreciation time for buildings to at least 100 years? Or should appreciation of real estate for taxation be taken as a given rather than its depreciation? Should all office buildings be automatically listed for preservation upon completion? Should they, like trees in many urban areas, come with a non-destruction clause, with demolition requiring a (very) special exemption?

- How can we encourage a reassessment of cleaning, steering towards a cultural re-appreciation of its craft and importance? Can we, at the same time, modernize it? Should cleaners share in the profits of the building's owner? Could we ban outsourcing of services such as repair and cleaning and reintroduce building- or company-based staff for it? Should repair and re-use services be exempted from (income) taxation to create a level-playing field compared to new extraction of resources? Should learning how to clean buildings become standard in all school curricula from a young age?

- Can we convince clients to consider building as an opportunity that stretches further than the accommodation of workers? Show clients how to go beyond economic metrics and connect their physical footprint with an architectural vision without resorting to cookie cutter icons? How can these clients be supported in looking beyond their own temporal horizons, beyond the short-lived and temporary? Can a wild-card system be added to the tendering regulations to allow smaller and more innovative parties to participate? And when a building is completed, should there be a minimum age for buildings to be awarded a prize?

- Finally, and perhaps most importantly, how can office discourse refocus from serving industry interests to facilitating longevity (with its associated ecological and climate benefits)? In order to actually sustain ourselves, does this mean building new models that incentivize appreciating no-change? Instead of designers picking the latest fashion colors, isn't' this the type of creativity this century really needs? Isn't that the real great reset we long for?

CREDITS & ACKNOWLEDGMENTS

biography

Ruth Baumeister is an architect and writer. Since 2014, she holds a professorship of architecture history and theory at Aarhus School of Architecture/DK. Previously she taught at TU Delft, Bauhaus-University Weimar, the Willem de Kooning Academy Rotterdam and she held the position of a visiting professor at the University of Cagliari, Italy. Her research on the impact of globalization on the building culture and the 20th century avant-gardes in art and architecture has been published internationally in 8 languages. Her current interest focuses on cultures of repair and maintenance in architecture.

Stephan Petermann holds a Master's degree in the History of Architecture and the Theory of Building Preservation from the Utrecht University (2001-2007) and studied Architecture at the Eindhoven University of Technology (2001-2005). From 2006 onwards he has been a long-term collaborator of Rem Koolhaas assisting him with research, strategy, editing, and curation. Petermann was an associate at OMA's thinktank AMO from 2010 until 2019. He is the editor-in-chief of *VOLUME* and a visiting professor at the Central Academy of Fine Arts in Beijing. With Marieke van den Heuvel he founded the design, research, and strategy studio Probe.

Marieke van den Heuvel graduated at the Design Academy Eindhoven (1999), followed by a scholarship at Benetton's Fabrica in Treviso (Italy, 2000-2001) and a master Cultural and Social Anthropology at VU University Amsterdam (2007). Her approach to design is intrinsically interdisciplinary and combines spatial and graphic design with research and strategy. Her current interest and work is focused on implementing circularity in design. With Stephan Petermann she collaborates in their studio Probe.

photo credits

FRONT MATTER (p.5–35):
p.4: Architectural Record (left middle)
p.9: Stember, Historic Images
p.15: *top row*: Fine Art Images/Heritage Images (left), *second row*: Jens Frederiksen (right), *fourth row*: Balthazar Korab (left); Jim Haefner (right)
p.17: *second row*: Ezra Stoller / ESTO (left), *third row*: Archives Muncipales Le Havre (left); Gilber Fastenaekens (right)
p.18: *first row*: Michael Carapetian (left); Alamy (right), Second row: Marcel Gautherot (left); Diego Baraveli (right)
p.20: *bottom row*: Foster + Partners (3rd from the left); Lars Hallén (4th from the left)
p.22: *bottom row*: Ian Lambot (3rd from the left); Jens Frederiksen (4th from the left)

BACK MATTER (p.483–514):
p.486: Floorplans of Melli bank by Inter-Esse studio
p.492–93: Bertelsmann Corporate Archive
p.495: John Deere Corporate Archive
p.497: Amsterdam City Archives; Oscar van Leer collection
p.499: Canadian Centre for Architecture; Phyllis Lambert fonds
p.500–01: Mierle Laderman Ukeles
p.504–05: Imataki Tetsuyuki
p.513: Graphic by Donald Ryan

colophon

Texts: **Ruth Baumeister, Stephan Petermann** (with additional contributors)
Design: **Marieke van den Heuvel**
Editor: **James Westcott**
Research studio directors US and Japan: **Ashley Schafer** (Knowlton School of Architecture), **Keigo Kobayashi** (Waseda University, Department of Architecture)
Contributors: **Shaun Fynn, Marieke van den Heuvel, Rem Koolhaas/AMO/Nicholas Potts, Manfredo di Robilant, Kenneth Ross, Solmaz Sadeghi Khasraghi, Ashley Schafer, Ali Tavakoli Dinani**
Copy editor: **David Cross Kane**
Editorial assistant: **İdil Gökgöz**

Principle photography: **Jens Frederiksen, Ossip van Duivenbode**
Further photography: **Iwan Baan, Cameron Campbell, Mario Carieri, Pietro Carieri, Shaun Fynn, Jules Gorce, HGEsch, Andrea Jemolo, Parasto Nowruzi, Milad Panahifar, Richard Pare, Juhani Niiranen, Sandra Schubert, Emanuele Scorcelletti, Phillip Sinden, Patrick Tourneboeuf**
Artist support: **Mierle Laderman Ukeles**
Image rights: **Stephan Petermann with Nanna Hagedorn Olsen**

This publication was made possible by financial support from:
Dutch Creative Industries Fund, Abe Bonnema Foundation, Dreyersfond, Danish Arts Foundation, Oslo Architecture Triennale, Aarhus School of Architecture, Nationalbankens Jubilæumsfonden Denmark

Printing and lithography: **Die Keure, Brugge**
Paper: **XPer 140/120 gram, PlanoScript 80 gram**
Production: **Laurence Ostyn, nai010 publishers, Rotterdam**
Publisher: **nai010 publishers, Rotterdam**

© 2022 nai010 publishers, Rotterdam.
All rights reserved. No part of this publication may be reproduced, stored in a retrieval system, or transmitted in any form or by any means, electronic, mechanical, photocopying, recording or otherwise, without the prior written permission of the publisher.

For works of visual artists affiliated with a CISAC-organization the copyrights have been settled with Pictoright in Amsterdam.
© 2022, c/o Pictoright Amsterdam

Although every effort was made to find the copyright holders for the illustrations used, it has not been possible to trace them all. Interested parties are requested to contact nai010 publishers, Korte Hoogstraat 31, 3011 GK Rotterdam, the Netherlands.

nai010 publishers is an internationally orientated publisher specialized in developing, producing and distributing books in the fields of architecture, urbanism, art and design. www.nai010.com

nai010 books are available internationally at selected bookstores and from the following distribution partners:
North, Central and South America - Artbook | D.A.P., New York, USA, dap@dapinc.com
Rest of the world - Idea Books, Amsterdam, the Netherlands, idea@ideabooks.nl

For general questions, please contact nai010 publishers directly at sales@nai010.com or visit our website www.nai010.com for further information.

Printed and bound in Belgium

ISBN 9789462086524
NUR 648
BISAC ARC011000, ARC000000

This book is chiefly a product of others. It was edited with creative rigor by James Westcott. The designer is Marieke van den Heuvel who steered and pushed the content into a digestible format, adding attraction and style, and turning a heap of before/after shots it into a captivating sequence. Biggest thanks to chief photographers Jens Frederiksen and Ossip van Duivenbode, who scrupulously worked on reenacting many of the photos you see in the book.

Big thanks to Ashley Schafer for organizing the 2017 Scrupulous research studio at Knowlton School of Architecture (Ohio State University) and her support in developing the prototype of this book for the 2019 Oslo Triennale. To Keigo Kobayashi and the members Kobayashi Lab at Waseda University, Architecture Department.

At Aarhus School of Architecture: Torben Nielsen, Thomas Bo Jensen, Betinna Odgaard, Henning Grauballe, Jonathan Foote, Peter Mandal Hansen, Carolina Dayer, Robert B. Trempe Jr., Niels Martin Larsen, Christian Koch Ramsig, Lone Bønløke, Kätte Bonløkke, Hanne Foged Gjelstrup, Nanna Hagedorn Olsen.

For the support of many along the road in helping us pursue and access precarious documents, images, and data, even when sometimes they could not be found or never existed:
Nicolas Besond, Giovanna Borasi, Chris Boyens, Anna Bronovitskaya, Jan Carlzon, Paul Cournet, Maria Antonella Crippa, Neil Dahlstrom, Matthew Dalziel, Charlotte Bundgaard/Academia Danimarca, Helmut Dippold, Joel Eberhardt Engblad, Gregory Ernst, Andrea Ferrari, Hugo Frey, Bjørn Frivold, Mariam Gegidze, Thomas Girst, Ekaterina Golovatyuk, Alexander Gorlin, Maria Gouerieva, Michelle Gulickx, Tinatin Gurgenidze, Phineas Harper, Sami Heikinheimo, Timo Heikka, Jørgen Helstrup, Susanne Herde, Caroline Hirsch, Christel Leenen (HNI), Jacob Rubæk Holm, Mari Hotti, Nikoloz Japaridze, Céline Jeanne, Jiang Jun, Stephan Jung, Henrik Jussila, Bart van Kampen, Tim Klähn, Niels Knappe, Phyllis Lambert, Ralf Lange, Torsten Lange, Matthias Latzke, Eva Lintjes, Holste Markus, Iso van der Meer, Gili Merin, Luis Moreno-Fernandez, Manuel Orazi, Benny Holm Pedersen, Céline Pereira, Brooke Petrany, Jessica Quagliaroli, Julia Raschke, Reeta, Christian Richters, Timo Riekko, Mervi Roiha-Muilu, Werner Rose, Paolo Rosselli, Anne-marie van Schaik, Sandra Schubert, Marianne Sinemus-Ammermann, Lisa van der Slot, Cecilie Sachs Olsen and Maria Smith, Christin Svensson, Amy Thomas, Gabriele Toneguzzi, Niels Torp, Anko van der Werff, Victoria Woodside, Shi Yang.

For the Kagawa Prefectural Office building, special thanks to Tomo Inoshita, Seiji Kagawa, Norito Shimada, Photo Department at Shokokusha Publishing Co. Ltd, Makoto Taira, Tetsuyuki Imataki, Ryuma Sato, Chizuko Konishi. For the Palaceside building: to Sanae Tobita, Vincent Hecht, Shigeru Sakurai, The Mainichi Photobank., Ltd.. For Shizuoka Press and Broadcasting building to Koji Mochizuki, Sayako Kinoshita, Yuri Taniguchi and Tange Associates. For the Meguro City hall building: Meguro city hall officials and building management office, UNISON Co. Ltd., Kunihiko Miyachi, Inori Miyachi.

To Rem Koolhaas, Ellen van Loon, Chris van Duijn of the Office for Metropolitan Architecture for the initial push on this topic. For advice in the executive summary on real estate finance and deprecation, special thanks to Frits Witpeerd, Pim Arts, Hilde Remøy (TU Delft), Marleen Bosma (Bouwinvest), Mark Berlee (Cushman and Wakefield), Reinier Vrancken. For advice on building services and MEP, Rob Beijer (Stevens Van Dijck). For discussions on preservation, Jonas Malmberg (Aalto Foundation).

The concept and content of this book has been boosted at various stages through engagements with universities:
Aarhus School of Architecture, 2016/17
Students: Asger Aagesen, Christopher Germann Bæhring, Anne Staun Christiansen, Anne Sofie Schmidt Frydenlund, Anna Sophie Gille-Udsen, Anna Louise Hansen, Anne Kühl Hansen, Emma Valnæs Holck, Victor Bøgebjerg Josefsen, Natascha Jørgensen, Simone Lundtoft Jørgensen, Ditlev Feldballe Kardyb, Anna Ildrup Keller, Niels Ove Kildahl, Alberte Thorup Kjær, Hannah Knudsen, Jens Juel Thiis Knudsen, Peter Korshøj, Lasse Vejlgård Kristensen, Line Rohr Kristiansen, Amalie Ruth Okholm Kryger, Tom Kwitkovsky, Clara Holm Lange, Rikke Thyregod Langkjær, Christine Kjølhede Larsen, Brian Laursen, Emil Christoffer Rasborg Laursen, Frederik Kromann Laursen, Jaime Levin, Tian Liang, Simen Enkerud Lien, Helene Bredgaard Garde Lind, Isabell Lippert, Anne Mette Thisgaard Lund, Kimmernaq Wilhelmine Rakel Lyberth, Christian Vang Madsen, Ida Lundø Madsen, Simon Markfoged Madsen, Christina Kastalag Magnussen, Marius Makos, Liam Alexander Marosy-Weide, Louise Dreier Matthiesen, Aliis Mehide, Ane Hestenes Merli, Anne Bea Høgh Mikkelsen, Adam Linde Nielsen, Dan Ravneberg Nielsen, Christine Skjøt Pedersen, Andrea Sara Mariel Rados, Agnes Alvilde Esther Schelde, Anna Woge Sørensen
Contributors: Khadar Yussuf Awil, Rebecca Bego, Carolina Dayer, Birgitte Geert Jensen, Henning Grauballe, Allette L. Marcel Hansen, Thomas Lillevang, Karen Olsen, Nikil Saval, Amanda Breum Skovsted, Anne Elisabeth Toft, James Westcott
Management: Torben Nielsen, Chris Thurlbourne, Rasmus Grønbæck Hansen, Claus Peder Pedersen, Trine Berthold

Knowlton School of Architecture, 2017
James Amicone, Jared Younger, Clark Sabula, Ali Sandhu, Brent Hall, Patrick Small, Rachael Dzierzak, Christina Tefend, Stephen Angus, Danny Yontz, Bethany Roman, and Kayla Eland

Keigo Kobayashi Laboratory, Waseda University Architecture department, 2020/21
Hiroki Senda, Yae Faye, Abudjana Babiker, Hiroki Kotagiri, Tomomi Nakanishi, Euridice Oliveira de Paiva, Erika Kakinoki, Kai Yoneyama, Yifu Zhang, Konstancja Kusiak, Ruriko Ueda, and Shoko Muranaka

April 2022